THE SCHOLASTIC ROOTS

OF THE

SPANISH AMERICAN REVOLUTION

The Scholastic Roots of the Spanish American Revolution

O. Carlos Stoetzer

FORDHAM UNIVERSITY PRESS
NEW YORK
1979

© Copyright 1979 by FORDHAM UNIVERSITY PRESS
All rights reserved
LC 77-075797
ISBN 0-8232-1027-8

Printed by
CULTURA PRESS
Wetteren, Belgium

TO RONA

CONTENTS

PREFACE		ix
I.	Introduction	1
	1. The Proprietary Character of the Indies	1
	Civil Government	4
	Ecclesiastical Government	5
	2. Political Liberty and the *Cabildo*	6
II.	The Medieval Tradition in the Spanish World, 1492–1700	16
	1. Medieval and Renaissance Thought in the Sixteenth Century	16
	Viceroyalty of New Spain	32
	Viceroyalty of Peru	34
	2. The Thought of the Baroque in the Seventeenth Century	39
	Viceroyalty of New Spain	44
	Viceroyalty of Peru	45
III.	The Enlightenment in the Spanish World, 1700–1808	60
	1. Enlightenment and Scholasticism in the Peninsula	60
	2. The Echo of the Enlightenment in the Indies	79
	Viceroyalty of New Spain	89
	Viceroyalty of New Granada	92
	Viceroyalty of Peru	96
	Viceroyalty of the River Plate	100
	The Spread of Divine Right Theories	103
IV.	Implementation of and Reaction to the Enlightenment in Spanish America, 1700–1808	113
	1. The Bourbon Reforms	113
	2. The Scholastic Tradition	121
	Viceroyalty of New Spain	123
	Viceroyalty of Peru	125
	Viceroyalty of New Granada	127
	Viceroyalty of the River Plate	131
	Scholastic Works in Libraries	138
	3. Important Events of the Period Relevant to the Spanish American Revolution	139
	The Revolt of the *Comuneros* in Paraguay (1723–35)	140
	The Expulsion of the Society of Jesus (1767)	141
	The Indian Uprising of Tupac Amarú in Upper Peru (1780)	143
	The Conspiracy of the Three Antonios in Chile (1780–81)	143
	The Revolt of the *Comuneros* in New Granada (1781)	144
	The Plot of Gual and España in Venezuela (1797)	144
	Miranda's Landings in Venezuela (1806)	145
	The British Invasions of the River Plate (1806–1807)	146
V.	The Spanish Late Scholastic Foundation of Independence, 1808–1823	151
	1. The Immediate Causes of the Revolution	151

2. The First Act: The Constitutional Crisis and the Establishment of Juntas (1808–14) 167
   a. The Holder of Sovereignty in a Territorial Sense . . . 168
     i. The Spanish or Loyalist Approaches 168
       aa. The Viceregal Case 168
          Viceroyalty of New Spain 168
          Viceroyalty of the River Plate 172
          Viceroyalty of New Granada 174
       bb. The Provincialist Case 176
          Viceroyalty of the River Plate (Uruguay) . . . 176
          Viceroyalty of the River Plate (Paraguay) . . . 184
     ii. The Spanish American Revolutionary Approaches . . . 185
       aa. The Unity Case 185
       bb. The Viceregal or Confederacy Case 187
          Viceroyalty of New Spain 188
          Viceroyalty of the River Plate 194
          Viceroyalty of New Granada 209
       cc. The Provincialist Case 214
          Viceroyalty of the River Plate (Upper Peru) . . 214
          Viceroyalty of the River Plate (Uruguay) . . . 216
          Viceroyalty of the River Plate (Paraguay) . . . 221
          Viceroyalty of Peru (Chile) 222
          Viceroyalty of New Granada (Quito) 225
          Viceroyalty of New Granada (Venezuela) . . . 227
          Viceroyalty of New Granada (Cartagena, Cali, Mompox, Pamplona, Socorro; Cundinamarca and Tunja) . . 229
   b. The Legitimate Basis for the Political Organization . . . 232
     i. The Peninsula or Conservative Formula 232
     ii. The Native or Spanish American Formula 233
   c. The Sovereign or Delegated Character of the Civil Authorities in Spanish America 234
     i. The Royalist or Loyalist Solution 235
       Viceroyalties of Peru and the River Plate 235
     ii. The Autonomist Solution 235
     iii. The Solution of the Followers of Independence . . . 237
       Viceroyalty of New Spain 237
       Viceroyalty of the River Plate 238
3. The Second Act: The Absolutist Reaction (1814–20) . . 238
   Viceroyalty of New Spain 242
   Viceroyalty of New Granada (Venezuela) 242
   Viceroyalty of the River Plate 243
   Viceroyalty of Peru (Chile) 244
4. The Third and Final Act: The Return of Liberalism (1820–23) 246
   Viceroyalty of New Spain 246
   Viceroyalty of Peru 247
   Viceroyalty of New Granada 248

CONCLUSION 258
BIBLIOGRAPHY 265
INDEX NOMINUM 293

PREFACE

The research upon which the present book is based was begun in the late 1950s at Georgetown University. The results of that research were translated into Spanish, and the Instituto de Estudios Políticos in Madrid published it as *El pensamiento político en la América española durante el período de la emancipación (1789-1825): Las bases hispánicas y las corrientes europeas* in two volumes in 1966. Though the present study uses material from the former work, it reflects much additional research and deals with a different problem.

This study seeks to prove that the Revolution which began in Spanish America in the years after 1808, and especially in 1810, and continued for the next fifteen years amid mounting political anarchy and intellectual confusion, had little to do with either the Enlightenment or the North American or French revolutions. It attempts to show, rather, that the Spanish American Revolution was a typically Hispanic family affair not influenced by foreign ideology, that it had a profoundly Spanish and medieval foundation, and that the political thought which unleashed it was Scholasticism, especially in its modern form, the Late Scholasticism of Spain's Golden Age. In order to prove this, the study has had to trace the roots over the centuries of Spanish domination in America and could not be limited to the few decades before the famous events of 1808-10.

The present study covers the period from 1492 to 1821—i.e., from the beginnings of the Spanish discovery and conquest to the independence of New Spain and Peru, the most traditional viceroyalties. Though the main argument—the *pactum translationis*—refers primarily to the years 1808-10, to end there, with the establishment of the *de facto* independent Spanish American juntas at the beginning of the Revolution, would sever a significant and necessary link. Thus the study includes the years 1810-21 because the historical developments in the Peninsula—the return of Ferdinand VII in 1814 with the imposition of absolutism and the revolt of Rafael del Riego in 1820 with the re-establishment of liberalism—cannot be omitted from the general thesis. The return of Ferdinand VII is closely linked to the earlier establishment of juntas in view of their claim that they ruled provisionally for the absent king; the return of liberalism is important in order to show the continuity of Spanish traditions, particularly in the case of the more traditional areas: New Spain, where the second Spanish liberal regime brought about the final political break with the Peninsula; and Peru, where the city of Lima reacted in favor of the revolutionaries when it heard the news of Riego's revolt and the return of constitutionalism. The choice of 1821 is thus linked to the independence of the traditional areas of New Spain and Peru, even though some countries had already achieved independence earlier (Venezuela and Paraguay, 1811; Argentina, 1816; and Chile, 1818).

In the view of this writer the so-called Spanish American Revolution was in reality no revolution at all, but simply an echo, a projection, of the historic events in the Peninsula—a profound cry of loyalty to Ferdinand VII as the symbol of resistance against Napoleon and the French Revolution and against the general influx of alien ideas—which only in view of the continued presence of anti-traditional forces (absolutism and constitutionalism both rooted in the Enlightenment) finally led to a spirit of total independence by 1819–21. In view of the general acceptance of the term Spanish American Revolution the author decided not to raise any objections to its use in this study but at the same time wishes it to be understood that he rejects the implication of the term as running counter to historical truth.

When dealing with the various parts of Spanish America, I have designated the countries by the names in use during the Spanish period of government and also largely during the Spanish American Revolution—i.e., the names of the four viceroyalties of New Spain, Peru, New Granada, and River Plate. Also, my subject is treated in line with the historic Spanish American division of these four viceroyalties. However, the following clarification is necessary. The discussion of New Spain covers only Mexico, unless the areas of the Captaincy General of Guatemala, Cuba, and Puerto Rico are specifically included. My treatment of Peru covers only Peru proper; Chile is treated separately within that section. As for New Granada, where the name of the country was often changed, I have retained the old name only for what is today Colombia and Panama, thus giving separate treatment to Venezuela and Quito within that particular section. Finally, in the case of the River Plate, I have preferred to use the name of the four countries which split from the viceroyalty. When dealing with the separate areas of the Viceroyalty of the River Plate, I have used the name Paraguay, and for what is today Bolivia the older name of Upper Peru, while preferring for the sake of clarity to use the modern ones of Argentina and Uruguay (although in the latter case I have also used in the text the name of *Banda Oriental*).

I have made a serious attempt at giving proportionate treatment to the various geographical areas, but a different historical and cultural evolution in the four viceroyalties and special regional circumstances made it impossible to observe this rule strictly. This is especially true of such a great area as the River Plate where the revolutionary spirit was stronger and where the various regions offered a greater challenge in comparison with the area of New Spain which remained loyal to the Peninsula until as late as 1821, and where the different regions (Captaincy General of Guatemala, Cuba, and Puerto Rico) were rather passive. The same perspective is also true of Peru proper which did not have any revolution at all and where the spirit of emancipation was imported.

The present study is not strictly speaking an historical one and does not claim to be complete. Because of the vastness of the subject matter, which covers most of the Spanish-speaking nations of the American continent and the interrelationship of political theory with the fields of philosophy, history, constitutional law, and economics, it is to be expected that lacunae will be found. The book is intended to show the main lines and to draw conclusions regarding the Spanish American Revolution.

Finally, I might mention that the translations of the source material are my own.

I wish to express my deep appreciation to Fordham University Press for bringing this project to publication. To my wife, Rona, I owe a great debt of gratitude for her patience, understanding, and help.

Wilton, Connecticut
Columbus Day, 1978

THE SCHOLASTIC ROOTS
OF THE
SPANISH AMERICAN REVOLUTION

I

INTRODUCTION

1. THE PROPRIETARY CHARACTER OF THE INDIES

TO UNDERSTAND THE INTELLECTUAL BACKGROUND of the Spanish American Revolution one must keep in mind certain features of the civil and ecclesiastical government in the Indies, since the Scholastic thesis forms the basis for these legal and institutional foundations. The Spanish conquest meant essentially the founding of towns and cities, of new provinces and kingdoms, and by the end of the sixteenth century the various Spanish provinces or kingdoms in the Indies possessed a political reality—as their various founders had envisioned —within the missionary and federative monarchy of Spain, with its special political institutions modeled along traditional Castilian lines. The new lands in Spanish America were established on two typically Hispanic medieval concepts: faith in God and loyalty to the king. These concepts were to have as much juridical validity in the Wars of Independence as they had in the days of the Spanish conquest.

Loyalty to the king meant loyalty to the Crowns of Castile and León, rather than to the Crown of Aragon, since the new lands were incorporated specifically into the two former Crowns. Castile became the standard-bearer in the Indies, not as a form of compensation for Aragon's Mediterranean titles but as a consequence of some very practical political facts. Aragon and Castile differed in their constitutional pattern because of historical developments caused by geographical and cultural factors: Aragon had had a Mediterranean outlook with Italian and Greek influences, and Castile had been relatively isolated from the rest of Europe until the Age of Discoveries. In Castile and León the Crowns had grown strong through alliances with the cities against the nobility, who lost voting rights in the Castilian *Cortes*;[1] but in Aragon the nobility had won against the monarchy, retaining its feudal rights and *fueros* as had no other country in Europe, with the possible exception of Poland.[2]

The decision to incorporate the new lands into Castile rather than into Aragon had two important results: (*a*) it did not create an oligarchy, thereby avoiding a repetition of the anarchical situation in Aragon, and (*b*) it strengthened the position of the colonizers. Until 1596 only Castilian emigrants were permitted to go to the Indies[3] (though actually the main body of emigrants were Extremadurans and Andalusians); after that date permission was extended to people from all parts of Spain.

The incorporation of the Indies into the Crown of Castile meant that they became provinces, not colonies, and represented integral parts of the monarchy; the kings were obliged to retain them in perpetuity by virtue of the work of the discoverers and settlers and a royal promise that the lands would never be transferred. This declaration implied the principle of legal equality between

Castile and the Indies,[4] and is a significant fact which will be stressed by the patriots at the time of the Revolution. Richard M. Morse has stated that

> the theoretical premise for royal centralization was not colonial subjugation of the Indies, but the assumption that the New World Viceroyalties were realms coequal with those of Spain, having equal claims to redress from the crown.[5]

Furthermore, the new lands were the property, not of the Spanish nation, but of the king of Castile personally—another important fact which will be used by the revolutionaries for the establishment of their respective governments. Therefore, "the Castilian Cortes, councils, and audiencias were not to have an atom of power in America," which the Crown intended to manage "as another hereditary domain, through a totally new set of institutions, without doubt closely similar to, and in fact modelled on, those of Castile, but entirely separate from them."[6]

The proprietary character of the Indies was stated specifically by Emperor Charles V in Barcelona on September 14, 1519, and by both the emperor and Queen Joan in Valladolid on July 9, 1520; and repeated in Pamplona on October 22, 1523. It was restated by the emperor and the governing prince in Monzón de Aragón on December 7, 1547, and by Philip II in Madrid on July 18, 1563,[7] and finally incorporated in the *Recopilación de leyes de las Indias* of 1680 by King Charles II and the queen, as follows:

> By donation of the Holy Apostolic See and other just and legitimate titles, we are Lord of the West Indies, islands and mainland of the ocean sea, those discovered and those to be discovered, and [they] are incorporated into our Royal Crown of Castile. And because it is our will, and because we have promised and sworn that they will always be retained in perpetuity, and for their greater strength, we prohibit their alienation. And we order that they can never be separated from our Royal Crown of Castile, nor can they, or their cities, towns, villages, under any circumstances or in favor of any person, be separated totally or divided in part. And in the light of the fealty of our vassals and the trials which the discoverers and settlers have undergone in their discovery and settlement, [and] in order for them to have greater security and to be assured that they will always exist and remain united to our Royal Crown, we promise and pledge our faith and our royal word on behalf of ourselves and the kings, our successors, that neither they, nor their cities or villages, for whatever cause or for whatever reason, or in favor of any person, will ever be alienated or separated in whole or in part; and if we, or our successors, should make some donation or alienation contrary to this [law], be [that donation or alienation][8] null and void, and we so declare it [Book III, Title 1, Law 1].

Juan de Solórzano Pereira, the famous lawyer of the Indies, reiterated this judicial meaning when he stated that the provinces of the Indies are part of those of Castile and are united to them in an accessory character.[9] A utilitarian and mercantilist concept in regard to the Indies will appear only in the eighteenth century.

Thus the relationship between the Spanish Crown and the Indies was proprietary:

The New Laws of 1542, the various *Ordenanzas sobre Descubrimiento*, and above all the great Colonial code—the "Recopilación de Leyes de las Indias" —form the most impressive of all monuments to an absolute imperial sovereignty based upon the formal assumption that the Indies were the private estate of the rulers of Castile.¹⁰

This can also be seen in such events as when Emperor Charles V sold his claims to the Moluccas to Portugal, although the *Cortes* of Castile had previously extracted from him a promise that he would not part with the islands, or when, bypassing the monopoly of Seville, he allowed Aragonese and Flemings to trade with the Indies. The right to travel or to trade in the Indies was reserved to him and continued to depend, "as it did throughout the colonial period, on individual royal license."¹¹ The proprietary theory would never have been accepted in the Peninsula in such a naked form, but in the Indies it was a fiction which enabled the Crown to exercise in theory "a maximum of political authority with a minimum of political responsibility" and tended to produce an idea of sovereignty much closer to the concepts of Sir Robert Filmer than to the constitutional theories of the Spanish school;¹² it was made necessary at the same time when in the Indies great distances, difficult topography, and human problems clearly indicated that in practice the royal will was rarely effective.¹³ The formula "Se acata, pero no se cumple" paid lip service to absolutism but allowed all the leeway so dear to the Spanish individualistic soul.

Neither the Council of Castile nor the *Cortes* had anything to do with the shaping of policy and the administration of the new lands; these were the sole right of the king, whose power was later vested in specially designed organizations.¹⁴ These administrative units were in part new creations, in part successors of Spanish traditions.

The earliest government appointment, in 1493, was Juan Rodríguez de Fonseca, the first "colonial secretary," and bishop of Burgos (1514-24). In 1503 the Crown established the *Casa de Contratación* in Seville with Fonseca as its head; it held authority in regard to the Indies in the preliminary stage of the Spanish Empire in America. It directed economic policy for the Indies, although its power was largely curtailed when the Council of the Indies was established.¹⁵ To reduce its workloads the Crown set up two more institutions: the *Juzgado de Indias* (Cádiz, 1535), to solve problems arising between sailors and merchants, and the *Consulado* of Seville (1543), a guild of merchants, and the *Consulado* of Seville (1543), a guild of merchants, to settle civil suits between members of the body.¹⁶ In 1707 the *Casa de Contratación* was transferred to Cádiz.

In 1524 the Crown created the Council of the Indies, which established policy and had jurisdiction over juridical matters overseas. "It was not a mere colonial office, but had ministerial status."¹⁷ Its competence in the affairs of the Indies was "literally all inclusive; it had exactly the same powers as the Council of Castile in home government—all other officials and tribunals were explicitly excluded from intervention in the Indies."¹⁸ It was the council which corresponded with all officials in the Indies, prepared candidates in both the temporal and spiritual realms, and acted as the superior court of appeals. The first president of the council, and thus the successor to Bishop Fonseca, was Francisco García de Loaysa, the Emperor's confessor, and the head of the

Dominican order in Spain—"a fact which bears eloquent testimony to the genuineness of Charles' zeal for the propagation of the faith, and for his determination to Christianize the inhabitants of the New World."[19]

Civil government. The cornerstone of civil administration in the Indies was the administrative and judicial positions of viceroy, captain general, and president of the *audiencia*. The first viceroyalty was created in Española but was of short duration. The system was renewed in New Spain in 1535, and in Peru (1542), to be followed later by two more: New Granada (1717 [1724], 1740) and the River Plate (1776). Since the viceroys never exercised their authority at any one place for any length of time—the normal assignment was for a period of three years, after which the viceroy was either recalled or reassigned—Spanish America was unable to develop a deep tradition of the monarchical principle. Government there was, rather, the application of a republican principle within a monarchical framework.

The captaincies general were a kind of small administrative territorial division, dependent on the viceroyalties, while the *audiencias* were the smallest administrative units of a legal character. Both were copies of similar administrative organs in the Peninsula.[20]

In spite of the fact that the viceroy was at the top of the hierarchical pyramid in Spanish America, the key position of Spanish rule was held by the *audiencia*, since it had the right of direct communication with the Council of the Indies through its *reales acuerdos*.[21] The *audiencia* was not only a court as in the Peninsula but also an administrative unit. Their presidents—in Mexico and Lima the post was held by the viceroy himself—were the executive officers of the region. In their judicial capacity the *audiencias* were courts of appeals and in legal matters they were supreme, since the viceroys were forbidden to interfere in their affairs and could not vote in their legal meetings. In administrative and executive matters, however, the situation was quite different: the *audiencias* had to follow the will of the highest representative of the Crown[22] and acted as advisory councils to the executives who presided over them. It was in this capacity that they exercised powers which their Peninsular models never had. They also assumed all political powers whenever a vacancy occurred in the office of viceroy. This was especially decreed in the case of the *audiencia* of Lima in 1550.

During the period of the Catholic rulers and of Emperor Charles V seven *audiencias* were established in the Indies: Santo Domingo, 1511 (all the Caribbean islands and Venezuela); Mexico, 1527 (heartland of Mexico and coast up to the Floridas); Panama, 1535 [1542], and 1563–64; Lima, 1542 (Quito, Peru, Upper Peru, Chile); Guatemala, 1543 (Central America, including Yucatán, from the Isthmus of Tehuantepec to the Isthmus of Panama); New Galicia [Guadalajara], 1548 (Northern Mexico and present Western United States), and Santa Fe de Bogotá, 1549.[23] Four of these *audiencias* (Santo Domingo, Guadalajara, Mexico, and Guatemala) formed part of the Viceroyalty of New Spain; the other three, of the Viceroyalty of Peru. Another seven *audiencias* were established after the death of Emperor Charles V: Charcas, 1559; Quito, 1563; Manila, 1583; Santiago de Chile, 1609; Buenos Aires, 1661; Caracas, 1786; and Cuzco, 1787.[24]

In theory, all the *audiencias* possessed the same powers; in practice, those of Mexico and Lima far outstripped the others. The viceroys had the right to give orders to the lesser *audiencias* within their viceroyalties, and although each *audiencia* was regarded as sovereign in its territory under the Council of the Indies, all were subordinated to the viceregal administration. Generally, the *audiencias* were coterminous with the captaincies general, the military areas, so that the president of a lesser *audiencia* who was virtually the governor of the region held at the same time the post of captain general.[25]

Ecclesiastical government. The special privileges which the Spanish Church enjoyed were of decisive importance in the shaping of ecclesiastical developments in the Indies.[26] Granted by several papal bulls issued between 1493 and 1508, and rendering the Spanish Church much less dependent upon Rome than any other European Church, these privileges constituted the *Real Patronato de Indias* and were the results of a struggle which began in Castile under Alfonso X, the Learned. The *Patronato*, which was based on the precedent of the Sicilian monarchy (Normans and Hohenstaufen) and of the *Patronato* of Granada, originated and developed in the midst of Spanish America, and was geared primarily toward the Christianization of the New World.[27] The *Patronato* meant that the Spanish Crown had the right to present candidates for ecclesiastical vacancies, levy the ecclesiastical tithes, and impose a royal *placet* for papal bulls; that no church could be built without the authorization of the king; that neither monasteries nor religious orders could be founded without prior royal consent; and that the monarchy was to finance all costs of the Church's works. "Thus, the King, represented by his Council, was in reality the supreme judge of the national clergy."[28] Indeed,

> practically all the points over which the temporal and spiritual powers of Western Christendom had fought throughout the Middle Ages were here decided at the outset in favor of the temporal. The Pope could really do nothing in Spanish America without the consent and cooperation of the Spanish crown; it was a situation without precedent.[29]

During the reign of Emperor Charles V two archbishoprics were established (Mexico and Lima, 1546) and twenty-two bishoprics; the earliest bishoprics had been established in Española and Puerto Rico in the years 1512–13.[30] By the time Alexander von Humboldt visited the New World, eight archbishoprics had been created: Mexico, Guatemala, Santo Domingo, Havana, Caracas, Bogotá, Lima, and Chuquisaca.[31]

The best symbol of the union of Church and Crown was the Castilian flag of the Golden Age, which carried, on one side, the royal coat-of-arms and, on the other, a cross or picture of the Virgin Mary, the apostle James, or another saint. "Spain never advanced in its incomparable push toward the subjugation of peoples without the Church's doing likewise."[32]

By the end of the sixteenth century, "the dominant influence of the Church on spiritual, intellectual, and social life, which was maintained throughout the entire colonial period, was plainly evident."[33] Moreover, the entire civil and ecclesiastical government in the Indies was an echo of the Middle Ages:

> The state was of a corporate character. Within it, there were independently defined privileges and jurisdictions for broad groups (Indians, Europeans, ecclesiastics, Negroes) as well as for smaller component groups, such as: Indians in missions, *pueblos de indios*, Indians in encomiendas; merchants, university students, artisans; regular clergy, secular clergy, inquisitorial officials; Negro slaves, colored freedmen, and so forth. The medieval im-

print which the system as a whole bore was not that of parliamentary representation but that of pluralistic, compartmented privilege and of administrative paternalism.³⁴

2. Political Liberty and the Cabildo

This paternalism notwithstanding, political liberty was a fact, manifest in the lax enforcement of censorship, certain personal freedoms protected by the Crown, and the development of the *cabildo*, an institution which was instrumental in the application of the Scholastic theory during the Spanish American Revolution. For the control of ideas, there existed a regulation of April 4, 1531—a directive by the queen (acting in the absence of her husband) to the *Casa de Contratación* at Seville—repeated in 1543 and signed by the prince, the future Philip II,³⁵ which forbade the importation into the Indies of any books other than Christian works. This regulation was still in effect in 1680 at the time of the *Recopilación de leyes de las Indias*, but was only nominal.

The censoring of books was among the duties of the Inquisition, a royal and civil court established in Spain in 1478 by Ferdinand and Isabella. In 1551 the *Index expurgatorius* appeared, and in 1558 details were published regarding the Inquisition's authority in the light of the increasing flood of printed materials. The lack of adequate personnel and the increase in the publication of books explain why often ridiculous and absurd matters passed without objection and others much less offensive were stopped.³⁶ Actually, the censorship which the Inquisition and the *Casa de Contratación* exercised was extremely generous and much less severe than in Europe. The fact that these laws were repeated within a few years clearly shows that the censorship was ineffective. As a matter of fact these royal orders were regularly ignored; "at no time did the royal commands seriously affect the exportation of the proscribed literature, and a similarly lax enforcement of the laws was the rule among the receiving officials in the colonial ports."³⁷ Had the Crown or the Inquisition wanted to protect the Indies from the intellectual ideas and literature of Catholic Europe (which was not their purpose), this effort would have been thwarted by commercial elements eager for profit.³⁸

This laxity in the enforcement of laws was a direct result of policy of assimilation in keeping with the philosophy of the Spanish monarchs to respect the rights of the vanquished, as long as doing so did not contradict the interests of the Crown.³⁹ It resulted in the Indian legislation and in a divorce between law and reality, a situation symbolized so well by the formula "Se acata, pero no se cumple."⁴⁰

Although political liberties were curtailed in the Indies during the period of the Catholic rulers and the Hapsburgs, they nonetheless existed in the following manner:

1. Through the right of personal appeal to the king as the source of justice; and
2. Through such substantial freedoms as:
    (*a*) the integrity of honor;
    (*b*) the protection of property; and
    (*c*) the intrinsic right to levy only those taxes approved by the people.⁴¹

The Crown was always the regulating factor which protected legitimately obtained rights, and the power which corrected abuses, punishing transgressors for their unlawful and immoral actions. The latter work, over the course of centuries, marked one of the greatest humanitarian accomplishments in Spanish America.

No accurate interpretation of Spanish rule in America can overlook the existence and development of political liberty which is closely linked to the *cabildo*. Indeed, the evolution of Spanish America from Peninsular rule to independent nations is inconceivable without this institution, which played an important role in the countries of Spanish domination at all times but particularly during the Revolution. In Spain political liberty traditionally manifested itself in the *Cortes*, and no doubt would have done so in the Indies, but this medieval Hispanic institution, no longer a source of popular freedoms during the Hapsburg rule, was never introduced there. The *cabildo* thus became the arena for the exercise of political freedom.

The *cabildo*—town council—was a typically Spanish medieval institution, and as the representative voice of municipal government it was intrinsically linked to the rise of towns and cities. According to Eduardo de Hinojosa, the town council is the forerunner of the modern state, and its history one of the most remarkable achievements of Western civilization, since it laid the foundation for many of today's liberties: personal freedom, freedom of property, freedom of work, inviolability of one's home, equality in civil and political rights, and, finally, intellectual and scientific progress.[42] For very special reasons, however, the rise of towns and cities was an even greater achievement in the Iberian Peninsula than in the rest of Western and Central Europe.

Municipal government in Spain is closely linked to the *Reconquista*, which really began in the tenth century. As more and more areas were freed from Moorish control, a process of repopulation, *población*, developed; soldiers were settled in the new areas, to be followed, slowly, by other immigrants. The kings, to pursue the *Reconquista* and to consolidate the recaptured areas, offered tempting rewards to those who would live within a new town, which was then allowed to build defenses, including the usual *alcázar*, and to manage its own affairs without royal interference. This repopulation of vast areas through small holdings soon created an important class of free men whose spirit of liberty would echo in the famous *cabildos*.[43]

The question of the origin of the medieval Spanish town council is still open to interpretation, but it is generally agreed that the source of the Castilian town council was the *concilium*, the *concejo* (which after the tenth century meant all free men in a given area), and the judicial assembly, the *conventus publicus vicinorum*; these institutions were eventually combined since the same persons participated in both.[44] In time the council expanded its jurisdiction to include rural areas, and a certain community of interests grew. Frontier conditions, the isolation of royal power, the necessity of dealing effectively with matters of security and supply, the need for protection from the nobility, and at the same time a certain royal policy favoring an alliance with the towns (the laws of León of 1188, for instance)—all these factors contributed to the rise and strength of town government, which achieved truly democratic power in the twelfth and thirteenth centuries and produced considerable improvements in rural areas and emancipation in civil and political matters.

Municipal government was in reality the voice of the third estate, since certain town-council positions—*alcaldes* (mayors), *justicias* (justices), *merinos* (representatives of royal authority), and *jurados* (officials entrusted with the roll of citizens)[45]—were filled by popular election (Moors and Jews were, however, denied the vote). In this aspect of municipal government Spain anticipated similar developments in the rest of Europe, since delegates from the towns were admitted to the medieval Spanish *Cortes* a century earlier than were commoners to the English Parliament and two centuries before Philip the Fair convoked the first French States General.[46]

After the fourteenth century, this brilliant period of medieval town councils came to an end. Internal dissensions, struggles between the nobles and the weakening towns, the rise of royal power, and encroachments by both Crown and nobility led to a decline in municipal government and to the end of its independence. The intervention of the Crown began under Alfonso XI of Castile (1312–50) and increased in the fifteenth century.[47] The towns, forced finally to choose between submission to the Crown—which was interested in controlling the important municipal political units—or acquiescence to the nobility—which continued to seize the towns' communal lands—elected royal control, which was offered through the offices of the *asistentes*, *adelantados*, and *corregidores* (all representatives of royal authority). But not until the reign of Isabella, when *corregidores* were assigned to all Castilian towns and cities (1480), was royal power successfully imposed on the towns, and the liberties of municipal government curtailed.[48]

The insurrection of the *comunidades*, in the years 1520–21, represented the last effort of the Castilian towns to defend their common interests and rights at a time when little of the prestige and power which had been theirs in the twelfth, thirteenth, and fourteenth centuries remained. The victory of Emperor Charles V over the Castilian freedoms represented not only the end of a glorious evolution in municipal government but a further intrusion of the spirit of the Renaissance into Spanish politics.[49]

Yet, "the old Castilian self-government permanently survived in the nascent cabildos of the Indies."[50] By a strange historical development, the *cabildo* recovered its vigor in the Indies during the early period of colonization—that is, until the reign of Philip II—thus becoming a true mirror of the Castilian town council of the Middle Ages. This recovery represents a logical development, since the conquests of new provinces and the founding of new towns resembled similar developments in Spain during the twelfth and thirteenth centuries. The epic ventures of the Spanish conquistadors in the Indies required a generous policy on the part of the Crown just as somewhat different conditions had during the *Reconquista*. The parallelism of the evolution of the *cabildo* in the Peninsula and in the Indies is best illustrated by the fact that the first institution of the conquistadors was the *cabildo*, with all its inherited traditions of self-government.[51] The powers and privileges granted to the *cabildo* by Emperor Charles V revealed his political openmindedness and vision,[52] yet he may have been counseled, as John Preston Moore pointed out, "by the gravity of the last uprising in Spain."[53]

The *cabildo* attained enormous significance in Spanish America during the first half of the sixteenth century.[54] It became the representative voice of the third estate, the colonizers, and *the* institution through which the commoners could channel their social aspirations and speak out against royal interference and the abuses of the great discoverers and their descendants.[55] Very much in keeping with the best Iberian traditions, the population of the countryside expanded "to meet the needs of the towns" whereas "in the English colonies of America the town grew up to meet the needs of the inhabitants of the country."[56]

> Even in the very seats of the central government, the *cabildos* constantly asserted their freedom, resisting attempted dictation whether by viceroys, governors, or *audiencias* . . . ; in the colonies, as had formerly been the case in the mother country, it was in the towns that the political activity of the race found expression. The central administration may have been stagnant; local administration was not.[57]

Yet in time the *cabildo* decayed in Spanish America—just as it had in Spain itself—because of the sale of official positions and of the ever increasing authority of the governors. The Crown was entitled under the system of *regalías* to reward deserving subjects with positions in the municipal government, and because of financial problems during the reign of Philip II, it introduced into the Indies, as it had into the Peninsula, the practice of auctioning the most lucrative positions to the highest bidder. By this harmful method, important positions on the town council were soon filled by members of the moneyed class and bequeathed to their descendants. The popular town council of the early-sixteenth century gradually turned into an oligarchic regime in which the interests of the members of the *cabildo* did not always coincide with those of the people, with the result that the Spanish American *cabildos* in the seventeenth century no longer had the vitality which they possessed the century before.

Though it declined after 1650, the *cabildo* left a strong foundation for municipal authority and self-government, which had been laid in the period of Emperor Charles V, and "the memory of it was to prove potent in the New World as well as in the Old, at the time of the revolutions of the nineteenth century."[58] By the beginning of the eighteenth century, "the heroic age of the cabildos was a thing of distant memory in all parts of the Spanish empire," and their plight could be traced to two basic causes: lack of popular representation and lack of adequate financial resources.[59] And yet, "if the *cabildos* in the seventeenth century lost the possibility of exercising political authority, they always retained the role of censure, even to the extent of instigating the removal of tyrannical governors."[60]

However, a surprising development occurred in the eighteenth century. The *cabildo*, which had deteriorated to a low level of efficiency and prestige,[61] reflecting the general decline of Spain in the same period,[62] underwent certain internal changes prior to independence, which one observer sees as coinciding with the period of the *intendencias*.[63] Although the advent of the Bourbons and the rising centralism and absolutism of the eighteenth century did not result in a revival of the old liberties of the *cabildos*, a significant evolution nonetheless took place. With the increased immigration of Basques and northern Castilians, many of whom were nobles, or considered themselves as such, and were imbued with pride in their traditional liberties, a shift in the character of the *cabildos* was noticeable. Earlier, the main body of immigrants had been Extremadurans and Andalusians who were interested mainly in agriculture and mining. The new immigrants, who devoted themselves to administrative and commercial careers, quickly achieved power in the *cabildos*, particularly after Philip V ordered the concentration of all Spaniards in the extended cities (1703).[64]

The new immigrants soon formed a second social stratum of landed aristocracy whose influence was to be felt as a more vigorous voice in municipal affairs. During the eighteenth century, this new class replaced the former members of the *cabildo*, giving the town council new prestige and influence, echoing the feelings of colonial society against royal officialdom. This was, indeed, an interesting development, since in Spain itself the institution had weakened even further with the advent of the Bourbons.[65] Because of these social changes in the Spanish American *cabildo*, the creole element had a bureaucratic hegemony on the eve of independence of Spanish America. It is a fact, not always stressed, that after the middle of the eighteenth century the creole element no longer merely sought preference, but tried to exclude European Spaniards in the filling of government positions. This local exclusion coincided with the policy in Madrid of limiting important positions overseas to Peninsular officials.[66] These factors partially explain the revival of the *cabildo* on the eve of independence.[67] It was with this renewed vigor that in the period of 1808–10 the *cabildos* started the independence movement (except for the strongholds of New Spain and Peru), and it was through them that the evolution from Crown lands to independent republics took place.

An interesting case of the *cabildo*'s renewed strength in the eighteenth century occurred during the British occupation of Havana (August 1762–July 1763). The Cuban capital surrendered to Sir George Keppel, Count of Albemarle, on August 14, 1762, and though the *cabildo* did not meet during the long siege, it was convened by the Spanish governor, José de Prado Portocarrero, on the day of the surrender, to acknowledge the terms. The *cabildo* then received upon request from the departing Spanish governor a certification that it had loyally served the Crown and had done everything to defend the city. It was also the *cabildo* which officially notified Charles III of the city's fall to the enemy (August 25). The *cabildo*, though weak for a long time, suddenly revived in this crisis. Francisco Carrera y Justiz comments that the measures of the Havana *cabildo* for reorganizing the city showed "that the municipal government knew how to fulfill its functions since it assumed the representation of the people and outlined the proper conduct in the very moment of natural confusion."[68] The *cabildo* continued its work during the British occupation under the most acute awareness that it represented the collective political entity of the Cuban people, and Albemarle recognized it as the town's representative.

Just as the *cabildo* had been the responsible Cuban voice during the occupation, so it continued when the Spaniards returned with the governor, the Conde de Ricla. The day he took possession of the city (July 6, 1763) he appeared before the *cabildo* to express the gratitude of the king to the town council, and as customary, to swear before it that all laws, ordinances, *fueros*, and privileges would be faithfully observed.[69]

Initially, the *cabildo* in Spanish America was composed of the first settlers; it was later (April 21, 1554) expanded by Emperor Charles V. The size of the town determined the number of officials, who comprised essentially two groups: the *regidores* and the *alcaldes ordinarios* (mayor-justices). In the first ordinances of Emperor Charles V concerning municipal government, it is clearly stated that the *regidores* should be elected annually by the *vecinos* (citizens) of a town and could be re-elected only after a year had elapsed. The *alcaldes*, elected annually, dealt in matters of civil and criminal law, and were not legally permitted to serve as *regidores* at the same time, but this law was not always strictly followed. Appeals against the decisions of the *alcaldes* were made to the local governor and finally to the *audiencia* of the respective kingdom or province. Viceroys and governors were forbidden to interfere in the elections of the *alcaldes*, but even in the best of circumstances higher influences were sometimes used to effect the desired results in an election.

The *cabildo* was born by appointment, a right reserved to the king and delegated to prospective conquistadors and colonizers and later given to the Council of the Indies and incorporated in the *Recopilación de leyes de las Indias* in Book IV, Title 8, Law 6. The *cabildo* developed by election, not popular election but succession, and therefore, should not be compared with modern democratic institutions. In the *cabildo* only between twelve and twenty were actually eligible to vote, and, hence, the *cabildo*, in its composition and in its intention to follow the medieval *bonum commune* without any recognition of estates or social classes, could be considered popular; yet its origin and its actions were more aristocratic: the rule of the few, chosen by the few.[70]

It should be borne in mind that the *cabildo*, like the *audiencia*, underwent a vast metamorphosis when it was transplanted to the Indies. On American soil the town council had more rights and powers than the Castilian *cabildo* ever had. The Spanish American *cabildo* could elect its own magistrates and members of the town council, send delegates to court for presentation of grievances, and hold procuratorial assemblies in the various regions.[71] It also represented the highest authority whenever there was no king's representative, and if a local governor died without delegate, it assumed responsibility for the administration of the entire region until the viceroy appointed a permanent successor. A decree of 1560 in favor of cities in Venezuela was interpreted to mean that they could govern themselves as city states in the event of the death of a governor.[72] The examples of the way in which Cortés in New Spain and Domingo Martínez de Irala in Paraguay gained legal recognition through the *cabildos* of their respective authority are well known, as are similar cases in Tunja and Santa Fe de Bogotá;[73] likewise the famous case of the *cabildo* of Darién which would not recognize the authority of Martín Fernández de Enciso and appointed Vasco Núñez de Balboa as governor. Or, similarly, at the time of the revolt in Paraguay (1725-35), when the *comuneros* not only dominated the cities and the province but adopted republican forms, the *cabildo* of the provincial capital arrogated to itself the authority for the entire province,[74] thereby foreshadowing the events of 1808-10.

It was the rule that the governor be invested with his position by the king; even so, there were certain legal procedures which linked him to the *cabildo*. As the representative of the monarch in Spanish America, the governor was responsible for the Crown's duties toward the people. Just as the king had to take an oath before the *Cortes* that he would comply with all divine and human laws before he could receive the *plenitudo potestatis* from the people, so likewise in Spanish America the governor had to take his oath before the *cabildo*. In Chile, the case of Valdivia is famous:[75] Valdivia had to promise by oath before the *cabildo* to be loyal to the king, to maintain peace and justice in his name, and to safeguard the town's liberties and privileges—a procedure symbolizing the medieval pact between the king and the community, which all governors who followed Valdivia were to carry out in like manner.[76] Or, in Puerto Rico, there is the case of Governor Antonio de Mosquera, who, after arrival on the island, proceeded in December of 1596 with the traditional custom of giving his oath to the *cabildo* of San Juan, a practice to which other governors adhered, both before and after him.[77]

The *cabildos* were responsible for those matters which usually fell under the jurisdiction of municipal government, but the Spanish American town councils, which dealt with enlarged towns and cities and hence had all the characteristics of small states, had much greater and broader powers: distributing lands, collecting taxes, controlling local police and militia, issuing building permits, maintaining roads, inspecting prices, and regulating holidays and processions.

It was the exclusive right of the *Cortes* to levy taxes in Hispanic medieval times, but in Spanish America—where the *Cortes* were never established—this responsibility was assumed by the *cabildo*, since the right belonged to the community. When the taxes were of a traditional nature, the consent of the governed was taken for granted, since—as with the famous *alcabala* granted by the *Cortes* of Burgos of 1342—it was presumed that the old Castilian law was applicable to the Indies.[78] A case in point were the rebellions in Tunja in 1592, when the *cabildo* rejected the *alcabala*, and in 1641, when it refused to accept new taxes for the establishment of a special navy, the *armada de barlovento*, to increase security in the Caribbean; and of Vélez, in 1740, again in view of the imposition of taxes without the consent of its *cabildo*.[79]

Certain meetings of the town council which dealt with such grave matters as the defense of the city and of the area in time of war were called *cabildo abierto*. The open *cabildo* was simply an enlarged *cabildo* with the most prominent citizens participating in the meeting and having the right to speak and to vote, although the regular *cabildo* was not forced to follow their resolutions. The open *cabildo* was thus more of a consultative body; it was convoked on the initiative of the governor, but the regular *cabildo* could well request the governor for such a meeting.

Even the Indians were affected by the institution of the *cabildo*. A *cédula* of 1549 established judges, *regidores*, and *alguaciles* (law enforcement officers)[80] in Indian towns, with the express order to run their affairs according to local traditions. Some cities, like Mexico, Cuzco, and Potosí, which contained large numbers of Indians, were run by Spaniards; but districts with a predominantly Indian population were in turn governed by Indian mayors. In the case of Mexico, more *regidores* were added to the city council so that the natives might be represented. There were also Indian towns, such as Tlaxcala, Cholula, and Tzintzuntzán in New Spain, which had Indian *cabildos* with their *alcaldes*, *regidores*, *escribanos* (secretaries),[81] and *alguaciles*. As in the Spanish *cabildo*, elections were determined not by popular vote, but by those who succeeded to a given town position; later, positions were also offered for sale. These Indian *cabildos*, experimental and not always successful, were nevertheless a step toward full integration of the Indian into Spanish-Christian life.[82]

The Spanish American *cabildo*—in reality, the government of a vast area based on a given administrative center and speaking as the local or provincial voice screening royal policies—represented real, small republics whose existence across the continent made up the Spanish Empire in America. This Spanish Empire in America was actually built on the federative basis of its many towns and provinces. With the Spanish American Revolution this concept will officially come to the fore when Francisco de Miranda calls for the implementation of a federation of all Spanish American *cabildos* headed by an Inca—in reality what had existed in the previous centuries with the metaphysical link to the Spanish Crown.

NOTES

[1] The fact that the cities were so intimately related to the Crown, since both needed each other against the nobility, explains their early (thirteenth century) representation in the *Cortes*. Logically, the cities' representation was stronger in Aragon than in Castile. For a comparison with the policy of the French kings after Louis VII, see Pirenne, p. 490.

[2] Merriman, I 460–62. See also Jackson, pp. 81–154; Vicens Vives, pp. 40–95; Livermore, pp. 132–58, 162–203.

[3] The term Castile and Castilians must be understood here in the widest sense—i.e., including Castile proper or Old Castile, León, Asturias, Galicia, Navarre, Extremadura, Toledo (New Castile), Murcia, Seville, Córdoba, Jaén, and Granada, in contrast to the territories belonging to the Crown of Aragon. See Merriman, II 221.

[4] Levene, *Historia del derecho argentino*, II 26–29. Ravignani claims (*Historia constitucional*, I 15–16) that the Indies were considered by the Hapsburgs as "dominions of the Castilian kings"; yet, taking a different point of view, he states that under the Hapsburgs the Spanish American regions were not considered to be on the same level as the Spanish provinces, while under the Bourbons "the colonies were assimilated to the metropolis." See also Gómez Hoyos, I 189–92.

[5] Morse, p. 141.
[6] Merriman, II 222.
[7] Consejo de la Hispanidad, I 523.
[8] Ibid.
[9] Gómez Hoyos, I 191.
[10] Parry, p. 71.
[11] Ibid., p. 54. See also Merriman, III 627ff.
[12] Parry, pp. 71–72.
[13] Ibid., p. 74. See also Pfandl, *Cultura*, p. 65.
[14] Civil and judicial power was vested in councils, directly responsible to the king: Royal and Supreme Council of Castile, Supreme and Royal Council of Aragon, Supreme Council of Italy, Council of Flanders, Supreme and Royal Council of the Indies, Council of State, Royal Council of Finance, Council of the Chamber of Castile, Supreme Council of War, Royal Council of the Orders, and Supreme Council of the Holy Inquisition (ibid., p. 66).
[15] On the *Casa de Contratación* and the Council of the Indies, see Schäfer.
[16] Merriman, III 624–26.
[17] Morse, p. 141. Before the establishment of the Council of the Indies it was the Royal Council which became the central organ of government and the cornerstone for the administration in Spanish America. Established in a definite form by John I before he left for Portugal and implemented upon his return in 1385 by the *Cortes* of Valladolid, it was composed of twelve persons—four prelates, four nobles, and four representatives of the cities (Merriman, I 211, 213, 217).
[18] Ibid., III 620.   [19] Ibid., 621–22.

20 See Ots Capdequí, *El estado español*, pp. 67, 64–65. The captaincies general of Guatemala and Chile as well as the presidency (*audiencia*) of Quito were always referred to as *reinos* (kingdoms). See Humboldt, *Relation historique*, I 577n2.

21 A royal agreement meant that the *audiencia* was acting as a body, and as such could control the actions of the viceroys; see Ots Capdequí, *El estado español*, p. 64.

22 Merriman, III 645–48, 653.

23 Ibid., 640–44.

24 At the end of the eighteenth century there were twelve *audiencias*: Mexico, Guadalajara, Guatemala, Havana, Caracas, Santa Fe de Bogotá, Quito, Lima, Cuzco, Chuquisaca, Santiago de Chile, and Buenos Aires (see Humboldt, *Relation historique*, I 576–77n2).

25 Merriman, III 645.

26 The Spanish clergy acquired its great power during the Visigothic period, when the monarchy was converted from Arianism and Catholicism expanded. It was enhanced by the parallel growth of both monarchy and Church during the *Reconquista*, and reached its summit during the Hapsburg period, when the Church became the most solid support of the Crown (Pfandl, *Cultura*, p. 96).

27 Egaña, *La teoría*, pp. 291–92, 100; see also pp. 1–100.

28 Pfandl, *Cultura*, p. 98.

29 Merriman, III 654–55. See also Egaña, *La teoría*.

30 Merriman, II 231.

31 Humboldt, *Relation historique*, I 576n2.

32 Bayle, *La expansión misional*, p. 7.

33 Leonard, *Books of the Brave*, p. 214.

34 Morse, p. 144.

35 Leonard, *Books of the Brave*, pp. 81, 82.

36 Pfandl, *Cultura*, p. 82.

37 Leonard, *Books of the Brave*, pp. 84, 85, 88.

38 Ibid., p. 317.

39 This is specifically mentioned in Book II, Title 1, Law 4 of the *Recopilación de leyes de las Indias* of 1680 (Consejo de la Hispanidad, I 218).

40 Ots Capdequí, *El estado español*, pp. 12–15, especially p. 14. The meaning of this saying is derived from the authorization which the viceroys received from the Spanish monarchs to the effect that, when a royal decree did not suit the circumstance, the viceroys were entitled to modify or suspend it through the formula "Se acata, pero no se cumple" (Angulo y Pérez, p. 3). Regarding the application of laws, the *Recopilación de leyes de las Indias* stated in Book II, Title 1, Law 2 that in case of doubt the law of Castile in accordance with the Laws of Toro was applicable. The Laws of Toro (1505) established an order of preference of Castilian law in the following sequence: *Ordenamiento* of Alcalá de Henares, promulgated under Alfonso XI (1312–50), the *Fuero Municipal* of the respective town, the *Fuero Real* of Alfonso X (1252–84), and, in the final instance, the *Código de las siete partidas* (Consejo de la Hispanidad, I 218). See Ots Capdequí, *El estado español*, pp. 9–12; Merriman I 237–46.

41 Tejada, *El pensamiento*, pp. 45–46. The right of personal appeal to the king includes liberty of correspondence, sending of messages, liberty of movement, and possibility of appeals (see pp. 46–78).

42 P. 5.

43 See Merriman, I 184–97; Ravignani, *Historia constitucional*, I 46–48.

44 Blánquez Fraile, p. 108.

45 See Merriman, I 186–89.

46 Mariéjol, p. 287.

47 Ibid., pp. 288–89.

48 Ibid., p. 289; Moore, *Cabildo in Peru Under the Hapsburgs*, pp. 26–27.

49 Pfandl has pointed out (*Cultura*, p. 75) that the restriction of municipal freedoms and the absolutism which Emperor Charles V introduced and bequeathed to his successors were the causes of the succeeding decline.

50 Merriman, II 229. See also Ravignani, *Historia constitucional*, I 48.

51 Merriman, III 638.

52 Ibid., 666–67.

53 *Cabildo in Peru Under the Hapsburgs*, p. 31.

54 See Gómez Hoyos, II 366–92 for the historic origin of the *cabildo* and its actions on behalf of municipal freedoms and the interests of the people, and for the *cabildo* in New Granada. See Ravignani, *Historia constitucional*, I 48–51 for the *cabildo* in Argentina.

55 Ots Capdequí, *El estado español*, pp. 68–69.

[56] Moses, *Spanish Dependencies*, II 370.
[57] Jane, *Liberty and Despotism*, p. 57.
[58] Merriman, III 639.
[59] Lynch, "Intendants and Cabildos," 338, 340; see also his *Spanish Colonial Administration*, pp. 202, 205.
[60] Eyzaguirre, p. 31.
[61] See Moore, *Cabildo in Peru Under the Hapsburgs*, pp. 265–84; and his *Cabildo in Peru Under the Bourbons*.
[62] See Davies, *Spain in Decline*.
[63] Lynch, "Intendants and Cabildos," 343.
[64] Schoen, p. 187. Here, the author probably meant the extended city.
[65] Ibid., pp. 186–187. See also Moore, *Cabildo in Peru Under the Bourbons*.
[66] See Eyzaguirre, p. 57, for the case in Chile. See also Moore, *Cabildo in Peru Under the Bourbons*, pp. 130–95.
[67] See the statements of Víctor Andrés Belaúnde, Cristóbal L. Mendoza, and Julio Alemparte in Congreso Hispanoamericano de Historia, pp. 56–58, 60–61.
[68] II 161. See also Roig de Leuchsenring.
[69] It is true that after 1763, and for the next 35 years, the authority of the *cabildo* declined, but still in all-important questions it was consulted.
[70] Bayle, *Los cabildos seculares*, p. 102.
[71] Moore, *Cabildo in Peru Under the Hapsburgs*, p. 44.
[72] Haring, pp. 200–201.
[73] Tejada, p. 64.
[74] Madariaga, *El ocaso*, p. 256.
[75] See Alemparte, *El cabildo de Santiago*, pp. 39–41, as well as his *El cabildo en Chile*, pp. 53–61.
[76] Eyzaguirre, pp. 29–30.
[77] Brau, *Historia de Puerto Rico*, p. 107.
[78] Tejada, *El pensamiento*, p. 77.
[79] Gómez Hoyos, I 155–60.
[80] Bayle, *Los cabildos seculares*, p. 366.
[81] Ibid., pp. 367–68.
[82] Ibid., p. 377.

II

THE MEDIEVAL TRADITION IN THE SPANISH WORLD, 1492–1700

1. MEDIEVAL AND RENAISSANCE THOUGHT IN THE SIXTEENTH CENTURY

THE SPANISH DISCOVERY AND CONQUEST of the Indies was carried out at a time when the Peninsula was still in the Middle Ages. Not only was the Spanish venture into the Americas the continuation of the *Reconquista*, it was accomplished in the spirit of a true crusade.[1] The idea of holy war meant,

> for every Spanish king, the duty of defending and propagating the faith—which was also the chief means of acquiring new territory, power and fame. Ferdinand, as Gracián (d. 1658) declared, "joined Heaven and earth" by combining the two objectives, the religious and the political—to his own immense profit.[2]

In 1509 Francisco Cardinal Jiménez de Cisneros took Oran in his campaign against the Turks, thus beginning Ferdinand's African policy later continued by Emperor Charles V. Ferdinand's ultimate goal (summarized in 1516 by his secretary of state, Pedro de Quintana, and reaffirmed by the Emperor in 1528 in Madrid in a speech drafted by Friar Antonio de Guevara) was a general Christian peace in Europe and a crusade against the Moslems; he wished to transmit to Europe the sense of Christian crusade which had been the life and breath of Spain for centuries, but would not aspire to the mastery of the entire world.[3]

The sixteenth-century Spanish idea of the state was still medieval, containing only in embryo the possibility of the "statist" state of seventeenth-century mercantilism, the bourgeois free enterprise state, or the nineteenth-century "imperialist" state.[4] The medieval character was perhaps best symbolized by the papal donation—the four papal bulls of the year 1493 (*Inter caetera* and *Eximiae*)—by which Pope Alexander VI, acting as *Dominus orbis* in keeping with the Gregorian doctrine, established the legal foundation for an ecclesiastical grant to the Spanish Crown, i.e., giving a legal sanction to a political claim; he did not divide the world between the Spaniards and the Portuguese as is generally maintained.[5]

Spain and Portugal were the first countries to establish empires of worldwide dimension, and in so doing they united distant lands on many continents under a single sovereignty. The Spanish Empire, which was formed in the course of the sixteenth century, represented

> one of the greatest political creations of European humanity, which projected to a high degree Europe's cultural mission in the world. Moreover, not only was this Empire a singular and limited fact, but the forces which created it and the way of life which it gave to the new world still persist after its fall in the states and peoples of Hispanic America.[6]

The spirit which animated the Spanish venture—the Christian struggle for an ideal and for a better and loftier world—and made it so successful that it carried the Spaniards from victory to victory and united a great variety of peoples of different races and languages within an immense universal Catholic monarchy was centered in God and is best symbolized in the saying: "One God, one Faith, one Empire."[7]

No empire in modern times has been built upon such solid and extensive theological and philosophical foundations as the one which the Spanish conquistadors carved out in the sixteenth century. For reasons deeply rooted in Spain's past and especially in the *Reconquista*, Spanish thought of the sixteenth century had a strongly medieval and legalistic tinge. No other country in Europe had such a robust and vital Scholastic basis, which served both as a philosophical system and as a means for the solution of public and private problems.[8] The need to make royal and civil actions conform to the natural law explains the great official concern with the ethical foundation of Spain's policy in the Indies.

Scholasticism furnished the key, not only in the period of the Catholic rulers and the Hapsburg dynasty, but well into the eighteenth century, and to a large extent was still a vivid reality at the time of the Spanish American Revolution. In its older forms Scholasticism is highly important because at the time of the Spanish discovery, conquest, and early colonization of the Indies the theories which were applied were chiefly those of the Hispanic fifteenth century. Not until the sixteenth century were other influences felt, which resulted in a fusion known as Late Scholasticism.

In the fifteenth century, Spain followed the pattern of contemporary Europe: classicism and Christianity were the basic traditions, and Aristotle and St. Augustine headed the list of authors. Almost all foreign political treatises in one way or another influenced Hispanic political theory, but of the medieval writers by far the greatest influence was exerted by St. Thomas, Marsilius of Padua, William of Auvergne, Hugh of St. Victor, John of Salisbury, and in particular by Giles of Rome. Some of the great Spanish figures in political theory before the *Conquista* were Pedro Campostelano, Pedro Gallego, Domingo Gundisalvo, Juan Hispano, Pedro Hispano (Pope John XXI), Ramón Lull, Guido de Terrena, Nicolás Eymerich, Alvaro Pelayo, Francisco de Exímenis, Jaime Caillís, Pedro Juan Belluga, Sánchez de Arévalo, and Juan Cardinal de Torquemada, to name only a few.[9]

In Scholasticism the basis of political thought is to be sought in the nature and source of law, since in medieval times the state was seen primarily in terms of law. Scholasticism based itself on the Christian natural law, the origin of which is to be found in antiquity and in the Greek and Roman Stoics —Zeno, Cicero, and Seneca—in particular. Christianity molded this natural law into a Christian law of nature, which attained remarkable intellectual heights in St. Thomas.

According to the medieval version of the natural law, God rules the world through His divine reason, and "all true laws are manifestations of the essential principle of things, existing from eternity in God as divine reason, and employed through his will and providence as a 'rule or measure' for the governance of all his creatures."[10] Natural law is the participation of a rational creature in the eternal law.[11] Since man is made in the image of God, he is subject to this law, not under blind compulsion but as a free agent. Man, then, shall act in accordance with his rational nature. Reason was the first rule for judging the ethical content of an act; hence, the highest norm of natural law is *to do good and to avoid evil.*[12]

It was logically deduced from this premiss that positive law—i.e., the law made by man—must conform to the precepts of natural law as the projection of eternal law. The existence and universal acceptance of natural law did not mean that the positive law now became superfluous, but that positive law had to follow natural law and could not contradict it. This meant in essence that an unjust and immoral law—the *ius naturale prohibitivum* or *negativum*—was not to be obeyed. On the other hand, the subject had to obey the positive law even though unjust if his resistance to it would cause even greater harm (the *ius naturale affirmativum*).[13]

But natural law can remain the yardstick of positive law only if it is connected with the doctrine of the immutability of natural law and of the continuing essence of man, and to the preference of reason to will in God and in man.[14] Just as medieval political thought in general and St. Thomas in particular held to this doctrine, so also Francisco Suárez and the Spanish Late Scholastics believed that the natural law was absolutely immutable in its fundamental principles. Hence, on the basis of this intellectual premiss, the political ideal of medieval Scholasticism—especially in St. Thomas—was a monarchy founded on natural law as the mirror of eternal law and thus subject to duties and limitations, and created by the people for the common utility of all and for the purpose of securing peace. It was a concept which was not very different from that of Isidore of Seville in the sixth and seventh century.

Just as in other parts of Europe, fifteenth-century political thought in Spain concerning kingship can be summarized as follows:

1. Power *in abstracto* is derived from God.
2. Power *in concreto* must be exercised with the consent of the people, through various theories regarding the divine origin of political authority (*translatio, designatio*).[15]
3. The king holds an office whose end is the *bonum commune*—the welfare of all members of the community for which he is responsible to God.
4. The king must rule in justice and in harmony with the laws and customs of the country.
5. The king must have a council in which the three estates (nobility, clergy, commoners) are represented.[16]

Spanish colonial practice reflects this political theory faithfully in every aspect of civil and ecclesiastical government, but especially in the establishment of the *cabildo*. In keeping with the transfer of traditional medieval political institutions to the new lands, several definite interpretations were given to such subjects as the council, the tyrant, the doctrine of resistance, and the *fueros* of the people, which clearly reflect the character prevalent in the Peninsula.

The obligation to take cognizance of the opinions of the ruled[17] is as evident in the Indies as it was in the Peninsula in the theory of the *consejo*. The theory of the tyrant was similarly important, since it made a clear distinction between lawful and unlawful authority. In Spanish medieval political theory tyrants were those who attempted to rule without legal title, the *tyrannus ab origine* (for instance, revolting against the king), and those who abused authority legally granted to them, the *tyrannus a regimine*.[18]

It should be emphasized that the political ideology of the conquistadors was more in keeping with the high period of Castilian political theory than with the later currents of the Spanish Renaissance—i.e., the traditional Castilian concepts of kingship, its free *consejos* and *Cortes*—to such a degree that, as Francisco Elías de Tejada has shown in the case of New Granada,[19] attempts were made to call *consejos* or *Cortes* in times of emergency. The fact that they were not called, however, also shows the impact of the Renaissance projected from the Peninsula.

With the sixteenth century new influences made themselves felt. The spirit of the Renaissance and of humanism crossed the Pyrenees, but neither had as strong an impact there as in other parts of Europe, though their influence was greater than is commonly believed.[20] In the great struggle of sixteenth-century Europe, Spain continued its medieval traditions, but was by no means opposed to those modern currents which were incorporated through the reforms of Cardinal Cisneros and the newly established University of Alcalá (1498/1508); these reforms represented a link to the influence of Erasmus of Rotterdam and the Spanish humanist Juan Luis Vives (1492–1540).[21] Thus the Renaissance in Spain (and Portugal) was a Christian Renaissance from all points of view.[22]

The fusion of Scholasticism and humanism found its greatest expression in Emperor Charles V, in the sense that elements of Dante and Erasmus—the ideas of the universal monarchy and of a unified and triumphant Christianity—were combined with the Hispanic concept of a Christian empire based not on conquest but on a high moral duty among Christian princes, as Ruiz de la Mota expounded to his imperial master.[23] Bishop Mota stated his providential doctrine at the *Cortes* of León and Castile in 1520 when he visualized the Emperor as waging a holy war against the enemies of the faith and stated that "'the Empire of the world cannot be obtained by counsel, industry, or human diligence. Only God is the one who gives it and can give it . . . .' It was a language which was perfectly understood by his Castilian subjects."[24]

The European, African, and American policies of Charles V bear the mark of Dante's universalist influence,[25] which the Emperor received from Mercurino Arborio di Gattinara, along with certain humanistic aspects, some of which originated in his native Flanders. Gattinara, inspired by Dante's *De monarchia*, hoped to establish a universal Christian empire, and, as a humanist and man of learning, was imbued with the idea of world empire: "for a dozen years he preached his doctrine to Charles and guided his steps, as far as he could, to the realization of his bold dreams"[26]—a doctrine symbolized by the verses of Pedro Barrante Maldonado "cuanto más lejos más fe," and Hernando de Acuña's "One king, one empire, and a single sword."[27]

Because Erasmus was not the prophet of a Renaissance which would make man divine, promising superhuman triumphs to his intellect and energy, his influence in Spain reached in particular an elite of humanistic priests.[28]

> The Erasmian reform had derived its power and life from its opposition to Protestantism's intransigeance and its struggle to prevent a schism, as well as from its effort to set limits to Catholic intransigeance by offering a double reform: of the Church as an institution and of the Church's faith, which had strayed too far from the teachings of its Founder.[29]

Erasmianism was simply a rationalistic piety but not a movement looking forward to eighteenth-century-style free thought.[30]

Yet the ideas contained in the writings of Erasmus were, obviously, not unknown in the Peninsula, since they can be found in the *Siete Partidas* of Alfonso the Learned, in the chapter dealing with the duties of the ruler toward his subjects. It is known that Alfonso X had also been thinking of an empire with a spiritual origin which would be realized historically,[31] which explains this ready acceptance of Erasmus' thinking, and points to a typically Spanish tendency to recognize a certain parallelism between a contemporary ideological movement and similar though older roots of traditional conception. This trend repeated itself during the Spanish American Revolution when revolutionaries, such as Mariano Moreno or Antonio Nariño, upheld concepts of popular sovereignty which were at once deeply rooted in the Spanish past and at the same time appeared rather modern on the surface. Perhaps the boldest expression of Spanish Erasmianism in its religious, moral, and political aspects was the interpretation which Alfonso de Valdés, Emperor Charles V's Latin secretary, gave to the Sack of Rome—"the judgment of an offended and angry God."[32]

An understanding of the currents of religious liberty in the Spain of Emperor Charles V cannot be grasped without a knowledge of the Erasmian influence there between 1522 and 1533.[33] While the Sorbonne censored and prohibited all Erasmian works, in Spain there was an intellectual elite which not only admired them, but actually helped them to reach large audiences. No country showed more tolerance and a greater spirit of Christian liberty than the Spain of the first half of the sixteenth century.

The sixteenth century marked an impressive development in the field of theology, and the new spirit radiated in particular from Salamanca where Francisco de Vitoria (1480–1546), following the model of the University of Paris, reorganized the study of philosophy by replacing Occam's Nominalism with Thomism. The Spanish Renaissance as it developed in the sixteenth century was essentially the work of Dominicans and Jesuits: it was linked first to such Dominicans as Vitoria, Domingo de Soto (1494–1560), Melchor Cano (1509–60), and Domingo Báñez (1528–1604), and then to the Jesuits, especially Francisco Suárez (1548–1617), Luis de Molina (1535–1600) and Juan de Mariana (1535–1624). In the sixteenth century the Dominicans were the great champions throughout Europe both of missionary enterprise and of Scholastic thought, and in spite of differences among them, steadily held to the principles of individual liberty and free conversion, for which position they also received support from other circles.[34] Dominicans and Jesuits, alike, together with other Spanish and Portuguese theologians, felt the need to repeat in the sixteenth century what St. Thomas had done in the thirteenth, "bringing factual knowledge and theological belief once more into harmony."[35] Thus

> Spanish theologians—Cano, Soto, Suárez—understood the great task of bringing Scholastic philosophy up to date, a task they performed so successfully that their writings have in our own time become the object of a renewed interest, as they were an important object of interest to Spinoza and to Leibniz.[36]

The Spanish Renaissance thus continued the great traditions of the Middle Ages without compromising basic principles, and upheld the Christian natural law of earlier periods which remained the basic yardstick well into the eighteenth century.³⁷ The following statement by St. Ignatius Loyola was regarded as an axiom, one to which Spanish culture clung with tenacity and stubbornness:

> Man is created to praise, revere, and serve God our Lord and by this means to save his soul; and all the other things on the face of the earth are created for man, to help him achieve the purpose for which he is created.³⁸

Thus skepticism had no place in the *siglo de oro*, and those philosophers who were not totally orthodox, such as Vives, Pedro de Valencia, and Francisco Sánchez, were still eminently Catholic.³⁹

The Spanish Renaissance found expression in the work of Fernando de Córdoba, Antonio de Nebrija, Marineo Sículo, and Pedro Mártir; in Greek and Latin studies (Fernández de Heredia, Arias Barbosa, Hernán Núñez, Juan Ginés de Sepúlveda, Gonzalo Pérez; Vives and Hernán Pérez de Oliva); and in Hebrew studies and archaeology. The study of ancient writings represented the ideal life preparation for the man of distinction whether he chose a career for personal interests or of service to the Church or Crown (*mar, Iglesia o Casa real*).⁴⁰ The Spanish sixteenth century produced soldier-priests, some of them of the very highest order, all of them steeped in the poetic lore of the classical world and guided in their self-expression by a classical sense of form. Thus, Spain expressed in the sixteenth century religious, cultural, and intellectual expansion which went parallel to her extraordinary exploits in exploration and colonization.⁴¹

Spain in its medieval choice during the European division of the sixteenth century initiated its own Reformation, which had begun with the establishment of the Inquisition in the fifteenth century, continued with the reforms of Cardinal Cisneros, and extended without interruption throughout the century—an indication that religious revival was no idle dream and that the Spaniard kept his preference for religious and orthodox Catholic values. Friar Alonso de Madrid, with his *Arte para servir a Dios* (1521, 1526), is an excellent example:

> diametrically opposed to Luther in his insistence on free will; deeply imbued with the doctrines of traditional philosophy and theology; . . . [he] gave an effective and personally conceived summary of traditionalist doctrine: the Gospels, the Fathers, Thomas Aquinas, Cajetan, Dionysius the Areopagite, Gregory of Nyssa, Gregory the Great . . . .⁴²

For the ordinary Spaniard, who was neither theologian nor philosopher, there was an unquestioned and blind acceptance of dogma, not because of any intellectual conviction, but simply because the Church declared it, and his parents and elders before him had accepted it. Morality may often have been lax, but the belief in rewards and punishments in the other world remained firm.⁴³ Religion was not only a matter of daily practice or of religious practice during holy days, but the essential ingredient of the inner life of the Spanish people. This is why, in addition to the extraordinary number of religious orders, there existed vast organizations of *cofradías*—a kind of sixteenth- and seventeenth-century version of today's *Opus Dei*—and *disciplinantes*—an adaptation to ordinary life of the disciplinary life which had been practiced in monasteries since the eleventh century.⁴⁴

This intense interest in religion explains the growth and fervor of the cults of the saints, especially of St. James, Teresa, and Isidore; yet none reached the heights of the cult of the Virgin, which arose in the Middle Ages on a predominantly regional basis and would flourish in a similar manner in the Indies. Closely linked to these cults was a faith in miracles and legends which increased in Spain while similar beliefs were undergoing a crisis in the rest of Europe. This faith was expanded to include historic, popular, and patriotic legends, and from this apparently unending fountain of tradition, legends, and popular poetry, Spanish art nourished itself to extraordinary heights in the fields of drama and novels.[45]

The great outburst of mysticism in Spanish culture in the sixteenth century was accompanied by an interest in asceticism, and together they represented the apex of Spanish spirituality. Both had their roots in special circumstances during the period of Philip II: the tendency to an interior renewal, the latent spirit of the Council of Trent, and Counter Reformation zeal. The best illustrations of this spirit were St. Ignatius Loyola for asceticism; Friar Luis de Granada and Friar Luis de León for ascetic mysticism; and St. John of the Cross and St. Teresa de Jesús for the highest form of mysticism.[46] The mystic spirit which they symbolized will have an important influence on Friar Alonso de la Vera Cruz and Sister Juana Inés de la Cruz in New Spain.

Currents of asceticism and mysticism kept alive the enthusiasm for the struggle against heretics, strengthened the institution of the Holy Office, and inspired Spanish painting and psychology.[47] Still, in spite of the fact that Spain—that country of contrasts—produced the great ascetics and mystics, its was, by no means, a people of ascetics and mystics.[48]

Religious life thus had its greatest period in the second half of the sixteenth century at the time of Spain's most extensive political, social, and economic expansion, when the Spanish nation, founded by Ferdinand and Isabella and consolidated by Emperor Charles V, reached its greatest magnificence under Philip II. During his reign Catholicism was nationalized and politics used as a defensive element of religion for the attainment of an unreal idealism.[49]

> [Philip's] unshaken seriousness, his balanced stoicism, his profound piety, his marked inclination to mystic life, his ideal of conquest and crusade, his wishes for Catholic unity, are qualities which pertain to the pure, specifically Spanish, patrimony, and which brought him closer than any other Hapsburg king to the heart of the Spaniards.[50]

The best symbol for the period, for the Spain of the second half of the sixteenth century, remains the Escorial: "the glorious formula of its character, of its spiritual and dominating greatness, of its noble and severe religiosity, of its literature and arts."[51] And although customs declined in the next century at the time when the *Don Quixote* and the picaresque novels appeared, clearly showing the symptoms of decay,[52] religion kept its strength undisturbed.

Spanish philosophy developing in the sixteenth and seventeenth centuries as Late Scholasticism was obviously not monolithic, though traditional elements predominated. In addition to the Spanish School proper (Suárez, Soto, Covarrubias, Vitoria), Late Scholasticism covered a variety of currents, such as: the Thomism of the Dominicans; the Scotism of Cardinal Cisneros and the Franciscans; Nominalism, which to some extent had influenced Vitoria in Paris;

the humanism of Hernando Alonso de Herrera, whose *Brief Dispute* . . . *Against Aristotle and His Followers* appeared in 1517; the Syncretism of Juan de Lucena, Luis de Granada, Francisco Sánchez de las Brozas, and Francisco de Quevedo, which combined elements of Aristotelianism, Platonism, Neoplatonism, Stoicism, and Christianity; and the Augustinianism of Gonzalo Jiménez de Quesada, Cervantes, and Quevedo. The same two centuries also witnessed in the Peninsula such currents as: the skepticism of Francisco Sánchez de las Brozas, Juan Luis Vives, Francisco Valdés, Pedro de Valencia, and Quevedo; the pantheism of Miguel Servet; the Platonism of Pedro Núñez, Sebastián Fox Morcillo, León Hebreo, Huarte de San Juan, Bernardino de Rebolledo, Friar Juan de Pineda, and Juan Eusebio Nieremberg; and the stoicism of Garcilaso de la Vega, Luis de Granada, Luis de León, Quevedo, Baltasar Gracián, Jerónimo de la Cruz, and Antonio Núñez de Castro.[53]

Yet the Aristotelian tradition remained so strong that it was confirmed at the Council of Trent and has lasted until the present. The philosophical system survived as well all the attacks of the anti-Aristotelianism of the Renaissance. Indeed, in some ways the tradition of Aristotelianism increased rather than declined in this period.[54]

Spain became the leading power in the sixteenth century, and its political and military strength kept pace with its cultural and ethical development. It led Europe "not only in the practice of law and government, but also in the abstract field of jurisprudence."[55] Building on the political thought of the European Middle Ages, but going beyond its more narrow concept, Spanish jurists evolved theories which were, in effect, those "of a constitutional State,"[56] in spite of the fact that the Spanish Empire tended already in the sixteenth century toward more absolutism. All the great names of the Spanish School of the sixteenth century—men like Suárez, Vitoria, Soto, Molina, Mariana—not only denied absolute powers to the king, but also refuted papal claims to dispose of the temporal possessions of infidels.[57]

> Sixteenth-century Spain then remained essentially medieval, and saw a great Thomist revival; its scholasticism was humanized by the literary bent of the Renaissance and directed by nominalist influences to apply morality to political problems. The theory taught in the universities of the Peninsula was that of a Christian state: no longer the old imperial dualism, but an adaptation to fit the realities of the nation-state.[58]

The summit of Late Scholasticism was reached with Francisco Suárez whose political thought was of particular import for Spanish American independence since justification for the start of the revolution was based on his contract theory.[59] He gave to the new Scholasticism "a renewed vitalistic and dynamic character, mitigating its tendency to become extreme in its intellectualism."[60] Suárez successfully re-established in the sixteenth century the Thomistic ideal of the thirteenth[61] by reformulating the philosophic problems of the past in a "very modern search for a metaphysics that would be epistemologically autonomous."[62] Furthermore, the importance of Suárez for Spanish American political theory depended not so much on whether he provided a Spanish pre-Enlightenment precedent for contract theory and popular sovereignty but rather on the fact that his fresh marshalling of scholastic doctrines, under powerful influences of time and place, encapsulated certain assumptions about political man and certain political dilemmas that pervade Hispanic political life to this day,[63] such as: (*a*) natural law is clearly distinguished from conscience; (*b*) sovereign power originates with the collectivity of men; (*c*) the people alienate, not delegate, sovereignty to their prince; (*d*) in certain cases the law of the prince loses its force; and (*e*) the prince is bound by his own law.[64] The doctrine of Suárez "won increasing attention in New Spain during the seventeenth century," and "the evidence . . . suggest[s] . . . that his writings are symptomatic of a post-medieval Hispano-Catholic view of man, society, and government which is by no means superseded in modern Spanish America."[65]

Suárez followed Robert Cardinal Bellarmine's theory of the indirect power of the Church in temporal matters—a theory which had already been suggested by Juan de Torquemada, and which John Maior used as the basis of his theory of conquest and Vitoria elaborated into a juridical system[66]—and thus adjusted the Scholastic theories of St. Thomas to the new reality which arose with the coming of the national state, the Renaissance, the Reformation, and the natural sciences. While the papacy was thought of as a universal and divine institution (St. Thomas' view), the state—though a moral organism—was considered to be only a human institution, national and particular. Suárez pointed out that the type of government heading the state was of little importance, since all political power was derived from the community, to which it was responsible.

The intent of his theory was to combat the contemporary political theories of Machiavelli and his followers by emphasizing the natural law, and to exalt the spiritual power of the pope—which had lessened as a result of the conciliar movement and the rise of national states—against the human and secular power of the kings. He also emphasized the rights of the people against the absolutism of the monarchy and particularly the divine-right theories of James I of England.

Suárez took over from the earlier Scholastics the concept that the principle of authority is derived from God because of the social nature of man,[67] whose will originates the social compact and in turn decides who is to exercise civil authority. He pointed out that to establish a civil authority which has full legality, the free consent of the governed must be obtained. In order for the inorganic, individual wills to constitute a political *civitas* which gives them an organic character, there must be free consent of the components. It is the *pactum* which establishes this unity. This social contract, whether tacit or expressed, precedes the political *pactum*. Hence, for Suárez, no civil authority can come into existence without the consent of the people, expressed in the social contract.

The alleged similarity between Suárez and Rousseau (as maintained by Otto von Gierke) is an important element which should be clarified, in spite of the fact that Heinrich Rommen has already disproved the theory.[68] First of all, the difference lies in the whole finality of Suárez' compact in its metaphysical condition. This pact is impossible if it is not molded by natural law, the reflection of eternal law in man, and oriented toward a definite end, the *bonum commune*. Furthermore, from a purely formal perspective the two social compacts have nothing in common: the Rousseauan compact is a formal union, that of

Suárez is not. In other words, the movement toward union, from the families —not isolated individuals—toward the *polis*, can be accomplished expressly or tacitly. Juan Salaberry has demonstrated the difference between the political ideas of Suárez and of Rousseau; this is of the utmost importance for the study of the movement for independence which began in Spanish America in 1808–10.

1. The authority or sovereignty of the people, according to Suárez, can and ought to be transferable and to be exercised by someone else. According to Rousseau, it is not transferable and can be represented only by itself.
2. According to Suárez, sovereignty is the attribute only of the whole perfect community, not of every individual. According to Rousseau, sovereignty is of all and everybody.
3. According to Suárez, man as such is civilized and social; from his culture and society the need to unite derives; once this union is made into a political bond, then *ipso facto* the supreme authority in the community is born, something which emanates naturally, and is the result whether the men who united in a perfect society wish it or not. According to Rousseau, man is naturally savage, and authority is only the effect of an entirely artificial pact, not an emanation from nature.
4. According to Suárez, God gives supreme authority directly to the perfect community by the mere fact that it was established by the union of wills, just as he creates the soul by itself since the germinal matter is prepared without the necessity of a new interpretation of human will. According to Rousseau, authority is the simple sum of wills taken materially.
5. According to Suárez, the community does not always deprive itself of all its authority, but ordinarily transmits it to the prince in a limited way. According to Rousseau, the individuals lose all their natural liberty and acquire civil and political liberty so that the sum of wills converts itself into the source and origin of all rights without any limitations.[69]

According to Suárez, the state is set up with the social contract; it is not simply a plurality of individuals and families, in an amorphous, atomistic, individualistic, and mechanical way, but an organic union brought about free upon mutual consent for the realization of the *bonum commune*. The result is a united *corpus politicum mysticum*.

Great confusion has resulted from Suárez' theory of the social contract and his assertion that the natural form of government is pure democracy. However, this assertion referred only to the abstract, since through the principle of *translatio*—not *designatio*—the social contract gave him the means of constructing a theory of government which could successfully oppose absolutism[70] and a political doctrine which allowed civil authority to rest in the hands of one, a few, or many under the following principles: (*a*) the fundamental equality of all men vis-à-vis the holder or holders of power in the state, (*b*) the lack of any special divine intervention at the transfer of authority to the person upon whom it is conferred, and (*c*) the necessity of popular consent for such transfer through the social contract.[71] He based the establishment of the state on the equality and liberty of man to prove that it was the whole nation, the people only, from whom the state could be derived: *Potestas dominandi, seu regendi politica homines, nulli homini in particulari data est immediata a Deo.*[72]

It was clear to Suárez that, once a society has been established and an authority designated to govern it, the people who comprise that society abandoned a state of shapelessness to become what really deserved to be called a society. When such a society invested authority in a ruler, it expressed a collective will. The fact that some individual possessed certain qualities to rule did not mean that he had a right to this position; only the people can confer that right upon an individual. According to Suárez and other Late Scholastic thinkers, however, once civil authority is established it is no longer based on the people but located and represented in the person or persons designated to exercise power. In sum, the ruler is invested with the power given by God with the consent of the people through a true compact, and the people cannot throw off this power so long as this pact is not broken or dissolved.

While the people cannot act as it wishes once authority has been transferred to the ruler, they can do so when there is sufficient reason for such action—in the case of the *tyrannus a regimine*, for example—and they must act when the ruler disappears without any legitimate successor. When the ruler through the *translatio* theory receives the *potestas*, there actually exist two authorities, one in the king and another in the state (Martín de Azpilcueta's distinction regarding constituent and constituted sovereignty[73]), the latter being *impedita in actu*—i.e., it does not function while the king asserts the rights given by the people. But should royal power be abolished or left vacant, the nation can make free use of its rights and can resist the ruler if he governs contrary to the medieval concept of the *bonum commune*.[74] The powers of *translatio* are not absolute; they are valid only as long as the ruler governs rightly. Passive and even active resistance is lawful if the ruler turns toward tyranny; but under no circumstances are the people exempt from obedience to the ruler, once he has been invested with authority through *translatio* and so long as he adheres to the common ideal: the *summum bonum*.[75] This theory was taught in Spanish America from the sixteenth century, and became the lever with which the Spanish American Revolution began. It should also be borne in mind that Suárez' political theory contained traditional Spanish concepts deeply rooted in the medieval past: (*a*) monarchy and democracy (king and people); (*b*) popular origin of sovereignty; (*c*) resistance to tyranny; (*d*) limitations to royal power; (*e*) taxes only with consent of the people; (*f*) king subject to laws; (*g*) defense of municipal freedoms, as stated in this case by Mariana.[76]

This theory was first applied in Spanish America in the sixteenth century. After the death of Pedro de Valdivia, Chile's conquistador, the *cabildo* of Santiago decided that his authority reverted to the people because the holder of that *potestas* had disappeared; hence, the *cabildo*, as the expression of popular will, took back into its hands full political power for the whole of Chile. For a short time the *cabildo* designated Rodrigo de Quiroga as captain general and lord justice (*justicia mayor*), and submitted the designation to the town members for approval. The *cabildo* was faced with the rivalries of Francisco Aguirre and Francisco de Villagra for this same position; it tried to be impartial and, though it agreed to grant full authority to Villagra as captain general in order to quell an Indian revolt, it shrewdly did not issue a permanent appointment; thus, it avoided civil strife by retaining its authority until the new governor of Chile, García de Mendoza, arrived from Spain in 1557.[77]

With the publication in 1597 of the *Disputationes metaphysicae*, the reputation of Suárez spread to all corners of Europe, helped by the circulating of his works by his numerous Jesuit followers. Aristotelian and Thomistic metaphysics no longer seemed to provide a satisfactory answer in a nascent modern world; only in Suárez did metaphysics appear to be a discipline separating metaphysics from theology in an essentially modern manner—in spite of the fact that Suárez intended his metaphysics to be propaedeutic to theology.[78] For this reason, certain authors have argued that Suárez was in reality a modern thinker.[79] Suárez and the Spanish School of Salamanca, then, provided the metaphysical basis which was essential to the European thought of the scientific revolution and which was to lead "to Newton and to Darwin, to William James and to Einstein."[80] But Spain clung tenaciously to her Dominican–Jesuit tradition—i.e., a Christian Renaissance and a continuation of that same spirit in the seventeenth century while the rest of Europe abandoned the medieval tradition more and more.[81] For two centuries Europe learned metaphysics through Suárez, though not necessarily Suarezian metaphysics. In the early sixteenth century the Sorbonne was dominated by the Spanish spirit in the teaching of logic, and some three or four generations later Spanish theologians held positions in the faculties of the major European universities. The Protestant school of natural law (Grotius, Pufendorf, Thomasius, Althusius, Wolff) was directly inspired by Suárez and the Spanish School.[82] It seems that "seventeenth-century philosophy needed what Suárez offered."[83]

Even greater than the influence of the Spanish School in Europe was the impact of Late Scholasticism in Spanish America. Thus, the Spanish conquest of the Indies had immense repercussions in the field of political theory. It was felt in numerous subtle theological and philosophical disputations, all within the wider context of sixteenth-century Scholasticism, though they hid rather practical political issues affecting various groups and interests which had great stakes in royal decisions on Indian policy. Generally speaking there were three groups. The first was exemplified by Juan Ginés de Sepúlveda, of nationalist and imperialist leanings and stressing the Spanish civilizing mission, and by Francisco López de Gómera, the chaplain of Hernán Cortés, who hailed the epic ventures of his master in his *Historia general de las Indias* (1552) to such an extent that it provoked an answer by the old soldier Bernal Díaz del Castillo.[84] The second group was essentially dominated by the Dominicans and was headed by Bartolomé de Las Casas and Francisco de Vitoria, who defended the Indians and were opposed to their exploitation and enslavement. The third viewpoint represented the mystic interpretation of the Spanish conquest and was led by the Franciscan Friar Gerónimo de Mendieta. His writings reflected an impact of the Renaissance on Spanish thought of the sixteenth century: the ideal of constructing a perfect Christian society free from the apparent defects of earlier periods.[85] The formula of this group meant simply a return to the basic precepts of Christianity in its pure form, as it existed in the apostolic age. Many of the mendicant friars of the sixteenth century had a conscious apostolic idea of their own mission in the New World, and they looked back to the age of the original twelve apostles not only as a source of inspiration, but as the prototype of their own missionary labors. This formula explains much of the missionary activity—especially that of the mendicant period with the arrival of Peter of Ghent and the twelve Franciscan friars, who had earlier been engaged in the spread of the gospel of "primitive" Christianity in southern Spain[86]—and reflects an ideal similar to that motivating the utopian reformer and Christian mystic Vasco de Quiroga in New Spain.

The Spanish conquest of America opened an extraordinary debate on both sides of the Atlantic which lasted for more than fifty years and formed part of the Spanish political thought of the period. This famous controversy concerned the treatment of the Indians, the concept of a just war, and the titles for the *Conquista*. It was also in this context that Erasmus and St. Thomas More became influential in the Indies.

The treatment of the Indians was related to the question of unbelievers and to the general problem of slavery.[87] It led first to a discussion of the *repartimiento* and the *encomienda* (established by Columbus in 1499 in Española), to the first outcry against abuses by the conquerors,[88] and to the Laws of Burgos of 1512,[89] and was followed by an inquiry into the question of the just war and the titles for the *Conquista*.[90]

At first the title for the conquest was the papal donation, though as early as the Junta of Burgos in 1512 this was not considered to be a sufficient argument (Juan López de Palacios Rubios, Matías de Paz),[91] and, hence, led to the *requerimiento* (1513).[92] It was then that two main positions emerged. The absolutist, Romanist position, taken by Ferdinand, and seconded by bureaucrats and *encomenderos*, was later defended at the height of the great debate by Sepúlveda, humanist and friend of Erasmus; he used the medieval theories of an *Orbis Christianus*, which no longer served Western Christendom but did further the interests of the Spanish national state. The more liberal position, based on the Christian ideas of freedom, proclaimed by Isabella and defended by, among others, Las Casas and Vitoria, stressed the eternal principles of the Gospel and the Christian conscience.[93]

Las Casas and Sepúlveda represented two opposite, though complementary, trends in sixteenth-century Spanish thought: Sepúlveda was more nationalistic and feudal, and Las Casas more constitutional and ecclesiastical, but both were firmly rooted in the Middle Ages.[94] The key to the thought of Las Casas was his insistence on liberty, based on St. Thomas' definition of natural law; the free exercise of reason was a right in accordance with natural law and, hence, it belonged to infidels as well as to Christians.[95] In considering the nature of the lordship which the Castilian monarchs exercised in the Indies, Las Casas acknowledged only the rights of the monarchs, as subjects of the papal grant; the settlers had no rights except as agents of the Crown. His ideal of colonial government referred, not to natural superiority, but to kingship, which was based on the medieval idea of divine ordination, not on some kind of secular election: "the kingly rank was ordained by God for the sake of justice and was never the property of the man who held it . . . but an office, with high and difficult duties."[96] Following the old rule of St. Isidore—"he who abuses authority is unworthy to rule"—Las Casas maintained that the Crown had permitted Spanish vassals in the Indies to blemish the realm: the *encomienda* was contrary to reason, natural law, and the laws of Castile.[97]

The greatest opposition to the treatises of Las Casas—the *Very Brief Account of the Destruction of the Indies*, and the *Apologetic History*—came from New

Spain where Las Casas believed conditions to be less oppressive than in other parts of the Indies,[98] and where the Franciscan Toribio de Motolinía, in a letter from Mexico to Emperor Charles V, charged Las Casas with stirring up animosity and discontent.

Yet nowhere in the New World were the treatises of Las Casas more popular than in the Viceroyalty of Peru—to such an extent that the viceroy of Peru, Francisco de Toledo (1569-82), used the Inquisition against those ecclesiastics who had fallen under the spell of Las Casas. In his struggle against what he considered an extremely dangerous ecclesiastic, the viceroy urged the composition of treatises rejecting Las Casas' theories, began an investigation to prove that the Incas were tyrannical and unjust, and arranged for what he considered an accurate history of Peru: Pedro Sarmiento de Gamboa's histories, the *Crónica del Perú* (1550) and the *Señorío de los Incas*.

The *requerimiento* was valid until 1543 when it was replaced by an epistolary message to kings and princes whom the expeditionaries might meet.[99] It amounted to nothing less than the total displacement of the older theories of the papal donation, putting in their stead the ability to enter into a political pact (*pactum subjectionis*). Thus, in Yucatán, according to Las Casas, agreements were made in which some twelve or fifteen Indian lords submitted themselves by their "own free will to the kings of Castile, acknowledging the emperor as king of Castile, as the supreme and universal lord."[100]

This new doctrine did not end the controversy between the absolutist and liberal positions, however. Las Casas, the champion of the Indian cause, received significant intellectual help from Vitoria whose interest in the affairs of the Indies was highlighted at the time the great debate on the Indies reached its peak between 1530 and 1550. In 1539, when his lectures on the Indies were held, Vitoria elaborated the fundamental rights of all men and peoples,[101] criticized the Spanish conquest, and defined the rights of the Indians. He created a theory of liberty and thus established modern international law by attacking not only the temporal power of the pope, but also that of the emperor—the *imperator dominus orbis*—though he did acknowledge the traditional view of the *imperium*.[102] Spain thus became the cradle of international law,[103] for with Vitoria's refutation of universal temporal power and blind nationalism —the latter trying to absorb the former—the modern community of nations was actually born.[104]

Vitoria was among the earliest of the thinkers who applied natural law to international law; this was a middle-of-the-road theory which held the field and actually determined the future against the concept of a superstate organized on republican lines (Gentile, Boxhorn) and the concept which rejected *in toto* any idea of a natural community uniting all states (Bodin, Hobbes). For Vitoria and Suárez and the Spanish School in general, there was a natural-law connection among nations, and this connection, though it did not issue in any authority exercised by the whole over its parts, at any rate involved a system of mutual rights and duties. From this point of view international law was conceived as binding *inter se* upon states which were still in a state of nature in virtue of their sovereignty, and binding upon them in exactly the same way as the pre-political law of nature had been binding upon individuals when they were living in a state of nature.[105] Thus it was not so much the idolatry or barbarity of the Indians as their transgressions of this newly conceived international law which in Vitoria's view gave the Spaniards a right to the conquered lands of the Indies.[106]

Las Casas and Vitoria represented in the highest degree the union of Scholasticism and humanism. The debates they engendered resulted in important historical developments in Spain, the Indies, and in the far-distant Philippines, which were affected as well by other partisans of moderation such as Domingo de Soto (d. 1560), Fernando Vázquez de Menchaca (d. 1569), and, later, José de Acosta (d. 1600), Domingo Báñez (d. 1604), and Francisco Suárez.

The controversy finally led to the historic dispute in Valladolid between Las Casas and Sepúlveda (1550–51)[107] which was indecisive; if it seemed at one moment that Sepúlveda had emerged as the hero—since the *encomienda* was not definitely revoked until the eighteenth century—the real victors were Las Casas and Vitoria, for the institution was reformed and the Indians declared free. Moreover, Sepúlveda failed in his attempt in Valladolid to publish his book, the *Democrates alter*, not only because of his imperialist theory that natural aristocracy held sway over the less perfect but also because the *encomienda* represented a form of private property over the Indians, which was frowned upon by a centralized monarchy and by the missionary orders.[108]

The problem of the Indies—Spanish sovereignty in America and freedom—received significant contributions from Vitoria's disciple Melchor Cano (1509–60), who taught at Alcalá, and from Bartolomé Carranza (1503–76), Diego de Covarrubias (1512–77), and Juan de la Peña (1513–65). The writings of these four thinkers clearly demonstrated their clamor for human rights. They stated unequivocally that (*a*) all peoples were free, independent, and sovereign; (*b*) they could freely choose the form of government they considered appropriate; (*c*) a political regime was legitimately established if constituted by the free will of the subjects; and (*d*) all peoples, regardless of race, culture, and religion, were equal.[109] They condemned conquest in international politics and defended the individual against the Machiavellian *raison d'état*, a trend which was to be continued in the seventeenth century. They also proclaimed the right of free people to intervene in the affairs of sovereign states to avenge crimes against humanity and to correct offenses against the fundamental rights of the people.[110]

On the basis of these ideas, a political theory for the Indies developed. More realistic than Las Casas, these four political scholars believed in social evolution. Spain could occupy the Indies, even against the natives' will, until the Indians were able to attain complete political capability. Spain could not subdue them but would instruct them and respect their customs and territories. These doctrines were crowned by the concept of a confederacy with those peoples who had freely consented to Spanish protection, based on the principle derived from the free election by the people. Its political relationship was vassalage to the Crown of Spain, but Spain never acquired an absolute *dominium* over these lands. The doctrines of Carranza, Cano, Covarrubias, and Peña, together with those of Vitoria and Suárez, represent the most important dialectical effort to define the Spanish mission in America.[111]

After the famous dispute, several important historical events ended the epoch. In 1567, the Council of Castile was reorganized into an organic institution by Juan de Ovando, who proclaimed the primacy of the spiritual realm and the basis for good and just government—the primacy of the *summum bonum*

—in the *Consulta al Rey* (June 9 to August 28, 1571) and in the *Real cédula magna* (1574).[112] The period ended symbolically when Philip II substituted in 1573 the title "Pacification" for that of *Conquista*, the term used until that time.

The legal highlights of the Indian dispute were the famous New Laws of 1542[113] and the *Ordenanzas sobre descubrimiento* of 1573.[114] "Both extremely liberal and human colonial codes for their time, [they] illustrate well the influence which humanitarian theory exercised upon the Spanish Crown throughout the sixteenth century."[115]

> The colonial ethics of the *siglo de oro*, based on Scholastic theological and political thought, was a theory perfectly thought out and methodical. It nourished itself from two great sources: natural law and Christian revelation.[116]

The Late Scholastic spirit was obviously reflected in the vast legislation with which the Indies were ruled from the Peninsula, the highlight of which was the *Recopilación de leyes de las Indias* with its 6,289 articles. Its goal was to establish a vast civilized community where law was effective and justice was done without arbitrariness. This legislation was based on immutable ethical values, and followed the Christian natural law as a reflection of divine law, in keeping with the teachings of St. Thomas: *Leges quidem justae a lege aeterna, a qua derivantur*.[117] Again religion was the foundation of Spanish legislation; the entire first volume of the *Recopilación* is aimed at establishing the religious basis of government. This is especially evident in its first article:

> And we order the natives and the Spaniards and other Christians from different provinces and nations, transients or established on these, our kingdoms and domains, islands and mainland, who, regenerated by the holy sacrament of baptism have received the Holy Faith, that they firmly believe and simply uphold the mystery of the Holy Trinity, Father, Son, and Holy Spirit, three persons and one true God, the articles of the Holy Faith and everything which Holy Mother, the Roman Catholic Church, holds, teaches, and preaches. If with stubborn and obstinate intention they should err and die hardened in not accepting and believing what Holy Mother Church holds and teaches, they will be punished with the penalties imposed by law in accordance and in the cases covered thereby [Book I, Title 1, Law 1].[118]

In this aim it was in agreement with the old Spanish legal tradition which, if in its end—to produce political unity—set up the absolutism of central authority over regional rights, did so always subject to the discipline of law; for the law of the *Fuero Juzgo* which said "Rey serás si fecieres derecho, et si non fecieres derecho, non serás rey" was never abolished.[119] This same Spanish legislation, including the *Fuero Juzgo*, the *Fuero Real*, the *Partidas*, and the laws of the Indies, was the legal basis in Argentina until January 1, 1870, and its spirit influenced to a great extent the civil and penal laws and the judiciary of Argentina thereafter.[120]

The reflection of the Scholastic fifteenth-century and Late Scholastic sixteenth-century ideas of Spain is evident in the early Spanish American philosophers and political thinkers. In general two basic Scholastic positions emerged in Spanish America: Thomism, followed mostly by the Dominicans and Augustinians, and Suarezism, defended primarily by the Jesuits. The Franciscans followed their traditional system, that of Duns Scotus, but it was not as influential as the main tendencies. Also, generally speaking, many of the ecclesiastical leaders and teachers in Spanish America were disciples of the great Late Scholastic personalities of the Peninsula.

Viceroyalty of New Spain. The sixteenth century in the Indies was the century of New Spain, and the philosophic trends which predominated there were the different Scholastic versions of the various religious orders. New Spain and Peru also reflected the freedom of thought prevalent in the Peninsula. The Crown encouraged free expression, particularly during the reigns of the Catholic kings and of Emperor Charles V, as is evident from the reports of Hernán Cortés and the writings of Bernal Díaz del Castillo, Martín Fernández de Enciso, Gonzalo Fernández de Oviedo, Francisco López de Gómara, Friar Bernardino de Sahagún, Friar Toribio de Motolinía, Bartolomé de las Casas, and others.[121]

Before Late Scholasticism swept the entire continent, certain unorthodox currents were introduced into Spanish America—especially into New Spain. Thus, Juan de Zumárraga, New Spain's first archbishop, was much influenced by Erasmus; his *Doctrina breve* (1544) is modeled on Erasmus' *Paraclesis*. Bishop Vasco de Quiroga attempted to put More's *Utopia* into practice and to create an ideal society for the Indians under his care; the village hospitals in Santa Fe, Mexico, and Michoacán were supposed to bring them closer to Spanish-Christian civilization through a work ethic and protect them from abuses.[122] Francisco Cervantes de Salazar introduced the criticism of Juan Luis Vives (1554) into New Spain, and the Spanish Protestant Constantino Ponce de la Fuente had his catechism printed anonymously in Mexico (1546).

From the end of the sixteenth century, the Jesuits had the greatest impact and "therefore the reformed Scholasticism of Molina and Suárez predominated there."[123] The common ground of the different doctrines was Aristotelian philosophy the elements of which had been reformulated by the Renaissance. Thus, a great part of philosophy until the eighteenth century was limited to commentaries on the works of Aristotle, especially in the fields of logic, psychology, and physics. Among the most famous commentaries used as textbooks were those from Coimbra directed by the Jesuit Pedro de Fonseca and those which were published by the Dominicans of Alcalá. In the second half of the sixteenth century several works on Aristotle were published in New Spain; among the most important was the *Introducción a la dialéctica de Aristóteles* by Francisco de Toledo, which was ordered published by the Jesuits in 1578.[124]

The influence of Scholasticism in New Spain centered in the colleges and universities. The year 1551 marked the date when the universities in Mexico and Lima were established as a symbol and practical step for the execution of Emperor Charles V's directive that not only the religion and institutions of the Iberian Peninsula but also Spain's culture be transplanted overseas. The universities were set up for the service of God, the public welfare of the kingdom, and the protection of the inhabitants against the darkness of ignorance.[125]

Founded in 1551 and beginning its teaching in 1553, the University of Mexico, from the beginning, felt the force of the Counter Reformation.[126]

The new institution gave pre-eminence to the chair of Scholastic theology. Some of its occupants held the highest degrees from Spanish universities and some had studied under such eminent masters as Domingo de Soto. Their task was "to impugn, to destroy, to vanquish, and to extirpate that which does not conform to the faith."[127]

In addition to the University of Santo Tomás (Santo Domingo, 1538), and the Universities of San Pablo (Mexico, 1551) and San Marcos (Lima, 1551), two others were established in the sixteenth century: Santiago de la Paz (Santo Domingo, 1558) and Santo Domingo (Santa Fe de Bogotá, 1580).[128]

The Royal and Pontifical University of Mexico was founded by decree of Emperor Charles V, following the model of Salamanca and Alcalá.[129] Its department of philosophy had chairs devoted exclusively to St. Thomas and to Duns Scotus, and after 1572, and the arrival of the Jesuits, there was a chair dedicated to Suárez. The first Mexican philosopher was an Augustinian friar, Alonso de la Vera Cruz (d. 1584). Although he was born in Spain, he set the trend of philosophy in the New World by introducing Aristotle into New Spain. In his works *Recognitio sumularum, Dialectica resolutio* (1554), and *Physica speculatio* (1557) he projected the Spanish spirit of the Golden Age and that special union of Scholasticism (Thomism) and the modern spirit of the Renaissance.[130] He was no doubt the greatest mind in New Spain during the sixteenth century. He came to Mexico in 1537, became an Augustinian, and in 1540 founded the first Augustinian college in Tiripitío. When he died in 1584, Scholasticism was well established. It was he who had given it its greatest stimulus, although he was also linked to the mysticism of Luis de León and to other humanistic currents of the Spanish Renaissance.

He was succeeded by Friar Bartolomé de Ledesma, a Dominican theologian who later taught at San Marcos in Lima and wrote a *Suma de casos de conciencia* (1570), *De septem ecclesiae sacramentis* (1585), and *De justitia et jure*.[131] Friar Ledesma and Friar Domingo de Mendoza, the author of several books on theology, had been disciples of Vitoria's in Salamanca.

Others who taught philosophy at the University of Mexico after Ledesma included the Augustinian José de Herrera and the Dominican Tomás de Mercado. The latter translated Aristotle's *Dialectics* and was the author of a *Suma de tratos y contratos* (1569)[132] and of a commentary on Pedro Hispano.[133]

Among the Jesuits who taught philosophy in the sixteenth century in New Spain was Antonio Rubio Rodensis (1548–1615), who arrived in 1576 and remained for twenty-three years. His *Commentarii in universam Aristotelis dialecticam* (1603) and his *Lógica mexicana* (1605)—a compendium of the former commentary—were republished several times. The *Lógica mexicana* became a textbook at the University of Alcalá at the time he was teaching there (1601–15). His other works include *Commentaria in octo libros Aristotelis de Physico auditu* (1605), *Principia de anima* (1611), *De coelo et mundo* (1617), and *De ortu et interitu* (1619).[134] His influence was substantial throughout Hispanic America and was instrumental later in the formation of a group of thinkers which included the eighteenth-century Jesuits Francisco Javier Alegre, Diego José Abad, and Agustín de Castro.[135]

Other Jesuit philosophers in sixteenth-century New Spain were: Antonio Arias (1562–1603), also an Aristotelian, who wrote *De physica, De generatione et corruptione, De sphera mundi, De coelo*, and *De rebus meteorologicis*;[136] Pedro López de Parra, the first philosophy teacher at San Pedro and San Pablo (1575); and the Mexican Juan Contreras whose philosophy lectures were widely read in New Spain.¹³⁷ The Asturian Dominican Pedro de Pravia, a scholar in theology at the University of Mexico and author of many works which have unfortunately been lost, was another illustration of the great cultural level of sixteenth-century New Spain. Thus, through erudite men, priests and lawyers, culture penetrated Mexican society: "Philosophy was the privilege of the clergy, who used it in a Scholastic sense as an auxiliary of theology; it was also the fundamental principle of law."¹³⁸

Other important scholars influential in New Spain in the sixteenth century were the following Dominicans: Friar Pedro de Córdoba, author of a *Catecismo para instrucción de los indios*; Friar Antonio Montesinos, author of the *In Indorum defensionem*; Friar Andrés Moguer, author of *Sermones de tempore et de sanctis*, *Historia de Santo Domingo de la Provincia de Méjico*, and *Liber exemplorum*; Friar Domingo de Lora, bishop of Guatemala and author of a *Diccionario del idioma chiapense*; Friar Antonio Remesal, author of an *Historia general de las Indias occidentales*; Friar Tomás de la Torre, Dominican provincial of Guatemala and author of an *Historia* which has been lost; Friar Domingo Vico, the author of many works, among which are *Teología de los indios*, *Fábulas y errores de los indios*, *De magnis nominibus*, *Paradiso terrenal*, and several *Historias*; and Friar Bernardo Albuquerque, author of *Tratado de doctrina cristiana para utilidad de los misioneros*.¹³⁹

The University of Mexico was not the only academic institution influenced by prevailing philosophic currents. Other colleges followed similar Scholastic trends: the College of Santa Cruz de Tlaltelolco, founded by Friar Peter of Ghent and Viceroy Mendoza, and famous for the attempt at establishing a native church; the Colegio Mayor de Santa María de Todos los Santos; the College of San Pedro y San Pablo, founded by the Jesuits in 1574 and combined in 1575, with that of San Ildefonso y San Gregorio, a school for young Indians, whose first philosophy teacher was Pedro López de Parra (1575); the Colegio de San Nicólas de Vasco de Quiroga (1540), and those in the towns of Oaxaca, Puebla, Veracruz, Guadalajara, Zacatecas, Durango, and Guanajuato, among others.¹⁴⁰ All these institutions had vast libraries; the first and largest belonged to Alonso de la Vera Cruz, who brought some sixty cartons of books to New Spain on his second voyage there in 1573. The libraries of the colleges, of the cathedral, and of the convents held thousands of books, including many classic works of Scholasticism.¹⁴¹

Viceroyalty of Peru. Peru followed essentially the same trends in the sixteenth century as New Spain. Here again the religious orders were the vanguard of culture. The early period was highlighted by the Augustinians, Franciscans, Dominicans, and Mercedarians, while at the end of the century the Jesuits predominated.

Although Peru was conquered in the 1530s (especially after the capture of the Inca Athahualpa on November 16, 1532), and most of its towns were founded in these years—including Piura (1532), Jauja (1533), Lima, Trujillo, Quito, Puertoviejo (1535), La Plata [Sucre], Chachapoyas (1538), Huamanga [Ayacucho] (1539), and Arequipa (1540)—the great Indian rebellion and the various civil wars (the "War of Salinas" in 1537–38, the "War of Chupas" in 1541–42, and the "War of Quito" in 1541–42)¹⁴² slowed the progress toward organized and stable government. The University of San Marcos in Lima was founded by royal decree on May 12, 1551, at the time when the second viceroy of Peru,

Antonio de Mendoza, took office; it was followed by two more universities (Cuzco and Huamanga) and several colleges, all established by the religious orders: Santo Toribio, San Martín, San Felipe, San Pablo, and San Ildefonso. As in New Spain, the religious orders followed their own masters and directed their teaching accordingly: thus, Dominicans and Mercedarians expounded the theories of St. Thomas; the Augustinians followed St. Augustine; the Franciscans, Duns Scotus; and the Jesuits, Suárez.

> In spite of rather serious divergencies, which sometimes exceeded the limits of mere debate and became conflicts for academic power, there remained, of course, a unified body of Catholic thought which every order helped to disseminate.[143]

The most noted Scholastic teacher and philosopher in sixteenth-century Peru was the Spanish Jesuit José de Acosta (1540–1600). Born in Medina del Campo, Acosta, a member of the Society of Jesus since 1552, arrived in Peru in 1572. He became the rector of the College of Lima and provincial, and played the most important role in the Third Liman Council convoked by Saint Toribio. Not only a theologian, philosopher, and historian, but a natural scientist as well, with a special interest in anthropology and physiography, Acosta symbolized the Late Scholastic fusion of universal knowledge with faith. His *Historia natural y moral de las Indias* (1590) made him justly famous. Published in Seville and hailed on both sides of the Atlantic, Acosta's work comprises seven volumes, dealing with the sky, climate, and population of Peru, the plants, animals, and metals of the area, and the government, religion, and customs of the natives.[144] Although the observation of Spanish American nature made him depart from the strict notion of Aristotle, adopting a more critical and empirical approach, he always remained very moderate and within the theological and philosophical framework of traditional Scholasticism. He stressed "the supremacy of theological contemplation over the acquisition of scientific knowledge," though he was devoted to an "essentially scientific interpretation of the biological phenomena encountered in the New World."[145]

Acosta was also the author of *De la justicia conmutativa y distributiva: Reglas de buen gobierno dirigidas al Virrey D. Francisco de Toledo*,[146] and took part in the great debate on the Indians; he sided wholeheartedly with the humane ideas of Las Casas and Vitoria when he wrote the *De promulgatione Evangelii apud barbaros sive de procuranda Indorum salute* (1589).

Among the Peruvians who expounded the theories of St. Thomas were the Friars Rafael de Segura, Juan de Lorenzana, Francisco de la Cruz (author of a *Curso de artes*), and Domingo de Medina y Vega. The theories of Duns Scotus were imparted by the Franciscan Friars Juan del Campo, Lucas de Cuenca, and Benito Guertas. Friar Luis López was the main exponent of St. Gregory; St. Augustine's thought was disseminated by the Augustinian Friars Pedro de Avellaneda, Gabriel de Sarna, and Nicolás de Santa María. The main follower of Suárez at that time was the Jesuit Ignacio de Arbieto, a disciple of Suárez' and author of a *Suma de las obras teológicas del p. Suárez*. Finally, the doctrines of Vitoria, who was quite popular in sixteenth-century Peru, were taught by one of his pupils, Friar Juan Solano.[147]

While Scholasticism reigned supreme in sixteenth-century Peru, currents similar to those in New Spain also played a role, though obviously a minor one. The Spanish Renaissance was represented in particular by that great personality, the Inca Garcilaso de la Vega (1539–1616), with whom the Renaissance began in Spanish America and who represents "the triumph, in the lyric, of the Spanish Renaissance."[148] His Neoplatonism was evident in his translation of the *Dialoghi d'amore* of León Hebreo (Judah Abravanel). Certain types of mysticism and illuminism or quietism found expression in Miguel de Molinos, and the approaching scientific revolution could be seen in the chair of natural philosophy at San Marcos, held by the physician Antonio Sánchez Renedo (1518–79), and representing the main center for the promotion of scientific knowledge.[149]

Among the important works dealing with politics and government in the Viceroyalty of Peru must be mentioned Juan Matienzo's *Gobierno del Perú*, written in 1573 when the author was a judge of the *audiencia* of Charcas. The book deals with the Indians first under the Incas, then under the Spanish. Matienzo affirms the justice of the Spanish cause based on the papal donation and asserts that the Indians did not represent a civilized nation. After discussion of the status of the Indians under the laws of the Indies, he delves into the organization of Spanish rule, including laws and customs prevailing in the viceroyalty in the sixteenth century.[150]

Other writers in the Viceroyalty of Peru also participated—as did Acosta and Matienzo—in the great debate on the Indians. There was Melchor Calderón who arrived in Chile in 1555 and became a canon and treasurer of the cathedral of Santiago, a commissary of the Inquisition, and vicar general of the bishopric. Later, in 1579, he became a member of the *cabildo* of Santiago. His book entitled *Tratado de la importancia y utilidad que hay en dar por esclavos a los indios rebelados en Chile*,[151] published in 1607, attempted to show the advisibility of enslaving the rebellious Araucanians instead of killing them in battle. A different point of view was manifested by Francisco Falcón, of the ecclesiastical court in Lima (1582), who fought for Indian justice in the sense of Las Casas, even questioning the right of conquest and criticizing the policies of the Spanish conquerors.[152]

Peru attracted chroniclers. Among the early ones, the most important were Juan de Sámano (1528), the anonymous soldier who wrote "La conquista del Perú, llamada la Nueva Castilla" (1534), and Francisco López de Jerez and his *Verdadera relación de la conquista del Perú* (1534). Juan Polo de Ondogardo, known for his sincerity and impartiality, was one of the most extraordinary jurists ever to come to Peru; he joined Pedro de la Gasca after the latter's arrival and became governor of La Plata and, later, corregidor of Charcas. His work includes the *Informaciones acerca de la religión y gobierno de los Incas* (1571), the *Informe* on the perpetuity of the *encomiendas* (1561), and the *Relación de los fundamentos acerca del notable daño que resulta de no guardar a los indios sus fueros* (1571).[153] Others include Juan de Betanzos (1510–76), author of *Suma y narración de los Incas* (1551);[154] Cristóbal de Molina, author of *Relación de las fábulas y ritos de los Incas* (1572); Cristóbal de Molina (el Almagrista), author of the *Relación de la conquista y población del Perú* (1552);[155] and Diego de Fernández (el Palentino), author of the *Primera y segunda parte de la historia del Perú que se mandó escribir a Diego Fernández, vecino de la ciudad de Palencia* (1571).[156]

Finally, mention should be made of Pedro Sarmiento de Gamboa (1530–92), famous for his *Historia Indica*,[157] and of Pedro Cieza de León (1518–60), the prince of Peruvian historians. His description of the Peruvian civil wars, in the *Crónica del Perú* (1550) and *Señorío de los Incas Yupanqui*, is the best source for the history of the Incas, the conquest, and the Peruvian civil wars.[158] The most outstanding chronicle, from a literary point of view, was written by Agustín de Zárate (d. 1560s) who came to Peru with the first viceroy, Blasco Núñez de Vela, in 1543; his *Historia del descubrimiento y conquista del Perú* (1555)[159] recalled the famous picaresque novels which had inspired the conquistadors.

Although the River Plate was not so important in the sixteenth century as New Spain and Peru, cultural developments nonetheless brought trends to this area similar to those in the more important regions of Spanish America. Here, too, mendicant orders and, later, the Jesuits were the vanguard of culture. The first Franciscans came in 1538, led by Friar Bernardo de Armentía, and, together with the Dominicans, introduced Scholasticism into the area. The first Scholastic philosopher in the River Plate was Alonso Guerra, the fifth bishop there and first teacher of philosophy in Buenos Aires after its second founding in 1580; he came to the city from Asunción in 1586 and established a modest academic center in which he taught the preferred theories of the Dominicans, such as Soto and Báñez.

Friar Reginaldo de Lizárraga (1545–1615) was equally famous. A Dominican theologian, and, hence, a Thomist, he became known in the River Plate for his *Descripción breve de toda la tierra del Perú, Tucumán, Río de la Plata y Chile*, written between 1560 and 1602. Chapter XVII, in particular, manifests the thought of Late Scholasticism:

> During the time the most generous Marquis [de Cañete, Viceroy Andrés Hurtado de Mendoza] governed, he proved himself [to be] a great republican; whoever is such merits the name of Father of the Country, but does not when he fails to look after the good of the country, since the prince exists for the kingdom, not the kingdom for the prince. It follows from this that the good prince with all his power tries to preserve his republic and increase it, to do justice, and to make his vassals rich and prosperous.[160]

Two more names conclude the Scholastic thinkers of the River Plate in the sixteenth century: the aforementioned José de Acosta and Francisco González Paniagua, who came with the expedition of Cabeza de Vaca in 1540, and was the author of a famous *Memorial* on conditions in the River Plate (lack of freedom, polygamy among Spaniards, sale of Indian women, political intrigues, character of Irala).[161]

In the area of New Granada, we might mention Gonzalo Jiménez de Quesada, the conquistador of today's Colombia. The writings of this Renaissance humanist reflect the great Spanish ideas of the Golden Age. His *Antijovio*,[162] written as a reply to Paolo Giovio (1483–1552), is a refutation of the theories of the Italian, a follower of Machiavelli's new ideas. Jiménez de Quesada sketched an idealistic picture of the new Christian universal polity whose head was Emperor Charles V. Leading a rich intellectual life and full of spiritual passion, Jiménez de Quesada represented an echo of Don Quixote in the New World; his wild imagination carried him away from reality, enabling him to view himself and the Spanish conquest as a modern version of St. Augustine's *civitas Dei* and Spain's rivals as the embodiment of the *civitas terrena*. His entire anti-Giovian struggle corresponded to the "Augustinian metaphysical vision of universal history as a battle between the two cities or two mystic armies of God and Satan . . . ."[163] The conquistador of New Granada tried to establish St. Augustine's City of God on earth in a way similar to Vasco de Quiroga's attempt to set up an Indian utopia on the teachings of More. His Augustinianism came forth as an absolute power, including the idea of the predestination of the elect and of the damned, as convincingly shown by Frankl.[164] In a treatise called "Indicaciones para el buen gobierno,"[165] written in the best traditions of the Scholastic period in Spain, he took up the defense of the Indians, reflecting the spirit of Las Casas in the sixteenth century and anticipating that of St. Peter Claver in the seventeenth.

Similar Scholastic theories were expressed by Juan de Castellanos (1552–1607) in his *Elegías*,[166] which contrasted the English, French, and Dutch colonization with that of Castile and León, in which new kingdoms were based on devotion to God and fealty to the monarchy. Castellanos, like Jiménez de Quesada before him, stressed the federative character of the Spanish monarchy and its universal nature. The *Conquista* was a service to God and king, and its legal title was based on the pope's decision. Castellanos also praised such Hispanic institutions as the municipal liberties (the *cabildos*), since in his view *potestas* did not reside solely in the king.

Friar Pedro de Aguado, author of the *Historia de Santa Marta y Nuevo Reino de Granada*[167] and the *Historia de Venezuela*,[168] showed traits similar to those of Jiménez de Quesada and Castellanos. Aguado's thought faithfully reflected fifteenth-century Castilian theories, since his arguments are patterned on those which the Tostado (Alonso de Madrigal) adduced in Castile or which Francisco de Exímenis used in Valencia citing the lively institution of the *cabildo* as an echo of Hispanic liberties.[169]

Finally, Bernardo de Vargas Machuca (1555–1622), author of the *Milicia y descripción de las Indias*,[170] is—his birth and death in Spain notwithstanding —the father of Colombian political thought; he was the first to mention a philosophy of government applicable only to the Indies. Vargas Machuca saw in Hispanic America several kingdoms (Peru, New Spain, New Granada, and Brazil), all members of the commonwealth, united to the Crown of Castile,[171] and three links of unity around this federation: the Spanish (Portuguese) language, Catholic faith, and loyalty to the king. The juridical personality of these kingdoms required two things: (*a*) from the legal point of view, a justification of the *fueros*, and (*b*) from the political, a justification of the political development of each individual American kingdom.[172]

In the field of philosophy two deserve mention: Friar Gregorio de Beteta, a missionary in New Granada, and Pedro de Ona, author of *Commentaria super universam Aristotelis Logicam* (1588), *Super primum librum Physicae auscultationis Aristotelis* (1592), and *Dialecticae introductio* (1593). Both likewise delved into the field of religion and theology in New Granada.[173]

To sum up: "the colonial culture possessed a true philosophical formation";[174] it showed the penetration of Scholasticism into all areas of Spanish America, although New Spain represented by far the greatest achievement in that direction.

2. The Thought of the Baroque in the Seventeenth Century

The Spanish sixteenth century, as was evidenced by the great debates on the Indies, recognized the problem of freedom and authority, and many of the greatest thinkers tried to foster a union between them.[175] But the union of Scholasticism and humanism decreased in importance after the Counter Reformation developed; for an understanding of Hispanic seventeenth-century political thought, it is necessary to bear in mind the changes which occurred in Spain after the Council of Trent (1545–63) and resulted in a stiffening of attitude toward unorthodox views.

Spanish ideas in the seventeenth century were still based on the religious concept of spiritual unity; the long struggle of the seventeenth century was caused by the widening of the abyss between the Spanish determination to remain close to the theocentric world view of Aristotle and St. Thomas and the new world view of force and matter which was gaining ground in the rest of Europe. The quixotic dreams which Spain had tried to impose on the world —the ideas of the universal monarchy and of a triumphant and unified Christianity in its specifically Spanish mold, symbolized by both Emperors Charles V and Philip II—were continued in the seventeenth century against increasing odds. In 1609, as in 1492, the *moriscos*—regarded as a possible threat in view of the Alpujarras revolt of 1568—were expelled, and religious unity became absolute. But by 1609 as well Spain had to acknowledge the independence of the Low Countries, and on March 19, 1643, at Rocroy, Spain's enemies triumphed, ending Spanish imperial goals in Europe. Still, in spite of the fact that Spain's political power was diminishing, the old ideal was not abandoned, though there was an increasing awareness that some kind of adjustment would be made. These old ideals are seen in José Pellicer's *Defense of Spain against Calumnies of France* (1623), and even in mid-century, after Rocroy, Pellicer maintained his religious and political idealism.[176]

Thus the Spaniards in this century clung tenaciously to the Scholastic world;

> they did not suffer appreciably from the upsetting astronomical discoveries of the time; nor did they find a comfortable new world view that enhanced the resulting changes in cosmological theory.[177]

The best example is Calderón, the dramatist of Scholasticism; when he died (1681) he believed in a Ptolemaic, a geocentric, universe, governed by a rational God to whom man's reason gave him access.

> He did not share Pascal's sense of desolation in infinity: *nous sommes si terriblement petits*. Between the years 1140 and 1681 the alliance of faith and "right reason" is not disrupted in Spain.[178]

At all times,

> reason (understood as "right reason," illumined by grace) was regarded as a noble thing—the best friend we have, as Gracián said. The Spanish Church had no fear of science, of knowledge, since God's truth is one. The Church's fears were two: heresy, the elaboration of mistaken dogma by the "blind intellect" (without grace); and certain types of mysticism.[179]

The seventeenth century in Spain was essentially no different from the preceding century: the concept of the Baroque, of the *seconda scolastica*, of Late Scholasticism, did not involve a conception of the world different from that of the Renaissance. It was still a world governed by a good and rational God in which man's place, with its responsibilities and duties, was firmly fixed; it was still a world in which means were available to man for his self-realization and salvation, where there was a clear distinction between good and evil, where the nature of evil was clearly recognized, and where personal and national failure and disaster were seen as the result of sin. It is a concept maintained unreservedly through the age of Calderón. The Spaniards

> did not see themselves faced with the basic dilemma of accepting simultaneously the theism of tradition and the emerging mechanism of natural philosophy. The scrutiny of nature did not supplant the scrutiny of man.[180]

And therein lay the great difference between the European Renaissance and Baroque and the Spanish versions: England produced a Hobbes and a Locke, Spain clinging to her Aristotelian-Thomistic universe did not.[181]

The seventeenth century brought to the Spanish world a wave of interest in the new natural sciences, awakening the love of knowledge, expanding the intellectual horizon of the contemporary Spaniard and Spanish American, and laying the foundation for the development of the Enlightenment.

While the Peninsula participated in the general movement of scientific research as did other countries, it showed the same pattern: it tried successfully to assimilate the revolutionary spirit which the sciences evoked all over Europe, but it did not develop a natural system in the sense of Descartes, Bacon, Newton, and other principal thinkers of the century, or, in political science, the absolutism of Hobbes. For such was the strength of Late Scholasticism that it was able to absorb but would not be absorbed.

In other parts of Europe religion diminished as the centuries advanced, aggravated by the Christian schism, but in the Peninsula there was no inclination to change things, to switch from the specific Spanish brand of Catholicism to the concept of humanity. As Green stated,

> Calderón is the end product of a Catholic culture, preserved in essential purity. Perhaps for that reason it seems incredible that he was a contemporary of Thomas Hobbes and Baruch Spinoza, and a partial contemporary of John Locke and Gottfried Leibniz.[182]

And thus it happened that Spain, always somewhat different from the rest of the European and Mediterranean countries, turned her back on the contemporary currents of Bacon and Newton, Hobbes and Locke, Galileo and Kepler, Descartes and Copernicus, and chose instead the traditional way of medieval Scholasticism adjusted to the realities of modern society; it followed the *seconda scolastica* of Suárez.[183]

Spanish political thought in the seventeenth century continued the basic philosophy of the previous century, drawing largely from four sources:

1. Late Scholastic philosophy as contained in Francisco Suárez' *De legibus* and *Defensio fidei*.
2. The Scholastic tradition headed by St. Thomas' *De regno ad regem Cypri* and the *Summa theologica*.[184]

3. The anti-Machiavellian reaction in the Peninsula.[185]
4. The ascetic–mystic outburst in Spain, which touched all social classes.[186]

The basic harmony between faith and reason is the philosophical, political, and constitutional ground on which all Hispanic political thinkers constructed their theories. It dominated political life in the Hispanic seventeenth century, and was by far the most important source of the anti-Machiavellian currents dominating Hispanic political writings until the end of the Spanish Hapsburgs in 1700.

Yet Spain also had to counter the influence of Jean Bodin, who advocated a state of religious neutrality dominated by an absolute sovereign. The absolute monarchy which Bodin envisioned in France because of the very special conditions there did not apply to the same extent in Spain, where religious unity had been preserved. It was therefore looked upon as somewhat dangerous and not consonant with the medieval traditions of Hispanic political thought. Hispanic political thinkers all adhered to the basic medieval concept of religious unity, particularly after they witnessed the devastation which a division of faith had effected in France and other European countries.

They visualized the republic, based on the elements of justice and unity, as an organism composed of individuals, estates, and dignitaries which cannot be absorbed totally by the state.[187] There was no possibility in the Hispanic seventeenth century of bringing into political theory in the philosophical sense any notion of individualism, on the one side, or of idealism, on the other. The Hispanic mind suspected elements of heresy in the notion of the state which Machiavelli, Bodin, and Hobbes formulated. The amoral teachings of Machiavelli could not develop in the Hispanic world because of the impressive strength of Scholasticism, nor could Bodin's—with whom they would agree somewhat more—since the Frenchman's state, with its religious neutrality, already bore within it the danger of decomposition.

The Hispanic seventeenth-century political order was a hierarchical system in which peace and tranquillity could be achieved only when things were put in their proper place, as medieval political theory ordained. This order called for political authority, since harmony among individuals cannot be attained without it, and the absence of such authority would be equivalent to lack of liberty. Society's end must be political, and the highest organ—the state —must have great authority, particularly in times when religious dissent results in widespread upheaval. Thus, Spanish political thought of the seventeenth century called for a strengthening of authority—which was in line with the general European political thought of the period—but without going to the extremes of a Bodin or a Hobbes, since the foundation of the whole political structure was still Scholastic. Furthermore, within Spain itself there was no equivalent of the Edict of Nantes, because Church and State were harmoniously united; their interests were parallel, and they were successful in preventing dissidents from threatening religious unity.

What is interesting about the political thought of the seventeenth century in Spain, in contrast to that of the sixteenth, is that it tended toward a more absolute pattern, resulting from the religious revolution of the preceding age and giving religion a more political character. The defense of religion, begun with the Counter Reformation and Philip II, presupposed a greater amount of political authority. Therefore, the right of resistance and of tyrannicide, so popular in the literature of the sixteenth century (Mariana, Molina, Soto), did not receive approval in the seventeenth. In this respect Bodin exerted a definite influence on the Spanish mind, insofar as the right of resistance against a monarch was inconsistent with the monarch's supreme role as unifier of the country—with the reservation that the prince was to be a Christian ruler in every sense of the word. And yet, the great books of sixteenth-century Spanish political thought circulated freely, including Mariana's *De rege*, and even a book like Hobbes' *Leviathan*, which at the time was publicly burned in England, was allowed to enter the Spanish world.[188] It is interesting in contrast that Suárez' *Defensio fidei* was publicly burned as dangerous to the state—but not in Spain. The burning occurred in England and France.[189]

The seventeenth century produced several famous lawyers whose legal works contributed significantly to political thought and government in the Indies. They included Gaspar de Escalona y Agüero, Antonio de León Pinelo, and, in particular, Juan de Solórzano Pereira. All these writers (as well as Matienzo in the sixteenth century) described the government as they saw it, not curbing their criticism when it was warranted, as in the case of Escalona, who condemned the exactions of the *corregidores* of Indians and other abuses resulting from the dishonesty of officials and their remoteness from the centers of higher authority.[190] All represented the political legal thought of the Late Scholastic period.

Escalona y Agüero was a native of Peru; he became *corregidor* of Jauja and, later, judge of the *audiencia* of Chile. His main work, *Gazophilatium regium Perulicum*, appeared in Madrid in 1647 and dealt with all aspects of government and politics in the Indies.[191]

Another great lawyer was León Pinelo who spent his life in Lima, studied at San Marcos, and went to Spain where he was appointed *relator* of the Council of the Indies. His works dealt with government and politics, as well as bibliography, and included *Política de las grandezas y gobierno del supremo y real consejo de las Indias* (1625), *Epítome de la biblioteca oriental y occidental* (1629), and *Aparato político de las Indias occidentales* (1653).[192]

The most important of these lawyers was Solórzano Pereira. Born in 1575, a student and, later, professor at Salamanca (1587), Solórzano Pereira came to Peru in 1609 on orders of Philip III as a member of the Lima *audiencia*; he later became governor of Huancavelica. He became a member of the Council of the Indies, in 1629, retired in 1644, and died in Madrid in 1655. His major work, dedicated to Philip IV, is the *Política indiana*, which followed an earlier Latin version entitled *De Indiarum jure et gubernatione*. It delved into a variety of subjects related to the Indies: discovery, acquisition, and retention of the Indies; physical condition of the New World; the Indians and their government; Indian services to the Spaniards, including the *encomienda*; and ecclesiastical and civil government.[193]

Solórzano Pereira marked a further step toward royal absolutism, though basically he still followed the philosophical precepts of the earlier century. In keeping with the Scholastic traditions of the past he believed that absolute kingship was not the best government, but at the time (because of the religious disunity in Europe) was seemingly the only solution. His traditionalism was based not on a simple repetition of already consolidated positions of the past, but on a fearful distrust of the future.[194]

Halperín Donghi sees in the Spanish political thought of the seventeenth century, and especially in Solórzano Pereira, a hidden naturalism, as he calls it, which in his view had been anticipated by Vitoria in the sixteenth century. Vitoria, forced (like Suárez) to compromise with modern times, had recognized that the ideal of the Middle Ages was unattainable: the *civitas Christiana* was gradually giving way to national entities, further divided by religious disunity. Vitoria's adjustment was the basis of his international law. In the sixteenth century, civil authority remained legitimate as long as it was geared toward an end, which "in turn meant a complex hierarchical structure of what was real based on the continuity of what was natural and supranatural";[195] it was this image of reality which represented in that century a living legacy of the Middle Ages in the Hispanic world. This was the reason why problems which otherwise appeared as insoluble could constantly be resolved on a very high intellectual level.[196] But Vitoria realized the need for greater authority, a trend which in view of the widening of the abyss from the medieval world was strengthened a century later by Solórzano Pereira and other writers of the Hispanic seventeenth century.[197]

In the opinion of Enrique de Gandía, however, Solórzano Pereira refuted Vitoria's thesis, since his position, as a seventeenth-century lawyer, was that of a "perfect absolutist,"[198] eager to defend the authoritarian monarchy of his king.[199] His was a providentialist theory favoring the Spanish monarchy, a somewhat baroque version of Ginés de Sepúlveda and contrary to the more liberal ideas of Vitoria of a century earlier;[200] he defended both the universal authority of the papacy and the universal monarchy of his kings, and based the conquest of the Indies on the papal donation. He thus reflected the spirit of the Spanish seventeenth century.

In Spanish America sixteenth-century political ideas were very much alive in the seventeenth century in spite of the new emphasis on authority, resulting, no doubt, from the strong influence of Francisco Suárez. The impact of Suárez in Spanish America was not sporadic; it began gradually at the end of the sixteenth century and then increased, with the result that Suárez became the undisputed intellectual influence there during the late-sixteenth and the seventeenth centuries, in spite of the occasional opposition of Thomism.[201]

The Jesuits arrived in Peru in 1568 and in New Spain in 1572. After the establishment of the College of San Pablo in Lima (1568), they opened others in Cuzco and La Paz, followed by a Jesuit house in Potosí in 1577; in 1624 they founded the University of Chuquisaca. The Dominicans, rivaling the Jesuits, established colleges in New Granada, Chile, and the Philippines; in 1655 they founded a Thomistic university in Santa Fe de Bogotá. There were twenty-three universities—ten classified as major, all of which were "royal and pontifical." Three of them were modeled after Salamanca; one, on Alcalá; others, on the Spanish American ones of Mexico, Lima, and Santo Domingo.[202] Of the minor universities, most were Jesuit, four were Dominican, one was Augustinian, and one was Franciscan. "In reality,"

> they were the very warp and woof of the church, without which a trained clergy could not have survived and the very solid rock upon which colonial structure, in all its formal aspects, rested in closest parallel to that of Europe.[203]

The list of these universities is impressive, as one after another was founded in the seventeenth century, following the first five in the sixteenth century: San Fulgencio (Quito, 1603), Santa Catalina (Mérida, 1618), Universidad Javeriana (Santa Fe de Bogotá, 1622), San Ignacio (Córdoba, 1622), San Ignacio (Cuzco, 1623), San Javier (Charcas, 1624), San Miguel (Santiago de Chile, 1625), San Borja (Guatemala, 1625), San Ildefonso (Puebla, 1625), Nuestra Señora del Rosario (Santa Fe de Bogotá, 1651), San Carlos (Guatemala, 1676), San Cristóbal (Huamanga, 1681), San Pedro y San Pablo (Mexico, 1687), Santo Domingo (Quito, 1688), Universidad Jesuítica (Guadalajara, 1696), and San Antón (Cuzco, 1696).[204]

Viceroyalty of New Spain. In New Spain the seventeenth century continued the philosophical trends of the sixteenth, but with a greater emphasis on orthodoxy, and thus followed the general lines of the Peninsula. Late Scholasticism, nurtured by the currents of the sixteenth century, so dominated the cultural life of New Spain that no other philosophical system had a chance to develop. Again, as in the previous century, the main Scholastic versions were those based on Saint Thomas (Augustinians and Dominicans), and on Suárez (Jesuits).

> In the arts course, in which the majority of undergraduates enrolled, the logic, metaphysics, and physics of Aristotle dominated until the late eighteenth century. In theology St. Thomas Aquinas and Duns Scotus reigned supreme.[205]

Nominalism and the thought of Ramón Lull were unpopular.[206] However, a less formalistic approach and a greater flexibility of the mind was found in New Spain among the Jesuits who did not shield themselves from the modern winds: they were the ones who raised Mexican culture to high standards in both the seventeenth and eighteenth centuries.

> In the knowledge of scientific and philosophic novelties, the shrewdness of the Jesuits to conciliate even the most incompatible ideas was highly useful to the culture of New Spain. From the very beginning they left Scholastic orthodoxy, teaching the doctrine of the Society's philosopher, Francisco Suárez.[207]

Among the philosophers best known in New Spain in the seventeenth century were: Juan Pedro Celi (1587–1617), a Mercedarian, who attempted to reconcile Plato and Aristotle, and who, known as the Spanish St. Augustine, was the author of *Tractatus theologici in primam partem divi Thomae* (1615) and of a *Laurea mexicana* (1615);[208] the Dominican Antonio Hinojosa, a well-known authority on St. Thomas in New Spain and author of *Clypeus thomistarum* and other works;[209] Friar José Calderón, likewise a Dominican, and a native of Mexico, who followed St. Thomas and Soto and was the author of a *Compendium philosophiae thomisticae*;[210] Friar Diego Villarrubia, an Augustinian, and the author of a *Philosophia scholastico-christiana* and of *Lectiones theologiae ad mentem Sancti Thomae Acquinatis*;[211] Alonso Guerrero, a Mexican Jesuit, the author of *Commentarii in universam Aristotelis philosophiam ... De physico auditu* (1623) and *Commentarii in universam Aristotelis doctrinam De anima* (1623);[212] the canon Marcos Portu, who wrote three volumes of commentary on Aristotle (1639);[213] the Spanish Augustinian, Friar Diego Basalenque (1577–

1651), author of a *Philosophia ad usum scholae, Summa summularum et totius dialecticae Aristotelis, De coelo et mundo*, and a *Crónica de la provincia de San Nicolás de Toletino de Michoacán*, and various books on native languages;[214] the Franciscan Francisco Cruz (d. 1655), author of a course on Scholastic philosophy;[215] Franciscan Friar Juan de Almanza, who wrote *Disputationes* on Aristotle (1660);[216] Diego Caballero, a Mexican Jesuit, who held a chair at Guadalajara College and wrote on Aristotle;[217] and the Franciscan Andrés Borda, who wrote a *De qualitate qualificabilium propositionum* and a commentary on Duns Scotus.[218]

Other influential Scholastic thinkers in New Spain included several Jesuits: the Peruvian Juan Pérez de Menacho (1565–1626), author of *De virtute castitatis* (1600), *Commentarii in I. 2ae. D. Thomae: De virtutibus; De peccatis* (1606), and of several other commentaries on the *Summa theologica* of St. Thomas;[219] and the brothers Alonso and Leonardo de Peñafiel—Alonso (1594–1657) wrote a *Cursus integri philosophici* (León, 1653–70) and a *Theologia scholastica naturalis* (1666), while Leonardo (1597–1657) was the author of *Disputationes theologicae* (1663), *Disputatione scholastica et morali de virtute fides divinae* (1673) and *Commentaria in Aristotelis Metaphysicam* (1632, 1693) (both the *Cursus* and the *Theologia* were published in Europe).[220] Finally, Diego de Avendaño, a native of Segovia, and teacher in Lima, Cuzco, and Chuquisaca, was the author of such theological and philosophical works as the *Problemata theologica* (1668), the *Cursus consummatus sive recognitiones theologiae expositivae scholasticae* (1686), and the *De Deo uno et trino*.[221]

Among the most representative figures of the seventeenth century in New Spain was Carlos de Sigüenza y Góngora (1645–1700), the symbol of the scientific revolution in the New World. He showed an extraordinary intellectual curiosity and independence of mind, which "set him apart from the tradition-bound society of theocratic despotism surrounding him."[222] Interested in mathematics, astrology, astronomy, mechanics, and history, he had a reputation for great erudition and was far above his intellectual environment and far ahead of this time. In spite of his interest in rationalism and the natural sciences, he loyally served Church and Crown, and remained close to religious orthodoxy as manifested in his *Indian Spring* (1662), "a fervent hymn to the Virgin of Guadalupe," and his *Evangelical Oriental Planet*, a posthumous panegyric of St. Francis Xavier.[223] His other works include the *Manifiesto philosóphico contra los cometas despojados del imperio sobre los tímidos* (1681), *El Belerofonte matemático contra la quimera astrológica*, and the *Libro astronómico y philosóphico* (1681) written against the astronomical viewpoints of the Jesuit Eusebio Kino.[224]

Sigüenza y Góngora is thus very close to the mind of Feijóo in the eighteenth century in his attempt to promote modern science and at the same time remain a devout and pious follower of traditional Catholicism. In this, of course, he reflected the typical Spanish genius:

> If Sister Juana Inés' secret sorrow was the impossibility of escaping into a world of wider horizons, Sigüenza's private grief was the impossibility of returning to the strict rule of a religious community.[225]

Viceroyalty of Peru. The seventeenth century in Spanish America was the century of Peru. Lima was the unrivaled center of an intellectual flowering, made possible by the return of peace after years of civil discord in the preceding century and by the material prosperity created by the rich economic resources of the country.[226] All cultural activities were deeply marked by the century's religious imprint and thus totally in harmony with the Spanish spirit. The religious orders brought knowledge to Peru, and it was in their midst that the great names of seventeenth-century Peru arose. The mendicant orders and the Mercedarians were the first to arrive, soon after the conquest, to be followed by the Jesuits in 1568. And thus "the seventeenth was the most Spanish century in the history of Peru, but probably also the most Peruvian as well."[227]

The century followed in the same footpath as New Spain but it surpassed its own sixteenth century as well as the great period of philosophy in the sixteenth century in New Spain. It thus represented the most distinguished period of Peruvian Scholasticism. The majority of the Peruvian Scholastics were Jesuits, and as in other parts of Spanish America education had gradually come into their hands after the second half of the sixteenth century.

The center of Peruvian cultural life in the seventeenth century was the University of San Marcos. It had been founded by Dominicans in 1551, under the leadership of Friar Tomás de San Martín, and it remained in Dominican hands for the next twenty years. In 1568 the Jesuits founded the College of San Pablo, which rivaled that of the Dominicans and led in 1571—at the time of Viceroy Toledo—to greater freedom of the university, to the extent that others besides Dominicans were allowed to teach there. The College of San Pablo was followed in 1575 by the Royal College of San Felipe, and those of San Martín in 1582 and Santo Toribio in 1591. In the seventeenth century, one college after another was founded: the Augustinian San Ildefonso in 1608, the Franciscan San Buenaventura in 1611, and the Mercedarian San Pedro Nolasco in 1626. In 1645 the Dominicans founded the College of Santo Tomás.[228]

As in other parts of Spanish America the Dominicans defended the theories of Duns Scotus, St. Bonaventure, and St. Thomas; the Augustinians showed a predilection for the Bishop of Hippo, the Jesuits for Suárez. The university more or less officially upheld the philosophy of St. Thomas; not until 1701 was a chair of Duns Scotus established, and not until 1725 was there a chair of Suárez.[229]

Four main groups should be distinguished in regard to the Scholastic studies: the Franciscan group, the Thomistic followers, those more inclined toward the Spanish Renaissance, and those tending toward mysticism.[230] Those who are generally classified as Thomists were all Jesuits, and this meant that they not only knew Suárez but followed him in those areas where he differed from St. Thomas.

The Franciscan Friar Jerónimo de Valera (1568–1625) was the most renowned follower of Duns Scotus in seventeenth-century Peru. A mestizo and nephew of the historian Blas Valera, he had a distinguished career in the Franciscan order. In 1601 he published in Lima the *Commentarii ac quaestiones in universam Aristotelis ac subtilissimi doctoris Johannis Duns Scoti logicam*, which became the text of Franciscan studies in Peru.[231]

The Thomist group was obviously the strongest. It included Esteban de Avila, s.J. (1549–1625), who arrived in Lima in 1577. He was linked to both the Inquisition and the University of San Marcos, and taught theology at the

College of San Pablo. He was the author of a *Compendium summae seu manualis doct. Navarri* (1620) and of a *Censuris ecclesiasticis tractatus* (Lyons, 1608).[232] His most famous pupil was Juan Pérez de Menacho, who was born in Lima and succeeded him at the University of San Marcos. A prolific commentator on the works of St. Thomas, Pérez de Menacho is said to have memorized the *Summa theologiae*,[233] and was

> undoubtedly the most brilliant figure in colonial philosophy. His extraordinary memory and tremendous learning earned him the admiration of his contemporaries and the most important educational and ecclesiastical positions in the viceroyalty.[234]

The brothers Alonso and Leonardo de Peñafiel also belonged to this group. Both were criollos, born in Riobamba. Alonso studied and taught at the College of San Pablo and in Cuzco; Leonardo taught theology at the University of San Marcos, became a professor at San Pablo and provincial in 1656, and died a year later in Chuquisaca. Martín de Jauregui, s.j. (1619–1713), was a pupil of Leonardo's; also a professor at San Pablo and twice the rector of the University of San Marcos, he was the author of a treatise on philosophy and of an unpublished *Tratado de teología*.[235] Juan de Alloza (1597–1666), a nephew of Pérez de Menacho's, likewise belonged to this group, though he was better known as a preacher and missionary.[236]

The most important name in Peruvian philosophy of the seventeenth century was, however, the Jesuit Diego de Avendaño. Besides the works mentioned earlier, he also wrote *Amphitheatrum misericordiae* and *Epitalamium Christi et sacrae sponsae*, which were commentaries on the psalms. His philosophy is contained in the two-volume *Problemata theologica*; in the first volume, which represents a metaphysical study of natural theology, he follows a Thomistic line of thought, but in the second volume, in regard to the orientation of the solutions, Avendaño inclines toward the Spanish School, making references to Valencia, Vázquez, and other famous Jesuits. Although his philosophy appears to be inspired by Suárez, he mentions him only a few times. The *Problemata theologica* is a serious work, which makes a great contribution to Scholastic philosophy at a time when the Christian philosophy was declining. From that point of view the importance of Avendaño and the impulse which he gave to Scholasticism in far distant Peru become even more significant.[237] Avendaño was also interested in the practical side of Peruvian politics and sociology. He wrote the *Thesaurus indicus* (Antwerp, 1668) in which he followed in the footsteps of Vitoria and Las Casas, defending the Indians, fighting slavery, and proclaiming the Suarezian origin of the state on the basis of the Late Scholastic social contract.[238]

Other Jesuit Scholastics included Cristóbal de Cuba y Arce (1648–1711), author of a *Panegyris cum adesset thesibus universae theologiae*; José de Buendía (1644–1727); Ignacio de las Roellas (d. 1690), who wrote a treatise *De incarnatione*; and Juan Espinosa Medrano, "El Lunarejo" (1632–1688), a native of Cuzco, whose works include a *Philosophia thomistica seu cursus philosophicus* (Rome, 1688), *Apologética en favor de Don Luis de Góngora* (Lima, 1662) and *La novena maravilla nuevamente hallada* (Valladolid, 1695).[239] Finally, other Thomists in seventeenth-century Peru were José de Mendarra y de la Serna, Juan Sebastián de la Parra, Diego Alvarez de Paz, Bernardo de Peñafiel,[240] and Juan Perlín, who, before his death in 1638, resided in Alcalá, Madrid, and Cologne, and taught the philosophy of Suárez in Peru and Quito.

The humanism of Erasmus and Vives, especially that of Vives, made itself felt, in the *Discurso en loor de la poesía*—published in Diego Mejía de Fernangil's *Parnaso antártico* (Seville, 1608)—and in the *Definición de amor* of Diego de Avalos y Figueroa, both of the seventeenth century.[241] Nicolás de Olea and José Aguilar are also linked to the Renaissance tendency in Peru. Olea (1635–1707), a Jesuit scholar, studied at the College of San Martín, became a member of the Society in 1652, and taught at the college in Cuzco. His most famous work was the *Summa tripartita scholasticae philosophiae* (1693), and his link to the Renaissance was his *Compendium universae veteris recentisque theologiae*, in several volumes (which may have perished);[242] he also published a *Cursus philosophicus* (Lima, 1687) and a *Curso de artes* (1693), and represented an early Cartesian influence in Peru.[243] He delved into other religious questions with his work *Tractatus de visione Dei, ad quaest. 12 et 13 S. Thomae*.[244] Aguilar (1652–1708), also a Jesuit, published a *Cursus philosophicus* in three volumes (1701), and the *Tractationes posthumae in primam partem divi Thomae* in five volumes (1731).

Mystic currents were represented by the Augustinian Friar Fernando de Valverde. Born in Lima, a theologian and a poet, Valverde was the author of a theological treatise *De trinitate* and of a *Vida de Jesucristo* (1657).[245]

The College of San Pablo in Lima was particularly important for cultural development in Spanish America. Its establishment in 1568 opened the gates for the spread of the philosophy of Suárez throughout the viceroyalty. The college itself soon had a profound effect in Lima, as it became "the training ground of an army of Jesuits who went forth to fight for justice and Christian love in America,"[246] covering an area of influence from Lima to Trujillo, Chachapoyas, Pisco, Ica, Arequipa, and Cuzco; Santiago de Chile; La Paz, Oruro, Charcas, and Potosí; and Tucumán, Córdoba, and the River Plate. Among the Jesuits linked to the early college were José de Acosta, thinker and theologian; José de Arriaga, humanist; and Alonso de Barzana, linguist. Other great teachers linked to the college included the aforementioned Esteban de Avila, Juan Pérez de Menacho, and Diego de Avendaño, as well as Pedro de Oñate, Diego Alvarez de Paz, and Juan Zapata.

Suárez' influence in Peru was accentuated with the arrival of the Jesuit Juan de Atienza at the end of the sixteenth century. Atienza was a fellow student of Suárez' and one of his most fervent admirers. As the Jesuit provincial of Peru, he was the founder of the Jesuit province of Paraguay, sending priests from Peru to organize that new province (1585). When the famous Diego de Torres, the first provincial of Paraguay (1607–15), founded the *Colegio máximo* of Córdoba in 1612, he specifically informed his superiors that the new studies were being carried out in accordance with the teachings of Suárez.[247]

In 1624, Pedro de Oñate arrived at San Pablo; "an extraordinary intellectual personality,"[248] he was to become one of the professors of the college. He had been a student at Salamanca and Alcalá and had studied directly under Suárez whose system he followed as a teacher at San Pablo and thereafter as Jesuit provincial of Paraguay, and whose spirit can be seen in his work *De contractibus* (1646).

The great controversies on the problem of human freedom which arose in Europe as a consequence of the Reformation also had their effect on the New World, and the Jesuit College of San Pablo used the theories of Suárez and Molina in its defense. Moreover, the college not only contained the works of Suárez—*De legibus*[249]—and Mariana, Gracián, Andrés Mendo, Torquemada, Avendaño, León Pinelo, Solórzano Pereira, but also had some twenty-one portraits of the best Jesuit writers, including Suárez, Bellarmine, and Canisius.[250] Indeed, the books of Suárez and his disciples had come to the library of San Pablo direct from the printing presses of Europe,[251] and even as late as 1767 the works of St. Thomas and Suárez still instructed the Jesuits in philosophy and theology, although the works of the new philosophers were also read at San Pablo.[252]

Since the seventeenth century in Spanish America was the century of Peru, there were echoes of Peru in the region of the River Plate. The first teacher to come to Córdoba was the Jesuit Juan de Albiz (1588–1630), who taught philosophy at the College of Córdoba (1613) after having carried out similar duties at the College of San Javier in Santiago de Chile. Later in his life he returned to Chile where he became the rector of the colleges of Santiago and Concepción and founded a new institution, the Colegio de Buena Esperanza, in the south of the country. Others who came to Córdoba at the time of Albiz were Francisco Vázquez and Juan Pastor.[253]

The University of Córdoba was established in 1613, and Albiz was its first professor of philosophy (1617, 1619). He was the author of a *Dissertatio theologica* (1613) and of a *Relación sobre la armada que envió a Chile el marqués de Mancera*, and became well known and popular.[254] He was succeeded by Miguel de Ampuero. Later in the century (1660) the chairs of philosophy were occupied by two other Jesuits: Cristóbal Gomera (1600–80), who was rector of the Jesuit colleges of Tucumán, Buenos Aires, and Córdoba, and later provincial of Paraguay, and Cristóbal Grijalba (1613–86).[255] Others who taught philosophy at Córdoba in the seventeenth century included the Jesuits Lauro Núñez and Ignacio de Frías. Núñez (1632–1718) was a famous theologian whose books concerned the intrusion of the *bandeirantes* and Guayra; Frías was rector of the colleges not only of Córdoba and Buenos Aires but also of Santiago del Estero. In 1671 he was succeeded by the Jesuit Francisco Burgés (d. 1725), known in the River Plate for his *Cursus philosophicus ad usum scholarium, ad mentem eximii doctoris*—which clearly demonstrated the intellectual hegemony of Suárez in the region—and for several other theological works.[256]

In 1676 the chair of philosophy was occupied by the Jesuit José de Saravia, followed by other members of the Society: Diego Ruiz and Francisco Medrano (1681–84), Joaquín González and Francisco Bazán (1684–87), and Ignacio de Arteaga and Juan Espinosa Medrano (1687–89). In 1689 Felipe de Espínola replaced Medrano, followed by José de Aguirre, Javier Tejedor and José López. Perhaps more important was Agustín de Aragón (1609–78) who became rector of the university and provincial of Paraguay (1669–72) and was well known for a *Cursus philosophicus dictato in Collegio Carmonensi* (1640–43), some *Conclusiones philosophicae defendendae in urba Palmensi* (1643), and a *Tractatus theologico-moralis de poenitentia* (1643–44).[257]

The most significant figure in the River Plate during the seventeenth century was Antonio Rubio Rodensis. A man of the sixteenth century, he was linked essentially to New Spain where he spent almost his entire lifetime (1576–1601), yet he had an extraordinary influence throughout Spanish America reaching far into the eighteenth century. His *Lógica mexicana*, ordered as a textbook by the University of Alcalá, had a wide dissemination and was used from 1613 to 1657 as far south as the University of Córdoba. Although there is no visible evidence of a Suarezian influence in the works of Rubio, the core of his philosophy coincided basically with that of Suárez, whom he often mentioned; as a member of the Society of Jesus, he worked within one and the same line of thought.[258] In the area of Buenos Aires the works of Suárez were disseminated during the rule of its first bishop, Pedro Carranza (1620–32), and in Chuquisaca under Ignacio Arbieto, the rector of the university, who was a great admirer of the Spanish theologian[259] and had been professor of philosophy in Lima, Quito, and Charcas.

The influence of Suárez arrived in New Granada with Diego de Torres, who for many years had served as rector of the colleges in Cuzco and Quito. In 1604 he brought forty-two Jesuits to the Indies, twelve of whom he left in Cartagena. Appointed the next year as vice provincial of New Granada, he organized the newly founded College of San Bartolomé in Santa Fe de Bogotá, which became the focal point for Suarezian philosophy under Torres and his successor, Gonzalo de Lyra, who founded the College of Tunja. In a very short time the three centers—Cartagena, Santa Fe de Bogotá, and Tunja—disseminated Suarezian thought.[260]

The first Colombian philosopher to expound Suarezian theories was Jerónimo de Escobar, s.j. (1596–1673). He was the author of several works, such as *In logicam* (1628), *Disputationes theologicae* (1637), *Proemiales sacrae theologiae* (1641), *Controversia de operationibus immanentibus Dei quae ad eum ut unum pertinent* (1658), and *De divina voluntate*.[261] He was followed by José de Urbina, s.j., rector of San Bartolomé, who in 1647 published his *Disputationes in octo libros physicorum artis Stagyritae*, in which Suarezian philosophy predominated.[262]

Other Scholastic thinkers in New Granada, some of whom followed Suárez, included, in mid-century, Alonso de Sandóval, s.j., a great defender of the blacks, and Jerónimo Marcos, o.f.m., author of *Domus sapientiae doctoris subtilis Joannis Scoti* (1692),[263] and, at the end of the century, Mateo Mimbela (1663–1736) and Juan Antonio Varillas. Mimbela taught at the Universidad Javeriana and was author of a *Tractatus de physica* (1693) and of a *Tractatus de essentia et attributis* (1698), while Varillas published a *Tractatus de conscientia* (1697).[264]

Scholasticism also played a significant role in Venezuela, as a result primarily of the efforts of the famous Chilean Franciscan Juan Alfonso Briceño (1590–1668). Theologian and philosopher, Briceño, in the course of his lifetime, moved throughout Spanish America: around 1636 he taught theology in Lima, was appointed bishop of Nicaragua in 1644, and arrived in Caracas in 1659.[265] (In the early nineteenth century Venezuela would pay a long overdue debt to Chile; for then what the Chilean Briceño had represented in the mid-seventeenth century to Venezuela, the Venezuelan Andrés Bello would mean to Chile.[266]) Briceño's main work is the *Prima pars celebriorum controversiarum in primum Sententiarum Iohannis Scoti ... principis excitatis saepe e re theologica metaphysicis* (1638), which follows Duns Scotus' philosophy against Thomism and Suarezism. Briceño also wrote an *Apologia de vita et doctrina Ioannis Dunsii Scoti*.[267]

The influence of Suárez and of other Late Scholastic thinkers was not only a theoretical matter limited to colleges and universities, but a very practical affair related to politics and government. Thus, when fundamental rights had been violated, resistance was initiated, as in the case against the viceroy of New Spain, Diego Carrillo de Mendoza y Pimentel, marqués de Gelves and conde de Priego, in 1624; or against the governor of Paraguay, Francisco de Mendiola, in 1691; or when the people of Concepción (Chile), sickened by the nepotism of Antonio de Acuña y Cabrera, rose in 1655 in open *cabildo* to depose the governor and install Francisco de la Fuente Villalobos.[268]

In spite of poor communications and official red tape, Spanish Americans had access to a substantial amount of sixteenth- and seventeenth-century literature. Book fairs—notably those in Mexico in 1576, in Lima and Manila in 1583, and in Mexico in 1600[269]—supplied a great variety of literature, ecclesiastical, secular, and belles-lettres. At the Lima fair in 1583, for instance, the works of Friar Luis de Granada and Friar Luis de León abounded.

> Works of jurisprudence, law codes and manuals present a larger variety, though quantities ordered are small. The most notable title representing the first-named group is undoubtedly the *De Justitia et jure* of the great Salamancan professor Domingo de Soto . . .;[270]

the law codes of Castile were also included, as well as the *Siete Partidas* of Alfonso the Learned.[271] As far as philosophy was concerned, Soto again topped the list, together with the works of St. Thomas and the commentaries on them and on the works of Aristotle "by such pure Thomists as Bartolomé de Medina and Francisco de Toledo."[272] The Lima book fair in 1583 matched the high level of the one in Mexico in 1576 and demonstrated that in

> hardly more than a generation the rough community of extrovert conquerors had almost wholly given way to a society binding its highest esteem to works of the spirit and the mind.[273]

The list of books which Luis de Padilla sent from Seville in 1600 clearly shows that neither Mexico nor any other colonial center was cut off from the chief currents of European thought of the period, and demonstrate convincingly that the New World had men of solid culture and catholic interest who were closely concerned with the same moral and scientific problems which interested the great European minds of the late Renaissance.[274] The books which could be found in Cuzco—the second city in Peru after Lima—included not only the obvious *Don Quixote de la Mancha* and the works of Lope de Vega but also such books as Juan de Torres' *Filosofía moral de príncipes*, chronicles of Emperor Charles V and Alfonso the Learned, and histories of Spain by Mariana.[275] It is interesting that an examination of the two book lists covering a shipment of books by a certain Juan de Sarria to Cuzco in 1606 for sale in that city—the first had 438 volumes with some 123 titles—was predominantly of an ecclesiastical nature (about 75%), secular literature and belles-lettres accounting for the balance.[276]

To sum up the political thought in the Spanish world prior to the eighteenth century: it was essentially Scholastic and based on St. Thomas' *De regno ad regem Cypri* and *Summa theologica*, and Francisco Suárez' *De legibus* and *Defensio fidei*, as well as on such sixteenth- and seventeenth-century writers as Domingo de Soto,[277] Diego de Covarrubias,[278] Domingo Báñez,[279] Friar Juan Márquez,[280] Francisco de Quevedo y Villegas,[281] Diego Saavedra Fajardo,[282] Juan de Mariana,[283] Luis de Molina,[284] and Francisco de Vitoria.[285] It was successfully applied in the Indies, in faithful imitation of the Peninsula, by the various Spanish monarchs and their eminent servants: Ferdinand V, with Melchor Maldonado and Bishop Juan Rodríguez de Fonseca; Isabella, with Francisco Cardinal Jiménez de Cisneros; Emperor Charles V, with Francisco de Vitoria and Bartolomé de Las Casas; and Philip II, with Juan de Ovando and Juan de Solórzano Pereira. These doctrines were a vivid reality of Spanish government in the Indies,[286] and can be summarized as follows:[287]

1. Any political authority is of human law, not divine law, and therefore can legitimately be chosen by the people (thus Vitoria in his *De potestate civili*, Soto in his *Defensio Catholicae confessionis*, and Juan de Torquemada in his *Monarquía indiana*).
2. By natural law, sovereign authority originating in God belongs to the people, who cannot totally reject this authority (thus Soto in *De iustitia et iure*, Azpilcueta in his *Opera omnia*); if the governors cannot create an order for the common good, then the people can take steps to remedy the situation.
3. Civil authority is legally acquired only with the consent of the people (whether express or tacit, prior or posterior), since the people are the only subject of sovereignty (thus Bellarmine's *De laicis*, Alfonso de Castro's *De potestate legis poenalis*, and Covarrubias, president of the Council of Castile under Philip II, in his *Opera omnia*).
4. Authority thus conferred on the king cannot be despotic; otherwise the right of resistance and tyrannicide is legal (St. Thomas, Báñez, Mariana, Juan de Santa María in his *República y política cristiana*).[288] It thus includes personal rights based on natural law, the norms of prudence and justice, and positive law, for the enforcement of which power is invested in the king (thus Covarrubias' *Variae*, Suárez' *De legibus*, Molina's *De iustitia*).
5. And last, but not least, if the king dies or abdicates, or is deposed without a legitimate successor, sovereignty reverts to the political community (thus Molina's *De iustitia*, Suárez' *Defensio fidei*).

These were the official theories of government prevailing in Spain and in the Indies; they were practiced by government officials, preached and taught in churches, universities, and colleges, and governed the mind of the kings and the opinion of the people in both Spain and the Spanish lands overseas. Juan de Ovando, lawyer and president of the Council of the Indies under Philip II, impressed these ideas on the government in the Indies—ideas which were published a century later, before the end of the Hapsburg rule in the Spanish domains, through the famous *Recopilación de leyes de las Indias* (1680), and contained four basic elements: providential order, social justice, personal liberty, and Christian charity.[289]

NOTES

[1] See Scott, pp. 3–63. [2] Green, *Spain*, III 85. [3] Ibid., 86.
[4] Morse, p. 140.
[5] See Merriman, II 200–202. These papal bulls are not to be confused with the Treaty of Tordesillas (June 7, 1494), which extended the line of demarcation from 100 leagues to 370 leagues west of the Azores and the Cape Verde Islands in favor of Portugal (pp. 203–204). See also Konetzke, *El imperio*, pp. 237ff., esp. pp. 242–45; and Weckmann, pp. 229ff.
[6] Konetzke, *El imperio*, p. 10.
[7] Ibid., p. 15, with quotation from Karl Vossler, "Die Bedeutung der spanischen Kultur für Europa," in *Deutsche Vierteljahresschrift für Literaturwissenschaft und Geistesgeschichte*, 8 (1930), 58.
[8] Zavala, *New Viewpoints*, pp. 5–6, and Hamilton, passim.
[9] Beneyto, *La ciencia política*, pp. 92ff.
[10] McIlwain, p. 326. See also Rommen, *Die ewige Wiederkehr*, pp. 41–42.
[11] McIlwain, p. 327.
[12] Hamilton, pp. 12–19. See also Morrall, pp. 19–20, and Rommen, *Die ewige Wiederkehr*, p. 54.
[13] Rommen, *Die ewige Wiederkehr*, p. 67. [14] Ibid., p. 58.
[15] See Rommen, *State*, pp. 440–50. [16] Beneyto, *La ciencia política*, p. 202.
[17] Tejada, *El pensamiento*, p. 80. The author gives as an example of the projection of the old Castilian theory of the council in New Granada the "Relación de lo que hacía en Santa Marta el gobernador García Lerma," in *Colección de documentos inéditos relativos al descubrimiento, conquista y colonización de las posesiones españolas en América y Oceanía, sacados en su mayor parte del Real Archivo de Indias* (Madrid, 1865), III 499. See also Solórzano Pereira's concept of the *consejo* in Ayala, *Solórzano*, pp. 247–76, and Angulo y Pérez, pp. 1–2.
[18] Tejada, *El pensamiento*, pp. 80–86.
[19] Ibid., pp. 45–78.
[20] Vossler phrased it well (p. 39) when he said that Spain was the country which has had its own Reformation and its own Renaissance, and not those of the other European peoples, and experienced in its own way the fundamental renewal of Christian faith and of human culture and education.
[21] Ramos, *La filosofía en México*, pp. 18–19.
[22] Green, *Spain*, III 226–27, 248–49, among others.
[23] See Menéndez Pidal, *Mis páginas*, pp. 232–53. In contrast to the theories of Brandi (pp. 90–94, 112)—expressed earlier in his "Eigenhändige Aufzeichnungen Karls V. aus dem Anfang des Jahres 1525: Der Kaiser und sein Kanzler" (*Nachrichten von der Gesellschaft der Wissenschaften zu Göttingen* [1933]) and in "Karl V." (*Preussische Jahrbücher*, 214 [1928], 23ff.), of Rassow, and of Schwarzenfeld (pp. 52, 111–113), who pointed out the importance of Gattinara's influence on Charles V, Menéndez Pidal maintains that the imperial ideology of Charles V had different sources. It was not Dante's ideas of the universal monarchy, but Mota's Hispanic concepts of a Christian empire which influenced him. Of interest is Beneyto Pérez' thesis (*Las doctrinas políticas*, pp. 213–14) that the Emperor's imperial idea derives from the religious sentiments inherited by Queen Isabella and from the doctrines of Mota, Alfonso de Valdés, and Antonio de Guevara: Charles V combined Roman, German, and Hispanic concepts regarding the imperial idea. As so often in Spanish history, a fusion seems to have occurred between the various currents; we cannot deny the great influx of Erasmian thought in Spain in the early years of the emperor's reign, though Bataillon (*Erasmo y España*) might have exaggerated it. For the relationship of Gattinara and Erasmus, see Brandi, pp. 128, 258; Schwarzenfeld, pp. 119–20.
[24] Fernández Alvarez, 401, with quotation from *Actas de las Cortes de los antiguos reinos de León y de Castilla* (Madrid, 1882), IV 294.
[25] See Penna, pp. 3–5, 8; Heer, pp. 292–93; Ritter, pp. 92–93.
[26] Keniston, p. 50. [27] Green, *Spain*, III 100–101. [28] Bataillon, passim.
[29] Green, *Spain*, IV 138. [30] Ibid., III 183.
[31] Fernández Bonilla, *El tiempo*, pp. 113–15.
[32] Green, *Spain*, III 104.

[33] See Bataillon, II 429–33; Heer, pp. 286–305.
[34] Ramos, *La filosofía en México*, pp. 20–24; Parry, p. 12.
[35] Green, *Spain*, II 11. [36] Ibid., III 169. [37] Ibid., II 174–75.
[38] Ibid., p. 157, quoted from J. M. Gallegos Rocafull, *El hombre y el mundo de los teólogos españoles de los siglos de oro* (Mexico, 1946), p. 18.
[39] Green, *Spain*, II 185. [40] Ibid., III 115–40, 122. [41] Ibid., 140.
[42] Ibid., III 231–32. [43] Pfandl, *Cultura*, pp. 158–59, 161–62.
[44] Ibid., pp. 147–48. [45] Ibid., pp. 149–54.
[46] Ibid., pp. 162–64; see also Davies, *Golden Century*, p. 290.
[47] Pfandl, *Cultura*, pp. 164–65. [48] Ibid., p. 165. [49] Ibid., p. 35.
[50] Ibid., p. 36. [51] Ibid., p. 42. [52] Ibid., p. 176.
[53] Green, *Spain*, III 301–24. [54] Ibid., pp. 283–93. [55] Parry, p. 2.
[56] Ibid. [57] Ibid., p. 4. [58] Hamilton, p. 4.
[59] His works include the *Tractatus de legibus, ac Deo legislatore* (Coimbra, 1612), the *Defensio fidei Catholicae et apostolicae adversus Anglicanae sectae errores* (Mainz, 1655), and the *De opere sex dierum* (Lyons, 1635).
[60] Green, *Spain*, II 193, quoting Mauricio de Iriarte, s.j., *El hombre Suárez y el hombre en Suárez* (Madrid, 1950), p. 34.
[61] Korn, pp. 29–30. [62] Morse, p. 153. [63] Ibid., pp. 153–54.
[64] Ibid., p. 154. [65] Ibid., p. 155. [66] Parry, p. 18.
[67] Rommen, *Die Staatslehre*, p. 105.
[68] Ibid., pp. xiii, 1, 111–15, 154–55, 158, 187–88, 193, 206–207.
[69] Pp. 29–30.
[70] Suárez applied the *designatio* theory to the papacy, while the *translatio* theory referred only to the state.
[71] Lanseros, p. 241; see also Gómez Robledo, p. 143.
[72] Suárez, *De legibus*, III.ii.3. [73] Lanseros, p. 237.
[74] Luis de Molina, *De iustitia et iure* (Mainz, 1602), II.26. Suárez in his *Defensio fidei* (III.III.3) specifically refers to Robert Cardinal Bellarmine and to Navarro (Martín de Azpilcueta) when he says: "Quod vero Bellarminus ex Navarro dixit populum nunquam ita suam potestatem in principem transferre, quin eam in habitu retineat, ut ea in certis casibus uti possit...." The "certain cases" to which Suárez referred are those of a positive-law character (abolishment or vacancy of the throne) or violations of natural law, as mentioned above. In regard to Molina, who followed this thought of Azpilcueta, see Costello.
[75] Suárez, *Defensio fidei*, III.III.4, where he points out: "Postquam rex legitime constitutus est, supremam habet potestatem in his omnibus, ad quae illam accepit."
[76] Gómez Hoyos, I 78–85. The theory can also be found in Mariana's *De rege et regis institutione* (Toledo, 1599), I.ii, v, vi, viii, ix, and III.vii.
[77] Eyzaguirre, p. 31. [78] Green, *Spain*, III 281–82.
[79] For example, Korn, p. 30: "Francisco Suárez, a strong and original mind, even if he does not greatly depart from St. Thomas' teachings, not only changes the traditional method, but attempts to state the old ideas in a new form"; or somewhat differently, Halperín Donghi, pp. 52–72, who concludes (p. 72): "In this manner the work of the political thinker Suárez, which appears to us so solidly rooted in its time, nonetheless closes a period of the history of Spanish legal and political thought: the new needs will bring about a style of political thought [which will] also be new during the seventeenth century."
[80] Green, *Spain*, III 282–83. [81] Ibid., 283. [82] See Reibstein.
[83] Green, *Spain*, III 282.
[84] López de Gómara, p. 275, and Díaz del Castillo. See also Tudela, I 255–56.
[85] Mendieta, *Historia eclesiástica indiana* (4 vols.; Mexico, 1945).
[86] See Phelan, esp. pp. 5–77.
[87] Konetzke, *Colección de documentos*, includes many decrees with regard to the good treatment which is to be given the Indians: I.19, pp. 28–29; I.24, pp. 36–38; I.39, pp. 78–80; I.44, pp. 87–88; I.46, pp. 89–96; I.47, pp. 96–97; I.48, pp. 97–98; I.55, pp. 107–108; I.59, pp. 113–20; I.64, pp. 129; I.66, pp. 131–32; I.68, pp. 134–36; I.72, pp. 138–39; I.96, pp. 171–76; I.114, pp. 188–89; I.122, pp. 197–98; I.123, pp. 198–99, among others.

Henry of Susa (Hostiensis, d. 1271), an extreme supporter of the papacy, advanced the idea in his *Summa aurea* that the pope was the universal vicar of Christ and held *plenitudo potestatis* not only over the Christians, but also over all unbelievers, since the *potestas* had been granted by God *in plenitudine*. According to the Cardinal of Ostia, whose theme was fully elaborated half a century later by Giles of Rome, after the coming of Christ, every principality, *dominium*, and jurisdiction had been taken from the unbelievers and by the pope's *plenitudo potestatis* transferred *de iure* and justly to the Christians. Thus, any title which unbelievers might have advanced through *ius naturale* and *ius gentium* to their kingdom automatically disappeared with the coming of Christ and fell to the temporal power of the pope, who could claim at any time *potestas* over the infidels. In the meantime, the latter held only a precarious rule as a concession from the papacy.

Innocent IV (d. 1254) had declared that unbelievers could have *dominium* because possession is inherent in all rational beings; hence, the pope or the Gentiles were not allowed, without sin, to appropriate the goods and jurisdiction which unbelievers possessed. But Christ, and hence the pope, has *potestas* over all men *de iure*, although this may not be *de facto*. This theory, based on the rationality of man and not on religious beliefs, was apt to give greater support to the rights of the unbelievers.

Although the Middle Ages also produced other theories on slavery, none had greater influence than that of St. Thomas, particularly since it reflected the summit reached by Scholastic philosophy. In his view, even the distinction between Christians and infidels did not cause the disappearance of a *dominium* of infidels over Christians. He somewhat mitigated this theory in asserting that this superiority could be limited by order of the Church which exercised the authority of God on earth, since unbelievers, by virtue of being infidels, merit losing the *dominium* over the Christians, who are sons of God.

Another expounder of theories connected with the title to the Indies and the treatment of the Indians was Thomas Cardinal Cajetan (1469–1534), a follower of Thomistic doctrines. He stated that there were three kinds of infidels: (*a*) those who *de iure* and *de facto* were subjects of Christian kings (Jews, heretics, or Moors living in Christian lands); (*b*) those who *de iure*, but not *de facto*, were subjects of Christian kings (the Moors who invaded Christian lands); and (*c*) a group which neither *de iure* nor *de facto* was subject to Christian rule, since they never heard or knew about Christianity. These people (like the Indians) are not deprived of the rights of *dominium* by reason of being infidels, since the right to rule is derived from positive law, and infidelity from divine law which does not destroy positive law. To wage war against such infidels would be unjust; the Christian princes who enter such a conflict would be committing a gross offense, *magna latrocinia*, for which restitution is necessary (Zavala, *La filosofía política*, pp. 26–35).

[88] Cf. Joseph Höffner, *La ética colonial española del siglo de oro. Cristianismo y dignidad humana* (Span. ed.; Madrid, 1957), pp. 235–303. See also Hanke, *Spanish Struggle*, pp. 17–22, and Parry, pp. 27–56.

[89] Konetzke, *Colección de documentos*, I.25, pp. 38–57. See also Hanke, *Spanish Struggle*, pp. 23–27, and Merriman, II.234–35.

[90] The Spanish title is linked to the four bulls granted by Pope Alexander VI in 1493. They were based on three fundamental principles: *donatio*, *concessio*, and *assignatio*. The first and second bulls dated May 3, 1493—*Inter caetera*—granted, assigned, and invested the kings of Spain with the sovereignty of the discovered lands, mentioning the concessions already given to Portugal. The third bull (May 4, 1493)—third and fourth bull: *Eximiae*—specified the well-known demarcation line of 100 leagues west of the Azores and the Cape Verde Islands. The pope specifically charged the Spanish Crown to send able men to propagate the faith, and forbade anyone else to trade or to intervene in these regions without their consent. The fourth bull (September 26, 1493) amplified the grant. Zavala, *La colonización española*, pp. 44–61. See also Ayala, *Solórzano*, pp. 345–81, and Hanke, *Spanish Struggle*, pp. 23–30, 111–79. The theory of the papal grants was upheld in various documents: Isabella's codicil to her will, November 1504; King Ferdinand's order to Governor Ovando, February 10, 1505, referring to him as perpetual administrator by apostolic authority; King Ferdinand's order of June 6, 1511, to Diego Columbus, charging "that the Indians be baptized and instructed in our Holy Catholic Faith, for this is the principal foundation upon which we base our conquest of these regions" (Hanke, *Spanish Struggle*, p. 26).

[91] Matías de Paz's "De dominio regum Hispaniae super Indos," now available in the *Archivum Fratrum Praedicatorum*, 3 (1933), 131–81, was first published in Heredia; the "Libellus de insulanis oceanis quas vulgus Indias appellant" (1512) of Juan López de Palacios Rubios, is preserved in the National Library of Madrid in MS 17.641 (see Pereña Vicente, p. 5). The two treatises are the only ones known to have survived. As early as the *Siete Partidas* of Alfonso the Learned, it is emphatically stated that a just war can be waged only for the propagation of the faith, and that the destruction of those who oppose it is justified. This concept became one of the principal ideas behind the Spanish *Conquista* of the Indies, since the conversion of the Indians was, at least officially, its main purpose—an objective prefigured by the conversion of the peoples of the Canary Islands.

[92] The first to use this "Requirement" was Pedro Arias de Avila (Pedrarias) in 1514, and subsequently all conquistadors, including Hernán Cortés in New Spain and Francisco Pizarro in Peru, applied it. For the text and for further commentary, see Lowery, pp. 147, 177–81, 387, who refers here to the use of the "Requirement" by Juan Ponce de León and Pánfilo de Narváez.

[93] Höffner, passim, esp. pp. 235ff.

[94] Parry, pp. 55–56. See Hanke, *Aristotle*, pp. 17, 55–61.

[95] Parry, p. 48. [96] Ibid., p. 50. [97] Ibid., pp. 52–53.

[98] Zavala, *Human Rights*, p. 46. See Hanke, *Spanish Struggle*, p. 89.

[99] Manzano Manzano, pp. 134ff., esp. pp. 139–43.

[100] Ibid., pp. 147–48.

[101] In his *De Indis prior* and *De Indis posterior, sive de iure belli Hispanorum in barbaros*, expounded in 1539, Vitoria denied that Spain had a right to conquer the lands of the Indians and to force conversion upon them. Expressing a thesis contrary to the official policy of the Catholic rulers and of such theologians as Palacios Rubios, he condemned the false titles for Spanish rule, proclaiming legitimate ones. Among the false titles were:

1. The emperor is not the master of the whole universe.
2. Even if he were, he could not on this account become the master of the provinces of the American Indians, install new masters and remove the old ones, or impose tributes.
3. The pope is neither the civil nor the temporal master of the universe, in the proper sense of sovereignty and civil authority.
4. Even if he had secular power over the entire universe, he could not grant it to secular princes.
5. The pope has temporal authority whenever it is at the service of spiritual matters.
6. The pope has no temporal power over the Indians or over other infidels.
7. Should the Indians decline to recognize any *dominium* of the pope's, war cannot be waged against them for this reason, nor their goods be appropriated.
8. The Indians are not guilty of the sin of infidelity, since they cannot believe in Christ before hearing about him (Pereña Vicente, pp. 7–8).

Some of the legitimate titles included:

1. The Spaniards have the right to travel across the lands of the Indians, who cannot prohibit it unless the Spaniards do them harm.
2. The Spaniards have the right to trade with the Indians without damage to their State, and can export excess goods without interference from the princes of the infidels, as the kings of Spain cannot prohibit the Indians from trading with the Spaniards.
4. The Spaniards have the right to hospitality from and residence in the cities and towns of America.
5. Should the Indians prevent the Spaniards from enjoying these rights, and should words, reasoning, and all other peaceful means be of no avail, the king of Spain may seek recompense for the injury by force, resorting even to war. An injury shall be considered as committed whenever anything due by *ius gentium* is denied.
6. Once all other peaceful means have been exhausted, the Spaniards may occupy the cities of the Indians, if such be necessary for their security and the guarantee of their rights, always respecting the Indians' property and their forms of government.
7. Should the Indians, in spite of these violent methods, decline to live in peace and continue to attempt the ruination of the Spaniards, the Spaniards have the right to apply the laws of war against unjust enemies, to seize their territories, alter their forms of government, and subject them to the Crown of Castile.
8. The Spaniards have the right to preach the Gospel to the barbarian peoples and may declare war on those who violently prevent the preaching and conversion of the infidels, it being understood that such missionary activity be done with moderation and without abuse, and with the intention directed more toward the good of the infidels than to their own interest (ibid., pp. 8–9). See Monica, p. 103; Parry, pp. 19–26; Hanke, *Spanish Struggle*, pp. 150–52; and Manzano Manzano, pp. 63–82.

[102] The *Imperium* meant only a sort of *regnum magnum* without implying any concrete hierarchical overlordship, in keeping with the thesis of the Spanish exemption (Beneyto Pérez, *Las doctrinas políticas*, p. 222). See Scott, pp. 117–25.

[103] See Scott, passim.

[104] Beneyto Pérez, *Las doctrinas políticas*, pp. 222–23.

[105] Gierke, pp. 85, 283. [106] Parry, p. 21.

[107] This controversy is all the more remarkable since the New Laws had earlier condemned slavery and dismissed the *encomienda* system as a result of Las Casas' struggle in defense of

the Indians and the high principles of international law proclaimed by Vitoria. See Sepúlveda, pp. xxxvi–xl. For a favorable opinion on Sepúlveda, see Marcos.
[108] Parry, p. 43.   [109] Pereña Vicente, p. 309.   [110] Ibid., p. 310.
[111] Ibid., pp. 311–12.
[112] Giménez Fernández, *Las doctrinas populistas*, p. 19.
[113] Konetzke, *Colección de documentos*, I.144, pp. 216–20, I.146, pp. 222–26.
[114] Ibid., I.341, pp. 471–78.
[115] Parry, p. 26.   [116] Höffner, p. 509.   [117] Korn, pp. 31–32.
[118] Consejo de la Hispanidad, I.1.   [119] Korn, p. 32.   [120] Ibid.
[121] See Hanke, *Spanish Struggle*, pp. 8–10.
[122] Tudela, I.213–14. See also Ramos, *La filosofía en México*, pp. 28–30, 24–25.
[123] Ibid., pp. 27–28.   [124] Ibid., p. 28.   [125] Merriman, III.663–64.
[126] Lanning, *Academic Culture*, pp. 21–22.
[127] Ibid., p. 18; Green, *Spain*, III, 72.
[128] Abad de Santillán, I 324. See also Tudela, II 439–46, and Lanning, *Academic Culture*, pp. 3–22.
[129] Ramos, *La filosofía en México*, pp. 30–31; Lanning, *Academic Culture*, pp. 14–15. "The 'seven columns' of learning in the Mexican university, the seven chairs, were theology, scripture, canons, arts (logic, metaphysics, physics), laws, decretals, and rhetoric—all upon a base of Latin language" (ibid., p. 18). See also Ramos, *La filosofía en México*, p. 31.
[130] Tudela, I 216. See Ramos, *La filosofía en México*, pp. 33–39, and Redmond, p. 105.
[131] Redmond, p. 52. See Ramos, *La filosofía en México*, p. 39, and Furlong, *Nacimiento*, p. 56.
[132] Redmond, p. 59; Ramos, *La filosofía en México*, p. 39; Tudela, I 216.
[133] Ramos, *La filosofía en México*, p. 39; Redmond, p. 59.
[134] Tudela, I 216; Ramos, *La filosofía en México*, p. 40; Furlong, *Nacimiento*, pp. 57–58; Redmond, pp. 84–85.
[135] Furlong, *Nacimiento*, p. 58.   [136] Redmond, p. 13.
[137] Ramos, *La filosofía en México*, pp. 32, 40. See also Redmond, p. 134.
[138] Ramos, *La filosofía en México*, p. 31.
[139] Furlong, *Nacimiento*, p. 56.
[140] Ramos, *La filosofía en México*, pp. 31–32.
[141] Ibid., p. 32.   [142] Lockhart, pp. 3–7.   [143] Salazar Bondy, p. 59.
[144] Acosta, pp. 1–247; see too the "Introducción," pp. vii–xlix, and "De procuranda Indorum salute o Predicacción del evangelio en las Indias," pp. 387–608. See also Salazar Bondy, p. 60; Vargas Ugarte, *Manual*, pp. 172–73, 298–99; Tudela I 217; Furlong, *Nacimiento*, pp. 87–94; Green, *Spain*, II 11–14, 187–88, and III 110–11, 331–33; Martín, pp. 22–27.
[145] Green, *Spain*, III 243.   [146] Redmond, p. 3.
[147] Salazar Bondy, pp. 60, 87–88. See also Redmond, p. 134.
[148] Green, *Spain*, III 21.
[149] Salazar Bondy, pp. 59–60.
[150] Moses, *Spanish Colonial Literature*, pp. 467–71.
[151] Ibid., p. 463.   [152] Ibid., pp. 464–65.
[153] Vargas Ugarte, *Manual*, pp. 114, 143–44, 354–55.
[154] Ibid., p. 145.   [155] Ibid., p. 143.   [156] Ibid., pp. 235–36.
[157] Ibid., pp. 244–45.   [158] Ibid., pp. 232–34, 227.
[159] Ibid., pp. 225–27. See also Imbert, pp. 27–28.
[160] Lizárraga, II 134.   [161] Furlong, *Nacimiento*, pp. 85–87.
[162] The full name of Jiménez de Quesada's *El Antijovio* (Bogotá, 1952) is "Apuntaciones y anotaciones sobre la Historia de Paulo Jovio, Obispo de Nochera, en que se declara la verdad de las cosas que pasaron en tiempo del Emperador Carlos V, desde que comenzó a reinar en España hasta el año mdxliii con descargo de la Nación Española. Lo cual escribía y ordenaba Don Gonzalo Jiménez de Quesada, Adelantado y Capitán General en el nuevo reino de Granada." This fact is mentioned here for the first time by Bayle, "Un libro nuevo," 338–46.
[163] Frankl, "Agustinismo," 1.
[164] Ibid., 1–32, esp. 12–13. See also Green, *Spain*, III 289–90.
[165] Jiménez de Quesada, "Indicaciones."
[166] Castellanos, *Elegías de varones ilustres de Indias*. For his complete works, see Castellanos, *Obras*.
[167] Aguado, *Historia de Santa Marta y Nuevo Reino de Granada*.
[168] Aguado, *Historia de Venezuela*.

[169] Tejada, *El pensamiento*, pp. 214–16. See Beneyto, *Los orígenes*, pp. 387–90, for Exímenis, and pp. 386–87 for the Tostado; see also Asís, pp. 143–60.

[170] Vargas Machura, *Milicia y descripción de las Indias*.

[171] See Parry, p. 72, concerning Friar Nicholas de Witte, a Dutchman, who argued, in a letter to the Emperor, that since "distant possessions are the most easily lost," only a system of decentralization would save the Spanish Empire.

[172] Tejada, *El pensamiento*, p. 252; and pp. 91–256, for the political thought of Jiménez de Quesada, Castellanos, and Aguado. See also Porras Troconis, pp. 25–33.

[173] Furlong, *Nacimiento*, pp. 56–57. [174] Tudela, I 217.

[175] See Beneyto, *Espíritu*, passim, esp. pp. 13–19.

[176] Green, *Spain*, IV 9.

[177] Ibid., p. 75. See also Menéndez y Pelayo, II 327–68.

[178] Green, *Spain*, II 210–11. [179] Ibid., 209–10. [180] Ibid., I 208.

[181] Ibid., 209. [182] Ibid., II 158. [183] Ibid., III 325–27.

[184] This current produced the *Libro primero del Espejo del príncipe christiano* (Lisbon, 1571) by Francisco de Monzón, and Francisco Patricio's *De regno et institutione regis*, translated into Spanish by Enrique Garcés, a Portuguese living in Peru (Madrid, 1591). To this current belongs as well Friar Juan de Torres' *Philosophia moral de príncipes para su buena crianza y gobierno y para personas de todos estados* (Burgos, 1596). See Maravall, *La philosophie*, pp. 39–40, 42, 158, 192, among others. See further Salazar, pp. vii–x.

[185] By far the best example is Pedro de Rivadeneyra's work *Tratado de la religión y virtudes que debe tener el príncipe cristiano para gobernar y conservar sus estados: Contra lo que Nicolás Maquiavelo y los políticos de este tiempo enseñan* (Madrid, 1595), based on the three fundamental princely virtues: prudence, strength, and moderation. Others in this line are Juan Fernandez de Medrano y Sandoval, *Republica mixta* (Madrid, 1602); Alvia de Castro, *Verdadera razón de estado. Discurso político* (Lisbon, 1616); Friar Juan de Santa María, *Tratado de república y política christiana: Para reyes y príncipes y para los que en el gobierno tienen sus veces* (Valencia, 1619); Friar Juan de Salazar, *Política española* (Logroño, 1619); Diego Felipe de Albornoz, *Castilla política y christiana* (Madrid, 1666); and Friar Francisco Garau's works *El sabio instruido de la naturaleza en cuarenta máximas políticas y morales* (Valencia, 1690), *El olimpo del sabio instruído de la naturaleza y segunda parte de las máximas políticas y morales* (Valencia, 1690), and *Tercera parte del sabio instruido de la naturaleza, con esfuerzos en el tribunal de la razón; alegados en cuarenta y dos máximas políticas y morales. Contra las vanas ideas de la política de Machiavelo* (Barcelona, 1700), to name but a few. See further Salazar, pp. xi–xix.

[186] Following in the tradition of Friar Luis de León are Castillo de Bobadilla, *Política para corregidores y señores de vasallos, en tiempos de paz y de guerra, y para prelados en los espiritual y temporal, entre legos, jueces de comisión, regidores, abogados y otros oficiales públicos* (Barcelona, 1624); Tomás Cerdán de Tallada, *Verdadero gobierno de esta monarchía, tomando por su propio subiecto la conservación de la paz* (Valencia, 1581), and *Veriloquium en reglas de estado, según derecho divino, natural, canónico y civil y leyes de Castilla* (Valencia, 1604); Friar Juan Márquez, *El gobernador cristiano, deducido de las vidas de Moysés y Josué, príncipes del pueblo de Dios* (Salamanca, 1612); and Francisco de Gurmendi, *Doctrina physica y moral de príncipes* (Madrid, 1615), to name a few. See Salazar, pp. xx–xxxv.

[187] Maravall, *La philosophie*, p. 103. [188] Hamilton, pp. 9–10. [189] Green, *Spain*, IV 155.

[190] Moses, *Spanish Colonial Literature*, pp. 467ff. [191] Ibid., pp. 473–76.

[192] Ibid., pp. 476–79. [193] Ibid., pp. 471–73. See Ayala, *Solórzano*, passim.

[194] Halperín Donghi, pp. 92–93, 94. [195] Ibid., p. 96. [196] Ibid.

[197] Ibid., pp. 96ff. [198] *Las ideas políticas*, I 126. [199] Ibid.

[200] Ibid., 128–33, esp. 130. [201] Furlong, *Nacimiento*, pp. 61, 201–19.

[202] Lanning, *Academic Culture*, p. 33. [203] Ibid.

[204] Abad de Santillán, I 324. See also Tudela, II 439–55; and Lanning, *Academic Culture*, pp. 3–33.

[205] Lanning, *Academic Culture*, p. 43.

[206] Ramos, *La filosofía en México*, p. 41.

[207] Ibid., pp. 45–46, esp. p. 46.

[208] Ibid. See also Redmond, p. 27.

[209] Ramos, *La filosofía en México*, p. 46. See also Redmond, p. 135.

[210] Ramos, *La filosofía en México*, p. 46. See also Redmond, pp. 21–22.

[211] Ramos, *La filosofía en México*, p. 46. See also Redmond, pp. 107–108.

[212] Ramos, *La filosofía en México*, pp. 46–47. See also Redmond, pp. 47–48.

MEDIEVAL TRADITION

213 Ramos, *La filosofía en México*, p. 47. See also Redmond, p. 135.
214 Ramos, *La filosofía en México*, p. 47. See also Redmond, p. 17.
215 Ramos, *La filosofía en México*, p. 47. See also Redmond, p. 134.
216 Ramos, *La filosofía en México*, p. 47. See also Redmond, p. 8.
217 Ramos, *La filosofía en México*, p. 47. See also Redmond, p. 21.
218 Ramos, *La filosofía en México*, p. 47. See also Redmond, p. 134.
219 Redmond, pp. 73–74. See also Tudela, I 218.
220 Redmond, pp. 72–73. See also Tudela, I 218.
221 Tudela, I 218. See also Redmond p. 14; Martín, pp. 60–61, 65–66, 68–69, 72.
222 Leonard, *Baroque Times*, p. 193. See also Ramos, *La filosofía en México*, pp. 49–53.
223 Leonard, *Baroque Times*, p. 200.
224 Redmond, p. 92.   225 Leonard, *Baroque Times*, p. 208.
226 Guil Blanes, p. 167.   227 Ibid., 169.   228 Ibid., 169–71.
229 Ibid., 172.   230 Ibid., 174.
231 Ibid., 175. See also Redmond, p. 101; Salazar Bondy, pp. 60, 88.
232 Guil Blanes, 176. See also Redmond, p. 14; Martín, pp. 56, 60, 72, 78, 147; Salazar Bondy, pp. 60, 88.
233 Guil Blanes, 177. See also Salazar Bondy, pp. 61, 89; Martín, pp. 56–57, 60, 73, 78.
234 Salazar Bondy, p. 61.   235 Guil Blanes, 177–78.   236 Ibid., 178.
237 Ibid., 179–82.   238 Tudela, I 218.   239 Salazar Bondy, p. 88.
240 Furlong, *Nacimiento*, p. 63.   241 Salazar Bondy, pp. 60, 87.
242 Guil Blanes, 178. See also Redmond, pp. 67–68.
243 Furlong, *Nacimiento*, pp. 62–63.   244 Redmond, p. 68.   245 Guil Blanes, 178–79.
246 Martín, p. 73.   247 Dell'Oro Maini, p. 14.   248 Martín, p. 57.
249 Ibid., p. 90.   250 Ibid., p. 86.   251 Ibid., p. 95.
252 Ibid., pp. 93–96, 147.   253 Furlong, *Nacimiento*, p. 95.   254 Ibid., p. 96.
255 Ibid., pp. 96–97.   256 Ibid., pp. 97–98.   257 Ibid., pp. 99–100.
258 Ibid., pp. 101–109.   259 Ibid., p. 206.   260 Gómez Hoyos, I 133ff.
261 Ibid., 138. See also Redmond, p. 36.
262 Gómez Hoyos, I 138. See also Redmond, p. 99.
263 Gómez Hoyos, I 138–41. See also Redmond, p. 56.
264 Gómez Hoyos, I 141. See also Redmond, pp. 60, 102–103.
265 García Bacca, p. 17.   266 Ibid., p. 18.
267 See ibid., pp. 27–178, in regard to Briceño's philosophy. See also Redmond, p. 20.
268 Eyzaguirre, p. 37.
269 See Leonard, *Books of the Brave*, pp. 183–257.
270 Ibid., p. 220.   271 Ibid., p. 221.   272 Ibid., pp. 221–22.
273 Ibid., p. 211.   274 Ibid., pp. 256–57.   275 Ibid., p. 298.
276 Ibid., p. 299. See also pp. 290–312.
277 *De iustitia et iure* (Salamanca, 1553), I, q. 1, a. 3; I, q. 6; III, q. 4; IV, q. 4, a. 1.
278 *Practicarum quaestionum liber unus* (Venice, 1566), I, 2 and 6.
279 *Commentaria in Secundum Secundae D. Thomae* (Salamanca, 1685), q. 60, a. 1.
280 Márquez, *El gobernador cristiano*.
281 *Política de Dios, gobierno de Cristo y tiranía de Satanás* (Saragossa, 1626). See Gómez Hoyos, I 103–107.
282 Saavedra Fajardo. See Murillo Ferrol, who pointedly brings out the Christianization of the *raison d'état*.
283 "Tratado y discurso sobre la moneda de vellón," *Obras*, II 463–593; and *De rege*, I.8.
284 *De iustitia*, II.20, col. 94, and n. 74.
285 *De potestate civili* (Lyons, 1586), n. 8. See also *Relecciones teológicas del maestro Fray Francisco de Vitoria*, trans. Luis G. Alonso Getino (Madrid, 1934).
Other thinkers of the Spanish School who followed similar doctrines included: Fernando Vázquez de Menchaca, *Controversium illustrium aliarumque usu frequentium libri tres*, III.xliii.1; xliv.4; xlvii.2–5, 12; Pedro de Aragón, *De iustitia et iure* (Lyons, 1596), q. 63, a. 2; Gregorio de Valencia, *Commentaria in Secundum Secundae D. Thomae* in *Opera* (Lyons, 1609), iii 277D–E; Martín de Azpilcueta, *Relectio capitis novi, de iudiciis*, in *Opera* (Cologne, 1616), II.iii.85; Alfonso de Castro, *De potestate legis poenalis* (Lyons, 1556), I, I, pp. 14–16. See Lanseros, pp. 189–210.
286 Höffner, pp. 305–524; Hanke, *Spanish Struggle*, pp. 88–105, 109–79.
287 Giménez Fernández, *Las doctrinas populistas*, pp. 10, 13, 14.
288 Santa María, *Tratado de república y política christiana*.
289 Giménez Fernández, *Las doctrinas populistas*, p. 21.

III

THE ENLIGHTENMENT IN THE SPANISH WORLD,
1700–1808

1. ENLIGHTENMENT AND SCHOLASTICISM IN THE PENINSULA

A NEW ERA BEGAN WITH THE EUROPEAN ENLIGHTENMENT: it was a further step toward monism built logically on the rationalism of Descartes and the scientific revolution, and emphasizing progress, nature, and science. The Enlightenment announced a new belief in the perfectibility of the human race and the ennobling effects of modern civilization. In Carl Becker's view the *philosophes* demolished "the Heavenly City of Saint Augustine only to rebuild it with more up-to-date materials."[1] Although this view is untenable, as shown in the revisionist interpretations of Peter Gay, Frank Manuel, and J. L. Talmon, among others,[2] it could be argued that the philosophers "were the secular bearers of the Protestant and the Jansenist traditions."[3]

"Having denatured God," the *philosophes* "deified nature," and attempted to establish a new morality and virtue which could replace the Christian Middle Ages—"those unhappy times . . . , when mankind, corrupted and degraded by error, wandered blindly under the yoke of oppression."[4] They thus presented "another interpretation of the past, the present and the future state of mankind" which was most subjective and in keeping with the rationalistic *Zeitgeist*. In Becker's view

> The new heaven had to be located somewhere within the confines of the earthly life, since it was an article of philosophical faith that the end of life is life itself, the perfected temporal life of men; and in the future, since the temporal life was not yet perfect. But if the celestial heaven was to be dismantled in order to be rebuilt on earth, it seemed that the salvation of mankind must be attained, not by some outside, miraculous, catastrophic agency (God or the philosopher king), but by man himself, by the progressive improvement made by the efforts of successive generations of men . . . . Thus the Philosophers called on posterity to exorcise the double illusion of the Christian paradise and the golden age of antiquity. For the love of God they substituted love of humanity; for the vicarious atonement the perfectibility of man through his own efforts; and for the hope of immortality in another world the hope of living in the memory of future generations.[5]

In time, many of the ingredients of the Enlightenment became part of the ideas of 1789 and received a quasi-religious meaning—the faith in progress and science, with its own "soldiers, apostles, and martyrs,"[6] very much like Positivism and Marxism later.

One of the main changes which came over Europe with the Enlightenment and was associated with the Age of Reason was the development of antireligious attitudes,[7] what Gay has termed the rise of neo-paganism, with its appeal to antiquity and its tension with Christianity: the retreat from reason —the adulteration of antiquity, the betrayal of criticism, and the rehabilitation of myth.[8] No doubt a chief characteristic of the Enlightenment was a critical and skeptical attitude toward religion. Yet Ernst Cassirer has pointed out that if one looks more deeply into the European Enlightenment it becomes clear that such a sweeping judgment would apply, with strong reservations and limitations, only to the English and German cases, "though it may be more in accord with the French type in view of its materialism, atheism, and sensualism,"[9] and what Germaine de Staël has called a philosophy favoring an ethic based on interest and an irony and disdain of lofty ideals.[10] In Cassirer's view, the religious attitude changed toward a new ideal of faith: a universal humanist religion which interpreted human nature as capable of elevating itself toward the divine by its own forms.[11]

The French Enlightenment—as Daniel Mornet pointed out—grew out of the progress of the sciences especially after 1690, and this progress was seen as the progress of humanity. It meant an attack on Christianity, since

> Man was not merely a fallen creature, devoted to sin, expiation, and self-sacrifice. He could create, conquer, dominate nature. Reason, or at least a certain type of reason, revealed to him immense horizons of activity and hope.[12]

It was on this basis that the French Enlightenment developed certain characteristics, such as optimism, *joie de vivre*, and an uneasy skepticism, the result of which was Deism, tolerance, and a natural or lay morality, which, being only social, was not a source of restraint. The decisive struggle, again according to Mornet, occurred in France between 1748 and 1770 with such intellectual leaders as Montesquieu, François-Vincent Toussaint, Helvétius, Voltaire, Diderot, Rousseau, and with the *Encyclopédie* (1751, 1772) "as the most striking victory of the philosophers."[13] Thus,

> Voltaire, Mably, Condorcet, and the rest never cared to see in the Crusades (following the abbé Fleury in this respect) anything but wars of adventure and of gross cupidity; Voltaire, d'Argens, and Helvétius spoke of the great mystics and, among others, of St. Francis of Assisi as ridiculous fools; Voltaire dealt with Joan of Arc in a mock epic, the *Virgin Maid*, that is a masterpiece of coarse stupidity.[14]

And Raynal's interpretation of the Spanish Conquest was one of cruelty, nothing else.[15] It was the spirit of obscene irreligiosity in some of the foreign versions of the Enlightenment which the Peninsula found so unacceptable.

The new European philosophy was based on a different interpretation of natural law—individualistic, mechanistic, atomistic—which had little in common with the Scholastic version. These new natural law theories, which had begun to spread in the seventeenth century in northern Europe, represented an extraordinary departure from the natural law theories of the past. Their exponents included Johannes Althusius (1557–1638),[16] Hugo Grotius (1583–1645),[17] Thomas Hobbes (1588–1679),[18] Algernon Sidney (1622–82),[19] John Locke (1632–1704),[20] Samuel Pufendorf (1632–94),[21] and Christian Thomasius (1655–1728).[22]

A gradual change in the interpretation of the law of nature, which had remained essentially the same during the Middle Ages and the period of Late Scholasticism, occurred in the seventeenth century through the work of Hugo Grotius. He symbolized the transition from the metaphysical to the rationalistic interpretation, though he was still too much indebted to the Spanish Late Scholastics to formulate drastic innovations in the direction of a total autonomy of human reason as the origin of the law of nature.

For some time it was generally thought that the modern natural law theories began with Grotius, since his system of international law was based on the *ius naturale*. But natural law for Grotius was still the mirror of eternal law, and God still the highest source of the law of nature; Grotius was still linked to tradition, but being a child of the times, he transmitted to following generations elements which contributed to the new version of natural law.

It was with Samuel Pufendorf and his interpretation of the work of Grotius that this new version arose. A totally different law of nature emerged, which in time became the modern natural law theories of the Enlightenment and reflected the new trends in religion and philosophy: Deism and rationalism.

The new natural law was the result of cultural and political causes. Humanism had died and with it the exaggerated deference toward antiquity, and toward Roman law in particular; Deism led to a greater appreciation of the lawful in nature and a horror of witchcraft and of any mystical influence on the part of a transcendent deity. To recognize the borders between the real and the imaginary, so the new school argued, it was necessary to use a true enlightenment, which could be achieved only through reason, not through faith.[23] Human reason thus became the guiding principle of the Enlightenment, thereby building on the preparatory work of the Renaissance, the Reformation, and humanism. It was now believed (as the logical consequence of developments of the Renaissance and of Cartesianism) that human reason was able to discover and define all laws. The autonomy of human reason was now the source of all morality and of all law; and the *lex aeterna* ceased to be the guiding principle it had been when Scholasticism reigned supreme.

The new natural law theories were no longer developed on organic lines as such theories had been in the Middle Ages and in antiquity; they were based on the growing individualism of the age. With this new individualism, there was injected into the interpretation of the law of nature a rather remarkable idealism, strongly in opposition to the realism of earlier natural law theories. This led to the theoretical construction of an imaginary state of nature, a natural law concept which in the Middle Ages had been of importance only from a speculative theological point of view.

In the vast field of law, the new school tried to elaborate a system founded exclusively on purely rational reflection, turning its back on history. Since the historic multiformity of positive law is but the proof of man's failures, its exponents argued, the only authentic law is the natural law which pure reason discovers.

To establish natural law, it was necessary to determine what was authentically human; one, therefore, needed to discover man's primitive condition, his state of purity, which had been degraded and deformed by the historic process. Then idealism was injected into natural law: man in the prehistoric, natural stage was pure and as yet undeformed.[24]

Instead of building on the immutable essence of man's human nature and developing organically on the basis of the individual, the family, the association, the state, and the community of nations, and thus growing logically from an *imperfecta societas* toward a *societas perfecta*, the new natural law was of an empirical nature found through abstract thinking—which then clearly explains the egoism of Hobbes, the sociability of the purely formal *socialitas* of Pufendorf, or the agreeable and confortable life of Thomasius.[25]

The new natural law, as the typical philosophy of the Enlightenment, implied that the state had the duty to educate the subject, to make him rich —which in reality meant a political program defined in two slogans: equality and liberty. Concealed in this modern natural law was the new morality of Deism which, disregarding the *lex aeterna*, was to end ultimately in Kant's total moral autonomy.[26] To be sure, the new natural law tried to subject the Church to the control of the State.

For all natural law theories of even the most divergent kind, political authority was the product of a fusion of the many original individual authorities, which could be total or limited. Likewise, the community was only an aggregate of the wills and powers of individual persons. But in spite of the fact that the individualistic foundation of the new natural law theories was identical in all its thinkers, the political consequences varied; individual rights were stressed by Locke, Rousseau, and the North American and French Revolutions, but not in the systems of Hobbes, Pufendorf, or Thomasius. All in all, the modern natural law school in Europe represented a most vigorous intellectual movement which would culminate—after Rousseau—in the French Revolution, which symbolized the apex of Enlightened natural law.[27]

The Enlightenment entered Spain and its Empire like a fresh wind, European and un-Spanish. The new century began, symbolically, with a new dynasty. The succession of the Bourbons to the Spanish throne in 1700 opened new horizons to the country and brought into Spain and its Empire the general European spirit of the times at a greater pace than might have been permitted by the Spanish Hapsburgs.

There were, nonetheless, a number of differences between the Spanish Enlightenment and its Western European counterpart. The Enlightenment which developed on Spanish soil had a typical Hispanic character insofar as it attempted to harmonize Spanish traditions with the prevailing European system and to repeat in the eighteenth century what had been successfully accomplished in the sixteenth in the fusion of Scholasticism and humanism. The Spanish Enlightenment was very much the work of a small elite whose main concern was the practical application of useful knowledge and whose members were basically religiously orthodox and politically monarchical.[28]

The psychological impact of a real or supposed Spanish decadence implied a will to overcome this decay and the "black legend" from abroad. The way to overcome these real or supposed deficiencies, in the view of all the Enlightened writers of the Peninsula, was to apply reason to a program of reform, the instruments of which were to be royal authority and education. In this sense, the Spanish Enlightenment followed the same currents as did other parts of Europe. Royal authority—enlightened despotism—was the main instrument, and was untouched by criticism or revolutionary tendencies until at least 1789. After that date, a different wind was blowing, but even the most ardent admirers and followers of the French Revolution, such as Count Francisco de Cabarrús,[29] preferred to wait a generation to carry through a political reform.

The minority began to educate the people in order to eradicate from their midst all superstition and error and to find truth through reason. But this attitude toward the people had very complex aspects, since some subjects were considered suitable, and others not. Among the latter was the correspondence between members of the Enlightened minority, and included subject matters which could be confided in a letter to a minister, since the writer knew the addressee belonged to the same group of Enlightened friends. There were, therefore, in the Spanish Enlightenment two different attitudes: one represented the knowledge of the minority and circulated in the higher stratum of society, in their academies, economic societies, and Parisian-type *salons*; the other was the one which the elite thought safe enough to present to the people.[30] One of the reasons why the Spanish Enlightenment has so often been misunderstood, and wrong conclusions deduced, is that the above characteristics lend themselves well to misinterpretation.[31]

In the Peninsula the new ideas of the Enlightenment, of science and progress, of reason and the perfectibility of the human race, were not devoid of religion. Faith was not questioned; religious faith and rational enthusiasm found in the Spanish Enlightenment an extraordinary harmony and balance quite unknown in the other countries of Europe. Even in the later period—with the exception of Cabarrús, the Spanish Rousseau—most of the Enlightened thinkers were quite devout Catholics.

> Neither in the reign of Charles III, nor in the mind of its most distinguished statesmen was the religious life of the Spaniards [no longer] their first political preoccupation.[32]

Charles III represents a fine example of what was typical of the Spanish Enlightenment, particularly if he is contrasted with his fellow-kings abroad. The Spanish monarch led a model family life and his rectitude was exemplary, while Louis XV led a frivolous and irresponsible life, dominated by the gallant dictatorship of favorite ladies. The French king prepared the French Revolution while Charles III actually interrupted the Spanish decline.[33]

As far as political matters were concerned, the regime was not attacked by the Spanish Enlightened thinkers; they battled more against the papacy, since they thought that Rome was trying to undermine the Spanish monarchy. The attack on monarchy, however, which was inspired by Rousseau, did not have an effect in Spain until after 1789, and later was only more effective than in the eighteenth century.

Spain thus attempted to mold the new ideological winds, the new European spirit of the eighteenth century, into its usual Catholic framework. It may not have been as successful as it was at the time of the Renaissance or during the Baroque period; but the attempt was again made, and again it was sincere, though it may have been rather incomprehensible or too simple. It was this type of Spanish Christian Enlightenment[34] which echoed in the Indies, though the really political repercussions of Enlightened liberalism would develop after Spanish America had broken its political ties with the mother country: "the Enlightenment in Spanish America was not only not a 'cause,' but rather a consequence of the independence movement."[35]

The Spanish Enlightenment may be divided roughly into two periods: the early part, from the advent of the Bourbon dynasty (1700) to the middle of the century, is best represented by the Benedictine Benito Jerónimo Feijóo (1676–1764);[36] the later part, marking the high point of the Spanish Enlightenment, has as its main figure Gaspar Melchor de Jovellanos (1744–1811).[37]

The Age of Reason began in Spain with the great figure of Feijóo, who sowed the seeds of this specifically Hispanic Enlightenment, and whose influence was to be found on almost all other Hispanic thinkers of the period. Examining the decadence of Spain, he saw its cause in the lack of the application of modern scientific inventions; this brought him in turn to sharp criticism of the Spanish nobility, though he praised labor and urged the stimulation of agriculture. He attacked Scholastic physics by taking sides with the experimental physicists, but he was a foe of Descartes and the new rationalists. He was largely responsible for the introduction and application of the critical and scientific approach, without losing the religious basis.

Feijóo believed that the king, rather than waging war for ambition's sake, should be the guardian of peace and the promoter of economic development. While he granted the just measure of power to the king, he did not agree with the absolutist theories derived from Hobbes, but insisted that the king is a man like everyone else, equal by nature and superior only by fortune. Like others before, Feijóo stated clearly the Scholastic idea that God did not create the kingdom for the king, but the king for the kingdom.

Feijóo was not insensitive to the times when European superiority, especially French, over Spain was too obvious to be hidden, yet he never became an *afrancesado*; he admired some French writers such as Montaigne, Gassendi, Descartes, Bossuet, Fénelon, and Fleury, but distrusted Cartesianism and the ideas of Voltaire and Rousseau.[38] Like Jovellanos, Feijóo admired certain English intellectual elements, and as a Galician he was sympathetic to many English qualities. Bacon, Newton, and Locke were among his favorite authors.[39] In spite of the fact that the French encyclopedist spirit penetrated the Peninsula at the end of the century after Feijóo had unintentionally prepared the ground, it was nonetheless his aim to strengthen religion and belief in God, enhance the prosperity of the kingdom, and halt Spanish decay.[40]

In sum, Feijóo coupled a profound love of country with an enthusiasm for universalization; an interest in science and respect for freedom of thought with the negation of all progress which was not of an evolutionary and disciplined nature; a pure religious faith with an ardent struggle against fanaticism.[41] Highly idealistic, he was actually a great realist whose philosophy was based on the profound roots of Spanish traditional thinking, to which he added the modern European thought of the century. Feijóo

> is the great Spanish representative, not so much of the eighteenth century, but of what the eighteenth century might have become. He symbolizes, indeed, that ideal Spanish possibility which could not fully crystallize in the eighteenth century.[42]

Finally, Marcelino Menéndez y Pelayo observed: "What a modern spirit and at the same time how Spanish was Father Feijóo!"[43]

Although Feijóo was neither the first nor the last of the Spanish followers of modern philosophies, he was the popularizer *par excellence* of these modern ideas. His literary success in Spain was unrivaled; no other Spanish writer was read as much as this Benedictine monk. In his own century the various editions and reprints comprised some 420,000 copies.[44] Feijóo's works contributed largely to counter the stereotyped views which foreigners had of Spain, but it was in Spanish America in particular that his works attained the greatest fame.[45] In one way or another his *Teatro crítico universal* and his *Cartas eruditas* were vehicles through which eighteenth-century philosophy reached Spanish America.

While the first part of the Spanish Enlightenment was associated with Feijóo (until about 1750), the actual height of the Spanish Age of Reason came with the advent of Charles III to the Spanish throne. In his entourage were several Enlightened Italians, including the Marqués de Esquilache and the Marqués de Grimaldi, who found their way to Madrid and had a marked influence on the destinies of Spain.

The adherents of the Spanish Enlightenment in this second half of the century included: Pedro Rodríguez de Campomanes, conde de Floridablanca, Cabarrús, conde de Aranda, ministers of Charles III; such writers as José Cadalso, Juan Meléndez Valdés, and Jovellanos; scientists like Antonio Cavanilles; economists like Ignacio Jordán de Asso, Antonio de Capmany, Bernardo Ward, and Gerónimo de Uztáriz; and many other intellectuals of lesser influence. Church and university took part in this movement and were in many cases the vanguard of the new ideology.

The greatest representative was Jovellanos, who successfully sought to rid the Age of Reason of its most extreme forms and to find a balance and a harmony with the traditions of his country. He was, as Valentín Andrés Alvarez has observed, "encyclopedic" without being an "encyclopedist,"[46] and loved his country with a plutonic rather than a Platonic spirit.[47]

Jovellanos, a contradictory mind, who was at the same time profoundly Catholic and yet tinged with Jansenism, Spanish in the traditional sense and yet the most representative figure of the Enlightened men of the century, suffered from the very contradictions which animated the political system of the age, absolutism and Enlightenment. He continued at the end of the century what Feijóo had begun earlier: educational reform, the struggle against ignorance, the application of the practical sciences in accordance with the precepts of the century—namely, economic liberalism, freedom from all medieval limitations on the stimulation of private enterprise, and government interference for the welfare of the nation whenever it was required by the principles of reason and nature.

Jovellanos showed a predilection for things English, an inclination strengthened by his friendship with Alexander Jardine and Lord Vassall Holland and by the influence which Adam Smith, John Locke, Adam Ferguson, William Ogilvie, and William Godwin exerted on him. It was in the economic field that Jovellanos followed the Enlightenment in general and the English economists in particular. He fought the mercantilists and physiocrats, and believed in private property (as a necessary evil) and in self-interest, though always with the limitations imposed by Scholasticism and in keeping with justice and humanity. He was against civil entails, ecclesiastical mortmains, latifundia, and communal lands, viewing them as obstacles to the free circulation of land.[48] He envisioned an agrarian reform which would create independent farmers at the expense of the Church, aristocracy, and the *Mesta*, and opposed the guild system and any restraint on free trade.[49]

His traditionalism was clearly shown in his ethics: he was against utilitarianism and hedonism, in which he included not only Aristippus, Epicurus, and Carneades but also Hobbes, Spinoza, and Helvetius, and believed in such Christian values as the *summum bonum*, a religiously oriented ethics, hope in eternal salvation as the basis of happiness, body and soul as the two substances of individual and social morality, and sociability as the essential dimension of man.[50] In philosophy, on the other hand, he fought Scholastic syllogism in favor of the experimental and inductive method (Bacon, Locke, Condillac). But believing that politics was not a science and thus could not have principles (its maxims could always be ascertained in theory but not always in practice[51]), Jovellanos could not accept the idea of a social contract. He was no follower of the eighteenth-century school of natural law but believed instead in an organic society more in tune with medieval philosophy. He rejected Raynal and Robespierre (irreligiosity and terror), but Rousseau, whom he considered impertinent and full of contradiction and pride, was a special target.[52]

In spite of his idealism concerning reason and nature, Jovellanos became perhaps the greatest critic of the French Revolution and of the exaggerations of the philosophic system which inspired it. He dubbed the spirit of the French Revolution modern sophistry, particularly when referring to the principle that all men are born free and equal. The persecution of the clergy he termed "a horrible and inhuman ferocity"; Danton and his friends were "savages," Robespierre a "whip of the human race," and his partisans "an infamous gang of thugs."[53] In a letter to the British consul in La Coruña, Hardings, who himself had caught the revolutionary enthusiasm of the ideas of 1789, Jovellanos wrote:

> Never ... will I help to sacrifice the present generation in order to better the future ones. You approve of the spirit of rebellion; I do not, I disapprove of it openly. I believe that a nation which enlightens itself can effect great reforms without bloodshed.[54]

His emphasis was always on education and virtue, and he argued that aristocracy in the modern world can be justified only on the basis of merit.[55] His concept of a country's constitution—that it should not be an artificial creation but something which reflects the essential elements of the country: climate and geography, religion and history, customs and laws—was in line, not only with Aristotle, Bodin, Montesquieu, Burke, and Ferguson, but also with Spanish traditionalism.[56] This traditionalism was particularly clear in his attitude toward monarchy, which he considered still the best form of government, and was highlighted at the time of the establishment of the *Suprema Junta Central* (1808) when he sought justification in medieval law, especially the *Partidas*, using arguments not unlike those of the Spanish Americans. Moreover, in the face of the French invasion Jovellanos, denying a natural right to rebellion, proclaimed that any people suddenly attacked from abroad and abandoned by its rulers had an extraordinary and legitimate right to rebel.[57] This too was a point of view advanced by the Spanish American revolutionaries and was Scholastic in essence.[58] Yet Jovellanos favored the two-chamber house, an Anglo-Saxon influence, as the only way to balance the constitution. Thus, Jovellanos' strong traditionalism in basic philosophical and political values but at the same time modern basis make him a true representative of a Christian Enlightenment at the turn of the century just as Feijóo had been in the earlier part of the eighteenth century.

With the exception of Feijóo and Jovellanos, few intellectuals had as much influence as Pedro Rodríguez de Campomanes in shaping the Enlightenment in Spain. Although his position was not so high as Aranda's or Floridablanca's, he was extremely adept at making the royal power amenable to his ideas. A man of immense erudition and universality of knowledge and interest, Campomanes was a true representative of the Enlightenment. Thoughout his life he was guided by the idea of overcoming Spanish decline, which he believed was to be accomplished on the basis of Spanish traditional elements and the new European philosophical trends.[59]

History and tradition determined his political outlook; he based the justification for the Spanish monarchy on national rights, and the defense of the *regalías* on the medieval *Partidas* and canons of the Visigothic councils. Yet neither the new natural law theories nor humanitarian cosmopolitanism had much impact on him, since he considered himself a subject of the Spanish Crown and had a strong national conscience. He seemed to be influenced by French ecclesiastical thought of the seventeenth century, which had its ramifications in the eighteenth (Gallicanism, Josephinism) and included a reaction against Scholasticism and Aristotelianism, an interest in the primitive Church, regalism, radical opposition to ultramontanism, defense of the divine right of kings, and criticism of the excessive wealth of the clergy.[60] As a lawyer he was the author of an anonymous work, *Tratado de la regalía de amortización* (1765), in which he claimed that the Church had no right to an unlimited accumulation of property.[61] His ideal was thus a Spanish church subordinated to the Crown. This attitude also characterized his relations with the Jesuits, since their political ends (Suárez, Mariana, Molina) and their links to Rome were in opposition to his absolutism, centralism, and regalism.

A fervent believer in Enlightened despotism, Campomanes called for the establishment of rational structures in his country, the opening of Spain to modern science and technology, and the mobilization of all economic power. This meant a more secularized view of history, an identification of happiness with well-being, a conviction that government had the duty to contribute to the growth of the state and to the happiness of its subjects, the idea that institutions had to be justified by their socially useful functions, an enthusiasm for political economy and for science in general, a reaction against the guild system, and a defense of free trade.[62] Thus, as a royal adviser, he urged drastic land reforms, and, like Jovellanos, he believed that the state should manage the economy. But he was aware that Spain lacked the human element for all these undertakings, an Enlightened middle class, and so he appealed to the old nobility to rise to the occasion.

Campomanes viewed Spain's decline in the seventeenth century as the result of two factors: (*a*) an absolute ignorance of economic reality, expressed in such measures as the expulsion of the *moriscos* (1605–10), the rise of the *alcabala*, the taxation of grains, the trade monopoly enjoyed by Seville to the detriment of the national economy, and the discouragement of agriculture; and (*b*) a fundamental error regarding the concept of national wealth based on metal extracted in the Indies.[63] To overcome these factors Campomanes proposed reforms in the areas of agriculture, industry, and trade, encouraging an increase in production. In agriculture, this meant the expansion of the amount of land under cultivation and the modification of production methods; in industry, a greater appreciation of manual work and the multiplication of family tasks;[64] in trade, the free circulation of goods for export if they were needed for industrial purposes and the prohibition of foreign goods if they could be produced domestically, and as much freedom as possible in foreign trade, within the mercantilist program for intra-imperial trade. In Campomanes' view, the true principles of a country's greatness were the useful occupation of all its inhabitants and the wealth of the people, and his preoccupation was to harness the energies of the many people—women, for instance—who were not incorporated into the productive process. Campomanes relied on the economic societies and on the Crown for the means: the former for research and information, the latter for direct and indirect action on the conditions of production.[65]

Campomanes, thus, represents a symbol of the Spanish Enlightenment in the sense that he tried to harmonize tradition with eighteenth-century rationalism; but he was not successful in his attempt and the various elements simply coexisted side by side.[66] From this point of view he differed from Feijóo and Jovellanos, who recognized the problem and came closer to a solution. A comparison of Campomanes and Feijóo clearly demonstrates how the spirit of the Enlightenment had changed from the early part of the century to the time of Charles III: Feijóo's political thought was still based on limitations of power in the classic Spanish tradition, of which little was left by the time of Campomanes—at least in his writings and in those of the ruling minority.

The Enlightenment reached Spain through various channels. One method of contact was travel to such countries as France, England, Austria, and Holland. This, of course, was limited to the few who could afford it. The many foreigners who visited Spain—the Irishmen Ward, Guillermo Bowles, Ricardo Wall, Alejandro O'Reilly, Dowling; the Italians Grimaldi and Tanucci—brought with them the same spirit of the eighteenth century which foreign books tried to convey.

Foreign books themselves were, of course, another way to introduce the Enlightenment from abroad. This was not easy, since the importation of books was prohibited, particularly after the French Revolution. Yet foreign books did circulate widely, but almost uniquely within the small elite. Indeed, there was a bookstore opposite the University of Salamanca—Alegría y Clemente—which dealt exclusively in French books. The Inquisition was not as vigilant as it had been in earlier times, and even Juan Antonio Llorente—who must be quoted with caution—refers to the Holy Office in the eighteenth century as "models of sweetness," of "extreme prudence and of a singular moderation."[67] Of greater importance was the fact that the Inquisition had lost favor under Charles III. Still, in spite of the fact that such books as the *Encyclopédie* and the works of Voltaire, Montesquieu, Condillac, and Mably were prohibited,[68] most of the elite had read them and admitted having done so when questioned by the Inquisition.

Among the foreign ideas which reached Spain were those of Rousseau and Locke. No doubt Spain received some Enlightened ideas through the impact of Rousseau,[69] though it was limited in the years before the French Revolution. In general Spaniards were not favorably inclined toward his ideas, and Feijóo was among the first to take a strong stand against him. Still, the influence of Rousseau came to the Peninsula relatively early in the eighteenth century, and through its diffusion in Spain it eventually found its way to the Spanish territories overseas. But this influence was more of a literary than of a political nature at that time.

The Enlightened circles all knew Rousseau, but only the *afrancesados*, especially Cabarrús, embraced him; others followed only his literary or pedagogic ideas.[70] Only the political ideas of Montesquieu and Pufendorf were considered respectable by the Spanish elite. That Rousseau's political influence in Spain was minimal in the eighteenth century does not mean that his main idea, the social contract, was not studied and debated. Yet it was never brought up as a theory against the monarchy or as a foundation for popular sovereignty.

Manuel Ignacio Altuna was a vehicle for the introduction of Rousseau's ideas in Spain; in 1762 "José Clavijo y Fajardo" (the pseudonym of Alvarez de Valladares) received permission to publish *El pensador*—a famous periodical which was imitated throughout Spain and in Spanish America—and he contributed extensively to the circulation of Rousseau in Spain; in 1814 Valentín de Foronda published a Spanish version of the *Contrat social*; José Marchena y Ruiz de Cueto became the great circulator of *Émile* and *Julie* in Spain and Spanish America.

The most significant figure was Aranda, a personal friend of Rousseau's who was involved in the expulsion of the Jesuits from Spain (1767), perhaps partly as a result of Rousseau's influence. Cadalso, largely influenced by Rousseau, was also important in both Spain and Spanish America, and through his *Noches lúgubres* and *Cartas marruecas* transmitted Romantic ideas to both Spain and Spanish America in the early-nineteenth century.

The Lockean influence in Spain was both direct and indirect, since the first knowledge of him came through France. It was projected into Spain by the French writers who to a greater or lesser extent had drawn on Locke, particularly Diderot, Turgot, and especially Montesquieu.

Among the Enlightened Spanish thinkers so influenced was León de Arroyal. In his *Cartas político-económicas* (1778)—although his authorship is disputed[71]—Arroyal constructed a political theory based on the Lockean assumption that in the state of nature man must protect his property as best he can, and therefore government is established. Civil liberty is the right which every subject has to act according to his will as long as his action does not oppose the society of which he is a member through the social contract. Other writers influenced by Locke (and Montesquieu) were Cabarrús, Jovellanos,[72] Alvaro Flores Estrada (directly inspired by Locke),[73] Francisco Martínez Marina, Ramón de Salas,[74] Meléndez Valdés,[75] Marchena, and Nicolás Alvarez de Cienfuegos.[76]

One of the greatest accomplishments of the Spanish Enlightenment was the founding of the so-called Economic Societies of the Friends of the Country. The Basque Society was the first of these to be established, in 1765 by the Count of Peñaflorida, following the establishment of similar economic societies in Bern, and in Brittany, Paris, and other parts of Europe. Its purpose in part, as stated in its statutes, was to cultivate the inclination and enthusiasm of the Basque nation for the sciences, *belles lettres* and art, to correct and to embellish its customs; to banish hate, ignorance, and their dismal consequences.[77]

With these societies, more French influence penetrated Spain. It was noticeable in "Clavijo y Fajardo" (Rousseau), José de Yereguí, Félix María de Samaniego (Raynal, Rousseau), Tomás de Iriarte, Nicolás Azara, Salas (Rousseau, and later Bentham), Manuel de Valbuena, and Cabarrús (Rousseau, Montesquieu).

French and English economic ideas of the century had a significant impact in Spain and Spanish America; as a matter of fact, the Peninsula, like the rest of Europe, followed the mercantilist theories and, later, fell under the spell of the physiocratic movement. The influence of the physiocrats Turgot, Mirabeau, and Quesnay, and of the Scottish economist Adam Smith, can be seen in Vicente Ferrer Gorráiz, José Alonso Ortíz, Ramírez, Asso, Cabarrús, Jovellanos, and Ward, and in such actions as the opening of many additional Peninsular ports to trade with ever wider areas of Spanish America (1765–78).

The ideas of the French economists of the end of the seventeenth century and the beginning of the eighteenth began to penetrate the Peninsula after the Bourbons ascended the throne in Madrid. French economic thought thus progressively influenced the Spanish scene as the century evolved. This was particularly true in the case of Uztáriz whose *Teórica y práctica de comercio y de marina* (1724) affected the thinking of the fiscal authorities in Spanish America, as well as such economists as Bernardo de Ulloa, Ward, and others,[78] for whom Colbert was the model to follow.

Among the most important Spanish economists in the first half of the century (1700–60) was José del Campillo y Cossío. Along with Jovellanos in the second half of the century, he exercised considerable influence in Spanish America. Campillo opposed the mercantilist system, considering it responsible for the decline of the Spanish Empire. His antipathy toward it extended to the entire system of colonization; and he viewed not only countraband but excessive duties and taxes, and the pernicious effects of Spanish American silver, as detrimental to the Spanish economy. His solution was to reduce taxes so that Spanish goods could compete with foreign countraband merchandise. Campillo also opposed the convoy system which he viewed as justifiable only in time of war, and he called for a greater integration of the Indians, with social equality between them and the Spaniards. Yet Campillo did agree with the mercantilist opinion of not allowing the rise of industries in Spanish America, a position also held by such eminent men as the Count of Revillagigedo in New Spain (1793).[79]

The Enlightenment in Spain—which was, above all, a stocktaking, a vigorous examination of the Spanish conscience[80]—led to many practical applications, especially to badly needed reforms. There was no doubt that Spain at the beginning of the century was a country financially bankrupt—largely because of the inflationary consequences of the silver brought to the Peninsula from America—and highly in need of reform, particularly after the mediocre rule of Charles II (1665–1700).[81] The Enlightenment effected this reform in Spain half a century later under Charles III and his ministers; but it was characterized by a number of measures which ran counter to the fundamental traditions of the country, in both Spain and Spanish America, and which were quite un-Spanish and more typically French, even Bourbon French.

In the course of the eighteenth century many changes occurred in the fields of administration and government. The Spanish Bourbons attempted in essence the centralization and nationalization of political life: it began with Philip V when the administration was rationalized, and under the later kings, Ferdinand VI and Charles III, the aim went more deeply into the rationalization of the state. But it would be wrong to assume that absolutism and centralism in the Spanish Empire reached the proportions they reached in France, even if by Spanish standards they represented the highest form of authoritarianism ever attempted in its long history.

The rationalization of public life meant a political struggle against the privileges of the aristocracy which by the eighteenth century were no longer justified.

> Without doubt, the decrees regarding the functions and the work of the *intendentes* and royal *corregidores,* which in large part annulled local power and considerably reduced the role of the *regidores* and mayors, were of greater efficiency,[82]

since they restricted the powers of the nobility. When the nobles became simple landowners, they lost "the idea of service, the reason of command, and were reduced to the condition of rich people,"[83] but this was due more to the rise of the middle classes than to ideological factors.

As it advanced, the eighteenth century gradually changed the old social order in the Peninsula: the new wealth, as a consequence of economic reforms, brought about the rise of the bourgeoisie, which challenged more and more the role of the aristocracy and received the decided support of the monarchy in its struggle against the nobles. This rise of the middle classes took shape under Charles III when the bourgeoisie increased its participation in agriculture, trade, and industry, though the question of a greater political participation will actually not be posed until the reign of the next king, Charles IV. In the second half of the century statesmen and economists alike belonged to the middle class and represented their victorious march toward power. They saw themselves, at least as far as the literature of the period depicts them, as the instrument for popular education, criticizing the nobility and their privileges as being of no real value for the nation. Eliminating these privileges, which had been based on the idea of service, now became a goal of the bourgeoisie, and one which it gradually achieved.

The era of Charles III also moved in the area of trade and industry as a result of liberal influences, in particular the ideas advanced by Colbert concerning the freedom of trade and protection of national trade in regard to foreign countries. In this period the Crown made a distinct effort in the economic field, which included establishing economic regions, formulating population and distribution policies, and promoting industry.

The rule of Charles III was characterized in particular by the attempt at building a modern state: Spain abandoned the patrimonial state of the past in order to become a truly national state. The transformation ordered from above represented a change in the internal structure of the old Spanish kingdoms, and, as a consequence, the Spanish bureaucracy acquired a certain uniformity. With this goal in mind the State intervened more and more in spheres which until then had been rather private, such as welfare and education. The areas of greatest challenge were in the armed forces and in public administration. Though the steps taken were slow, they were taken with great sureness, and the result was that the Catholic monarchy of the Peninsula, that old federation of Hispanic kingdoms, became what today is called Spain.

One of the measures by which the State became more powerful in the eighteenth century was the increased control of the Church through the regalist movement. It began with the *fiscal* Melchor de Macanaz in the early decades of the century and ended with Campomanes in the period of Charles IV; the movement turned to the Indies in order to bring to the Peninsula the ecclesiastical institutions, i.e., the *Real Patronato de Indias*, which in Spanish America were more favorable to the Crown. The first book of the *Recopilación de leyes de las Indias* represents a veritable code of ecclesiastical law and was based on the Alexandrine bulls, though with secular sources. When this foundation eroded, the Crown looked for a different solution, which presented itself with the arrival of the Bourbons. This aim was then achieved during the reign of Ferdinand VI when Pope Benedict XIV through the concordat of 1753 consented to the transfer of parts of the *Real Patronato* to the Peninsula.[84]

Yet more important than the simple transfer of the *Real Patronato* to Spain was the metamorphosis which the institution underwent in the second half of the eighteenth century. A unique opportunity arose when the Bourbons desired to introduce new legislation for the Indies in keeping with the changed spirit of the century rather than simply to reissue the old Hapsburg legislation of 1680. Charles III accepted the idea and ordered the elaboration of a new code of the laws of the Indies, a task which was carried out by a *Junta codificadora*, composed of a group of reformers (Lanz de Casafonda, Antonio Porlier).[85]

But the work was finished by another junta whose ideology was considerably more traditional than the reformist zeal of the first, and the result was a proposal simply to modify the *Recopilación* instead of introducing major changes in the entire ecclesiastical legislation. Consequently, there was a further increase in royal absolutism in regard to the Church—manifested, for example, in the prohibition against communicating to Rome any information concerning the State in the respective dioceses; the king only was to receive this information and would decide what was suitable for transmittal to the pope[86]—but at the same time the old aim of the propagation of the faith in America was kept alive.[87]

The strength of the Enlightened State could also be seen in the attack on tradition made by the Spanish *philosophes*. It was particularly strong after the expulsion of the Jesuits and the closing of their schools in 1767. That the Inquisition which the *philosophes* established should prove more effective than the tottering genuine institution is not at all paradoxical. The works of Suárez, Molina, and Mariana were forbidden, since a doctrine of tyrannicide and of resistance to the usurpation of power was, in the eyes of the new despotism, merely seditious and contrary to good law and order, "monstrous ideas against the king's authority."[88] Thus, without mentioning names, the *intendente* of Seville attacked the teachings of Suárez and Mariana in regard to tyrannicide, and Pablo de Olavide did likewise when he fought the old Jesuit doctrines he considered subversive since they implied the right of the people to make the king accountable to the nation. Olavide's ideas regarding the exclusion of the poor from higher education and the elimination of the medieval restrictions on royalty amounted to a marked consolidation of royal absolutism, which received its support from the rising bourgeoisie and a declining nobility, and completely excluded the poor.[89] The result of this policy was the destruction of the old legal foundation linking the king to his poor vassals, and the immobilization and loss of an enormous intellectual reservoir. The academic discrimination and the destruction of the old populist Castilian laws, "elevated to positive doctrine by Suárez and Mariana, had incalculable consequences in the Spanish Indies."[90]

> The system of *intendencias*, which destroyed the imperial federalism of the Hapsburgs, as well as other foreign elements, concluded the break of Spain with America, just as Peninsular regalism and Jansenism ended the break with the Church.[91]

In sum,

> The reform movement seemed to favor Spain in the material sense, since international trade increased substantially, communications improved, and the merchant marine and the navy were enlarged. Numerous ports of the Empire were fortified, and cattle and industrial production, particularly in the Indies, increased; but the French invasion, with the bloody struggle which it unleashed, put the country back to 1717.[92]

The year 1789 added a new element to the general ascendancy of Enlightened influence in Spain. The French Revolution, the highlight of the Enlightenment in Europe, had its first repercussion in the Spanish world in governmental action against such influence. The Spanish government enforced stricter censorship and prohibition against French books which were smuggled in in increasing numbers; Charles IV, king since 1788, took precautionary measures in Spain[93] which were also ordered in Spanish America.

J. E. Léger Cottin, deputy for the third estate for Nantes, was the first to be named by a royal decree of September 24, 1789, as having proposed the introduction of seditious material on the Revolution into the Spanish Empire. With the rupture of relations between Bourbon Spain and Revolutionary France in 1792, the influence of the French Revolution became indirectly stronger, since one of the reasons for the war was the protection of Spain from revolutionary contamination. France also prepared the Kersaint Plan, followed by others, in which Spain was to serve as a base for the expansion of the new political ideas.[94] In general, however, although the ideas of the French Revolution had some impact upon Spain and its Empire, the government was able to weather the storm.

Still in spite of the measures taken by the court in Madrid, the public managed to follow the course of the Revolution with interest, avidly reading the books inspired by liberty. The new ideas spread rapidly to all the provinces, aided perhaps by the prohibitive measures of Floridablanca, which only served to heighten curiosity.[95]

From then on, the monarchy itself became involved, abandoning its earlier position of remaining outside any debate on Spanish reform. In time the modern forces gained more strength in their attacks. After the Revolution, the new ideas continued to develop, surfacing at Cádiz. The times had changed from the days when "the kings owed the Crown and the scepter to God alone," when "the will of the prince is the universal law of the people."[96] But these changes in attitude toward the old regime in Spain cannot be attributed solely to the new currents of the Enlightenment, Spanish and foreign, and to the ideas of the French Revolution. There was no such monopoly; the relative revival of Scholasticism also clamored for a re-establishment of traditional liberties against the regime of enlightened despotism.

Jefferson Rea Spell, in describing the situation in Spain, notes that freedom of speech and of the press were urged, and social equality advocated. Abolition of the nobility was even suggested. The educational system was severely criticized. The Church was subject to attack, though its supporters came to its defense with speeches and writings. At first, the attack was launched by the upper classes, followed by younger intellectuals who opposed the evils of absolutism in government. From the kingdoms overseas came rumblings of independence. But the onslaughts of these groups were met by the entrenched majority, who rose to prevent quick changes in education, government, or religion.[97]

But there was a small minority among the Spanish elite which was fascinated by the revolutionary trend. This minority was composed of those who had gone into exile in France and were to return to Spain with the Napoleonic armies, as well as some who then went over to Joseph Bonaparte: men like Cabarrús, Gonzalo O'Farrill y Herrera, José de Mazarredo, Meléndez Valdés, Miguel José Azanza, and Mariano Urquijo. These men, the real *afrancesados* or Jacobin Quislings, hoped to effect reforms in Spain through revolution, with the aid of Napoleon's brother with whom they were to cooperate; they only manifested thereby the great rift already evident in the eighteenth century between the people and the governing Enlightened groups—a rift which with time widened and became so apparent in the period of Napoleon's usurpation of the Spanish throne.[98]

This group in particular was greatly influenced by Rousseau. His ideas filtered into the upper classes in the Peninsula through news items, articles, and reviews, which enjoyed an ever increasing circulation. These ideas received a great impulse, particularly at the turn of the century, and were to converge with the more conservative trends of a Jovellanos and a Floridablanca toward the goal of the eighteenth-century Enlightened liberals, the Constitution of Cádiz of 1812.

The concepts expressed in the first half of the eighteenth century still constituted the basis of the argumentation, though now they were stressed more emphatically and wore a Romantic veneer. Thus, the century completed a cycle which began with a critical, businesslike, and aseptic stocktaking of the state of Spain and ended with political Romanticism (Alvarez de Cienfuegos, Meléndez Valdés, Manuel José de Quintana).

But by no means did this imply that Scholasticism had disappeared. It is true that, as the eighteenth century advanced, Scholasticism diminished in the Iberian Peninsula, but its impact could still be seen in such late eighteenth-century thinkers as Antonio Javier Pérez y López, Fernando de Ceballos y Mier, Lorenzo Hervás y Panduro, Pedro de Peñalosa, Pedro José Pérez Valiente, Martín Sarmiento, Joaquín Marín, and Juan de Cabrera.[99] The moral concern of the sixteenth and seventeenth centuries, so strongly expounded by the Spanish theologians and philosophers in the face of the enrichment which capitalism entailed—a point of view inherited from the Middle Ages—was still expressed, though with less vigor, in the eighteenth century (as the writings of Friar Antonio Garcés attest), but did not affect the general tendency in this century toward state control of the economy.

Actually, in spite of the fact that the advent of the Bourbons to the Spanish throne in 1700 meant an increasing influence of the European spirit on Spain, the traditionalist currents maintained their strength, even beyond the middle of the century. While Europe moved logically into the Enlightenment from the earlier Renaissance, the situation in Spain was quite different. José Ortega y Gasset has pointed out that Spain lacked the educating eighteenth century,[100] and Francisco Puy, going even farther, claims that Spain lacked a religious crisis without which it was impossible to arrive at rationalism. Spain maintained its religious posture in the eighteenth century, at least until the time of Charles III, and only after the death of Feijóo in 1764 were there two currents: (a) the authentic and traditional Spanish thought, and (b) a reformist trend, led by a smaller minority, which became dissident not by evolution but by foreign influence.[101]

In France itself, there existed a somewhat similar situation, though it was much more removed from the Middle Ages than in the Peninsula, since the Jesuits directed most of the colleges until 1762, and their teaching methods at that time were about the same as they had been a century earlier.[102] The spirit of reform swept over France after 1762,[103] just as the Enlightenment in Spain really took shape in the period of Charles III. As Daniel Mornet says in regard to France,

> Thus, in spite of the *Encyclopedia*, philosophy, and "revolutions" in thought, the classical spirit, or at least a certain classical spirit, subsists throughout the century.[104]

For Puy a Spanish Enlightenment did not exist because there was no school of thought which could justify such a label: in theology there was no Spanish thinker; in philosophy scarcely half a dozen; in political thought nobody.[105] If the Enlightenment meant a concept of life with man independent from traditional principles, especially religion, and believing in his own means —reason and science—to master life and dominate nature (optimistic and progressive humanism), then, in this sense, there existed no Enlightenment in Spain until the end of the eighteenth century.[106]

Until the long reign of Charles III Scholasticism remained the strongest current, as Puy has convincingly shown.[107] In his study Puy lifted "the law of silence" which attempted to interpret the Spanish eighteenth century as a purely Enlightened period, and demonstrated instead the extraordinary strength of Scholasticism in the first sixty years. He agrees with Menéndez y Pelayo's term "decaying Scholasticism" only insofar as Scholasticism did not produce a really dominating personality, but not in the sense that traditional philosophy was moribund.[108]

As earlier, in the sixteenth and seventeenth centuries, Scholasticism was represented in the eighteenth century by three rather homogeneous tendencies: Thomism, Scotism, and Suarezism, which was essentially also the division in Spanish America. Among the most important Scholastic representatives in the first sixty years of the eighteenth century were: José de Aguilar, Miguel Viñas, Julián García Vera, Luis de Lossada, Juan de Ulloa, Gabriel de Henao,

Diego de Quadros, Juan de Montalván, Froilán Díaz, Francisco Palanco, Juan de la Trinidad, Juan de la Natividad, González de la Peña, Biedma, José del Espíritu Santo, Aguilera, Juan Martín de Lessaca, Bernardo López de Araujo y Ascárraga, Vicente Calatayud, Francisco Rábago, and Manuel Bernardo de Ribera.[109]

Scholasticism even enjoyed a revival at the end of the century—a very interesting phenomenon of great importance to Spanish America. The increasing influence of the *philosophes*, the Encyclopedists, Rousseau, and the French Revolution did not nullify the Scholastic influence; nor was it greatly hindered by the expulsion of the Jesuits or the increasing impact of regalism, physiocratic ideas, or modern natural law theories.

Although many of the new eighteenth-century doctrines were based on rational arguments, they were largely derived "not [from] Rousseau, but [from] Vitoria, Suárez, and the traditional line of the Spanish Baroque, always adjusted to rational norms."[110] The criticism which Ceballos y Mier made of atheism and of the impious French influence, which Marín leveled at rationalist natural law, and which Pérez y López applied to the dangerous doctrines of Rousseau, showed the strength of Scholastic ideas even in the second half of the century.[111]

Evaluating the eighteenth century in Spain is extremely complex because of the many currents of thought which overlap. Until the early 1760s Scholasticism was the most powerful philosophy, but this position changed later in the century and rationalism increased at the end of it.

In the view of Rodríguez Casado, the French influence in Spain in the eighteenth century was essentially one of form. It was there, and in many cases in an overwhelming manner, but it was only superficial.[112] He points out that the reform movement in Spain did not impose itself without a struggle: "the defenders of traditional and purely Spanish values are legion."[113] In other words, there were two tendencies: the reformers and the conservative forces, and each has its extremists. Achieving a harmony between reason and tradition is the great contribution of the conservative element and explains why the reformers based much of their argumentation on traditional principles and why so many works from the Hapsburg period were reprinted in the eighteenth century.[114]

For Rodríguez Casado there were actually four intellectual groups in the Spanish eighteenth century: the conservatives who were hostile to any reforms; the traditionalists who were opposed to some but open to other reforms (Juan Pablo Forner, Andrés Piquer); the "traditional progressives" or Enlightened Christians (Feijóo, Floridablanca, Jovellanos, Campomanes), and the revolutionary reformers who followed modern trends (Olavide, Samaniego). The general characteristics of the Spanish Enlightenment were its weak philosophical basis, and its enthusiasm for the application of useful knowledge—economy, education, government. Other traits common to the reformers were their shortsighted view of history and their unbelievable optimism.[115]

The four groups agreed on three basic issues: (*a*) the need for religious education as the best means for character formation, in keeping with Scholastic methods; (*b*) the urgency of putting all educational systems at the service of the new social structure; and (*c*) turning all this into the adequate instrument for the benefit of the individual as an important means for obtaining his human and transcendental happiness. Perhaps the best example of the attempt to harmonize reason with faith, this program was strengthened when Charles III, in his *Instrucción reservada a la Junta de Estado*, expressly stated that religion and ethics were the foundation of the building.[116]

In the view of one recent writer, the Spanish eighteenth century must be viewed, not from the black and white point of view of Eugenio d'Ors (the century of reason and enlightenment, of the European spirit in Spain)[117] and Ortega y Gasset (a century in which Spain did not participate),[118] but from a middle-of-the-road view. Spain attempted a great deal in the eighteenth century, and though it did not reach the goal it had set for itself, still it tried to modernize and to approach the level of the rest of Europe without at the same time losing its Spanish character.[119]

The eighteenth century brought to the Peninsula a certain prosperity and an impressive administrative reform and was

> one of those moments of history to unite and harmonize the two contradictory tendencies of Spanish life: isolation and communication, tradition and progress, inwardness and European orientation.[120]

With all its errors and successes the eighteenth century in Spain represented above all a great effort at reform and at Europeanization, the aims of which, however, were mostly not attained.[121]

That the new ideas arrived in Spain as they did elsewhere in Europe but reached only a selective minority, while the country at large was either hostile or indifferent to them, is a point of view accepted by most scholars, including Friedrich Heer.[122] The old medieval political theories survived in the Spain of the eighteenth century, and men like Feijóo, Jovellanos, Macanaz, and Cabarrús tended to adjust them to their modern times in keeping with the needs of the new age. What was at stake was nothing more than the incorporation of Spain into the general European current, but this goal was never reached.[123]

Broadly speaking, the European spirit of the century — especially French rationalism — was projected into Spain and into its Empire overseas, though this spirit never touched the people, remaining on the surface with the upper classes. Heer maintains that this foreign "Enlightenment," which reached a small elite, was an artificial creation.[124] The consequence of this alienation was such that Charles III may be called the real liberator of Spanish America, or at least an actual forerunner of Spanish American independence, as Cecil Jane does.[125]

The eighteenth century thus gave rise to that unholy child : a divided Spain. Heer described the two Spains as follows : the one, an inflexible, conformist, dominating Spain in which the king and the upper classes, in deep inner agreement and alliance with the lower people (whose inner chaos was dominated, secured, and glorified), stood together against the "Other Spain" of a handful of intellectuals, savants, and artists who through three centuries had maintained the heritage of the Jewish–Moorish intelligentsia from the "World of the Three Rings," the heritage of the Cisnerian and Erasmian reform.[126] The schism in Spain's soul was to have its eruption in the years 1812 and 1869 and its continuation in the twentieth century. Absolutism in the political field, true to the age of Enlightenment, and Gallicanism and Jansenism had certain repercussions in Spanish governing circles, although they were only superficial.

The modern philosophies did not reach the people, as the rise against Napoleon (1808–12) and the rejection of liberalism in 1823 were to show.

The eighteenth century cannot be seen merely as a century of enlightened liberalism; it meant the greatest height of governmental power carried to the extremes of usurpation.[127] In this century, particularly as it advanced, classic theories from the former Spanish centuries, which dared to put limitations on royal power, were attacked by the Spanish *philosophes*. It is useful to remember this in viewing the situation in Spanish America. The rejection of the ideas of the Spanish elite — belief in science and progress, rationalism, centralism, and absolutism — was one of the main causes of Spanish American independence, in the sense that the Revolution fought the centralism and absolutism of the Enlightened regime.

2. The Echo of the Enlightenment in the Indies

After the sixteenth, the eighteenth century ranks as the most important historical period in Spanish America, and, as one critic has commented, in the eighteenth century the national spirit in all American countries matured, preparing itself for separation from the great European powers.[128] No doubt, the achievement of Spanish American independence was assisted by the cultural preparation of the Enlightenment, which should not be construed, however, as the intellectual foundation of the Revolution.

As in the Peninsula, so in Spanish America, the eighteenth century produced a special type of Enlightenment. This Spanish American Enlightenment — an echo of the Peninsular — was linked to the Spanish decay in the century, as the decline of Spain and the simultaneous rise of Western Europe brought new influences which both directly and indirectly — through the Peninsula — reached the Spanish lands overseas.

The simple story that Enlightened ideas reached Spanish America surreptitiously has long been discounted. The Spanish Enlightenment, on the contrary, was projected into Spain's overseas territories; there was no need of indirect infiltration. Spanish America was of interest to the Enlightened *philosophes* not merely in terms of the "noble savage";[129] nor was it, as the Western European *philosophes* (Montesquieu and Voltaire, among others) asserted, a stronghold of reactionary ecclesiastical and civil rule, and of obscurantism and superstition. This assumption was never shaken, and the popularized version of the Black Legend[130] served to re-create in the eighteenth century an erroneous and falsified interpretation of the Spanish American reality. It was diametrically opposed to the facts, since in the early eighteenth century Feijóo had contributed largely throughout the Hispanic world to the dissemination of one of the Enlightenment's greatest achievements: the promotion of useful knowledge. These critics would have been closer to the truth had their interpretation of the Spanish American situation considered the strength of traditional values: side by side with the currents of modern philosophies there existed a strong attachment to traditional values, notably those of religion and government.

The idea that Spanish America lagged far behind Europe intellectually is a serious misconception which has taken a long time to disappear. Based in part on exaggerated facts, the legend was perpetuated by Spaniards and Spanish

Americans themselves.[131] Though Spain had declined since the early seventeenth century and was attempting a renewal in the second half of the eighteenth, Spanish America had not witnessed a similar development: the eighteenth century, far from being a period of decline, provided an extraordinary example of progress in both cultural and material fields.

Scholasticism, no doubt, declined in Spanish America as the century advanced; the collection of some 5,000 manuscript and printed theses from the university archives of Mexico, Guatemala, Caracas, Chile, and Córdoba demonstrates that "all possible philosophies [were] held from 1750 to 1810," though they were all "within the scholastic formulae," and indicates an increasing intellectual fermentation.[132] Yet the special character of the Spanish American Enlightenment again manifests itself in the case of the Venezuelan ecclesiastic A. de Valverde, who while opposing Aristotle was a partisan of Saint Thomas,[133] or in the policy of the Viceroy of Peru, Manuel de Amat y Junient, who insisted that "at least one author in modern philosophy should be taught." But in order to have a greater choice he decreed intellectual freedom, in the sense that the students could choose "any system of philosophy, or combination of philosophies, which appealed to them."[134] A similar policy was enacted in the River Plate by Viceroy Juan José Vértiz (1777–84).[135]

Alexander von Humboldt observed that civilization in America (except in the places where it had existed before the Spanish conquest) began on the coast, following rivers and mountain valleys which offered a temperate climate. He divided South America into three social stages, although he made it clear that this division of cultivated coast, followed by the great *llanos*, and the marginal jungle, was not the same everywhere, but in no part was it so clear as in Venezuela. In general terms, Humboldt observed that the more one would penetrate into the interior the more the population, trade and industry, and intellectual activity would decrease. The first stage, that of the coastal regions, was largely made up of whites who engaged in trade with Europe and North America and comprised the Peninsular Spaniards and the Spanish Americans; most important positions were retained by the *peninsulares* while the *criollos* kept their social distinctions but few of their political ones. This area was more politically minded than other regions farther inland because of its closer links to Europe. The second stage referred to the great plains, less civilized areas than the coast, containing a mixed population, a kind of buffer between the coast and the true interior of the country. Finally, the third stage, the marginal jungle, was really Indian territory. Although the situation was somewhat different in Mexico, Peru, and Quito — where the high plateaus and the central mountains offer greater population, commercial activity, and intellectual life — the pattern was consistent and thus there developed a great disparity of interests between the people of the interior and those who lived along the coast.[136] The Enlightenment was thus more highly developed along the coast than in the interior.

A further characteristic of the Enlightenment in Spanish America was that it was stronger in the larger towns than in the provinces, as Humboldt observed in his *Political Essay on the Kingdom of New Spain*:

> Spanish laws prohibit the entry into their American possessions of any European who is not born in the Peninsula. Thus, the words "European" and "Spanish" have become synonymous in Mexico and Peru; the inhabitants

of the remote provinces conceive with difficulty that there are Europeans of another language [and] consider this ignorance [of Spanish] as a sign of humble lineage, since where they live only the lowest class of people cannot express itself in Spanish. Knowing more the history of the sixteenth century than that of our days, they believe that Spain continues to exercise a pronounced domination over the rest of Europe; and for them the Peninsula is the center of European civilization. This is not the case with the [Spanish] Americans who live in a capital. If they have read works of French or English literature, they easily fall into the contrary error; they have a more unfavorable idea of the mother country than the one which was held of Spain in France when communications were less frequent between Spain and the rest of Europe. They prefer the foreigners coming from other countries to the Spaniards; and abandon themselves to the belief that intellectual culture is effecting more rapid gains in the colonies than in the Peninsula.[137]

Although the first half of the eighteenth century in Spanish America was affected more by Spanish thought, the second part shows increasing influence from France. In the first half of the century, the Enlightenment made progress as far as natural sciences and useful knowledge were concerned, but with the second half the new ideas, already consolidated, started to batter the bastions of Aristotelianism. The rise of rationalism was coupled with growing attacks on Scholasticism, the challenge of dogmatism and traditional authority, and the promotion of empiricism. But this should not detract from the fact that during this period faith in God, loyalty to the king, and Scholastic philosophy maintained their fundamental validity — a fact recognized by John Tate Lanning when he states in regard to the impact of Baruch Spinoza (1632–77) and his "so-called pantheism" that "not once, apparently, in the eighteenth century was there an ardent defender of the last of the 'Hebrew prophets.'"[138]

The French Revolution increased the influence of the Enlightenment in Spanish America, as it had in the Peninsula, and the elite groups continued to adhere to Enlightened liberalism and its political institution, Enlightened despotism. Loyalty to the Bourbon monarchy was still unquestioned after 1789, though the degree of absolutism became a different problem which eventually ended in the constitutionalism of Cádiz (1812). José Luis Romero observed, in regard to the Spanish American elite prior to the Spanish American Revolution, that

> indeed, as in Spain, the urban [Spanish] American minority was anti-Jacobin, except for very rare cases. What predominated in the mind of the [Spanish] Americans were the principles set forth by the official Bourbon liberalism, with its respect for monarchy and its no less vigorous respect for religion. The liberalism of Jovellanos, for instance, the inspiration of the [Spanish] American liberals, was kept alive in the minds of all. This liberalism was still further refined when, in 1806, the English invasions of the River Plate occurred. Even if they precipitated the forces which were partisans of independence, they contributed with efficacy to clarifying the character of the [Spanish] American liberal movement.
>
> Indeed, in spite of the sympathy which some of these ideas—particularly the economic ones—awakened in the midst of [Spanish] American society, the English appeared to their eyes guilty of religious heterodoxy which created an insuperable obstacle to direct and definite understanding.[139]

Although the cultural atmosphere of Spanish America largely resembled Spain's, the impact of the Enlightenment was weaker in Spanish America, since Scholasticism had succeeded there, in spite of the expulsion of the Jesuits in 1767, in maintaining its strength to an even greater extent than in the Peninsula. That the atheistic aspects of the Enlightenment had a smaller impact in Spanish America was the result of the impressive Jesuit influence and the slighter penetration of foreign ideas from neighboring countries than was the case in Spain. Another factor was that Spain produced Enlightened giants,[140] whereas the thinkers of Spanish America were less original and, hence, less influential.

The Enlightenment arrived in Spanish America through various channels: the influence of Feijóo and other thinkers of the Spanish Enlightenment; the influence of Cartesian doctrines and of French and English philosophy; the impact of the *regalista* literature; and travelers, scientific societies, and scientific knowledge. In every part of Spanish America modern ideas were promoted through eminent men, scientific societies, the universities, and journals.

The influence of Feijóo — "who, as a temperate Cartesian, familiar with Newton and assailant of authority, became a good philosopher of transition"[141] — touched all areas of Spanish America and all spheres of academic life. Although Feijóo neither referred in his works to the New World nor visited the Spanish Empire in America, he was very much concerned with it, and his impact across the Atlantic was extraordinary in every sense of the word. His works reached a total of 528,000 copies in the eighteenth century,[142] and although it is difficult to state how many reached the overseas areas, most libraries contained his works. In many instances these copies came from exiled Jesuits who often agreed with his philosophic position; in others, through the many shipping companies which sailed to Mexico, Venezuela, and the Antilles.[143]

Feijóo's influence was twofold: on the one hand and in the short run, he was followed by a group of Spanish American enthusiasts; on the other hand and in the long run, and in a more complex manner, he had an indirect impact on the revision of scientific research, such as the medical reforms of 1780 and Hipólito Unanúe's studies in Lima.[144] He was also the writer primarily responsible for the *criollos'* gaining greater faith in their intellectual ability against prevailing European views. He also aided many Spanish Americans in their struggle for modernity against many old fashioned positions of Scholasticism.[145]

Feijóo, like Carlos de Sigüenza y Góngora in New Spain earlier, understood that progress could be achieved without a concomitant loss of the Christian concept of man and of culture[146] — he was thus the best example of the Spanish Enlightenment. The awakened interest in the experimental sciences and a philosophical eclecticism, both the result of Feijóo's influence, characterize the second half of the eighteenth century in Spanish America.[147]

The key to his extraordinary impact on Spanish America has to be found in his attempt at ideological renewal and intellectual modernization, and in his great concern for America. His impact was stronger in some countries than in others; he was particularly influential in Peru, Quito, and New Spain, but he also left a mark on New Granada and Cuba, where the attempted reform plans of the University of Havana may be credited to his influence.[148] The scientific voyages (Ruiz López, Sessé, and Mociño), the works of Jose Celestino Mutis, and the initiation of Peru's first great scientists (José Baquíjano, Hipólito Unanúe, Rodríguez de Mendoza, and Vicente Morales), the unsuccessful study plan of 1783 for the University of San Marcos in Lima, the plans for the Real Convictorio de San Carlos of 1785, Father Liendo y Goicoechea's in Guatemala, and those of Moreno Escandón in Bogotá (1779), the economic societies and the improvements in medicine and pharmacy — all clearly link Spanish America to the dominant trends of the Enlightenment, thanks to the works of Feijóo.

Friends and foes alike admired Feijóo. Among the former were Francisco Javier Eugenio de Santa Cruz y Espejo in Quito, José Ignacio Bartolache in Mexico, and Ignacio de Escandón in Lima; among the enemies who respected and praised him were the Dominican Cristóbal de Coriche, the Jesuit José Mariano de Vallarta y Palma, the Cuban Jesuit Francisco Ignacio Cigala, all followers of Scholasticism. Even the controversies which raged in the Peninsula in regard to Feijóo had repercussions in Spanish America, as in the case of Francisco Soto Marne's sermon "Las grandezas del poder en la concepción de María," preached in Lima in 1755.[149] In sum, whether praised or pilloried, Feijóo was the greatest promoter of the Enlightenment in Spanish America without, however, leaving Christian orthodoxy.

The influence of the Spanish Enlightenment was not restricted to Feijóo but extended as well to the economic ideas dominating the great minds in Spain. Ramón de Posada, the *fiscal* of the Royal Treasury of New Spain, is a good example. In his view only agriculture and industry were the means to keep a country independent, and a wealth based on gold and silver was precarious. Like his Spanish counterparts he believed that the Spanish decay was due primarily to the fact that agriculture had been allowed to decline. Posada is thus an excellent case not only of the influence of Jovellanos and other Spanish economists of the century but also of the general influx of physiocratic currents into the Spanish Empire.[150] These currents also found expression in the encouragement of interprovincial trade, of the increase of industry and production, and of free trade as a means to attain these goals. The example of Posada in New Spain (1781) and the reports of the *Oficiales reales* of Veracruz and of the *Consulado* of Mexico[151] demonstrate that physiocratic ideas influenced

> unquestionably the economic thought and practice of New Spain, and of the whole of Spanish America, but without exercising an absolute dominion in the field of theory. The new ideas of the French school mixed with the old Spanish traditional ideas from which not even the most advanced Peninsular thinkers of the eighteenth century could free themselves.[152]

However, the physiocratic ideas, which by the end of the century seemed to be more influential in the Indies than in the Peninsula, found opposition in Spanish America not only in the mercantilist tradition but also in the Spanish American institutions. The result was what Eduardo Arcila Farías has called "a hybrid thought," which did not fit any of the classic definitions, since it had mercantilist ingredients, modern thought, and the stamp of the Spanish American institutions.[153]

Besides the influence of Feijóo and of other Spanish currents of thought, there was the European influence of René Descartes (1596–1650), Gottfried

Wilhelm von Leibniz (1646–1716), and Sir Isaac Newton (1642–1727), whose ideas were taught in Quito as early as 1736,[154] and that of Johann Gottlieb Heineccius (1681–1741),[155] and Christian Wolff (1679–1754),[156] two of the many Protestant natural law thinkers deeply influenced by the earlier Spanish school. To the influence of these thinkers came also that of Pierre Gassendi (1592–1655), Nicholas Malebranche (1638–1715), Etienne Bonnot Condillac (1715–80), and John Locke (1632–1704),[157] to which must be added the influence of Luiz Antonio Verney (1713–92), "the Portuguese intermediary and eclectic so popular in the Indies."[158] Other important foreign influences were those of Pufendorf, Montesquieu, Rousseau, Voltaire, Abbé Guillaume-Thomas de Raynal, and Humboldt.[159]

The Enlightenment was prepared by Descartes whose rationalism "came to be accepted, if not actually followed, everywhere in America between 1736 and 1800."[160] Thus, by 1785, "it was common academic doctrine throughout the Indies that sensation . . . became the basis of knowledge and the warp and woof of mental operations."[161]

The wind of change which spread with the rationalism and skepticism of Descartes, the empiricism of Locke, and the sensualism of Condillac was apparent. It was not isolated and by the end of the century could be found in the University of Mérida, in Venezuela, as well as in the University of San Carlos de Guatemala, and in the universities of Caracas, Mexico, and Lima.[162]

Pufendorf was known in Spanish America in two ways: in the seventeenth century, prior to the Enlightenment proper, and later with the encyclopedists, through Jean Barbeyrac's French translation of the *De iure naturae et gentium*.[163] However, Pufendorf did not represent a powerful intellectual influence before the Spanish American Revolution.

Locke's influence in the eighteenth century generally was limited to the realm of philosophy, and even here it was rather restricted. The assimilation of Locke's and Montesquieu's principles into Spanish American political thought was evident in the constitutional forerunners which appeared after 1811. The full influence of Locke's philosophy emerged in the latter phase of the Spanish American Revolution, however, when it flourished along with the Spanish liberalism of the 1820s, Bentham's utilitarianism, Condillac's sensualism, and the materialism of the *idéologues*.

The French ideas of the Enlightenment, particularly those of the encyclopedists, reached Spanish America as the century advanced. This French influence was even more restricted to the ruling classes than the Spanish Enlightenment, which itself borrowed heavily from France. But the Spanish Enlightenment was linked more to tradition, while the French was of a more revolutionary character. The French influence, personified particularly in Rousseau, Voltaire, d'Alembert, Raynal, Montesquieu, and Diderot, came to Spanish America slowly at first, but with gathering momentum, arriving directly from France, or indirectly through the Peninsula. It reached Spanish America through various channels, of which one was the well-organized book trade. Destined for the elite, shiploads of Enlightened literature were unloaded with the permission of the authorities. The Franco-Spanish alliance and the proximity of French colonies made it easier to get French and other foreign books not introduced directly from Spain.

It is known that Esteban de Enderica in New Spain borrowed two of Rousseau's works and parts of the *Encyclopédie* from a French seaman; that José Antonio Rojas had copies of Bayle, Holbach, and Montesquieu which circulated in Chile; that the Baron von Nordenflicht lent his Voltaire's *Henriette*, Montesquieu's *Esprit des lois*, and other works to Peruvian readers; and that the Argentine Juan Baltasar Maciel was the owner of a large collection of unorthodox books (although his library also contained the works of St. Augustine, St. Thomas, and Spanish classical literature).[164]

During the second part of the eighteenth century, the works of Voltaire and Rousseau, Montesquieu's *Esprit des lois*, Buffon's *Histoire naturelle*, Condillac's *Traité des sensations*, and the *Encyclopédie* were read by the upper classes of Spanish America. The prohibition by Church and State was very lax, and was enforced only toward the general public. The spirit of tolerance toward the elite is evident in the many dispensations which leading men received from the pope to read the French *philosophes* — Manuel Belgrano, for example, who received permission in 1784 to translate Rousseau, Voltaire, and Montesquieu.

The extensive reading of Feijóo, the spread of the spirit of science and progress, the establishment of economic societies on the Spanish model contributed to a climate in which Rousseau was read and discussed. The economic societies and the literary periodicals known as the *mercurios* were important vehicles for the dissemination and penetration of Rousseau into Spanish American intellectual circles.

The spread of Rousseau throughout Spanish America was aided by the many intellectuals in Spain who held ideas similar to those fashionable in Western Europe, by the many foreigners who traveled in Spanish America or became residents, by Spanish administrators who came to the territories overseas and spread liberal ideas in their circles, and by contrabandists who found an easy and prosperous market for forbidden books.[165]

But by far the greatest disseminators of Rousseau were the young Spanish Americans whose travels and study in Europe put them in touch with the liberal doctrines of the eighteenth century in both Spain and Western Europe, particularly in France. They were stimulated by personal contacts, freedom of speech, and the prevailing spirit of inquiry.[166] Many were drawn to the works of the Genevan, and a great proportion of them returned to their homelands converted to Rousseau's ideas and the revolutionary creed. Rousseau and Raynal were by far the idols whose precepts were most closely followed, and whose works helped to create the prerevolutionary spirit within the liberal frame of the eighteenth century.

Rousseau's influence throughout Spanish America was important, though in varying degrees in the different countries, and comprised in the colonial period three spheres: political, educational, and literary. From the unsuccessful plans for a Chilean constitution of 1781 through a large part of the nineteenth century, the *Contrat social* inspired many Spanish American leaders, particularly Francisco de Miranda, Simón Bolívar, and Bernardo de Monteagudo; yet it was not the real intellectual force of the Spanish American Revolution. Rousseau's influence was more literary and educational; in politics, it was somewhat marginal even at the beginning of independence, gaining in momentum the more the Revolution neared its close, and more through the indirect influence of the Spanish liberal movement of the *doceañistas*.

Although the influence of Voltaire should not be exaggerated, it found a place among the currents of the Enlightenment coming from Spain, France, and England; not comparable to that of Rousseau and Montesquieu, it was more of a cultural type. In general, the Spanish American environment was not favorably inclined toward Voltaire and his message, although he did encourage those who for one reason or another were opposed to the Jesuits. Romero mentions that Alexander Gillespie called the River Plate area "a land of fanaticism and of ecclesiastical predominance," and recalls that even during the period of independence the popular masses would react against Protestants,[167] as the Spaniards had rejected French ideas during the Napoleonic invasion. Believers in Voltairian thought were few, such as Pablo de Olavide, and Miranda, to some extent. Yet the *philosophes* — and Voltaire among them[168] — were partisans of Enlightened despotism, to which the upper classes throughout the Hispanic world adhered: "from the court of Madrid and its viceroys in the Indies the entire Spanish world breathed the air of the century."[169]

Raynal, a friend of Diderot's and Voltaire's, was also influential in Spanish America; his *Histoire philosophique et politique des établissements et du commerce des européens dans les deux Indes*[170] had an extraordinary vogue in both Europe and Spanish America. Much of the material for the book was gathered for Raynal by Spanish Americans. At least this is alleged by Miranda, who knew Raynal personally and who himself gave Raynal Spanish American documentation for the work. Raynal told Miranda that he had also received such information from Ignacio de Heredia and the marqués de la Torre in Havana.[171]

This work, with its distinctly irreligious sentiments, may be classified as an eighteenth-century anti-colonialist book: his target is the Europeans, including the French. The work was published in 1770 and, though it was soon banned, new editions appeared in 1774 and 1780. The Paris *parlement* and the Church condemned the book, and Raynal had to flee abroad.

Raynal's book was widely read in Spanish America in the original French and in the Spanish translation by Pedro de Góngora y Luján, duke of Almodóvar del Río. The book could be found in many libraries in Spanish America, particularly in the area of Cuzco, and may have appealed to many Spanish Americans because of the flattery it bestowed on them in the face of Peninsular Spanish "colonialism."[172] Even Humboldt, during his scientific expedition to Spanish America at the turn of the century, mentioned how widely Raynal was known, and commented on the popularity of his writing.[173] Although Raynal's book does not contain any direct political philosophy, it belongs to the general current of Enlightened liberalism.

The famous authors on *regalismo*, the Spaniard Melchor Rafael de Macanaz and the Portuguese Antonio Pereira de Figueiredo, had an extraordinary impact on Hispanic America, as had Campomanes, whose two treatises on this topic influenced Santa Cruz y Espejo.

The Enlightenment also arrived in Spanish America through famous scientific expeditions, such as that which Jorge Juan and Antonio de Ulloa made in 1735 together with Mutis, or that of the Ulloa brothers organized by the Parisian Academy together with Pierre Bouger, Louis Baudin, and Charles de la Condamine in 1736. Also noteworthy here are the expeditions of the botanists Dombey, Hipólito Ruiz, and José Pavón in 1778, the famous enterprise of Juan

Bautista Muñoz, and the politico-scientific Malaspina expedition in 1789–90. Finally, at the close of the century, Alexander von Humboldt and Thaddeus Hänke went to Spanish America to begin their long residence, which, in Humboldt's case (1799–1804), was to furnish the material for his classic accounts of that region.

> And it is to be noted that, although Humboldt was the spiritual heir of the philosophers, personal acquaintance with Spanish America emancipated him from their stock ideas about it, and he painted a portrait of it that was perhaps more generous than just, but which was at any rate strikingly different from the stereotype popularized by Raynal, and different mainly because it presented Spanish American culture in a far more favorable light.[174]

Of all the many aspects of the Enlightenment which echoed in Spanish America, none had more immediate or visible results "than the one associated with the phrase 'the promotion of useful knowledge' and more particularly with the natural sciences."[175] It enabled Spain not only to catch up with foreign countries, "but also to transmit the new knowledge and techniques to Spanish America."[176] A case in point was the Spaniard Félix de Azara, who lived for twenty years in the New World, was a forerunner of Cuvier and Darwin, and made great contributions to the natural sciences and to modern scientific trends in the evolution of Enlightened Spanish America.

In the advancement of science, Fausto and Juan José de Elhuyar and the Baron von Nordenflicht gave mining a great impetus in New Spain and Peru. While the brothers Elhuyar organized two missions of famous scientists and miners in New Spain, the German baron spent about twenty years in Peru furthering both modern science and scientific methods.[177] The three mining missions left Spain in 1788, and the credit for them had been given either to José de Gálvez, the Spanish Colonial Secretary from 1772 to 1778, or to Mutis.[178]

The modern spirit of science was not only spread by the intellectuals, but fostered by clergy and State as well. From the beginning, the Jesuits in particular showed great interest in the sciences, especially in astronomy, chemistry, and experimental physics.

> Few of the high officials of the Church and State sent to America in the last half century were reactionary men and so many of them revealed modernism, and insistence on experimental science in their comments on education, that they must have belonged entirely to the Enlightenment. Archbishop-Viceroy Caballero y Góngora in Bogotá remarked (1789), in regard to the new university there, "all the object of the plan should be directed to substituting the useful exact sciences for those merely speculative, in which up to now time has most regrettably been lost." Viceroy Revilla Gigedo advised his successor in Mexico (1794) that "much reform is needed . . . in the method of studies [in the university] . . . . There is no *gabinete*, nor collection of *máquinas* for studying modern experimental physical sciences; the library has few good works, especially modern ones." Such comments were typical. Viceroy Guirior even brought books to Mutis (1773) as a gift from Linnaeus.[179]

Thus the Enlightened thinkers in Spanish America by no means had a monopoly.

Another important vehicle of Spanish Americain Enlghtenment was the establishment of the many economic and scientific societies which sprang up in the Spanish American kingdoms in imitation of the ones already set up in the Peninsula.[180] These learned societies were rapidly founded in every major town and soon acquired an important place in the community, using their influence for the promotion of the Enlightenment. The first economic society in the Spanish Empire was founded in Manila in 1781, to be followed by those of Mompox in New Granada in 1784, and Santiago de Cuba in 1787, and Veracruz (briefly), also during those years.[181] Lima had its "Society of the Lovers of the Country" (1793), Quito its "School of Harmony" (1791), Havana its "Patriotic Society" — later called "Economic Society of the Friends of the Country" (1791) — and Buenos Aires its "Patriotic, Economic and Literary Society of the Country" (1812), to name but a few. All these Enlightened clubs were founded with the acquiescence and protection of the Spanish overseas authorities, although the approval lessened somewhat when the excesses of the French Revolution became known in Spanish America.

Poverty and prosperity were the main concerns of the economic societies. The production of both agricultural and industrial goods was their great objective, and in this aim they inherited ideas from Feijóo, Campomanes, and other exponents of the Spanish Enlightenment, and were inspired by the statutes of the Madrid Society. Particularly was this the case with the specific repudiation of bullionism, the axiom that money is not wealth, and the hope that increased trade would result from a greater production of goods.[182] They also took from Campomanes his ideas on popular education and industry.[183]

The belief in progress, science, and rationalism was the basis of the economic societies, but they did little to further the formal study of political economy. They concentrated on local problems, and in this sense encouraged a regional patriotism, though they occasionally tended to embrace a wider American "fatherland." But the development of the local economy was their main goal, which they sought through publicity, education, example, and experiment.[184]

It was not the object of these societies to foment revolutionary ideas or to fight the existing political order. Nevertheless, it was natural in a way that they should eventually veer in that direction, since association of ideas between scientific progress and political progress helped this evolution. Arthur Whitaker maintains that

> these associations were not merely literary and scientific, but had a strong political, social-liberal, anti-military and anti-clerical tendency, rooted in foreign ideas and institutions. In other words, they challenged the greatest part of the traditions of the people and threatened the vested interests of the higher classes of the country.[185]

But Robert Jones Shafer, who does not take such an extreme view, says:

> The members had some interest in maintaining the strength of the Spanish world, and some distaste for contributing to that of its rivals.... The numerous Spanish members of [Spanish] American Societies were not promoting revolution, but trying to strengthen the Spanish world: such Spanish founders of [Spanish] American Societies as Villaurrutia and Ramírez wanted to use modern ideas and methods to improve the [Spanish] American economy. The creole members were generally moderate men of

property and position, sometimes intellectually "advanced," but socially and politically moderate; many in the coming years of independence were to be conservatives, like José Cecilio del Valle of Guatemala. The publications of the [Spanish] American Societies may have been potentially dangerous to unchanged continuation of the old regime, but they were not inflammatory. At most, this was occasionally a literature of complaint, not of protest. . . . the [Spanish] American Societies neither brought useful change, nor reinforced the status quo, but helped widen the gulf between points of view already separated by other issues.[186]

Viceroyalty of New Spain. The new spirit which had been prepared by Sigüenza y Góngora began with a Jesuit priest, thus symbolizing as in the case of Feijóo in the Peninsula the Hispanic ideal of harmonizing faith with reason. Andrés de Guevara y Basoazábal, with his *Institutiones elementariae philosophiae*,[187] initiated the distinction between pure philosophy and the natural sciences, and thus showed the influence of Bacon, Descartes, Locke, and Condillac. His mind was eclectic; he attacked Scholasticism, yet remained within religious orthodoxy.[188] There were also at the time a group of Jesuit scholars who followed similar trends and were no doubt influenced by rationalism: Diego José Abad, José Agustín de Castro, Francisco Javier Alegre, and Francisco Javier Clavijero.[189]

José Antonio de Legaria was among the first Mexicans who were enthusiastic followers of Feijóo. In 1730 he published in Madrid the *Congratulación al P. M. D. Benito Feijóo por sus panegíricos discursos; y nuevas pruebas que apoyan su Mapa intelectual o discurso 15 del tomo 2*. Two other followers of Feijóo in New Spain were Mariano Gregorio de Elizalde Ita y Parra, who in 1734 praised Feijóo's work in Madrid, and Andrés de Arce y Miranda, who in 1746 advised the famous Juan José de Eguiara y Eguren concerning several of Feijóo's observations about the Spanish Americans, as was evident in 1755 when the first volume of Eguiara's *Biblioteca mexicana* was published.[190]

In 1757 the Royal College, the former Colegio de San Ildefonso, reprinted some writings of Feijóo's, perhaps as a result of the interest of Clavijero, the dean of students at San Ildefonso.[191] In 1760, the Aristotelian Cigala published in Mexico a *Carta segunda* in which he disagreed with some of Feijóo's ideas.[192] Cigala later fought Feijóo against his countryman Coriche, rector of the Colegio de San Luis; as a Scholastic he attacked the modern trends of Feijóo.[193] Yet in his *Oración vindicativa del honor de las letras* (Mexico, 1763) Feijóo provided the basis for an attack on Rousseau by Coriche.

The general idea of Feijóo was also followed by Juan Benito Díaz de Gamarra y Dávalos (1745–83), an Oratorian *(filipense)*, who is considered the greatest figure of eighteenth-century New Spain. He studied in Mexico and after 1786 resided in Madrid and Rome after graduating from the universities of Pisa and Bologna. On his return to New Spain, he reorganized the study programs of the Colegio de San Miguel el Grande. His most important work was the *Elementa recentioris philosophiae* (1774),[194] which was praised by both the viceroy and the university. He attacked Scholasticism, propounding an eclectic blend of modern philosophy and the natural sciences with traditional Scholasticism. Although he was not original, his contribution and influence in Spanish America were great indeed. He represented an important element in the evolution of Mexican thought, but with him the intellectual leadership in New Spain, which in the sixteenth and seventeenth centuries had generally been monopolized by *peninsulares*, passed into the hands of the Mexicans.[195]

The new spirit which fought Aristotelianism found its greatest champion in José Antonio de Alzate (1729–90), who, in the *Gaceta de literatura de México* (1788–95), wrote some of the greatest satires against Aristotle ever published in New Spain.[196] He was a naturalist, famous for his knowledge of and scientific research into natural history and geography. Another famous foe of Aristotelianism was José Ignacio Bartolache (1739–90)[197] in his *Mercurio volante*. Both these men were influenced by the writings of Feijóo, and through them Feijóo made his greatest impact in New Spain.[198]

No non-Spanish writer ever attained the importance of Feijóo. This was particularly true among the Mexican Jesuits — influenced earlier by Sigüenza y Góngora — such as Castro, Abad, Alegre, Clavijero, López Portillo, Dávila, Parreño, Pedro Bolado, Juan Luis Maneiro, Mariano Soldevilla, Raimundo Mariano Cerdán, and José Rafael Campoy, and was reflected in the rise of Mexican nationalism and the formation of a Mexican mind.[199] Among those who read and commented on Feijóo were many of the exiled Jesuits who after 1767 resided in Italy, such as Clavijero and Castro, and Rafael Landívar, in particular, who in 1782 published the definitive edition of his *Rusticatio mexicana*, mentioning Feijóo in a poem ("El famoso Cola"). No doubt, the group of modern Jesuits in New Spain reflected the inspiration of Feijóo when they proclaimed freedom and fought against slavery.[200]

In 1789 in Madrid Juan de Escoiquiz published his poem *México conquistada*, drawing a fine distinction in the preface about love of country and national passion based on the teachings of Feijóo. Feijóo also influenced the great Romantic writer José Joaquín Fernández de Lizardi (1776–1826) — to such an extent, in fact, that one critic has claimed that "Without Feijóo, Lizardi would not have been what he was."[201] Lizardi, who was greatly influenced, among others, by the Peninsular writers Jovellanos, Father Isla, Torres Villarroel, Macanaz, and such Mexican authors as Díaz de Gamarra, Alzate, and Sister Juana Inés de la Cruz, was also deeply influenced by Feijóo. Lizardi followed in many aspects the ideas of the Benedictine monk (on patriotism, agriculture, work, university studies, economy, science, and superstition) and has even been called the Mexican Feijóo. Feijóo's influence can be seen in the first number of *El pensador mexicano* (1813), in Lizardi's defense of certain modern and critical trends in the *Periquillo Sarniento* with its reference to the *Teatro crítico* and its "illustrious" author; and in such minor works as the *Impugnación de los gatos Barbilucio y Machucho*, where the reading of Feijóo is recommended over "that red writer [Raynal]."[202]

The rise of the Enlightenment — though it did not destroy Scholasticism — expressed itself in 1786 when the ecclesiastical authorities replaced the older texts with the *Instituciones* of Jacquier, which represented an adjustment to the modern rationalistic currents of thought as characterized by Descartes, Bacon, Locke, Condillac, and Gassendi.[203]

The Enlightenment in New Spain manifested itself not only in new philosophical currents but also in an extraordinary interest in the natural sciences. The high standards of scientific research conducted in the face of all kinds of difficulties were praised by Humboldt in 1803 during his visit to Mexico when he stated that "no city of the new world, including the United States, presented such great and solid [scientific] establishments as the capital of Mexico."[204]

In 1787 Charles III established a commission for the scientific exploration of the whole of Spanish North America; Martín de Sessé y Lacasta funded it, and was joined by Vicente Cervantes and by the Mexican naturalist José Mariano Mociño, who had studied the Mexican flora, founded a botanical garden in 1788, and explored the area from California to Guatemala.[205] Mociño's works *Flora mexicana* and *Plantae Novae Hispaniae* were later published, as were such philosophical treatises of his as *Institutiones logicae* (1781) and *Elementa metaphysicae selectae* (1781).[206]

The symbol of the scientific advance in New Spain was the above-mentioned Alzate, who pursued all the branches of the natural sciences with the greatest enthusiasm. A member of the Royal Academy of Paris, of the Basque Society, and of the Royal Botanical Gardens of Madrid, he set the example. Other famous Mexican scientists were Joaquín Velázquez Cárdenas and Agustín de la Rotea, both famous in geometry, the astronomer Antonio de León y Gama, and the previously mentioned Bartolache, known as a distinguished chemist and mathematician.

The College of Mining was perhaps the greatest institution symbolizing the changes which the Enlightenment brought to the Indies. Founded by the Spaniard Fausto Elhuyar (who discovered tungsten) and continued by Andrés Manuel del Río (who discovered vanadium), the college was an instrument for research, but much more: it made Mexicans conscious of themselves as Mexicans.

This rising nationalism — which Humboldt discovered in his voyage to Spanish America — found expression in the new tone of histories, such as Clavijero's *Historia antigua de México* or in José Agustín Aldama's *Arte de la lengua mexicana* (1754), in Mariano Fernández de Echeverría y Veytia's studies of pre-Colombian and colonial Mexico, and Landívar's *Rusticatio mexicana*. The same nationalistic spirit expressed itself in an inventory of all books written in New Spain since the arrival of Cortés by the previously mentioned Eguiara y Eguren, the *Biblioteca mexicana*.[207]

Foreign influences were also represented in the Enlightenment in New Spain. Thus, as in other parts of Spanish America, there is evidence of the influence of Pufendorf. An edict by the Inquisition in Mexico in 1745 banned a book entitled *Le droit de la nature et des gens, ou système général des principes les plus importants de la morale, de la jurisprudence, et de la politique*. It is none other than Pufendorf's main work in the French translation by Jean Barbeyrac which had been introduced into the area of the Viceroyalty.[208]

Lockean influence reached New Spain as early as 1730 when the philosophy of Locke was attacked in a book entitled *Fides et ratio* by the abbé Pierre Poiret.[209] Copies of Locke's main work, in Latin, *De intellectu humano*, were found in New Spain in 1758 and 1762.[210] The *Essay on Human Understanding* was quoted several times in 1772, and in 1794 the previously mentioned Enderica was condemned by the Inquisition for having read Locke, and the *Essay* itself was confiscated.[211]

In New Spain the influence of Rousseau was similar to that in other parts of Spanish America. But it was enhanced by the cession of Louisiana,[212] which enlarged the stream of revolutionary literature and ideas pouring into the

Spanish realms overseas, and prompted the appointment of a liberal Frenchman — the marqués Carlos Francisco de Croix — as viceroy in 1766.

After the French Revolution, the same drastic measures which Spain enacted toward foreigners and literature were repeated in the Spanish American territories. Following the general prohibition of all the works of Rousseau by the Spanish Inquisition in 1764 and by Rome in 1766, Mexican officials published on December 16, 1803, in *La gaceta de México*, a renewed prohibition, and were later forced to issue a circular in which they warned that the ideas of Rousseau and Montesquieu and similar philosophers were forbidden.[213]

Though modern philosophies gained ground as the century advanced, this did not represent a total break with the past. In a traditional society such as that of New Spain, which was dogmatically supported by both Church and Crown, it was impossible to have quick changes. Thus, it is an error to attribute the ideological revolution in Spanish America to Voltaire, Rousseau, or Montesquieu, since the really important philosophers were not these French *philosophes* but such thinkers as St. Thomas, Descartes, Newton, Condillac, Gassendi, and Malebranche, without whom the Spanish Americans would not have understood Raynal, Condorcet, Rousseau, Voltaire, Diderot, Franklin, and Paine.[214]

The most representative figure of the Enlightenment in Central America was the earlier mentioned Friar Antonio de Liendo y Goicoechea, professor at the University of San Carlos de Guatemala. Influenced by the Cartesian currents he fought the old Scholasticism and was instrumental in the introduction of the vast reform plans of the University of San Carlos.

The island of Cuba did not have the cultural development of the mainland, but a cultural evolution, which was very much the work of the Enlightenment, occurred there at the end of the eighteenth century. The great figure was the priest José Agustín Caballero with whom Cuba began a remarkable start in philosophy. This cultural rise was largely centered in the Colegio de San Carlos, which had initiated a reform in keeping with the modern currents of philosophy.

Viceroyalty of New Granada. In New Granada José Celestino Mutis (1732–1808) and Francisco José de Caldas (1770–1816) were outstanding projections of the Spanish Enlightenment, and particularly of the spirit of Feijóo. Mutis, an important naturalist, was born in Cádiz but came to New Granada in 1760 where he taught mathematics and physics at the Colegio del Rosario of Bogotá. He soon got into trouble, because he based his teachings on Newton and Copernicus, and attacked the Ptolemaic system. His monumental work on the *Flora de Bogotá o de Nueva Granada* and his botanical expedition of 1783 contributed to his fame, as did his efforts in organizing the astronomical observatory.

His great pupil, Caldas, continued his work in New Granada in the fields of astronomy, botany, geodesy, and physics. He showed the influence of Feijóo (and of Jovellanos and Quintana) in his *Seminario de Nueva Granada*.[215] Other pupils of Mutis were José Manuel Restrepo, Francisco Antonio Zea, José Domingo Duquesne, Eloy Valenzuela, Joaquín Camacho, Jorge Tadeo Lozano, and Francisco de Ulloa.

It was in Quito, the "key country of colonial life,"[216] that there was perhaps the deepest influence of Feijóo and the new sciences. The popularity of Feijóo's *Teatro crítico* was so great in Quito that prices were forced up to truly fantastic levels. The *Teatro crítico* arrived in Quito in 1728 and provoked some intellectual changes in the country. Juan Pablo Espejo, who introduced Feijóo's works to Quito, was largely influenced by the Benedictine monk. By the end of the century, because of the influence of Feijóo, there will be a reaction against Aristotelianism and Scholasticism in favor of more modern educational methods.[217]

A great representative of the Enlightenment in Quito was the Franciscan Friar Francisco Solano, whose ideas were close to those of the Spanish Benedictine. Like other outstanding men of his century, he refused to accept anything which had not been proved by experiment. He tried in the manner of Feijóo to introduce science and rationalism into his country, and in good Rousseau-like style [218] he asserted that work means everything. Solano's belief in modern sciences, education, and progress was similar to Feijóo's, though perhaps not so universal.

Other scientific men in Quito who followed this trend of the modern sciences were Pedro Franco Dávila, Juan de Velasco, and Pedro Vicente Maldonado, the geographer whose scientific reputation was well established in Europe. Cartesian rationalism was introduced by Manguín and Tomás Larraín.

But by far the most outstanding figure of eighteenth-century Quito was Francisco Javier Eugenio de Santa Cruz y Espejo (1747–96), the "Reformer" and "Forerunner " as he is now called. This eminent man was also guided by the cult of science, a passion for free-thinking, and all the other ideas which made up the century. He, like the Peruvian Peralta Barnuevo, was a Spanish American Feijóo. He was influenced by Campomanes and his treatise on *regalismo*, and mentioned Locke in his periodical *El nuevo Luciano* (1779) and in *La ciencia blancardina*.

An enthusiast for any novelty, Santa Cruz y Espejo became a physician, lawyer, writer, and philosopher, and brought Spanish America farther along the road of Enlightenment. *El retrato de golilla*, a satire against the Viceroy, the marqués de Sonora, brought him imprisonment. In Bogotá thereafter he met Antonio Nariño and Francisco Antonio Zea, and upon his return to Quito was appointed director of the public library. He was also very active in the Society of the Friends of the Country. Santa Cruz y Espejo belonged to the more radical elements of the Enlightenment: he advocated complete independence, the establishment of a republic, the nationalization of the administration with the exclusion of all Spaniards, the nationalization of the clergy, and the confiscation of all Church property.

The Enlightenment was represented in Venezuela by Friar Juan Antonio Navarrete and Salvador José Mañer. Navarrete, a Franciscan like his Scholastic compatriots Quevedo y Villegas and Valero, represented the Spanish Enlightenment in the manner of Feijóo. He taught theology, philosophy, and the arts, and became a theologian at the University of Santo Domingo.[219] In 1770 he joined the Franciscan order and in 1783 wrote his work *Arca de letras y theatro universal de fuentes, questiones, noticias, experimentos, secretos, descubrimientos, sucesos y varias cosas pertenecientes a diversas ciencias, artes, facultades, assumptos, y materias de toda clase* (1783), in some seventeen volumes, dealing with all kinds of topics.[220] In his *Auto filosófico-teológico* he eulogizes St. Thomas (although he does not agree with him on every point) and Duns Scotus, and later was happy that Venezuela suppressed the Inquisition in 1813 (following the special decree of the Spanish *Cortes*).[221]

Mañer (1676–1751) was born in Cádiz and came to Venezuela in his youth, though he later returned to Spain (1729). He became known for his *Voz del pueblo* resulting in a polemic controversy with Feijóo.[222] Another force hostile to Scholasticism was Baltasar de los Reyes Marrero (1752–1809), who, in 1788, was the first to explain the modern philosophies in Caracas. His influence led to changes in education in Venezuela. Actually, the University of Caracas became a center of Enlightened ideas, influenced no doubt by the private companies, such as the *Compañía Guipuzcoana*, known as "the ships of the Enlightenment," with their shiploads of books which they helped to unload in Venezuela.

Feijóo's influence, so strong in New Granada proper and in Quito, was also apparent in Venezuela. Humboldt, in his *Personal Narrative to the Equinoctial Regions of the New Continent*, stated at the time of his visit to Venezuela how surprised he was to find at the Capuchin monastery of Caripe Feijóo's *Teatro crítico* and his *Cartas eruditas* (together with the *Traité d'électricité* of the abbé Nollet): "on dirait que le progrès des lumières se fait sentir jusque dans les forêts de l'Amérique."[223]

Of the foreign influences the most important was that of Rousseau. In New Granada proper, Rousseau's ideas influenced Antonio Nariño. His indebtedness to Rousseau is manifest in portions of the document which he presented in his defense, particularly in such statements as "man is born free" and "men are equal and all should enjoy the delights of liberty."[224]

No doubt Rousseau's impact was strongest on Venezuela's greatest heroes. Francisco de Miranda, the forerunner of independence, was the prime exponent of Rousseau's ideas in Spanish America. After a good education in Caracas, he was sent to Spain in 1771. Very early in his life he became acquainted with the Enlightenment — particularly with the thought of Rousseau — to such an extent that he participated in the revolt of the British colonies and, because of a resultant charge of illicit trade in the West Indies, went to the United States and Europe. In his *Diary: Tour of the United States*, Miranda mentions a conversation with John Tracey in Newburyport, Massachusetts, which centered on the doctrines of Rousseau ("emelio compareció en la mesa"[sic]).[225]

Miranda's visits in various parts of Europe left the mark of Rousseau's influence on him. He bought the *Confessions* in 1788 in Amsterdam or during his visit to Neuchâtel, Bern, and Vevey; Rousseau was the reason for his visit. In Vevey he bought the *Nouvelle Héloïse*, and at Madame de Karn's in Geneva he was drawn toward a copy of the *Emile*. In Marseilles he visited another writer of influence on Spanish American independence: Raynal. The end of his journey was in London to plead with British ministers for aid in bringing about Spanish American independence.[226]

Miranda's active participation in the French army,[227] his visits to Switzerland, and the fact that at the capture of Antwerp he "ordered the name of Rousseau and of Helvetius, as emblems of liberty, substituted on conspicuous columns for those of Spanish despots,"[228] showed him a great propagandist for Rousseau. Miranda wrote an interesting paper in 1795 on the political situation of France.[229]

Miranda's activities against Spain were in keeping with Rousseau's and Raynal's teachings: he cooperated with everyone in his plans for independence;

the most spectacular instance of this was the cooperation between Miranda and the Peruvian Jesuit Vizcardo y Guzmán. In the proclamation which he issued at Coro on August 2, 1806, Miranda specifically refers to the *Letter* of Vizcardo y Guzmán attached to the proclamation.[230] In 1797, he worked with Olavide. His two expeditions to Venezuela failed, but the seed he planted was to grow soon after he was forcibly transported by the Spaniards to La Carraca (Cádiz).

Perhaps Rousseau's greatest effect among the intellectuals and the youth of Spanish America was his impact on Simón Rodríguez, tutor and teacher of Simón Bolívar. Born in Venezuela in 1771, Rodríguez lived successively in Spain, Germany, and France before returning to his homeland. On reading *Emile* he became enthusiastic about Rousseau's ideas, especially in regard to pedagogy, and he subsequently wrote a treatise on education, and popularized Rousseau's ideas in politics and education in the hope of having them applied.

> The subversive ideas of Jean Jacques [Rousseau]—his revolutionary metaphysics, his sentimentalism, and the seductive, declamatory, and, nonetheless, magnanimous emphasis of his style—had to reach the very heart of the liberal youth of the New World and to stir up its enthusiastic and fiery imagination. To these qualities, which were as rooted in him as in his compatriots, Rodríguez added special characteristics which made him throughout his life a sort of caricature of Jean Jacques.[231]

Jules Mancini gives an excellent account of Rodríguez' Rousseauan impact on the young Bolívar:

> entrusted with absolute authority over his favored pupil, Rodríguez then thought of carrying out a project particularly dear to his heart: to put into practice the system of education *par excellence* advocated by Rousseau. The child was as Emile ought to be: "rich," "of good family," "orphan," "robust and healthy"; [at the same time,] did Rodríguez not fulfill the ideal of the teacher desired by Jean Jacques? "Young," "prudent," "bachelor and independent," "a sublime soul," qualities or attributes which Simón Rodríguez could claim, since at that time he was twenty-one, reputed to be the best professor in the city, a more than neglectful husband, and one whose extreme independence of taste and character permitted intimate contact with the most ample thoughts .... He dedicated himself then "to the difficult task of teaching nothing to his pupil!" In order for his pupil to remain in the "natural state" and prepare himself to justify the axiom according to which "the reason of the wise man tends to associate itself with the vigor of the athlete," Rodríguez prolonged his stay in the country and succeeded at least in developing in Bolívar a marvelous aptitude for corporal exercise, making of him a tireless walker, a notable horseman, an intrepid swimmer with whom none of his later comrades-at-arms could compete. On reaching the age of thirteen, Simón had, following the rules of the educator, fulfilled absolutely "the first part" of the *Emile*.[232]

After his tutor had to leave because of implication in revolutionary activities, Bolívar became a cadet; he was then sent to Europe in 1799, where he showed eagerness to study. In Madrid he came in close contact with the Enlightenment and delved into literary and scientific works. He married at the age of nineteen and sailed with his wife in 1802 to Venezuela, but on the way she died. He then remembered the plan to tour Europe with his former tutor. Rodríguez had advised him to study Helvetius, Holbach, and Hume; Bolívar, for his part, admired Hobbes and was fascinated by the philosophical speculation of Spinoza. Before joining his teacher, he read Montesquieu, Voltaire, and Rousseau, who were to leave a lasting influence on him.[233] Just as Humboldt instilled in Bolívar the greatness of nature on the American continent and the important destiny of South America, so Rousseau led him to picture immense visions of the future, particularly the Romantic idealization of liberty.

Bolívar's letters of this period are pure Romanticism — the influence of Rousseau as conveyed through Rodríguez;[234] and if any one work contributed directly to the accomplishments of Bolívar's life purpose — the independence of Spanish America — it was the *Contrat social*.[235]

Viceroyalty of Peru. As it was in other parts of Spanish America, the Enlightenment was reflected in the Viceroyalty of Peru. Modern trends in philosophy were favored by the government in regard to the promotion of useful knowledge and by the many foreign scientists who came to Peru during the eighteenth century (Jorge Juan, Antonio de Ulloa, Pierre Bouger, Louis Baudin, Charles de la Condamine, Dombey, Ruiz López, Malaspina, Hänke, and Humboldt). The impact of Feijóo and the reforms of Charles III echoed in Peru and were accelerated by the foundation of academies and societies like the *Sociedad de amantes del Perú* in Lima, in 1790, and the School of Medicine in 1808.

Among the main representatives of the Enlightenment in Peru was Pedro de Peralta Barnuevo (1663–1743), who, critical of Scholasticism, taught the doctrines of Copernicus, Descartes, and Gassendi.[236] He is by far the best example of Feijóo's influence on the Spanish American mind and of the introduction of scientific and Enlightened ideas. Feijóo knew Peralta Barnuevo and spoke highly of his talents and erudition; Peralta Barnuevo returned the compliment in his epic poem "The Conquest of Peru." Like Feijóo, he was a man of wide interests, combating bigotry, obscurantism, and all kinds of superstition. He was the representative in Peru of that scientific zest characteristic of the changing times, and, as professor and sometime rector of San Marcos University, he was able to exert great influence. He wrote a variety of books, of which forty-eight have been preserved — dealing with philosophy, history, mathematics, chemistry, biology, physics, medicine, and other sciences — the most important of which was, perhaps, the *Observationes astronomicae* published in Lima in 1717.[237] His fame was such that the Parisian Academy made him a member.

The influence of Cartesian doctrines and Newtonian philosophy in most cases accompanied the impact of Feijóo. Cosme Bueno (1711–98),[238] a Spanish naturalist and cosmographer famous for his *Descripciones de provincias*, succeeded Peralta Barnuevo and abandoned Aristotelian physics to become a promoter of Newtonian. He is considered the first follower of Newton in Peru.

Because of Bueno's pioneering work, it was possible for others such as Hipólito Unanúe and Father Isidoro de Celis to pave the way for official acceptance of Newton's philosophy.[239] Unanúe, influenced by Newton and Descartes, "personified a new type of scholar, interested not only in empirical knowledge but in its application as well";[240] but in spite of his excursions into rationalism Bueno did not break with religious orthodoxy and in keeping with the Spanish temperament tried a reconciliation between faith and science.[241]

José Eusebio de Llano Zapata (c 1720–80), a follower of Feijóo's, is another outstanding example of scientific development in Peru. A declared enemy of Scholasticism, he focused his interest on the fields of the natural sciences, history, philosophy, and public education. He followed the pattern set by Peralta Barnuevo and was the author of *Resolución físico-matemática sobre la formación de los cosméticos cuerpos* (1744) and *Filosofía moral de Séneca, o el Catón cordubense, expurgado de muchos errores, y ajustado a la debida mensura*.[242]

Other Peruvians indebted to Feijóo were José Pardo de Figueroa, Pedro Bravo de Rivera, Father Tomás Polo, the Jesuit Gian Domenico Coletti, and Ignacio de Escandón, who hailed Feijóo in a work called *Un corto panegyrico . . . al querido Adonis de la América, a su adorado Maestro: el ilustríssimo Señor, y Rmo. P. Mro. D. Benito Gerónymo Feijóo*, published in Lima in 1765.[243] Escandón, one of the greatest disseminators of Feijóo in Peru, Quito, and New Granada, called him "the teacher of America," and compiled the names of his great friends and admirers.

Other famous Peruvians linked to the Enlightenment included José Baquíjano y Carrillo, conde de Vistaflorida (1751–1818), who following a position similar to Unanúe's, attempted a balance between tradition and progress, and the famous Pablo de Olavide (1725–1803). As a typical representative of the Spanish American Enlightenment, Baquíjano became particularly well known through the establishment of the above-mentioned Economic Society of Lima (1790), and through his liberal mouthpiece *El mercurio peruano* (1791), both in imitation of Peninsular examples, and both important in Peruvian history. The continuous campaigns of the *Mercurio peruano* against the old theories in favor of the new Enlightened ideology were unsurpassed in Spanish America. On the other hand, Olavide, as a more radical thinker, was linked more to the foreign elements of the Enlightenment.

Besides Lima, other active centers of the Enlightenment in Peru were Huamanga, Arequipa, and Cuzco. Ignacio de Castro, rector of the Real Colegio de San Bernardo in Cuzco, fought Scholasticism in favor of modern physics, and under Bishop Pedro José Chávez de la Rosa (1740–1819), the Seminario de San Jerónimo in Arequipa became a strong center of the Enlightenment.[244]

The Enlightenment found further strength in the Convictorio de San Carlos, founded in 1771 to fill the vacuum in education after the expulsion of the Jesuits. The Peruvian Toribio Rodríguez de Mendoza (1750–1825) and the Spaniard Diego Cisneros (d. 1812), both secular priests, revised the curriculum in 1786 and introduced European thought (Descartes, Leibniz, Locke, Condillac).[245] Rodríguez de Mendoza, the Bacon of Peru, as he was called, was much influenced by European rationalism. In his *Informe* of 1791 he stated that students were opposed to any rigid system such as the Aristotelian. Actually, the study of rationalism, empiricism, and sensualism tended toward eclecticism. The natural sciences which Rodríguez de Mendoza fostered were also encouraged by two other priests, Mariano Rivero Aranibar (1765–95) and José Ignacio Moreno (1767–1841). Rivero Aranibar was famous for his *Pro publico juris naturae et gentium examine* (1787) and *De theologiae preambulis*, while Moreno was the author of a *Programma propositionum ad logicam et ethicam pertinentium* (1789) and *Certamen universae philosophiae quod nunc primum ad recentem et accuratiorem studiorum rationem instituent . . .* (1793).[246]

The modern scientific trends were continued, in spite of some official and academic obstacles, by José Gregorio Paredes (1778–1839), who followed in the footsteps of Bueno and Unanúe. Viceroy Abascal sponsored the establishment of the medical school in San Fernando in 1808 and later requested the establishment of scientific chairs.[247]

A few comments are necessary in regard to the Enlightenment in Peru. In the first place, the existence of strong currents of the Enlightenment did not mean "that modern thought was in complete control and that Scholasticism had lost all prestige in educated circles in the second half of the eighteenth century."[248] Secondly, the modern intellectual movement in Peru was favored by certain factors: a government inclined toward reforms which the Enlightenment proposed, a group of young teachers fostering the study of the exact sciences, and the many European scientists visiting Peru during the eighteenth century. Therefore it is legitimate to speak of a Peruvian Enlightenment,[249] which is in reality an echo of the Spanish Enlightenment with its specific characteristics, as is clear from such great names as Peralta Barnuevo, Llano Zapata, Bueno, Unanúe, and Baquíjano, to say nothing of the many priests, such as Celis, Rodríguez de Mendoza, Cisneros, Rivero Aranibar, and Moreno, who were partisans of modernity without losing their religious orthodoxy. Finally, the political consequences of the Enlightenment actually manifested themselves only in the early 1820s as in other parts of Spanish America. The great liberal names of Francisco Javier de Luna Pizarro and José Faustino Sánchez Carrión as well as those of Manuel Lorenzo de Vidaurre (the Peruvian Rousseau),[250] Francisco Javier Mariátegui, José Manuel Valdés, and Manuel Pérez de Tudela[251] reflected the Enlightened liberalism of the *doceañistas* at a time when the Spanish American Revolution was coming to an end.

The Viceroyalty of Peru also had its share of the foreign Enlightenment. Thus, Lockean thought was diffused in Peru by the famous *El mercurio peruano* and by such Enlightened thinkers as Baquíjano and Olavide.[252] But by far the best example of the influence of French and English Enlightened thought before the Spanish American Revolution was Olavide. Born in Lima, he was a collaborator of the Count of Aranda, a friend and correspondent of Holbach's and Voltaire's. He passed through many stages, going from one extreme to another; from an admirer of the more radical ideas of the French Revolution, he became in later life the writer of apologias for religion.[253]

Because of an accusation regarding the disposal of funds for the recovery of Lima from an earthquake, he left for Madrid to justify himself and there associated with the leading men of the Spanish Enlightenment. He had a brilliant career, translating the latest major theatrical works.[254] While in Spain he put into practice two of his pet projects: reform of the university and colonization of the Sierra Morena. His Enlightenment, coupled with a critical approach to the Church, and his correspondence with Rousseau and Voltaire were denounced to the Holy Office, which sentenced him to eight years' seclusion in Murcia. He later fled to France, where he was hailed as a martyr of science, liberty, progress, and reason. Soon after the Revolution began he suffered persecution from the same Revolution he had so hailed, and he lost faith in the Enlightenment. He returned to Spain and to the Church. His influence in both Spain and Spanish America was very great, since he was an echo of French thought contributing to the popularization in the Spanish world of the writings of Voltaire, Rousseau, and the encyclopedists.

Baquíjano was another disseminator of Rousseau. In 1773 he became acquainted with Olavide and Jovellanos in Seville. Although wealthy and in a high position, Baquíjano was denounced to the Inquisition in 1789, but he continued to circulate French books and other works of the Enlightenment.

Chile was not a stronghold of the Enlightenment, which did not penetrate the traditional atmosphere at the University of San Felipe. By far the most representative figure of the Chilean Enlightenment was Manuel de Salas, a lawyer and sociologist instrumental in the establishment of the Academia de San Luis.

An interesting case of the Enlightenment in Chile was the Jesuit Francisco Javier Caldera, exiled to Italy after 1767. His *Exposiciones selectas tomadas de todas las partes de la filosofía* (1780) dealt with logic, metaphysics, physics, and ethics. He stated that he was neither a Scholastic thinker nor a follower of Descartes and attacked Bayle as a renewer of Manichaeism. Though favoring Copernicus over Tycho Brahe, he explained the origin of ideas in keeping with Scholasticism.[255] He was, thus, an example of the eclectic trend often followed by the Jesuits in their quest to harmonize tradition with progress.

Chile was especially famous for some of its Jesuit naturalists. There was, first of all, the natural scientist and historian Juan Ignacio Molina (1770–1829), who enjoyed a great reputation on both sides of the Atlantic, as a result of the many works comprising the *Compendio de historia geográfica y natural del Reino de Chile* and the *Ensayo sobre la historia civil de Chile*,[256] both of which were published in Bologna in 1787. Other naturalists included the Jesuits Diego Alquízar Herrera, known for his *Elementos cosmológicos*, and José Zeitler, a Bavarian, whose pharmaceutical studies (1762, 1767, 1768) were renowned; his library of 130 volumes was among the best in Chile at the time.[257]

A great name in historical studies was Felipe Gómez de Vidaurre Girón (1740–1818), who wrote a *Historia geográfica, natural y civil del Reino de Chile* (1776) in which he intended to cover the entire spectrum of Chilean history, thus following in the footsteps of the earlier sixteenth-century Jesuit José de Acosta and his *Historia natural y moral de las Indias*. As a man of the eighteenth century, however, he was also interested "in sketching the customs, society, civil events, culture, and education."[258] The work has an eighteenth-century flavor, emphasizing the useful and productive qualities of nature and using history as a vehicle for eighteenth-century progress.[259] Another historical work was the *Compendio de la historia geográfica, natural y civil del Reino de Chile* (Bologna, 1776), published anonymously, which apparently was the first study printed by the exiled Jesuits in Italy.[260]

There were also Jesuit scholars devoted to geographical, linguistic, and literary studies, such as Manuel Morales and Bernardo Havestadt. The former was famous for the *Observaciones sobre la cordillera de los Andes y llanuras de Cuyo* (1787), while the latter wrote a most important linguistic work, the *Chilidugu sive res Chilenses vel descriptio status tum naturalis tum civilis, cum moralis regni populique Chilensis, inserta suis locis perfectae ad Chilensem linguam manuductioni* (1777). Finally, the anonymous *Noticia breve del Archipiélago de Chiloé, de su terreno, costumbres de los indios, misiones* (1769/1770)[261] was also evidence of the great interest in the natural sciences.

The foreign Enlightenment was represented by José Antonio Rojas, who introduced Pufendorf's *De iure naturae et gentium* in Chile, and especially by Camilo Enríquez, the forerunner of Chilean independence, who felt the influence of Rousseau. He was denounced for having read the *Contrat social* in 1802. As editor of the *Aurora de Chile*, Enríquez was to become a strong influence for Rousseau in Chile after 1810. Thus, as in the River Plate, the real impact of the ideas of Rousseau and the French Revolution arrived after the establishment of the junta in Santiago and was to increase later in the 1820s.

Viceroyalty of the River Plate. The Cartesian spirit arrived in the River Plate at the end of the seventeenth century and the beginning of the eighteenth. As in other parts of Spanish America it engendered great polemics: since some people adopted the new philosophies, others fought them, and still others adopted middle-of-the-road positions. Many Jesuits in the Indies accepted much of Cartesianism when it came to the experimental sciences, as we have seen in New Spain, New Granada, and Peru, and it was no different in the River Plate, although it was not the pure rationalism of Descartes but the Cartesianism of Leibniz, Wolff, and Newton.[262]

The works of Gassendi, Descartes, Wolff, and Newton were available at the University of Córdoba from the turn of the century, as was the famous *Tableau méthodique des mémoires de Trévoux* (1701–75), edited by Jesuits until 1762, a real fountain of knowledge in all scientific fields.[263] Among other influences which contributed to the propagation of the new trends in philosophy in the River Plate were the works of Juan Caramuel y Lobrowitz of Madrid. His *Rationalis et realis philosophia* (1642), though read in the River Plate in the second half of the seventeenth century, had its greatest impact in the early eighteenth century. Anti-Aristotelian and primarily a mathematician, Caramuel followed Descartes and greatly encouraged the spreading of Cartesianism.[264]

In the River Plate as elsewhere Feijóo was the greatest disseminator of the new spirit; in Córdoba the Jesuit Francisco Javier Miranda praised the great Spanish Benedictine.[265] The *Teatro crítico* and the *Cartas eruditas* were as well known here as elsewhere in the Spanish Empire; and in fact, "No Spanish author was more popular in the River Plate during the eighteenth century than Feijóo."[266]

The famous Jesuits of the University of Córdoba, Tomás Falkner, Domingo Muriel, Mariano Suárez, Benito Riva, José Rufo, and Ramón Rospigliosi, were both Scholastic and followers of the Cartesian philosophy in the sense that they adhered to religious orthodoxy and Scholastic philosophy but followed modern trends in physics and mathematics. This trend was also followed by Franciscans. Thus, Fernando Braco followed Descartes and Newton in the natural sciences, though he did not accept the law of gravity; Manuel María Truxillo, in his *Exhortación pastoral, avisos importantes y reglamentos útiles para la mejor observación de la disciplina regular e ilustración de la literatura en todas las provincias y colegios apostólicos de América y Filipinas* (1786), praised the experimental sciences, and Newton and Descartes, in particular; and Pablo de Cires, in a report to the viceroy in 1802, favored the new trends in the area of the experimental sciences.[267]

But the most important Franciscan scholars in the River Plate were Friars José Cayetano Rodríguez and José Elías del Carmen. Rodríguez, born in 1761 in San Pedro, in the province of Buenos Aires, was the author of a number of famous works, including the *Institutiones philosophicae praecipuae philosophiae partes complectentes logicam nempe, metaphysicam, physicam, et ethicam* (1796) and the *Secunda physicae pars physica particularis quae in rerum naturalium contemplatione versatur juxta recensiorum placita.*[268] Religiously orthodox and generally Scholastic, Rodríguez adopted an independent philosophy in regard to physics, sometimes following Descartes and Gassendi, sometimes following Aristotle. In regard to logic, he adopted a position which was at variance with the old Scholastic version but which at the same time followed neither Condillac nor Thomas Reid and was in reality the old position of Duns Scotus.[269] Elías del Carmen (1760–1825) of Córdoba entered the Franciscan order in 1776 and held the chair of philosophy at the University of Córdoba from 1783 to 1790. He favored the modern trends in physics but rejected the political and philosophical thought of Pufendorf along with that of Rousseau and Voltaire.[270]

Among the scholars who were heavily influenced by the extraordinary development of the natural sciences in the eighteenth century were a number of thinkers who also tried to reconcile their Scholastic philosophy with the results of their experimentation in the new sciences. Some of these scholars were Juan José Paso, professor of San Carlos (1781–83) and author of *Universae physices theses* (1784); Melchor Fernández, author of *Theses ex universa philosophia* (1792) and, though theologian and philosopher, a great physicist familiar with Descartes, Newton, Gassendi, Copernicus, Guericke, Black, and Priestley; two Newtonian physicists, Manuel Gregorio Alvarez and Mariano Medrano, who was the author of *Conferencias filosóficas sobre toda la facultad de filosofía* (1793) and *Secunda philosophiae pars* (1793); José Valentín Gómez, who in physics held some original ideas in regard to the earth and the stars; Diego Estanislao Zavaleta, who also engaged in the study of physics; Franciscan Friar Juan Fernández whose disciple Friar Manuel Buenaventura Villegas defended in 1803 a *Conclusiones público-histórico-dogmático-escolástico-físico-teológico* in favor of Tycho Brahe's system; Friar Juan Antonio del Valle whose system of physics both agreed and at times opposed Aristotle, Newton, and Descartes; and the Jesuit Manuel Gervasio Gil (1745–1807), who became one of the greatest physicists in the River Plate and was the author of several books (*Theoria Boscovichiana vindicata et defensa ab impugnationibus, quibus impetitur in dissertatione quadam: De singulari systemate aut hypothesi P. Boscovich circa legem continuitatis et contractum corporum, ab aliorum quoque difficultatibus in eamdem oppositis, hac occasione expeditur* [1791], *Dissertatio de viribus repulsivis in natura existentibus* [1798], *Disquisitio in causam physicam recentium chemicorum pro elasticitate aeris admospheaerici, et aliorum fluidorum elasticorum, quae gas nuncupatur cum appendice de causa fluiditatis* [1799]).[271]

Finally, the naturalists José Sánchez Labrador, José Godoy, Sebastián Díaz, Manuel Morales, and Lázaro de Ribera conclude the list. Sánchez Labrador was author of a famous encyclopedia; his articles on the most varied themes concerning the natural sciences were published between 1755 and 1767, and again between 1771 and 1776 when he was in exile; Godoy lectured at the University of San Felipe in Santiago de Chile in the late 1770s, while the Chilean

Díaz devoted his studies to the flora and fauna of Cuyo Province. Of greater importance was the previously mentioned Chilean Jesuit Morales for his observations on the Andes and Cuyo Province, and Ribera "star of the Lima classrooms, where he proved his vocation for mathematics and [became] an enthusiast of Descartes."[272]

Another follower of the Enlightenment was Miguel Rubín de Celis, famous for his Spanish translations of many French works and author of a variety of studies, such as *Egloga pastoril: lamentos a la muerte de María Ladvemont, primera dama del teatro* (1765), *Discursos políticos sobre los proverbios castellanos* (1767), *Parábola entre la juventud y la vejez* (1768), *Carta histórico-médica sobre la inoculación de la viruela* (1773), and *Oración fúnebre de Carlos Manuel de Cerdeña* (1774).[273] Celis was, no doubt, one of the most distinguished encyclopedists of the River Plate.

Among the rationalists in the last decade prior to independence was Joaquín Millás, a Jesuit missionary in Paraguay and Tucumán. Born in Saragossa and educated in theology at the University of Córdoba, he lived in Italy after the expulsion of the Jesuits and held the chair of science at the Royal College of Saint Peter at Piacenza (1796–98). He was the author of the Cartesian *Propositiones praecipuae logices* (1797), *Introductio ad metaphysicas disciplinas* (1798), and *Psychologiae institutiones* (1797), all of a markedly anti-Scholastic bias he derived from Wolff.[274] He tried to harmonize Condillac's sensualism with the Scottish school of thought.

The viceroyalty of the River Plate had a greater share of the foreign Enlightenment. Among these currents was, first of all, Pufendorf. An early example of one who knew his theories is the Franciscan Friar Elías del Carmen who, as has been mentioned, rejected them. Deán Gregorio Funes referred to Pufendorf in his autobiography,[275] and Canon Juan Baltasar Maciel furnishes evidence of the interesting influence of Pufendorf's theory of natural law; Pufendorf's *Le droit de la nature et des gens* was among the books in Maciel's library.[276]

Locke appears to have been known in the River Plate as early as 1701 through the Jesuit teachers at the University of Córdoba. During the middle of the eighteenth century the above-mentioned Jesuits Domingo Muriel and Joaquín Millás showed an interest in Locke in their studies and lectures; Millás was a follower of empiricism and accepted Locke's pedagogical theories.

At the end of the century Pantaleón Rivarola quoted Locke in his lectures at the Colegio de San Carlos where Juan José Castelli was one of his pupils. Luís José Chorroarín, a Scholastic thinker as was Rivarola, also showed some influence of Locke, although in both cases it was not substantial. The famous Deán Funes, a follower of Scholastic ideas, quoted Locke on several occasions, although a strong Lockean influence must be denied. Funes was well acquainted with the modern rationalist and sensualist philosophy, but not to the extent of becoming a follower of Locke. Much more serious attempts to introduce Locke were made by Francisco Sebastiani, who held the chair of logic at the same college from 1791 to 1793, and by Juan Manuel Fernández de Agüero y Echagüe in his early courses (1805–1806).

The works of Rousseau were also known in the River Plate area, but there is no evidence that his views, particularly those concerning the social contract, were influential before the revolutionary days of 1810.

It cannot be denied, . . . that the principles of the *Social Contract* were known and had penetrated deeply, thanks to the reading of Rousseau; but it is also undoubtedly true that if these ideas were accepted by so many intellectuals and found so many followers it was because these principles floated in the environment, were known as Spanish legal and traditional norms, and had been sustained by old and notable authors of the Peninsula.²⁷⁷

In any case, Rousseau's impact during this period, prior to the May Revolution in Argentina, was very limited, though it will play a greater role after 1810, and in the 1820s, in particular, at the time of Bernardino Rivadavia.

When the French revolution occurred, there were some who sympathized with the ideas of 1789. One of these was José María Caballero, a miner and former student at the Colegio de México.²⁷⁸ Another partisan of the Enlightenment who fell under the spell of the ideas of 1789 was Luís Ramírez Vidal, a priest, of the *Banda Oriental*. He knew Miguel Rubín de Celis and the former Jesuit Cosme Antonio de la Cueva who had felt strongly the impact of the North American Revolution; Vidal had arrived from Spain as an astronomer in 1781 and was ordered back to the Peninsula in 1785. In 1791, in France, he fell under the spell of the Declaration of the Rights of Man and the Citizen and worked against the Spanish government. The *Impromptu, o espontánea declaración de un español admitido por aclamación y por unanimidad al Club de los Amigos de la Constitución de Bayona* is thought to have been written by him, and perhaps the *Discurso sobre los principios fundamentales de una constitución libre* as well.²⁷⁹

But these ideas penetrated only a limited circle in the River Plate area: mostly Frenchmen, other foreigners, and certain intellectual *criollos*, whose sympathy toward events in France cooled considerably after the king's execution. Still some ideas which came from the French Revolution were accepted, and thus Manuel Belgrano could say:

> At the time of 1789 when I found myself in Spain, the French Revolution accounted for a variety of ideas, particularly among the educated men with whom I had contacts; thus the ideas of liberty, equality, security, property took hold of me, and I saw only tyrants in those who opposed [the principle] that man, wherever he be, should enjoy the rights that God and nature had given him.²⁸⁰

Belgrano, largely a follower of the Enlightenment, had sympathized in his early studies (at Buenos Aires and Salamanca) with Locke and Condillac, although he remained religiously within the strictest orthodoxy.²⁸¹ The French revolutionary influence was also noticeable in that unstable character Bernardo de Monteagudo, a student in Córdoba and Charcas, who later in Buenos Aires became the soul of the *Sociedad Patriótica y Literaria* and of such publications as *La gaceta de Buenos Aires* and *El grito del sur*.

The Spread of Divine Right Theories. At the very time the echo of the Spanish Enlightenment pervaded the cultural atmosphere of Spanish America the government was aided by the spread of divine right theories; these theories were encouraged by the regime, though they often appeared independently of such action.

But just as the Enlightenment did not mean that the Scholastic tradition had been abandoned, so the spread of divine right theories did not imply that medieval political thought had come to an end. Actually, the spread of these theories gave a rather distorted view of the situation in the sense that it made it appear as if Spanish traditional thought, with its medieval limitations on royal power, had been forgotten, which was not the case at all. Thus, we find the *Catecismo real*[282] of the Carmelite José Antonio de San Alberto, bishop of Córdoba (1779–84) and later archbishop of Charcas, a book highly reminiscent of Sir Robert Filmer's earlier *Patriarcha* insofar as it extolled divine right and the duty of passive obedience. San Alberto may be considered a Spanish Robert Filmer; he was a most conspicuous reactionary,[283] and his absolutism was much stronger than any writer in the seventeenth century ever admitted.[284] It was based on an uncompromising religious orthodoxy, though politically he was far removed from the medieval tradition and the Late Scholastic experience, and yet his roots in the seventeenth century are unquestionable. His was a divine right theory based on the Bible and interpreted in an absolutist manner difficult to reconcile with medieval philosophy.

Similar doctrines are found in the *Breve cartilla real* which Lázaro de Ribera, as governor of the Province of Paraguay, wrote for the children of that area. Ribera, the governor of Mojos from 1783 to 1792 and of Paraguay from 1794 to 1805, was a great reformer in the spirit of the late Spanish Enlightenment, encouraging popular education, and the application of useful knowledge, and favoring agriculture and industry. He was a kind of Spanish American Campomanes, carrying his reforms to all administrative spheres, taking over the civil government from the priests who had been in charge of the Indian reservation, and attending personally to improving agriculture and industry in the area.[285] Yet he allowed neither free trade with nor free access to the Indians of Mojos, a practice which went contrary to the economic ideals of the Spanish minister.[286] Essentially, Ribera followed the political theories of Enlightened despotism as did the above-mentioned bishop of Córdoba, San Alberto, and his successor, Manuel Abad Illana.[287]

Other examples are the *Memoria* presented in 1790 by the viceroy of Peru (formerly of New Granada), Francisco Gil de Taboada y Lemus, in which kings are portrayed as the sacred substitutes of God for the temporal government of His people,[288] and the stance taken by the Capuchin Joaquín de Finestrad, an ideological opponent of the revolution of the *comuneros* (1780) in New Granada, in teaching "the true doctrine which assures the thrones, supports fidelity, strengthens obedience, and establishes the peace of the republic."[289]

The previously mentioned Juan Baltasar Maciel, born in 1727 in Santa Fe, a rather eclectic and controversial scholar, also took a somewhat absolutist point of view in his *Reflexiones sobre la famosa arenga* (1781)[290] consonant with Charles III and the political thought of Bishop San Alberto. Maciel's *Reflexiones* represent a report on the attack delivered by José Baquíjano in Lima against the Spanish minister José de Gálvez on August 27, 1781, which the *superintendente* of the Royal Treasury, Francisco de Paula Sanz, had forwarded to him in 1783 with the request for a legal opinion; in the *Reflexiones* Maciel refuted the Peruvian intellectual and sided with Gálvez and the Spanish government. In philosophy, Maciel was somewhat confused. He believed that students could follow, especially in physics, any system — either in accordance with Descartes, Newton, or Gassendi, or without any determined line, following simply the dictates of experience or observation; but in the event that they followed Aristotle it had to be within the framework of St. Thomas.[291] There have been attempts to cite his vast library as proof that he was a modern thinker, but the library, like the *Reflexiones*, does not yield much evidence. Though the works of Hobbes, Bayle, Grotius, Pufendorf, Montesquieu, Voltaire, Gassendi, and Wolff, as well as Rousseau's *Discourses*, found a home there, so did the works of Cano, St. Augustine, Bossuet, St. Thomas, and Feijóo.[292] Maciel was a foe of the Jesuits and quite influential in his time. Enrique de Gandía has called him an obedient servant of Enlightened despotism dedicated "to defending the unlimited authority of the sovereign and the duty of the subject to remain silent regarding 'the specious principle of natural liberty,'" and disagreed with Juan Probst's ideas that Maciel was the father of the May Revolution in Argentina. Actually Maciel was more in line with Solórzano Pereira and the absolutism of the seventeenth century than with the more traditional thought of Vitoria in the sixteenth century.[293]

Finally, another representative of this type of thought was Fernández de Agüero y Echagüe, whose famous *Discursos varios dirigidos a conservar la autoridad de los soberanos, y la fidelidad debida a sus sagradas personas* was published in Buenos Aires in 1799. This interesting work drew on the scriptures and on history; it contained a word neither of the foreign Enlightenment nor of the French Revolution, but referred to St. Augustine and Jean Gerson; it opposed Mariana's theories of tyrannicide and discussed a thesis propounded by Giambattista Vico (who had died in 1774) in regard to the changes which occur in men and in nations. Fernández de Agüero's political theory followed in essence the divine right theory of kings:

> Based on the most solid foundations, we state that subjects can neither legitimately attack the legitimate prince, even though his rule be the most impious and tyrannical, nor *de facto* try or legally plot anything against his position, honor, life, or dignity, since subjects have no jurisdiction whatsoever over the monarch; he does not depend on the people's *potestas*, and, therefore, the people can neither decide against him nor give him orders.[294]

Gandía considered Fernández de Agüero the highest expression of Enlightened despotism in the River Plate area and, thus, together with Maciel, at the opposite pole from the leaders of the May Revolution in Argentina.[295]

Obviously, the Enlightenment was a strong intellectual and cultural movement in the Indies in the eighteenth century and prior to the Spanish American Revolution. Yet the Enlightenment in Spanish America is the Spanish version, with its eclectic elements and Christian foundation, and it operates largely within a Scholastic framework — i.e., with Scholastic formulas — drawing more on the thought of the scientific revolution of the seventeenth century than on the French and English philosophy of the Age of Reason. Conservative in its support of Church and Crown, the Spanish American Enlightenment in no way indicates the end of Scholasticism in the Indies — as is evident in the negative reaction to the Bourbon reforms and in the remarkable vitality of and extraordinary upsurge in Scholastic thinking, which occurred in the early eighteenth century, and especially at the end of it, and which will be linked symbolically with the great renaissance of the *cabildo* at the turn of the century.

NOTES

[1] Becker, p. 31.
[2] Gay, *Enlightenment*; Manuel, *Age of Reason*; Talmon, *Origins of Totalitarian Democracy*. See Whitaker, "Interpretations," pp. 42–57.
[3] Becker, p. 42.   [4] Ibid., p. 63.   [5] Ibid., pp. 129–30, 123.
[6] Ibid., pp. 154–55, quoted from Alexis de Tocqueville, *L'ancien régime et la révolution*, I.3.
[7] See Mornet, *French Thought*, pp. 60–78, 305–16; Mornet, *Les origines intellectuelles*, pp. 37–41, 52–58, 105–12, 137–41, 240–43, 270–77, 364–74, 471.
[8] Gay, passim.   [9] *Die Philosophie*, p. 178.   [10] *De l'Allemagne*, II 105–17, 181–94.
[11] Cassirer, *Die Philosophie*, pp. 179–82.
[12] Mornet, *French Thought*, p. 48.
[13] See ibid., pp. 54–78; and Mornet, *Les origines intellectuelles*, pp. 37–44, 105–12, 71–96, esp. p. 75.
[14] Mornet, *French Thought*, pp. 68–69.
[15] Ibid., p. 67.
[16] *Politica methodice digesta et exemplis sacris et profanis illustrata*, 3rd ed. (Herborn, 1614); *Dicaiologicae libri tres totum et universum jus, quo utimur, methodice complectentes* (Herborn, 1617).
[17] "De iure praedae commentarius" (unpublished MS, 1604), published for the first time in The Hague, 1864; *Mare liberum, sive de iure quod Batavis competit ad Indicana commercia, dissertatio* (Amsterdam, 1609); *De iure belli ac pacis* (Paris, 1625); *De imperio summarum potestatum circa sacra* (Paris, 1646).
[18] *De cive* (Paris, 1642); *Leviathan* (London, 1651).
[19] *Discourses Concerning Government* (Edinburgh, 1750). This was first printed in 1698.
[20] *Two Treatises on Government* (London, 1690); *Letter on Toleration* (London, 1690).
[21] *De statu Imperii Germanici ad Laelium fratrem, dominum Trezolani, liber unus* (Geneva, 1667), published in The Hague under the pseudonym of Severinus de Monzambano; *De iure naturae et gentium* (London, 1672); *De officio hominis et civis prout ipsi praescribuntur lege naturali* (London, 1673); *Le droit de la nature et des gens, ou système général des principes les plus importants de la morale, de la jurisprudence, et de la politique*, trans. Jean Barbeyrac (Amsterdam, 1712).
[22] *Institutiones jurisprudentiae divinae in positiones succincte contractae, in quibus hypotheses Pufendorffii circa doctrinam juris naturalis apodictice demonstrantur et corroborantur, praecepta vero juris divini positivi universalis primum a jure naturali distincte secernuntur et perspicue explicantur, libri tres* (Frankfurt, 1688). *Fundamenta juris naturae et gentium ex sensu communi deducta, in quibus ubique secernuntur principia honesti, justi et decori, cum adjuncta emendatione institutionum jurisprudentiae divinae* (Halle, 1705); *Dissertationes academicae varii imprimis juridici argumenti*, 4 vols. (Halle, 1773–80).
[23] Rommen, *Die ewige Wiederkehr*, p. 76.
[24] Recaséns Siches, pp. 266–67.
[25] Rommen, *Die ewige Wiederkehr*, p. 78.   [26] Ibid., p. 81.   [27] Recaséns Siches, p. 232.
[28] Whitaker, "Elhuyar Mining Missions," 557; Rodríguez Casado, "La nueva sociedad burguesa," 2–3. See also Herr, passim, and Sánchez Agesta, *El pensamiento*, passim.
[29] Francisco (conde) de Cabarrús, *Cartas sobre los obstáculos que la naturaleza, la opinión y las leyes oponen a la felicidad pública* (Vitoria, 1808).
[30] Sánchez Agesta, *El pensamiento*, pp. 89–91.
[31] Sarrailh, for instance, in his otherwise excellent book *L'Espagne éclairée*, has not brought out this dichotomy.
[32] Rodríguez Casado, "El intento español," 145.
[33] Tapia, pp. 293–96.
[34] This point of view has been maintained in Spain by Luis Sánchez Agesta, Vicente Rodríguez Casado, and Patricio Peñalver. For Rodríguez Casado even the expulsion of the Jesuits from the Spanish Empire in 1767 cannot alter this judgment since that unfortunate

event was applauded by sincere Catholic laymen and ecclesiastics who were simply enemies of the Society—José Nicolás de Azara and Francisco Lorenzana, the archbishop of Toledo, for instance ("El intento español," 146).

[35] Whitaker, "Interpretations," p. 54.

[36] *Theatro crítico universal*, 9 vols. (Madrid, 1726–40) and *Cartas eruditas y curiosas*, 5 vols. (Madrid, 1742–60).

[37] *Informe a la ley agraria* (Madrid, 1795).

[38] Pérez-Rioja, pp. 153–62.   [39] Ibid., pp. 163–69.   [40] Ibid., p. 176. See also pp. 189ff.

[41] Marañón, "Visión," 20.   [42] Pérez-Rioja, p. 45.

[43] *Historia de las ideas estéticas en España* (Madrid, 1947) III.i.75, quoted in ibid., p. 20. See also Delpy, p. 111, where he expresses Feijóo's ideas: "Science is a living source of humility. Science and religion! No antithesis, but quite the contrary, the most holy harmony .... The discoveries of science will go to infinity; and this appetite will never be satisfied. Even at the end of centuries there will remain unsolved riddles; what we need is immortality, the beyond, to penetrate them; and it is our best reason to believe in the beyond, in immortality."

[44] Pérez-Rioja, p. 130.

[45] Ibid., pp. 131, 133–35.

[46] "Prólogo", in Jovellanos, p. 10.

[47] Ibid., p. 12.   [48] Polt, pp. 28–29.   [49] Ibid., pp. 34–40.

[50] Peñalver, pp. 118–19.   [51] Polt, p. 53.   [52] Peñalver, pp. 123–27.

[53] "Darios" of December 23, 1795; September 11, 1794; May 9, 1794; and November 1, 1794, in Jovellanos, *Obras: Diarios (Memorias íntimas), 1790-1801*, published by the Instituto de Jovellanos de Gijón (Madrid, 1915), quoted in Sánchez Agesta, *El pensamiento*, p. 208.

[54] "Carta a persona desconocida," *Obras publicadas e inéditas*, 2nd ed., 2 vols. (Madrid, 1926), II 366, quoted in ibid., p. 212.

[55] Polt, p. 59.   [56] Ibid., p. 61.   [57] Ibid., pp. 64, 62–63.

[58] Ibid., p. 64. Polt asserts that in this case modern currents (Locke, Hutchinson) may have converged with similar ideas of a more traditional foundation—a trend which quite often is also to be found in other thinkers of the Hispanic world.

[59] See his *Discurso sobre el fomento de la industria popular* (Madrid, 1774), passim; and Krebs Wilckens, passim.

[60] Ibid., pp. 274–75.   [61] Herr, pp. 18–19.   [62] Krebs Wilckens, p. 275.

[63] See Decouflé et al., pp. 111–24, which is based on Campomanes' *Respuesta fiscal sobre abolir la tasa y establecer el comercio de granos* (1764), *Discurso sobre la educación popular de los artesanos* (1775), and *Apéndice al discurso sobre la educación popular de los artesanos*, 4 vols. (1775–77) and on the *Discurso sobre el fomento de la industria popular*. The expulsion of 160,000 Jews in 1492 and of 300,000 *moriscos* in 1610 deprived Spain, in the first case of merchants and bankers, and in the second, of excellent farmers and artisans who not only took their secrets with them but were not replaced (Decouflé et al., pp. 97, 113–14).

[64] [Campomanes] *El fomento de la industria*, passim.

[65] Decouflé et al., pp. 125–36, 137–44, and [Campomanes] *El fomento de la industria*, pp. 143–58.

[66] Krebs Wilckens, p. 279.

[67] *Histoire critique de l'Inquisition d'Espagne depuis son établissement par Ferdinand V jusqu'au règne de Ferdinand VII*, trans. Alexis Pellier, 2nd ed., 4 vols. (Paris, 1818), I xxv, IV 92, as quoted in Sarrailh, p. 289.

[68] Sarrailh, pp. 293–94, contains a listing of the foreign books forbidden in Spain during the second half of the eighteenth century.

[69] Spell, passim; Herr, pp. 63–65; and Sarrailh, passim, among others.

[70] Spell, pp. 177–87; Sánchez Agesta, *El pensamiento*, passim, esp. p. 241.

[71] Sarrailh, p. 554. Menéndez y Pelayo, II 590, attributes the *Cartas* to Cabarrús; for him they could not be written by Campomanes, "ni por las ideas, ni por el estilo." Sánchez Agesta attributes them to Arroyal, which seems more likely (*El pensamiento*, pp. 305–308).

[72] Polt, p. 7.

[73] Rodríguez Aranda, 122ff.   [74] Ibid., 125.   [75] See Polt, p. 7.

[76] Meléndez Valdés, Arroyal, Marchena, and Cienfuegos drew more on French ideas, though to some extent Locke's influence is discernible from the indirect impact of the French writers Montesquieu, Diderot, Turgot, and Rousseau.

[77] Motten, p. 5. See in this respect the excellent work of Shafer, pp. 3–119.

[78] Arcila Farías, p. 7.   [79] Ibid., pp. 7–12.

[80] Sánchez Agesta, *El pensamiento*, p. 39. Feijóo had led the attack, and he was followed by such men as Diego Torres Villarroel, Ignacio de Luzán, and Gregorio Mayáns y Císcar. Authors Torres Villarroel and Jovellanos criticized education; José Francisco de Isla, Luzán, Antonio de Capmany, Juan Pablo Forner, Nicolás Fernández de Moratín, and Mayáns wrote literary criticism; José Cadalso and Antonio Javier Pérez y López criticized society; Campomanes, Arroyal, Jovellanos, and Cabarrús found fault with the political and economic situation as did such minor figures as Gerónimo de Uztáriz, Nicolás de Arriquibar, Manuel Sisternes y Feliú, and Bernardo de Ulloa (ibid.).

[81] See Davies, pp. 92–108, and Gaettens, pp. 52–73. Some symptoms of change had begun to manifest themselves at the end of the seventeenth century with the establishment of the Royal Society of Medicine (1697), and in the accomplishments of the astronomer Vicente Mut and the mathematicians Friar Vicente Tosca and Antonio Hugo de Omerique (author of an *Analysis geometrica*, praised by Newton). This was followed in the eighteenth century by the establishment of a series of societies: the National Library (1712), the Royal Academy of the Spanish Language (1714), of Medicine (1734), of History (1738), and of Literature (1752). See Fernández Bonilla, "La polémica filosófica," 109–11.

[82] Rodríguez Casado, "Del estado," 114.

[83] Ibid., 115.

[84] Hera, 241. The Enlightened spirit obviously had its effects on the relation of Church and State. The older theories of the unity of Church and State were now interpreted with an eighteenth-century French application, putting the Church under the supervision of the State.

Contributing, no doubt, to this trend was the fact that the papacy had often sided with Spain's enemies (France) and had supported the losing Austrian cause during the War of the Spanish Succession; thus the Spanish Court viewed any priest appointed by the pope as a potential enemy. At that period Philip V, the new Bourbon ruler, did not hesitate to close the Tribunal of the Nunciature (created by Pope Clement III as a court of appeals for matters dealing with the controversial subject of the *regalías*). This disagreement between Madrid and Rome was finally settled in 1753 when that year's concordat gave the Crown an overwhelming victory over the rights of the Church, to such an extent that E. P. I. Miguélez (p. 211) has called it a virtual separation of the Spanish Church from Rome. The Enlightenment in Spain found it an easy task, therefore, to make the necessary inroads into the political relations between Church and State after historical developments had laid the foundation, and in spite of the fact that the Late Scholastic theories were, after all, still predominant. But it may be, as Sánchez Agesta points out (*El pensamiento*, p. 177), that Suárez' theory was too flexible as far as practical application was concerned, admitting various interpretations according to the interests which were supposed to be defended. See in this respect Halperín Donghi, pp. 52–72.

The Hispanic *regalismo*, a movement which did not necessarily mean animosity toward the Church and religion, actually began in the sixteenth century, though at that time it was countered by the Late Scholastic theories of the indirect *potestas*. The movement which culminated in 1767 in the expulsion of the Jesuits was connected with the general ideological currents of the Enlightenment and the special trends in the Peninsula of the so-called *regalista* literature.

See Macanaz, *Regalías*, and *Pedimento*; as well as "The Concordat between Spain and Benedict XIV," in Hargreaves-Mawdsley, pp. 113–21.

[85] Hera, 243–44. [86] Ibid., 250. [87] Ibid., 250–51.

[88] Sánchez Agesta, *El pensamiento*, p. 112.

[89] Fernández Bonilla, "La polémica filosófica," 123.

[90] Ibid. [91] Ibid., 124. [92] Ibid., 126.

[93] See Herr, pp. 243, 295, 297–315 passim, and 321 regarding opposition to the French Revolution. For the influence of the French Revolution, see pp. 244–45, 271–96 passim, 318–20, 323–24, 336, 360, 374–75, 438–41, 444; see also Sarrailh, pp. 573, 600–11.

[94] The projects of Stephen Sayre, Péreyrat and Beaujoil, Odet, Flassan, and Jeaubon de Saint André.

[95] Sarrailh, p. 604. See also Herr, pp. 243, 438.

[96] Sarrailh, p. 610–11. See Martínez Mariana, *Teoría de las Cortes*, I 38, 232; and Fugier.

[97] Pp. 137–39. [98] See Houdaille, passim.

[99] This is strikingly evident in the title of Ceballos' work: *La falsa filosofía o el ateísmo, materialismo y demás nuevas sectas convencidas de crimen de estado contra los soberanos y sus regalías, contra los magistrados y potestades legítimas. Se combaten sus máximas sediciosas y subversivas de toda sociedad y aún de la humanidad* (1774–76).

See also Hervás y Panduro. This treatise was written so that the Spaniards could learn from the French events. The author argued that one of the causes of the French Revolution was Jansenism, as were Calvinism, encyclopedism, and Freemasonry. It is interesting to note that the book, though finished in 1794, could not be published in Spain because of the opposition of the Spanish Jansenists, led by Joaquín Lorenzo Villanueva, and circulated there only after 1807. These details are of significance insofar as they reveal quite a different picture from that generally drawn of the Spanish eighteenth century. Hervás y Panduro's book fell under the general prohibition leveled against the works of Suárez, Molina, and Mariana.

See too Pérez y López, *Principios del orden esencial de la naturaleza establecidos por fundamento de la moral y política* (Madrid, 1785), and *Discurso sobre la honra y deshonra legal* (Madrid, 1786); Peñalosa, *La monarquía* (Madrid, 1771), and *El honor militar: Causas de su origen, progresos y decadencia* (Madrid, 1795); Pérez Valiente, *Varios libros elocuentes sobre materias políticas* (Valencia, 1700), and *Apparatus juris publici hispanici: Opus politicumjuridicum* (Madrid, 1751); "Sarmiento" (pseudonym of Pedro José García Balboa), *Demonstración crítico apologética del* TEATRO CRÍTICO, 2 vols. (Madrid, 1732); Marín, *Historia del derecho natural y de gentes* (Madrid, 1776); and Cabrera, *Crisis política: Determina el más florido imperio y la mejor institución de príncipes y ministros* (Madrid, 1719). See also Sánchez Agesta, *El pensamiento*, pp. 251–79.

[100] "El siglo xviii educador," *Obras*, II 600.
[101] P. 31.   [102] Mornet, *French Thought*, pp. 5–6.
[103] Ibid., p. 6. A definite change in French thought occurred between 1670 and 1770: until about 1740 people argue, from 1740 to 1760 the experimental sciences gain the upper hand, and after 1762 "men's souls are moved and exalted by sensibility." But "French thought in the second half of the eighteenth century is neither rational nor philosophical, neither scientific nor experimental, neither sentimental nor mystical. It represents all these tendencies, according to the environment or the individual, and at times in the same environment and in the same individual" (ibid., pp. 329, 333–34).
[104] Ibid., p. 16.   [105] Puy, p. 31.
[106] Ibid., pp. 31–32, quoted from Luis Hirschberger & J. Martínez Gómez, *Historia de la filosofía*, 2 vols. (Barcelona, 1956), II 419.
[107] Passim, esp. pp. 95–133, 135–94; see too the impressive Spanish bibliography from 1700 to 1760 in Appendix I (pp. 241–81).
[108] Pp. 55–56, referring to Menéndez y Pelayo, *La ciencia española: Polémicas, proyectos y bibliografía*, 3rd ed., 3 vols. (Madrid, 1887–88), III 199–205.
[109] Puy, pp. 56–57, referring to Menéndez y Pelayo, *La ciencia española*, III 199–205.
[110] Rodríguez Casado, "La nueva sociedad burguesa," 3.
[111] Sánchez Agesta, *El pensamiento*, pp. 262–70.
[112] "El intento español," 147.
[113] Ibid., 148–49.   [114] Ibid.   [115] Ibid., 152–55.
[116] Ibid., 155–59.   [117] Pp. 228–30.
[118] Ortega, II 600. Thus, while Ortega deplored the fact that Spain had actually jumped ahead of the eighteenth century into the nineteenth and twentieth centuries, d'Ors joined Marañón in pointing out that modern Spain was actually born in that century. Marañón maintained that the Spanish eighteenth century was not a century of further decline but one in which Spaniards on both sides of the Atlantic witnessed a certain spiritual revival, the diametrically opposed political consequences notwithstanding. For Marañón (pp. 20–21) the French influence on Spanish culture in that century remains largely a legend based on anecdote. Sarrailh commented (p. 709): "It is Dr. Marañón, good commentator of Feijóo and his time, who seems to express it best when he writes: 'Spain as a nation perhaps did not join the encyclopedist movement, which no doubt everywhere was an attitude of chosen minorities. But, as always, she had among her sons isolated great titans, charged with the task of preventing the line of continuity of civilization from breaking.' Let us make giants of these titans, and we shall accept the judgment of Marañón and its whole in terms of this study."
[119] Pérez-Rioja, p. 29.   [120] Ibid., pp. 30–31.   [121] Ibid., p. 37.
[122] Pp. 324ff.   [123] Pérez-Rioja, pp. 35, 33, 36.   [124] P. 330.
[125] Pp. 63–64. Jane very pointedly called Charles III the Diocletian of Spain (p. 63). This point of view is also taken by Giménez Fernández, *Instituciones jurídicas*, I 216, and *Las doctrinas populistas*; by Fernández-Bonilla, "La polémica filosofica"; and by Sousa, "Formación brasileña," 278, among others.
[126] P. 324.   [127] Sánchez Agesta, *El pensamiento*, pp. 98–99.   [128] Marañón, 19.
[129] See Zavala, *América*, passim, esp. pp. 157–66, 204–207.

[130] The Enlightenment marked a new stage in the development of the so-called Black Legend. As Whitaker says ("Dual Role of Latin America," p. 8): "In its first stage, its founder, Las Casas, had used it to discredit secular government in America in order to establish the control of the Church over it. In the second stage, the Legend had been exploited by the foreign enemies of Spain, among whom many were Protestants seeking to discredit Roman Catholicism. Now, in the third stage, the philosophers of the Enlightenment used the Black Legend as a weapon in their assault on all revealed religion." See also Juderías, pp. 145–54, 165–76, 223–29; and Carbia, *La Leyenda Negra*, pp. 97–155, 214–38.
[131] Lanning, *Academic Culture*, pp. 61–64.
[132] Ibid., pp. 71–72.   [133] Ibid., p. 67.   [134] Ibid., p. 69.
[135] Ibid.
[136] *Relation historique*, I 565ff.
[137] *Ensayo político*, II 123.
[138] *Academic Culture*, p. 83.   [139] Pp. 58–59.   [140] Sarrailh, p. 709.
[141] Lanning, *Academic Culture*, p. 65.
[142] Palacio Atard, "La influencia del P. Feijóo," I 22.
[143] Ibid., 23–24.   [144] Ibid., 25.   [145] Ibid., 26.
[146] Ibid.   [147] Ibid., 27.   [148] Delpy, p. 318.
[149] Pérez-Rioja, pp. 134–35.   [150] Arcila Farías, pp. 13–16.
[151] Ibid., pp. 16–17, 17–21, 13.   [152] Ibid., pp. 20–21.   [153] Ibid., p. 21.
[154] Lanning, *Academic Culture*, p. 65.   [155] Ibid., p. 67.
[156] See Gay, pp. 328–30; Laaths, p. 460; Wolf, pp. 309ff., 334ff., 364, 379, 387f., 400ff. 414, 436, 456, 475, 661. See also Gierke pp. 113, 121, 125, 147–48, 175, 185, 196; and Furlong, *Nacimiento*, pp. 52, 66, 76, 175, 178, 184, 192, 199, 287, 351, 400, 437–38, 512, 551–61.
[157] Lanning, *Academic Culture*, pp. 66, 79, 69, 78.
[158] Ibid., p. 80.
[159] See Madariaga, *El ocaso*, pp. 279–307, for the influence of Montesquieu, Rousseau, Voltaire, and Raynal.
[160] Lanning, *Academic Culture*, p. 74.   [161] Ibid., p. 81.   [162] Ibid., p. 84.
[163] *Le droit de la nature et des gens*; for Pufendorf's influence in Spanish America, see "Alegato de Quiroga en el primer juicio iniciado contra los próceres en febrero de 1809," in *Memoria de la Academia Ecuatoriana correspondiente de la Real Española, número extraordinario dedicado a la memoria del Gran Mariscal Antonio José de Sucre, con motivo del centenario de la batalla de Pichincha* (Quito, 1922), pp. 62–100.
[164] Hussey, pp. 31–34; for Maciel, see Gandía, *Las ideas políticas*, I 180.
[165] Spell, p. 129.   [166] Ibid., p. 130.   [167] Romero, p. 59.
[168] See Madariaga, *El ocaso*, pp. 298–303. Madariaga, however, seems to exaggerate Voltaire's influence in Spanish America.
[169] Ibid., p. 297.   [170] Published in Geneva in 1780.   [171] Madariaga, *El ocaso*, p. 303.
[172] Ibid., pp. 305–306.   [173] Ibid., p. 306.
[174] Whitaker, "Dual Role of Latin America," pp. 15–16. See also the appendix listing the main government-sponsored scientific expeditions of Latin America before 1800.
[175] Whitaker, "Elhuyar Mining Missions," 557.
[176] Ibid.   [177] Ibid., 557–85.   [178] Ibid., 559–60.
[179] Hussey, pp. 28–29.   [180] See Shafer, pp. 123–249.   [181] Ibid., pp. 145–57.
[182] Ibid., p. 273.
[183] This is the reason why Baquíjano in Peru, Santa Cruz y Espejo in Quito, José Cecilio del Valle in Guatemala, among others, enthusiastically praised Campomanes (ibid., p. 287).
[184] Ibid., p. 352.
[185] Whitaker, "Las sociedades científicas latino-americanas," pp. 99–109.
[186] Shafer, pp. 272, 355.
[187] See Redmond, p. 48.
[188] Ramos, *La filosofía en México*, pp. 74–75.
[189] See Redmond, pp. 1, 8, 31; and Díaz-Plaja & Monterde, pp. 459–64, 471, 481.
[190] Cruz, I 47–48. See also Díaz-Plaja & Monterde, p. 468.
[191] Cruz, I 48.
[192] Ibid., 49. See also Redmond, p. 30.
[193] Pérez-Rioja, p. 180.
[194] Cf. Redmond, pp. 33–34; and Cruz, I 50.
[195] Ramos, *La filosofía en México*, p. 87.
[196] Ibid., pp. 64–67. See Redmond, p. 10.

[197] Ramos, *La filosofía en México*, pp. 64–67. See Redmond, p. 17.
[198] Cruz, I 49. See Monguió, pp. 217–19.
[199] Pérez-Rioja, pp. 179–80. See Redmond, pp. 19, 93, 28.
[200] Cruz, I 49–50.   [201] Ibid., 49, 51.   [202] Ibid., 51.
[203] Ramos, *La filosofía en México*, p. 74.
[204] *Ensayo político*, I 231. See also Ramos, *La filosofía en México*, p. 90.
[205] Ibid., pp. 90–91.   [206] Redmond, pp. 60–61.
[207] Ramos, *La filosofía en México*, pp. 92–97. See also Díaz-Plaja & Monterde, pp. 464–65, 466–67.
[208] Pérez-Marchand, p. 71.   [209] See ibid., p. 58.
[210] Rodríguez, "Locke en el Río de la Plata," 50.
[211] Ibid.
[212] In the Treaty of Paris (1763), France ceded Louisiana to Spain.
[213] Hernández y Dávalos (ed.), "Exposición de los fiscales contra las opiniones de los novadores," *Colección de documentos*, I 756, August 9, 1808, Document 260, pp. 672–80.
[214] Lanning, *Academic Culture*, pp. 62–63.   [215] Pérez-Rioja, p. 183.
[216] Marañón, *Evolución*, p. 13; idem, "Visión."
[217] Pérez-Rioja, p. 182.   [218] Marañón, 21.   [219] García Bacca, p. 439.
[220] Ibid., p. 441. See also Redmond, p. 66.
[221] García Bacca, pp. 506–10.   [222] Ibid., pp. 513–22.
[223] *Relation historique*, I 410.   [224] Pérez-Sarmiento, pp. 83–84.   [225] P. 136.
[226] Spell, pp. 131–33.
[227] See Rojas (ed.), *Miranda en la Revolución Francesa*, passim.
[228] Spell, p. 221.
[229] "Opinión de Miranda sobre la situación actual de Francia y los remedios convenientes a sus males," in Rojas, *Miranda en la Revolución Francesa*, esp. pp. 339 and 342 for the influence of Rousseau.
[230] "Proclama de Miranda fechada en Coro á 2 de Agosto de 1806," in Instituto Panamericano de Geografía e Historia, publication No. 9, p. 75.
[231] Mancini, pp. 118–19.
[232] Ibid., pp. 119–20. (The quotations were taken from Rousseau's *Emile ou de l'éducation*, Bk. II, passim.) See also André, pp. 5–11, 15–16. André very fittingly called Rodriguez a tropical Rousseau (p. 5).
[233] See Madariaga, *Bolívar*, p. 63; Leturia, *El ocaso*, pp. 64, 70, 72, 87, 134.
[234] See "Composición de fragmentos de cartas de Bolívar para Fanny du Villars," in Bolívar, *Obras*, I 20–24.
[235] It is interesting to note that in his will Bolívar left his copy of the *Contrat social* to the university of his native city. This copy, which he had received some years before from his friend Sir Robert Wilson, had belonged to Napoleon; it is symbolic of the link of Bolívar's thought and actions with those of Rousseau and Napoleon. See his letter "Al General Sir Robert Wilson," dated November 15, 1824, in ibid., II 43–44.
[236] Salazar Bondy, p. 63.
[237] Redmond, p. 73; Pérez-Rioja, pp. 182–83.
[238] See McPheeters.
[239] Salazar Bondy, pp. 63–64.
[240] Ibid., p. 66.   [241] Ibid., pp. 66–67.   [242] Redmond, p. 52.
[243] Pérez-Rioja, pp. 182–83; Lanning, *Academic Culture*, p. 66n13.
[244] Salazar Bondy, pp. 65–66.   [245] Ibid., pp. 67–68.
[246] Ibid., pp. 68–69. See Redmond, pp. 79, 64–65, and Monguió, pp. 221–22.
[247] Salazar Bondy, pp. 69–70.   [248] Ibid., p. 69.   [249] Ibid., pp. 61–62.
[250] Spell, p. 253.   [251] Salazar Bondy, p. 70.
[252] See Monguió, pp. 220–31, in regard to the *Mercurio peruano*; and Tapia, p. 290, Fernández-Bonilla, "La polémica filosófica," 122–23, and Deforneaux in regard to Olavide.
[253] *El evangelio en triunfo o historia de un philósopho desengañado* (Valencia, 1798), *Poemas cristianos* (Madrid, n.d.), *Salterio español* (Madrid, 1800).
[254] Such as Racine's *Phèdre*, Sédaine's *Le déserteur français*, Lemierre's *Hiperménestra et Lina*, Favart's *Ninette à la cour*, Voltaire's *Zaïre*, Maffei's *Mérope*, and others.
[255] Hanisch, p. 211.
[256] Ibid., pp. 213–15, 223.   [257] Ibid., pp. 218–22.   [258] Ibid., pp. 228–31, esp. p. 230.
[259] Ibid.   [260] Ibid., p. 231.   [261] Ibid., pp. 232–33.
[262] Furlong, *Nacimiento*, p. 170.

[263] Ibid., pp. 170–72. [264] Ibid., pp. 172–73. [265] Ibid., pp. 175–77.
[266] Ibid., p. 177n28. [267] Ibid., pp. 239–43. [268] Redmond, p. 80.
[269] Furlong, *Nacimiento*, pp. 245–56. [270] Ibid., p. 257.
[271] Redmond, pp. 71, 40, 58, 9, 46, 109–10; Furlong, *Nacimiento*, pp. 488–515.
[272] Furlong, *Nacimiento*, pp. 515–22, 481.
[273] Ibid., pp. 532–33.
[274] Redmond, pp. 59–60; Furlong, *Nacimiento*, pp. 551–67.
[275] Argentina, Biblioteca Nacional, pp. 9–10; see Furlong, *Nacimiento*, pp. 591, 649.
[276] Juan Probst, "Juan Baltasar Maciel, el maestro de la generación de Mayo," *Instituto de Didáctica* (Buenos Aires, 1946), quoted in Narancio, "Las ideas políticas," 116; see also Furlong, *Nacimiento*, pp. 437–38.
[277] Gandía, *Las ideas políticas*, I 103.
[278] See Furlong, *Nacimiento*, p. 527. [279] Ibid., pp. 530–32.
[280] Caillet-Bois, 39.
[281] Furlong, *Nacimiento*, pp. 581–83.
[282] *Catecismo real . . ., en que por preguntas y respuestas se enseñan catequísticamente en veinte lecciones las obligaciones que un Vasallo debe a su Rey y Señor* (Madrid, 1786). See Tejada, "Fray José Antonio de San Alberto." See also Eyzaguirre, pp. 49–50; and Gandía, *Las ideas políticas*, I 269–92.
[283] Korn, p. 114.
[284] Halperín Donghi, pp. 110–23, esp. pp. 118, 122.
[285] Furlong, *Nacimiento*, p. 481. [286] Ibid. [287] Korn, p. 114.
[288] Eyzaguirre, p. 50.
[289] Gómez Hoyos, I 199. For Finestrad, see 168, 170, 197–202.
[290] The full title of the opinion given by Maciel is *Reflexiones sobre la famosa arenga, pronunciada en Lima por un individuo de la Universidad de San Marcos, con ocasión del recibimiento que hizo dicha Universidad a su Virrey, el Excelentísimo Señor don Agustín de Jáuregui y Aldecoa, el día 27 de agosto de 1781* (see Gandía, *Las ideas políticas*, I 185ff.).
[291] Furlong, *Nacimiento*, p. 436. See also pp. 430–39.
[292] Gandía, *Las ideas políticas*, I 180–81.
[293] Ibid., 193, 195, 186.
[294] From the *Discursos varios*, included as an appendix in ibid., 460. See also 320–39.
[295] Ibid., 338.

IV

IMPLEMENTATION OF AND REACTION TO THE ENLIGHTENMENT IN SPANISH AMERICA, 1700–1808

1. The Bourbon Reforms

THE ENLIGHTENMENT HAD OPENED NEW HORIZONS in the Spanish world leading to a greater influence of modern philosophies, which reached the political field, in particular. This is illustrated especially by the famous Bourbon reforms of the eighteenth century which were much resented by the Spanish Americans and actually opened the gates for the future revolution in the Indies. It is ironic that the Spanish Americans disliked these reforms, in spite of the fact that they were supposed to benefit the entire Spanish Empire.

An important element linked to the Bourbon reforms was a famous report called the *Noticias secretas de América*[1] written by Jorge Juan and Antonio de Ulloa while they resided in Quito and Peru. Compiled for the Spanish Crown at the specific request of Ferdinand VI, this report apparently remained a guideline for the kings and their Council of the Indies in all policy decisions during the second half of the century.[2]

The report described the oppression of the Indians, especially at the hands of the *corregidores* but also under the system of the *repartimientos*, and stated that protests by the Indians not only had not brought relief but often had even resulted in their punishment as rebels. The report went on to point out that the lot of the Indians, hard enough on the plantations, cattle ranges, and wool-growing estates, was worse in the factories.[3] These hardships included corporal punishments in which, it was alleged, parish priests also participated, thus joining in the general spoliation, since Indian property allegedly was often seized.

To support this charge, the report cited the case of the Indian town of Pinampiro where the behavior of the priests had driven the Indians to desperation and rebellion, and mentioned that the towns of Logroño and Guariboya had disappeared because of such oppression.[4] The report charged that Spanish rule in the Indies was arbitrary and oppressive and that the Church was corrupt—though it exempted the Jesuits from this general indictment, nonetheless emphasizing their accumulated wealth in the Indies — and called for a complete change in administrative policies.[5] Indeed, it is most likely that the *Noticias secretas* was used as evidence to support putting the Church under the greater control of the Crown and introducing administrative reforms, such as the *intendencia* at the end of the century.

The *Noticias secretas* was intended to depict the situation as the king and his Enlightened entourage wanted it to be: within the spirit of the Age of Reason, and with the obvious conclusion that the traditions which so far had been followed in the Indies had been morally wrong and politically ill-advised.

Written from this subjective point of view, the report magnified out of proportion certain abuses which had probably occurred, while at the same time ignoring totally the extraordinary achievements of the Church, especially the missionary activity with its remarkable success in Paraguay. Thus, the *Noticias secretas* did not represent the real situation, and neither in form nor in substance was it in keeping with tradition. In the first place, the *Noticias secretas* was a sharp break with the past since the report itself did not originate within the administration of the Indies. Up to that time the authorities in Spanish America had compiled similar reports for their superiors in the Peninsula which essentially defended conditions as they were and any suggestions for change "were suggestions for change from within and by means of the ordinary action of constituted authority."[6] But now a report of conditions in Spanish America had been commissioned from the Peninsula outside the regular channels and with a different spirit. Indeed,

> The *Noticias Secretas* was inspired not by religious fervour, as had been the most denunciatory pamphlets of Las Casas, but by that eighteenth-century humanitarianism which had little regard for Christianity. The attack contained in it was also officially authorized, and was probably even commanded. It is very unlikely that it would have been what it was, had not its authors been assured in advance that the royal wish was that they should produce as scathing an indictment as possible of everything Spanish in Spanish America.[7]

Thus, in sum, the *Noticias secretas*, like the many administrative reforms which the Bourbon regime introduced in the eighteenth century, far from pleasing the Spanish Americans, was apt to anger them, since the report broke with tradition, demonstrating little appreciation of the past, imposed a spirit which was intrinsically alien to the *criollos'* idealism, and showed a lack of understanding of the true climate of the Indies.[8]

The Bourbons introduced various political innovations into Spain and the Empire which they took from France. Though they were intended to put an end to Spain's decline, they proved counterproductive and actually disastrous to Spanish interests. As early as the reigns of the first Spanish Bourbons (Philip V, Louis I, Ferdinand VI), the government had tightened the administration and centralized it from Madrid in imitation of the French system and in keeping with the general policies in contemporary Europe.

> The Enlightened monarchy then opened the last phase of a unique process: namely, the Spanish Catholic monarchy, which was prophesied by a widespread hope in the fifteenth century; established for a more-than-national mission in the sixteenth century; and nationalized thanks to a progressive, but never totally acknowledged, renunciation of that mission in that century, and the following, which now attempts to adapt itself to the political realities, to the new spiritual requirements of European life.[9]

This marked tremendously important changes in political methods toward overseas territories, which in turn brought about several significant innovations. In the first place, the government established two new viceroyalties (New Granada [1717, 1740], and River Plate [1776]) — measures which had become necessary for several reasons, including military, in the case of the viceroyalty of the River Plate. With it came the establishment of new administrative subdivisions, the captaincies-general of Chile, Venezuela, Guatemala, and Cuba, within the former viceroyalties. These measures were carried out to introduce efficiency; but they represented an encroachment on the Hispanic concept of freedom, insofar as they entailed a greater centralization and control while at the same time exempting the smaller administrative areas from viceregal supervision.[10]

A second reform concerned the introduction of the *intendencia* (Havana, 1764, in a more limited form; River Plate, 1782; Peru, 1784; Chile and New Spain, 1786; and in the remaining areas in 1790), a typically French administrative institution, which had literally been translated and adapted from France. Inspired by José de Galvez when he was *visitador general* in New Spain, the *intendencia* was meant as a reaction to the Hapsburg tendencies toward decentralization. The rise in trade and the increase of population demanded new tasks and prompt attention, and the system of the *intendencias* was supposed to solve these problems.

The *intendentes* held competency in the field of finance, but they soon carried out other administrative duties, such as military affairs (*milicias*), which had been the responsibility of the *audiencias* and the viceroyalties; they also dealt with matters of police and justice. Since many abuses had allegedly been committed by the *corregidores*, the *intendentes* were a check on these and were in fact more favorably inclined toward the Spanish Americans. In many cases, administrative, judicial, and ecclesiastical divisions had not coincided, and confusion resulted. The *intendencia* was supposed to correct this jurisdictional anarchy,[11] modernize and streamline Spanish administration overseas, and end alleged abuses. Indeed, with the introduction of more than thirty *intendencias* in Spanish America (12 in New Spain, 8 in Peru, 8 in the River Plate, and a lesser number in New Granada), many of the functions of the governors, *corregidores*, and *alcaldes mayores* were assumed by the *intendentes*, and in New Spain alone some two hundred *corregidores* and *alcaldes mayores* lost their positions. Though undoubtedly successful from a financial point of view, the system of *intendencias* had a very harmful effect on the entire Spanish administration overseas: from the viceroys down to the members of the *cabildos*, all felt discriminated against.[12] It was a great political error to replace the *criollos* — who, in the course of time, had attained high position as governors, *corregidores*, and *alcaldes mayores* — with *peninsulares*, and the Crown unnecessarily made enemies for itself. The *intendencia* was a symbol of the French spirit of order which Charles III wanted to force upon the freedom-loving Spanish Americans, without realizing that this measure contained typically European traits; geared toward efficiency, it simply bypassed the cleverly divised system of the Spanish Crown overseas.

John Lynch has expressed an interesting point of view in regard to the relationship of the *intendencia* and the *cabildo*. In contrast to the opinions of Cecil Jane and of Emilio Ravignani,[13] Lynch feels that in view of the legal and practical weakness of the *cabildos* on the eve of the intendant system, it was "unreal to consider the problem in terms of local institutions being absorbed by centralizing officials," but to see it instead in the context of whether the *intendentes* made the *cabildos* in the new era more active and allowed them to cooperate in the work they were doing."[14] The freedom of the *cabildos* was restricted, not from "any conscious anti-municipal policy, but simply in the interests of greater efficiency and by the creation of a more detailed administrative machinery."[15] Thus, Viceroy Croix of Peru stated that the *intendentes* "had completely alienated the municipalities by an intolerant intrusion into their affairs."[16] But in Lynch's view the system of *intendencias* solved the problems of the past, with better representation and financial stability. Thus the *cabildos* "entered upon a period of greater activity in public administration,"[17] a period of cooperation between the two institutions which lasted for fifteen years after the introduction of the *intendencia*, and was symbolized best — in the case of the River Plate — in the work of the *intendente* and Governor Rafael de Sobremonte. Describing him as its *nuevo fundador*, the *cabildo* of Mendoza requested from the Crown his continuation in office in view of his great contribution to prosperity and general progress in the area.[18]

But while this support of the *intendencias* by the *cabildos* in the River Plate and in Peru was the norm in the 1780s and '90s,[19] it vanished at the beginning of the nineteenth century. The reawakening of political consciousness on the part of the *cabildos* during this period resulted from the decrease in the quality of the *intendentes* and an increase in self-assurance of the *cabildos*, which had been encouraged by the respect the *intendencia* had shown them. Though this revival was not directed against the *intendencias*, it gave evidence of the *cabildos*' resistance to any kind of continued tutelage.[20] Thus, in the River Plate the antagonism of Chuquisaca began in 1796, in Córdoba in 1798, and in La Paz by 1805.[21] But by far the most vigorous defense of municipal freedom and opposition to arbitrary government came from the *cabildo* of Buenos Aires, whose confidence had been further strengthened by the role it played during the British invasions; it in turn appealed to the towns of the interior, which had become more conscious of their rights and duties.[22]

Furthermore, the changes which occurred with the introduction of the *intendencia* resulted in another consequence in keeping with Bourbon centralism:

> the ordinances which were published in this respect extended not only to Spain but to America as well This represents quite a constitutional evolution insofar as *it assimilates the colonies to the metropolis*, in contrast to the practice at the time of the Hapsburgs. Thus, the dominions are elevated to the rank of the other provinces. "The monarchy of Spain and of the colonies is one," since from this time on they are governed under a system of equality. ... Hence, we can say that under the Bourbons any reform born in Spain has repercussions in America. When the juntas are set up in Spain, they are also established in America; when the metropolis disintegrates, the disintegration [of the area] which once represented the colonies follows almost immediately.[23]

Another administrative act derived from France was the sending of Peninsular officials to positions in the Indies, which had largely been reserved to native Spanish Americans. This trend lasted until the end of the rule of Charles III, when a reversal of this policy set in — a measure which like many others came as something too little and too late. The Spanish Hapsburgs had followed the Spanish tradition of filling administrative vacancies with natives of a particular region, and had continued this political practice both in the mother country and throughout the Empire.[24]

In the economic sphere the general policies of Charles III envisioned a better utilization of the Indies through the development of its wealth and the growth of its population. They aimed at an increase of trade, production, consumption, and navigation, and at the centralization of revenue, protection of national industries, and a more equitable distribution of wealth. From a purely economic point of view, these policies were obviously successful in a very short time. The increase in production and trade and an improvement in working conditions and the distribution of capital were their immediate consequence.[25]

This growth occurred in spite of the fact that economic ideas in the Indies lagged behind those prevalent in the Peninsula, though there were such officials as Ramón de Posada, the *fiscal* of the Royal Treasury of New Spain who, influenced by the thought of Jovellanos — the *Informe sobre la Ley Agraria* — advocated free trade.[26] But there were powerful groups in New Spain who at the end of the century continued to support certain monopolistic positions of mercantilist tendency (such as the restrictions of cargoes to New Spain and the return to the abolished convoy system, and the reaction of businessmen against free trade and the commerce with foreigners) which had been abandoned earlier by the Peninsular government. This reaction against liberalism was not restricted to New Spain, but found a place as well in other parts of Spanish America, such as Venezuela and the River Plate. Thus

> while Spain was evolving toward liberalism, in [Spanish] America there were interests which resisted these new currents aimed at giving a greater and more active participation to more numerous social groups.[27]

In the pursuit of these economic policies, the monopoly of Cádiz and Seville was destroyed when several private companies were formed and many ports in metropolitan and overseas Spain were opened to foreign interests, giving rise to the suspicion that the Crown was willing to sacrifice the interests of the Spanish Empire.[28] To break the monopolistic role of Seville, of which the convoy system was a part, the Crown encouraged the establishment of private trading companies. In spite of many projects which failed because of opposition by the Council of the Indies — such as the Franco-Spanish plan of 1703, proposed by Pontchartrain, the French Minister of the Navy, and that of 1707 proposed by the marqués de Montesacro — the companies included the famous *Compañía de Caracas* or *Compañía Guipuzcoana* (1728), the *Compañía de Galicia* (1734), and at the end of the rule of Philip V, the four companies called *Cinco Gremios Mayores de Madrid*, and those of Havana, Seville, and Granada.[29] The *Compañía de Caracas* traded with Venezuela; that of Galicia traded with Campeche; the Company of the *Cinco Gremios Mayores de Madrid* — linked also with the biggest Spanish trading company, the Casa de Uztáriz — traded with all areas of the Spanish Empire and was allowed in 1784 to set up a trading establishment in New Spain. The companies of Havana, Seville, and Granada had close relations with New Spain, but the biggest trading company was that of the Philippines.[30] Among the foreign trading companies which did business with Spanish America was the French Company of Guinea (1701) which obtained the *asiento* right up until the Peace of Utrecht (1713), when the right passed to the Royal Company of England giving the British enterprise an important advantage in its trade with New Spain. This advantage at times was so strong that the English even set up factories in the very heart of Mexico and in other parts of New Spain. They became isolated, however, since society in general as well as the authorities, merchants, and religious orders, all for different reasons, viewed this intrusion as extremely dangerous.[31]

The increase of wealth was a direct consequence of the policy allowing greater freedom to navigation and trade, which culminated in the royal decree of 1789 incorporating New Spain into the system of free trade. This incorporation led to a flight of old trade capital into agriculture and mining, the growth of the middle class, a rise in the consumption of foreign merchandise, an increase in the volume of business, demand for greater capital, and the end of the Mexican trade hegemony. Yet another of the consequences of free trade was the shift in the center of business from Mexico to Veracruz.[32]

The new system, as Arcila Farías observes, dealt a severe blow to the interests of a small group of businessmen who enjoyed a privileged position, who were represented in the *Consulado de México*, and who tried by all means to keep it that way. Free trade was not welcome in New Spain. In his report of 1793, the viceroy of New Spain, the conde de Revillagigedo, stated that, with the exception of two individuals, all wanted a return to the old restrictions. And the *Consulado de México* echoed these feelings when, representing 105 businessmen, it voiced an identical opinion.[33] The government attempted to break this opposition by establishing two new *consulados* (Veracruz and Guadalajara) in 1795.

When free trade was introduced in New Spain, businessmen, believing that their privileges were being eroded by the import of foreign merchandise, withdrew funds from trade and invested them in agriculture and mining. This in turn opened the gates to newcomers who had been prevented from entering the field of trade, and resulted in a level of competition previously unknown in New Spain.[34]

The rise of commercial interest in a growing number of new individuals as well as a growing volume of transactions produced a demand for capital, which was not available; the situation was aggravated by the sidetracking of what capital was available into other activities. When the government of Revillagigedo tried to alleviate the problem with a low interest policy, resentment was widespread. During the earlier period of mercantilism, no doubt few would have objected, but within the new system of free trade, it seemed rather contrary to the spirit of the times.[35]

The religious orders owned a great deal of land and leased considerable portions of it; for this reason they remained extremely powerful in spite of the social changes of the period.[36] Few credit institutions existed in New Spain at the time, and when the Indians, in particular, tried to buy on credit, the *corregidores* seized the opportunity to become great purveyors to them; when this position was removed from them by law in 1787, the *corregidores* had yet another cause for resistance to authority.[37] These economic factors thus also influenced future developments and explain much of the conservative reaction, so strongly displayed in New Spain and in other parts of the Indies, during the Spanish American Revolution.

But the break with tradition was not confined to politics and economics. Perhaps most important was the overt tendency toward secularization and the typical eighteenth-century attempt to put the Church under the control of the

Crown. In earlier centuries the Spanish administration had been permeated by a deep religious spirit, which characterized the Golden Age of Spain and manifested a unique harmony of interests linking the Church to the Crown. Now all this had changed or seemed to have changed. Through the doctrine of *regalismo*, the Crown began to control the Church according to the new trends of the Enlightenment, and gave at least the appearance of being less interested in religion than in earlier times. The expulsion of the Jesuits was but one example, though perhaps the most dramatic.

In addition to the purely administrative measures of the Bourbons in Spanish America, which represented a centralist trend as they did in France, there were other shortcomings of an even more serious character: with the exception of a few great men like Floridablanca, Jovellanos, and Campomanes, the reformers were to a large extent arbitrary administrators. Their work resulted in the destruction of the organic structure of the nation (councils, universities, colleges, orders, brotherhoods, and corporations), the culmination of which was represented by the expulsion of the Jesuits. When the Enlightened regime began to reconstruct, it was unable to build according to tradition and the true sentiments of the people; instead, it imposed — as the Romantics and the Positivists in Spanish America would later — artificial constructions not aimed at the common good.

Among those questionable tendencies was the creation of a caste of rather self-centered military viceroys (Manuel Oms y Santapán, marqués de Castell dos Ríus, viceroy of Peru [1707–10]; Baltasar de Zúñiga, marqués de Valero, viceroy of New Spain [1716–22]; Pedro Cebrián y Agustín, conde de Fuenclara, viceroy of New Spain [1742–46]; Carlos Francisco de Croix, viceroy of New Spain [1766–71]). This was followed by another group (Manuel Amat y Junient, viceroy of Peru [1761–76]; Miguel de la Grúa Talamanca, marqués de Branciforte, viceroy of New Spain [1794–98], and José de Iturrigaray, viceroy of New Spain [1803–1808]), who lowered Peninsular prestige.

Another such tendency was the raising of increased funds to meet the serious need of economic resources for the pursuit of dynastic interests in peace and war and for implementation of the general mercantilist theories of the century. The result was a strain on the proprietary corporations, which contributed to their destruction and had detrimental effects on Spanish American trade and industry. To all this was added the sad picture of the Spanish monarchy under Charles IV when favorites, such as Manuel Godoy and Mariano Urquijo, or flatterers such as José Antonio, marqués de Cavallero, and Pedro de Cevallos, held influential positions, while eminent men like Floridablanca and Jovellanos in Spain, or Juan Vicente de Güemes Pacheco de Padilla, conde de Revillagigedo, viceroy of New Spain (1789–94), Manuel de Guirior, viceroy of New Granada and later of Peru (1776–79), and the Mexican Juan José de Vértiz, viceroy of the River Plate (1778–84), in Spanish America, were removed from their high posts. All in all, it characterized a development absolutely at variance with the traditional government which Spain had projected to its domains in the New World during the reigns of Isabella and the Hapsburgs.[38]

The Spanish system of government may have been defective from an Enlightened French or European point of view, but the colonists were satisfied with it, for the simple reason that it allowed them a maximum of freedom, particularly in the field of local liberties. The *cabildo* was free from the *au-*

diencia, the *audiencia* was independent of the governor, the governor could constantly escape the control of the viceroy; local autonomy was the rule, subordination to the central government the exception.[39] To change all this was the purpose of the vast reforms undertaken in the spirit of Enlightened absolutism; though the goal was not really achieved, freedoms which had existed earlier were so curtailed that it can truly be said that

> under the rule of the Hapsburgs, the colonists . . . enjoyed practical liberty while enduring theoretical restraint; under the Bourbons, they rather endured practical restraint, while enjoying theoretical liberty.[40]

In all these reforms a European spirit was manifest, which found expression particularly in the very French-inspired and French-oriented centralization which ran counter to the Spanish temperament. Indeed, the attempt of Charles III to reform the Spanish Empire in a French–European sense destroyed the spiritual foundation on which the Empire had been built and upon which it had been able to last for so long. Thus,

> the *regalismo* of the Bourbons aimed at destroying the work of centuries, and, what is more important, at setting straight the spontaneous manifestations of the physical and moral nature of the peoples of [Spanish] America.[41]

Or, as Richard Graham has recently pointed out,

> Perhaps the most important alterations made by the Bourbons were the result of their views of the relationship between king and subjects, which sharply differed from that of the Hapsburgs. The Hapsburgs thought of themselves as patriarchs who occupied their position, not because of the divine right of kings, but because of the divine right of fathers. According to the Hapsburg view, God had ordained the family as the basic unit of society, and the family was hierarchically structured with the father as its head; therefore the king was also the head of a similarly structured family with every member of society occupying a place within it that was fixed by God. In a sense, the Hapsburgs ruled over a family, not a state. The basic political philosophy, which permeated the entire social organism, elicited and depended upon relationships of authority–dependency, benevolence–loyalty. No legislation could change the deeply meaningful link between king and subject, just as no law could alter the biological connection between father and son. The Bourbons thought somewhat differently about the relationship between king and subject. Although not entirely free of such a familial viewpoint, the Bourbons were more apt to think of the king as a ruler than by his love for his subjects. The Spanish American clung to the Hapsburg image of the patriarchal state and resisted the Bourbons' political philosophy.[42]

When the Enlightenment revealed a shameless irreligiosity, the end was reached. For the Spaniard and the Spanish American the question of religion and of the Church was of primary significance — i.e., Christian tradition was more important than any reform. The question of religion was to play a great role in the Spanish American Revolution, and independence would come between 1820 and 1823 as a conservative reaction to liberal Spain. Spanish America became independent because it wanted to remain Spanish in temperament and character, and because Spain seemed to have lost this character through the Bourbon regime and the influence of the European Enlightenment: while Spanish America wanted to continue Spanish tradition, Spain seemed to have become un-Spanish. Ultimately, the Spanish Empire lasted as long as it satisfied the ideals upon which it had been built; it began to collapse when the Bourbons in their zeal toward efficiency gave no heed to these ideals and thus weakened them.

2. The Scholastic Tradition

The negative results of the Bourbon reforms of the eighteenth century were further aggravated by the prevailing strength of Late Scholastic ideas. To understand the actual picture of the Spanish American reality in the eighteenth century and on the eve of independence, it should be borne in mind that Enlightened despotism waged a relentless campaign against the "subversive" theories of Suárez. At the time of the expulsion of the Jesuits, the bishopric of Santiago alone accounted for fourteen Jesuit educational centers serving more than a thousand students. When after the expulsion the Jesuit boarding school of San Francisco Javier was reopened by Governor Guill y Gonzaga under the direction of two secular priests, it was expressly stated that the philosophy of Suárez would not be taught.[43] Also, a *real cédula* of October 18, 1768, repeated a few days later, forbade in all Spanish American centers of higher learning the teachings of the Jesuit school, particularly Suárez, Mariana, and Molina. An illustration of this policy was the cancellation in 1795 by Viceroy José de Espeleta in New Granada of the chair of natural law (which dealt with such Late Scholastics as Covarrubias and Vázquez de Menchaca).[44] Moreover, the banning of Late Scholastic theories, which Campomanes called subversive and heretical, was followed by the spreading of such absolutist theories as those proclaimed in New Granada by the Capuchin Finestrad, in Peru by Viceroy Taboada y Lemus, and in the different areas of the River Plate by the Carmelite Bishop San Alberto, Governor Ribera, Fernández de Agüero, and Maciel.

But this does not reflect the actual situation in Spanish America in the eighteenth century; as Marcelino Menéndez y Pelayo said, government censorship used the mixed jurisdiction of the Inquisition to silence all opposition, including the defenders of ecclesiastical orthodoxy. The government would not allow the printing of documents unfavorable to civil authority or defending positions inimical to the Jansenists, regalists, and Masons, the real beneficiaries of the Enlightened despotic system. Thus the governments of the eighteenth and early-nineteenth centuries used the Inquisition not only to ban certain works of the Enlightenment but in particular to suppress Spanish sixteenth-century political literature. Commenting on the taking control of the Inquisition by such Jansenists as Villanueva, Espiga, Santa Clara, canon of San Isidro, Menéndez y Pelayo exclaims sarcastically "¡ En buenas manos había caído la Inquisición!"[45] Their opposition to Enlightened despotism was the reason behind the expulsion of the Jesuits, as was the persecution by magistrates like Domingo Valcárcel or Pedro de Tagle y Bracho, by bishops like the Carmelite José Díaz Bravo, or by ministers like Jovellanos.[46]

The political theories of Suárez were fought as much as were certain political theories of the Enlightenment — Rousseau's, for example, though he had very little political influence in Spanish America during the period. One need only read the correspondence (kept in the Archivo de Indias of Seville) of such enemies of the Jesuits as Archbishop Lorenzana (November 13, 1774; November 19, 1774; December 1, 1775; May 11, 1789) and Bishop Francisco Fabián y Fuero (February 1, 1773; February 19, 1773) or to read Vicente La Fuente[47] to discover the books, articles, pamphlets, and other "surreptitious" publications of a Scholastic bent opposing Enlightened despotism. To combat these publications the regime went so far as to censor dissertations (September 6, 1770) and to burn histories of the expelled Jesuits.[48]

The strong opposition on the part of authorities to Late Scholastic ideas is also evident in the inquiries of the attorneys general of the councils requesting reports on seditious doctrines; the limit was reached in the royal decree of December 3, 1769, ordering the confiscation of goods and the imposition of the death penalty for the mere possession of a picture of St. Ignatius Loyola.[49] Yet Enlightened despotism had no objection to the publication of new editions of sixteenth- and seventeenth-century Scholastic writers whenever such publication suited its interest. Witness the new editions in the eighteenth century of the most important works of Solórzano Pereira, which furthered regalist theories.[50]

In spite of all the efforts to combat the Jesuit teachings concerning the right to rebel and the right of tyrannicide, Scholasticism continued to be taught in the philosophy courses in the universities and colleges. After the Jesuits were expelled, they were replaced not by adherents of the modern philosophies but by their own students who, in most cases, were even more strongly imbued with traditional thought. Examples of this occur in the universities of Charcas and in the Carolinian College in Upper Peru where the theories of Suárez were taught by such former Jesuit pupils as Salinas, Segovia, Montoya, and Herrera.[51] The same was also true of Chile[52] and of other learning centers in Spanish America.

Scholasticism was still so strong at the end of the eighteenth century and prior to independence that it was responsible for the educational background of most of the leading men of the Spanish American Revolution. John Tate Lanning has pointed out that

> Anyone examining the record of the South American wars of independence will be amazed at the critical acumen and philosophical audacity of Sánchez Carrión, Antonio Nariño, Bernardo Monteagudo, Andrés Bello, José Joaquín Olmedo, and Hipólito Unanúe. They were not leaders who sprang fully educated from the brow of Zeus. They were the fruits of an educational discipline which was thoroughly scholastic, although it was in a free society that their mature intellects unfolded.[53]

Lanning goes on to observe that a student of the theoretical foundation of the Spanish American Revolution would come to the conclusion that the Enlightened thought of "Rousseau, Voltaire, Montesquieu, or even Raynal" would not be so significant, and that

> the names which would seem of transcendant importance... would be, instead, St. Thomas Aquinas, Descartes, Newton, Condillac, Pierre Gassendi, and Malebranche. Without them Raynal, Condorcet, Diderot, Benjamin Franklin, and Thomas Paine would scarcely have been heard and certainly not understood.[54]

Not only was the echo of the older currents of thought consistent with the role of the Church, it explains as well the "political conservatism of men like Unanúe, Monteagudo, and even Bolívar."[55] The old Spanish tendency of attempting a fusion between faith and reason, tradition and progress, is evident here too.

> The same desire to embrace the new with little corresponding sacrifice of their heritage marked the Americans as clearly as it did Descartes. Hence Cartesianism and natural law seem scarcely more than advanced stages of scholasticism.[56]

Lanning gives a few examples of what he has so aptly called "The Last Stand of the Schoolmen":[57] the prolonged disputation between Thomists and Scotists in the last two decades of the eighteenth century in Mexico; or those "academic Quixotes" who insisted, in Venezuela in the early nineteenth century, "that the sky was a great solid canopy and that the planets passed through its portholes in their periodical movements," or in Guatemala, in 1816, who were still "qualifying the law of universal attraction."[58]

Viceroyalty of New Spain. The strong influence of Late Scholasticism in New Spain in the seventeenth century continued unabated in the eighteenth. The Enlightenment, which had gradually penetrated the Peninsula, also came to New Spain in the course of the eighteenth century; the new spirit arrived mostly through the clergy, which in one form or another was the agent of modernity, particularly after 1750 when Feijóo had opened the gates to the new currents. Yet in spite of the attacks on Aristotelianism, especially those by the famous Alzate, Scholasticism remained a viable and strong philosophy, particularly in the first half of the century, and formed the basis for the entire legal structure.[59]

> Scholastic education was a reality with which the inhabitants of New Spain lived for three centuries and [an understanding of the] influence of which is necessary for an appreciation of the formation of the Mexican mind.[60]

It should also be pointed out that even as early as the nineteenth century the Revolution in New Spain was begun by priests who had received a Scholastic training.

Thus, the eighteenth century in New Spain, though obviously not devoid of modern philosophical trends — exemplified, for instance, in Díaz de Gamarra — witnessed a strong revival of Scholasticism parallel to similar trends in the Peninsula and the River Plate. And in spite of the criticism leveled against Scholasticism, it was the Scholastic philosophy which had stimulated thinking and awakened a critical approach among Mexicans.[61] The inroads of the European spirit notwithstanding, the different versions of Scholasticism — Duns Scotus for the Franciscans, St. Thomas for the Dominicans, and Suárez for the Jesuits — continued to be relevant, though they undoubtedly weakened as the century progressed; even in the last decade of the eighteenth century there were still serious polemics between the followers of St. Thomas and of Duns Scotus in New Spain.[62]

A true Scholastic in New Spain was the Franciscan Miguel Díaz, who was known as the Duns Scotus of New Spain and taught at the Colegio de Tlaltelolco.[63] Other Scholastic thinkers in New Spain during the eighteenth century included the Franciscan José Antonio de Aldalur, who taught philosophy at the Colegio de Querétaro and wrote on Aristotle and theology, *Cursus completus philosophiae Aristotelicae* (1716–19), *Cursus theologicus iuxta celeberrimam et acutissimam mentem divi Thomae et Scoti* (1719–20), *Tractatus de scientia Dei* (1721–22), *Disputationes theologicae amplectens tractatum de admirabili Dei voluntate* (1723), and *Tractatus de hominis ultimo fine, et de beatitudine* (1725–26);[64] several Jesuits like Antonio de Peralta (1668–1736), who wrote some fourteen volumes on law and theology, but became famous for his *Dissertationes scholasticae de divina scientia media* in 1724 and his *Dissertationes scholasticae de divinis decretis* (*Disertaciones escolasticas*) in 1727;[65] Lucas Rincón (1685–1741), who taught at the Colegio de México and was the author of a *Cursus philosophicus integer*;[66] Pedro Zurita, teacher of philosophy at the same college and later rector of the Colegio de Oaxaca, who wrote an *Exposición de la filosofía natural* (*Naturalis philosophiae explanatio*) in three volumes and delved into theological writings with his *Funiculus theologiae scholasticae*;[67] Gregorio Vázquez de Puga (1677–1747), who was a well-known teacher of philosophy in Mexico and Puebla and author of a *Cursus philosophicus* (1715) and of *Disputationes in octo Aristotelis libros Physicorum* (1715?);[68] Francisco Javier Lazcano (1702–62), who taught philosophy in Puebla, held the chair in Suárez for some twenty-six years at the University of Mexico, and was the author of *Opusculum theophilosophicum de principatu seu antelatione Marianae gratiae . . .* (1750);[69] the Colombian Juan Antonio Oviedo, rector of the Colegio de San Ildefonso, who also wrote on philosophy (*Cursus philosophicus*) and religious subjects;[70] the Cuban Francisco Ignacio Cigala, who wrote his *Cartas al Ilmo. Rmo. Mro. F. Benito Gerónimo Feijóo Montenegro* against the Spanish Benedictine and in defense of Scholasticism;[71] and, finally, the Dominican José Gallegos, a follower of Melchor Cano, who became famous for his *Breve apología del método de estudios* (1774).[72]

Others who continued Scholasticism in New Spain but tried to renew it with the infusion of modern currents of thought included Andrés de Guevara y Basoazábal (1748–1801) whose *Institutiones elementariae philosophiae* was also studied in the Peninsula. Among the most famous writers who attempted this Scholastic renewal with a more modern tinge were the famous Jesuits: the philosopher Rafael Campoy (1723–77) and the philosopher–historian Francisco Javier Clavijero (1731–87), who wrote the *Phisica particularis* and *Diálogo entre Filaletes y Paleófilo, contra el argumento de autoridad en la física*; the philosopher, lawyer, and theologian Diego José Abad (1727–79), who wrote a *Tractatus unicus de summulis: Disputationes in universam logicam Aristotelis* (1754), *Philosophia naturalis* (1756), *Disputationes in libros Metaphysicorum Aristotelis: De rerum ortu et interitu, De anima* (1754), and *Musa americana seu de Deo carmina ad usum scholarum* (1769); the philosopher Agustín de Castro (1728–90), and the historian and philosopher Francisco Javier Alegre (1729–88), author of the *Institutionum theologicarum libri XVIII* (1789).[73] These formed the nucleus of a group of Jesuits who, without leaving the path of religion and theological orthodoxy, tried to follow a humanistic path toward modernity, though their neo-Scholasticism was not well received by their more orthodox companions. They tried successfully to inject into their historical studies a more nationalistic Mexican point of view, which they continued to do in exile in Italy after 1767; they remained influential in New Spain in spite of their physical separation.[74] This group also included the historian

Andrés Cavo (1739–1803), Pedro José Márquez, Manuel Fabri, and Juan Luis Maneiro, who were also exiled to Italy in 1767. Clavijero's *Historia antigua de México*, Alegre's *Historia de la Compañía de la Nueva España*, and Cavo's *Anales de la ciudad de México desde la conquista española hasta el año de 1767*, and the many works of Abad are ample evidence of the strength of Scholasticism in New Spain during the eighteenth century.

Viceroyalty of Peru. The influence of Scholasticism in its various forms was not restricted to New Spain. Scholasticism also continued to be a powerful intellectual force in the eighteenth century in Peru, though it gradually declined in the face of the increasing pressure of the Enlightenment. The inroads of the Enlightenment, especially after the middle of the century, put Scholasticism on the defensive, though by no means was it defeated. As a matter of fact, in spite of widespread adherence to the Enlightenment within elite groups, including academic circles, modern currents of thought were far from controlling the situation completely. Scholasticism maintained a strong position, existing alongside Cartesianism and the Enlightenment proper, as happened in the case of the Convictorio de San Carlos, which was founded in 1771 to fill the vacuum in education left with the forced departure of the Jesuits in 1767.[75]

One of the main representatives of Scholasticism in eighteenth-century Peru was the Franciscan Francisco de Soto y Marne (d. 1755), who tried to revive Scholastic philosophy by bringing together its different tendencies.[76] Scholastic thinkers in Peru included the Jesuits Francisco Javier Salduendo, who wrote a *Tractatus de scientia Dei ad primam partem divi Thomae a quaestione 14 usque ad 18^m* (1708); Marco de la Vega, author of *Philosophia peripatetica in tres partes divisa: Pars tertia sive metaphysica* (1727), *Philosophia peripatetica in tres partes divisa: Pars secunda seu physica* (1746), *Tractatus scholasticus de divina scientia* (1750), and several other studies; Gaetano Velasco, known for his *Summa tripartita scholasticae philosophiae* (1727) and his *Summa tripartita scholasticae philosophiae. I. Tractatus in dialecticam* (1729); Isidoro Loll, who wrote *Cursus philosophici ad mentem Aristotelis* (1738); Félix de Silva (1703–68), known for his *Tractatus in octo Aristotelis Physicorum libros* (1738); Firmino Ximénes, author of a *Tractatus theologicus de visione Dei supernaturali* (1765), and José de Armas, who wrote *Septendecim supra tercentas ex philosophia et mathesi desumptae propositiones* (1786). Other Scholastic writers included Agustín de Aragón y Cardona, author of a *Tésis de filosofía* (1735); Juan de Basurco y Zagal, who wrote a *Pro publico totius philosophiae examine . . .* (1781); Manuel Calderón de la Barca, author of a *Pro publico examine in . . . has ex philosophia et mathesi desumptas propositiones* (1788); Pablo Castañeda, who wrote a *Tractatus de divina scientia* (1715); Gabriel Helguero y Gorgolla, known for his *Theses ex universa philosophia depromptae* (1799); Silvestro Hostas, author of *Ex historia philosophiae logicae et ethicae excerptas propositiones . . .* (1792); Juan José Manrique, author of *Theses ex universa philosophia atque ex primis mathesis elementis desumptae* (1782); Juan Pablo de Porras, known for his *Theses ex logica universa, simulque metaphisica*; Luis de Rodríguez, author of *Commentaria in octo Aristotelis Physicorum libros* (1729); Pedro Ruiz, known for his *Disputationes circa Aristotelis dialectica* (1759); Marción Soto Florido, author of *Theses ex universa philoso-*

phia selectae (1790), and José Joaquín de Vicuña e Ibáñez, who wrote *Universae philosophiae theses* (1774).[77]

Yet those who followed Enlightened tendencies were by no means willing to break with Christian tradition: they followed the Enlightenment — i.e., the Spanish version of it — as far as science was concerned but maintained a vigorous Catholic orthodoxy in regard to theology and religion. In keeping with Spanish tradition, they sought a reconciliation, a fusion, of religion with science. This was certainly true of such scientists as Hipólito Unanúe and José Baquíjano y Carrillo. And even such an unbalanced, though highly idealistic, figure as Pablo de Olavide repudiated at the end of his life both anticlericalism and free-thinking and turned to the defense of Christianity, as is evident in his *El evangelio en triunfo* and his *Poemas cristianos*.[78] Moreover, science and mathematics were fighting a losing battle against academic traditionalism and were not popular subjects among students.[79]

The Chilean Scholastics included Jesuits Juan de Puga with his *Disputationes scholasticae* (1710–11); Juan de Sorozábel, author of a book on physics and a *Cursus philosophiae scholasticae* (1724); and Miguel de Ureta, well known for his *Disputationes in omnes Physicorum libros Aristotelis* (1726) and *Disputationes in metaphysicam* (1728); the Mercedarian Francisco Bello who wrote on Scholastic philosophy (1753–55), and the more eclectic José Francisco Echaurren whose *Philosophia eclectica ad mentem et methodum celeberrimorum nostrae aetatis philosophorum comparata* (1796) showed the inroads of modern philosophies.[80]

The famous Jesuit scholars also included Manuel Lacunza Díaz (1747–1801), who wrote the *Venida del Mesías en gloria y majestad*,[81] and several eminent theologians. Among these were Diego José Fuenzalida, who wrote *Observaciones crítico teológicas sobre el Análisis de las prescripciones de Tertuliano* (1783) defending the papacy and attacking Jansenism; Pedro Mogas Fiol, author of the *Cartas dogmático críticas sobre los negocios presentes en torno a la religión* (1791) and of a *Compendio del libro de las leyes del doctor eximio Francisco Suárez*; Bernardino Jerónimo de Boza y Solís, author of the *Triunfo teológico del Sacratísmo Corazón de Jesús* (1744–72); Juan Manuel de Zepeda, who wrote the *Cartas apologéticas en favor de la verdad, piedad y religión* (1789); Domingo Antomás, from Navarra, author of *El cristiano de este siglo iluminado e instruído divinamente por la carta de N. S. Jesucristo escrita en el Apocalipsis capítulo III* (1784) in which he attacked the Age of Reason.[82]

Philosophy was represented by Juan Félix de Arechavala, author of the *Proposiciones filosóficas* (1770) in which "one notices an openness to modernity";[83] though opposed to Descartes and Malebranche, he accepted some ideas of Leibniz and Wolff, and gave considerable attention to modern physics.[84] In the field of history there was Miguel de Olivares (1713–93), whose *Historia militar civil y sagrada de lo acaecido en la conquista y pacificación del Reino de Chile hasta la mitad del siglo décimo octavo de nuestra redención* served as a source for other historical studies such as those of Molina and Gómez Vidaurre.[85]

Among the Jesuit scholars devoted to literary studies must be mentioned, in particular, Andrés Febrés Oms (1734–90), author of the famous *Seconda memoria cattolica contenente Il trionfo de la Fede o Chiesa, de' Monarchi e Monarchie, e della Compagnia di Gesù e sua Apologia, con lo sterminio de' lor nemici: da presentarsi a Sua Santità ed ai principi Cristiani* (1783).[86] This work, in three volumes, resulted from the persecution he suffered for the publication of the *Memoria cattolica* written by Carlos Borgo and published by a former Jesuit without the author's permission. Febrés Oms then conceived of the *Seconda memoria cattolica*, an apologetic work of the Jesuits, in which he attempted to show the fantastic plot against the Church, Spain and its Empire, and the Society of Jesus by the liberal Spanish ministers. It is a prophetic book in which he claims that the plot was directed at monarchical governments and their empires overseas, and foresees the Spanish American separation. No doubt, history has proved him right in his assessment of the expulsion of the Jesuits as an injustice and a grave political error.[87]

Viceroyalty of New Granada. Late Scholasticism dominated the studies in the Viceroyalty in the seventeenth and early-eighteenth centuries. St. Thomas and Aristotle were the leading philosophers of the Jesuits and Dominicans; St. Augustine, through his disciple Giles of Rome, was followed by the Augustinians; and Duns Scotus was the favorite of the Franciscans. But in contrast to the River Plate, where modern philosophies were well known, neither New Granada nor New Spain gave evidence of the impact of Descartes, Spinoza, Bayle, Locke, Hume, Berkeley, Condillac, Newton, Kepler, or Wolff, whose influence did not appear at that time.[88] The new philosophies would come to New Granada (and to New Spain) only later, through Feijóo in the second half of the eighteenth century.

Scholasticism was represented in New Granada proper by such Jesuits as Juan Martínez de Ripalda (1646–1727), famous for his *De usu et abusu doctrinae divi Thomae* (1704); Ignacio Meaurio (d. 1751), who wrote *Tractationes physicae* (1706); Luis Chacón, author of *Disputationes metaphysicae* (1736), *Disputationes in libros Aristotelis de anima* (1737), and *Tractatus scholasticus et theologicus de divina scientia* (1738); José Molina, author of a *Tractatus scholasticus et theologicus de divina providentia, et praedestinatione* (1737) and a *Tractatus theologicus et scholasticus de divina scientia*; José Rojas, who wrote a *Tractatus scholasticus de proemialibus theologiae et disputationibus gratiae actualis* (1738–39); Jerónimo Godoy, author of *Summunculae* (1742); Nicolás Candela, who wrote a *Cursus philosophicus in quinque tractatus et ad Aristotelis mentem consignatus* (1747); Manuel Balzátegui (d. 1792), who wrote several works, such as *In summula* (1749), *Logica universa iuxta Doctoris eximii mentem* (1749), *Disputationes in universam Aristotelis Physicam* (1750), *De meteoris* (1751), *De principiis extrinsicis* (1751), and *De anima* (1752); José Vals, author of a *Tractatus theologico-moralis de conscientia* (1752); Francisco Javier Trías, who wrote *De metaphysicis quaestionibus* (1755) and *De anima et generatione* (1755); José Fernández (1725–1801), author of a work on physics (1761); Juan Antonio Ferraro, who wrote *De justitia et iure* (1762/1764); Lorenzo Tirado, author of a *Tractatus theologico-moralis de iustitia et iure* (1763); Julián Antonio (d. after 1788), who wrote a *Tractatus scholastico-theologicus de Deo uno et trino* (1765) and a treatise on habitual grace (1765); Francisco Escobar, who wrote a *Synopsis logico-thomistica* and *Logicae dissertationes secundum exactam, veram, et genuinam cherubici doctoris mentem* (1770), and Pedro Choperena, the author of a *Tractatus scholasticus de divina voluntate* (1793) and a *Tractatus theologicus de divina providentia* (1796).[89]

The Dominicans included such scholars as Juan Duarte with his *Naturalis philosophiae iuxta mentem angelici doctoris sancti Thomas Acquinatis et Aristotelis tractatus* (1733) and *Juxta mentem angelici doctoris commentarium ex variis tractatibus* (1733); Jacinto Antonio Buenaventura, a prolific writer who composed a *Tractatus in octo Physicorum Aristotelis libros . . . ad mentem divi Thomae Aquinatis angelici praeceptoris* (1755), *De generatione et corruptione* (1757), *De anima* (1757), *Tractatus de actibus humanis desumptus ex lucidissimo phoebo angelici nostri doctoris divi Thomae Aquinatis in 1.2 a quaestione 6 usque ad 21* (1759), and *De scientia Dei respectu futurorum contingentium*; Rafael Mancera, author of a *Tractatus in tres summularum libros* (1759) and *De anima iuxta mentem angelici doctoris divi Thomae et Aristotelicam doctrinam* (1762); Francisco Huelga, who wrote *De praedestinatione sanctorum et impiorum reprobatione* (1762) and a *Tractatus de voluntate Dei* (1763), and Antonio Cabrejo (b. 1733), author of *De iure et iustitia* (1762). Finally, there was also the Augustinian Gregorio Agustín Salgado, author of a *Peripatetica phylosophia*; Antonio José Guzmán y Monasterio, with his *Tractatus de visione beatifica de quo divus Thomas 1ª part. a quaestione duodecima usque decimam tertiam mirifice pertractat* (1753), and Agustín Manuel de Alarcón y Castro (b. 1713) with his *Tractatus de dialectica* (1758) and his *Philosophia thomistica* (1761).[90]

Suárez also maintained his influence in the viceroyalty during the eighteenth century. Thus, Martínez de Ripalda followed Suarezian thought in his *De usu et abusu doctrinae divi Thomae*, quoting Suárez with respect on every page; and Buenaventura, though a Thomist, quotes Suárez extensively in his *Tractatus de actibus humanis*. Even after the expulsion of the Jesuits, Suárez continued to be studied, especially at the Colegio del Rosario.[91]

Scholastic influence was evident in some of the pre-revolutionary leaders in New Granada, among them Antonio Nariño, Pedro Fermín de Vargas, and José Félix de Restrepo. Born in 1765 of a noble Spanish family, Nariño had some formal schooling at the Colegio de San Carlos of Bogotá, though in reality he was a self-educated man. Idealistic, romantic, and of noble character, Nariño felt attracted to the ideas of the Enlightenment and attempted to turn his home into an intellectual center in which prominent members of Bogotá's society were welcome. *On Education*, his first attempt at writing, betrayed the influence of Feijóo and Rousseau.[92] Because of his social standing and intellect, he was soon offered an important government post by the viceroy of New Granada. A man endowed with great privileges, one of which was the ownership of a printing press, Nariño was able to publish *Los derechos del hombre* in 1794. Since the times were not propitious, and trouble was brewing in many places in Spanish America, the viceroy ordered all copies seized and Nariño imprisoned. There are evidences of Scholastic thought in the document which Nariño presented in his defense, though he was careful not to mention Suárez, Mariana, or Molina, claiming that

> no man has received from nature the right to command others; the authority of kings is derived from the people; the prince receives authority from his subjects; he cannot use it without the consent of the nation; the Crown, the Government, public authority, are property of the nation; the nation is the owner and the princes usufructuaries.[93]

Nariño was sent as a prisoner to Spain, but escaped to France and Britain. After failing to interest these governments in the independence of Spanish

America, he returned to Bogotá in 1797, and surrendered to the court. He then became a loyal adviser and the author of the *Essay on a New Plan of Administration for the New Kingdom of Granada*, in which he called for reforms, specifically the end of the *alcabala* and the monopolies controlling tobacco and alcohol. Nariño had no influence on the events of 1810 when the junta was established in Bogotá, though he later became the president of Cundinamarca.

Pedro Fermín de Vargas was born in San Gil in 1762. Educated at the Colegio del Rosario, he later became a good friend of Mutis', was appointed to the office of the viceroy, and in 1789 became *corregidor* of Zipaquirá. His scientific collaboration with the botanical expedition gave him a great insight into the problems of the country which he expounded in various treatises: *Pensamientos políticos sobre al agricultura, comercio, y minas del Virreinato de Santafé de Bogotá, Memoria sobre al poblacion del nuevo reino de Granada, Discurso sobre el estado actual del río de la Magdalena*, and *Reflexiones acerca de las principales fuentes del reino*. Vargas became the first Colombian economist and sociologist, and his ideas were revolutionary: anti-Indian, anti-aristocracy, and anticlerical; the views he advanced manifested a progressive social thinking which would later be expounded by Pope Leo XIII, Proudhon, and Marx against the liberal state of Locke, Adam Smith, and the physiocrats. His revolutionary feelings forced him to flee abroad in 1791 where he worked openly for independence and sought British help (1799). Though no doubt greatly influenced by Rousseau, Montesquieu, and the Spanish Enlightenment, he manifested a considerable acquaintance with Scholasticism in upholding such principles as the supremacy of the common good, the limitations of private property in order to fulfill social ends, the intervention of the state in economic matters, conflicts of capital and labor, and problems of social security.[94]

José Félix de Restrepo was perhaps the patriot who best represented the philosophical ideas of the Revolution in New Granada in 1810. Educated at the Colegio de San Bartolomé, in 1780 he became a professor of philosophy and later taught art and law. His writings — *Oraciones, Lecciones de física*, and *Lecciones de metafísica* — which are based on the Spanish Late Scholastic school of the sixteenth and seventeenth centuries of Suárez, Vázquez de Menchaca, Covarrubias, Vitoria, Las Casas, Saavedra Fajardo, refute the modern philosophies of the Enlightenment. His philosophy of traditional Aristotelian imprint, based on the Christian notion of justice and freedom, was very influential at the time, and molded innumerable pupils who prepared the ground for the events of July 20, 1810, in Bogotá. He was a true creator of culture and one of the greatest forerunners of the movement for independence in New Granada.[95]

Scholasticism was also quite a vivid reality in eighteenth-century Venezuela — to such an extent that of the four most important philosophers two were Scholastic: the Franciscan Friars Agustín de Quevedo y Villegas and Tomás Valero. Quevedo y Villegas was born in Coro at the beginning of the eighteenth century. After his theological studies, he taught for some fifteen years, became censor of the bishopric of Caracas, and later of the archbishopric of Santo Domingo. His *Opera theologica*, a commentary in the medieval style of Peter Lombard's *Four Books of Sentences*, was published in Seville in four volumes between 1752 and 1756 and followed the philosophy of Duns Scotus.[96] His treatise on God in the first volume contained all those questions which Suárez had considered earlier in his *Disputationes metaphysicae*.[97] Juan David García Bacca makes the fascinating comment:

> Indeed, in eighteenth-century Spain, not only was Duns Scotus dead, and dead a matter of centuries, but the lack of theologians was so extensive and felt so keenly by the censors of Madrid that they could not suppress surprise that in the West Indies works appeared which, by the topics, language, length, and severity of the ideas and style, were so divorced from what was then fashionable in the "Frenchicized" Spanish intellectual and political life. In opposition to a Feijóo, Spanish America — the creole [towns of] Coro and Santo Domingo — came up with a *Theological Course* in four volumes.[98]

Valero was another Franciscan friar on the Scholastic horizon of Venezuela, born probably in the early eighteenth century. In his early youth he entered the monastery of Santa María de los Angeles of Tocuyo, and later became theologian of the Holy Office and retired as lector of the province of Santa Cruz de Santo Domingo and Caracas.[99] Like Quevedo y Villegas, he too took up the pen in defense of theology; his two-volume *Theologia expositiva in sacrosanctum evangelium Domini nostri Jesu Christi secundum Matthaeum: Modo historico, concionatorio, et scholastico* was published in Seville in 1756.[100] In the part dealing with natural law, Valero states some very traditional views: such as "the power which men have to give themselves laws is derived from God" (first conclusion, question xiii) and "civil authority comes directly from men, indirectly from God" (third conclusion).[101]

Scholasticism continued in eighteenth-century Quito with the same strength it had manifested earlier, and, more than other areas, Quito had a very impressive list of Scholastic thinkers. The Jesuits comprised the largest group of scholars, including: Antonio Genaro Garófalo, with his *Tractatus de ente supernaturali* (1702); Jacinto Basilio Morán de Buitrón, author of several works, *Cursus philosophicus triennalis in Logicam, Physicam, et Metaphysicam Aristotelis* (1706), *Commentaria in octo libros Aristotelis* (1707), *Scholastica commentaria in Aristotelis libros De ortu et interitu* (1708), among others; Juan Bautista Mújica, author of a ... *Pars prima in logicas enodationes* (1708) and a *Divinae providentiae disputationes scholasticae* (1712); Antonio Andía, who wrote a *Tractatus de iustitia et iure* (1709); Joaquín Alvarez, with his *Tripartitus philosophiae Aristotelicae tractatus* on various aspects of Aristotelianism (1710–49) and his *De essentia et attributis Dei* (1753); Andrés de Cobos, author of several books on physics, metaphysics, psychology, and grace (1711–12); José Nieto Polo, who wrote a *Philosophia peripatetica* dealing with logic, metaphysics, and psychology (1712) and a *Tractatus de peccatis* (1720); Francisco Ravago, with his book on logic (1715); Pedro de Campos, with a course on philosophy (1715); Esteban Ferriol, who wrote on different aspects of Aristotelian philosophy (1719–21); Fernando Espinosa (1696–1742), author of a *Triennalis scholasticae philosophiae cursus* on logic, physics, and metaphysics (1721, 1728, 1729), an *Universa Aristotelis philosophia* (1727), and a *Tractatus I, de principiis intrinsecis entis naturalis* (1732); Marco de Escorza (1690–1767), who wrote several philosophical works: *Quaestiones in universam philosophiam, Philosophia naturalis in octo Physicorum libros Aristotelis* (1722), *Libri tres in hoc tertio philosophiae cursu peragendi de metaphysica, animastica, generatione et corruptione* (1723), and a *Tractatus de moralitate sive de bonitate et malitia actuum humano-*

rum (1724); Jacinto Serrano, author of a *Physicae Aristotelicae tractatus primus* (1722) and a *Cursus philosophicus* on logic; Luis de Andrade (1690–1742), who wrote a *Course on Philosophy* (1731), a treatise on logic, and a *Miscellanea theologica: Tractatus de vitiis et peccatis*; Pedro Tobar, author of a *Tractatus de conscientia seu de principio interno humanarum actionum* (1732–33); Jerónimo Herze, who wrote on Aristotelian metaphysics (1734); José Baca, author of a *Cursus triennalis in universam Aristotelis philosophiam: Cursus secundus, in physicam* (1736) and a *Materia de bonitate et malitia*; Marco Arévalo, who also wrote a *Cursus triennalis in universam Aristotelis philosophiam: Cursus secundus, in physicam* (1739); Tomás Larraín, with several theological works: *Tractatus primus: De decretis divinis* (1743), *Tractatus scholasticus de divinae providentiae praedestinatione sanctorum et impiorum reprobatione* (1743), *Liber in quo agitur de divinis decretis* (1744), and *Tractatus de divinis decretis* (1744); Gregorio Mora, author of a *Tractatus theologicus de divina caritate* (1745); Juan Magnin, who wrote a *Millietus amicus cum Cartesio seu "Cartesius reformatus." Responsio nempe ad refutationem hypothesis Cartesianae a R. P. Claudio Francisco Milliet de Chales, S.J. editam, quae sub finem primi tomi ejus "Mundi Mathematici" invenitur, ubi tria elementa Cartesii dilucidantur et novo systemate fungiuntur cum pluribus aliis noviter excogitatis* (1747); Pedro Garrido, author of several works: *Philosophia: Pars secunda in physicam* (1751), *Pars secunda Aristotelicae philosophiae* (1751), *Pars tertia Aristotelicae philosophiae* on metaphysics and psychology (1753), and a *Tractatus theologicus scholasticus de divina voluntate* (1756); Sebastián Rendón, author of *Tractatus theologicus* (1753); Francisco Javier de Aguilar, who wrote a *Cursus philosophicus ad Aristotelis mentem* on logic, physics, metaphysics, and psychology (1753–55) and a *Tractatus scholasticus de praedestinatione sanctorum*; Mateo Folch, with several works: *Tractatus theologicus: De quo divi Thomae angelice disputavit 1ª parte a quaes. 50 ad 64 et alibi*, *Metaphysica Aristotelica iuxta mentem utriusque doctoris angelici et eximii jesuitico methodo* (1754), *Liber primus physicorum* (1754), and *Tractatus theologicus de divina scientia media* (1760); Fernando Vergara (1690–1750), author of a *Resoluciones morales o esplicación de los contratos en común y en particular* (1756); Juan Bautista Aguirre, with several works: *Cursus philosophicus* on logic, physics, and metaphysics (1756–58), *Physica ad Aristotelis mentem* (1758), *Universae philosophiae theses* (1759), and a *Tractatus theologicus-canonicus de contractibus* (1761); and Sebastián Imbert, author of *De imperio intellectuali* (1761), a *Tractatus scholastico-moralis de actibus humanis*, a *Tractatus theologicus de divina voluntate sanctorum praedestinativa et impiorum reprobativa*, and a *Tractatus theologicus de scientia Dei optimi maximi*. The most important Franciscan scholars included Gregorio Tomás Enríquez de Guzmán (1706–87), who wrote on logic, physics, and metaphysics; Clemente Rodríquez (d. 1760), author of a *Cursus philosophicus ad mentem nostri subtilis magistri Dunsii Scoti*, and Pedro Ceballos y Tena, who wrote a *Brevis in sumulas exaratio iuxta subtile numen subtilioris ducis*, a *Philosophia naturalis Aristotelis*, and a *Tractatus super metaphysica* (1741–42).[102]

Viceroyalty of the River Plate. Scholasticism, which had been so powerful in the seventeenth century in the River Plate, continued along the same path in the eighteenth. The University of Córdoba, the third oldest university in the Indies,[103] was the center of academic life, and its many

Jesuit scholars continued the Scholastic tradition until 1767. Worthy of particular note are Antonio Machoni, known for his *Palatium eloquentiae* and *Buen gobierno de las comunidades religiosas*, and Antonio Torquemada, who taught his students (as is evidenced in the student documents preserved in the Regional Seminary of Catamarca) such Suarezian concepts as: "the political activity of a prince emanates from God," but "the political kingdom comes not directly but indirectly from God," since "God only delegates the supreme authority to the community," and it is "the perfect community which transfers this authority to the prince"; but "even if it has been transferred to the ruler, it is retained *in habitu* by the people, who can restrict or abrogate it only in certain cases."[104] Important were also Joaquín Torre, author of a *Cursus philosophicus: Pars prima*,[105] and Manuel Vergara, one of the last great Jesuit scholars prior to the expulsion in 1767. Vergara taught theology for some fifteen years and was known for his many works, such as *In universam philosophiam Aristotelis juxta mentem eximii doctoris, Philosophia peripatetica, Cursus tripartitus in universam Aristotelis philosophiam, In libros decretalium* (1746), *Tractatus theologicus de perfectionibus Christi, Tractatus de angelis, De perfectionibus Christi Domini, De trinitate* (1754), *De sacramento Eucharistiae,* and *De merito vitae aeternae*.[106]

An interesting group of Jesuit scholars included the English physician and surgeon Thomas Falkner, who lectured at the University after 1732. Though he was a proponent of the new Cartesian trends, he demonstrated the flexibility of Scholastic philosophy in the sense that he abandoned it only wherever he considered it antiquated.[107] He was thus close to the group of Mexican Jesuits in New Spain who renewed Scholasticism in the second half of the eighteenth century and to the Jesuit Domingo Muriel, who lectured at the University of Córdoba after 1749.[108]

A similar flexibility was demonstrated by the last Jesuit philosophers at Córdoba: Mariano Suárez, Benito Riva, José Rufo, and Ramón Rospigliosi. They too adapted Scholasticism to the new realities of the eighteenth century. Though Suárez, in his *Dialectica rationalis* (1758), opposed Duns Scotus and Ramón Lull while remaining within the general lines of Late Scholasticism,[109] Riva was attracted by the modern thought, which in his view was not necessarily in conflict with traditional philosophy. What Falkner and Muriel began in the River Plate Riva deepened. Rufo wrote two treatises on psychology and metaphysics — *Philosophiae tripartitae tertia pars: Commentaria in tres libros De anima juxta mentem Aristotelis* and *Tripartitae philosophiae tertia pars: Commentaria in artis metaphysicam, in libros De anima necnon De ortu et interitu* (1766) — though he readily abandoned Aristotle, St. Thomas, and Suárez in favor of Gassendi and Newton when it came to physics, as shown in his two other works, on the experimental sciences, published in 1765 and 1773.[110] Finally, Rospigliosi, a colleague of Rufo's at the University of Córdoba in 1765, was the teacher of Gregorio Funes and Pedro Vicente Cañete.[111] As Guillermo Furlong has observed:

> they knew how to and could effect an appreciable assimilation, more or less perfect, of the metaphysical knowledge, which they had inherited from Aristotle and Aquinas, with the physics which came from the French of Descartes, the English of Newton, and the German of Wolff.[112]

After the expulsion of the Jesuits, many Franciscans assumed the teaching positions which the Jesuits had formerly held. Among the followers of Duns Scotus was Fernando Braco, known for his *Cursus philosophiae complectens logicam, nempe ethicam, physicam* (1795) and *Pars tertia philosophiae seu metaphysica*. Though he upheld certain Cartesian positions, Braco came close to Suárez when defending traditional Scholasticism in regard to free will.[113] Though he was not the only Franciscan during the eighteenth century to approach the Jesuits, he was by far the most outstanding example of the tendency.

Among the most famous Franciscans were José Cayetano Rodríguez and José Elías del Carmen. Both similarly followed trends established by eighteenth-century Jesuits favoring modern experimental sciences, especially physics, though they did not necessarily always side with Descartes, Newton, and Gassendi; at the same time they maintained a Scholastic attitude (Duns Scotus) when it came to pure philosophy, ethics, and political theory. Elías del Carmen was the author of several works, such as the *Physica generalis nostri philosophici cursus pars tertia* (1784), the *Certamen litterarium, quo sequentes e logica ethicaque decerptae theses disputationi subjiciuntur* (1785), the *Conclusiones ex universa philosophia quibus disputationes criticae, dogmaticae physiologicae, historicaeque, praesertim adversus atheistas, deistas, fatalistas, atque libertinos accessere* (1786) and the *Conclusiones ex universa philosophia cui dissertationes criticae, dogmaticae, historicae, et physicae logicae maxime adversus deistas, fatalistas, atheistas, materialistas aliosque pejoris ordinis philosophos accessere* (1790).[114] As a good Scholastic, he maintained that political authority was derived from God but *in concreto* given to the ruler according to traditional theories of *translatio* and *designatio*. He opposed such writers as Voltaire and Pufendorf, and maintained the existence of a natural law which was both absolute and immutable, and thus traditional.[115] He likewise asserted that popular acceptance was not required for laws to be legal, as long as they were in accord with the natural law. His doctrine in criminal law was similarly Scholastic. In metaphysics, Elías del Carmen followed Thomism in regard to what is "one and multiple," "similar and dissimilar," but became Suarezian when he denied

> the real distinction between essence and existence and when he stated that even if he admitted the identity of the one and the other, there was an abyss in regard to the creature, whose metaphysical essence does not include existence, and the creator whose metaphysical essence includes it.[116]

Anastasio Mariano Suárez and Manuel Suárez de Ledesma were two other Scholastic thinkers in the Franciscan order; both taught at the University of Córdoba, and both took decisive stands against rationalism. The former's works included the *Asserta ex universa philosophia deprompta* (1792) and the *Cursus philosophicus veterum recentiorumque philosophorum doctrinas complectens, quatuorque continens partes, logicam, nempe ethicam metaphysicam et physicam*, the philosophic basis of which was rather Thomistic and Suarezian; the latter's *Philosophia pars quarta vulgo metaphisica* closely followed Duns Scotus.[117]

The Mercedarians and the Dominicans, whose teachings were based on St. Thomas, also played a rather conspicuous role in the River Plate. Until 1774 the Dominicans maintained two colleges in the River Plate region (Buenos Aires and Córdoba); in that same year a third college was founded in Asunción.

The Dominicans established special Melchor Cano chairs (also called *loci theologici*), such as those held in 1779 by Friar Cipriano Negrete in Buenos Aires and by Friar Angel Bahía in Córdoba. Similar chairs were held in 1783 by Juan José Chambo in Buenos Aires and by Friar Andrés Pereyra in Córdoba. Friars Carlos Molina (1787), Pedro Antonio Ordóñez (1791), and Manuel Cañiza (1793–1803) held such chairs in Asunción.[118]

Of the Dominicans, however, the most important were Isidoro Celestino Guerra (1747–1820), Juan Antonio Cruz del Valle, and Melchor Fernández, all three of whom based their philosophy on Thomism and opposed Cartesianism. Guerra in his *Plan de estudios* (1795) tried to revive Scholasticism; he accepted Melchor Cano as long as his views did not contradict St. Thomas'.[119] Cruz del Valle's *Theses ex universa philosophia* (1803) — a compendium of logic, metaphysics, natural theology, and physics — opposed the philosophies of Voltaire, Hobbes, Spinoza, and, to an extent, Leibniz. Fernández, like Cruz del Valle a Spaniard, in his *Theses ex universa philosophia* (1792) and his *Theses ex universa theologia* (1795) showed an eclectic tendency insofar as he pursued a modern trend in physics while remaining Scholastic in ontology and logic, actually often following Suárez.[120]

At the end of the eighteenth century Scholasticism underwent a revival, the greatest names of which were Mariano Medrano, Diego Estanislao Zavaleta, and José Valentín Gómez,[121] all of the Colegio de San Carlos (founded in Buenos Aires in 1783). It was a revival which, though limited in comparison to sixteenth-century Late Scholasticism, was still powerful and extended to other parts of Spanish America. Of interest is the fact that it was more concentrated in Buenos Aires than in Córdoba, where the Franciscans were often more inclined to follow modern rationalistic trends.

Medrano, Zavaleta, and Gómez were able to give traditional philosophy a new and solid foundation. From 1793 to 1795 Medrano (1767–1851) taught at San Carlos and later, from 1832 to 1851, held the highest ecclesiastical position in Buenos Aires. In his teaching he particularly opposed the philosophies of Descartes, Malebranche, Leibniz, and Locke.[122] His *Cursus* or *Conferencias filosóficas sobre toda la facultad de filosofía, . . . , preparadas para el trienio con método claro y escolástico, según las sentencias selectas de los filósofos actuales* (1793)[123] clearly indicated Scholastic continuity. His other works, also dated 1793, dealt with physics, logic, and ethics.

Zavaleta, like Medrano a great patriot, received his education under the Dominicans and later at San Carlos. He later taught philosophy at San Carlos from 1795 to 1797, and served as congressional deputy in 1817 and 1825, and as a member of the ecclesiastical *cabildo*. A greater philosopher than Medrano, he left several works: *Elementa philosophiae universae: Secunda pars seu physica generalis* (1795), *Institutiones philosophiae universae: Pars 4 metaphysicam continens*, which also deals with psychology and natural theology, and the *Elementa philosophiae universae: Pars III seu physica particularis* (1796). In metaphysics he departed from St. Thomas to follow Suárez, whom he quotes, and like Medrano he opposed the theories of Descartes, Malebranche, and Leibniz. A similar point of view is expressed in his treatise on physics, though in some cases, where he deemed it warranted, he praised Descartes, Gassendi, and Newton.[124]

Gómez (b. 1774) also studied at the Colegio de San Carlos and graduated in theology in Córdoba. Upon his return to Buenos Aires, he became a lawyer of the *audiencia* and in 1799 decided to teach philosophy. Later in his life he served as governor of the bishopric and as a deputy at the Constituent Assembly of 1813. The foundation of his thought was deeply Scholastic, whether in logic, metaphysics, or ethics — as is evident from his *Conclusiones ex universa philosophia* (1802); yet in physics he maintained that modern knowledge did not contradict the scriptures.[125] In politics he was a fervent centralist and monarchist. Furlong characterized Gómez's thought well when he said:

> Such is the philosophy of Gómez: robust, firm, vigorous, and luminous, just like that of the best Scholastic thinkers who at the time honored the speculative sciences throughout educated Europe.[126]

Other Scholastic representatives in the second half of the eighteenth century were Pantaleón Rivarola, Luis José Chorroarín, Pedro Miguel Aráoz, José de Reyna, and Manuel de Labardón. Rivarola (1757–1821) studied law in Santiago de Chile and Córdoba, and in 1778 became a priest. He taught law at the University of San Felipe in Santiago de Chile and, later, philosophy and theology at Córdoba University. Among the most famous pupils of Rivarola were Juan José Castelli, Ramón Vieytes, and Melchor Fernández. He was the author of a *Tertia philosophiae pars sive metaphysica scholastico methodo* (1781), which clearly showed the Scholastic roots of his thought, although he accepted Newton's law of gravity and praised him for it.[127] According to Furlong,

> The mere reading of these notes of one of the professors of San Carlos at the end of the eighteenth century proves clearly, once again, that the thinkers of the River Plate at the time were on a level with those of educated Europe, and thanks to a Scholastic tradition rooted in the country since the end of the sixteenth or beginning of the seventeenth century, were able to separate the wheat from the chaff. . . . Aristotle and St. Thomas continued to be for Rivarola, as they are still today for all great Scholastic philosophers, indispensable guides, but in all calmness Rivarola knows how to distinguish between metaphysical and physical problems, opting in the latter [case] for the guidance of Newton, Descartes, Wolff, Leibniz, Gassendi, etc.[128]

For twenty-five years, Chorroarín (d. 1823) was rector of the Colegio de San Carlos, and to a greater or lesser degree the leaders of the May Revolution, such as Manuel Belgrano, were influenced by him and by the Scholastic philosophers Zavaleta and Gómez. His *Institutiones philosophiae* (1783) showed him profoundly rooted in Scholasticism.[129]

Aráoz (1759–1832) took over the chair of philosophy at San Carlos in the year 1785. Author of a *Triennalis philosophicus cursus*, he also followed the Scholastic philosophy with no concession to the empiricism of Locke, the sensualism of Condillac, or the rationalism of Descartes or Gassendi.[130] Reyna (1787) and Labardón (1788) followed a similar philosophic orientation.

Another exponent of Scholasticism was Juan Manuel Fernández de Agüero y Echagüe, a rather versatile Spaniard who came to Buenos Aires in 1794 where he joined the Colegio de San Carlos. Having graduated in law and theology from the University of San Felipe in Santiago de Chile in 1801, he joined the priesthood in 1802. He was the author of a *Disciplinae philosophicae institutiones ad captum juventutis* (1805), the contents of which were assembled in some forty-seven conclusions under the title *Theses pro deponendo philosophiae tyrocinio, ex logica et ethica publice propugnandae* (1805), and with one exception were all of a Scholastic nature.[131] Fernández de Agüero's ideas at that time were Scholastic in spite of the fact that he had also shown interest in Locke and that, in 1799, he had been the author of a political discourse based on the divine right of kings opposed to the political tenets of sixteenth-century Spanish thought and more in keeping with the authoritarian ideas of a Solórzano Pereyra in the seventeenth. His versatility will come fully to the fore in the 1820s at the time of Bernardino Rivadavia when he will become the champion of Destutt de Tracy's *idéologie* on the River Plate.[132]

Besides Córdoba and Buenos Aires, the Scholastic tradition was continued in the eighteenth century by the colleges of Asunción, Salta, Mendoza, and Montevideo. After the departure of the Jesuits in 1767, it was the Dominicans in particular who played an important role in Asunción.

Because of favorable location, between Córdoba and Charcas, Salta in the second half of the eighteenth century became an important cultural center. Filiberto de Mena stated in his chronicle written near the end of the eighteenth century that the Province of Salta enjoyed a good reputation because of its teachers, who included many excellent theologians, philosophers, moralists, canonists, and Scholastics.[133] Among the best were Manuel Antonio de Acevedo and Aráoz.

The Jesuits had been in Mendoza since 1616 and in the middle of the eighteenth century established a chair of philosophy. After 1767 both Franciscans and Augustinians in Mendoza and Dominicans in San Juan taught theology, philosophy, and canon law: among them, in 1771, Friar Agustín Ramírez y Barroso.[134]

Montevideo had its first formal chair of philosophy in 1782 when the Franciscans established it in the friary of San Bernardino. Among the greatest teachers there was the famous Mariano Chambo (1762–1833), author of *Largifluí logicalis scientiae rivi ex subtilis Marianique doctoris Joannis Duns Scoti promanentes* (1789), one of the earliest patriots, and, like Vieytes, Castelli, and Moreno, a partisan of the regency of Carlota Joaquina.[135] In 1790 a chair of theology was added so that the young students had no need to continue their studies in either Buenos Aires or Córdoba.

Thus, until 1767, the Jesuits, together with the other religious orders, continued the Scholastic tradition in the River Plate and in the other parts of Spanish America. In many cases they adjusted Scholasticism to the new trends in the natural sciences while at the same time remaining orthodox in faith and religion and traditional in theology, philosophy, and political thought. The majority of their pupils — Mariano Medrano, Pantaleón Rivarola, Luis José Chorroarín, and, in the case of the Colegio de San Carlos, Carlos José Montero and Vicente Anastasio Juanzaras, to name but a few — received this kind of education, and it was in this philosophical environment that the great men of the Argentine Revolution of 1810 — Cornelio de Saavedra, Mariano Moreno, Juan José Castelli, Hipólito Vieytes, Gregorio Funes, Juan Ignacio Gorriti, Pedro Ignacio de Castro Barros, Cayetano Rodríguez, Miguel Calixto del Corro, Juan Perdriel, and Vicente López y Planes — found their cultural background and scientific education.

The influence of Suárez was so great that in some instances the University of Córdoba in 1730 ordered Suarezian doctrines to be taught to the exclusion of all others.¹³⁶ Although there was some opposition to his theories, it was through Suárez and his disciples that Scholasticism during the eighteenth century maintained an extraordinary hold over the intellectuals, the university centers, and the colleges in Spanish America.

The domination of Suarezian theories was so widespread in the middle of the century that the bishop of Asunción wrote on August 30, 1757, to Minister Wall that the Jesuits of the River Plate had in their hands all necessary goods, being the masters of all resources.¹³⁷ It was so deep and durable an influence that it lasted far beyond the famous date of 1767. If after that date this influence waned somewhat, it was the result not only of the expulsion of the Jesuits and their replacement by followers of other philosophical systems, but of the eruption of Cartesianism. Nevertheless, much evidence exists which shows that at the end of the eighteenth and the beginning of the nineteenth centuries the theories of Suárez actually had not been forgotten at all after the famous order of 1767. Intellectuals such as José Valentín Gómez (1802) and the Franciscans Elías del Carmen (1786) and Anastasio Mariano Suárez (1792) maintained and defended philosophical theories the contents of which were taken from Suárez rather than from St. Thomas or Duns Scotus.¹³⁸

Other examples may be seen in the sermons of the priest of Guandacol, José Francisco Echenique, when he preached that in this world the power of kings was subject to that of peoples. The governor, alarmed at such a political novelty, which had so little in common with the ideas of Enlightened despotism, mentioned this to the ecclesiastical *cabildo*, then presided over by Gregorio Funes. In order to explain the ideas of Echenique, Funes told the governor that "in the University the same doctrines were taught, as were others even more destructive to the powers of the kings, that laws receive their strength not from the authority of kings but from acceptance by the people, for instance."¹³⁹ To get to the truth of the whole matter, the governor then wrote to the rector of the University of Córdoba, Guitián, who acknowledged that these political ideas had been taught, and that at that very moment were being set forth by the Franciscan Friar Juan José Casal.¹⁴⁰

In 1779 a certain jurist in Chuquisaca maintained before the courts that the law was legal only with the consent of the people.¹⁴¹ Gabriel René-Moreno mentioned the strength of Scholastic teachings at Chuquisaca, and noted with special interest that the students were taught the right of resistance against tyrannical rule, the nullity of unjust laws, and the supposed right of conquest.¹⁴² These same Scholastic ideas twenty years later will be upheld by all the members of the very *audiencia* which earlier had condemned the lawyer who dared to express ideas contrary to the policies of enlightened despotism.

The bishop of Buenos Aires, Manuel de la Torre, wrote to the king after the expulsion of the Jesuits in 1767, claiming that, though it was true that the Jesuits had gone from Spanish America, their expulsion certainly did not mean that their ideas were eradicated from Spanish American soil. The bishop, obviously no friend of the Jesuits, added that he was quite sure that they had left behind some very dangerous and explosive political theories.¹⁴³ José Ingenieros, who admits what he calls the really formidable resistance in Buenos Aires to the expulsion of the Jesuits, mentions the remarks of Friar Antonio

María Bucareli y Ursúa, viceroy of New Spain, who said in a letter that the Jesuits' power in the River Plate was absolute.[144]

Moreover, at the time of the first British invasion of the River Plate, certain anonymous writings appeared in Buenos Aires in August and September, 1806, attacking Viceroy Sobremonte who had fled to the interior; these were based on traditional Spanish legislation and political theory and invoked not only the *Siete Partidas* of Alfonso the Learned, but the Laws of the Indies and the political thought of Late Scholasticism as well, stating, for example:

> It is known that government positions have been created in Spain not to accommodate persons but in order for the persons to serve and perform the functions . . . . when the law prohibits a person who has been mayor for a year from succeeding himself until a period of two years shall have elapsed, the law and the practice allow dispensation if he is acclaimed by unanimous vote . . . . Similarly, when in Spain the *corregidor* is dead (and the same may be said of the governor), the jurisdiction of the deputy expires and he cannot assume the position of the one who appointed him, [but] the prohibition has no effect if the people elect him. The same thing occurs whenever there are no surviving kinsfolk of the king; should no one of his dynasty remain to whom the crown would legitimately belong, it is the responsibility of the people to elect the one whom they think best fit.[145]

Thus, the conclusion is clear: these political doctrines were as popular at the end of the eighteenth century and on the eve of independence as during the sixteenth and seventeenth centuries, a fact which becomes apparent in several historical developments, such as the wars of the *comuneros* in Paraguay and in New Granada.

Scholastic Works in Libraries. It is not surprising that the works of the Spanish Late Scholastics formed a part of the private libraries of many teachers, lawyers, and public officials. Even after the expulsion of the Jesuits, many collections of the works of Suárez were to be found in the libraries of Santa Fe, Córdoba, Buenos Aires, Asunción, and Mendoza. Even today it is not unusual to find copies which carry an *ex libris* dated before 1767, such as the *In tertiam partem divi Thomae, tomus secundus* in the library of the Colegio del Salvador in Buenos Aires, which had belonged to the Jesuit College of Córdoba.[146] In the library of Pedro Antonio de Arias de Velásquez Saravia in Salta could be found at the time works of St. Thomas, Suárez, and Leibniz.[147]

In Chile, for instance, José Teodoro Sánchez owned Suárez' *De legibus*; Molina's *De iustitia et iure* could be found in the libraries of Sánchez, of Santiago de Tordesillas, and of Bishop José de Toro Zambrano; Azpilcueta's *Opera omnia* could be seen in Manuel de Salas' collection of books.[148] Other libraries belonging to lawyers, bishops, and Jesuits in Chile and ranging from the late seventeenth century to the early part of the nineteenth showed that the following works were available: Solórzano in 14 libraries, Covarrubias in 14, Menchaca in 6, Matienzo in 11; St. Augustine's *City of God* in 3, Saint Thomas in 6, Vitoria in 1, Soto in 6, Suárez in 8, Molina in 10, Azpilcueta in 3, Cajetan in 2, and Bellarmine in 1. Quevedo could be found in 7, Feijóo in 9, Olavide in 1, while Pufendorf was available in 1 and Rousseau only through *The New Heloïse*.[149] These collections totaled some 20,000 volumes, which later came into the possession of the University of San Felipe in Santiago de Chile and belonged to the following owners: Canon Francisco Machado de Chávez (1661), Basilio Echeverría (1731), *Oidor* Juan del Corral Calvo de la Torre (1737), Bishop José de Toro Zambrano (1746), Bishop Manuel de Alday (1755), Tomás Durán (1759), Santiago de Tordesillas (1766), *Oidor* Domingo Martínez de Aldunate, the rector of the University of San Felipe (1778), Fernando Bravo de Naveda (1778), Pascual Silva Bohorquez (1790), José Sánchez Villasana (1790), *Oidor* Juan Verdugo (1779), *Oidor* Francisco Antonio Moreno Escandón (1792), Alonso de Guzmán, rector of the University of San Felipe (1792), Agustín Seco y Santa Cruz (1795), Jerónimo Hurtado de Mendoza Salinas (1811), José Teodoro Sánchez (1812), and Canon Miguel Rafael Palacios (1818).[150]

The National Library in Bogotá is full of Spanish classical works — Soto, Báñez, Vitoria, Azpilcueta, etc. — but Suárez, with 152 volumes, is especially prominent; these include the *Opera omnia* in the Venice edition of 1749, and the *De legibus*, in its first (Coimbra) edition of the year 1612, the Antwerp edition of 1613, and two copies of the Lyons edition of the same year. Gómez Hoyos points out that all sections dealing with the theory of popular sovereignty in these works not only were underlined but included handwritten marginal notations as well.[151]

Other famous libraries in New Granada also contained the classical Spanish works. The library of Fernando de Castro y Vargas, canon of Bogotá (d. 1665), included the works of Suárez, Vázquez de Menchaca, Bellarmine, Báñez, Soto, Saavedra Fajardo, and Azpilcueta;[152] that of the wealthy widow, the condesa de Torre Velarde — according to an inventory made in 1801 — held the works of Suárez, Molina, Fernández de Navarrete, Vitoria, Covarrubias, and Feijóo. The library of Archbishop-Viceroy Caballero y Góngora included the works of Fernández de Navarrete, Mariana, Bellarmine, Soto, and Vitoria, while that of Camilo Torres contained all the classic works of Spanish and Indian law, including Soto's *De iustitia et iure*;[153] Nariño's could boast the most important works of classical antiquity and the Spanish Golden Age — especially Solórzano Pereyra, Covarrubias, Soto, Bellarmine, and Saavedra Fajardo — as well as important works in French (Raynal, Rousseau, Voltaire, Montesquieu, Pascal, and Condillac).[154]

3. Important Events of the Period Relevant to the Spanish American Revolution

Several historic developments with important consequences for the future Spanish American Revolution occurred before the period ended. Though most of these took place in the second half of the century, there was the revolt of the *comuneros* in Paraguay, which lasted for the twelve years between 1723 and 1735. Of the events occurring in the latter part of the century, the expulsion of the Jesuits heads the list, followed, in the 1780s, by a series of happenings which include, in particular, the revolt of the *comuneros* in New Granada and the Indian uprising of Tupac Amarú in Upper Peru. The plot of Gual and España in Venezuela at the end of the century, and the significant landings of Miranda in Venezuela and the British attacks on the River Plate at the beginning of the nineteenth century, foreshadowed some of the events which would occur in the years 1809 and 1810.

The Revolt of the Comuneros *in Paraguay (1723–35).* This strange revolt is linked to the uprising of Antequera and involved what Salvador de Madariaga has characterized as a typical Spanish story. The viceroy of Peru appointed Diego de los Reyes governor of Paraguay, but after a considerable number of complaints arrived in Lima, a *pesquisidor*, José de Antequera y Castro, the *fiscal* of the *audiencia* of Charcas and *protector* of Indians, was sent to Asunción to investigate. As a result of Antequera's inquiries, Reyes was imprisoned. He later escaped and reassumed his position as governor. Returning to Asunción, Antequera, with the backing of the *cabildo* and the *audiencia*, opposed this reinstatement, in spite of the fact that Reyes enjoyed the support of the viceroy, who had dispatched García Ros to assume the post temporarily until calm returned. But Antequera was able to recapture Reyes and have him arrested. When Ros arrived with troops, Antequera sought and obtained the support of the *cabildo abierto*. In reality, the Antequera–Reyes controversy concealed a more important problem: the opposition of the Jesuits, the protectors of the Indians, to the desire of the *vecinos* and *encomenderos* for increased Indian labor. In the ensuing battle, Antequera defeated Ros with the promise of Indian slave labor and booty; when Antequera later turned against the Jesuits, his victory was overturned and he was forced to return to Asunción.

A new viceroy, the marqués de Castelfuerte, together with an able bishop, José de Palos, took steps forcing Antequera to flee, while a new governor, Martín de Barúa, took over and released Reyes. Antequera was finally captured in Lima (1726) where he spent five years in prison; yet he enjoyed so much freedom that he was able to send another rebel to Asunción — Fernando de Mompox — at a time when the viceroy had sent a new governor and a new *pesquisidor*. Mompox organized a second uprising, known as the revolt of the *comuneros*. It was joined by the resentful Barúa and the *vecinos* (eager for Indian labor) and was directed against the Jesuits. The *comuneros* ruled Asunción and the countryside for months, and, when Barúa stepped down, they adopted republican forms: they established a *junta de justicia*, the chairman of which, José Luis Barreyro, was called the *presidente de la provincia*. The struggle continued, with further strange developments — Barreyro turned out to be a loyal royalist who took hold of Mompox, and was later replaced — including the execution of Antequera in Lima in 1731. Although the beginning of the struggle in 1723 was linked to the wealthy and aristocratic, the revolt developed into a more democratic and popular movement, the republican tendencies of which attracted those members of other religious orders who were unfriendly to the Jesuits, such as the Franciscan bishop of Buenos Aires, Arregui, who replaced the earlier Palos. The revolt was finally suppressed in 1735 by the governor of Buenos Aires but not without difficulty, and even at that time foreshadowed the forces of regionalism and growing nationalism which came to the fore in an explosive manner in 1809 and 1810.[155] It is important to note that both the rebels and the clergy, who sympathized with their aims, based their stand on Hispanic concepts derived from the *Etymologiae* of Isidore of Seville, and repeated by the famous Councils of Toledo, the tenets of Late Scholasticism, and such plays as Calderón de la Barca's *Life Is a Dream* and *The Mayor of Zalamea* — i.e., that in case of an unjust law the king ought not to be obeyed.[156]

The Expulsion of the Society of Jesus (1767). The expulsion of the Jesuits — in the Portuguese Empire in 1759, in France in 1762, and in the Spanish Empire in 1767 — was one of the most significant events of the eighteenth century in the Indies.

Instigated by Pombal in Portugal and by Aranda and Tanucci in Spain, the order of expulsion had very serious repercussions, actually cutting the history of Hispanic America in two. In their missionary work and in their colleges, the Jesuits had maintained very high standards. In education, Hispanic American colleges could well rival those of the Old World, and the Jesuits' work in Paraguay had to be acknowledged even by their foes. Hispanic American culture, the Scholastic tradition of which the Jesuits upheld in the eighteenth century without neglecting the sciences, truly owed a great debt to these men suddenly exiled from their homelands.

But in spite of their brilliant achievements the Jesuits in Spanish America often encountered opposition from civil and ecclesiastical authorities. Many envied their power; some coveted their wealth. The manifestations against the Society by Bishop Juan de Palafox y Mendoza of Puebla in New Spain and the inimical stand of the Mexican Archbishop Francisco Antonio Lorenzana are justly famous, as is the case of Miguel García de Tagle in the River Plate, who was condemned to death for conspiring for the Jesuits.[157] Yet New Spain, among others, witnessed several riots by the people protesting the order of expulsion.

The expulsion of the Jesuits signaled the ruin of the Paraguayan mission and opened a new chapter in the academic history of Hispanic America. When the more than two thousand Jesuits were forced to leave the Spanish American provinces,[158] one hundred and twenty colleges had to be closed, and a considerable number of natives were left without spiritual guidance.[159] Thus, the culture of New Spain declined from the end of the eighteenth century until the first half of the nineteenth. A large group of the exiled Jesuits went to Bologna where they became a powerful force in the movement for Spanish American independence, since they loved their native countries and hoped one day to return. To their opposition to the *philosophes* and the materialistic currents of the century was added their emotional enmity toward the Spanish and Portuguese monarchies.[160] The Ecuadorean Ramón Insúa Rodríguez has said of their expulsion that

> these men, among whom served many of the best spirits and most powerful intellects of the time in Spanish America, were victims of one of the most unjust explosions of collective passion recorded in history . . . . In Spanish America, the cultural damage caused . . . was immense. Since higher education rested almost entirely in their hands, they departed leaving a vacuum which contemporary society was not able to fill. The Jesuits in America aspired to obtain for everyone a higher and more extensive culture. They loved knowledge most ardently. They created in the New World an intellectual zone, ample and harmonious, formed by educated men, among whom the Spanish American element predominated in the final years.[161]

The expulsion of the Jesuits added another element in the struggle against Enlightened despotism, since the exiled Jesuits engaged increasingly in political activities against the Spanish monarchy.[162] They often used French eighteenth-century pre-Revolutionary phraseology in their Scholastic theories, which followed Suárez much more than Rousseau. The exiled Jesuits wished to return to their homelands and left no stone unturned. They cooperated with Francisco de Miranda in his Venezuelan plans. They issued a manifesto on December 22, 1797, in which appear the names of the Jesuits José del Pozo y Sucre and Manuel José Salas as Spanish American deputies. The Argentine Jesuit Juan José Godoy — resident in the United States since 1782 — collaborated in plans for the Venezuelan expedition. Finally, the famous *Letter Addressed to the Spanish Americans*[163] by the Peruvian Juan Pablo de Vizcardo y Guzmán, which Miranda distributed in French and Spanish (June 10, 1799, and 1801), shows the Jesuit opposition to Enlightened despotism. The *Letter* is an interesting document insofar as it reveals not only the emotions of the exile toward his lost country, but the continuation of Scholastic thought at the turn of the century. Thus it states:

> that any law which is opposed to the universal good of those for whom it is intended is an act of tyranny and that to demand its observance is tantamount to [imposing] slavery; that a law which has as its purpose the destruction of the prosperity of a people would be a monstrosity beyond expression; ... that a people deprived of its personal freedom and of the right to dispose of its property, when all other nations under the same circumstances strive to extend it, will find itself in a state of slavery greater than that imposed by a foe drunk with the spirit of victory. ... It was, thus, a fundamental disposition of the constitution of Aragon that if the king violated the rights and privileges of the people they could legitimately banish him and appoint another in his place, even if he be a pagan, according to the same Gerónimo Blanca.
>
> To this noble spirit of liberty our ancestors owed the energy which enabled them to carry out such great enterprises, and which in the midst of such burdensome wars made the nation flourish, and which heaped up prosperity such as we observe nowadays in England and Holland. But after the king exceeded the limits set by the constitutions of Castile and Aragon, the decay of Spain was as quick as the power acquired — or, in other words, usurped — by the sovereigns had been extraordinary. And this proves sufficiently that absolute power joined always to arbitrariness is the ruin of states.[164]

Miguel Batllori denies any influence by the exiled Jesuits on the Spanish American Revolution,[165] claiming that the supposed Jesuit participation is a myth which through the ages has become magnified and in any case is true of only one Jesuit, Vizcardo y Guzmán. According to Batllori, the exiled Jesuits searched in a Romantic way for a Spanish American national conscience, which represented "the true and historic intervention of the Jesuits in the independence of Spanish America."[166] The influence of the exiled Jesuits may have been exaggerated,[167] but their active participation was by no means restricted to Vizcardo y Guzmán and Godoy. Thus, only in the case of Spanish South America was there the previously mentioned Andrés Febrés Oms, a Catalan and former missionary in Chile who in the years 1783 and 1784 published the *Seconda Memoria Cattolica* in which he warned the Spanish monarch of the future independence of Spanish America in view of free trade and the expulsion of the Jesuits at the instigation of what he termed "Spain's liberal traitors."[168]

There were also the Peruvians Pedro Pavón, author of a *Trattato della civiltà* (1791), and Manuel Baeza, who agitated for both republicanism and independence.[169] The Asturian Jesuit of Paraguay, Cosme Antonio de la Cueva, who was imprisoned for three years in Genoa for revolutionary activities, and the Chilean Diego León Villafañe, who returned to Chile in 1800 and engaged in similar plots for Chilean independence, belong as well to the group of exiled activists.[170] Finally, Javier Caldera and Felipe Gómez de Vidaurre both participated actively in the independence of their Chilean fatherland.[171] Thus, Batllori's point of view must be rejected. Furthermore, the Jesuit influence cannot be measured solely in terms of political activity; it must be viewed as the accumulation and continuity of a great philosophical and political tradition which appeared at the end of the sixteenth century and continued even after the expulsion of the Society from the Indies.

The Indian Uprising of Tupac Amarú in Upper Peru (1780). At the end of the century several historic events occurred, the first of which was the famous Indian uprising under Tupac Amarú. José Gabriel Condorcanqui, who called himself Tupac Amarú II and was the lineal descendant of Tupac Amarú I, executed by Viceroy Toledo in 1571, led an uprising of some 50,000–70,000 Indians in 1780 who in a short time occupied an area comprising southern Peru, Upper Peru, and parts of northwestern Argentina. The revolt, which opposed certain abuses by the *corregidores*, was seen as a threat to Spanish power and dealt with accordingly.

After six months, the uprising was quelled, and Tupac Amarú II, together with his family, was publicly executed by quartering. The revolt failed for several reasons: (*a*) as a possible movement for emancipation (which it was not), it was premature; (*b*) as a purely Indian affair, it did not interest the *criollos*; and (*c*) the excesses which the Indians under Tupac Amarú committed within their areas of control frightened Spanish American society. The net result was a hardening of attitudes resulting in a conservatism which could still be felt twenty years later in Lower and Upper Peru and which was similar to the consequences of Father Hidalgo's revolt in New Spain in 1810.

The Conspiracy of the Three Antonios in Chile (1780–81). Another interesting event, though of much less importance than the revolts in Paraguay and Upper Peru, was the unsuccessful revolutionary attempt known as the "Conspiracy of the Three Antonios" in Chile. An abortive plot, planned by the Frenchmen Antoine Alexandre Vergne and Antoine Gramusset with the aid, it is alleged,[172] of José Antonio Rojas, Mariano Pérez Saraiva, Juan Agustín Beyner, and the Spaniard Pacheco, was to be staged in 1781. Simon Collier has called the conspiracy "a picturesque episode, though completely concealed from the vast majority of Chileans at the time,"[173] and thus hardly significant for the future independence of the country.

Yet the plot is perhaps more interesting for the history of ideas than as evidence of revolutionary activity. Up to now the conspiracy has been attributed to the influence of Rousseau insofar as the leaders were French and the final goal the establishment of a Chilean republic, the end of slavery, and agrarian reform. But Vergne's republic was based on natural law and on the scriptures and aimed at the establishment of a popularly elected junta-type regime with the title "Sovereign Senate of the most noble, most strong, and most Catholic Chilean Republic."[174] The main ideas for this republic were derived from history, and, like the later *Catecismo politico-cristiano*, represented a political program favoring a republican system and opposing the form of monarchy.[175] Thus, though it was not devoid of some Rousseauan concepts, the roots of Vergne's republic were, rather, medieval and Spanish. They will be echoed later in the *Catecismo politico-cristiano* and in the works of Juan Egaña.[176] It is worthy of note that the conspiracy was formed at a time when the contents of the *Noticias secretas* of Juan and Ulloa were "becoming generally known; the two facts are definitely and closely related."[177]

The Revolt of the Comuneros in New Granada (1781). Like the earlier uprising in Paraguay, this revolt of the *comuneros* was also rooted in republicanism and in medieval philosophy, and took its inspirations from the rebellions of Tunja in 1592 and 1641; based on the concept of popular sovereignty, it foreshadowed also the political independence of New Granada in the early-nineteenth century.

This serious revolution began in Socorro as a result of the imposition of taxes (tobacco, navy) and soon blossomed into a league of towns — the *común* — the political ideology of which was "the defense, or advantage, care, and good government of the republic"[178] and opposition to what it termed the despotism of the authorities. Again the revolution of New Granada in 1781, as seen, among others, in the revolutionary slogans, the thought of the revolutionary leaders Juan Francisco Berbeo, Salvador Plata, Antonio Monsalvo, and Diego de Ardilla or Francisco Rosillo, the *Cédula*, and the preamble of the *Capitulaciones*, was based philosophically on the Late Scholasticism of Suárez, with its concept of the popular source of the state and its limitations, the social contract, resistance to tyranny, invalidity of unjust laws, popular consent for the imposition of taxes, the primacy of the common good, and the Christian natural law.[179]

The Plot of Gual and España in Venezuela (1797). In 1797 a group of Spanish revolutionaries arrived in La Guaira. Participants in the republican conspiracy of San Blas in Madrid, they had been condemned to death but were later exiled to Spanish America. These revolutionaries included the ringleader Juan Picornell, Sebastián Andrés, and Manuel Cortés. On arrival in Venezuela they joined forces with Venezuelan plotters, especially Gual and España. The Spaniards were able to flee from prison to La Guaira and Picornell had a pamphlet printed in Guadeloupe on the Rights of Man and the Citizen and even a song called "the American Carmagnole."[180]

Though the plot of Gual and España failed, it is an interesting episode from the point of view of political thought. From papers which were found, it is clear that the revolutionary movement wanted the re-establishment of liberty to the Spanish American people — its goal was, thus, an independent Spanish America linked to Spain solely on the basis of language and history, and as such similar to the Romantic concepts of Miranda. The documents began with a religious invocation: "In the name of the Most Holy Trinity and of Jesus, Mary, and Joseph, Amen."[181] They proclaimed the protection of religion and of the Church, promising to punish any insult against either; abolished any tax contrary to consumption and trade; opened Spanish America to all the nations of the world; invited all Spanish American areas to an assembly to declare independence; prohibited the extraction of gold and silver; and ordered severe punishment to all armed forces which would oppose the revolutionary movement, at the same time offering a safe-conduct to all those who wanted either to return to Spain or to join the rebellion — thereby excluding the *peninsulares*.[182] Perhaps the most important provision was Article 32, which declared "natural equality among all the inhabitants of the provinces and districts," and called for the establishment of

> the greatest harmony between whites, Indians, mestizos, and mulattoes, who should look upon each other as brothers in Christ equal under God, [and] who should attempt to be different only through merit and virtue, which are the only two true and real distinctions which exist between man and man and which will exist in the future among all individuals of our republic.[183]

Madariaga sees in these documents an influence of French revolutionary ideas because of their egalitarian character — finding "strong reminiscences of Rousseau under its Christian forms" — which came to Venezuela at least in part through the Spanish republican revolutionaries and through the influence of Spanish freemasonry.[184] However, as in other documents which have similar contents and which appeared before and during the Spanish American Revolution, it is difficult to link the religious invocation and Article 32 to the ideas of 1789. Rather, this part has an undeniable Scholastic character the philosophical foundation of which is rooted in the Spanish tradition of Late Scholasticism and in the most elementary notions of medieval philosophy.

The plot failed, in Madariaga's view, because of its social implications, prompting the wealthy and the elite groups to join the government in suppressing it. This may indeed be true, since the conservative reaction in Venezuela to the social threat was similar to that in Peru and Upper Peru to the rebellion of Tupac Amarú and to that in New Spain to Hidalgo's and Morelos' revolts.

Miranda's Landings in Venezuela (1806). None of the events prior to the crisis of Bayonne was as important as Miranda's landings and the British attacks on the River Plate in the years 1806 and 1807. Miranda's Venezuelan landings in 1806 (Puerto Cabello, Coro), which failed to rally the people to independence, proved, instead, that the Spanish Americans of that region were loyal to Spain. Yet there is a further note of interest in the endeavors of the Venezuelan patriot: when he landed, Miranda was aiming at the independence not only of his native Venezuela, but of an entire continent. Thus he was a forerunner not only of Venezuelan independence, but of a united and independent Spanish America. His ideal — proclaimed at the landings — was a federation of free townships working toward a common Spanish American fatherland: the community approach based on medieval Spanish thought. In his proclamation of August 2, 1806, Miranda addressed the peoples of the "American-Colombian Continent" and specifically referred to the *cabildos* which were to exercise all the functions of a provisional government, and to send one or two deputies to army headquarters to meet in a general assembly.[185] It is fascinating to note that Miranda, undoubtedly influenced by the ideas of the Enlightenment, Rousseau, and the French and North American Revolutions, actually based himself primarily on solid Spanish traditional ground. By proposing a federation of free townships, he was following traditions which had been stated in the same area of New Granada by Bernardo de Vargas Machuca (1555–1622) some two centuries earlier, when Vargas Machuca justified the political development of each American kingdom.[186] Even though the landings in Venezuela failed, they were to some extent a foretaste of further events; as a matter of fact, when the opportunity of forming a junta in Caracas (1810) presented itself, it was not long before a general assembly was convoked as Miranda had requested.

The British Invasions of the River Plate (1806–1807). The British had been interested in the River Plate for some time when a British force of 1,000, under the command of Sir Home Popham and William Carr Beresford, returning from Cape Town (which it had seized from the Dutch), decided without official orders to capture Buenos Aires; the city fell in June 1806. Unfortunately for their cause, the British had not taken Montevideo, and it was from there that Santiago de Liniers y Brémond, a Frenchman in the service of Spain, marched to the rescue of Buenos Aires, forcing the British to withdraw (August 12, 1806). At this point the *cabildo* of Buenos Aires proposed on August 14, 1806, independent of any Peninsular action, to depose the viceroy, the marqués de Sobremonte, because he had fled to the interior at the time of the British invasion. The *cabildo* then appointed Liniers military chief, and the removal of the viceroy was effected by a special war junta on February 10, 1807; this action signified, prior to the fateful events of Bayonne, the beginning of the legal crisis in Spanish America. Although the British made a second attack in 1807, with 12,000 men under General John Whitelocke, and by first capturing Montevideo were able to take Buenos Aires a second time, they were soon forced by Liniers to surrender. As a result Liniers was appointed acting viceroy by Charles IV.

The British invasions are important for several reasons: (*a*) they proved — as did Miranda's in Venezuela — that the River Plate area was fervently loyal to the Spanish cause and to the unity of the Spanish Empire; (*b*) the war effort had been carried out by the *criollos* — entirely an Argentine affair, it received no aid whatsoever from Spain — which gave a tremendous boost to Argentine self-confidence and signified the birth of Argentine nationalism; (*c*) the *cabildo* had acted like the *Cortes* in medieval Spain and like many *cabildos* in Spanish America in the past: it had deposed the highest authority for incompetency and had appointed a *caudillo* who had shown himself worthy of the citizens' trust. The *cabildo*'s action was to inspire the events of May only a few years later which led to independence.

The actions of the *cabildo* of Buenos Aires are more easily understood in the light of its regained prestige in the last decade. Thus, the *cabildo* of Buenos Aires, the viceregal seat of the River Plate, became the most conspicuous defender of municipal liberties in the early nineteenth century and had been leading all other municipal governments in Peru and the River Plate. The victorious struggle against the British resulted in Buenos Aires' gaining a reputation as "leader and protector of municipal politics";[187] its constitution became the model for the *cabildos* of Asunción and Córdoba.[188] And, conscious of its ascendancy, Buenos Aires petitioned in December 1807 for the title "Defender of South America and Protector of the *Cabildos* of the Viceroyalty of the Plata." The petition to the Crown was written by Mariano Moreno who stated:

We learn by bitter experience in these dominions the constant practice followed by governors in general of humbling and depreciating the *cabildos*. Ignorant of their noble origin . . . they openly boast of vilifying them, and there is hardly a governor or subdelegate who does not consider it a supreme demonstration of his authority to scorn and despise the *cabildos*.[189]

In the same petition he called the *cabildo* of Buenos Aires "the organ by which complaints of the *cabildos* reach Your Majesty and through which they receive your graces."[190]

Thus, the British attacks and the actions of the *cabildo* of Buenos Aires were a clear and unmistakable sign of the future events in the area, foreshadowing the strong actions of Buenos Aires in 1810 in the face of the Napoleonic usurpation in the Peninsula — actions which were rooted in Spanish medieval thought and in Spanish political tradition.

The evidence is clear that Scholasticism continued to play an impressive role in Spanish America throughout the eighteenth century. In the first half, it largely dominated; in the second, when the Spanish Enlightenment made itself felt, it even enjoyed a revival, particularly in the River Plate. Far from ending with the expulsion of the Jesuits, Scholasticism continued, through the work of the other religious orders and the pupils of the former Jesuit teachers. Permeating the atmosphere in the eighteenth and early nineteenth centuries as it had in previous centuries, Scholasticism had a marked impact on social and political thought, which, in essence, was an attitude of mounting opposition to Enlightened despotism and its liberal reforms under Charles III. Even in those cases where Scholastic thinkers adopted a modern point of view toward the natural sciences, there was no deviation from the fundamental philosophic tradition as far as pure philosophy, ethics, and political theory were concerned. For this very reason such basic tenets as the religious foundation of Spanish political thought, loyalty to the reigning house, the metaphysical bonds linking the Indies to the Crown of Castile and León, the spirit of liberty and independence under well-established institutions and very distinct rules concerning the right of rebellion against tyranny — which had left such an indelible stamp on Spanish America — were as valid at the beginning of the nineteenth century as they had been in earlier times.

The general picture, thus, revealed a remarkable continuity of the medieval tradition in thought and in action, in spite of such exceptions as the divine-right theories, which obviously represented a deviation from this medieval past.

NOTES

[1] See Juan & Ulloa. See also Moses, *South America*, pp. 167–92, and Jane, pp. 86–90.
[2] Moses, p. 168.
[3] Juan & Ulloa, pp. 181–257. See also Moses, pp. 169ff., esp. pp. 171, 180. See also Herring, pp. 200–201, 209.
[4] Juan & Ulloa, pp. 258–73, esp. p. 265. See also Moses, pp. 185ff., esp. pp. 189–90.
[5] Juan & Ulloa, pp. 274, 387, 407–408, 405–406. See also Herring, pp. 179–80.

⁶ Jane, p. 86.
⁷ Ibid., p. 87.
⁸ Ibid., p. 49.
⁹ Halperín Donghi, p. 103.
¹⁰ Jane, pp. 85–86.
¹¹ Levene, *Historia del derecho argentino*, II 243.
¹² Haring, pp. 171–76, and Ots Capdequí, *El estado español*, pp. 76–77. See also Moore, *Cabildo in Peru under the Bourbons*, pp. 130–51, 152–72.
¹³ See Jane, pp. 81ff., esp. pp. 92–93, and Ravignani, *Historia constitucional*, I 70–84, esp. pp. 75–76, and pp. 46–51.
¹⁴ "Intendants and Cabildos," 345.
¹⁵ Ibid., 348.
¹⁶ To Valdés (May 16, 1789), ibid., 337.
¹⁷ Ibid., 357.
¹⁸ Ibid., 354–55.
¹⁹ Ibid., 355–56.
²⁰ Ibid., 357.
²¹ Ibid.
²² Ibid., 337, 361–62. See also Lynch, *Spanish Colonial Administration*, pp. 201, 234–36.
²³ Ravignani, *Historia constitucional*, pp. 16–17.
²⁴ See Konetzke's contribution to Congreso Hispanoamericano de Historia, pp. 250–61, esp. pp. 257–61.
²⁵ Arcila Farías, p. 255.
²⁶ Ibid., pp. 13–16.
²⁷ Ibid., p. 256. See also Molinari, passim.
²⁸ Jane, p. 85.
²⁹ Arcila Farías, pp. 22–27.
³⁰ Ibid., pp. 32–38.
³¹ Ibid., pp. 39–55, esp. p. 45.
³² Ibid., pp. 257–58, 116.
³³ Ibid., pp. 114–15.
³⁴ Ibid., pp. 258–59.
³⁵ Ibid., pp. 261–62.
³⁶ Ibid., p. 262.
³⁷ Ibid., p. 263.
³⁸ Giménez Fernández, *Las doctrinas populistas*, pp. 25–26.
³⁹ Jane, pp. 92–93.
⁴⁰ Ibid., p. 90.
⁴¹ Levene, *Historia del derecho argentino*, I 296n2.
⁴² Pp. 6–7.
⁴³ Eyzaguirre, p. 47.
⁴⁴ Gómez Hoyos, II 21. See also I 142–45.
⁴⁵ See Menéndez y Pelayo, II 547-48.
⁴⁶ Giménez Fernández, *Las doctrinas populistas*, pp. 24, 27–28, 30. See Cuevas, *La iglesia en México*, IV 515, in regard to Friar José Díaz Bravo, bishop of Durango, who died on his way to Spain as a prisoner.
⁴⁷ *La corte de Carlos III* (Madrid, 1868).
⁴⁸ Giménez Fernández, *Las doctrinas populistas*, p. 29.
⁴⁹ Ibid., pp. 28–29.
⁵⁰ Thus there are several editions of the *Política indiana, sacada en lengua castellana de los dos tomos del Derecho y Gobierno municipal de las Indias Occidentales* (2nd ed., Antwerp, 1703; 3rd ed., Madrid, 1736–39; 4th ed., Madrid, 1776), a second edition of *De Indiarum iure, sive de iusta Indiarum Occidentalium gubernatione* (Madrid, 1777), and a second edition of the *Emblemata Regiopolitica in centuriam unam redacta* (Madrid, 1779).
⁵¹ Giménez Fernández, *Las doctrinas populistas*, p. 35. Furlong, *Nacimiento*, pp. 410, 479. See also pp. 217–19, 585ff. and Tudela, I 233–34.
⁵² Hanisch Espíndola, pp. 100–101.
⁵³ *Academic Culture*, p. 86.
⁵⁴ Ibid., p. 87.   ⁵⁵ Ibid., p. 88.   ⁵⁶ Ibid.
⁵⁷ See ibid., pp. 61–89.   ⁵⁸ Ibid., p. 89.   ⁵⁹ Tudela, I 219.
⁶⁰ Ramos, *La filosofía en México*, p. 68.
⁶¹ Ibid., p. 72.   ⁶² Ibid., p. 62.   ⁶³ Redmond, p. 134.

[64] Ibid., p. 7. [65] Ibid., p. 73. [66] Ibid., p. 135.
[67] Ibid., p. 110. [68] Ibid., p. 103. [69] Ibid., p. 51.
[70] Ibid., p. 70. [71] Ibid., p. 30.
[72] Ibid., p. 43. See Ramos, La filosofía en México, pp. 72–73.
[73] Redmond, pp. 48, 31, 1, 8. See also Díaz-Plaja & Monterde, pp. 459–64, 471, 481.
[74] Tudela, I 222–23. [75] Salazar Bondy, pp. 69, 67. [76] Ibid., p. 69.
[77] Redmond, pp. 87, 103–104, 104, 53, 92, 108, 13, 11–12, 18, 22, 26, 48, 49, 55–56, 75, 80, 87, 94, 106.
[78] Salazar Bondy, pp. 566–67.
[79] Barreda y Laos, pp. 207–208.
[80] Redmond, pp. 76, 93, 99–100, 18, 35.
[81] Hanisch, p. 292. [82] Ibid., pp. 183–208. [83] Ibid., p. 210.
[84] Ibid. [85] Ibid., pp. 223–27, esp. p. 225. [86] Ibid., pp. 251–54, 277.
[87] Ibid., pp. 252–54. [88] Gómez Hoyos, I 314n2.
[89] Redmond, pp. 57, 28–29, 61, 82, 45, 24, 15–16, 102, 98, 39, 40, 96, 11, 36, 29.
[90] Ibid., pp. 34–35, 20, 55, 47, 21, 87–88, 48, 6. See also Porras Troconis, pp. 123–310.
[91] Gómez Hoyos, I 141. [92] Ibid., 215–17.
[93] Pérez Sarmiento, Proceso de Nariño, p. 84.
[94] Gómez Hoyos, I 311. [95] Ibid., 375–76.
[96] García Bacca, pp. 185–87; for Quevedo y Villegas' philosophy, see pp. 209–324. See also Redmond, p. 76.
[97] García Bacca, p. 203. [98] Ibid., p. 191. [99] Ibid., p. 327.
[100] Ibid., p. 328. See also Redmond, 101.
[101] García Bacca, pp. 338, 395–97.
[102] Redmond, pp. 44, 63–64, 65, 11, 8–9, 31–32, 66, 77, 41, 38, 37, 91, 11, 96–97, 49, 15, 12, 50–51, 63, 54, 44–45, 77, 3–4, 41–42, 105–106, 5, 49–50, 35, 80, 26–27.
[103] Moses, South America, p. 143.
[104] Furlong, Nacimiento, pp. 143–47, 147–48. [105] Redmond, p. 97.
[106] Ibid., p. 136; Furlong, Nacimiento, pp. 155–56.
[107] Furlong, Nacimiento, pp. 177–78. [108] Ibid., p. 180. [109] Ibid., p. 186.
[110] Redmond, pp. 78, 86; Furlong, Nacimiento, pp. 193–95.
[111] Furlong, Nacimiento, p. 196. [112] P. 199.
[113] Redmond, p. 19; Furlong, Nacimiento, p. 239.
[114] Redmond, pp. 24–25; Furlong, Nacimiento, pp. 257ff.
[115] Furlong, Nacimiento, p. 263. [116] Ibid., p. 264.
[117] Ibid., p. 277–90. See also Redmond, p. 95.
[118] Furlong, Nacimiento, pp. 297–312. [119] Ibid., pp. 313–16. [120] Ibid., pp. 320–27.
[121] Redmond, pp. 58, 109–10, 46. See also Furlong, Nacimiento, pp. 359–78.
[122] Furlong, Nacimiento, pp. 359–64. [123] Redmond, p. 58.
[124] Furlong, Nacimiento, pp. 364–70. [125] Ibid., pp. 370–77. [126] Ibid., p. 377.
[127] Ibid., pp. 398–400; Redmond, p. 79.
[128] Furlong, Nacimiento, p. 400.
[129] Redmond, p. 30; Furlong, Nacimiento, pp. 400–10.
[130] Furlong, Nacimiento, pp. 410–12; Redmond, p. 12.
[131] Redmond, p. 40; Furlong, Nacimiento, pp. 572–77, esp. pp. 574–75. See also Gandía, Las ideas políticas, I 320–39.
[132] Furlong, Nacimiento, pp. 579–80.
[133] Ibid., p. 384. [134] Ibid., pp. 386–87. [135] Ibid., pp. 390–94.
[136] Abad de Santillán, I 387. See also Furlong, Nacimiento, pp. 210–11. This was in application of Constitution 18, one of the many university statutes, elaborated by Father Andrés de Rada, which had governed the university since 1664.
[137] Furlong, "Suárez," p. 81. [138] Furlong, Nacimiento, p. 218.
[139] Furlong, "Suárez," p. 97. [140] Ibid. [141] I 66.
[142] Ibid. René-Moreno says, however, that the students learned these ideas from St. Thomas and that many copies of the Summa theologica could be found in Upper Peru. He himself found many in Sucre (n70).
[143] Furlong, "Suárez," p. 100. [144] I 81.
[145] Narancio, "Las ideas políticas," 108, 110–11.
[146] Furlong, "Suárez," p. 82; idem, Nacimiento, p. 216.
[147] Ibid., p. 384. [148] Eyzaguirre, p. 82. [149] Hanisch Espíndola, pp. 98–100.
[150] Ibid., pp. 98–99. [151] I 146; 146n28. [152] Ibid., pp. 146–47.

[153] Ibid., p. 147. [154] Ibid., pp. 208–10. [155] Madariaga, *El ocaso*, pp. 252–59.
[156] Furlong, "Suárez," p. 98n54. [157] Gandía, *Las ideas políticas*, I 176.
[158] New Spain, 562; New Granada, 261; Quito, 226; Peru, 413; Chile, 315; and Paraguay, 437.
[159] New Spain, 122,000 natives were left without Jesuit priests; Peru, 55,000; Chile, 7,586; Paraguay, 113,716; New Granada: 6,594. Total: 304,896 natives (Becher, p. 303).
[160] P. 150. [161] Ibid. [162] Jane, pp. 85–86.
[163] *Carta dirigida a los españoles americanos* (London, 1801), appendix to Giménez Fernández, *Las doctrinas populistas*. See also Gómez Hoyos, I 148–54, who, like Gímenez Fernández, sees a Suarezian impact on the *Carta*.
[164] Vizcardo y Guzmán, appendix to Giménez Fernández, *Las doctrinas populistas*, pp. 130, 139.
[165] *El abate Viscardo*. The book also contains Vizcardo y Guzmán's *Carta* (pp. i–lxxxviii).
[166] Ibid., p. 171. [167] See Madariaga, *El ocaso*, pp. 308–53.
[168] Hanisch Espíndola, pp. 102–103. Cf. also Hanisch, pp. 251–54.
[169] Hanisch Espíndola, p. 103. [170] Ibid., pp. 103–104. [171] Ibid., pp. 104–105.
[172] P. 82. [173] Ibid., p. 42. [174] See Hanisch Espíndola, p. 111.
[175] Ibid. [176] Ibid., p. 112. [177] Jane, p. 90.
[178] Gómez Hoyos, I 175. See pp. 155–202.
[179] Ibid., p. 200. [180] Madariaga, *El ocaso*, pp. 322, 419. [181] Ibid., p. 420.
[182] Ibid. [183] Ibid., p. 421. [184] Ibid., pp. 420–21.
[185] "Proclama de Miranda fechada en Coro a 2 de Agosto de 1806," in Instituto Panamericano de Geografía e Historia, pp. 73, 75.
In another proclamation, Miranda pointed out that his main objective was the independence of the Colombian Continent ("Proclama a los habitantes de Aruba a 17 de Agosto de 1806 e instrucciones para una comisión a Curazao," ibid., p. 80). Miranda frequently used the term "Colombia" for the whole of Spanish America (see Robertson, "Introduction," p. xxvi).
[186] See Moses, *South America*, pp. 254–99; Abad de Santillán, I 351–73; Levene, *History of Argentina*, pp. 191–202, and Ravignani, *Historia constitucional*, pp. 102–108, esp. p. 108.
[187] Lynch, "Intendants and Cabildos," 361. See also Lynch, *Administration*, p. 236.
[188] Lynch, "Intendants and Cabildos," 361–62. See also Lynch, *Administration*, p. 236.
[189] Lynch, "Intendants and Cabildos," 337. See Also Lynch, *Administration*, p. 201.
[190] Lynch, "Intendants and Cabildos," p. 362.

V

THE SPANISH LATE SCHOLASTIC FOUNDATION OF
INDEPENDENCE, 1808-1823

1. THE IMMEDIATE CAUSES OF THE REVOLUTION

ALTHOUGH THE INDEPENDENCE of Spanish America would have come sooner or later, that it occurred between 1810 and 1826 was the result of certain historical circumstances. The reforms of the Bourbon regime during the reign of Charles III[1] prepared the way for the Revolution; the Napoleonic invasion of the Iberian Peninsula was its immediate cause. But the so-called Spanish American Revolution was no revolution at all, merely the echo of events which began in Spain on May 2, 1808. As in Spain itself, so in the territories overseas, citizens acted in defense of the fatherland, in the name of the deposed King Ferdinand VII and against the Napoleonic usurpation, with deepest loyalty and in keeping with old and accepted traditions.

The Spanish Empire developed over the centuries in a framework built essentially on consent, which was precisely the reason why it lasted as long as it did. A remarkable fact about this Empire is that the more Spain's power declined, the more loyalty to the Empire increased, since its foundations were the medieval concepts of belief in God and fealty to the Crown. There was, in general, no tendency to have things changed,[2] and ideas of political independence and of republican government were entertained by only a very few individuals, such as Francisco Javier Eusebio de Santa Cruz y Espejo and Francisco de Miranda. Moreover, when the Revolution began, there were no such radical concepts, although it finally led to these goals around 1819.[3] To be sure, the Revolution never involved the Indians and the blacks, whose lot was much better in Spanish times than thereafter; they in no way benefited from independence, since under Spanish rule they had enjoyed the protection of both Church and Crown. Thus, race problems played no important role, and social revolution was neither achieved nor visualized. Social and economic structures were maintained and even strengthened, for the Spanish American Revolution was an aristocratic affair and the controversy with Spain a typical Spanish civil war.

There would have been a number of opportunities for Spanish America to engage in a revolution had there been a genuine desire for political independence; nor could Spanish military might have stemmed such a movement, for Spain had no sizable army to counter such an endeavor and Britain controlled the seas. Puerto Rico's heroic defense against the French and the English in the sixteenth century, against the Dutch in 1625, and against the English in 1797; Cartagena's stand in 1740, and Cuba's in 1762; the River Plate's repulsing of the British attacks in 1806 and 1807, and Venezuela's handling of Miranda's landings in 1806 — all clearly demonstrated Spanish

American loyalty to the Empire. Obviously, many rebellions occurred in the Spanish Empire — the Spanish world could hardly exist without them! — but these were directed against officials who had misused their authority or against abuses of the administration in general rather than against the Crown, and should not be interpreted as signs of disloyalty to or revolution against Spain. On the contrary, as Cecil Jane has observed:

> If an edict, promulgated by the authorities in America, were flagrantly violated, it was asserted, and was perhaps really believed, that the edict did not in truth emanate from the crown and that the royal will had been misrepresented; disobedience became, in fact, the truest obedience.[4]

If during the Revolution a struggle was waged in certain parts of the area for liberty and republicanism, none of the patriots ever envisioned the type of government which existed in the United States, England, or France; this is evident from both the statements and the actions of the revolutionary leaders. Jaime Delgado has pointed out, in contrast to nineteenth-century interpretations, that there was no one solution to the monarchical crisis of 1808, nor was this solution at the beginning and in all parts of the Spanish Empire the establishment of republican governments. On the contrary, the problem was extremely complex and the solutions offered gave rise to an unusual galaxy of political experiments.[5]

The Bourbon reforms, however, had gradually eroded this fealty, in spite of the demonstrations of loyalty in 1806 in Venezuela and 1806–1807 in the River Plate — to such an extent that the grievances of the *criollos* against the *peninsulares* increased in the decades prior to the actual Revolution. As Octavio Paz stated:

> The reforms undertaken by the Bourbon dynasty, particularly Charles III, improved the economy and made business operations more efficient, but they accentuated the centralization of administrative functions and changed New Spain into a true colony — that is, into a territory subject to systematic exploitation and strictly controlled by the center of power.[6]

This opposition of the *criollos* to the *peninsulares* had its origin in the structure of the patrimonial state, in which every subject is linked to the king but in no way feels himself connected to the subjects of the other kingdoms of the monarchy whom he actually regards as foreigners and intruders; it is this foundation which the Bourbons attempted to change by giving their empire a centralist, modern outlook.[7] Richard Konetzke has clearly proved that Spanish legislation did not establish a distinction between *criollos* and *peninsulares*,[8] but Spain always favored native rule, in keeping with traditional precepts which the Hapsburg dynasty continued. The *Reglamento* of December 12, 1619, repeated this general policy in stating that both *criollo* and Indian natives "as patrimonial sons must and ought to be preferred to all others who do not have the same qualities and requirements."[9] At that time the monarchy was a royal patrimony formed by kingdoms and lordships, all equal but independent, each retaining its *fueros*, privileges, franchises, and liberties.[10]

This concept began to change when the Bourbons attempted to establish a modern state. The policy remained the same in the first half of the eighteenth century, though there was greater centralism, but changed during the period of Charles III. Konetzke has shown that the change began with the meeting of March 5, 1768, under the chairmanship of the count of Aranda, in which Pedro Rodríguez de Campomanes and José Moñino, later Count Floridablanca, reported on the subject of "a policy to combat fanaticism in the city of Mexico as a result of the doctrines of the exiled Jesuits." The new policy, suggested by the two *fiscales*, amounted essentially to giving the Spanish subjects of both hemispheres the notion that they belonged to one and the same nation, but in order to encourage the new liberal spirit it was necessary to awaken a Spanish national spirit. Hence, the basis was laid for the transition from the patrimonial to the modern centralist state, which the Bourbon reforms tried to accomplish.[11] But in Europe the French Revolution marked the transition from Enlightened despotism to liberal constitutionalism, yet Spanish America remained faithful to the patrimonial state.[12] The *criollos* officially indicated their opposition to the change from Hapsburg patrimonial to the Bourbon modern state in the famous *Representación al Rey del Cabildo de la Ciudad de México* in 1771; in this report the *criollos* asked for the same rights as the *peninsulares* enjoyed and emphasized traditional feelings for autonomy. It is a theme which is often repeated in other circumstances, especially in the years 1808 to 1810.

The consequence was the persistence of medieval political thought: (a) the obligation of the king to rule with justice and to act for the *bonum commune*, and his risk of deposition if he should become tyrannical; (b) should the ruler for any reason be absent, power would revert to the people, the source of all sovereignty.[13] Thus, in sum, the Spanish American Revolution had purely Spanish and medieval origins and little, if anything, to do with economic and social matters, with foreign intellectual currents, or even racial conflicts; to the extent that these factors did in part exist, they reflected only secondary elements.[14] The various rebellions in Spanish America before the events of 1808 were always fought for the king and against the despotic behavior of some of his lieutenants, while the Revolution resulted from the application of another medieval concept, the *pactum translationis*, and led to the establishment of juntas in Spanish America between 1808 and 1810.[15]

There were other factors which were of prime importance and which aided the revolutionary movement. First, because of the distance from the mother country, authorities in the Indies wielded vast powers which in a geographically different situation would have been more limited. The importance of the geographical factor was highlighted by the British blockade at the time of Spain's alliance with France (1796–1808), and particularly after the naval engagement off Trafalgar when Spain's decaying sea power was almost totally destroyed.

Secondly, the extent of the Empire, and, in particular, the immense size of the interior, and the dependence of vast regions on urban centers, had created a strong regionalism accompanied by a vigorous local patriotism[16] all too often antagonistic to the viceregal capitals (Charcas, Asunción, and Montevideo toward Buenos Aires; Santiago de Chile toward Lima; Quito, Panama, and Caracas toward Bogotá; Guatemala toward Mexico). This local nationalism was strong enough to cause the formation of independent units quite apart from the viceregal political jurisdiction to which they once belonged. Indeed, it was so strong that the viceroys and captains general of the eighteenth century, in contrast to their predecessors, were actually in a subtle way more symbolic personifications of the various nationalities over which they presided than, strictly speaking, the king's representatives in the Indies.[17]

Thus, when the Revolution came, it represented in reality a long-smoldering protest against "the abandonment of the old, and Spanish, system of colonial administration and the attempt to substitute for it a new system, of which the spirit was not Spanish."[18] Only a new approach — a reversal of the Bourbon centralist policies of Madrid — which took into account the factors which geography and the new political realities dictated and which the count of Aranda had foreseen, could have saved the Empire, or postponed and lessened its fragmentation. In his famous Memorandum of 1783, Aranda, with prophetic insight in regard to both a possible independence of Spanish America and the encroachment of an expanding United States, had proposed three independent Spanish American kingdoms (New Spain, Peru, and Costa Firme) headed by the three *infantes* and linked to Spain only dynastically.[19] A similar plan was proposed later by Manuel Godoy, the Prince of Peace, in 1804. The proposal was later revived by the liberals of 1820 when Spain proposed the division of Spanish America into three sections with capitals in Lima, Bogotá, and Mexico City (the River Plate area was by then considered lost). Each section was to be headed by a regent selected by the Spanish king and *Cortes* and subordinated to the latter. Each part was to contribute to the support of the Spanish government by a payment of an annual subsidy. Trade between Spanish America and the Peninsula was to be an internal matter. The project was not revealed because public opinion was considered unprepared for such a transformation; the *pronunciamiento* of Agustín de Iturbide in New Spain in 1821 canceled the entire matter.[20] Actually, Aranda's plan itself had a forerunner in the suggestion by a Dutchman, Friar Nicolás de Witte, a friend of Emperor Charles V, who wrote to his sovereign in 1552 to suggest the appointment of a prince of the blood to govern the Indies independently of Spain. As those at the time of the Revolution would, de Witte argued as early as the mid-sixteenth century that only decentralization could save the Spanish Empire.[21]

The Revolution was helped by the existing social stratification, with a noticeable division of the upper classes, and aggravated by financial instability, certain negative consequences of agrarian policies, and the fiscal policy of Charles III with its oppressive multiplication of taxes and commercial monopolies. In the political realm, the fact that high positions were seldom conferred by the Crown on Spanish Americans aroused a typical Hispanic reaction of hurt pride.[22]

The Revolution also included certain economic, socio-political, and psychological elements, such as the conservative desire to remain in power (strongly represented in the *consulados* of Lima and Mexico), or the endeavor of those who favored free trade to eliminate the monopolies of Cádiz and Lima (greatly entrenched in Venezuela and Buenos Aires). Furthermore, there were autonomists, such as Manuel Abad y Queipo in New Spain, or Francisco José de Caldas and Antonio Nariño in New Granada; Juan José Segovia and Jaime Zudáñez in the River Plate; and the Franciscan Friars Diego Barranco and José Gabriel Aguilar, the Jeromyte Father Diego Cisneros and Toribio Rodríguez de Mendoza, a priest in Peru,[23] who envisioned only certain reforms. And there were still others whose actions resulted in consequences they did not seek, such as Juan José Castelli's invasion of Charcas, the Royalist terror in Quito, José Tomás Boves' terrorism against the Spanish American bourgeoisie and the tragic attack on the Alhóndiga de Granaditas which in the end paralyzed Miguel Hidalgo y Costilla's revolt in New Spain. The psychological element also included idealists, such as Miranda, Simón Bolívar, José de San Martín, Bernardo O'Higgins, and Bernardino Rivadavia on the Spanish American side, and Francisco Javier de Venegas, Mariano Osorio, and General Calzada on the Royalist, who later were sacrificed, and the usual pragmatists and opportunists — some such as Viceroy José Fernando de Abascal y Sousa, Viceroy Félix María Calleja del Rey, and Pablo Morillo left Spanish America before the drama's end, while others such as Iturbide and Governor Gabino Gainza changed sides at an opportune moment.[24]

But all these elements alone would not have brought about the independence of Spanish America. Indeed, independence there is inconceivable without the fundamental link to historical developments in Spain itself. In an attempt to strengthen the blockade of England, Napoleon tried to gain control of the Iberian Peninsula, in which plan he was greatly aided by the scandalous situation at the Bourbon court in Madrid. Thus, Napoleon furnished the direct cause of the Spanish American Revolution by forcing the abdication of the Spanish Bourbons, Charles IV and Ferdinand VII, on May 5, 1808, in Bayonne. These abdications led in turn to a constitutional crisis throughout the Spanish Empire and opened the question of succession and of sovereignty in its widest sense.

The constitutional crisis resulting from Napoleon's intervention not only led to the Spanish War of Independence, but was instrumental in effecting a far-reaching and thorough political and constitutional reform of the entire Spanish Empire. The Napoleonic usurpation thus produced a revolution which transformed the institutional structure of Spain itself and found an extension in Spanish America. Julio V. González advanced this point of view in the 1930s[25] and Enrique de Gandía took it over, rejecting the term "revolution" to describe what in his opinion was simply an expansion of institutional transformation.[26] Marcelino Menéndez y Pelayo aptly sketched the situation in Spain when he said that

> Never, in the long history of Spain, did a nation so gloriously awaken after such a dull and heavy dream as Spain did in 1808. Spain had gone through a century full of misery and moral debasement, of an administrative despotism with neither greatness nor glory, of disgraceful impiety, of disastrous peace treaties, of wars favoring the children of the royal family or our greedy neighbors, of accelerated ruin or miserable disuse of what remained of old freedoms, of tyranny by the Church under the deceiving title of *protection* and *patronage*, and, finally, of decayed art, sick philosophy, and a literature with neither power nor efficiency — all dissimulated with a certain glitter of material civilization which even the very same historians of the Positive School explain as shallow, artificial, deformed, and false.... To recover the national conscience too long atrophied by the office fetishism of the *most august and most beneficent person of His Majesty*, it was necessary that a sea of blood run from Fuenterrabía to the Bay of Cádiz, and that in these red waters we could regenerate ourselves after having been abandoned and sold out by our kings.[27]

Obviously, then, the Spanish War of Independence represented both a struggle against an invader and a political revolution. The war was not only resistance to the French armies, but a religious war against the ideas of the French Revolution — a crusade in the real sense of the word — yet at the same time an internal purification. Spain's glorious past would be invoked, and foreign models of the period would be an inspiration in this outspoken domestic reform. This was another attempt, as was so often the case in Spanish history, to find harmony and balance between religion and rationalism, between Spanish traditionalism and the modern European spirit. It is ironic that the many reforms which the free Spanish government introduced in a moderate manner and with the cooperation of very distinct and varied ideological and political forces paralleled those decreed in a more extremist way by the illegal regime of Joseph Bonaparte and his radical liberal Spanish friends who now returned to Spain with the Napoleonic armies (the Urquijos, Ceballos, Cabarrús, O'Farrils, Piñuelas, Mazarredos, and Azanzas).[28]

The crisis of Bayonne had interrupted normal life: representative institutions had disintegrated, the political constitution had been suspended, and the authorities had disappeared. Neither the people nor the elite groups were really prepared to take the steps required. As Enrique Lafuente Ferrari pointed out:

> The Spaniards had no opinion on anything, no collective sentiments other than those very noble and elementary [emotions] of loyalty to their monarchs and of rebellion against an alien power.[29]

The people did not follow the politicians, French ideas were not accepted, and the primitive reactions of the Spanish people soon were to eliminate the "subtle and artificial building set up in Cádiz."[30] This situation was repeated on the other side of the Atlantic: the *criollos* attempted to capitalize on the situation in the Peninsula but the problem was the same: "To aspire to too much but [to be] capable of little."[31] Unable to understand subtle political forms, the people in Spanish America reacted with an emotional response, which was aggravated by the specifically American environment, with the result characterized so well by Bolívar at the end of the struggle: "He who makes a revolution plows the sea."[32] A misguided government in the Peninsula failed to recognize the similarity of the situations on both sides of the Atlantic. Both the *Suprema Junta Central* and the Regency attempted to maintain the centralist policies of the Bourbons and thus missed the opportunity to straighten out the situation in keeping with the *criollos*' grievances regarding traditional Hispanic regionalism.

Thus the events of Bayonne, when Napoleon forced the two kings to abdicate and placed his brother Joseph on the Spanish throne, had extraordinary consequences in the Peninsula and in the Indies, since the king was the nominal source of all legislation. The Spanish people, not wishing to betray their legitimate kings and to recognize a foreign ruler without being consulted, refused to recognize the arrangements of Bayonne. Their glorious resistance received support mainly from the *cabildos*, which similarly were the instruments of freedom after 1809–1810 in the Spanish American Revolution.

The political developments in the Peninsula led implicitly and explicitly to the application of constitutional theories, which were in accordance with

Spanish individualism and idealism and with the whole Spanish tradition. Upon the abdication of the legitimate king, the *pactum translationis* was applied; civil authority reverted automatically to the people who had designated the king their ruler.[33] The people were now legitimately empowered to take civil authority in their own hands, since there was no legitimate Spanish monarchy as long as the king did not return. This the juntas proclaimed, using the very terminology of the Scholastic writers of earlier periods.

The Scholastic influence is beyond any doubt operable during the Spanish and Spanish American Wars of Independence, and represents a part of the Spanish liberal movement, which reached its summit in the Spanish Constitution of 1812, the common work of Spaniards and Spanish Americans.

Just as Charles III had prepared the ground for the coming Spanish American Revolution with his French-inspired reforms, Napoleon in his turn provided the catalyst which in time became the intellectual key to Spanish American independence. When the government council created by Ferdinand VII fell in April 1808, the Spanish people took up arms against the French invaders (May 2, 1808). The uprising led to the establishment of juntas throughout the country, a political device soon to be followed in Spanish America. The first places to establish juntas in the Peninsula were Murcia, Santander, and Seville.[34] These raised their defiant voices and negotiated with their respective neighbors as if they represented sovereign states or republics, and thus followed the traditions of the *Reconquista* when the local town councils exercised similar powers. On May 25, 1808, the Junta of Asturias officially declared war on France, which meant that Spain and its Empire were in a state of war with Napoleon. This event not only determined the future actions of the various juntas but pitted *afrancesados* and traditionalists against each other, as in the case of Martín de Alzaga and Santiago de Liniers in the River Plate.[35]

The establishment of juntas was in the best Hispanic tradition; they were made up of men of the higher classes — from among the nobility, the clergy, the religious orders, and the universities. Their diversity and their spread to all corners of the realm were also in keeping with Hispanic regionalism and separatism. The establishment of the juntas was an expression of Scholastic theories regarding the origin of civil authority — the Suarezian *pactum translationis*. Since "people" in Spanish was connected with both people and town — the double meaning of *pueblo* — and was in keeping with Spanish urban civilization and its psychological traditions, the concept of popular sovereignty was linked to the major towns, i.e., the provincial capitals. This popular power was thus inherent in the juntas which represented Spain in its struggle against Napoleon for the legitimate rights of King Ferdinand VII.

The multiplication of juntas led finally to the establishment of the *Suprema Junta Central* of Aranjuez, on September 25, 1808, which later was transformed at Seville into a Regency (January 29, 1810). Composed of two delegates from each of the established juntas, the *Suprema Junta Central* tried to set up an organized central authority, although many of the other juntas remained in existence. Both the *Suprema Junta Central* and the later Regency led the war of resistance in the name of the deposed King Ferdinand VII against Napoleon and the regime of Joseph Bonaparte, and at the same time called for a political and constitutional reform in which all Spaniards of both hemispheres were to participate.

The *Suprema Junta Central* and the later Regency demanded the loyalty and obedience of the various parts of the Spanish Empire and were prepared within the spirit of Spanish liberalism to put the constitutional relations of the Peninsula with overseas Spain on a new basis. To introduce the liberal spirit in a moderate way into Spain and its Empire, and to modernize the country politically and constitutionally, the Spanish *Cortes* was to be convoked as soon as possible, and one of its first tasks was to draft a charter. The new spirit found expression in the declaration of equality of rights between Spain and Spanish America (January 22, 1809)[36] which called for Spanish American representation in the *Cortes*, and included procedures for representation of the overseas provinces — New Spain, Peru, New Granada, River Plate, Guatemala, Chile, Cuba, Puerto Rico, Venezuela, and the Philippines — in this junta.[37] Each of these provinces was to elect a deputy, who was to be chosen from among three candidates proposed by the larger towns. The names of the deputies thus elected were to be presented to the royal *acuerdo*, presided over by the viceroy, so that the *audiencia* could elect three persons one of whom would represent the political views of a viceroyalty in Spain. A similar procedure was to be followed in the captaincies general. These procedures were decided upon on January 22, 1809, and were then adopted in Puerto Rico (July 17, 1809) and New Granada (September 16, 1809). That other provinces did not follow suit may well be the result of the desperate military situation in Spain, as an outcome of which the *Suprema Junta Central* was forced to flee to Seville, where it was transformed into a Recency which finally established itself in Cádiz. That the Spanish American provinces were to send one delegate each (a total of nine), while the Spanish provinces were allowed two delegates each (a total of thirty-six), was an inequality, as Camilo Torres was to point out in his *Report of Grievances* to the *Suprema Junta Central* on November 20, 1809.[38]

On January 1, 1810, the first modern Spanish *Cortes* was convoked in Seville for assembly on March 1, 1810. The liberals pleaded for the re-establishment of the old liberties, for the legal representation of the Spanish people as known in the constitutional system during the Middle Ages; such assemblies had last met during the early years of the reign of Emperor Charles V. The calling of the *Cortes* was a reaction to Enlightened despotism.

On February 14, 1810, a new call was made to Spanish America to send deputies to Cádiz (though with a smaller numerical representation), to participate in the common task of providing the entire Spanish Empire with a new political and constitutional structure, in keeping with the decree of equality of rights. The actual delegation from Spanish America to Cádiz was limited in numbers, since not all the overseas provinces accepted this invitation; half the Spanish American delegates were elected in that city.[39]

The *Cortes* (Regency and deputies) assembled on March 25, 1810, in Seville, where the *Suprema Junta Central* had withdrawn because of the war, solemnly declaring by oath to uphold certain principles — later incorporated into the Constitution — such as the Catholic religion, integrity of the nation, and the dynastic rights of Ferdinand VII — and to comply faithfully with the political representation received from the people. It had 107 members, of whom twenty-seven were Spanish American delegates. A decree of September 24, 1810, was read in which the Assembly declared that the deputies were constituted in general and extraordinary *Cortes* in which the national sovereignty resided, and that the legitimate king was Ferdinand VII whose renunciation in favor of Napoleon was null and void.[40]

When the *Cortes* issued the decree of equality of rights between Spaniards and Spanish Americans on October 15, 1810, it confirmed and sanctioned

> the unquestionable concept that the Spanish dominions in both hemispheres form one and the same monarchy, one and the same nation, and one and the same family, and that therefore those born in said European or overseas dominions are equal in rights to those of the Peninsula.[41]

However, this decree signified a total break with the concept which had linked the Indies with their different kingdoms to the Crown of Castile and León. With the elimination of this link and the replacing of the metaphysical union with a purely rational construction, another step was taken in the direction of Spanish American independence. Thus the captivity of the king and the proclamation of the new link between Peninsular and overseas Spain were two significant historical and constitutional developments which were to be of great importance in the further evolution of Spanish America.

The liberals of Cádiz — who were following the Bourbon policies to create a modern state by destroying the old patrimonial state — had overlooked the important fact that the unity of the Spanish Empire was of a metaphysical nature, linking the Indies to the Crown, but not to the Spanish nation, the Spanish people, or Spain as such. They failed to see that by destroying this metaphysical link and by placing the union of the different parts of the Spanish Empire on a rationalistic foundation — equality of rights — in keeping with modern views and thus in disagreement with tradition, they themselves opened the gates of revolution, already ajar with the abdication of the legitimate kings.

They likewise failed to realize when they established the juntas that this constitutional right could just as well be invoked by Spanish America, since the concept of the equality of both metropolitan and overseas Spain was not a new idea in 1809–10 — Juan de Solórzano Pereira had mentioned it in the seventeenth century.[42] Actually the proclamation of these rights by Spanish America occurred soon afterward, in direct application of the *pactum translationis*, not of Rousseau's *Contrat social*, or of any other foreign political theory. The fact that all successors to Ferdinand VII in the Peninsula (Joseph Bonaparte, the Juntas of Asturias and Seville, and the *Suprema Junta Central* and the Regency) requested acknowledgment of their authority from the Spanish American territories created confusion and "indirectly granted a *de facto* sovereignty to the Spanish Americans."[43] To these facts must be added the decisive element of the entire "revolution" in Spanish America: "the absolute lack of comprehension on the part of the Spanish rulers."[44]

Melchor Fernández Almagro maintained, with good reason, that Spain did not need to imitate Rousseau or Locke for popular sovereignty: it could look to its great tradition of Late Scholastic thinkers, particularly Suárez.[45] Julio Alemparte offered the view that the establishment of republics in the former Spanish American Empire could not possibly be linked to the ideology of the Enlightenment, particularly the French manifestation, but only to the Late

Scholastic thought of Suárez, Mariana, and all the other *magni Hispani* of the period.

> Indeed, the Voltaire of monarchical ideas admired the Chinese despotism about which Quesnay had written a complimentary treatise; Montesquieu was a partisan of the English monarchy; Rousseau, of the monarchy or the aristocracy depending on whether it concerned larger or medium-sized peoples; Mably, of the monarchy; and " . . . even those who like d'Holbach, Helvetius, Diderot go further and even abhor the royal institution do not count, more or less expressly, with the possibility of a French Republic." Only in small communities did Rousseau believe in the republican system. Nor should it be forgotten that this system triumphed in Spanish America — as it did in Anglo-Saxon America — in spite of the strong opposition of the Spanish American monarchical currents and even of patriots and eminent personalities such as San Martín, Bello, Belgrano, Egaña, etc. — partisans of constitutional monarchy.[46]

The application of the *pactum translationis* was considered just as dangerously revolutionary in 1808–10 as it was during the eighteenth century. It began not only the Spanish American Revolution but also the division between absolutists and liberals who in Spanish America were later to call themselves Royalists and followers of independence, respectively. Logically, it also led to the Balkanization of the old Spanish Empire in America.

When the crisis of Bayonne found an echo in the Spanish Empire and led to the Spanish American Revolution, it was not necessarily leading to the severing of political ties with Madrid. The so-called Revolution aimed at certain political and constitutional reforms but not independence. Had the Peninsula been more farsighted and understanding, the Spanish Empire could have remained intact for many years, since

> it was not until a number of years after Napoleon's deposition of the Spanish king that the goal of independence became clearly defined and was pursued in the military campaigns conducted separately by Simón Bolívar and José de San Martín.[47]

But even then the balance tipped toward independence only by the end of the 1810s and early 1820s. Nationalism was not an ingredient of the Spanish American Revolution.[48]

> Simón Bolívar, the *líder máximo* of independence, was torn between the generous vision of a transnational amphictyony of the Hispanic American peoples and a keen perception of the feuding local oligarchies and earthbound peasantries from which only phantom nations could be formed. One surmises that Bolívar's use of the term "amphictyony," dictated by the Enlightenment fashion of neoclassicism, was a surrogate for his instinctive sense of a Hispanic unity rooted in a political and religious heritage having medieval coloration.[49]

Spain and Spanish America alike agreed that the regime of Joseph Bonaparte did not represent the legitimate government, and that the forced abdication of the legitimate king could result only in a provisional solution. But the Spaniards interpreted the *pactum translationis* simply, understanding it to mean that the Spanish people on both sides of the Atlantic could exercise power, and they thus wanted all regions of the Spanish Empire to recognize the *Suprema Junta Central*, or the Regency, respectively, until the return of the king. The Spanish Americans, on the other hand, declared that with the abdication in Bayonne overseas Spain was free from all obligations toward the Peninsula and could legally establish its own separate governments; these governments would first provisionally and then permanently solve the immediate constitutional problem of the various parts of the Spanish Empire, since authority reverted to them in accordance with the agreement entered into in the sixteenth century between the Spanish Crown and the conquistadors.

The constitutional foundation of the dispute between Spain and Spanish America was clearly recognized by the agent of the United States, Henry M. Brackenridge, who was sent to South America in 1817 and 1818 to report on political conditions in the various countries. There is no clearer testimony for the entire controversy than Brackenridge's report:

> The Spanish Americans, as the descendants of the first conquerors and settlers, ground their political rights on the provisions of the code of the Indies. They contend that their constitution is of a higher nature than that of Spain; inasmuch as it rests upon *express compact*, between the monarch and their ancestors. They say, it was expressly stipulated, that all conquests, and discoveries, were to be made at the expense of the king. In consideration of which the first conquerors and settlers, were to be *the lords of the soil*; they were to possess its government, immediately under the king, as their feudal head; while the Aborigines were given to them as vassals, on condition of instructing them in the Christian religion, and in the arts of civilization. It was in virtue of this compact, that the American junta denied the right of bodies similarly constituted in Spain, to exercise authority over them, as this right alone appertained to the king, in his council of the Indies. They objected, on the same grounds, to the Spanish Cortes, which proposed to act in the name of the captive king; and admitting that it was regularly constituted, its authority could not lawfully extend over any other than the European part of the empire. There appears to be nothing clearer than this reasoning. Spain had no right to assume the sovereign's name for any other purpose, *than to provide for her own safety*, there being no conexion between her and the Indies, but through the sovereign; that conexion ceased the moment the sovereign was in a situation where his acts were null, and the royal authority for a time completely interrupted. The Peninsula, as a component part of the empire, was entitled from necessity to establish a Cortes, for the purpose of taking care of its own concerns; and each viceroyalty of the Indies, had an equal right to erect its junta for the same purpose. Here is the foundation of the dispute between Spain and the Indies; the conduct of the Spanish in Europe, as well as those in authority in America, justly created disgust. The Europeans, instead of resorting to Cortes in the first instance, successively erected juntas in the provinces, which not only claimed sovereignty over the rest of the Peninsula, but likewise over the Indies.[50]

The Spanish Americans held the opinion that Spanish America was not obliged to recognize the *Suprema Junta Central* or the Regency: the paths of the two parts of the Spanish Empire diverged. But just as Spanish America as a whole was justified in separating from Spain in the absence of a legitimate ruler, so was it logical and justified that the different historical regions would use this same principle, not only against Spain, but against the capitals of the various viceroyalties as well. When the military plans of Buenos Aires against La Paz, Asunción, and Montevideo failed; when the endeavors of Lima toward Chile collapsed in 1818 through the actions of San Martín and O'Higgins; when the two-year occupation of Central America by Vicente Filísola in the name of the first Mexican Empire came to an end in 1824; and when Greater Colombia, the Bolivarian re-establishment of the old viceroyalty of New Granada, disintegrated after the death of Bolívar, the Balkanization of the old Spanish Empire was an accomplished fact.

The Spanish American juntas used the same terminology as the Spanish juntas and Scholastic thinkers, and they too were linked to the institution of the *cabildo*. In true Spanish spirit, the *cabildo* took power and at the first opportunity deposed viceroys and governors as representatives of a nonexistant authority, using the syllogistic statement on which the independence of Spanish America was intellectually based:

> The vassalage of the Indies was a tie which joined them, not to metropolitan Spain, but to the legitimate king of Castile and León [major premiss]; therefore, when Ferdinand VII renounced the throne, that political link was broken forever [minor premiss]; hence, the monarchical civil servants, representatives of a nonexistent power, have no right to political authority, and the community of the people, the customary holder of sovereignty, has to provide for the designation of its legitimate authorities [conclusion].[51]

It has been suggested that the establishment of revolutionary juntas in several parts of Spanish America in the name of the legitimate rights of Ferdinand VII was a mask, a camouflage, to hide the real goal of the revolutionaries: political independence from Spain. John Lynch, for instance, points out, in regard to the junta of Buenos Aires, that

> The formal deference to Ferdinand was a convenient device, a temporary tactic. By assuming the "mask of Ferdinand" the patriots hoped to make capital out of the remnants of royalist sentiment in the people of the Río de la Plata, to avert a Spanish counter-revolution and to secure the support of Britain, Spain's powerful ally. Moreover, it involved no great commitment, no real sacrifice, to invoke the sovereignty of a man who was no longer sovereign, to defer to a ruler who did not rule, to speak for a crown that was in captivity. The mask of Ferdinand was quickly torn off when, after the defeat of Napoleon, Ferdinand was restored to power, indeed to despotism, in Spain. Then the creole revolutionaries had to admit that they did not want him;[52]

in a short time the policies of the new regime had reached a point of no return:

> In short, the *de facto* change was so revolutionary that it is relatively unimportant whether the insurgents deceived themselves or others with the "mask of Ferdinand."[53]

This opinion does not seem to be warranted; it, unfortunately, is a continuation of a liberal point of view which cannot consider seriously such devotion to an unhappy and captive monarch. Enrique de Gandía stated it clearly when he said in regard to the same events in the River Plate:

> on May 25, 1810, Cornelio de Saavedra, Mariano Moreno, and the other members of the Second Junta, which some textbooks like to call the First, swore on their knees with their hands on the Bible, and in the presence of the crucifix and of the representatives of the people of Buenos Aires, to be loyal to Ferdinand VII and to return these lands as soon as he should recover the throne. This was the principal aim of May 25, 1810: to preserve these lands for the beloved Ferdinand VII until he should return from his captivity and could again govern them.[54]

Gandía commented further that it is inconceivable that in so many places and at the same time so many people would have maintained such a deceptive attitude.

> In other words: all the inhabitants of Buenos Aires, Caracas, etc., wished the independence of a new nation, but when the news of the loss of Spain arrived they falsely, hypocritically, manifested loyalty to Ferdinand VII. A unique case in the history of the world, with thousands of inhabitants all liars and traitors. Unbelievable history which so many historians have been teaching for more than a century.[55]

Not only was the devotion to Ferdinand VII sincere, it represented the extraordinary hatred of Napoleon and the French in the River Plate.[56] It also represented,

> on the one hand, the symbol of the anti-French reaction, and, on the other, [support for] the Crown [which] had for centuries upheld the claims of the people against the claims of the [Spanish] American *encomenderos* and oligarchs which had not always been reasonable.[57]

The crucial point in this debate was, obviously, the return of Ferdinand VII, but the question would apply only to Argentina, since all other areas were by that time no longer masters of their own destiny. Some regions had not rebelled at all: Peru, Guatemala (Central America), Cuba, Puerto Rico, and Santo Domingo, which by 1808 had freed itself from French rule; in Mexico Morelos' rebellion was under control and would be crushed by 1815. In Venezuela the Second Republic had ended in disaster by July 1814, and New Granada was slowly recaptured by the Royalists (Cartagena, December 1815; Bogotá, May 1816). Quito was already Royalist by 1812 and Upper Peru partially since Huaqui (1811) and totally after Sipe Sipe (1815). Finally, with the battle of Rancagua Chile was back under Spanish control by October 1814.

The River Plate was the only area where the willingness to return the government to Ferdinand VII could be tested. But here, too, Paraguay and Uruguay were exceptions. Both had become *de facto* autonomous and independent for essentially regional reasons: Paraguay because of its isolation, and the strategically more important *Banda Oriental*, far from terminating its ordeal, would be Portuguese by 1817. Thus, Argentina was the only area to test this willingness, and, indeed, there is evidence that the viewpoint of Lynch, John Edwin Fagg, and others is at least open to some question. That Manuel de Sarratea would offer, on behalf of the Argentine government, to return these territories to the control of Ferdinand VII after his release from captivity in 1814 provides conclusive evidence that the "mask of Ferdinand" was no empty talk, in spite of all the agonies which Argentina underwent after 1810: political differences between *criollos* and *peninsulares*, ideological struggles, territorial losses, and foreign intrigue and pressures. It is a fact that independence in Argentina was not declared until 1816, i.e., after all hopes of a reconciliation with the obstinate Ferdinand VII had failed. The blame for this situation has to be laid squarely on the king, who refused any concession toward a constitutional readjustment of his Empire just as he had in Spain itself. Hence, the chasm widened further.

Actually, Lynch indirectly admits that it was Spain and not Argentina which had refused to accept a compromise — that Argentina would remain within the Spanish Empire under a more autonomous constitutional framework which would have undone many of the Bourbon centralist policies — in quoting *El censor* of September 19, 1816:

> In 1810 we only wished to preserve freedom against foreign domination . . . . But the Spaniards began to make war on us and tried to impose despotism in America. We still placed all our hopes in Ferdinand. But these hopes were destroyed when he actually reached the throne, for he waged bloody war against America. And we began to detest so unjust a King.[58]

Bartolomé Mitre specifically mentioned the *pactum translationis* as the ideological basis of the Spanish American Revolution in referring to the diplomatic mission of Bernard de Sassenay to the River Plate, who was charged with persuading Santiago de Liniers to join the French cause. Mitre pointed out that the events of Bayonne and the fall of the Spanish monarchy were then used by both the *peninsulares* and the *criollos* for different political ends. The Spaniards wanted to stay in power, while the *criollos* prepared the ground for political change; but both groups, in spite of their profound divisions, were in agreement in resisting the French usurpation and remaining loyal to the legitimate ruler. It was thus that *peninsulares* and *criollos* happened to be united fatally in one and the same political thought though with different future goals; both believed Napoleon would win in the Peninsula and thus they organized themselves for their different goals, while Spain was setting the example in the partition of royal power when the various provinces resumed their sovereignty. A true revolution was operating within the constitution of the Spanish monarchy and especially between the people and the government.[59]

Mitre argued that following Roman law the old Spanish legislation linked the royal oath, not only to the person of the ruler but also to the territory in all its integrity of things and persons; in regard to the remaining matters, feudal law prevailed, which by such an act bound one man to another, not only by virtue of the area but mainly because of the person. It was on this basis that Solórzano Pereira, "the most profound Spanish lawyer" as Mitre called him, derived the right of the Spanish kings to the Indies, not so much from the right of discovery, conquest, and colonization, but from the papal donation of Pope Alexander VI, who, acting as the *dominus orbis*, had given the Indies to the Spanish kings as a personal feudal possession.[60]

It was this theory of personal rule which resulted in the proclamation of the concept that Spanish America owed personal obedience only to the legitimate sovereign on whom it alone depended, and that once the legitimate ruler was dethroned and found himself in captivity, Spanish America belonged to its loyal vassals. Once Spain had been conquered by a usurper, Spanish Americans, being bound to the absent ruler, who ruled though he did not govern, owed no allegiance to Spain, and, hence, in the absence of a legitimate monarch, Spanish America ought not to follow the fate of the Peninsula — an argument which grew in cogency once Spanish territory was conquered. Independence was the logical conclusion to this set of premisses.[61]

The opposing tendencies of the various groups lent different interpretations to this theory: the Spaniards considered themselves the only ones justified to rule over the Indies in the absence of the legitimate sovereign, while the settlers, maintaining the only legal bond which in fact was broken, proclaimed fealty to an imaginary king and prepared themselves for his inheritance in the Indies. These tendencies became manifest in 1808 within three forces: the legal authority of the colony, the *peninsulares*, and the *criollos*; the first aspiring to tranquillity, the others to predominance and autonomy or independence, respectively. In the River Plate the viceroy and the *audiencia*, as representatives of the old order and faithful to the traditional right of the delegated authority with which they were invested, wanted at any price to preserve the integrity of the Spanish monarchy according to the spirit of the written legislation, while Liniers as French by birth and Spanish by choice was more apt to follow a policy of wait and see. A slightly different situation arose in New Spain where the viceroy sided ambiguously with the Spanish Americans — the *cabildo* of the city of Mexico — while the *audiencia* represented the old regime. The result, as Mitre observed, was that at first both authorities in the River Plate proclaimed loyalty to Ferdinand VII in a rather lukewarm way (August 15, 1808, in Buenos Aires), exhorting the population to await the final outcome in the Peninsula.[62] But this in turn provoked the rise of the Spanish element, which was followed by that of the *criollos*, who preferred the old regime to a foreign yoke. Thus, the final reply to Sassenay was

> the solemn oath of allegiance to Ferdinand VII which was celebrated with all pomp in the midst of enthusiasm by both Spaniards and [Spanish] Americans, [an act] which was attended by General José Manuel de Goyeneche, the emissary of the Junta of Seville to the River Plate, hostile to Napoleonic influence.
>
> The [Spanish] Americans demonstrated with this act a new theory, which, though in perfect agreement with the spirit of the absolute monarchical government, was essentially revolutionary in view of the logical consequences deduced from it. They maintained, as explained, that [Spanish] America did not depend on Spain but on the monarch to whom they had sworn obedience, and that in his absence all his delegations had elapsed in the metropolis. This theory of government was to lead them later not to recognize the Spanish authorities in America and to reassume his rights and prerogatives by virtue of the absolute sovereignty converted into popular sovereignty.[63]

With the exception of New Spain, Peru, and Montevideo (which established a non-revolutionary junta), all areas of Spanish America set up revolutionary juntas; in New Spain, Peru, and Montevideo the Spanish element was stronger politically, and the viceroys and governors remained faithful followers of the new government in southern Spain. The *cabildos* of Buenos Aires, Santiago de Chile, Asunción, La Paz, Quito, Bogotá, and Caracas rejected the authority of the *Suprema Junta Central* and of the Regency and established local juntas for the defense of the legitimate rights of King Ferdinand VII.

The Spanish American *cabildos* actually represented the real foundation of future states. The movement which began in the year 1808 in favor of *de facto* autonomy or independence led gradually and logically toward independent republics. This development was again a symbol of that everlasting Spanish individualism, local patriotism, and regionalism, now linked to a provincial capital.

Because of the history and tradition which had molded the Indies so closely to Spain, Spanish America had by necessity to reflect the political development of the Peninsula in its three different historical phases between 1808 and 1820:

(a) The abdication of the Bourbon dynasty in Bayonne (May 5, 1808) was the key to the entire Spanish American Revolution. The monarchical crisis broke the link which united the lands overseas (New Spain, New Granada, Peru, and the River Plate) to the Spanish Crown, thereby creating an extraordinary political and constitutional problem. Local juntas arose in 1809 (La Paz, July 16; Quito, August 10) and in 1810 (Caracas, April 19; Buenos Aires, May 22; Santiago de Chile, July 16 and September 18; Bogotá, July 20; and Querétaro, September 16); though at first autonomous and monarchical, some declared independence (Caracas, July 5, 1811; New Granada [Cartagena], September 11, 1811; [Cundinamarca], July 15, 1813; New Spain [Chilpancingo], November 6, 1813), or implied it [Buenos Aires, January 31, 1813, in its General Constituent Assembly]).

(b) The king's return or absolutist reaction in Spain (1814–20) turned the tide in Spanish America against the revolutionaries and strengthened the Royalist position. Viceroy Abascal recaptured lost territory in Peru, Chile, and Quito; Calleja del Rey reconquered land in New Spain, as did Morillo in Venezuela and New Granada. Had the victories not turned the Royalists into extremists, they might have foreshadowed final triumph. But the immoderate policies of Morillo and Francisco Casimiro Marcó del Pont were followed by the somewhat conservative political course of San Martín and Bolívar, who with the Argentine Declaration of Independence at Tucumán (July 9, 1816) and the Congress of Angostura (February 15, 1819) gained popular support for the revolutionary cause.

(c) The liberal movement (1820–23), finally, was decisive for Spanish American independence. Authority was too weak and immobilized in Spain to be able to send the necessary soldiers to the Indies. Also, a liberal government in Spain, anticlerical and masonic, was repulsive to the traditional, conservative elements in New Spain and Peru. Iturbide's conservative *pronunciamiento* proclaimed independence in New Spain (February 24, 1821) and San Martín's entry into Lima (July 8, 1821) deprived the Royalists of all assistance.

Throughout these three different stages the Suarezian *pactum translationis* was used to justify several political solutions, in spite of the fact that some of them were diametrically opposed to others. Yet before the various experiments could be put into practice, there was an attempt to find a solution to the Bayonne crisis by applying the famous "Brazilian formula." This formula was simply to transfer the sovereignty of Ferdinand VII to his sister Carlota Joaquina, princess of Brazil, and wife of Regent Dom João. In the opinion of Manuel Giménez Fernández, the formula originated with Floridablanca and was supported in America by Goyeneche, the emissary of the Peninsular authorities, who was able to convince Archbishop Moxó y Francolí and León y Pizarro, the president of the *audiencia* of Charcas, of the viability of the solution, including its recognition of the *Suprema Junta Central*. Though this solution was well received by Admiral Sir Sidney Smith, commander of the British naval station in South America, Goyeneche's intrigues were unsuccessful, and formed part of the background for the establishment of the junta of La Paz of May 25, 1809.[64] It is interesting to note that the "Brazilian formula" found sympathy with the Argentine *criollos*, headed by Manuel Belgrano, who wanted to solve the constitutional crisis with the establishment of a monarchical government, since the principles of North American democracy had neither been popularized nor penetrated South America.[65] A constitutional monarchy which would embody absolute power was Belgrano's general idea, and he hoped to realize his project with the help of Carlota Joaquina. It was a plan which found support with such men as Castelli, Hipólito Vieytes, Juan José Paso, Juan Martín de Pueyrredón, Nicolás Rodríguez Peña, and others, but it failed because of the opposition of the Regent Dom João, Carlota Joaquina, and Lord Strangford, the British minister in Rio de Janeiro, who hated Ferdinand VII's sister.[66] It failed in particular because Carlota Joaquina pursued her own ideas of recovering absolute power for her brother; she was thus just as obstinate and unrealistic as her brother would be in 1814, not realizing that a return to absolutism would be counterproductive.

2. The First Act: The Constitutional Crisis and the Establishment of Juntas (1808–14)

The Napoleonic usurpation of the Spanish throne provided an ample opportunity for the application of the Scholastic theory, in the sense that the authority which God had given to the legitimate ruler with the consent of the people through a true compact had now been invalidated. As a matter of fact in any case where the lawful ruler disappears without a legitimate heir and the throne is usurped — *tyrannus ab origine* — the people have no option; they must act to recover that very authority which had previously been given to the legitimate monarch.

As soon as the events of Bayonne became known in Spanish America, this Suarezian *pactum translationis* was used for different purposes: (*a*) to determine the holder of sovereignty in a territorial sense, (*b*) to establish the legitimate basis for the political organization of sovereignty, and (*c*) to proclaim the sovereign or the delegated character of the civil authorities in Spanish America. But countries followed individual patterns; each area acted in accordance with its own historic traditions and political circumstances.

a. The Holder of Sovereignty in a Territorial Sense

This question arose as soon as juntas were established, and several different approaches were advanced. On the Spanish or Loyalist side there were, within the general lines of loyalty to the Peninsular authorities, two main positions: one followed the territorial area of the viceregal borders and succeeded in New Spain until the very end of the Revolution (1808–21) but failed in the River Plate; the other, a rather *sui generis* position, based on the smallest administrative unit and dictated more by regional and local conditions than by Peninsular events, triumphed temporarily in Montevideo (1808–14). On the Spanish American side there were three approaches: the community or unity approach based on the territorial integrity of Spanish America; the viceregal or confederacy approach, based on the borders of the old viceroyalties; and the provincialist, founded on the smallest administrative units. Both the community and the viceregal revolutionary approaches failed, and only the provincialist — the Balkanization of the Spanish American Empire — succeeded, the result, in large part, of historic, geographic, and, in some cases, economic reasons.[67]

In all these cases — whether on the Spanish or Spanish American side, and whether on a community, viceregal, or provincialist basis — the argument was essentially the same, the *pactum translationis*, in the sense that the parties who invoked this reasoning always justified their actions by claiming the right of the people to assume authority in the absence of the legitimate ruler. The provincialist case finally prevailed for the simple reason that the only link which had provided unity for so long had been severed; hence, in true Iberian fashion the various regions in Spanish America now demanded the same rights in regard to the viceregal capitals as the revolutionary capitals did toward the metropolis. Although some of the reasons the provincialists advanced had not only an historical and geographic foundation but also an economic basis, the justification for their actions and their legal challenge always rested on a Scholastic premiss.

i. *The Spanish or Loyalist Approaches*

aa. *The Viceregal Case*

Viceroyalty of New Spain. At the time of the events of Bayonne the viceroyalty was governed by José Joaquín Vicente de Iturrigaray y Aróstegui, who had arrived in Mexico in 1803. Iturrigaray, with whom the first act of the Mexican drama unfolded five years later, was a military man with quite a distinguished career, although as a favorite with Manuel Godoy, the powerful Prince of Peace, he was somewhat tarnished. In a short time he was able to gain the sympathy of the Mexicans, no easy task for a successor of brilliant envoys, some of whom — the second count of Revillagigedo, in particular — had left their mark on the country. Iturrigaray's arrival coincided with the famous visit of Alexander von Humboldt for whom New Spain was at the time the most cultured nation of Spanish America and who in 1804 had shown Iturrigaray the draft of his *Political Essay on the Kingdom of New Spain* praising the Mexicans and thereby increasing their national pride.

The new viceroy began his term with the installation of the famous statue of Charles IV by Manuel Tolsá — *el caballito* — and the introduction of vaccination. His popularity was quite high, as is evident from a document in the Mexico City town hall, citing his good qualities.[68] Yet the war against Britain required the raising of funds and led to the famous *Real Cédula de Consolidación* (December 26, 1804), which affected the religious orders; aimed against ecclesiastical properties, it thus hurt many people and fostered resentment. Another controversial problem was his plan for the defense of the viceroyalty, which called for the abandonment of Veracruz, but the town was able to intercede successfully in Madrid for an opposite point of view.[69]

Iturrigaray's virtues were generally recognized — even later by the insurgents — especially his interest in public works, but it became known that he was using his high office to increase his personal wealth. Iturrigaray's venality, and his ties with the unpopular Godoy and an undignified regime, made him an easy target of increased discontent; Spaniards on both sides of the Atlantic felt ashamed by this and looked to the future Ferdinand VII as the redeemer of the nation.

The year 1808 brought matters to a climax. With neither moral authority nor effective government, confused by a court interested only in its own selfish designs, and misled by the Napoleonic projects, the Spanish people suddenly arose in an almost blind fury against internal corruption and mismanagement and against the foreign foe. When the news of the plot of Aranjuez arrived in New Spain with the bark *Atrevida*, which had left Cádiz on April 21, 1808, it caused a sensation, since the country was not accustomed to palace revolts deposing an old king and installing his son.[70] The *criollos* in New Spain interpreted the plot as a rebellion against an immoral and hated government and considered their own situation in similar terms. Iturrigaray was put in an unusual situation: he was a *godoyista*, yet he had achieved considerable popularity among the Mexicans. He thus drifted toward the *criollo* cause, while the Spanish element expected a purification with the new king. As in other parts of the Empire, the Spanish American party had its strength in the *cabildos*, while the Spanish party was entrenched in the *audiencias*.

The events of 1808 propelled both *cabildo* and *audiencia* to action, though in opposite directions. The *cabildo* of Mexico took the initiative on July 16, 1808, and on July 19 it decided to follow the example of the capitals of the viceroyalties of the River Plate and New Granada, in arrogating to itself the right to speak on behalf of the entire viceroyalty. It then resolved to consider the abdication of the kings at Bayonne null and void, to assume provisionally the government for the area until the viceroyalty would make a final decision, and to allow the viceroy to remain in his post until further notice. It further decided that the government of New Spain should remain as it was before the events of Aranjuez, i.e., under the sovereignty of Charles IV and "the Prince of Asturias," with express orders that the viceroy should not alienate it to any power, including that of Spain, or to any person, including Charles IV or the Prince of Asturias, and that the viceroy ought to give an oath of allegiance to the kingdom to this effect.

The decisions of July 19 were officially communicated to the viceroy, who accepted them, and to the *audiencia*, which considered them scandalous and dangerous to the interests of the Spanish Empire. The *audiencia*, meeting as *Real Acuerdo* on July 21, then declared that: (a) the city government of Mexico had taken over the representation of the entire kingdom without any legal right to do so and without consulting the provinces — a position identical to that taken in 1810 in Buenos Aires in regard to the viceroyalty of the River Plate; (b) the proposals of the *cabildo* of Mexico were not in accordance with the laws; (c) the legally established authorities should continue, there being no need for a provisional appointment or an oath, since they had not witnessed any change from within; (d) an oath, which had already been sworn, was valid from both legal and sentimental viewpoints, and one for which they would shed their lives for their kings and natural lords, and (e) what was needed at the moment was the union of all without parties and factions for the sake of preserving these dominions for the royal house of Bourbon.[71] Finally, the *Acuerdo* also expressed his gratitude to the *cabildo* — although its feelings were quite different — called for thanksgiving to the Almighty, and asked for the repeal of the *Real Cédula de Consolidación*. Hence, by July 21, 1808, the disagreement among the most important branches of government in New Spain was complete: the viceroy siding with the city, while the *audiencia* was hostile to the moves of the *criollos*.

On the 23rd the *cabildo* again met, to put into practice the principles which it had announced on the 19th; it convoked a general congress of all established authorities to implement those decisions. The viceroy was fully aware of the *cabildo*'s intentions and, on the same day, without waiting for a legal opinion from the *audiencia*, called for the famous junta, which would be the representative of popular sovereignty. In Enrique Lafuente Ferrari's views, Iturrigaray never believed in the junta but felt that, in view of circumstances, it might keep him in his high position, though perhaps with a different title.[72] The junta, to be held shortly, would resolve only two rather harmless points agreed to by the viceroy: (1) to communicate the news received from the Peninsula, and (2) to express its indignation and to defend these dominions for the Spanish monarch.[73]

At the end of the month New Spain received the news of the revolt of the Spanish people against Napoleon. It gave renewed hope to the Spanish elements in the viceroyalty; and the people at large were caught in a frenzy for Ferdinand VII and against Napoleon and Godoy similar to that felt in Spain itself and in other parts of Spanish America.

On August 3, the *cabildo* sent to the viceroy its reply to the opinion of the *Acuerdo*, stating its surprise concerning the legal stance adopted by the *audiencia*; in regard to its assumption of the full sovereignty of the viceroyalty of New Spain, it cited several documents of the sixteenth century in its defense, and requested the convocation of a general junta, and even a *Cortes*, as was done later in the Peninsula, in order to have its decisions implemented.[74]

On August 5, the viceroy informed the *audiencia* about the petition of the *cabildo* and asked that it state its opinion in order to proceed in line with the wishes of the city of Mexico. The *Acuerdo* replied the next day, stating that of fourteen members thirteen opposed the holding of a meeting of a junta; that in the absence of the legitimate king the legally established authorities should continue their work; and that if in the Peninsula juntas had been set up it was a circumstance of war, a situation which did not exist in New Spain. The *Acuerdo* then pointed out that the grave danger in the announcement of the principle of popular sovereignty was its promotion of a division into castes.[75] With great perspicacity the *oidores* of the *audiencia* stated further that if the principle should be applied in all its logic, sovereignty would have to revert to the Indians of New Spain.[76]

The viceroy did not follow the opinion of the *audiencia*, however, deciding to go along with the petition of the *cabildo*; thus he called for the famous meeting of Tuesday, August 9, 1808, in spite of the express opposition he had received from two lawyers, Manuel del Castillo Negrete and Antonio Torres Torija, and from those representing the interior of the country (such as the conde de la Cadena from Puebla, Juan Antonio Riaño from Guanajuato, Nemerio Salcedo, commander of the internal provinces), and from the *audiencia* of Guadalajara.[77]

The meeting of the *junta general* of August 9, 1808, which was to prepare an assembly of the *Cortes* of New Spain, was a heterogeneous assembly of 82 members from the *audiencia*, the *ayuntamiento*, and the *consulado*, including the ecclesiastical authorities and the native governors of the districts in Mexico City. The meeting officially acknowledged the sovereignty of Ferdinand VII; recognized, at the request of the city, the Bourbon dynasty and the order of succession as established in the *Recopilación de Autos* of Castile in Book V, Title 7, Law 5; and stated that so long as the king did not return to his monarchy they would obey no order from the French emperor or from any authority which would not emanate from his legitimate rule, nor acknowledge any supreme junta of those or these kingdoms unless ratified by his Catholic Majesty.[78] A clash of opinions resulted. The Spanish or colonialist approach to the Bayonne crisis was upheld by the *oidor* Guillermo de Aguirre, the leader of the Spanish party, who then proclaimed the right of Spain and the Spaniards to rule over the Spanish American territories, a viewpoint echoed in Spain by Pablo Vicente, deputy to the *Cortes*:[79]

> As long as there exists a piece of land in Spain, Spain must rule over the Americas; and as long as there exists a single Spaniard in the Americas, that Spaniard must rule over the Spanish Americans, authority coming to the sons of the country only when there is no longer any Spaniard there.[80]

Opposing the views of Francisco Primo de Verdad y Ramos de Aguascalientes, who had proclaimed the right of New Spain, the Peninsular Spaniards, who formed the majority, thus ended the first, peaceful attempt at gaining autonomy for the area.

Neither the town council nor the *audiencia* was satisfied with the meeting and the official *Acta*. The *audiencia* had reluctantly agreed to the junta, while the *cabildo* had gone to the meeting with great hopes left unfulfilled. One of the main arguments upheld by the *audiencia* was the point advanced by the *cabildo* that the absence of the legal monarch meant a vacuum in sovereignty, and implied high treason; if the argument had been accepted, it would have meant that all officials no longer had any legal foundation.[81] The Spanish party was particularly upset since the final *Acta* specifically mentioned that New Spain would not recognize any *Junta Suprema* of the Peninsula; this wording increased its suspicions about the viceroy, and it determined to keep a watch on his further conduct and to take the necessary steps in defense of what it considered the Spanish imperial interest.

The victory of the Spanish cause found expression a few days later when Ferdinand VII was publicly given an oath of allegiance on August 13, 1808. Yet the Spanish party blamed Viceroy Iturrigaray for his embarrassing and highly questionable conduct. The situation was aggravated by incidents between the *audiencia* and the viceroy, one of which revealed the ambiguity of Iturrigaray's position and contributed to the crisis. The *audiencia* decided to stamp all documents with the head of Charles IV until new stamps with that of Ferdinand VII should arrive from Spain — a practice which had been followed after the death of Charles III in 1788 — and informed the viceroy accordingly. Iturrigaray responded that he had ordered a stamp "valid for the reign of Ferdinand VII" and that one with the head of Charles IV could not be used:

> no stamps with the head of Ferdinand VII can come from Spain since he will not return for many years; if stamps come bearing the coat-of-arms of the Duke of Berg, they should not be used much less those coming from the Junta of Seville.[82]

The abyss between *audiencia* and viceroy widened in subsequent weeks. Both *audiencia* and *consulado* had been opposed to the moves of the viceroy and felt that action was necessary to prevent the worst. In Gabriel de Yermo they found a leader, and on September 16, 1808, the Spanish party deposed Iturrigaray and deported him to Spain, putting in his stead Pedro de Garibay, who began a campaign of persecutions. Garibay was replaced by Archbishop Francisco Javier de Lizana y Beaumont on July 19, 1809, but since many of the archbishop's policies were disliked by the Regency, he was asked to turn over the government to the *audiencia* (May 8, 1810) until the newly appointed viceroy, Francisco Javier de Venegas, should arrive from Spain (September 13, 1810). The Spanish party, having won the contest for power in 1808, remained in control in spite of the revolutions of Hidalgo, José María Morelos, and Vicente Guerrero until the very end of the Spanish American Revolution, and successfully maintained the integrity of the viceroyalty.

Viceroyalty of the River Plate. The events of Bayonne divided opinion in the River Plate as they did elsewhere in the Spanish Empire. The call of the *Suprema Junta Central* for delegates to be sent to Spain was heeded only slowly and with little interest as long as Viceroy Liniers feared the possible establishment of juntas in his area.[83] Actually, Liniers was losing popularity, not because he had said he preferred to be French rather than Spanish, or of some letter he had written to Napoleon, but because he had voiced the opinion that whichever government should triumph in Spain ought to be recognized.[84] When the *Suprema Junta Central* was no longer in existence, the River Plate was still electing deputies to represent the region in the Peninsula.

The idea of a junta in the River Plate on the model of the Peninsular originated with the wealthy Spanish merchant Martín de Alzaga, the former mayor of Buenos Aires, leader of the Royalist group and hero of the defense of Buenos Aires. His idea was put into practice in Montevideo on September 21, 1808; as a friend to Governor Francisco Javier de Elío, and through him, Alzaga had actually prepared the establishment of this junta.[85]

Alzaga and his friends Esteban Villanueva, Olaguer Reinals, Juan Antonio de Santa Coloma, among others, endeavored to set up a junta in Buenos Aires on January 1, 1809, as had been done in Montevideo.[86] Interpreting Napoleon's march through the Peninsula as the final loss of Spain to the French emperor, the Alzaga group — which represented half of Buenos Aires — planned to form a junta in order to establish a kind of New Spain on the River Plate in which the Spanish element would be dominant, to demand the resignation of Liniers, and to call on the interior to send delegates to Buenos Aires for each provincial *cabildo*. They were thus separatists and had chosen the first day of January when the *cabildo* elected the new members for the coming year. They failed in their plot when Cornelio de Saavedra leading creole troops came to the aid of Liniers.[87] Hence, Buenos Aires had to wait for May 1810 before it had its junta. The failure to establish a loyalist junta on January 1, 1809, meant a victory for the *criollos*. Emilio Ravignani views this as the result of a combination of troop pressure and popular will[88] — neither the first nor the last of such actions.

Long before the May Revolution, the people had taken matters into their own hands, as a result of the increasing confidence and prestige which the *cabildo* of Buenos Aires had enjoyed since the last decade of the eighteenth century and, in particular, of the successful resistance to the British invasions. On August 14, 1806, the *cabildo* gave command of the troops to Liniers — what Ravignani calls the "first revolutionary *cabildo*";[89] on February 6, 1807, it deposed Viceroy Sobremonte; on September 20, 1808, it prepared the junta in Montevideo; and on January 1, 1809, it wanted another junta like those in Spain.[90] There were also the events of Chuquisaca and the junta of La Paz of July 16, 1809, when the people of Upper Peru feared they would be delivered to the much disliked Carlota Joaquina. Thus, at the time of the May Revolution the people of the River Plate was well accustomed to the system of juntas.

The First Junta of Buenos Aires was set up on May 24, 1810, and lasted one day. It was established as a result of deliberations of the general congress of May 22 and May 23, 1810, which in turn was the consequence of the news, received on May 13, 1810, that the Peninsula was almost totally in the hands of Napoleon.[91] This First Junta actually accomplished the earlier aims of the Alzaga group. Following in the footsteps of the abortive attempt of 1809, it wanted the interior to participate in a future general congress, although the views of the new viceroy Baltasar Hidalgo de Cisneros were not as firm as Alzaga's had been in this future assembly. Cisneros — who had arrived in the River Plate (Montevideo) on June 30, 1809, and who had been appointed viceroy by neither Charles IV nor Ferdinand VII but by what Ravignani called an "improvised government" such as the *Suprema Junta Central de Gobierno de España e Indias*[92] — wanted the formation of a Spanish American Regency with an exchange of views among all established political powers. Finally, Alzaga had planned the separation of the River Plate from an occupied Spain, while the Second Junta of May 25, 1810, ordered that all deputies who came to Buenos Aires must swear allegiance to Ferdinand VII and his legitimate successors.[93] Thus, there were profound differences in these three cases, but in all of them the *pactum translationis* was the basic principle.

An approach similar to that of the *oidor* Aguirre in Mexico City occurred in Buenos Aires at the famous meeting of the *cabildo abierto* of May 22, 1810, although in the Argentine case the Spanish party was not victorious. Events came to a head in 1810. As a result of the bad news from Spain which he did not hide,[94] Viceroy Cisneros issued a proclamation on May 18, 1810, which included the promise to consult local leaders and the interior, since the loyalists knew that the provinces were more conservative and loyal to Spain. It was a plan for a preventive counter-revolution.[95] On May 20, the mayor of Buenos Aires, Juan José Lezica, informed the viceroy about the serious agitation in the capital and among the troops, all demanding an open *cabildo*. The viceroy was told on that occasion that if the *cabildo* did not call for a *cabildo abierto* the people would take the initiative. Thereupon the viceroy held meetings with military leaders, and on May 21, the *cabildo* agreed to a *cabildo abierto* on the next day which moved toward a general congress (May 22 and 23, 1810).

In the famous meeting of May 22, 1810, attended by some 225 *vecinos*, the Spanish party lost, by a vote of 155 to 69, the different Spanish American positions.[96] The Spanish party, headed by Bishop Benito de la Lué y Riega, had voted for the continuation of the viceroy — alone or in association with others. It was in this meeting that the bishop, in justifying his vote, stated that there was no reason at all to discuss the position of the viceroy,

> since as long as there were Spaniards in America it was they who should be in command, and that authority could only come to the sons of the country when no Spaniard no longer resided in it.[97]

But the *criollo* majority had opted for other solutions, which amounted basically to the end of the viceroy's functions and the establishment of a local junta which would assume the authority until the provincial deputies should arrive.[98]

On the 23rd the *cabildo*, following the decisions of the general congress, resolved to establish the junta and to invest the viceroy with its chairmanship, arguing that it was entitled to do so on the basis of the general congress of the 22nd, which had left the composition of the junta to the discretion of the *cabildo*. When it discovered that the troops opposed this interpretation and that they had asked for publication of the election results and an end to the viceroy's functions, the *cabildo* issued a proclamation that it would immediately proceed with the election of the junta without giving any details. On May 24 the *cabildo* established what amounted to the First Junta of Buenos Aires, with the viceroy as president and associated with two Spaniards, the priest Juan Nepomuceno de Sola and the merchant José Santos Inchaurregui, and two *criollos*, Juan José Castelli and Cornelio de Saavedra. This junta, which had retained the deposed viceroy, was exactly the Spanish formula of Bishop Lué y Riega, the minority vote of the 69 of May 22, except for the names of two of the members.[99] The *cabildo* then proceeded to have this solution confirmed by the oath of the troops; it seemed that the Spanish party had won the day.

Yet the revolutionary element, which felt that it had been cheated — especially Domingo French and Antonio Luis Berutti — agitated so that the junta returned the authority given by the *cabildo* that same day and asked that it proceed to the election of persons who could merit public confidence. During the night, at the home of Nicolás Rodríguez Peña, the revolutionaries worked on the petition with the names of those who should be part of the new junta. In view of the strength of the sentiments reflected earlier in the majority vote of May 22, this petition was accepted and led to the events of May 25, 1810: the establishment of the Second Junta (which is officially called the First) and the forced resignation of the viceroy. Thus, the Spanish party failed, and with it the formula of Bishop Lué y Riega. In Buenos Aires, unlike New Spain, it was the *criollos* who prevailed.

Viceroyalty of New Granada. The events of Bayonne also had repercussions in traditional New Granada. As news came in from the Peninsula, the viceroy, Antonio Amar y Borbón, convoked a meeting of notables on September 5,

1808, which with the unanimous consent of both *criollos* and *peninsulares* proclaimed allegiance to the Peninsular authorities, declared war on France, and sent financial aid to Spain.[100] Amar y Borbón then proceeded to protect the viceroyalty from outside attack and to cope with possible internal subversion, though loyalty to Spain was overwhelming. Robert L. Gilmore has stated that

> It is well to emphasize that catastrophe in Spain caused in the empire an explosion of loyalty to king and empire and of grave fear for the safety of the Church. It is possible that these sentiments reached their peak in the viceroyalty of Nueva Granada.[101]

and that the

> Broad similarity of reaction in Spain and the empire to the imperial crisis is striking evidence of the strength of Spanish institutions and culture overseas.[102]

However, the revolutionary junta of Quito, set up on August 10, 1809, changed the atmosphere in New Granada proper. Although the Quito rebellion was not well received in other parts of the viceroyalty, it forced the viceroy to take some action and influenced *criollos* like Camilo Torres, the *asesor* of the *cabildo* of Bogotá, who, while supposedly condemning the action of the revolutionaries, ended by confirming their arguments — i.e.:

> that the rebellion was "the effect of the distrust of that kingdom in the authorities that govern it. They fear being handed over to the French and they complain because of it of the mysterious reserve of the government in communicating news, of the delay in preparing defenses, and of various unjust actions toward the Spanish Americans by those who command."[103]

On September 5, 1809, the viceroy called a meeting for the next day, composed of members of the *audiencia*, the *cabildo*, and the clergy, and including royal officials, *hacendados*, and notables of the city of Bogotá, in order to decide on measures in regard to Quito. In this meeting the *criollos* "approved the principle but not the means used by the *quiteños*,"[104] thus declining any strong action against the revolutionaries.

The meetings of September 6 and 11, 1809, in Bogotá, deciding to persuade rather than to strike, opened a Pandora's box, which eventually was to end the Royalist government in New Granada, since the arguments of the *quiteños* were essentially those of the *criollos* of Bogotá. The opinions expressed in the September meetings by important *criollos*, such as Torres, Frutos Joaquín Gutiérrez, and José Gregorio Gutiérrez Moreno, the *síndico procurador general* of the *cabildo* of Bogotá,[105] and similar viewpoints incorporated in Torres' *Memorial de Agravios* only foreshadowed the revolution in New Granada proper of July 20, 1810. Thus, the revolutionary junta of Quito crystallized the attitudes of the *criollos* and gradually led to conspiracy, which then erupted on that day with the deposition of the viceroy and the establishment of New Granada's new revolutionary junta.

The events in the years 1808–10 in Bogotá were not really different from those in the viceroyalties of New Spain and the River Plate. In all three cases, the *cabildo* was the instrument favoring the Spanish American cause while the *audiencia* interpreted the *pactum translationis* in a purely Spanish and colonialist sense. The debates of the Bogotá meetings of September 6 and 11, 1809, resemble those of the assembly in Mexico City of August 9, 1809, and those of the May Revolution in Buenos Aires a year later. In the end the Spanish cause lost in 1810 in Bogotá as it had in Buenos Aires, and Viceroy Amar y Borbón had the same fate as Viceroy Cisneros in the River Plate; yet in New Spain the greater strength of the Spanish party forced the resignation of Viceroy Iturrigaray in view of his ambiguous stand, and resulted in a totally different situation.

bb. *The Provincialist Case*
Viceroyalty of the River Plate (Uruguay). The provincialist case is linked to the *Banda Oriental* but comprises two different stages: the first, 1808–14, is connected with the town of Montevideo and is a loyalist affair; while the second, from 1811 to 1817, began in the interior under the leadership of José Gervasio Artigas and is a *criollo* affair. In both cases, however, the legal theory in the challenge of Montevideo to the viceregal capital first, and of the interior of the *Banda Oriental* against the Royalist stronghold of Montevideo later, was based on the Scholastic theory of the *pactum translationis*, even if in the case of the second challenge, certain constitutional documents like the *Instrucciones del año XIII* do contain different, i.e., Enlightened, ideological currents of thought. Both cases, moreover, are so Spanish in nature, that it would be hard to conceive of them in a different cultural environment.

Long before Uruguay became an independent country, there existed two tendencies in the area: one, of the *vecinos* of the town of Montevideo, who sensed the great future of the port and engaged in commercial activities; the other, of those interested in the conquest and colonization of the interior where they fought Indians and gradually established a cattle industry.[106] Both tendencies developed during the eighteenth century and led to separate revolutions at the time of Napoleon's usurpation of the Spanish throne. Moreover, Montevideo was neither an intellectual center nor a spiritual bastion like so many other places in Spanish America, but a growing port; in its hinterland there was no aristocracy — its settlers "never saw a viceroy, an *oidor*, or a bishop"[107] — and the economic system was not based on slavery.

In contrast to the older Spanish administrative centers (New Spain and Peru, and even New Granada), the River Plate was a rather heterogeneous creation, with different geographical regions and racial backgrounds, which since its establishment in 1776 had had insufficient time to mold its parts into one homogeneous whole.[108] The *Banda Oriental* was only one example, since by 1810 the entire area had disintegrated; even the main body, the future Argentine Republic, would not have succeeded in maintaining its unity if Juan Manuel de Rosas had not imposed it from above. In the opinion of Juan E. Pivel Devoto, the *cabildo* of Montevideo was characterized by such a strong local, autonomist, and provincialist stand that neither viceroy nor *audiencia* would have had much influence. Thus, in the *Banda Oriental*, geography, economic factors, and its military role in regard to the border with Brazil awoke in its people a typically Spanish attitude, which resulted in the autonomist and provincialist positions of both the *cabildo* and the guilds of ranchers and merchants of Montevideo.[109]

Although the Spanish cause had lost in Buenos Aires and Paraguay in the aftermath of Bayonne, it triumphed temporarily in Montevideo. The city had aided Buenos Aires during the British invasions when Santiago de Liniers freed the viceregal capital. But with the developments in Spain in 1808 Montevideo established a junta, since Governor Francisco Xavier de Elío in Buenos Aires had differences with Liniers, who in the meantime had been appointed acting viceroy. On September 21, 1808, the *cabildo abierto* established a junta which declared loyalty to Spain, a right which the viceregal authority in Buenos Aires did not recognize, since the city was the capital of the viceroyalty of which the *Banda Oriental* was a part.[110]

Underlying the situation was an historic rivalry between the two cities, a clash of interests, which erupted in 1808. Montevideo, as the capital of the *Banda Oriental*, was founded in 1720 in reaction to Portuguese encroachments centered in their base Colônia do Sacramento, which had been set up in 1680. The *Banda Oriental* was an important region of the Spanish Empire in various ways;[111] it commanded access to the River Plate and was a buffer between the two rivals, Spanish River Plate and Portuguese Brazil. But Montevideo's more favorable geographic position on the Atlantic brought about an increasing rivalry with Buenos Aires, particularly after the latter city was made the capital of the viceroyalty of the River Plate in 1776. From then on Buenos Aires became more aware of the increasing importance of Montevideo, which was further secured by the treaties of Madrid (1750) and San Ildefonso (1777), acknowledging the right of Spain to the *Banda Oriental* and eliminating Portuguese rule over Colônia. Just as Buenos Aires was to exercise control over its surrounding territory, it was logical that Montevideo would do the same in its area. Thus, when Montevideo, because of the importance of the *Banda Oriental*, was assigned its own governor, it acquired a national identity of its own, which was enhanced by its continuing political and economic development.

To these military and political aspects was added the economic. In the eighteenth century the area had become a haven for contraband, a fact which sorely distressed the mercantile interests in Buenos Aires; after 1778 and the *Pragmática de Libre Comercio*, the economic dispute worsened. Legal trade was no less distressing to Buenos Aires, for Montevideo enjoyed the benefit of a better geographic position. Thus, as the eighteenth century drew to a close, Buenos Aires attempted to control and even to reduce Montevideo's importance. Its own position was enhanced when it obtained a *consulado* in 1794, though it refused all requests from the neighboring harbor for similar rights.[112]

The establishment of a customs office in Montevideo in 1779 had stimulated especially the trade in hides. While these developments had broken the monopoly of the viceroyalty of Peru, it gave Montevideo an increasing edge over Buenos Aires by stimulating agriculture and trade, and decreasing contraband. When Montevideo obtained the privilege of introducing slaves into the River Plate, it became, in the years after 1787, the main center of the slave trade in the area; although this type of trade benefited mostly the Portuguese, it resulted in a fierce struggle for supremacy between Montevideo and the viceregal seat. The antagonism was heightened in 1795 when Montevideo was allowed to trade (on a trial basis) with the Portuguese areas of Brazil. In 1798 the *consulado* of Buenos Aires protested against these privileges on the basis that they were damaging to the commercial position of the viceregal capital.[113] Thus, the hostility between Buenos Aires and Montevideo existed long before the political controversy between Liniers and Elío exploded in the aftermath of Bayonne.

The commercial jealousies were further aggravated by administrative antagonism. The Buenos Aires *consulado* held jurisdiction over the entire viceroyalty, but the merchant interests in Montevideo refused to recognize it since doing so would mean the payment of taxes for use outside the *Banda*. They protested unsuccessfully in 1794 and petitioned the Crown in 1799 for the establishment of a *consulado* in Montevideo. Because of an unfavorable report by the viceregal authorities, the Crown rejected the request in 1803.[114] Moreover, the intendant system, introduced in the viceroyalty in 1782, had bypassed Montevideo and the *Banda Oriental*. The then governor of Montevideo, Joaquín del Pino, tried to remedy this situation in 1785 when he suggested the expansion of the administrative jurisdiction of the city. When this was denied, the *cabildo* of Montevideo, with full support of the local interests and the interior, petitioned the Crown in 1797 for the abandonment of its old borders of 1726, realizing that the city could hardly prosper without some kind of enlargement.[115]

By the nineteenth century it was obvious that Montevideo had evolved because of certain privileges which the mercantilist system had granted the city, though the new ideas of economic liberalism were gaining ground. The economic development, which included increased slave trade and contraband, and the growing disputes with Buenos Aires, combined to give a strong and permanent character to the two prevailing local interests, the Guild of Merchants of the city, and the Association of Ranchers and Cattlemen of the interior.[116]

Further polemics between the two cities regarding financial contributions ordered by the *consulado* of Buenos Aires and the general view in Montevideo that the viceregal authorities did not concern themselves with the problems of the *Banda Oriental* induced the city to find its own solutions. It made plans to improve its port with its own resources, and again petitioned the Crown for its own *consulado* and *intendencia* (1802–1804).[117] The justification for these measures on the basis of Montevideo's growing importance was clearly demonstrated when the Crown was also petitioned to abandon the customs office in Buenos Aires (1805).[118]

The British invasions of the River Plate introduced new tensions: Commodore Popham's blockade hurt Montevideo and benefited foreigners; Viceroy Sobremonte's measures for the *Banda Oriental* were received with mixed feelings. However, the conquest of Buenos Aires momentarily smoothed the differences between the two rivals in a spontaneous demonstration of loyalty to the mother country, and the commercial interests in Montevideo made a considerable contribution toward the liberation of Buenos Aires.[119] Furthermore, the first capture of Buenos Aires by the British added a significant political element to Montevideo's importance and again showed the vitality of the *cabildo*. Basing its decision on the fact that the viceroy had withdrawn to the interior, that the *audiencia* had been suspended, and the *cabildo* of Buenos Aires was under foreign control, the *cabildo* of Montevideo, on July 18, 1806, proclaimed its governor, Pascual Ruiz Huidobro, the "Supreme Chief of the Continent," with full powers to take all steps necessary for the liberation of the viceregal seat.[120] This measure was a prelude to the later establishment of the viceregal seat in Montevideo and a further indication of the area's increased unity and autonomy.

The second British invasion resulted in the capture of Montevideo (February 3–September 9, 1807) and the introduction of free trade. Buenos Aires did not aid Montevideo in its liberation, and, levying taxes on the *Banda Oriental*, later accused Montevideo of having welcomed the British occupation to further its own designs, citing as proof of this the goods the British had left behind which the merchants of Montevideo, to recoup earlier losses and sacrifices, tried to introduce into other parts of the viceroyalty. All this resulted in the resurfacing of the old antagonisms and the increasing of Montevideo's resistance against the domineering claims of the viceregal capital.[121] As a result of the aid which Montevideo had given to Buenos Aires, in 1807 it again petitioned to become the seat of a *consulado* and an *intendencia* — hence the mission of Nicolás Herrera and Manuel Pérez Balbás to Madrid — pointing out its own loyalty to Spain while Buenos Aires had so easily fallen into British hands.[122] The viceregal denial of these petitions convinced Montevideo that Buenos Aires was acting selfishly and in the worst traditions of colonialism as it was also doing in its own Argentine interior.

The liberation of Buenos Aires, and of Montevideo on September 9, 1807, resulted in the appointment of Santiago de Liniers as viceroy of the River Plate; he in turn designated Francisco Javier de Elío acting governor of Montevideo.[123] Serious conflicts between them led a few months later to Elío's resignation. But on December 2, 1807, a sizable number of people invaded the *cabildo* of Montevideo demanding the return of Elío. When Liniers viewed these procedures as rather revolutionary, the *cabildo* of Montevideo, arguing in defense of autonomy, replied that "popular juntas, far from being prejudicial, were convenient and should be rewarded," and that, in keeping with the popular wishes, the *cabildo* would have to ask that any procedures against these individuals be dropped.[124] It thus took an action foreshadowing the events of the following year.

When Elío was confirmed in his position in 1808, the king appointed him the commanding general of the entire *Banda Oriental* as well.[125] Hence, his government represented another stage in the evolution of the future Uruguay, and the unity of the *Banda Oriental* was thus achieved legally; but the situation between Buenos Aires and Montevideo could only worsen.

The constitutional crisis of Bayonne, the threat of a Napoleonic expansion, and the fears of further Portuguese encroachments added to the already existing antagonism between the two cities and the two men. It was thus unlikely that Montevideo and Buenos Aires would act in the same way when the news of Bayonne arrived in the River Plate. While Elío recognized the Spanish authorities fighting the Napoleonic invasion and maintained good relations with the Portuguese court in Brazil which had demanded cession of the *Banda Oriental*,[126] Liniers was more cautious and had actually agreed to confer with Sassenay, a personal friend of his and the emissary of Napoleon.[127] Thus each side was highly suspicious of the other: Montevideo believing that Liniers was going to side with Napoleon, Buenos Aires assuming that Elío was furthering the old aim of Portuguese policy in the River Plate. Liniers then attempted to depose his subordinate, but Governor Elío with the spontaneous support of the Montevideo *cabildo* resisted these efforts; the result was the establishment of a junta in Montevideo which proclaimed its loyalty to the Spanish authorities in the Peninsula.[128] Montevideo considered the establishment of a junta justified, not only because the Peninsula had set the example but also, and primarily, because it held Liniers — though erroneously — to be a traitor to the Spanish cause.

The Junta of Montevideo, established under the presidency of Governor Elío on September 21, 1808, was characterized by two main sentiments, an unwavering loyalty to Spain and the wish for freedom from the viceregal authorities by whom Montevideo always felt it had been harassed. The Junta of Montevideo only emphasized this situation when it severed relations with Buenos Aires; Elío, in taking this drastic action, converted himself into the typical Spanish *caudillo* who correctly interpreted the popular will. In this role, Elío was no different from many Spanish viceroys who at the time played a double role: loyal to Spain but also representative of new Spanish American regional entities. Viceroy Abascal in Peru and Viceroy Iturrigaray in New Spain are good examples of this, though each case was different: Abascal in Peru, where no domestic revolution developed, was loyal to the Peninsular authorities; Iturrigaray in New Spain was more ambiguous and unsuccessfully tended to side with the revolutionary movement.

It was around Elío and the Junta of Montevideo that such intellectuals as Lucas José Obés and Pedro Feliciano Cavia, the priest José María Pérez Castellanos, and Mateo Magariños y Ballinas rallied against those who objected to the junta's creation, Joaquín Ruiz Huidobro, colonel Juan Francisco García, and the priest Juan José Ortíz.[129] On January 14, 1809, the *cabildo* of Montevideo and other authorities swore allegiance to the *Junta Suprema Central*.

Montevideo was thus the first Spanish American town to establish a junta in accordance with the Peninsular model and on the basis of the *pactum translationis*, though it was not of a revolutionary nature. By applying the principle of popular sovereignty, Montevideo anticipated what most of the other Spanish American seats of government were to do. As María Julia Ardao and Aurora C. de Castellanos have pointed out,

> the conviction existed that the same [right] which the Spaniards had to constitute their government for want of the king was also a right of the Spanish Americans, and that the same justifications were valid for the defenders of this thesis in both parts of the Spanish world. This was precisely the doctrine which the *cabildo* of Montevideo assumed on September 21, 1808 — i.e., the concept that the Spaniards, whether Peninsular or American, had equal rights; thus, as subjects of one and the same king, the two Spains had the right in his absence to establish authorities worthy of his confidence.[130]

It was this principle of popular sovereignty and of the reversion of authority to the people which the *cabildo* of Montevideo expressly stated on the historic day of September 21, 1808:

> finally, ... this represents the vote of the people, at whose request the *cabildo* assembled on this day: that in the meantime and until with better advice a plan of government can be established which is most fitting to the circumstances and to the subsequent resolutions of the capital, this junta be recognized, presided over by Governor Francisco Xavier Elío, as the particular and subordinated [junta] of this people, constituted on the model which was ordered by the *Suprema* of Seville in all the towns of the kingdom

with more than 2,000 inhabitants from the very moment the sinister designs of the French Emperor, the imprisonment of our beloved King Ferdinand VII, and the violent abdication of the Crown of which the Royal family was the subject, became known.[131]

The priest Pérez Castellanos wrote an interesting letter (in response to a letter of the bishop of Buenos Aires suggesting that he ought not to participate in the new government of Montevideo, of which he was a member) in which he vindicated the right of the Spanish Americans to set up juntas like those in the Peninsula, stating that:

> The Spanish Americans are brothers of the Spaniards of Europe because we are children of the same family, are subject to one and the same monarch, are governed by the same laws, and have the same rights. Those [in Europe], being deprived of our beloved King Ferdinand VII, have faculties to provide for their common security and to defend the inalienable rights of the Crown, establishing governing juntas which have been the salvation of the country and setting them up almost at the same time and as if by divine inspiration. No doubt we can do the same, since we are equally free and we are involved in the same dangers.[132]

Furthermore, Lucas Obés, one of the main composers of the formula which the *cabildo* of Montevideo accepted on September 21, 1808, explained in a letter addressed to Vicente Anastasio de Echeverría and dated October 24, 1808, the bases justifying the creation of the junta, which centered on the legal and constitutional assumption that Spanish America had exactly the same rights as metropolitan Spain.

> Very much to the contrary, I am angered and become excited when I see that you and other countrymen of good mind and [even] better talents honor [Spanish] America so little when you think that it has no right to do by itself what the other peoples of Spain have done, and you encourage the Mohammedan who believes himself in every way superior to us, who considers us as conquered [peoples], as a *quid distinctum* of the Spaniard born in the Peninsula, because you imply nothing less when you say that we have no right to elect the governing juntas which have been set up here. You told me . . . that you agreed in the retrocession of rights to the people because of the dethronement of Ferdinand VII and all his royal family, and that this justified the changes introduced in the constitution. When you speak of the people, what are you talking about? Is it not the Spanish monarchy? And when the Spanish monarchy is meant, does it not include [Spanish] America as well? Hence, if the Spanish people or the Spanish monarchy resumed the rights transferred to the sovereign and for that reason is free to introduce changes in the government, [Spanish] America will also be an integral part of that people, nation, kingdom, or whatever you may call it.
>
> . . . how could you and my countrymen believe that the people of Seville have a right to establish a junta and confer rights upon it, to enable it to give orders not only in its district but also in all provinces and even in the colonies proper?

> ... I will always think that we are not only entitled to do what we have done but also to carry our vote to the junta which we acknowledge as *Suprema*, [and] that to think differently is to establish the most hateful distinction between the Metropolis and [Spanish] America.¹³³

Interesting also in this connection is the memorandum of the legal adviser to the government of Montevideo, José Eugenio de Elías, written at the request of the governor of that town to answer the question whether the establishment of the junta in Montevideo was legally correct or whether it should be dissolved, as had been ordered by the viceregal authorities in Buenos Aires. Elías replied that royal orders should always be complied with, provided they did not go against the welfare of the people. In the case of Montevideo, he was aware that the people supported the junta, and he therefore counseled its continuation, at least until Ferdinand VII or the *Suprema Junta Central* made a definite decision in the matter.¹³⁴

Another example is an anonymous proclamation written in 1808 by a citizen of Montevideo in reply to an article which had appeared in Buenos Aires over the signature of "Spanish American." It called for the breaking of relations with Buenos Aires, attacked the policy of Viceroy Liniers, and justified the establishment of the junta in Montevideo. It invoked for Spanish Americans the same rights as the Peninsular Spaniards enjoyed and said clearly:

> We believe that, once the reigning house was dethroned, the Spanish people resumed all the rights of sovereignty, and that using these [rights], just as in the first instant of a political being, it could create new authorities, new laws, new constitutions.
>
> ... I am a free man [and] belong to a society to which I subjected myself with the preferential aim of obtaining all possible benefits; I find myself in a political orphanage; I am emancipated through the civil death of the father of my great family; today I can dispose of everything; I reassumed the rights which I had conferred upon them; that is why I have turned everything upside down; and I will not stop one bit in the reform until my measures or the freedom of the beloved Ferdinand VII has restored order.¹³⁵

There is a connection between this anonymous proclamation of a citizen of Montevideo in 1808 and anonymous writings which had appeared in Buenos Aires in 1806.¹³⁶ What is most interesting about these Argentine writings is that the Uruguayan Magariños used them two years later to defend the establishment of the Junta of Montevideo. It is ironic that Magariños in urging the prosecution and dismissal of Liniers, and hence the establishment of a junta in Montevideo, should use the same arguments which two years earlier had been used in Buenos Aires for the elimination of Viceroy Sobremonte and his replacement by Liniers.¹³⁷

For John Lynch Montevideo's action was not so much in support of the cause of Spain as the only possible alternative to domination by Buenos Aires. It was, in his words, "only a means to an end, emancipation from Buenos Aires," "the Revolution against the River Plate,"¹³⁸ and meant freedom from traditional pressures from Portugal for control of the delta. Nonetheless the loyalty of this region to Spain under whatever constitutional change should not be doubted, even if in this case the local conflicts were undoubtedly of greater and more immediate concern. Obviously, the one did not exclude the other, but loyalty to Spain was generally unquestioned until about 1820 in the entire Spanish Empire, and the later developments in the *Banda Oriental* give no indication of a desire for total separation from the River Plate.

The Spanish government, believing that the crisis in the River Plate could be solved by dismissing both Liniers and Elío, in 1809 appointed Cisneros as the new viceroy; he in turn dismissed Elío and appointed him inspector and second commander of all troops in Buenos Aires. The arrival of the new viceroy occasioned a "brief and superficial reconciliation" between the two cities. Since the existence of the junta was no longer justified, it was dissolved on June 30, 1809. Though Cisneros was "more acceptable in royalist Montevideo than in dissident Buenos Aires,"[139] his support was soon lost when he dismissed Elío, thus widening still further the existing abyss.

The Junta of Montevideo, which had governed for eight months, was the first expression of self-government. The Spanish character of this action was further stressed when freedom of trade not only diverted contraband to Buenos Aires but gave foreigners greater influence. In its meeting of July 19, 1809, the *cabildo* of Montevideo stated that it considered the presence of foreigners harmful

> since they pervert tranquillity, religion, and moral virtues with perverse concepts and seduction; experience has shown that they alone are the reason why . . . contraband has been developed with great scandal, bad customs and other vices contrary to Christian morality and our laws.[140]

The initial reaction of Montevideo to the May Revolution in Buenos Aires was to acknowledge its *Junta Provisional*, but soon divisions occurred. One group, headed by Nicolás Herrera, Lucas Obés, and Pedro Feliciano Cavia urged the establishment of a similar junta in Montevideo, which to them was not in conflict with the oath given to the Council of the Regency. In any case, on June 2, 1810, the other group, headed by José de Salazar, forced the *cabildo* to make the recognition of the Buenos Aires junta subject to the latter's loyalty to the Spanish authorities in the Peninsula. Thus, what had occurred in Buenos Aires and in other parts of the Spanish Empire found an echo in Montevideo: the Spanish party centered in Salazar (and his marines), and the revolutionary — though just as loyal — in Prudencio Murguiondo (and his Corps of Volunteers).[141] It was the Salazar group which won in Montevideo, though the *juntistas* were by far not eliminated.

When Buenos Aires established its revolutionary junta, the old antagonism reappeared, with the difference that the authorities in Buenos Aires were now Spanish American and did not recognize Montevideo's right to secede, just as they did not recognize such a right in the cases of Paraguay and Upper Peru. The Buenos Aires junta, as heir to the viceroyalty, demanded recognition as such by the *Banda Oriental*, which all areas of the *Banda* had granted[142] except Montevideo after the coup of June 2, 1810; thus it resisted as it had on previous occasions.

The antagonism continued since the new military governor, Joaquín de Soria, supported by the *cabildo* of Montevideo, was opposed to recognition of the new authorities in Buenos Aires; these authorities meanwhile viewed the situation as a great threat to their own revolutionary course. It was obvious that Buenos Aires would do everything in its power to get control of Montevideo. The opening of the port of Maldonado and an offer to help the frontier areas were aimed at weakening allegiance to Montevideo, but the attempts were not successful. It was then that Montevideo became the leader of the entire area which it had always aspired to rule. On October 7, 1810, the undecisive Soria was replaced by Gaspar de Vigodet, who, in order to solve the mounting crisis, and to fill an empty treasury, set up a Junta of Finance and Arbitration. This action amounted to the establishment of an *Intendencia*, and thus completed the institutional process which had turned the *Banda Oriental* into an autonomous center of political, military, and financial authority.[143] And with the return of Elío on January 12, 1811, as viceroy, a chapter in the history of the River Plate closed, and a new one was soon to open: Montevideo had become the seat of the viceroyalty of the River Plate, even if the effective jurisdiction did not extend beyond the limits of the *Banda Oriental*, and even though it was to be but an interlude to the next chapter, the revolution of the interior.

Viceroyalty of the River Plate (Paraguay). The Paraguayan revolution, similar to events in the *Banda Oriental*, is also divided into two phases: the first, from 1810 to 1811, is linked to the loyalist cause; the second, beginning with the revolt of May 14, 1811, is revolutionary and is connected with Gaspar Rodríguez de Francia. Geography, history, economics, and geopolitics — Paraguay being situated much less in the crossroads of Spanish–Portuguese rivalry and foreign power interests than the *Banda Oriental* — explain why the two revolutionary phases succeeded one another rather quickly and with less involvement than the events in Uruguay.

Like the *Banda Oriental* Paraguay was a buffer region and exposed to pressures from the River Plate, which controlled its economic life, and the Portuguese areas of Brazil. But while the *Banda Oriental* played an increasingly significant role, Paraguay had always been more primitive and more isolated. "Half Indian, half Jesuit" — as M. A. Pelliza observed[144] — Paraguay resented progress because of its native masses, its Jesuit paternalism, and its remoteness.[145] Asunción had played a great role in the early conquest and colonization of the River Plate to which it was intimately linked; but when the province of the River Plate was set up in 1617, and the Jesuit missions were established in the new province of La Guayra — as it was then called — it became more oriented toward Lima. With the establishment of the viceroyalty of the River Plate in 1776 and Asunción's becoming the seat of one of the eight *intendencias* in 1782, its orientation shifted once again toward the River Plate.

Paraguayan regionalism had grown over the centuries, and Asunción became more conscious of it once it realized its increased dependency on Buenos Aires after the establishment of the new viceroyalty. Like the *Banda Oriental*, Upper Peru, and the interior of Argentina, Asunción resented the administrative and economic domination of Buenos Aires, particularly since the new intendant system gave the viceregal capital a greater control over Paraguayan affairs.

At the beginning of the nineteenth century the head of government in Asunción was Bernardo de Velasco. He had been appointed governor of the old Jesuit missions in 1803 — aside from the Paraguayan government — and in 1806 became the head of both areas which had been joined.

The events of Bayonne also reached the more isolated area of Asunción, and after 1809 revolutionary ferment increased. Since the *cabildo* was dominated by the Spanish element, which made up the urban class, loyalty to the

Peninsular authorities was unquestionable. Actually, "In 1810 this *cabildo* was more royalist than the intendant himself. And it was utterly incompatible with incipient creole nationalism."[146]

The events of May 1810 in Buenos Aires forced Asunción to take a stand. On June 26, 1810, Velasco called a *cabildo abierto* to define Paraguay's relations with the new regime in Buenos Aires. The Provisional Junta of Buenos Aires then sent a delegation to ensure that Paraguay would acknowledge the revolutionary authorities, but Paraguayan leaders like Iturbe, Gracia, and Cabañas now rallied to Velasco in resisting the Argentine pretensions. The *cabildo abierto* of July 24, 1810, decided to swear allegiance to the Peninsular authorities, to maintain good relations with Buenos Aires but not recognize its authority, and to take precautionary measures for the defense of the country.[147] Thus, Paraguay, while professing continued loyalty to the mother country, obtained autonomy in a manner similar to the *Banda Oriental*'s, although the struggle to achieve it was of shorter duration and less difficult here because of geography and lesser importance.

In October 1810 the government of Buenos Aires deposed Velasco, and "with characteristic folly the *porteño* revolutionaries decided to force the issue."[148] An Argentine army under Belgrano moved into Paraguay but was defeated twice (Paraguarí, January 9, 1811; and Tacuarí, March 5, 1811). Belgrano was forced to sign an armistice with the Paraguayan Manuel Anastasio Cabañas which *de facto* recognized the autonomy of Paraguay.

At the same time these victories eliminated the Argentine threat, they increased the self-confidence of the Paraguayans as the British invasions had for the Argentines. Thus, by winning over the Argentines, the Paraguayans had "in effect emancipated themselves from Spanish control and experienced the advantages of self-government."[149] Velasco, realizing the situation, followed the example of Governor Elío of Montevideo and appealed for Portuguese help, which was not forthcoming. Paraguay, safe from Buenos Aires, was safe from Spain since Elío did not succeed in recovering Buenos Aires for Spain.

The next step in the revolution in Paraguay came on May 14, 1811, when a junta was established. Including Velasco at first, it declared independence on May 17, 1811, from Buenos Aires and all foreigners. Thus the first act of the Paraguayan revolution ended in a declaration of loyalty to the Council of the Regency, and Paraguay, like Montevideo in 1808, applied the *pactum translationis* in the meeting of the *cabildo abierto* of July 24, 1810, without making specific reference to it. Like Montevideo, it employed the *pactum translationis* to assert a provincialist and autonomist stand in regard to the former viceregal capital.

ii. *The Spanish American Revolutionary Approaches*

aa. *The Unity Case*

Several leading Spanish American revolutionaries were convinced that, although the events of Bayonne justified the break with the Peninsula, the unity of Spanish America should not be impaired. This represented the Spanish American unity or community case which Miranda had attempted to adduce at the time of his ill-fated Venezuelan expedition of 1806.[150]

The unity argument was also followed — though unsuccessfully — by Simón Bolívar, and others, who in one way or another adhered to it, including Juan José Castelli, José de San Martín, and Bernardo de Monteagudo (Upper Peru) in the River Plate area, Martínez de Rozas and Juan Egaña in Chile, and José Cecilio del Valle in Central America. But the reality of Spanish America spoke against this solution from all points of view — geography, history, tradition. The union of the Spanish American area could be preserved only within a monarchical framework and along metaphysical lines; once that link was broken, it was difficult to maintain even the unity of the old viceroyalties. Thus, these leaders were forced to change their goals to more moderate ones — to the viceregal, and, ultimately, to the smaller provincialist concept. Bolívar and his Greater Colombia was the only viceregal exception, but his death in 1830 also signaled the end of this Neo-Granadine dream.

In Spain the creation of local juntas throughout the country ended in the establishment of one supreme junta, in Seville. At first glance there seems to be a difference in Spanish America, but the difference is more apparent than real.[151] For Spanish America too had plans to establish a *Suprema Junta Central* similar to the one in Seville, and the proposal was supported by several prominent persons, among whom were Viceroy Cisneros, Pedro Vicente Cañete, and Ignacio Tenorio.

In the River Plate, as agitation increased during May 1810, Viceroy Cisneros issued an order on May 18 in reaction to the bad news from the Peninsula and the political turbulence around him. The proclamation did not provide all the facts of the situation in Spain but it did suggest that should the Peninsula be lost Cisneros would not commit himself to any particular step without consulting leading persons in Buenos Aires and in the interior until the time that the four viceroyalties could act together to establish a government loyal to Ferdinand VII. This plan was aired at a time when a similar project arrived from Cañete, the legal adviser of the *intendencia* of Potosí. Cañete's proposal was contained in a letter to Cisneros suggesting the retention of a provisional government until the four viceroyalties could agree to convoke a Spanish American *Cortes* somewhere in Spanish America; the *Cortes* would in turn proceed to the appointment of a sovereign Spanish American Regency for the protection of the rights of Ferdinand VII.[152] But events moved so rapidly, there was not even time enough for the four viceroyalties to consult about such an action.

Tenorio, the *oidor* of Quito, likewise proposed the establishment of a Spanish American Regency, to which Torres replied in a letter dated May 29, 1810. Tenorio's proposal meant a Spanish American Regency elected by all the Spanish American provinces, which he based on the *Siete Partidas* (Partida III, Title 15, Law 2), and he stated further that in case the Spanish kings should follow the example of the Portuguese rulers, the *criollos* should continue in their obedience to the Peninsular authorities.[153]

The interesting proposal of a Spanish American Regency and of a Spanish American *Cortes* — also aired in New Spain prior to the meeting of August 9, 1808 — did not succeed because conditions were different from those in Spain. In the first place, geographic distances — those same distances which during the Spanish period of government made it necessary for the Crown to give special powers to the viceroys — made it impossible to create one junta for all of Spanish America. Moreover, regionalism, so strong in Spain at all times (indeed, in the midst of war against Napoleon, the juntas, such as those of Seville and Granada, concluded treaties which had all the characteristics of alliances among sovereign nations[154]), was even stronger in Spanish America; finally, in contrast to Spain, there was in Spanish America no direct danger of enemy invasion and occupation which necessitated a solution such as the establishment of a *Suprema Junta Central*. But even if the idea of such a Spanish American *Suprema Junta Central* would have gained ground, the question would then have arisen where to establish it, and on this point the entire problem would have collapsed. Spanish America would be and was loyal to the Spanish Crown, but no region in Spanish America would have accepted the rule of and the subordination to an area outside its historic region, particularly when even within a given viceroyalty the different areas would not acknowledge the rule of the viceregal capital. A similar question later concerned the Pan American movement (Inter American system): it was solved by establishing the seat of the organization from the very beginning outside the Latin American sphere, and at the same time by introducing administrative decentralization gradually; another solution, as it has been proposed from time to time, would have been counterproductive. Spanish individualism and regionalism gave the answer in both cases. A *Suprema Junta Central* for Spanish America in Buenos Aires would have had difficulties in obtaining acceptance in Chile or Peru, and certainly would hardly have been recognized in New Spain.[155]

bb. *The Viceregal or Confederacy Case*

This solution was adhered to by the leaders in the viceregal capitals which had established revolutionary juntas and who using the *pactum translationis* wished at least to preserve the unity of the respective old viceroyalty. The concept was taken up in Buenos Aires and Bogotá — and in the *cabildo* of Mexico City where it had not succeeded — and both capitals while severing ties with the authorities in the Peninsula frantically attempted by military force to keep the viceregal borders (Castelli in Upper Peru; Belgrano in Paraguay; José Rondeau, Manuel Sarratea, and Carlos de Alvear in the *Banda Oriental*; Nariño's attempted liberation of Quito; Bolívar's "admirable campaign" in Venezuela). This resulted in actually consolidating the autonomy of the provincial seats of government.

A good case for the confederacy or viceregal example was also the Treaty of Santa Fe de Bogotá signed on May 28, 1811, by the Chilean priest José Cortés de Madariaga on behalf of the Supreme Junta of Venezuela and by Jorge Tadeo Lozano de Peralta on behalf of the Electoral Constituent Power of Cundinamarca.[156] This treaty of alliance and federation is a further case in point for the close resemblance of events in Spanish America with those in the Peninsula: just as in Spain the various juntas behaved as sovereign states and concluded alliances against the common foe, the newly established juntas of Caracas and Bogotá did likewise against the Regency in Spain. The Spanish and Scholastic spirit behind this federation is clearly expressed when the canon wrote on December 11, 1810, to Archbishop Coll y Prat in Santa Fe de Bogotá, informing him about his diplomatic appointment in the following manner:

> The Supreme Junta of these Provinces, after having agreed on a confederation with the new Kingdom of Granada to preserve the rights of the King

and of our Holy Religion, has given me its confidence to travel to Santa Fe de Bogotá . . . .[157]

The confederacy case was also followed by Mariano Antonio Molas and Gaspar Rodríguez de Francia when in 1811 they expressed support for a confederation of the United Provinces of the River Plate "provided it was founded on complete equality of its parts."[158] Molas even went further when he proposed at the Paraguayan General Congress of 1811 — which agreed to it by a large majority — "that integration into Buenos Aires should be accepted only on terms of equality as part of a larger American confederation."[159] Likewise, Artigas, the *Jefe de los Orientales*, proclaimed similar concepts: a loose confederation of the United Provinces, "which in time perhaps might develop into a real federation,"[160] and in which the various provinces would be autonomous.

A typical example of the confederacy approach was also Juan Egaña's call in 1811 for a "Sovereign Diet of South America"[161] joining in a confederation the regions of Buenos Aires, Chile, and Peru, based on concepts which were the same as those contained in the preamble of his draft Constitution of 1811. It was an idea which had a certain similarity with the famous plans of Aranda (1783) and Godoy (1804)[162] and which also was launched by Buenos Aires in a variety of ways (Belgrano's and Rivadavia's plans for a kingdom uniting the River Plate, Chile, and Peru; and Pueyrredón's plan for a United Kingdom of Buenos Aires and Chile,[163] and it was also inherent in Bernardo O'Higgins' Pacific Confederation and in its intellectual continuation by San Martín and Bolívar. The establishment of Greater Colombia with Bolívar as President and Francisco de Paula Santander as Vice-President through the confederate Constitution of Rosario de Cúcuta of the year 1821 represented the only real example of the viceregal case. But even before the death of Bolívar it disintegrated into its three provincial parts — an invisible king had been able to keep the Spanish Empire united; even a great personality like Bolívar was unable even to keep the union of a much smaller area like the old viceregal borders of New Granada. Thus, the viceregal thesis failed, as the Congress of Panama (1826) was to show, although political developments before that date had already buried any hope for such an arrangement: New Spain, New Granada, Peru, and the United Provinces of the River Plate all split into the old and similar administrative units. The only exception to this was the development in Portuguese America.

Viceroyalty of New Spain. The plot of Aranjuez and the crisis of Bayonne became the catalyst for important historical developments. The stronghold of the Mexican party was the *cabildo* of Mexico City which now decided to play a significant role at a time when New Spain had already developed a strong national feeling. Among the most conspicuous leaders who aimed at autonomy or independence were the lawyers Francisco Primo de Verdad y Ramos and Juan Francisco de Azcárate who, together with the Peruvian Mercedarian friar Melchor de Talamantes Salvador y Baeza, and the marqueses de Uluapa and de Guardiola, colonel Ignacio Obregón, count de Santiago and canon José María Beristain, represented the core of Mexican nationalism.

When the fateful news from Bayonne was received in New Spain by the middle of July, the *cabildo* of Mexico City took the initiative and called for an extraordinary meeting for July 16, 1808, which did not come to any conclusions, so that another one was called for July 19th. For the *cabildo* the abdication at Bayonne was an act of force and an alienation of the monarchy in favor of a person with no right to it. All Spanish sovereigns had given an oath to "this most noble city as the Metropolis of the Kingdom without alienating it, or giving away what it owns in terms of privileges."[164] It concluded that monarchy was like an entailed estate — the order of succession could not be altered to the disadvantage of those entitled by law; hence, "there was a natural and legal incapacity to alienate what did not belong to it."[165] Monarchy, like an entailed estate, cannot be vacated; by absence or impediment, represented sovereignty resides in the kingdom represented in the metropolis, classes, and courts. It further stated that:

> Under no circumstances does monarchy remain without the sovereign, and in the present [case], the most critical which will be read in the annals of the history of [Spanish] America — note that America is meant, not Spain — there exists a royal and legitimate monarch even if force has . . . impeded Charles IV, the Prince of Asturias and the Royal Infantes D. Carlos and D. Antonio to unite with their royal vassals and beloved peoples, and they are due the respects of vassalage and fealty.[166]

It was the principle of popular sovereignty which was thus announced.

The *cabildo* then proposed the following steps: the government of New Spain would remain as it was before the events of Bayonne — New Spain would sustain the sovereignty of Charles IV and the Prince of Asturias, but while they recovered their freedom and the French troops evacuated the Peninsula, the city requested that Viceroy Iturrigaray continue in his post provisionally as viceroy, governor, and captain general, without handing the government over to anyone, not even Spain proper, even if he should receive orders from Charles IV in France, from the Emperor of the French, or from the Grand Duke of Berg, or to any viceroy appointed by Charles IV or the Prince of Asturias under the name of Ferdinand VII.[167] The viceroy should stay on by the mere fact of the popular will which the *cabildo* was now interpreting. This act of sovereignty would then be solemnly confirmed by an oath of the viceroy to the Kingdom of New Spain as represented provisionally in the *cabildo* of Mexico City.

These decisions were communicated to the viceroy and to the *audiencia*. While the viceroy sided with the Mexican party, thus representing a unique situation in the entire Spanish American Revolution — for that rising new conscience he represented at that moment a kind of king of New Spain — the *audiencia* was totally opposed to the course of the *ayuntamiento*.

On July 23, the *cabildo* met again and called for the convocation of a general congress, since in its opinion all authority in Spain had ceased to be legitimate. The *cabildo* also reminded the viceroy that he could not oppose a French invasion without the active defense of the Mexicans — it thus issued what amounted to be an ultimatum to the viceroy to put himself under the guardianship of the *cabildo*. At the same time several written requests for identical purposes were sent to the viceroy by the municipalities of Jalapa (July 20) and Querétaro (July 30), perhaps synchronized by members of the Mexican *cabildo*, as Lafuente Ferrari seems to think.[168] Thereupon, the viceroy decided to call the general meeting in Mexico City for early August, as urged by the *cabildo*.

On July 28, 1808, news arrived about the rise of the people in Spain and for a moment it confused the Spanish American party. It was also at that time that Talamantes sent his writings on the National Congress with a chapter on his "Idea of a Congress" to the *cabildo*.[169]

On August 2, the *cabildo* urged the viceroy to publish the decisions of the *cabildo* of July 19th, and the next day, the *cabildo* sent a long explanation to the viceroy responding to the legal opinions of the *audiencia* of July 21st. It is an interesting document which again showed the Spanish roots of the entire revolutionary argument: in the first place, the *cabildo* justified its actions as spokesman for the entire Kingdom of New Spain because it considered itself the head of Northern Spanish America and this had been specifically recognized by the sovereigns in the *reales cédulas* of October 22, 1523, and December 26, 1606. It also cited two other *cédulas* — June 19, 1568, and August 11, 1590 — in which the Crown also acknowledged the right of the City of Mexico to speak in the name of the entire Kingdom of New Spain. It also mentioned the case when on May 2, 1636, as a full *cabildo* and with the consent of the viceroy, it decided to levy an annual tax of 200,000 pesos on behalf of New Spain for the maintenance of the *armada de barlovento*. In the second place, the *cabildo* referred to the *Siete Partidas* when it called for a general junta, since this old Spanish legislation invoked such a remedy in case of an infant king, and in the view of the city fathers the present situation was identical, since neither a young king nor an imprisoned king can govern the nation. For this reason, the city had argued for the continuation of the viceroy in his present position, though on a temporary basis, and it compared its actions with those taken by Seville and Valencia, and others in the Peninsula, arguments which were to be used in an identical manner by other cities in Spanish America. The town council of Mexico then renounced what it requested in response to the negative reaction of the *audiencia*, but not without the most solemn protest that this temporary suspension of its rights did not prejudge its historic and legal rights.

Three days later, on August 5, the city again went over to the attack: since its first argument had not been accepted, the town council proposed a different solution also based on the Peninsular experience: in this "Exposición del ayuntamiento de Méjico al Virrey el 5 de Agosto de 1808,"[170] the city declared that its actions were inspired by those of Seville, Valencia, and others, and that its petition was guided by a desire to fulfill the law, since in such special circumstances as these, the people ought to be consulted. With the impediment of the monarchy, sovereignty was represented in the nation, and the city urged the convocation of a general junta presided over by the viceroy and composed of the *audiencia*, the archbishop, the city, the courts, the ecclesiastical and civil bodies, nobility, main citizens, and army, which would then decide the measures to be taken. It also proposed the convocation of a *Cortes* "to fill as soon as possible the immense vacuum between the authorities who order and sovereignty,"[171] and finally used for the first time the name of Ferdinand VII. Hence, the initiative of the City of Mexico, including that of a *Cortes* in New Spain, was in imitation of the events in Spain, except that in the Peninsula the movement would finally lead to a constitutional regime (Cádiz) while in Spanish

America it would lead toward independence. The entire argumentation was Spanish and had its roots in medieval legislation and philosophy.

On the same August 5, the viceroy forwarded the two declarations of the Mexican town council to the *audiencia*, which replied the next day that it was not in agreement with the *ayuntamiento*'s idea of a general congress. However, the viceroy went ahead, ignoring the opposite viewpoint from lawyers, from the *audiencia*, and from subordinate authorities. The meeting of the *junta general*, urged by the *cabildo* of August 9, provided the opportunity for the application of the *pactum translationis* on behalf of both opposing positions: by Aguirre, the spokesman for the *peninsulares*, and by Primo de Verdad, the speaker of the *criollos*. It was during this meeting that Primo de Verdad of Aguascalientes made his famous speech that the reason for the convocation of general *Cortes* was the simple fact that the legitimate metropolitan authorities had disappeared and that the people, source and origin of sovereignty, ought to resume its authority in order to establish a provisional government which would fill the vacuum created by the absence and apparent perpetual dethronement of the Spanish kings.[172] His arguments were based on the legislation of the *Siete Partidas* and represented the *pactum translationis*.

However, as soon as Primo de Verdad ended his speech, the Spanish party, headed by the inquisitors, the members of the *consulado*, and the Peninsular merchants whose opinion was that of the *oidor* Aguirre and of Miguel Bataller, overruled him and voted for recognition of the Peninsular authorities as the only legitimate political body in the absence of King Ferdinand VII.

Both the final *Acta* of the *junta general* of August 9 and the proclamation of the viceroy of August 11 were ambiguous and not happily received by either party. Feelings on the Spanish American side were well expressed by Talamantes who stated on that same day in his *Reflexiones sobre las ocurrencias del día*, among other things, that

> The King does not exist for us; the very same Viceroy has published his imprisonment and the difficulty that he get out of it; the same must be believed from the other members of the royal family who went to France;[173] ... Since there is no legitimate King, there cannot be viceroys.... The one who called himself, then, viceroy of Mexico, has ceased to be [viceroy] from the moment that the King was incapacitated to rule over the nation. If he has any authority at present, it cannot be any other than the one the people wanted to give him; and since the people is not King as it is also not Republic, the one who governs by consent of the people cannot call himself viceroy.[174]

On August 25, Talamantes sent a *Representación nacional de las colonias dedicada al ayuntamiento de México por Irsa, verdadero patriota* which, although influenced by eighteenth-century thought, was quite similar to the political writings which appeared in the Peninsula at the same time. However, in both Spain and New Spain, the mass of the people did not follow the politicians, as could be seen in the very Spanish action of the plot of Veracruz (August 16, 1808) when the people was aroused by the mere suspicion of treason at the arrival of two French ships sent by the Napoleonic authorities.[175] But reformist or independentist agitation was not confined to the politicized clergy: on August 19 there appeared a pamphlet which stated that "once the sovereignty of the

Bourbons had ceased, the people demanded the sovereignty of [Spanish] America."[176]

The crisis which had not been solved in the *junta general* foreshadowed actions by the two opposing parties: Hidalgo would start his revolution exactly two years after the Spanish party deposed Iturrigaray and had shipped him back. No doubt, the independence of New Spain (Mexico and Central America) could have been achieved in 1808, though not necessarily leaving the Spanish Empire, if the *criollo* party of Primo de Verdad had won in the deliberations of the *junta general*, particularly since Iturrigaray had sided with them. Was the action of Iturrigaray simply treacherous, as Lafuente Ferrari pointed out, or was Iturrigaray, as his contemporary and modern defenders stated, acting in the best Spanish interests — i.e., the independence of New Spain with him as king; could it have maintained New Spain within a reconstructed Spanish Empire?[177]

The assembly of 1808 had not produced the political changes which the Mexican party had envisioned, nor did the country become the scene of the heroic deeds of great liberators, like the South American continent. Instead, while the Spanish party maintained itself in power until 1821, a series of revolts shook New Spain which still did not produce the desired results.

The first of the series was linked to Father Miguel Hidalgo y Costilla and the Junta of Querétaro and became by accident more a social revolution than a purely political struggle; thus, "the Mexican War of Independence was a rehearsal for the War of the Reform and for the Revolution."[178] Father Hidalgo, parish priest of Dolores in the province of Guanajuato, who became the leader of the first revolt, had studied at the Colegio de San Nicolás of Valladolid (today's Morelia) under José Antonio Borda and with the methods of Clavijero who had initiated the philosophical reforms. Hidalgo was in the midst of his career when his Jesuit teachers were expelled; nevertheless, he preserved the ideological tendencies which he had received from them and which denied the divine-right theories of kings and defended the popular origin of the state. As Samuel Ramos observed, "Hidalgo's emancipation from the political tradition was not accompanied by the corresponding theological transformation, which reveals a typical mental accommodation of the Jesuits."[179]

Hidalgo formed part of a group of conspirators which included the *corregidor* of Querétaro and his wife, some Spanish officers of the regiment stationed there whose most prominent members were the young landowner Ignacio Allende, commander of the militia of Querétaro, and Ignacio Aldama and the manufacturer and former *corregidor* Miguel Domínguez. The conspirators were not for independence — "they were not republicans, nor were they opposed to the Catholic Church."[180] They wanted creole rule for New Spain and equality of their country within the Spanish Empire. They were thus reformists and not radicals.

It would be difficult to state categorically the philosophy which these men professed. Hidalgo (and Morelos) received his education at the Colegio de San Nicolás, and later studied at the University of Mexico where he obtained his bachelor's degree in theology in 1773.[181] He was familiar with the French literature of the period, but it would be erroneous to deduce from this that his philosophy was determined by the Enlightenment. Hidalgo, like Morelos, had been tutored by the Jesuits and their education was marked by the traditions of Suárez and the Spanish School. Aldama, too, received a philosophical training — he graduated from the Colegio de San Francisco de Sales in San Miguel el Grande and was not unfamiliar with the Late Scholasticism of the Jesuits and Dominicans. On the other hand, Ignacio López Rayón and Mariano Matamoros graduated from the University of Mexico which was closer to the cause of the *status quo*. In any case, when the uprising began, the leaders of the emancipation tried to justify their actions with a philosophy of liberty which paralleled the passionate debates on popular sovereignty and whose roots were Spanish medieval political thought. The debates of the *junta general* of New Spain of 1808 and the actions of Hidalgo in 1810–11 (and of Morelos in 1811–15) had a common link with Spanish tradition, or as Aníbal Sánchez Reulet commented: "the history of colonial thought ended as it had begun with a polemic stand on natural law."[182]

The conspirators had intended to declare Mexican independence in December 1810, during the fair of San Juan de los Lagos; instead the junta of Querétaro had to begin prematurely when it seemed that their plans had become known to the authorities, and they were forced to change them. Hidalgo then started the revolt — the *Grito de Dolores* — on September 16, 1810: he rang the church bells, and with the traditional slogan "Down with bad government, long live the King" and under the banner of Our Lady of Guadalupe, appealed to the Indians since he could no longer hope "to organize a creole rebellion" or "to seduce the army";[183] silver taken from the churches was then used for minting coins with the head of Ferdinand VII. The insurrection soon spread and could not be stopped. Moreover, Hidalgo, who had assumed leadership under the title of Captain-general of America, had aroused social forces which could not be controlled. They led to looting and plundering and to the massacre of the Alhóndiga de Granaditas, which damaged the movement. Still, the insurrection spread: to Zacatecas, San Luis Potosí, Jalisco, Saltillo, Nuevo León, and Texas; to win support of the population, Hidalgo promised an elected congress which should govern the country in the name of Ferdinand VII.[184] The movement became more and more a civil war "in which almost all the forces on either side were natives of Mexico,"[185] or, "under Hidalgo an inchoate crowd of humble Indians and mestizos in central Mexico was led to fight for land, for Mexican autonomy, and for an end to the caste system (1810–11),"[186] but not yet for independence. It was a purely Spanish affair in general and more Mexican in particular; it was in the best of Spanish traditions and in line with the revolutionary movements in other parts of Spanish America, and resembled the struggle which the Spanish people was carrying out against Napoleon, with priests leading fanaticized and uneducated masses.

In October 1810, Hidalgo's irregulars marched on the City of Mexico and forced the royalists to withdraw from the Monte de las Cruces. But Hidalgo decided not to press on with his attack on Mexico City and retreated, against the advice of Allende, to Guanajuato, and later set up a "government" in Guadalajara. Harassed by the royalist armies under the able Calleja del Rey, Hidalgo's insurgents then faced defeat at Calderón (January 1811) which then signaled the end of the movement. In the summer of 1811 all leaders were caught and shot except for Ignacio López Rayón.

Rayón, who had been the secretary of state in Hidalgo's "government" at Guadalajara, continued resistance and established a junta in Zitácuaro which, while continuing Hidalgo's struggle against Peninsular control of New Spain, proclaimed loyalty to Ferdinand VII. It was there that some intellectuals like José María Cos and Andrés Quintana Róo joined him. However, the continuation of resistance was linked not so much to Rayón as to José María Morelos y Pavón, a priest who had fought with Hidalgo and who had been sent by him to free Acapulco. It was Morelos who initiated the second insurrection right after the end of Hidalgo's in 1811, and by the end of the year was in control of today's state of Guerrero. With Morelos were also other leaders like the future presidents Vicente Guerrero and Félix Fernández (Guadalupe Victoria), Nicolás Bravo, and the village priest Mariano Matamoros.

The Spanish authorities, encouraged with the victory over Hidalgo, continued under Calleja to destroy the insurgents. They were successful at the end of 1811 in eliminating the junta of Zitácuaro, but could not deal with Morelos who in 1812 set up his headquarters in Tehuacán, southeast of Puebla, threatening vital communications to the viceregal seat. He then took Orizaba and in the fall of 1812 marched into Oaxaca, and in August 1813 seized Acapulco.

It was after the capture of Acapulco that Morelos felt he should give his movement a legal and constitutional foundation, even though Rayón and the junta of Zitácuaro still claimed the leadership of the revolt. Morelos summoned a congress at Chilpancingo in November 1813, whose participants were delegates from the areas under his control and soldiers from his army. Appointed generalissimo of the insurgent forces by this body — reminiscent of Hernán Cortés' appointment at Veracruz — he drew up a political program which called for independence and was largely based on Scholastic and traditional thought: Catholic religion, republican government, equality among all social groups of the country, abolition of the special privileges of the clergy and the army, as well as of slavery, taxes, and tributes, breaking up of the *haciendas* into small holdings, and seizure of Church lands.[187] When dealing with the Church Morelos spoke harshly of it, saying that it lacked men of integrity to defend its rights. He based his assertions on Suárez' *De Religione*,[188] a work he must have studied at the seminary of Michoacán, an institution which played a role in New Spain in the diffusion of Scholastic thought similar to that played by the University of Chuquisaca in the River Plate area.

The Congress of Chilpancingo represented the apex of this second insurrection; the tide had already turned when Calleja, now viceroy of New Spain since 1813 and taking a great risk, armed the *criollos* in the correct belief that the social message of Morelos and the continuous destruction by the *guerrilleros* were a serious handicap to peace and progress in the country. Two years later, in November 1815, after his movement filled with growing dissension was harassed by superior forces, Morelos was caught and executed. Like the first insurrection, the second was profoundly Spanish and Mexican in its thought and action, ideas and ideals. It was also typical, as Ricardo Majó Framis reminded us, that all of Mexico's heroes of independence were shot: Hidalgo and Morelos by the Spanish authorities, Iturbide and Guerrero later by the very same Mexicans, thus proving that Bolívar's verdict was also valid for New Spain.[189]

Viceroyalty of the River Plate. Innumerable examples can be shown to demonstrate the vitality of the Scholastic theory here. The ideas of the *pactum translationis* also came to the fore with the statement of Possidonio da Costa in Buenos

Aires in 1809 when he tried to induce the troops not to acknowledge Viceroy Cisneros and instead to set up a junta in defense of the rights of Ferdinand VII or of the prince upon whom would fall sovereign power in accordance with the constitution of the monarchy.[190] On the eve of the revolution, a townswoman of Córdoba announced that in September 1809 a gentleman passing from La Rioja en route to Santa Fe had mentioned to her that "the king having left Spain voluntarily, he thus had abandoned the kingdom, and, therefore, Spanish America was free to elect its government." In December of that same year the Deputy Governor of Santa Fe informed Viceroy Cisneros that rumors were circulating that, since Ferdinand VII was no longer in power and the *Suprema Junta Central* was alternately French or English, "it was up to the people to elect, appoint, and designate someone to govern them, because it was the people who make the king, and not the king who makes the people."[191]

As a result of the viceroy's proclamation of May 18, 1810, and in view of growing agitation for a *cabildo abierto*, Cisneros held meetings with military leaders, such as Martín Rodríguez, who stated that his oath to the legitimate authority no longer obligated him and that the people therefore rightly demanded a change in government. The next speaker was Colonel Merlo who stated his loyalty to the Peninsular authorities. Finally, Cornelio de Saavedra, commander of the regiment *Patricios*, told Viceroy Cisneros:

> Must this immense territory, its millions of inhabitants, perhaps acknowledge the sovereignty of the merchants of Cádiz and of the fishermen of the island of León? Have the rights of the Crown of Castile in which the Americas were incorporated passed to Cádiz and to the island of León which belong to Andalusia? ... He who gave Your Excellency the power to rule over us has ceased to exist, and therefore the forces upon which that authority was based do not exist either.[192]

On May 21, the *cabildo* agreed to a *cabildo abierto* for the next day — the general congress of May 22nd and 23rd — and issued the necessary invitations for some 450 people,[193] though in the view of Emilio Ravignani, if Castilian legislation had been followed to the letter, some 3000 to 4000 individuals should have been invited.[194] Some 250 *vecinos* actually attended the meeting although 26 withdrew without participating in the election.[195] The 224 *vecinos* who voted included 27 members of the clergy, 24 officials, 62 members of the army and 3 of the navy, 59 merchants, one professor, 15 district and brotherhood mayors, and 33 individuals specifically called *vecinos*.[196] The legal thesis of the revolution was stated by Castelli who declared that the government of Spain had fallen, and especially after the dissolution of the Junta of Seville which lacked the faculties to set up the Regency; hence, sovereignty reverted to the people which was freely entitled to establish a new government.[197] After Castelli had spoken, the floor was taken by Pascual Ruiz Huidobro, who declared that "he [Ruiz Huidobro] ought to be separated from the superior government, since in Spain the sovereign representation to which he owed his appointment had ended, [and] that the *cabildo* should resume it and transfer it to another person."[198] He was followed by a variety of speakers, like the *fiscal* Villota, who disagreed with Castelli's thesis, since in his opinion the people of Buenos Aires had no right to question the Regency — the people of Buenos Aires had no right to a sovereign government since this would break the unity of the country and establish as many sovereignties as there were peoples.[199] Juan Nepomuceno de Sola, parish priest of Our Lady of Montserrat, called for the *cabildo* to exercise power provisionally until a governing junta established with the participation of all interior provinces of the viceroyalty was set up. The text which finally was adopted stated, "if another authority is to be set up which is superior to that which H. E. the Viceroy receives, [and] dependent on the sovereign [power], that it be exercised legitimately in the name of King Ferdinand VII and [specified] in whom."[200]

As Diego Abad de Santillán comments, the majority of the participants were sincere in their loyalty to the king, and thus it was not a calculated camouflage;[201] Enrique de Gandía calls it "el entusiasmo delirante por Fernando VII."[202] When the final vote was taken, the results were that the Spanish party — continuation of the viceroy — had obtained, as mentioned previously, 69 votes, while the Spanish Americans, totaling 155, were divided as follows:

1. *The Ruiz Huidobro formula*: That authority should be resumed by the *cabildo* until a provisional government was established: 25 votes (among them Melchor Fernández, of the cathedral, Juan León Farragut, chaplain of the dragoon regiment, the lawyer Joaquín Grigera).

2. *Formula of Pedro Andrés García, Juan José Paso, and Luis José Chorroarín*: That authority should be assumed *ad interim* by the *cabildo* until the form of government to be set up had been decided upon: 20 votes.

3. *Formula of Saavedra*: That the authority of the viceroy should pass *ad interim* to the *cabildo* "until such time as the junta which should exercise it is established, and that the formation [of said junta] should be in the manner and form which the *cabildo* considers appropriate, and there should be no doubt that it is the people who confers the authority or the command."[203] This was also the position of Castelli, which included those who gave their favorable vote with the addition of a decisive vote to the trustee, the attorney general Julián de Leyva: 87 votes (including Belgrano, Vicente López, Moreno, Rivadavia, Francisco Antonio Escalada, Gregorio Tagle, José Darregueyra, Joaquín Campana).

4. *Formula of Juan Nepomuceno de Sola*: That the *cabildo* should provisionally assume the authority with the vote of trustee until the election of the junta with deputies of the entire viceroyalty: 18 votes (among them Manuel Alberti, Miguel Azcuénaga, Antonio José de Escalada, Cosme Argerich, Juan Pedro de Aguirre).

5. *Formula that the* cabildo *should take power once the authority of the viceroy had ceased*: 4 votes.[204]

The meeting of the general congress ended at midnight with the decision to continue the debate the next day when the votes would also be counted. No record of this first *cabildo abierto* was made and it was simply declared that the viceroy should relinquish his office while the *cabildo* would temporarily assume authority until a governing junta could be set up, also leaving the counting of the votes in the hands of the *cabildo*, whose result the revolutionaries accepted. The *cabildo* also received discretionary powers to proceed toward the establishment of a junta "as it deemed convenient." However, the *cabildo* canceled the next meeting and on May 24th appointed a junta of five members which included the deposed viceroy as president. The decisions of the *cabildo* of May 23rd and 24th thus reflected more the viewpoint of the conservative minority.

When the revolutionaries realized what had happened, they brought about the consequences of May 25. Late in the evening of the 24th, the *Patricios* with great active participation by the people went to the houses where the *cabildantes* lived and warned that unless the moves of May 23rd and 24th were rescinded the people would take matters into their own hands.[205] They were particularly displeased about the viceroy's still being included in the junta. It seems that the people were hostile to the inclusion of Viceroy Cisneros in the First Junta because it was known that he was a friend of Godoy, the enemy of Ferdinand VII, who had been chased away by the people in the famous events of Aranjuez. Hence, he was, as Gandía says, a "politician who had fallen in disgrace," who did not inspire confidence, and thus hostility to his presiding over the First Junta was for political reasons, "not for absurd reasons as so many historians have mentioned, of a racial character — for the crime of being Spanish — or of a patriotic character — the legend of the creation of a new nation — et cetera."[206] Finally, on May 25th a petition with 409 signatures demanded an acceptable junta which did not include Viceroy Cisneros. The *cabildo* agreed, and with the deposition of the viceroy the Second Junta of Buenos Aires was set up.[207] As Abad de Santillán commented:

> against the conservative minority, a patriotic minority moved. If the latter did not have the consent of the people, its life could not last long; if the conservatives could have disposed of an effective support, they would have regained power. But the truth was that the cause of Spain was then untenable and did not count with the necessary material force to maintain itself.[208]

Ravignani has summarized the Revolution with the existence of two periods, as follows:

> The *first* includes *two phases*: the 22nd, the deposition of the viceroy; the 23rd the maintenance of the viceroy who declares that he would not serve unless he had support; and the 24th, the open reaction of the Spanish party and the installation of a reactionary junta. Here ends the first period.
>
> The *second* period has *two phases*: the action of the people which demands and obtains the resignation of a reactionary junta, and the second phase, the establishment of a junta appointed by the people and the troops and whose members are revolutionaries.[209]

Ravignani contends that the decisions of May 1810 were brought about by popular action and military pressure — a kind of Napoleonic influence, an impact which many historians have viewed as an echo of the French Revolution (Ricardo R. Caillet-Bois, among others)[210] — when the people acted against the minority opinion of the *cabildo* which in his view attempted to circumvent the earlier decisions. This latter viewpoint which many historians have also followed (Lynch, among others)[211] does not take into account the fact that the *cabildo* felt it was legally entitled to establish *any* type of junta, including chairmanship by the viceroy, under the resolution of the general congress which stipulated "as it deemed convenient"; hence, no fraud was involved. In any case, Ravignani's point of view that the people outside the *cabildo* imposed the final decision does not alter the fact that the *pactum translationis* was applied, and any influence of the French Revolution has to be rejected, since the opinion of the people's leaders was clearly stated in the *cabildo* meetings. Finally, revolutionary or not, the junta of Buenos Aires of May 25, 1810, meant what it said when it proclaimed allegiance to Ferdinand VII — it was he who later did not acknowledge the loyal sentiments of the people of the River Plate. On the other hand, Lynch is correct when he says that "this was a patrician revolution, accomplished by an elite who spoke for the people without consulting them"; ". . . not a democratic movement. Like most revolutions, it was initiated by a minority who sought to mobilize — and manipulate — a majority."[212]

We should bear in mind that in the two years between the events of Bayonne and the May Revolution of May 25, 1810, in Buenos Aires, the River Plate had experienced a series of juntas. Actually there had been four juntas earlier: Montevideo (September 21, 1808), Buenos Aires (January 1, 1809 — which really never got off the ground), La Paz (July 16, 1809), and Buenos Aires (May 22–24, 1810). As Gandía points out, all these five juntas were born from the same principles as the Peninsular ones (*pactum translationis*) and for the same end: to fight the Napoleonic usurpation. For different reasons, however, they all vanished except the last one of May 25, 1810. Montevideo's junta ended by recognizing the Regency and ruling in the name of the Peninsular authorities; the Buenos Aires junta of 1809, set up by Alzaga and his friends, was annulled by Saavedra and the chief military leaders, since they disliked the junta system and were friendly to Liniers; that of La Paz was disbanded by the Royalist Goyeneche, and that of May 2, 1810, in Buenos Aires failed because its president was suspected of sympathy for Napoleon and Godoy.[213]

With the popular verdict of May 22, Buenos Aires set up a junta to take care of its own interests and with the goal of keeping intact all the territories of the viceroyalty. In the establishment of the juntas of 1810 it could look back to the actions of the *cabildo* of 1806 and to the earlier examples of Montevideo and La Paz as well as to its own attempts in 1809. The May Revolution was not for independence,[214] since that political goal began to circulate only secretly by 1812 with the arrival of San Martín and the establishment of the *Logia Lautaro*. The goal for independence will increase with the fall of Napoleon in 1814 and become an invincible force by 1816.[215] The May Revolution was the continuation of the events in the Peninsula, of the Spanish Revolution, with absolute and sincere loyalty to King Ferdinand VII as expressed by solemn oath.[216]

> The May Revolution was not anti-Catholic. It was not intended to mean nor did it mean, certainly in the beginning, a break with tradition, but a mere political change which represented an essential continuity; more, even: observing how in the mother country the freedom and the classical Spanish institutions were threatened, [Spanish] America rose up to save them. These and other factors were the reasons why in theory and in practice the immense majority of the secular and regular clergy declared itself in its favor. But the errors of a time so full of novelties succeeded in infiltrating it and in obtaining many of its goals.[217]

Guillermo Furlong, s.j., has shown that the social contract which was applied in Buenos Aires in the May Revolution was Suárez' *pactum translationis*, the same to which Castelli, Juan Hipólito Vieytes,[218] Mariano Moreno, Saavedra, and later Juan Gorriti, Gregorio Funes,[219] Pantaleón García, Mariano Medrano, and others referred. During the fateful days of May 1810

Pedro Andrés García had declared that "the supreme law [is] the well-being of the people"; Melchor Fernández, that "this people is in a position of freely exercising authority, since by default or lapse of the Supreme Junta to which it had given an oath of allegiance this authority had reverted to the people"; Juan León Farragut, that "once the Supreme Central Junta had ended, the right of the individuals of this city to appoint a chief must be resumed"; Cosme Argerich, that "once the Supreme authority had been extinguished, the latter must be resumed by the people"; Antonio Sáenz, that "the moment has come for the people to resume its original authority, and rights"; Antonio José Escalada, that "the people has the concept that the supreme power has been returned by lack of legitimate rule"; Francisco Seguí, that "the popular commotion regarding the knowledge that the moment has come to resume its primitive rights is common knowledge"; Joaquín Grigera, that "legitimate authority having expired, the people resumes its primary rights which belonged to it before it had conferred that authority"; and this principle remained dedicated as Dr. Roberto H. Marfany points out, in the written petition which was submitted to the *cabildo* on May 25 and where it can be read: "the people . . . once the authority and power which it had conferred were resumed . . . repeals and invalidates the established junta . . . ."[220]

This was not Rousseau's contract. In the first place, the contract which the revolutionaries used during and after the May Revolution is one which links the subjects to the ruler and not one which unites the citizens among themselves. This is a fundamental difference, since the first is the Suarezian formula which Rousseau not only denies but refutes. Rousseau considered as social contract only that by which a people really becomes a people, and attains this through public deliberation or convention. This is not the pact which the revolutionaries of the Argentine May Revolution or those in other Spanish American territories dreamed about; their political theories of popular sovereignty had to do with the link between the people on one side and the monarch on the other, between the kings of Spain and the peoples of Spanish America.[221] Besides, Rousseau was not popular in the River Plate area before the May Revolution and his theories were not applied before the end of 1810; moreover, Rousseau was not as well known as Suárez, who was popular for over two hundred years in the River Plate area and in the whole of Spanish America.

While Gandía denies any influence of Suárez — though not of Scholasticism, since he interprets the revolution as having a Thomistic foundation — Tulio Halperín Donghi sketches a different link between the Hispanic tradition and the Spanish American Revolution: he denies in a different way that Suárez represents the intellectual foundation of the Revolution. However, he does admit that "Suarezian thought (the concept that political authority has as its source the consent of the people) had been rediscovered within an ideological and historical framework which was different from the original."[222] And yet, Halperín Donghi does not contradict the main thesis which both Suárez and Vitoria proclaimed in the sense that power received by the ruler is not only just and legitimate, but that it originates in God and cannot be taken back or changed even with everyone's consent.[223] Civil authority which is not submitted to the temporal power of the popes is still submitted to his spiritual authority[224] — the indirect power proclaimed by Suárez and Vitoria. Halperín Donghi agrees also with the basic tenets of Hispanic political thought which, while adjusting to modernity, maintained its idealistic posture by repudiating the modern notions of Machiavelli; Late Scholasticism represented a medieval political theory mixed with certain trends of the European Renaissance and humanism but by maintaining its idealistic and spiritual nature became not only original for the seventeenth century but also superior to the thought of the other European nations.[225] On the other hand, he sees in Vitoria certain modern trends which separate him from Suárez: a naturalistic element. Instead of a continuity of Scholasticism, Halperín Donghi feels that the monarchical crisis brought about a new assessment of the legal and historic foundations of the Spanish monarchy when traditional points of view were then rediscovered, and thus "traditionalism and monarchical crisis are two aspects of one and the same process."[226]

Scholasticism lost ground during the eighteenth century, but this does not mean that it was completely eliminated from the scene and that a rediscovery of medieval thought for certain political goals suddenly arose at the time of Bayonne. In any case, Halperín Donghi recognizes the Spanish sources in the famous meeting of May 22, 1810, "in which it was not to establish a new law but to see what legal norms of valid legislation could be applied in the grave case of the monarchy,"[227] and he refers to *Partida* II, Title 1, Law 9, of the *Siete Partidas*, which shows clearly how from the thirteenth century the notion was present in the spirit of Spanish legislation that in case political power had disappeared it could only be reconstructed with the consent of those who had to obey it thereafter.[228] He concludes that "the presence of traditional ideological elements in Argentina are thus undeniable."[229] For him it is a gradual rediscovery of medieval values, particularly when independence is justified later on the basis of the Scholastic theory of the tyrant: three hundred years of Spanish rule are seen as *tyrannus ab origine*, since it had no legal title, thus denying the legality of the papal donation.

This traditional heritage must not be interpreted, in Halperín Donghi's view, as a thread which had never been severed, from medieval Castile to the events of Bayonne. For him it is a tradition rediscovered which owes its reappearance to the services it will render as a polemical instrument against the more recent tradition of absolutism, now seen as a foreign element introduced by Charles V and his Flemish advisers; seen in the light of the principle of rising constitutional liberalism this medieval tradition ends up identifying itself with modern teachings.[230] If this interpretation be accepted — and this writer does not — then this point of view would not be different for the events in Spain itself which led to the *Cortes* and to the Constitution of 1812 — again a link to Spain and not to foreign sources, since the delegates to the Spanish *Cortes* also looked in a Romantic manner toward the re-establishment of the medieval Spanish monarchy. Also, Halperín Donghi acknowledges that "behind three centuries of Hispanic and Catholic unity under the rule of an ever more mature absolutism one begins to notice the existence of older political liberties, hidden by the streamlining success of modern authoritarianism,"[231] but he sees it as linked to the Enlightenment itself: to Montesquieu, in his statement that in Spain freedom was old and despotism new; to Jovellanos, for whom the

Spanish monarchy was constitutional; to Martínez Marina, who looked at Spain's past as a solution for the problems of the present. The return of Jovellanos to Spanish tradition is seen more as a Europeanization of Spanish culture than as a return to purely Spanish roots.[232] But this attitude would seem to reflect, in the first place, clearly the strength of Scholastic ideas on the great thinkers of Spain's Enlightenment, especially Jovellanos who followed modern European ideas in economics but stuck in politics to traditional values, and, secondly, there are still the currents of Scholasticism which exist in the eighteenth and early nineteenth centuries and which Halperín Donghi does not want to recognize as prevailing in their own right. In my opinion the Spanish political tradition was so strong that it did not need any rediscovery, either directly or indirectly through the Enlightenment.

From the debates of the *cabildo abierto* of May 22, 1810, in Buenos Aires it is clear that only Suárez' contract-theory was meant; there is no evidence of any Rousseauan influence at this period. Besides Saavedra and all the other members who spoke at the meeting, Castelli's exposition was in line with Scholastic thought when he explained the existence of a pact between the Spanish kings and the peoples of Spanish America, and it was on this basis that his entire argument for the establishment of a junta in Buenos Aires was put forward. With the dissolution of the *Suprema Junta Central* the sovereign Spanish government had ended, and Castelli derived from this historical fact the resumption by the people of Buenos Aires of the rights of sovereignty, and their free exercise in the establishment of a new government, mainly because King Ferdinand VII had lost his authority over Spain. Castelli made a similar statement in Upper Peru on April 3, 1811, when he said that he did not recognize the authority of the viceroys and their subordinate authorities to negotiate for and on behalf of the peoples and for their welfare, since their destiny depended only on the people's free consent, "because the people is the origin of all authority and the magistrates are but a curator of its interests, and dependent on contingencies."[233]

Castelli, like many of his contemporaries, studied at the University of Córdoba and played a leading role in the *cabildo* of 1810. Like Moreno, he also has been associated with the ideas of the French Revolution because of his radical opinions and his fervent, enthusiastic revolutionary temperament. In the face of the events in Spain, Castelli did not act differently from the other leaders of Spanish America, *criollos* and *peninsulares*: he condemned the *afrancesados* such as "Godoy, Soler, Asansa, O'Farrel, Caballero, Mazarredo, Solano, Borja, and others" as traitors to the Spanish cause who had delivered the country to Napoleon.[234] Castelli wrote a statement in defense of Nicolás and Saturnino Rodríguez Peña and of the physician Diego Paroissien who were charged with treason after the 1806 British invasions of the River Plate area because they allegedly had conspired to set up a republic.

In its political part, the document maintains that the legal government does not exist, since the Regency which the king had left on his departure had ceased *mero jure et facto*. The nation first set up juntas, then a *Suprema Junta Central* — for which it had neither the approval of the king nor the express will of the people. This junta lacked jurisdiction over Spanish America but sought to exercise control over overseas Spain without power, title, and authority. The Spanish Americans have the same right to representation of sovereignty as the citizens of Seville; they have neither more nor fewer rights, but are on an equal footing as an integral part of the nation. The authorities in Spain have legitimate rights, but these rights cannot extend beyond the Peninsula. While the king is captive, and there is no Regency, no legal government exists as far as Spanish America is concerned. The government which may be formed cannot have any jurisdiction in Spanish America as long as the king has not returned, since this would mean the establishment of a vassalage of vassals over vassals. Spanish America remains *de facto* independent from Spain as long as the royal link which unites them is broken by the absence of the monarch; therefore, Spanish America has as much right as Spain to form its own government.[235] One may conclude with Ricardo Levene who made the following summary of the political doctrine of Castelli:

1. There was a crisis of Spanish political and constitutional law which started with the year 1808 when, because of the abdication in Bayonne, the people of the Peninsula established their own governing juntas and then the *Junta Central*;
2. This *Junta Central* had been dissolved and had no faculties to organize the Council of the Regency — among other reasons, because in its elections no Spanish American deputies participated;
3. Hence, the sovereign government of Spain had ended, and the result was the resumption of the rights of sovereignty by the people and the free exercise of the new government.[236]

According to Julio César Chaves, Castelli was the first to announce this doctrine a year and a half before the events of 1810. Castelli made known his ideas on popular sovereignty when he heard of the departure of the Infante Don Antonio from Madrid, which for him meant that the government had fallen.

Among the more important leaders of the May Revolution besides Castelli, were Mariano Moreno, Manuel Belgrano, and Gregorio Funes. Moreno was born in Buenos Aires in 1779; he had studied at the Colegio de San Carlos and the University of Chuquisaca (1799–1805) where he graduated as a lawyer. Moreno knew the Spanish and Spanish American legal tradition from these studies, although he was also influenced by the currents of the Enlightenment, particularly in regard to economic matters as witnessed in his *Representación de los hacendados y labradores* of the year 1809 in which he fought for freedom of trade and the end of all commercial obstacles. On the other hand, this document did not have the influence which has been attributed to it, and it played no role in the strictly political controversy of the May Revolution, especially in regard to Spain, since the economic problems were related more to the Spanish position in Peru.[237]

Among the most important documents which show the prevailing political thought with its medieval roots is the *Manifiesto de la junta*. This *Manifiesto* dealt with the execution of Liniers and other persons involved in the plot of Córdoba and was dated September 8, 1810. Written by Moreno, it is an interesting document which shows clearly the political thought current in those historic days in the River Plate area, a current which was to be found likewise in other parts of the Spanish American territories. It stated:

> Since the treacherous conduct of the Emperor of France extirpated from Spain the most beloved of its monarchs, the Kingdom became acephalous,

and the principle was dissipated around which alone the true rights of sovereignty could be concentrated. With our Monarch gone, there ended the foundation from which the magistrates derived their powers; the peoples lost the father who was supposed to look after their welfare; and the state, left to itself, began to feel the upheavals resulting from the opposition of interests which previously the hand of the King had kept united through the reins of government .... Ferdinand VII had a kingdom; but he could not rule it; the Spanish monarchy had a king, but it could not be governed through him; and in this conflict the nation had to resort to itself in order to govern, defend, save itself, and to regain its monarch.

The peoples from whom the kings derive all the power with which they govern did not entirely resume the authority which they had deposited in the Monarch: his existence prevented such resumption; but his captivity transmitted to them all the necessary authority to establish a provisional government without which they would run the risk of division and anarchy ....

Supreme Juntas were established in the main departments of the state [in the Peninsula] and continued to prosper until power was concentrated in one alone, at which point it was set up by the others as the representative of sovereignty. The magistrates who composed this respectable assembly supported without envy the provincial juntas, the stability of which rested on the public vote of the kingdom; the governors were already seen to cede command to the suggestions of the peoples who sought to establish another form of government, or become the victims of their ire when they believed that they had sufficient right to resist them.

Buenos Aires, attentive observer of these great events, did not wish to take part in the attempts of a number of individuals who conceived the plan of changing the government; since, though its consent could have legitimatized that enterprise, it was not considered then to be opportune and necessary. But when the *Junta Central* languished in the confidence of the nation, when it saw first a wavering and then that its authority and representativeness were suppressed; when it knew that the Pillars of Hercules were stirred up by strong fluctuations before the presence of a powerful army which, having penetrated into Andalusia, reduced the previous remnants of that province in most arduous conflict: when the free part of our Peninsula presented itself divided into fragments deprived of communications and the body of the state without a system of united association to concentrate its purposes, requirements, and forces: then it was that this great people, looking at its own situation and to the necessity to provide ... for the security of our future destiny, created, through the plenitude of its votes, the corporation of this Provisional Junta of Government, modeled after those which all the provinces of Spain had established.

The period of our installation was precisely that of the dissolution of the *Junta Central*; and if that could be established legitimately through the exercise of those rights which the absence of the King had caused to revert to the peoples, the same faculty had to be acknowledged for a new act which would secure the effects of the first [act] which unfortunately became dissipated. Those who derive from the recognition of the *Junta Central* an argument against the legitimacy of our government certainly ignore the true principles of its establishment. The peoples could set up in the *Junta Central* a sovereign representative of the absent King; once it is dissolved, the peoples resumed the authority which they had exercised before, so as to replace it with a new one, and the act of this surrogation conferred upon them a plenitude of faculties which was applicable as before to the preservation or removal of those magistrates who did not merit confidence . . . .

. . . never has any power been derived from a purer origin than the one which enlivens ours. These are as free as the peoples of the Peninsula [and] they must believe that they have powers equal to the latter; and if the capitals of Spain could set up juntas and separate their magistrates, such equal authority cannot be denied to those of America.[238]

It clearly demonstrated the Late Scholastic impact made upon Moreno in the University of Charcas where, despite the expulsion of the Jesuits and the prohibition of their teachings after 1767, Jesuit thinking was still a vivid reality. In many other writings of Moreno, composed while he was the Secretary of the Provisional Junta of Buenos Aires (until December 1810), similar Suarezian formulas are to be found, such as on the Congress Convoked and on the State's Constitution of November 2 and November 28, 1810:

Ferdinand VII being separated from his Kingdom and helpless to exercise the supreme dominion which is inherent in the Crown; the *Junta Central* dissolved which the Kingdom established to fill the lack of its Monarch; the acknowledgment of the Council of the Regency's being suspended because it could not show legitimate titles for its inauguration: who is the supreme chief of these provinces, the one who looks after the others, the one in whom the fundamental relations of the social compact are concentrated, and who executes the high rights of the sovereignty of the people? Congress has to appoint him. If the election would fall upon the Council of the Regency, the latter would take over the faculties which the *Junta Central* had exercised; if it would fall upon some person of the Royal family it would be a true regent of the Kingdom; if the example is preferred which Spain has given us, [viz.,] wishing not regents but an association of patriotic men with the denomination of *Junta Central*, then the latter will be the supreme chief of these provinces and will exercise over them during the absence of the King the rights of his person with the extensions or limitations which the peoples predetermine in its establishment. The authority of the Monarch returned to the peoples through the captivity of the King; hence, they are the ones who can modify or subject it to the form which they most desire . . . .[239]

The authority of the peoples in the present cause is derived from the resumption of supreme authority which through the captivity of the King has returned to the origin from which the Monarch derived it, and the exercise of said power is subject to new forms which freely may be given to it.[240]

Moreno, like Castelli, was of a revolutionary and adventurous temperament, and this may have been the reason that he has been associated with the ideas of the French Revolution and the thought of Rousseau. How this confusion came about is well demonstrated by Jaime Delgado when he said that "in the defense of the members of Córdoba, elected but afterward not confirmed in their positions," Moreno based himself on the ground that "the plurality of votes decided the election. Plurality, votes, elections — here we have the French influence." Furlong comments that

> evidently such an influence did not exist, since elections in the civil and ecclesiastical *cabildos* were already a tradition two centuries old in the River Plate area, and with the elections came the votes, and with the votes their plurality which influenced the balance in favor of one side or the other. We need only open the capitular agreements of Córdoba of the seventeenth century to find many cases of this electoral process.[241]

Thus confusion about simple elections is joined to confusion about the social contract, particularly because Moreno had translated Rousseau's work (although the chapters on religion had to be omitted). At the meeting of the *cabildo* of February 5, 1811, it was stated that the reprinted part of Rousseau's *Contrat social* was of no utility to youth; that, on the contrary, it could be harmful, since it lacked the principles it should contain to make it desirable reading; the members of the *cabildo* believed that the authorized purchase of two hundred copies of the work was useless, superfluous, and harmful. Therefore, they decided to call upon the printer, to propose returning the books.[242] Actually, Moreno's presumed link to Rousseau is similar to Nariño's supposed connection with the French Revolution; in both cases, the deeper influence is the Spanish Late Scholastic thought of Suárez and his sixteenth-century colleagues.

Moreno has been called the precursor; although that is not historically true, he was the greatest force of the May Revolution, at least in the first months. The revolution was a manipulated popular movement without a *caudillo*, as so often happens in Hispanic countries, and thus paralleled events in the Peninsula; however, it was Moreno who gave the movement direction and who imprinted his thought as a guiding force on the revolution. Moreno showed Scholastic traits, but no doubt he also represented another example of the fusion of old Hispanic thought with political ideas from a different source — a line of thinking which was applied after the May Revolution had taken roots. In this sense, as Delgado points out,

> Moreno's thought ... is a confluence of two different lines of thinking: the line of French tradition followed by him through the main philosophers of the great Revolution, Rousseau, Montesquieu, by way of Filangieri, Raynal, and others, and the Hispanic line, marked by the Spanish jurists of the Indies, such as Aguiar y Acuña, Pinelo, Solórzano Pereira whom the student of Charcas had consulted,

and, Furlong continues,

> Moreno thus takes nourishment from the French philosophers, since in them he finds the expression of what he seeks. Catholic-Christian equality, liberty, fraternity, reaffirmed by the Hispanic writers, find an echo in the French doctrines, and at the same time the latter leave in his mind the outline of a policy .... [243]

This point of view can be better understood if we realize that

> when the ideas of the Enlightenment and the thought of the French Revolution, especially the famous Declaration of the Rights of Man and the Citizen, arrived in the Peninsula, they were amply diffused, but at the same time

were modified and intertwined with Hispanic thought without generally causing a subordination to the French intellectual ideas. [This happened] because the ideas which at that moment invaded the world were not logically original .... One especially cannot forget, because of his influence in Spanish America, that one of the most profound political thinkers humanity has known, Suárez, had arrived in his *De legibus* of 1612 at a doctrinal elaboration which in many aspects, especially with regard to the Social Contract and the Rights of Man, is to be found later in political thought and, hence, in the constitutional texts.[244]

Belgrano was born in 1770, studied in Spain (Oviedo: 1782–88; Salamanca: 1787–88; Valladolid: 1789) and graduated as a lawyer. He was very much molded by the Spanish Enlightenment, especially Campomanes, and like Jovellanos was much influenced by Adam Smith — ideas which all determined his economic and political outlook. Belgrano was not a Scholastic thinker and cannot be associated with the *pactum translationis*. Instead he let himself be carried away by the Lockean philosophy; but it must also be said that Belgrano — whom Furlong calls a non-career military man, a confused politician, and also a superficial philosopher[245] — remained orthodox in faith in spite of the impacts of Locke and Condillac.

Among the intellectuals of the Argentine May Revolution was also dean Gregorio Funes. A native of Córdoba, he graduated from the University of Alcalá with a solid education. In 1785 he addressed the viceroy in regard to the situation at Córdoba University; though not discussing the philosophy taught, this document represented a most significant Report of Grievances and limited itself to contrasting the glorious past of the university with its present decay.[246] A few years later Funes made his famous *oración fúnebre* to the memory of Charles III at the Mercedarian Church in Córdoba (1790). In this he mentioned the social contract, which has been interpreted in favor of Rousseau (Mariano de Vedia y Mitre, Jefferson Rea Spell) while Furlong opted for Suárez.[247] Halperín Donghi linked him instead to Jovellanos and his similar address to the Royal Economic Society of Madrid (November 8, 1788), i.e., to the ideas of Enlightened despotism with its first duty, abundance and prosperity, although not in a total way; he summarized his ideology as anti-Machiavellian, anti-war, and anti-fanaticism[248] — the first would link him to Late Scholasticism and to Spanish seventeenth-century political thought, the second and third to the Spanish Enlightenment of Feijóo. This link to Jovellanos backfires, however, since the author of the *Informe sobre la Ley Agraria* had profound roots with Spain's past in the field of philosophy and politics. Alejandro Korn interpreted Funes well:

> The dean Funes thus is a man of the Enlightenment, open to the progressive trends of the period, who intends to preserve, as the basis of the reforms and changes whose necessity he acknowledges, his deeply rooted religious and Scholastic convictions which in his mind are compatible with a moderate liberalism.[249]

In 1808, when the old university was reorganized, Funes became its first rector, and at the time of the May Revolution he sided with the patriots as a member of the conservative party of Saavedra and opposed the counterrevolutionary movement headed by Juan Gutiérrez de la Concha, Liniers, and

Santiago Allende. A defender of the interior provinces, Funes was elected deputy by the *cabildo* of Córdoba, and together with Felipe de Molina (Mendoza) demanded the incorporation of the provincial representatives into the Buenos Aires junta to which Moreno was opposed. In the conference of December 18, 1810, attended by the provincial deputies, Funes defended the right of the provinces to participate in the government of the Junta of Buenos Aires, a goal which was achieved with the establishment of the *Junta Grande*. Funes had argued

> that the deputies felt compelled to claim the right which belonged to them of being incorporated in the provisional junta and of taking an active part in the management of those provinces until the meeting of the congress that had been convoked; that this right, besides being undisputed by the people, their constituents (for the capital city did not have the legitimate right by itself to elect rulers whom the other cities ought to obey), had been acknowledged by the junta itself, for, in the official circular of the convocation, it had expressly pledged the delegates that as soon as they arrived they would take an active part in the government and would be incorporated in the junta.[250]

In sum, there is no clear evidence that the social contract Funes mentioned is linked to either Suárez or Rousseau. Halperín Donghi's assertion that he was more a man of the Enlightenment and linked to Jovellanos definitely shifts the balance more to the Hispanic side than to Rousseau, particularly in view of Jovellanos' Scholasticism in politics and philosophy.

It must be borne in mind that the junta established in Buenos Aires in May 1810 was a purely urban affair: the interior had not been consulted in the fateful decision. Soon afterward negotiations were opened and the original junta of nine was enlarged by December with nine additional deputies from the interior of Argentina. This new body of eighteen (five were still missing by mid-December) representing the city and the provinces[251] called itself the *Junta Conservadora de la Soberanía del Señor Fernando VII* and meant a victory of the conservative elements (Saavedra) against the revolutionary faction (Moreno). Although not necessarily in favor of independence, these delegates also showed their familiarity with the popular doctrine which had set up the junta in Buenos Aires. The instructions which these provincial deputies carried with them when they arrived in Buenos Aires to constitute the *Junta Grande* or Congress were as Scholastic as the Memorandum which the former *oidores* of the royal *audiencia* sent to the king when they were expelled in that year. The *pactum translationis* was mentioned again on October 22, 1811, when this *Junta Grande* repeated the formula used in 1810. The proclamation of the junta stated in its introduction that as a result of the absence and the imprisonment of the king the state had become acephalous and the peoples had reasserted their sovereign power.[252]

It was this *Junta Grande* and the succeeding governments — the Triumvirates and the Directorate — in the River Plate which tried to extend their power beyond Buenos Aires and the interior of Argentina and bring back any area of the viceroyalty which had set up its own junta. This explains the military campaigns against the dissident areas, all of which successfully resisted the attempts of reincorporation into the old Viceroyalty of the River Plate for which Buenos Aires arrogated to itself the right of the viceregal capital and which it pretended to rule with the centralist style of the old regime. Castelli hastened to Upper Peru in 1810, but was beaten at Huaqui in 1811 by a Royalist army from Peru. Belgrano attempted the recapture of Paraguay, but his army was beaten by the Paraguayans at Tacuarí in 1811. The problem with Montevideo was complicated by the fact that the city was in Spanish hands, having established a junta in 1808 loyal to the Peninsula, and the interior was led by José Gervasio Artigas, willing to join a federal Argentine government but not a Buenos Aires bent on extreme centralism. Here too Buenos Aires lost out, even if by 1814 it was able to seize Montevideo; by 1817, however, Uruguay fell into the hands of Portugal. In the end Buenos Aires — like Mexico and Bogotá — was reduced to Argentina proper and the application of the *pactum translationis* remained provincial.

The same ideas which had inspired the May Revolution were repeated three years later by the Argentine General Constituent Assembly which took place in Buenos Aires, January 30–31, 1813. In the convocation of this Assembly, announced on October 24, 1812, it is stated:

> That after having consolidated the first step to freedom with an effort and a resistance as general as sublime; ... when Spain cannot justify its conduct before the court of impartial nations without confessing, despite itself, the justice and holiness of our cause; when the eternal captivity of Ferdinand VII made disappear its last rights with the last duties and the most ingenious hopes ...,[253]

and after a solemn Mass in the cathedral the government accepted the oath of the representatives, which demonstrates the continuity of Spanish traditions:

> Do you swear to God, our Lord, upon the Holy Scriptures, and do you promise to the fatherland to carry out truthfully and precisely the duties of the sublime positions to which the peoples have elevated you, upholding the Catholic religion and promoting the rights of the cause of the country for the good and the happiness of America?[254]

Moreover, a famous priest, Canon Domingo Achega, also referred to the *pactum translationis* during the early period of the Argentine Revolution. In 1813 he wrote

> that the authority of the kings emanates originally from the will of the people.... No one will dare to maintain that the authority of the kings is as natural as the *potestas* of parents over their children .... The respect, fealty, and obedience which [the people] owe to their sovereign are based upon the obligation which they themselves imposed. Their duties and their corresponding rights, as well as the rights and duties of the sovereigns, result from the contract which one party concluded with the other.[255]

Thus the picture of the Argentine situation does not warrant a statement that the prevailing intellectual influences must have been the ideas of Rousseau and the French Revolution or the European Enlightenment. The lever for the beginning of the Wars of Independence seems to have been the *pactum translationis*, and the whole foundation of the movement in 1809–10 was Scholastic. Admittedly, these theories were not in all cases expounded in a concise and coherent way, but were mixed with modern thought, particularly after the revolution had become an historical fact. Levene stated it well:

The Revolution of 1810 is rooted in its own past and nourishes itself from Hispanic and Spanish American ideological sources. It was formed during the Spanish domination and under its influence, though it went against it, and only in a peripheral way do the facts and ideas of the world alien to Spain and Spanish America, which constituted the native world of these ideas, have an impact. Philosophically and historically, it would be absurd to imagine the Spanish American Revolution as an act of ape-like imitation, as an ephiphenomenon of the French or North American Revolution . . . . In no part of Europe other than Spain was there such a prolific production of political literature of a markedly liberal and antimonarchical tendency . . . . The egalitarian idea prevails in this Spanish literature: the egalitarian idea of the states among themselves, which is the thesis of Francisco de Vitoria, the creator of public international law; the egalitarian idea of the members which make up the political society, which is the thesis of Father Mariana and of Suárez — who bases the existence of the state upon the consent of the governed, thus anticipating the theory of Rousseau's *Contrat social* — who with many others explain the right of resistance or of revolt against tyranny; the egalitarian idea of men among themselves whatever their race, which was the thought of Queen Isabella and for whose realization that apostle of the liberty of the Indians and of the blacks, Bartolomé de Las Casas, and that defender of the Spanish Americans, Juan de Solórzano Pereira, wrote and fought.[256]

Viceroyalty of New Granada. A royalist junta under the presidency of Viceroy Amar y Borbón had proclaimed loyalty to the Peninsular authorities on September 5, 1808, but the revolutionary movement in Quito (August 10, 1809) subsequently divided *peninsulares* and *criollos,* in the September meetings of 1809 in Bogotá which had dealt with that question. These September meetings had crystallized the opinions of the *criollos* and led to a conspiracy which was to depose the viceroy and establish a revolutionary junta of three members: Luis Caicedo, Pedro Groot, and Antonio Nariño. The conspirators met in the *hacienda* of Father Andrés Rosillo and also had contacts with *criollos,* such as Ignacio de Herrera and possibly Joaquín Camacho.[257] Though the plot did not succeed, it showed the changing times.

The bad news from Spain, the inability to cope with the revolutionary junta of Quito, and the establishment of the revolutionary junta of Caracas on April 19, 1810, brought matters to a climax in New Granada proper: Cartagena was the first to emulate this example when it set up its own junta on May 22. It was not so much the difference between *criollos* and *peninsulares* — which liberal historians continue to emphasize — but distrust of the authorities which might extend recognition in Spain to *any* government, including the hated Napoleonic regime. Thus, the distrust of the Argentine *criollos* to Viceroy Cisneros was repeated here in the person of Viceroy Amar. And thus, again, the so-called revolution in New Granada also arose from a deeply felt loyalty and was not a camouflaged pretext to use Spain's momentary weakness for the goal of independence.

On July 20, Bogotá followed the example given by Cartagena: it established its *Junta Suprema de Gobierno* and deposed Viceroy Amar. In its *Acta,* the *cabildo* stated clearly that the people had recovered its rights and had transferred them to the *Junta Suprema* of Bogotá, the holder of popular sovereignty, and that "New Granada would not abdicate the imprescriptible rights of the people's sovereignty to other than its august and unfortunate monarch Ferdinand VII any time that he would come to govern among ourselves,"[258] a political theory in line with the Spanish doctrines of the sixteenth century regarding the origin of authority and its return to the popular source.[259] The same *Acta* also expressed another concept which was one of the main causes of the revolutionary movement: the preservation of the Catholic religion, when it stated that

> we swear by God who exists in heaven that we shall religiously comply with the Constitution and the will of the people as expressed in this *Acta*; to spill our last drop of blood for the defense of our sacred Catholic, Apostolic, and Roman religion, our beloved monarch Ferdinand VII, and the freedom of the fatherland.[260]

This junta then attempted to unify the country and to re-establish sole authority over the entire viceroyalty. It convoked a national congress of all its areas on December 22, 1810, which was unsuccessful, since few heeded the call. Moreover, it separated into two major factions: the federalist majority of Camilo Torres, and the centralists of Antonio Nariño. The result was the fragmentation of New Granada proper with the centralist state of Cundinamarca under Nariño, and the federalists retreating with their congress to Tunja and setting up the United Provinces or Confederation of New Granada under Torres, while Cartagena, staunchly republican, remained outside both groups. Thus, to the constitutional and revolutionary dispute with the Peninsula was added the civil war in New Granada proper, further aggravated because the viceroyalty had split in the meantime: Venezuela had organized its own provincial junta in 1810 followed by its declaration of independence (the first republic: July 1811–July 1812); Quito after a short period of *de facto* independence in 1809 had returned to Spanish authority in 1812, while Cuenca and Guayaquil had remained loyal to Seville; Panama, together with Pasto and Popayán, was also in Peninsular hands.

When the Venezuelan first republic collapsed in 1812, Bolívar showed up in New Granada where the Confederation allowed him to organize an army which he was to use for the short establishment of the second Venezuelan republic (July 1813–July 1814) and which also ended in disaster by the time Ferdinand VII had returned to his throne in Spain.

Nariño in the meantime attempted to bring back to the fold the dissident areas of the south including Quito (1813); instead he himself was taken prisoner by the Spaniards (May 1814). When Bolívar had to flee from Venezuela in 1814 after the end of his "republic of wise and virtuous men,"[261] he was invited by Torres to fight for the Confederation and conquer the centralist state of Cundinamarca, which he accomplished by December 1814. Another attempt to liquidate the republic of Cartagena failed though he weakened its defenses to such a degree that the Spanish forces were later able to take it (December 1815). Although the Confederation set up its headquarters in Bogotá and now assumed the former role of Cundinamarca with Torres as President, the plunge came quickly with the absolutist return in the Peninsula. Pablo Morillo, the able Spanish commander, after capturing Cartagena, entered Bogotá in May 1816.

Thus, in contrast to Buenos Aires which made attempts to reconquer the dissident areas and was itself never reconquered by the Royalists, the situation in New Granada was even more complex: Bogotá could not even attempt the reconquest of Quito and Venezuela, and already by the end of 1810 it was no longer able to rule New Granada proper. Finally, amid growing internal Balkanization and anarchy (*la patria boba*), it was reconquered by the royalists. On the other hand, attempts to maintain the unity of the old viceroyalty were also pursued by Bogotá, as was demonstrated in the treaty of alliance and federation between the centralist state of Cundinamarca and the Venezuelan junta (Treaty of Santa Fe de Bogotá: May 28, 1811). The treaty was part of the struggle for supremacy in New Granada proper and remained a temporary solution, since by 1812 Venezuela was back in Spanish hands.

A discussion of some of the most eminent patriots of New Granada may clarify further their political ideology. Torres is the other great leader of the revolution in New Granada, besides Nariño. A man of great education, as acknowledged by Humboldt, he became in 1794 the lawyer of the Royal Council and of the *audiencias* in Spanish America. His political ideas are contained in two documents: the Representation of the *cabildo* of Bogotá to the *Suprema Junta Central* of November 20, 1809, and the letter he addressed to Ignacio Tenorio, *oidor* of Quito, on May 29, 1810.

The Representation of the *cabildo* of Bogotá, better known as the *Report of Grievances*, is in reality the voice of Spanish America airing its grievances and asking for the right of political equality.[262] In this treatise, Torres states that the establishment of the Spanish juntas was not done with the participation of the Americas and that the foundation of union between the two Spains could be achieved only by justice and equality. All provinces are "constitutional parts of one body politic," and hence, the establishment of an inequality (36 deputies for Spain, while only 9 for Spanish America) would result in a degradation.[263] Stating that the Spanish Americans are not foreigners, but Spaniards like the descendants of King Pelayo, he attacked Madrid's policy of providing positions for Peninsular Spaniards and for imposing unjust taxes without the consent of the ruled. Torres mentions the Castilian laws and those of the Indies to reinforce his legal argument that Spanish America was equal to Spain, and proclaims that in the periods prior to the Bourbons the Spanish American territories had such rights and that gradually during the Enlightened despotism they were taken away; a return to the original and constitutional foundation of the monarchy is thus necessary. Finally, Torres points out that had real equality been established or acknowledged in Spain, the sad events in Quito would not have happened, and he recalls that the *cabildo* of Bogotá in its meetings of September 6 and 11, 1809, had called for the establishment of juntas all over Spanish America, in accordance with the laws of the monarchy, which would represent a link of union from which everyone would benefit.

The *Report of Grievances* circulated widely;[264] although it never reached its final destination, it is a document which is inspired by the Spanish traditions of the Castilian and Indian laws and by such Spanish jurists as Puga, Aguiar y Acuña, Encinas, Diego de Zorilla, León Pinelo, and Solórzano Pereira.[265] It breathes the air of municipal freedoms, of justice and equality, of the great times of the Spanish and Spanish American *cabildos*.

Torres' other famous document is a reply to a letter from Ignacio Tenorio, the *oidor* of Quito, dated Bogotá, May 29, 1810. Tenorio had proposed the establishment of a Spanish American Regency, elected by all the Spanish

American provinces; Torres, however, objected to this proposal and stated in his letter, using the political concepts of the Late Scholastic Spanish school, that the oath to the king no longer counted since the bonds had been broken, and with the disappearance of the Spanish monarch civil authority reverted automatically to the people.[266] Tenorio in his letter had justified the establishment of a Spanish American Regency on the old legislation of the *Siete Partidas* (*Partida* III, Title 15, Law 2), but Torres replied that the abdication of Ferdinand VII was not covered by that law which deals only with a prince who is not of age or acts with fatuity. Thus, Torres argued that once Ferdinand VII was no longer the Spanish sovereign Spanish America was free to establish its governments in accordance with respective circumstances and necessities. He argued further that provincial juntas should have been set up from the moment that the events in the Peninsula became known, as required by the laws of Castile and the Indies[267] and by the urgent political situation, and that they should not be convoked by the Spanish authorities since their authority had entirely ceased and would not be recognized by the peoples. "*Any power, any authority, has returned to its primitive origin which is the people, and this is the one which ought to convoke.*"[268] Tenorio had also suggested that in case the Spanish government would come to America (as in the case of the Portuguese kings) the Spanish Americans should continue in their obedience to the Peninsular authorities, but Torres rejected this, contending that once the political link which united Spanish America to the legitimate kings was broken, the kingdoms and provinces which formed part of these vast dominions were free and independent and could not and ought not to recognize any government but that which these kingdoms and provinces have given themselves. The theory is clear: it was based on the Late Scholastic *pactum translationis* and had nothing to do with the concepts of either Rousseau or Locke.

In the memorable events of July 20, 1810, in Bogotá, Torres played a great role as political leader and secretary of the *Junta Suprema de Gobierno*, not unlike that of Moreno in Buenos Aires. The documents of those days always mentioned "the full recovery of the people's rights,"[269] and furthermore, Torres discussed the origin of society which in accordance with the doctrines of Suárez was an accord sanctioned by natural law — "a sacred agreement which had been transmitted to posterity by this natural action of some intelligent and moral beings which communicate their needs, participate in their pleasures, and correspond in their sentiments .... Thus, this divine law is the one that has formed societies and has been seen as basis and foundation of the political bodies."[270] Moreover, Torres attacked the Enlightened despotism of the Spanish monarchy in the name of Scholasticism: "In Spain there has been nothing but tyranny, ever *since the kings surrounded themselves with an absolute mantle which the nation did not wish and could not grant them.*"[271] Finally, Torres stated that religion had always been the support of the states, and that a religion "so holy, pure, and true as that of Jesus Christ, which particularly was followed by New Granada and Venezuela, is certainly the most appropriate for the new governments." Asking the Church to cooperate and support the republican authorities, he recalled the divine origin of legitimate authority, "since he who deviated from it deviates no less from the road which Jesus Christ has shown us."[272]

Other revolutionary leaders in New Granada proper were Joaquín Camacho, Frutos Joaquín Gutiérrez, and Ignacio de Herrera. Joaquín Camacho was the writer of several official reports, especially the *Instrucción del cabildo del Socorro al diputado del reino a la Junta Suprema* (October 20, 1809), influenced by Jovellanos — the happiness of the state depends essentially on the inviolability of its constitutional laws, suppression of sterile classes, reduction of unproductive employments, freedom of land and work — which was based on the eternal law. In a polemic with the bishop of Cuenca, Camacho defended the sovereignty of the new government — "It is called *Suprema Junta* with a very just title, by the sovereign authority which the people conferred upon her."[273] Like Servando Teresa de Mier y Nóbrega, o.p., the author of the famous *Carta de un Americano a el Español*, and the Mexican deputy to the Spanish *Cortes*, José Miguel Guridi y Alcocer, Camacho also believed that sovereignty was rooted *radically, originally*, and not *essentially* in the nation.[274] Hence, Camacho's political views were rooted in Scholasticism.

Frutos Joaquín Gutiérrez, professor of canon law, adviser to the Holy Office, and attorney of the *audiencia*, was author of several works dealing with bishoprics, cemeteries, and the *Cartas de Suba* of February and March 1809.[275] In the famous meeting in Bogotá on September 6 and 11, 1809, he

> thought the only means to retain Quito in the empire and convert distrust into confidence in the provisional Spanish government was to establish a junta in Bogotá composed of the first dignitaries of the viceroyalty and representatives of the provinces. Upon restoration of friendly relations with Quito, the defense of the viceroyalty and of the presidency could be placed in the hands of the respective juntas,[276]

but these views were not accepted. On July 20, 1810, he became one of the key personalities: he justified the establishment of the junta, stating that the people had the right to get rid of the yoke. On July 28, he called together the priests of the capital and explained the righteousness and legitimacy of the new government on the basis of the Scholastic teachings of the direct origin of political power which was *radically* retained by the people. On September 25, 1810, Gutiérrez, with the counter-signature of Torres, published the *Manifiesto* on behalf of the Junta, which cited the famous Augustinian formula *Remota iustitia quod sunt regna nisi latrocinia* and whose full title showed the Suarezian formula: Reasons which forced the New Kingdom of Granada to reassume the right of sovereignty, to remove the authorities of the old government, and to install a Supreme Junta under the sole title and in the name of our sovereign Ferdinand VII and with independence from the Council of the Regency and any other representation.[277] Finally, for the justification of the war with Spain, Gutiérrez quoted St. Thomas — there is no so well-ordained and legitimate power as that constituted by the will of the people — and cited the same articles of the *Summa theologica* which Suárez also had used in order to show the Thomist foundation of popular sovereignty and which Nariño used to defend the principles of the rights of men: Q. 40, 1, of IIa IIae; Q. 90, 3; Q. 95, 4; and Q. 105, 1, of Ia IIae. Far from being sedition, it was a just war for the common good (Q. 42, 2, of IIa IIae, confirming this further with Q. 68, 4, of IIa IIae, and with the comments of Cardinal Cajetan to Q. 64, 3, of the same IIa IIae).[278] He ends his comments on the ideological foundation of the revolution of 1810: *"This is the* conclusion which Saint Thomas proposes, [the one] which provides the guide for the ethics of our political transformation."²⁷⁹

Ignacio de Herrera, lawyer of the *audiencia*, was the author on September 1, 1809, of his *Reflexiones de un Americano imparcial sobre la legislación de las Colonias Españolas, 1810*, a document highly critical of Spanish policy — especially the inequality of the *criollos* to the *peninsulares* — in which he stated that the peoples were the sources of absolute authority and that they had transferred these rights to put them into the hands of a chief who would make them happy, and that he was to rule impartially as the source of justice, as a real *pater societatis*.²⁸⁰ As attorney of the *cabildo*, he wrote a report (January 15, 1810) to the Spanish government requesting an investigation against the abuses committed against the *criollos* and accusing the administration of Viceroy Amar of treason to king, country, and religion, with the possibility of even obeying Joseph Bonaparte.²⁸¹ He was soon imprisoned, though released prior to July 20, 1810, always emphasizing the return of sovereignty to the popular source. Herrera was one of those who planned the revolution of July 20, and whose participation was most distinguished. The *Acta* of the *cabildo* of July 20, 1810, records that in that meeting Herrera pointed out that "the new government had nothing to discuss, since the sovereign people had stated its will through the most solemn and august act with which free peoples utilize their rights in order to transfer them to those persons who merit their confidence."²⁸² Thus, not unlike leaders and events in other parts of Spanish America, the revolutionary actions in New Granada were deeply rooted in Spanish and Spanish American history, constitutional law, and philosophy.

cc. *The Provincialist Case*

This is the theory which was actually accepted by the majority and which succeeded in giving birth to the various independent republics within borders based on the theories of *uti possidetis iure*; the unity case of a single Spanish American political body was deemed utopian and idealistic, and the viceregal or confederacy case had also shown that it was unworkable. The provincialist case meant that sovereignty was determined in a territorial sense by the old Spanish American administrative units, or as Víctor Andrés Belaúnde stated: "Spain seeded *cabildos* and harvested nations."²⁸³

Viceroyalty of the River Plate (Upper Peru). The *pactum translationis* was here invoked by the lawyers who assembled from all over the country in Chuquisaca on January 12, 1809. They declared that they understood the colonial vassalage, not in regard to Spain or to any Spanish government or king, but personally in favor of a certain individual member of the Spanish ruling house who, in accordance with the constitutional laws of dynastic succession of the country, was the legitimate ruler.²⁸⁴ Two famous Spanish Americans who upheld Scholastic theories in this area were especially Pedro Domingo Murillo²⁸⁵ and Pedro Vicente Cañete — their ideas were close to those of the *fiscal* Celedonio Villota in Buenos Aires.

The disarray of the Spanish monarchy found its first revolutionary action in Upper Peru influenced largely by the intellectual activities of the University of Chuquisaca. For a long time a distinguished center of learning, the university played a most important role in the political ferment which had grown in the area, and as John Edwin Fagg commented: "While modern revolutionary writings enjoyed some circulation, of more importance were the doctrines of St. Thomas Aquinas and Francisco Suárez concerning the relations of rulers and subjects."[286] The events of Bayonne then ushered in "a veritable frenzy of discussion."[287] While several rival groups were now vying for power, the *audiencia* simply acted by imprisoning the President-Intendant and establishing a revolutionary junta in Chuquisaca on May 25, 1809, in which students and lawyers of the university, members of the *cabildo*, and dissident members of the *audiencia* were represented. This revolutionary junta which came to power by popular revolt and in which the students of the university had been the most important groups repeated now the arguments of the lawyers in early January in the sense that Upper Peru had the same right to set up its own junta in the absence of the legal king as did other areas of the Spanish Empire. Chuquisaca thus put into practice the traditional teachings of its university, the Scholastic thought which had permeated the whole Spanish world since the university's inception.

The junta of Chuquisaca was unable to cope with the growing fragmentation and anarchy in the area, however, and thus another revolutionary group, led by Murillo, seized power in La Paz on July 16, and deposed the Peninsular authorities, including the president-intendant and the archbishop, who were not popular since it was known that they had seriously considered the proposals of Princess Carlota Joaquina for a throne in the River Plate area and had followed the other Spanish American regions in acknowledging the Peninsular authorities. The revolutionary junta of La Paz then proceeded to declare autonomy from both distant Spain and closer Buenos Aires. While critical of Spain's economic system it was in reality more concerned with its dependency on Buenos Aires, and thus announced the end of silver remittances to the former viceregal seat.[288]

The revolutionary movement in both Chuquisaca and La Paz, too weak and too divided but clear in its determination to resist Peninsular pretensions, was caught between two fires, Peru and the River Plate, and was in reality not yet ready for independence. Moreover, Upper Peru's links to traditional Lima were too strong, and the Indian masses preferred Spanish rule to revolutionary experiments. The revolution in Upper Peru was thus a welcome opportunity for Lima to capture an area which had always been closer to Peru proper, whether in Incan times or in the Spanish period until 1776, when it was detached from it to be part of the new Viceroyalty of the River Plate. On the other hand, Upper Peru's importance to Buenos Aires because of silver production was such that the city could ill afford its secession. Military forces from both viceroyalties thus converged on Upper Peru: troops of Viceroy Abascal, headed by Goyeneche, defeated the insurgents on October 25 at La Paz, and an expedition ordered by Viceroy Cisneros fared likewise at Chuquisaca in the same month.

After the failure of the revolutionary movement a guerrilla resistance began operations against the royalists. Similar to the situation in contemporary Spain, it resulted in the establishment of six different *republiquetas* — the priest Ildefonso de las Muñecas at Ayata in the north; Juan Antonio Alvarez at Mizque and Vallegrande in the center; Miguel Lanza at Apopaya; José Vicente Camargo in the south; Manuel Ascensio Padilla at Chuquisaca, and Ignacio Warnes at Santa Cruz de la Sierra. They were more a nuisance factor than a serious threat to the royalist authorities, and by 1816 all but one had been destroyed.[289]

The guerrillas recognized the revolutionary regime in Buenos Aires, but things changed when the regime decided to seize control of the area. In 1810, in pursuit of the policy of Buenos Aires to assert its rights as successor to the viceroyalty, and given the importance of the area, one army after another invaded Upper Peru. On November 7, the Argentine expedition under Castelli won the battle of Suipacha but his repressive and arbitrary measures caused hostility. At Huaqui (June 20, 1811) his troops simply disintegrated at the sight of Goyeneche's army. In pursuit of the enemy the royalists now invaded Argentine territory but, having overextended themselves, were defeated in turn in the battle of Salta (February 20, 1813).[290]

The victory of Salta was then the background for the second Argentine invasion of Upper Peru, this time under Belgrano. Twice defeated by Joaquín de la Pezuela, the royalists again moved into Argentina, and again overreaching themselves were now defeated by San Martín.

A third expedition left for Upper Peru under José Rondeau in 1815 but at Sipe Sipe was annihilated on November 29. From then on Upper Peru remained firmly in royalist hands until the very end of the Revolution. The cause of the Argentines had been continuously weakened by their own doing — "it was undermined by their own reputation. They bore the unfortunate stigma of social reformers"[291] — while the revolutionary cause in Upper Peru suffered further from the rebellion of Mateo Pumacahua, descendant of the Incas and *cacique* of Chincheros, which following in the footpath of the earlier rebellion of Tupac Amarú (1780–81) with its atrocities also shifted opinion toward the royalist side.

In sum, the revolutionary movement in Upper Peru showed the persistance and political application of Scholastic theories in pursuit of a provincialist and autonomous stand while it also demonstrated the continuity of the idea of integrity of the viceregal territories on the part of Buenos Aires and the permanency of Upper Peru's older ties to Peru. The conflict in Upper Peru, outside of the wishes of the regional insurgents, was essentially a clash of interests between the revolutionaries of the River Plate and the traditional forces of Peru against whom the River Plate had shown increasing hostility in view of the mercantilist and monopolistic hold of Lima.

Viceroyalty of the River Plate (*Uruguay*). The provincialist case was expounded also by the interior of Uruguay in its revolution of 1811. The hinterland of Montevideo was quite different from its port with its merchant and shipping interests. In the interior, the feudal *estancia*, not unlike the *hacienda* or *fazenda* in other parts of Hispanic America, was the center of social order, and, in view of protection and working opportunities, its main attraction. Contraband was the other institution largely encouraged by the mercantilist policies of the Spanish Crown and the favorable geographic situation, close to the Portuguese border, as well as by the lack of government enforcement. Both the struggle for survival, since much lawlessness existed, and the contraband activities were part of the social and economic evolution of the *Banda Oriental*.[292] The constant Portuguese encroachments into the area, such as in 1796 when the treaty of Basel with Spain (1795) — a drift into the French orbit

— encouraged such actions, were an additional factor.[293] All these explain the establishment of a border patrol, the *Cuerpo de Blandengues*, in 1796.

To counteract Portuguese activities the Spanish authorities also ordered the founding of border towns, though this collapsed with a new Portuguese attack in 1801.[294] It was in this new invasion that the future leader of the *Banda Oriental*, Artigas, distinguished himself highly in the border patrol. The Portuguese invasion of 1801 had strengthened the will of the viceregal authorities, and, in turn, the ranchers and cattlemen of the *Banda Oriental* requested greater protection with the founding of more border towns and the establishment of a sole and indivisible province.[295] This led to a new plan for the founding of towns in 1805, which followed that of 1801, as part of a military campaign (the Viana expedition). However, the plan was badly received by the local interests of Montevideo: it was supposed to be carried out mostly with their financial aid.[296] Montevideo's governor, Pascual Ruiz Huidobro, sided with the ranchers and cattlemen of the *Banda Oriental* against the financial contributions ordered by the then Viceroy Sobremonte. It thus became manifest by 1805 that the ranchers and cattlemen of the *Banda Oriental* already represented a powerful interest group which was not willing to accept dictation by Buenos Aires.[297]

Both town and country which had been affected by the British invasions of the River Plate (1806–1807) were further aggravated by the arrival of the Portuguese royal family in Rio de Janeiro. This resulted in a renewed interest in the settlement of the border areas and in measures for the recapture of land lost to the Portuguese in 1801. Jorge Pacheco's colonization plan envisioned the end of contraband, the persecution of unlawful elements, and the regularization of the rural property, but failed in view of political uncertainties (fear of new British invasions, differences between Liniers and Alzaga in Buenos Aires, the events of Bayonne, and the dispute between Liniers and Elío).[298]

The antagonism of Montevideo to Buenos Aires was generally shared by the interior, and the Spanish junta which was established in Montevideo on September 21, 1808, was able to obtain the support of the *orientales* in its resistance to the viceregal seat, but this situation became more precarious after Buenos Aires had set up its own revolutionary junta in 1810. It seemed strange then that the *orientales* were siding with the Spanish royalist cause when everyone else in the River Plate and Chile was on the other side of the fence. When the unity of Spaniards and *criollos* cracked by 1811 a new revolution began which symbolized the second act of what Lynch called "the Revolution against the River Plate" — only this time it will be led by the *gauchos* of the interior of the *Banda Oriental* and by *criollos*, although its aims will be similar: autonomy.

The immediate causes of the revolution were linked to the last colonial administrations: Gaspar de Vigodet, who arrived on October 7, 1810, at a time when the prestige of the Crown was low and the treasury empty. The latter problem called for taxes to be obtained through the regularization of land properties, but the decisions of August 23, 1810, based on similar solutions in the past (royal *Acuerdo* of April 4, 1805, and Pacheco's plan of 1808), meant a real revolution in the interior since most land was occupied without legal title.[299] It was the wrong decision at the wrong moment, since the royal authorities lacked the earlier prestige and power to enforce it at a time when political circumstances were extremely precarious. In order to meet the emergency head-on Vigodet then set up the mentioned Junta of Finance and Administration with jurisdiction over financial and economic matters, which amounted to the establishment of the long-desired *intendencia*.

The return of Elío with the rank of viceroy did not improve matters. Though, no doubt, one of the best Spanish officials, he lacked knowledge about the conditions in the *Banda Oriental*, which then led to the revolt of the interior, first against Montevideo, later against Buenos Aires and Portugal. The troops of Montevideo acted in a heavy-handed way as if in conquered territory, the *cabildos* were bypassed by military necessities, the *gauchos* were persecuted, and the ranchers felt threatened by the system of contributions which were more radically enforced in 1811 than in previous months.

When peace negotiations with Buenos Aires failed, Elío declared war on Buenos Aires on February 13, 1811. Thus, in sum, the rather unclear situation of the frontier, contraband, the non-concentration of the native population in reservations, the administrative disarray, the antagonism between landholders and those who lived on land without legal title, the embryonic situation of the poor towns which had arisen, the resistance of the big landholders to the formation of towns, the lack of judges — all these social problems converged with the wrong measures of Vigodet and Elío, which irritated the interior in view of the sacrifices demanded, the culmination of which was the declaration of war on Buenos Aires.[300]

Montevideo's opposition to Buenos Aires had been a logical consequence of the old commercial rivalry symbolized in the Argentine *consulado*; on the other hand the merchants, so loyal to the Spanish cause and so burdened with financial contributions, expected Montevideo to be rewarded, as it indeed was, with the administrative measures of 1810 and 1811. But the situation in the interior was different: it had been severely hurt in the past by the British and the Portuguese and lately by the Spanish authorities of Montevideo itself, and, besides, loyalty to a distant king was weak. It explained then why the ranchers for economic reasons, the towns in view of the measures of Montevideo which had shown great disrespect for their *fueros*, and the *gauchos* for their love of freedom, joined a revolutionary movement against the new viceregal center of Montevideo.[301]

The revolt which started with the *Grito de Asencio* by Venancio Benavides and Pedro José Viera in February 1811 against Montevideo was in favor of the Buenos Aires Junta. Elío's declaration of war which had branded the revolutionary leaders traitors resulted in Artigas' rallying to the cause of Buenos Aires, and soon he became the *jefe de los orientales* who could successfully reconcile their different viewpoints and lead them to victory. Not without reason did Juan E. Pivel Devoto call him the last Spaniard, for his austere simplicity, his devotion to the *fueros* and to local rights;[302] the Uruguayan campaign was another typically Hispanic venture for an ideal of liberty, even if there also existed profound economic interests.

Victorious in San José and Las Piedras, Artigas' revolutionary forces laid siege to Montevideo while the latter was blockading Buenos Aires by sea. Elío then accepted earlier offers of help by Princess Carlota Joaquina. As a result Portuguese troops under Souza entered the *Banda Oriental*, thus establishing a new political fact. While Carlota had been intriguing with Argentine patriots like Saturnino Rodríguez Peña, for a throne in the River Plate area — an idea also followed by men like Belgrano, Castelli, Pueyrredón, and Vieytes — the Portuguese Regent had other ideas in line with Portuguese policy of expanding the frontier to the delta though pretending he was doing this to stamp out subversive agitation.[303] The Portuguese invasion thus offered many interpretations; in any case, Buenos Aires was shaken by the event since it also had to face royalist threats from Upper Peru. The first result was the collapse of the junta in Buenos Aires and the establishment of a stronger Triumvirate, and then, the conclusion of an armistice on October 20, 1811, with Elío, which stipulated that the *Banda Oriental* would be evacuated by Argentine forces, recognizing Elío's sovereignty over the *Banda,* and promising aid against Napoleon in Spain.[304]

The action of Buenos Aires dictated by the Portuguese occupation of the *Banda Oriental* and the threats from Peru were nonetheless a serious betrayal of Artigas and his cause. It thus opened fresh wounds between the *Banda Oriental* and Buenos Aires which seemed to have been closed with the *Grito de Asencio.*

While the Portuguese remained in the *Banda Oriental,* Artigas was forced to lift the seige of Montevideo and to cross the River Uruguay with his troops and their families (the *éxodo*): it gave him "the unmistakable stature of a leader, the head of an independent people."[305] From his encampment in Ayún (Entre Ríos) he unsuccessfully appealed for help from Paraguay. However, the situation changed, when the Portuguese government in Rio de Janeiro, realizing that it was difficult to pursue its aims against British wishes — Lord Strangford from 1808 to 1815 had consistently defended the Spanish cause (though from a view to protecting British interests and not from any romantic inclination toward either Spanish side)[306] — and disgusted with Elío's pressure to abandon the territory, negotiated with Buenos Aires an agreement of May 26, 1812, by which the Portuguese evacuated the *Banda Oriental.*[307] The result was that the *Banda* again became a theater of operations.

Buenos Aires, which by 1812 "was moving toward complete independence,"[308] now reopened hostilities, with the Portuguese out of the picture. It made its peace with Artigas, and though it was an uneasy alliance, appointed him Commander in Chief of the Patriot Army of the *Banda Oriental* but reserved the supreme command to Manuel de Sarratea with instructions to eliminate Artigas' influence. Despite different aims, the revolutionary armies re-entered the *Banda Oriental* and soon again laid siege to Montevideo, winning at the *Cerrito.*

Before a decision could be achieved, however, the superficial harmony between Buenos Aires and Artigas collapsed, again in view of Sarratea's aim to dissolve the forces of Artigas, calling him a traitor. The *jefe de los orientales* then demanded the dismissal of Sarratea and the recognition of the autonomy of the *Banda Oriental.* Buenos Aires accepted the dismissal of Sarratea, thus opening the way for a united army under the new Argentine general José Rondeau.

Artigas realized, however, that the final goal of Buenos Aires, which would be achieved after the fall of Montevideo, was quite different from his own. While he wanted the autonomy of the *Banda Oriental,* Buenos Aires insisted on his centralist position as heir to the viceroyalty, thus representing its simple incorporation. At a time when the River Plate was organizing a General Constituent Assembly, Artigas called for a local assembly to make his position clear and to receive the necessary support from his people. This assembly took place at Peñarol, close to Spanish-ruled Montevideo, on April 4, 1813,[309] in which he stated that "My authority emanates from yours and it ceases with your sovereign presence. You are in the full enjoyment of your rights . . . ."[310] These were populist concepts derived from medieval Spanish philosophy which had given greatness to the *cabildos* and to local and regional *fueros*.

The next day the Assembly of Peñarol worked on the famous *Instrucciones del Año XIII* with which the Uruguayan delegates would go to the General Constituent Assembly in Buenos Aires. These *Instrucciones* represented Artigas' terms for remaining within the United Provinces of the River Plate, and may be summed up as autonomy, republic, federation, freedom of religion, and freedom of thought. The *Instrucciones* were also influenced by the ideas of the Enlightenment and the French Revolution — Pufendorf's concept of confederation is to be found in Articles 7, 10, and 11 which were adopted from the United States Articles of Confederation and Perpetual Union of 1777; Articles 4 and 20 mentioned the principles of equality, liberty, and security — but came from deep Spanish roots only modernized in line with the growing *Zeitgeist*. The Assembly of Peñarol confirmed that the *Banda Oriental* would remain under the formula of confederation within the borders of the old viceroyalty if its autonomy were respected. It is interesting to note that at a time when Buenos Aires was still acting "in the name of Ferdinand VII" Peñarol was three years ahead of the Congress of Tucumán in proclaiming the emancipation of the various provinces.[311] Peñarol then led to the establishment of a local government on April 20, 1813, which was set up at Canelones, while its delegation tried to persuade Buenos Aires of its justice. It also appointed Artigas Governor of the *Banda Oriental*.[312]

The General Constituent Assembly refused to accept Artigas' terms and ordered Rondeau to convoke a congress in the *Banda Oriental* under his auspices which would be amenable to the centralist policies of Buenos Aires. This congress assembled on December 8, 1813, at Capilla de Maciel under highhanded measures from Rondeau and under pressure from the Argentine army. Artigas protested and referred to his free election in 1811 and the agreements of Peñarol. It was at this Congress of Capilla de Maciel that Pérez Castellanos repeated arguments used earlier in the establishment of the Junta of Montevideo and illustrated perhaps best how the *pactum translationis* was used as the legal basis for the autonomy of the entire *Banda Oriental* from the old viceregal capital of Buenos Aires, and how it was still a valid argument five years after the establishment of the Junta of Montevideo. Pérez Castellanos mentioned the lack of freedom at the congress and that in its election the welfare of the *Banda Oriental* had not been taken into account but only its subordination to Buenos Aires, and then said:

> Mr. President: When has the Government of Buenos Aires been recognized by that of this *Banda*? I do not know when. What I do know is that this *Banda Oriental* has the same right to withdraw from the Buenos Aires Government as Buenos Aires had to withdraw from the government of the Metropolis of Spain. From the moment when there was lacking the person of the King, who was the only link uniting everyone and to whom we were

all subordinated, the peoples became acephalous and had the right to govern themselves.[313]

The Congress of Capilla de Maciel had no effect: the Uruguayans did not recognize it and the delegates to the Argentine Constituent Assembly never went there. The authorities of Buenos Aires, realizing the resistance, now simply appointed a governor for the *Banda Oriental*. This in turn resulted in most *orientales'* abandoning the siege of Montevideo.

The Argentine government was determined to get control of both the city and the interior, eliminating Artigas. Montevideo finally fell to the Argentine forces under Carlos María de Alvear on June 22, 1814, with the express stipulation that, like all areas of the United Provinces of the River Plate, it would remain part of the Spanish monarchy and under the legitimate rule of Ferdinand VII. These stipulations were violated later, as were the promises to Artigas that the city would be turned over to him.[314]

The Argentine occupation of Montevideo led to the dissolution of the *cabildo* and was followed by domination of the *Banda Oriental*, but the arbitrariness of many Argentine measures increased Artigas' prestige. In opposition to the centralist position of Buenos Aires Artigas now openly campaigned in favor of a confederation, and such Argentine provinces as Corrientes, Entre Ríos, Santa Fe, Córdoba, and Mendoza followed his leadership. Hostiles between Artigas and Buenos Aires now turned into open warfare and led to the great victory of the *orientales* at Guayabo (January 10, 1815) and to the Argentine abandonment of Montevideo on February 26.

With the capture of Montevideo by Artigas' forces, the *cabildo* of Montevideo was asked to resume its full powers until the people would decide a more permanent solution. In line with Spanish traditions, it was then again the *cabildo* which on March 7, interpreting the popular will, gave Artigas the title of "Protector and Patron of the Freedom of the Peoples" and appointed him Captain General of the *Banda Oriental*.[315]

Although the final independence of the *Banda Oriental* did not come until 1828 and after many more convulsions, the year 1815 with autonomy fully achieved by the Protectorate of Artigas ended another chapter in the pursuit of the long-desired goal. The intellectual basis of this struggle, first in Montevideo and later in the interior, was deeply rooted in the Spanish and Spanish American past and especially in the rivalry between the two cities of the River Plate, thus again echoing typically Hispanic traits.

Viceroyalty of the River Plate (Paraguay). The coup which forced Velasco out of office on May 14, 1811, and established a revolutionary junta ended a process which had begun the year before with the confrontation between Asunción and the new regime in Buenos Aires. This revolutionary junta was supposed to rule in the name of Ferdinand VII, thus imitating the Provisional Junta of Buenos Aires,[316] but very quickly proceeded to declare independence on May 17, and on June 9 deposed the former Intendant.[317]

A Paraguayan Congress which convened in Asunción between June 1 and 20 stated its policy through its most eminent intellectual, Mariano Antonio Molas, who, following policies similar to Artigas', proposed integration within the old borders of the viceroyalty provided the principle of federation was accepted. The proposal failed as it did in the *Banda Oriental* and other Argentine provinces in view of the obstinate policies of Buenos Aires which continued to follow the Bourbon centralist line.

The first Paraguayan Congress then asserted that, pending an overall solution of the former areas of the viceroyalty, "this province would govern itself"[318] and set up a new *Junta Superior Gubernativa* on July 20 (Fulgencio Yegros, Pedro Juan Cavallero, and Dr. Francia): it ruled for two years and was "the last expression of the colonial ruling class."[319] In these years the only revolutionary leader who had the educational ability and strength to carry out a political program was Dr. Francia. He established his power by pursuing a tough policy toward Buenos Aires and succeeded in outwitting the other members of the junta. By the time the second congress assembled at Asunción in 1813 Francia was well on his way to ultimate authority in Paraguay.

Too isolated from the main political and economic centers like Buenos Aires, Montevideo, Santiago or Lima, Asunción–Paraguay played only a secondary role in the Spanish American Revolution. Led by an ambitious and farsighted man who made the best use of the political circumstances and who believed that isolation was the only possible policy to pursue, Paraguay was able to establish its autonomy and then its total independence. The *pactum translationis* was used in the actions of May 1811, which is not surprising given the traditional roots of the country and the educational background of Francia — who had studied theology and law at the University of Córdoba[320] — and his direct experience with the *cabildo* of Asunción as one of its elected members.[321] It may be pointed out that Francia's background is not necessarily in opposition to his future career in 1814 as Supreme Dictator of the Republic and in 1816 as Perpetual Dictator when he fell increasingly under the spell of the Napoleonic influences and became a symbol for the persistance of Enlightened despotism.

Viceroyalty of Peru (Chile). While Peru did not develop a homegrown revolutionary movement, the events in Spain also caused a debate in the Captaincy General of Chile, at that time a separate part of the viceroyalty. In Chile, two important pamphlets were the *Diálogo de los porteros*, attributed to Manuel de Salas, and the *Catecismo político cristiano*, written by "José Amor de la Patria." The first brought to light political doctrines of the Scholastics when it pointed out that everything came from God, and that the monarchs derived their divine rights from the people and for their common good. The pamphlet went on to say that the people, when they established the monarchy, had decided that kings were to be succeeded by their children; they also authorized in case of the rulers' absence or the succession of minors the appointment of a regency to govern the kingdom; finally, if these same kings were not able to appoint legal representatives, the dignitaries would choose three of five persons to take the reins of government — authority returns to the source whence it came. This is the Hispanic political theory already incorporated in the *Siete Partidas* (*Partida* II, Title 15, Law 3).[322]

An even clearer formulation of Late Scholastic political thought is found in the *Catecismo político cristiano*, whose author is believed to have been Bernardo de Vera Pintado.[323] The *Catecismo* begins with the statement that monarchy is not the best form of government, since it can easily lead toward tyranny, and recalls that the Spanish *Cortes* was destroyed by the kings in order to establish despotism. The origin of civil authority is seen in God's governing the universe and allowing all things to happen among human beings (first and universal cause); thus, all earthly things are derived from providence. On the other hand, all natural effects have immediate second and natural causes — this is what happens with the civil authority of kings and others who rule over man. It was the people who established the monarchy and who, by so doing, imposed upon the ruler certain limitations. The author of the *Catecismo* then points out that authority returns to the people whence it came, and the people alone has the authority to appoint or institute a new king or to establish a form of government which best suits its happiness. "José Amor de la Patria" then takes up the practical side of the thesis and declares that this is the doctrine which the Peninsular Spaniards had applied in their proclamations, acts, and manifestos, when their kings were detained in Bayonne and Napoleon invaded their country, through the establishment of juntas, all independent of one another until the provinces established the *Suprema Junta Central*. Continuing the argument, the author of the *Catecismo* explains that the inhabitants and the provinces of Spanish America had sworn allegiance only to the kings of Spain and were subjects only of these kings, just as the people and regions of Spain had been and were subjects of that same monarch. This oath, however, had never been given to either the people or the provinces of Spain; therefore the latter had no right to empower the *Suprema Junta Central* with such an authority over the peoples and provinces of Spanish America; hence, the *Suprema Junta Central* had no legal title to rule in Spanish America. Finally, the governors of Spanish America, like the governors of Spain, lost their authority and jurisdiction once the prince who delegated it was gone; in this case, the authority to appoint them or to establish the provisional government which best suited the common well-being reverted to the inhabitants, to the people and provinces of Spanish America — as was the case in metropolitan Spain.[324]

The theories expressed in both pamphlets, particularly in the *Catecismo*, showed very well what the political ideology was which prevailed in Chilean society, just as it did in greater or lesser degree in other parts of Spanish America. It also foreshadowed political developments in those parts of Spanish America where juntas had been or would be established. In Chile itself, the famous date was September 18, 1810, although the *pactum translationis* was a matter of discussion earlier among the members of the *criollo*-dominated *cabildo*, and between them and the Spanish-dominated *audiencia* and Acting Governor Count de la Conquista. The count resigned at the *cabildo abierto*, awaiting the decision of the people as represented in the town council. The legal foundation for the establishment of the Chilean Junta in defense of the rights of Ferdinand VII was given by José Miguel Infante, the attorney of the city of Santiago, based on the legislation of the *Siete Partidas* (*Partida* II, Title 15, Law 3), on the *pactum translationis*, and on the fundamental equality of rights between metropolitan Spain and overseas Spain — the only link which connected Chile to the Peninsula was the legitimate Crown.

> In a case like the present one, ... when the sovereign is captive and has not appointed beforehand a regent of the kingdom, Law 3, Title 15 of the Second *Partida* sets forth that a governing junta is to be established, appointing the members who ought to form it "through the representatives of the Kingdom, such as the prelates, the wealthy, and the other good and honest men." The Spanish nation, once it learned of the captivity of its

monarch, established the supreme junta of Seville, then the Central [Junta], and lastly the supreme council of the regency; although in the former as in the latter the sovereign authority is deposited, many provincial juntas were also set up with subordination to the Supreme [Junta of Seville]. I do not need to show you the reasons why the law adopts this kind of government in a case like the present one; because no one can fail to see that public confidence is better founded upon a government composed of some individuals than when only one obtains it . . . . If it has been said that the peoples of [Spanish] America form an integral part of the monarchy, if it has been acknowledged that they have the same rights and privileges as those of the Peninsula where provincial juntas have been established, are we not entitled to set them up too? There can be no equality when to some the faculty is denied to do what to others is allowed and has actually been done . . . .[325]

In 1835, the Franciscan José Javier Guzmán, who from the very beginning had joined the revolutionaries and was the brother-in-law of Domingo José de Toro, in whose residence the historic meeting of September 18 took place, stated the position of the Chilean patriots of 1810, a position in complete accord with the *Catecismo*:

The rights of the [Spanish] Americans being the same as those of the Spaniards and also the motives which they expressed for the establishment of their juntas, they decided to act in the same manner as the Peninsular Spaniards — that is, to organize a government junta which in the name of the King would take care and deal with all situations which might arise during the captivity of that ruler; since, although in Seville a junta had been established which called itself "Supreme," [Spanish] America ought not to submit to that authority because it is, in accordance with the laws of the Indies, independent of any submission to any province of Spain, even if it considered itself an integral part of the monarchy; because the cession which Pope Alexander VI made to the petition of the Catholic rulers regarding the Americas was neither to the Spaniards nor to the Provinces of Spain but to the same Kings and Sovereigns of Castile.[326]

The governing junta which appointed the former Acting Governor, Count de la Conquista, as its president, represented the victory of traditional Hispanic thought and had nothing to do with any political theory of foreign origin. It also showed a similarity with other revolutionary areas, such as the River Plate and New Granada, when it chose as president of the new revolutionary junta the highest authority of the former regime. The Scholastic theory is seen further when the same government junta was reminded by the *cabildo* of Santiago that the latter meant to retain those same rights and privileges which it had enjoyed in earlier times under the effective rule of the kings; the junta was to govern under the limitations which the people imposed on it in consenting to the junta's establishment. However, the junta was unwilling to abide by this traditional viewpoint, and used its authority without those limitations. In arguing for the *cabildo*'s rights, Infante, who spoke on behalf of the town council, used Scholastic doctrine. He stated that "when the peoples transferred all their authority to the sovereign, they reserved certain areas where they could strengthen their security and the preservation of their rights, thus establishing the *cabildos* to which they entrusted all their power, to represent them in their name...."327

Since the governing junta was only a provisional measure (as in all other parts of Spanish America where juntas had been established) it was decided on September 18 that this junta would remain in power only until a general congress was convoked which would decide the most adequate, permanent form of government. The Scholastic theory is repeated in a memorandum which was sent by Infante on behalf of the town council and which states specifically

> that it is an immutable fact that, once the right of sovereignty had been returned to the peoples because of the death of the monarch, the former, making use of the free will generally received, have to elect their representatives, so that united in a General Congress they may determine the kind of government which has to be set up, as long as the sovereign is not restored to the throne to resume his sovereign authority through right of postliminium.[328]

The *audiencia*, which disliked the idea of a congressional convocation, found in Colonel Tomás de Figueroa a useful weapon to fight the constitutionalist theory. On April 1, 1811, the day fixed for the election of deputies, a royalist plot led by Figueroa broke out; it was smashed by the forces of the junta, which justified its action on the basis of the *pactum translationis* — similar to Moreno's arguments in regard to Liniers and the Córdoba conspiracy in Argentina. It stated:

> There is on earth no authority which is based on more legal and solid foundations than the provisional junta. We have given an oath of allegiance to a Prince who from his captivity cannot govern the nation. In that unfortunate moment there returned to the peoples the authority which they had transmitted to their King [and] which in his absence they alone could administer: from this source of sovereignty emanated the provincial juntas of Spain, while the authority of the governors which the Court had appointed ceased; from that same principle followed the consolidation of sovereignty in the *Junta Central*, which by its dissolution returned [sovereignty] for a second time to the people. And have those of Chile perhaps not enjoyed the same rights to follow the example of the Peninsula? Or perhaps do they not have the same rights as the Peninsula to assemble and elect their representatives who determine their uncertain fate in this terrible monarchical crisis? Have the fundamental laws which govern us been violated so completely?[329]

Viceroyalty of New Granada (Quito). The revolutionary movement in New Granada began in Quito, although there existed no real sentiment for independence except among some members of the elite. The 1808 conspiracy of Chillo led to the movement of August 10, 1809, when some *criollo* leaders deposed the President of the *audiencia*, Ruiz de Castilla, and set up a revolutionary junta in the name of Ferdinand VII and under the Marquis de Selva Alegre and the Bishop of Quito. This was an aristocratic junta whose support emanated from control over the local militia[330] while, ironically, the people revolted in Guayaquil and Cuenca — whose *cabildos* were openly opposed to the revolutionary cause — in favor of the royalists and against the insurgents of Quito, thus demonstrating also the underlying local rivalries beneath the constitutional problem resulting from Bayonne and the different application of the *pactum translationis*.

Although Quito was a part of the Viceroyalty of New Granada, it was Viceroy Abascal of Peru, "the strong man of the empire,"[331] who took action against the revolutionaries, manifesting traditional Peruvian interest in that area. Abascal's military expedition, moving from both Guayaquil and Cuenca, soon captured Quito, and on October 28 Ruiz de Castilla was reinstated in his former position under conciliatory terms for the insurgent party, which included a future *quiteño* representation at the Spanish *Cortes*. This agreement, however, was broken by Ruiz de Castilla when the royalists were strengthened with more troops from Guayaquil, New Granada, and Peru. It was then that royalist repression accomplished what the revolutionary junta had so far not been able to do in 1809: it united the *quiteños* in their determination for freedom and autonomy.

The royalist massacre of August 2, 1810, caused a new revolutionary wave to break loose at a time when revolutionary juntas had already been established in Caracas and Bogotá. The strong popular support of this movement forced Abascal to withdraw his troops and to grant amnesty — measures which, however, no longer sufficed. The second revolution of October 1810 eliminated Spanish officials — including the assassination of Ruiz de Castilla — and set up a revolutionary junta which assumed a much more defiant attitude. In due course, a congress was convened which on February 15, 1812, declared independence from Spain and proclaimed the famous *Constitución quiteña* which, like so many other Spanish American constitutions, never took effect.

The new junta suffered from too many weaknesses: personal and ideological divisions, inability to carry the revolution into the whole country, lack of support by the Indians — who actually supported the royalist position more — and especially the fact that Guayaquil and Cuenca never went along.[332] Thus, on November 8, 1812, Toribio Montes dispersed the insurgents and royalist rule returned to Quito until 1822 when Antonio José de Sucre won the battle of Pichincha and captured it from Governor Aymerich.

Quito's revolutionary 1809 junta had preceded the events of Caracas, Cartagena, and Bogotá; its importance also lies in the fact that it brought about the collapse of the entire viceroyalty by exhausting the latter's resources.[333] Inherent in its actions was also the *pactum translationis*, and the junta justified its establishment on the same basis as those of other parts of Spanish America. The reasons most frequently given in speeches, proclamations, and correspondence were

> defense of king, religion, and country; thwarting conquest by France or preventing submission of peninsular officials to Napoleon; and the many-faceted quarrel between peninsular and criollo so strongly aroused by events in Spain. Accessory themes were Quito's critical situation, peninsular plans to assassinate the criollo nobility, the example of the Spanish provinces cessation of authority vested in officials appointed by Godoy, and the "fatal state" of Spain.[334]

As in other parts of Spanish America where revolutionary juntas were set up or would follow, the events of August 10, 1809, were not seen as disloyalty or rebellion but as a demonstration of support and allegiance to the cause of Spain against French influence in general and Napoleon in particular. The establishment of a junta was seen as a temporary device until the king would be restored to his throne.[335]

The same concepts were also expressed in the *Manifiesto al pueblo de Quito*, which stated, among other things, that the junta was set up for the defense of religion, king, and country; it "defended the role of the crown in imperial government and denounced the 'subaltern despotism' of generations of subordinate European officials. It deprecated the arrogant European assumption of sole right to debate and deal with major public problems."[336] Moreover, there also circulated in Quito a pamphlet, the *Catecismo en que debe estar instruido todo fiel vasallo de F. 7º*, whose message was that in view of the Napoleonic threat to America it was the duty of all loyal subjects to declare independence, make peace with Britain, and ransom Ferdinand from the traitor, implying — as in other documents and actions of the period — that the Peninsula was definitely lost.[337] Finally, one of the Scholastic leaders in this province was Ignacio Tenorio, who used the *pactum translationis* in a similar way as the *fiscal* Villota did in the River Plate and Pedro Vicente Cañete in Upper Peru — i.e., calling for the establishment of a Spanish American Regency and for the convocation of the kingdom's *Cortes* in overseas Spain.

Viceroyalty of New Granada (Venezuela). The news of Bayonne was not differently received here: it sparked the fuse of yet another revolution. Napoleon's emissaries arrived in La Guayra on July 15, 1808, and while the authorities seemed to hesitate, the people began to act. Two parties were then formed which agreed on the absolute rejection of Joseph Bonaparte.[338] The people of Caracas also demonstrated in front of the governor's house in favor of Ferdinand VII and sent a delegation demanding that he be proclaimed king, and while the French emissaries had to flee the country, the Venezuelans enthusiastically received the delegation of the Peninsular authorities who reported on the successful resistance against the French.

> Celebrations were held in their honor, masses were said in the churches, and the cities were illuminated. In their hats or belts the people wore the Spanish colors with the inscription: "Let us die or triumph for our King." The women donated their jewels, and millions of gold pesos were collected in a few days for the cause of Ferdinand VII . . . .[339]

The more important faction of Simón Bolívar held secret meetings at the latter's *El Palmito* estate aiming at an autonomous government for Venezuela. In November 1808 the notables of Caracas reaffirmed their loyalty to Ferdinand VII and to the holy faith and requested an assembly which together with the authorities would rule the country until the return of the king, but the government refused the petition.[340]

The arrival of the new governor, Field Marshal Vicente de Emparán, coincided with the bad news received from Spain. Events then escalated, with the *cabildo* setting up a junta on April 19, 1810. This junta offered Emparán the chairmanship, but later in the day this was declared null and void after the people in the streets had made known their feelings.[341]

The main leaders of the revolution in Caracas, besides Bolívar, were canon Cortés de Madariaga and Juan Germán Roscio, reflecting Scholastic theories. The junta was not bent on breaking ties with the Peninsula — it did only what it considered its right. However, the incomprehension and blindness of the

Peninsular authorities who misread the real and traditional meaning of the establishment of the Caracas junta, and thus were bent on crushing what they called the Venezuelan rebellion by imposing a blockade of the Venezuelan coast under a royal commissar in Puerto Rico, Antonio Ignacio de Cortabarria, as well as the arrival of Miranda and Bolívar — the latter had been sent to London by the Caracas junta together with Andrés Bello and Luis López Méndez — in late 1810, changed matters. A general congress assembled on March 2, 1811, which under the influence of Miranda proclaimed the famous Venezuelan Declaration of Independence and gave rise to the first Venezuelan Republic (July 1811–July 1812). Although this document also contains influences from Rousseau and the French Revolution, the entire basis for emancipation is the *pactum translationis*, as when it stated:

> We, the Representatives of the United Provinces . . ., considering the full and absolute possession of our rights which we recovered justly and legislatively from the 19th of April 1810 onward, as the consequence of the events of Bayonne and the occupation of the Spanish throne by the conquest and succession of a new dynasty which established itself without our consent . . .
>
> When the Bourbons agreed to the invalid stipulations of Bayonne, abandoning the Spanish territory against the will of the peoples, they failed, disregarded, and degraded the holy duty which they had contracted with the Spaniards of both worlds when with their blood and their wealth they had been put on the throne in spite of the House of Austria. Through this act they made themselves unfit or incapable of governing a free people whom they surrendered like a herd of slaves . . . .
>
> . . . calling upon the Supreme Being as witness to the justice of our actions and to the rectitude of our intentions, beseeching His divine and celestial aids and affirming to Him in the moment of our birth to dignity that His providence restores to us the wish to live and die freely believing in and defending the Holy Catholic and Apostolic religion of Christ, as the first of our duties . . . .[342]

It is also interesting that the new flag which the Republic of Venezuela adopted with its declaration of independence joined the traditional Spanish colors of red and gold to the blue of the *cabildos*.[343]

The Scholastic contents of the Venezuelan Declaration of Independence also formed the basis of Uztáriz' Republican Federal Constitution (December 11, 1811). While the spirit of the Enlightenment had penetrated Miranda and Bolívar, the patriots who had the greatest influence on this constitution were all adherents of the traditional and Scholastic ideas — e.g., Roscio, Fernando Peñalver, Francisco Javier Yáñez, Felipe Fermín Paúl, and Francisco Javier Uztáriz. The constitution lasted only five months because most of the federated provinces preferred the royalist regime of Miyares y Cajigal — it was one thing to set up a provisional junta, but another to declare independence, which the majority of the people did not approve. Moreover, Miranda clashed with all his friends because of his Jacobin views, so that finally Bolívar then profited from the anti-royalist atmosphere which Monteverde's high-handedness had created contrary to the wishes of the *audiencia*. Later, when it came to a political program (Angostura, 1819), Bolívar's ideas were quite different from Miranda's Jacobinism and from his own ultrademocratism of those days.

A further Scholastic example is given by Bolívar himself, although he cannot be classified as a Scholastic thinker. In a letter which Bolívar addressed on October 2, 1813, to the Governor of Curaçao, there is evidence of thoughts similar to those which animated patriots at that time in Venezuela and elsewhere in Spanish America. Bolívar revealed that he shared exactly the same legal and constitutional principles which had been the foundation for the establishment of juntas in Spanish America, and which were based on the equality of rights between metropolitan and overseas Spain — recently confirmed in the Constitution of Cádiz — and on the *pactum translationis*:

> Indeed, Venezuela adopted such a measure [the establishment of a junta], compelled by irresistible necessity. In circumstances which were less critical, provinces of Spain, less important than it [Venezuela], had established government juntas to save themselves from disorder and uprisings. Should Venezuela not likewise shelter itself from so many calamities and assure its existence against the rapid vicissitudes of Europe? . . .
>
> Venezuela, persuaded that Spain had been completely subjugated, as was believed in the other parts of [Spanish] America, took that step, which it could likewise have taken much earlier, authorized by the example of the province of Spain to whom it was declared equal in rights and political representation . . . .[344]

Viceroyalty of New Granada (Cartagena, Cali, Mompox, Pamplona, Socorro; Cundinamarca and Tunja). Cartagena was the first town in New Granada proper to act on behalf of the people. Through a *cabildo abierto* it deposed Governor Montes on May 22, 1810, and established a *Junta Superior de Gobierno* in line with the proposals of Cádiz and Book IV, Title 7, Law 2, of the *Recopilación de leyes de las Indias*. It justified its actions with the necessity of providing for its own government in the face of possible French threats.[345]

After Cartagena it was the turn of Cali: on July 3, 1810, it established its own provincial junta whose *Acta* of the *cabildo* of that same day stated clearly the clamor in the entire kingdom for the establishment of juntas like those which had been set up in Spain, and whose object was only "that of preserving the purity of our sacred religion, the loyalty due to our unfortunate Ferdinand, and the security and tranquillity of the country . . . ."[346]

The actions of Cartagena and Cali coincided with the ill-fated rise of the *cabildo* of Mompox and the successful events in Pamplona of July 4. This town deposed the Spanish governor Juan Bastus y Falla and also established a junta. The *Acta* of the *cabildo* of Pamplona records on July 31 that "such and such members . . . of the *cabildo*, having assembled in *cabildo abierto*, had by deposition of the governor Juan Bastus reassumed the provincial authority . . . for the country's salvation."[347] This was followed by another similar action: the revolt of Socorro, the town of the 1781 revolution. A *cabildo abierto*, of July 11, set up a *Junta de Gobierno* whose *Acta* ends: "Already we breathe with liberty, having re-established public confidence; we know that we can preserve our sacred religion and restore this Province to its legitimate sovereign, Ferdinand VII, without danger that the favorites of Godoy and the envoys of Bonaparte turn us into slaves by dividing us."[348] Finally, Bogotá itself established its own junta on July 20. This was the most important event in New Granada proper, but it is linked more to the confederacy case, although in the end it also remained a provincial junta.

The revolutionary *actas* of the various *cabildos* reveal two ideas shining clearly from their texts: the concept of popular sovereignty as the foundation of the various autonomist movements, and the preservation of the Catholic religion as one of the main causes of the revolutionary movements.³⁴⁹ Similar to these ideas contained in the *Acta* of the *cabildo* of Bogotá, the declaration of the *Acta* of the revolution of Socorro of July 11, 1810, stated that every people had the right by natural law to determine its own government and that no one ought to oppose the exercise of this right without violating the most sacred right which is liberty.³⁵⁰ The Junta proceeded to enumerate the principles of government, which followed the same concepts as those proclaimed in the 1781 revolution, and stated that the first basis of a constitution is the Christian religion.³⁵¹ Finally, it said that the Junta had reassumed for the moment all authority, since the king was absent and no national congress had been established; once the king returned or a national congress had been set up, the people of Socorro would deposit in that body those rights which it could sacrifice without loss of freedom.³⁵²

The *Acta* of the *cabildo abierto* of Pamplona of July 31, 1810, stated that the entire people "reassumed the authority which resided in our legitimate Sovereign, Ferdinand VII, and by its absence in the same people which had been confided to him."³⁵³ It also gave an oath to "the preservation of our holy religion, obedience to our legitimate monarch, support to the just cause of the entire nation and to the absolute independence of this part of the Americas from all foreign yoke."³⁵⁴

On February 1, 1811, Cali set up its *Junta Provisional de Gobierno de las Ciudades Confederadas del Valle del Cauca* for "its defense and security" and with the aim "of preserving these dominions for our legitimate sovereign, Ferdinand VII." It then proceeded to give an oath of allegiance for the defense of "our holy religion, without permission of any other, loyalty and vassallage to Ferdinand VII and perservation of these places for himself, sacrificing itself for the fatherland."³⁵⁵ The next day the Junta appointed Our Lady of Mercy as its patron saint and captain of its troops.

On February 23, the Representative, Constitutional, and Electoral College of the Province of Bogotá was established, which assumed the powers of the Junta of July 20, 1810, which it now annulled. All members of the new government then took an oath of allegiance to defend to the last drop of blood the preservation of the Christian faith as taught by the Catholic Church, the rights of Ferdinand VII, and the freedom of all the people of the Province from the so-called Council of the Regency and the *Cortes*,³⁵⁶ and it finished by stating that the *Colegio Constituyente y Electoral de la Provincia* had reassumed the rights of sovereignty in the absence of the king.

Cartagena, the first town to act in New Granada proper, was also the first to declare full independence. On November 11, 1811, it stated clearly that with the abdication of Ferdinand VII from the throne of Spain "the ties which linked the King to his peoples were broken, and the latter were left in the full enjoyment of their sovereignty and authorized to give themselves their own government."³⁵⁷ The declaration went on to state that the juntas in Spain owed their authority to their popular source and that Cartagena had proved by acts and deeds that it remained faithful to the mother country in face of the Napoleonic menace; however, it seemed incredible that the Peninsula while fighting the usurpation at the same time tried to enslave the Spanish American provinces — the naval blockade of the Colombian coast. For these reasons Cartagena justified its separation.

Other documents which contain similar Scholastic viewpoints were the independence declaration of July 16, 1813, of the *Colegio Electoral y Revisor* of Cundinamarca, under President Nariño; that of Antioquía, of August 11, 1813; of Neiva by its *Colegio Revisor Electoral* of February 8, 1814; and of Mariquita of December 26, 1814. In Cundinamarca's declaration it was stated that the emancipation was a result of the events and dissolution of the Peninsula and government from whom it derived, "having had long and mature discussion in which the old obligations which through solemn oaths united us to the mother country were mentioned."[358]

Thus the actions and declarations of the various juntas speak a clear language whose source is the Late Scholastic political philosophy of Suárez and his fellow thinkers. Moreover, in New Granada, the various governments issued some six constitutions: the monarchical constitution of Cundinamarca (April 4, 1811), the Federal Act of the United Provinces of New Granada (November 27, 1811), the Constitution of Tunja (December 9, 1811), the Constitution of the Republic of Cundinamarca (April 17, 1812), the Constitution of the State of Antioquía (March 21, 1812), and the Constitution of the State of Cartagena de Indias (June 14, 1812).

The Constitution of Cundinamarca is based on the Scholastic principles of popular sovereignty, resistance to tyranny, and of the social contract between the people and the king, as when it stated in Title I, Art. 1:

> The Representation, freely and legitimately constituted by election and consent of the people of this province which with its liberty has resurrected its primitive and original name of Cundinamarca, convinced and sure that the people whom it represents has reassumed its sovereignty, recovered the plenitude of its rights, in the same way that all those who form part of the Spanish monarchy, from the moment Ferdinand VII was made prisoner by the French . . . needs to give itself a Constitution which being a barrier to despotism may be at the same time the best guarantee of the imprescriptible rights of man and the citizen, establishing the throne of justice . . . .[359]

With the exception of "the imprescriptible rights of man and the citizen," the entire sentence is medieval and thus linked to the Spanish Late Scholastic school of thought. The Constitution also contained recognition of Ferdinand VII, the Catholic faith as the only one, and the oath which was based on the old oaths which the Spanish kings gave to the medieval *Cortes* with the explicit statement that they could lose their throne in case of basic violation of this oath.[360]

The Act of Federation of the United Provinces of New Granada, drafted by Torres and linking together the provinces of Antioquía, Cartagena, Neiva, Pamplona, and Tunja, of November 27, 1811, was one of the goals which the Junta of Bogotá of July 20, 1810, attempted to achieve. This constitutional document followed the previous Constitution, though it dealt more with the legal boundaries of the various members of the Federation.

The Constitution of the Republic of Tunja is most important since it is the most republican, but at the same time the most Scholastic document of the period in New Granada. The Constitution showed the Suarezian foundation when it stated that its authors were "persuaded of the dissolution and destruction of the social contracts with which South America found itself linked with that part of the nation, be it by the captivity of the king, be it by the other tragic events in the entire Peninsula." It proclaimed that government is established for the common good, for the protection, security, and happiness of the people and not for the benefit, honor, and special interest of any man, family, or class of men. It stated further that kings were equal to other men and that they had been put on the throne by the will of the peoples in order to maintain peace, justice, and happiness, and that if they do not comply with this sacred pact they can be deposed, or the peoples can chose another form of government. Resistance to tyranny is another concept which links this interesting constitutional document to the Spanish Middle Ages since the governor is forced to give an oath that he will not abuse power. And finally, the duty of the citizens is based on the purity of religion and of customs.[361]

Viceroyalty of New Spain (Puerto Rico). Although New Spain remained loyal to the Peninsular authorities and no revolutionary movement occurred outside the borders of Mexico, the case of Puerto Rico is worth mention. It reveals exactly the same principle which had dominated the minds of the Spanish Americans on the mainland. Puerto Rico had also been invited to send delegates to the *Suprema Junta Central* in Spain. The delegate to represent the island in Spain was Ramón Power y Giral, duly elected under the governorship of Salvador Meléndez. When the *Suprema Junta Central* was transferred to Seville and transformed into the Regency, it declared Power's appointment invalid, but he was re-elected in 1810.

The town council of San Germán sent Power after the last election a list of instructions for his work at the Spanish *Cortes*; the sovereignty of Ferdinand VII was recognized in the first item, but Power was reminded that, in case this sovereignty should be broken, the island would regain possession of its natural right to govern itself as it deemed best.[362] Nothing came of it since the royalist position on the island was too strong and Puerto Rico too important as the Gibraltar of the Antilles.[363]

b. *The Legitimate Basis for the Political Organization*

In view of the vastness of the Spanish American area and the different conditions and characteristics in the various parts of the Spanish Empire, it was obvious that the many juntas which had been set up would have different social backgrounds, political aims, and ideological goals. Hence, a legitimate, sovereign political organization developed in several different governmental forms, once the provincialist case regarding the area of control had been decided upon.[364] Essentially, there were two main positions: the Spanish formula, and the Spanish American which ran the whole gamut of political and ideological variations.

i. *The Peninsular or Conservative Formula*

Without solving the question of continuity and justifying the submission to the Peninsular Regency by an autonomist stand, this formula simply tended to perpetuate the old order. This was particularly the case of the able Viceroy

Abascal in Peru (1806–16); of Viceroy Venegas in New Spain (1810–15), where the revolutions of Hidalgo and Morelos had been destroyed so that New Spain remained loyalist until 1821; and of Viceroys Amar in New Granada (1803–10) and Cisneros in the River Plate (1809–10), and of such officials as Vicente Emparán in Venezuela, Count Ruiz de Castilla in Quito and Francisco Antonio García Carrasco in Chile, deposed by the revolutionary juntas where Spanish American control was strongest.

ii. *The Native or Spanish American Formula*

This can be subdivided into several varieties which all tended to replace the former authorities by Spanish American representatives:

1. The *monarchic* type included the possibility of offering the throne to a member of the Spanish royal family or a compromise solution in favor of a foreign dynasty (Brazil, England, Lucca, France). The monarchic type was linked to the efforts of Carlota Joaquina to secure for herself a throne in the Viceroyalty of the River Plate. It was also connected to the persistent Argentine efforts to find a monarchic solution in the River Plate for reasons of political stability and foreign recognition. The idea was also carried to Peru by San Martín. It succeeded only temporarily in the case of Iturbide in Mexico.

    The monarchic type could also be carried out under a republican disguise and as democratic Caesarism, as in the case of Saavedra in the River Plate and Bolívar in Greater Colombia, Peru, and Upper Peru. To some extent it also fitted the pattern of the Paraguayan Rodríguez de Francia; it lasted longer because of the country's isolation.

2. The *aristocratic* type, as in the case of Her Majesty the Junta of Quito, established on August 10, 1809, under the Marquis de Selva Alegre. The members of this junta represented an extreme monarchical concept without a king, projecting a caricature of the Bourbon court into Quito, and opposing the authorities of Guayaquil and Cuenca, who had recognized the *Suprema Junta Central* of Spain. It lasted until November 8, 1812, when Montes' small army dispersed it.

3. The *oligarchic* type, applied by powerful native economic groups: the Carrera brothers and the O'Higgins family, Martínez de Rozas and Friar Enríquez in Chile, and the Caicedo family in New Granada. These groups eliminated the Peninsular authorities in successful coups d'état, replacing them by oligarchic juntas with opposing political ideas. They succeeded in creating an atmosphere of independence, despite the fact that they were at times beaten, like the Carreras in Chile, by the returning royalists.

4. The *democratic* type, postulated by Celedonio Villota in the Buenos Aires *cabildo* (May 22, 1810), by Cañete in Potosí, and by Tenorio in Quito, with the idea of holding the kingdom's *Cortes* for the establishment of a legitimate government. This was also the case applied in New Granada by Nariño, Torres, and Lozano, which finally led to the Constitution of Cundinamarca, still promulgated in the name of Ferdinand VII (April 4, 1811), and which despite temporary failures (royalist return to New Granada — Morillo) became the basis of New Granada's future political organization. The idea of reviving the

Cortes in Spanish America followed the trend in the Peninsula, and also showed that the ideas of Francisco Martínez Marina[365] were not confined to metropolitan Spain.

5. The *demagogic* type, which succeeded in the River Plate area (Castelli Pazos, Monteagudo) with the application of French revolutionary techniques, the bayonets of Saavedra, and the appeal to the masses of Berutti and French. Despite well-intentioned reforms and eventual moderation (Director Pueyrredón, 1816-19 — Declaration of Independence [Tucumán, 1816], and "Constitution of the United Provinces in South America," 1819), it led to anarchy and, finally, to the tyranny of Rosas. It was also applied in the early period of the revolutionary movement in Venezuela under the eccentricities of Miranda and the radical views of the young Bolívar.

6. The *eclectic* types, some written but not applied, like Bolívar's later Constitution of 1826 (Bolivian Constitution); others applied but unwritten, like the federal pluralistic tyranny prior to Rosas (Federal League: Francisco Ramírez, Entre Ríos; Estanislao López, Santa Fe; Juan Felipe Ibarra, Santiago del Estero; Juan Bautista Bustos, Córdoba; Juan Facundo Quiroga, La Rioja; Martín Güemes, Salta; Bernabé Aráoz, Tucumán) in the River Plate area, and the many political struggles which took place among families, cities, and regions, under the guise of political parties. A political program which arose as soon as the juntas were set up was the issue of centralism and federalism, which became the great apple of discord in the River Plate and in New Granada, though it was also part of the political scene in New Spain and Chile. Federalism in the River Plate was especially strong in the *Banda Oriental* and Paraguay, and in the interior of Argentina; in New Granada it was linked to the United Provinces of New Granada (Antioquia, Cartagena, Neiva, Pamplona, and Tunja) and to the towns of the Cauca valley. Centralism, on the other hand, was essentially linked to the old viceregal seats.

Some of these political varieties represented typical Hispanic expressions of individualism and idealism, while others were influenced by foreign concepts. The monarchic type represented by far the most serious attempt to find a solution to the revolutionary chaos. It was in these different types that most of the foreign influences were found which often represented the fusion of Scholastic and Hispanic traditional thought with modern philosophies, though the currents of the Enlightenment did not furnish the basis for the Spanish American Revolution, and played only a role in the later evolution of the civil war when it became clear that a political union between the Peninsula and Spanish America was no longer possible. Modern thought was used increasingly after the revolutionary movement had established fully independent republics.

c. *The Sovereign or Delegated Character of the Civil Authorities in Spanish America*

This third application of Scholastic theories included three different positions, one in the Spanish royalist camp, and two on the Spanish American revolutionary side.[366]

i. *The Royalist or Loyalist Solution*

Viceroyalties of Peru and the River Plate. The promoters of this solution contended that civil authority in Spanish America was derived from a delegation of sovereignty which in Spain was exercised successively by the *Suprema Junta Central* and by the Regency according to the *pactum translationis*. It was expressed in the theory that the main duty of the people was fidelity to their representatives and sovereigns, since the *potestas* of the kings was derived from God. The solution was most strongly adhered to in Peru, and in traditional Lima it governed the actions of Viceroy Abascal as its most spectacular follower.

Others adhering to this Spanish interpretation included Lázaro de Ribera, *Intendente* of Potosí and former Governor of Paraguay, who in a letter dated September 1, 1810, to Bishop Nicolás Videla del Pino (who had been deprived of his diocese of Salta by Belgrano and taken to Buenos Aires), stated this concept as follows:

> The citizens of Lima are aware that the main duty of the subject toward their representatives and sovereigns is *fidelity*, expressly recommended by Saint Peter, because the authority of kings is derived from the same God and cannot be resisted without opposition to the order of Our Lord. They also know that the State affirms its political constitution on the same basis of the Gospel: that it is [based] on the natural law that in every well-established society there are chiefs who govern and a legitimate subordination to them . . . that every society may elect a supreme head of state when they do not have an hereditary chief or when, through an infamous perfidy, the latter is put in prison as happened with ours, and that all members participate with their vote in the election of the one or ones whom they have voted to obey. Here Your Honor has the origin of the sovereign authority which the Central Junta obtained and the inherent right of the *potestas* which the people conferred upon it through a solemn oath in order to elect and appoint a successor, when the interests of Ferdinand and of the nation so demand it. Your Honor sees that I am talking of the Supreme Council of the Regency which by a natural consequence of the clear and unquestionable principle which I mentioned has acquired a *plenitudo potestatis* equal to that of Ferdinand.[367]

In Upper Peru, the case of Archbishop Benito María de Moxó y Francolí is also interesting. In a pastoral letter dated February 22, 1810, the Archbishop of Charcas exhorted his parishioners to fidelity to the Council of the Regency after it had been established in Spain. This was the same council to which Viceroy Abascal had given his full support.[368]

ii. *The Autonomist Solution*

According to this solution, the right of the people to exercise civil authority after the abdication of the king is not limited to the Spanish juntas and the Regency, but is an inherent right of every province in the Spanish territories overseas: the logical conclusion derived from the link of these territories to the Crown. The autonomist stand was closely linked to the provincialist point of view and often overlapped. It was carried out with the establishment of the various juntas, revolutionary or not, as in the case of Montevideo (1808), La

Paz and Quito (1809), and Caracas, Buenos Aires, Santiago de Chile, Bogotá and Querétaro (1810). In a way it was also part of the revolt in the interior of the *Banda Oriental,* since it continued the earlier autonomist stand of royalist Montevideo. The autonomist stand was part of the political program of the revolutionary junta of Quito and is also expressed in the circular letter, confidential in character, which the Archbishop of Quito, José Cuervo y Caicedo, addressed to his parish priests, in which he exhorted them to be faithful in their subordination to the new government:

> You do not ignore the adversities which today surround ... Quito; its inhabitants ..., imbued with the highest sentiments of fidelity and patriotism, have consulted in good faith the surest means for maintaining themselves in the religion of Christ and in the vassalage of the captive Ferdinand, and they thought that they had found with the establishment of a government worthy of the confidence of the peoples a secure asylum against seduction, against the dangers, and against the frequent changes which are noticeable in the one which the people of the town of Cádiz had set up; but suddenly one of those tempests began .... The Governors of Lima, Guayaquil, and Cuenca, assembling a multitude of bandits without religious principles, have invaded our territory in order to separate by force of arms those magistrates whom the peoples had constituted .... Indeed, who can be persuaded to invade a free Province which enjoys the same rights as the people of the entire [Spanish] American [lands] and the Spanish Peninsula, only because it does not want to put up with the doubtful system adopted in some towns of Peru where the educated and literate inhabitants are suspicious with good reason of the conduct of their Governors? Upon what reason or law can this treacherous policy, offensive to the freedom of the peoples and to the obligations which they have [taken upon themselves] to conserve these lands to the true King and natural Sovereign, be based? In what code is it stated that the government constituted by the people of Cádiz is the only master during the captivity of Ferdinand VII, to create magistrates and give judges to the free Provinces of [Spanish] America? ...
>
> In such a sad state of affairs, and having heard the clamors of the peoples of this fertile and delightful Province, who dread to be sacrificed because they believe in truth and adhere to the system proclaimed by the learned [Spanish] Americans, there seems to be no alternative than that you comfort them with your teachings and encourage them to keep firm in their subordination to this Supreme Government whose legitimacy was recognized in its constitution by the Council of the Regency of Spain, which could not deny the freedom which the peoples had to elect their representatives, so that united they could take the necessary steps against Bonaparte's attempts ....[369]

The autonomist solution was also acknowledged in a different way, in that it explicitly gave to Ferdinand VII the right to be King of New Granada (Constitution of Cundinamarca, April 4, 1811) and of New Spain (Plan of Iguala, February 24, 1821), if he ever chose to set foot in either province. Finally, it is also a formula which Viceroy Abascal applied to Chile when, in the Treaty of Lircay (May 3, 1814), he expressly recognized the Chilean junta.

iii. *The Solution of the Followers of Independence*

In some cases autonomy led soon into independence as in the case of Caracas (July 5, 1811) and Cartagena (September 11, 1811) — largely the result of the unwise policies of the Peninsular authorities who, misreading the situation, began to blockade the Colombian and Venezuelan coasts since they refused to recognize the establishment of revolutionary juntas. It was followed in 1813 by other areas: Bogotá (July 15), and Chilpancingo, New Spain (November 6), or implied in Buenos Aires (January 31 — General Constituent Assembly), although in each case the reasons were different. But in all cases, the *pactum translationis* was the intellectual foundation for the overt or implied proclamation of independence.

Viceroyalty of New Spain. The best example for the persistence of Scholastic ideas among the followers of independence is the second Mexican movement for emancipation. Morelos continued in 1811 the insurrection begun by Hidalgo. In 1813 Morelos addressed the Congress of Chilpancingo and mentioned in his opening speech several principles which were all rooted in Scholastic political thought, including the *pactum translationis*:

> Sir: our enemies have persisted, up to the degree of evidence, in letting us know certain important truths of which we were not ignorant but which the despotism of the government, under whose yoke we have lived oppressed, endeavored carefully to hide from us; these are: that sovereignty resides essentially in the peoples . . . . That, transmitted to the monarchs, it reverts by their absence, death, or captivity to the peoples . . . . That no people has the right to subjugate another unless there is first an unjust aggression . . . .[370]

The Act of Independence of November 6, 1813, which the Assembly of Chilpancingo proclaimed under the guidance of Morelos, drawn up by Carlos María de Bustamante, followed Spanish traditional thinking when it stated:

> The Congress of Anáhuac . . . solemnly declares in the presence of God, our Lord, regulating arbiter of empires and author of society, who gives and takes them away according to His mysterious designs of Providence, that because of the present circumstances in Europe it has recovered the exercise of its usurped sovereignty; that under such concept the dependency upon the Spanish throne is broken forever and dissolved; that it is the arbiter to establish the laws which it considers desirable for internal settlement and happiness; that it may declare war and peace and conclude alliances with the monarchs and republics of the old continent no less than to sign concordats with the Holy Roman Pontiff with regard to the Catholic, Apostolic, and Roman Church, and to send envoys and consuls; that it neither follows nor acknowledges any other religion but the Catholic and it will neither permit nor tolerate the public or secret use of any other; that it will protect it with all its power and shall watch over the purity of faith and of its dogmas . . . .[371]

These declarations vary somewhat, but both have a general similarity to fundamental Scholastic thought: sovereignty of the people in the Scholastic sense and invocation of the Catholic faith (although the former may also permit a Rousseauan interpretation, since Morelos refers to sovereignty as residing *essentially* in the people).

Viceroyalty of the River Plate. An interesting middle-of-the-road position, based on Scholasticism, was assumed by those who did not support a specific government. This was the case, for instance, of Bishop Rodríguez de Orellana, of Tucumán, in his letter of October 12, 1811, to Saavedra after the latter announced the end of his confinement in Luján, and in which the bishop stated that:

> The holy religion which we follow not only adjusts itself to all governments, but consolidates and perfects them, because the celestial kingdom which Jesus Christ established on earth is a kingdom of charity, fraternity, and union of wills for everything which is good, honest, and just, and with detestation of everything which is bad. Human laws bind only because they are received, accepted, and published by the peoples; at the moment when the authority of the Supreme Governing Junta was received in Córdoba, I would have offered to recognize it myself, and such has been constantly the practice of the fathers of the Church who, guided by the spirit of the Gospel, were far from exciting revolt in the state, but eager to acknowledge the authorities admitted by the peoples . . . .[372]

Many more examples of Scholastic influence could be given for that period. Suffice it to mention the reports of the Peninsular Bishop of Trujillo, José Carrión y Marfil; of the Mexican deputy to the *Cortes* of Spain, Guridi y Alcocer; and the most valuable document for studying the Wars of Independence — the report of May 30, 1810, of the Mexican Abad y Queipo — all asking for reforms. On the royalist side, the Scholastic theory was used by the Spanish Bishop of Arequipa, Luis Gonzaga de la Encina (pastoral letter of February 22, 1811); by that of Cuenca, Andrés Quintián (letter to the Marquis de Selva Alegre, later president of the junta of Quito, February 29, 1809), and by that of La Paz, Remigio de La Santa y Ortega, to his *cabildo* (July 20, 1811).[373]

3. The Second Act: The Absolutist Reaction (1814–20)

The year 1814 marked the return of Ferdinand VII to Spain and the re-introduction of absolutism and reaction, culminating in the abolition of the Constitution of 1812. At the time of his return, some sixty-nine deputies had issued what later was called the *Manifiesto de los Persas* in which Ferdinand VII was urged to rule in the traditional manner, and introducing certain reforms, all of which was within the framework of Spanish tradition. Ferdinand VII, however, chose to return to the Enlightened despotism of the Bourbons and declared all acts and laws of the constitutional government null and void. On May 21, 1814, his new Minister of the Indies, Lardizábal, issued the famous manifesto which called on the Spanish Americans to desist from further "insurrection" and to lay down their arms. The policy was then followed with the shipment of new armies to America to subdue the existing "rebellions."[374] This not only opened the second act in the Spanish American drama but continued, though in a different way, the wrong Peninsular approach — a liberal policy totally devoid of reality and thus again misinterpreting the events which had led to the establishment of juntas in Spanish America between 1808 and 1810. In a way it was not surprising that the stubbornness of the king was not different from the misguided policies of the liberals, since both absolutism and constitutionalism had their roots in the Enlightenment.

The events of 1814 can only be understood if they are linked to the constitutional crisis of 1808. To the traditional forces which were stronger in Spanish America than in Spain itself, it seemed that Spain was lost or that it was at least in danger of being unable to resist foreign pressure. Thus the idea spread in the Indies that Spanish America had to resist Peninsular Spain in order to maintain its Spanish heritage; hence, it was not surprising that opinions gradually changed and turned against the Peninsula, and this for reasons which today are little understood: Spanish America wanted to be independent and free because it viewed the Peninsula as no longer a bastion of traditionalism but as a country and a people which had fallen prey to foreign cultural and political influence.

1814 could have offered a brilliant opportunity to correct past mistakes since until 1820 there was in general no tendency to break political ties with Spain.[375] But such a position presupposed in the returned king and his ministers a real understanding of political developments in overseas Spain. Had Ferdinand VII been imbued more with Spanish traditions and less with the liberal Enlightenment, and had he understood the true causes for the apparent disobedience of many parts of Spanish America, perhaps 1814 could have meant the re-establishment of unity in the Spanish Empire, despite the six full years of constitutional crisis and political disagreements. Much could have been saved if Ferdinand VII had realized that the Bourbon reforms of the eighteenth century had been received with misgivings in the Indies, as in many parts of Spain, and that the liberalism of the early nineteenth century — whether Enlightened or Romantic, within an absolutist or a constitutionalist framework — represented a continuation of the French-inspired Bourbon drive toward more efficiency. This was particularly so, because the establishment of the provisional juntas in both Spain and Spanish America was specifically meant to last only as long as the king was absent. Hence, from a legal point of view, the possibility existed that the areas in Spanish America which had set up such provincial juntas for the defense of the legitimate rights of their former king would recognize the return of their monarch and act accordingly. But this presupposed a clear understanding of the political situation in the Indies, and particularly of that typical Spanish contradictory trait that disobedience was essentially an act of obedience, as had happened so often in earlier periods. Jane mentions the great example of Bishop Pedro de la Gasca in the sixteenth century, who single-handedly and armed only with the authority of his office succeeded in ending the famous civil war in Peru.[376] This possibility could very well have been repeated if the king and his advisers had interpreted the events in the Indies as a movement to keep Spanish traditions alive, and not as a revolt to remove Spanish domination.

Historians have generally bypassed this situation, since few accepted the claims of the Spanish American revolutionaries who in 1809–10 set up provisional juntas "for the defense of the legitimate rights of our beloved King Ferdinand VII"; they interpreted it instead as a clever and cynical camouflage to mask their own political designs — taking advantage of the temporary weakness of Spain and its French domination, which they considered final, in order to achieve political independence.

However, the case of Manuel de Sarratea in the River Plate proves that the declarations and proclamations of 1809–10 had been sincere, and this could also be said of other revolutionary areas, although different conditions and circumstances forbid a complete generalization. The other revolutionary areas (Upper Peru, Chile, Quito, New Granada, and Venezuela) cannot be tested in this question, since by 1814 they were either back in royalist hands or in such turmoil that they would soon be under Spanish control. Sarratea was commissioned by the Argentine Triumvirate to negotiate with Ferdinand VII in an attempt to end what he himself called a civil war. On May 25, 1814, from London, he addressed the King as follows:

> Sir: Don Manuel de Sarratea, vassal of Your Majesty and deputy of the Government of Buenos Aires for the conciliation with the metropolis, even if [this is done] from foreign soil, has the honor to express to Your Majesty the sentiments of love and loyalty to Your royal person from the government from whom he is sent as well as his own.[377]

Sarratea explained in this letter the reasons for the establishment of the various revolutionary juntas in Spanish America — the absence of the king, the dissolution of the *Suprema Junta Central*, and the desire to avoid chaos through taking immediate measures. Unfortunately these measures had not been understood by the metropolis, and hence had resulted in civil war. Despite many failures to conciliate the supreme interests of the nation with regional interests, again British mediation had been asked, since Britain had been Spain's ally against Napoleon and she had succeeded in having Portugal evacuate the *Banda Oriental*.[378] Sarratea then stated that Buenos Aires was no less loyal to its king than other regions of Spanish America, and only aspired to some improvements in its situation "compatible with the national unity and the rights of the Crown,"[379] and explained further:

> Allow me, Your Majesty, to conclude, assuring you with the greatest respect, that the evil which has arisen in Your Americas was not born from a spirit of disloyalty as Your foes say, [and] had not Heaven permitted the absence of Your Majesty, not even an echo of insubordination would have been heard in Your lands. But, Sir, it is not surprising that those peoples could not look to the governments which successively appeared in Cádiz (however good and legitimate they may be) with the same respect and love as to their King; it is not [strange] either when it was considered to be loyalty in the Peninsula where the peoples ruled in the name of Your Majesty during Your absence, that those of the overseas [areas] were unwilling to cede them this privilege as [being something] exclusive; it is not surprising when they were themselves cruelly attacked and without stating [that it was] in the name of the most beloved and benign King who has ascended the throne of Spain, that they would not recognize as the true representatives of Your Majesty those who so badly imitated his paternal character, and lastly, Sir, [it is not surprising] when doctrines full of anarchy were protected in the Peninsula that some turbulent minds found the opportunity of having them spread through [Spanish] America, taking advantage of the stream of blood which in part had prepared her to receive the dismal seeds.[380]

Finally, the Argentine delegate concluded that Buenos Aires, although in 1813 it had suppressed the royal symbols, had never been against the king and had only fought against those who attempted to impose an illegal regime.

> But, Sir, let the [Spanish] Americans listen to the paternal voice of Your Majesty, and the evil of those unfortunate countries shall cease. I would dare to speak in the name of all of them if I had to judge from what I know of my own. The people of Buenos Aires had never raised its voice against its beloved King; if it has taken up arms it was to defend itself against the aggression of those who misusing such an august name have used it here only to hang Spaniards without listening to them. Your Majesty ought to speak out and you will see that if there is a people in Buenos Aires which does not submit to the injustice of others [who are] its equals, never shall it forget its profound respect with which it shall listen to its King; neither shall it abandon the name and the just duties of the vassal.[381]

The message is clear and confirms that the events in Spanish America were an echo of the heroic defense of the Peninsula against the French usurpation, that the revolutionary juntas in Spanish America acted with deep loyalty to their king, and that they expected, with the return of the king in 1814, to hand over those powers they had provisionally assumed in 1809-10 in return for reforms which would have put an end to the absolutist and centralist Bourbon policies of the past. The message also showed the strong continuity and the deep roots of Spanish tradition: nowhere is there evidence of foreign ideas in this entire political process of a possible reconciliation with the king.

Nothing came of these negotiations; nothing was achieved a year later when Sarratea was joined by Belgrano and Rivadavia in the sincere pursuit of identical goals.[382] Thus the return of Ferdinand VII, which coincided with another hopeful event, the liberation of Pope Pius VII, from which the Spanish Americans also expected a solution to their problems, did not have positive results. The hopes of the Spanish Americans were dashed by Pius VII as much as by Ferdinand VII; both the King of Spain and the Pope missed a great historic opportunity.[383]

It was a fact that Ferdinand VII saw in the establishment of juntas an act of defiance, challenge, and open rebellion to his rule: he and his advisers interpreted the events in Spanish America after 1808 as an echo of the French Revolution; therefore, the mutiny and disobedience should be met only by force. Hence, the return of the king meant not only the end of the constitutional period and the return to absolutism, but in the Indies the attempt to reconquer lost positions and to teach Spanish Americans a lesson. Indeed, in the Indies it marked the recovery of almost all lost territory (by Abascal in the Viceroyalty of Peru, Calleja del Rey in New Spain, and Morillo in New Granada), except for the River Plate region. However, while the royalists succeeded militarily almost everywhere, they lost politically, because they used wrong methods and continued to misinterpret the true basis of the Spanish American Revolution. The persecution of the revolutionaries led to terrorism (by Domingo de Monteverde in Venezuela, Francisco Casimiro Marcó del Pont in Chile), and succeeded in uniting the efforts of the patriotic forces which rectified past ideological errors, as in the case of Miranda and of the revolutionary brand of terrorism (Piar, Páez). Their actions led to the three national congresses of Apatzingán, New Spain (October 22, 1814), Tucumán, River Plate (July 9,

1816), and Angostura, Venezuela (February 15, 1819), largely helped by ecclesiastics, such as the Mexicans José María Cos and Carlos María de Bustamante, the Argentines Cayetano Rodríguez, Gregorio Funes, and Pantaleón García, and the Venezuelan Fernando Peñalver. These declarations represent a decline in Scholastic political thought and are characteristic of the evolution of political philosophy and of the rising Western European and North American influence.

The reactionary despotism of the period 1814–20 based its policies in Spanish America on the continuation of the principles which had been valid during the eighteenth-century Bourbon regime: absolutism and centralism (Marcó del Pont, Elío, Morillo, Calleja del Rey, among others), regalism (Vargas Laguna, Gómez Calderón, Hipólito Sánchez Ranjel, Fonte, Rodríguez Bergosa — it re-established the Inquisition in such a way as to discredit it, one instance occurring on December 22, 1815, in New Spain), militarism (Morillo, Calleja del Rey, Calzada, Canterac, Osorio, Olañeta, among others) — it failed as a political measure, and, as the future was to prove, laid the foundations for the disastrous system of military uprisings, not so much of the great leaders but of militarized petty politicians like Páez, Santa Ana, Belzú, Melgarejo); and it added terrorism.[384] The use of terrorism was begun by Bolívar, and the royalists answered with their brand of terrorism (Boves). During 1814–20, when absolutism had been restored in most parts of Spanish America, terrorism became a further principle of the royalist side, with very negative and counterproductive results (the Purification Committee in New Granada, for instance). The consequence of these policies was rising anticlericalism in the opposite camp, while the military necessities favored the system of *caudillismo*.

The reintroduction of absolutism helped the cause of the patriots, since it considerably narrowed their different factions. Militarism and terrorism were also elements on the revolutionary side, which was characterized by two main positions: Scholasticism and increasing republicanism. Despite inroads of modern currents of thought, Scholastic theories triumphed in several places.

Viceroyalty of New Spain. The influence of Suárez can be seen in the patriot Morelos and his secretary, Dr. Cos. Examples of this influence can also be found in Quintana Róo's *Semanario patriótico americano*, in the speeches given at Zitácuaro and Chilpancingo,[385] and in the defense of Mexican independence under Ferdinand VII and (after September 6, 1813) without him. These ideas finally converged in the ephemeral Constitution of Apatzingán (October 22, 1814)[386] which is both Scholastic and republican. Symbolic of the influence of Scholastic thought in the whole movement of Morelos is the re-establishment of the Jesuits,[387] a blow to the regalist policies of royalist Enlightened despotism; a movement which would have drawn from the ideas of the Enlightenment and the French Revolution would hardly have pressed for a return of the famous Society.

Viceroyalty of New Granada (Venezuela). At this time there developed a movement toward conservatism and away from the early demagogic excesses in Venezuela. The ideological errors which both Miranda and the younger Bolívar had committed, their radical Jacobinism which was an influence of Rousseau and of the ideas of 1789, made Bolívar modify his political plans. Learning from past experience, the Venezuelan leader announced his new political ideas at the Congress of Angostura (1819).[388] The convocation of the Venezuelan Congress was inspired by Peñalver, one of the most beneficially influential advisers of Bolívar — his Nestor, as Bolívar called him.[389] Peñalver was a convinced republican and an anti-Peninsular Venezuelan with deep religious convictions and a very conservative mind in ecclesiastical matters. It is interesting, in connection with Bolívar's famous draft Constitution, that the Congress of Angostura accepted a request presented by Ramón Ignacio Méndez, later the first republican Archbishop of Caracas, that all bishops be honorary senators in Bolívar's hereditary senate. Likewise, Congress, through the influence which Peñalver exerted upon Bolívar, agreed that in the next diplomatic mission to London direct negotiations should be entered into with Pope Pius VII. The instructions elaborated by Roscio, of the same spiritual convictions as Peñalver, represent an enlightening document which more than anything else will demonstrate the Catholic and Scholastic influences dominating the Angostura Congress. Thus, it states in

> *Article 31.* You shall open negotiations with the Pope as chief of the Catholic Church and not as temporal master of his Legations. Against the imputations of our enemies you will declare that the Catholic religion is the one which is professed in New Granada and Venezuela and in the whole of [Spanish] America which rose against colonial dependency and the tyranny of the Spanish Government. You will tell him that, even if that same government, oppressor and destroyer of [Spanish] America, boasts of being aided by the successor of St. Peter against the emancipation and happiness of these countries, its faithful inhabitants hold as apocryphal the documents of the Roman Curia, published and circulated as evidence of such aid . . . . You will demonstrate that no authority is more legitimate and worthy of being obeyed than that which is derived from the people, the only immediate and visible source of any temporal power, and since all those established in the Republic of Venezuela are of this nature they are the most deserving for the fulfillment of the doctrines of the Apostles St. Peter and St. Paul . . . .[390]

As Pedro Leturia, S.J., points out, the instructions of Roscio are worthy of a high place in the universal history of the Church in the nineteenth century: at a time when the spirit of the Holy Alliance was in full swing and when in Europe general opinion found it impossible to conciliate republicanism with Catholicism, there was heard from Angostura the voice of convinced Catholics who believed that in the spiritual crisis of religion in Spanish America the papacy could and had to be approached outside of the *Patronato Real*.[391] The above instructions represent an impressive demonstration of Scholasticism at such an advanced period of the Spanish American Revolution as the year 1819.

Viceroyalty of the River Plate. In Buenos Aires the demagogic excesses caused a reappraisal of the situation at the time of Director Posadas. Funes mentioned (sermon of May 24, 1814) that the tyranny of the citizens was as bad as the despotism of the chiefs, and the Franciscan Pantaleón García pointed out that "fidelity is not an abstract right which binds us in every circumstance: it is the obligation to stick to the social contract which binds the parts with the whole." He then continued by saying that

... its obligation is reciprocal: the head has to be as loyal to the colonies as the colonies to it. We have to respect and obey the King and the mother country, but the latter must guard our rights and promote our happiness, ... [since] authority emanates from the peoples sustained by Providence which leaves our actions to free will.³⁹²

Pedro Ignacio de Castro Barros in his speech of May 25, 1815, began by asserting that the Argentine people "had resumed its old dignity and rights. The person of the King or any other government is put on the throne for the good of the country and not the other way round, and if it is not for the good of the country then it can and ought to be corrected, even by deposing him if necessary."³⁹³

Others who maintained the Scholastic theory and its social contract were the Franciscan Juan Esteban Soto from the cathedral of Buenos Aires in 1816 and Julián Segundo de Agüero in 1817; although by that time — in fact, since the end of 1810 — theories other than Scholastic are mixed with Scholastic political thought. It was also from this Scholastic basis and not from any ideas of Rousseau and the French Revolution that the twelve clergymen and the majority of laymen who assembled at the Congress of Tucumán, patronized by San Martín and Belgrano, declared Argentine independence on July 9, 1816.

In Upper Peru, the Archbishop of Charcas, Moxó y Francolí, famous for his *Cartas mejicanas* and for his courageous stand against both the excesses of the *ancien régime* and the demagogic licenses of the new revolutionary order, pointed out in his *Carta a los americanos* (September 18, 1815) on his way into exile the true rights of men and the equality of Spanish Americans and Peninsular Spaniards, since the Indies were not a colony but an integral part of the monarchy;

> In that gloomy period I resolved to talk about the sacred and true rights of men, painting in vivid colors the unmerited depression into which they had fallen in those countries, and revealing the melancholic frame of the excessive red tape of their commerce, of the broken workshops, of their retarded agriculture. I dared to say that it was time the Spanish Government took away all these barriers, and that once the lights of our century made us acknowledge conscientiously that [Spanish] America was not a colony but an integral part of the monarchy, and that the [Spanish] Americans were equal in everything to other Spaniards, the integrity and good faith of our character ought accordingly to oblige us to make this truth known.³⁹⁴

Viceroyalty of Peru (Chile). The *pactum translationis* and with it the Spanish tradition of the *Siete partidas* and the philosophy of Suárez and Mariana had been the main intellectual forces during the fateful events of 1810. Thereafter, modern influences accounted for a gradually increasing element in the ideology of the leading patriots. However, Scholastic theories continued to come to the fore, if in an attenuated way, as in the instance of Juan Egaña, the author of the Constitution of 1823. Confined to the island of Juan Fernández by the government of Marcó del Pont when royalist power was re-established in Chile in 1814, Egaña wrote a book which represented not only his opinion but that of the majority of the political exiles. The book contains a significant memorandum which was written with the idea that it would reach the king; its intellectual foundation is based on the defense of religion and the traditional thought of Suárez, Soto, and Solórzano Pereira, and states:

> Spanish America, through the laws of the Indies,[395] is an integral part of the monarchy but independent from any submission to either a province of Spain or to its continent; united to the nation only through the link of the monarch, and with local and representative rights equal to the most privileged kingdoms which have been gathered to Your Majesty's crown. It has its council independent of that of Castile and with prominence equal to the latter to advise Y. M. of all its relations and rights. Through its fundamental laws[396] its natives are called upon to all ecclesiastical benefits of these countries and to positions in government, justice, and administration. Through the abdication of Y. M. in Bayonne and through that of your august father who ceded the crown to a foreign prince against the laws of the kingdom and against any social pact, the provinces of Spain rose up, established their governments which later set up a central junta, various regencies, and a cortes, ruled over the Peninsula, reformed the basic laws and the prerogatives which the king enjoyed as of right. Even if [Spanish] America was entitled to do likewise by its special laws, by the example, by distance, and in view of not being represented there, nothing changed these laws, neither the organic principles of the nation nor the royal rights of Y. M. An orphan without king, without council, with all ministers submissive to the usurping monarch, and seeing Spain nearly reduced to the area of Cádiz, [Spanish America] established provisional governments which without any change acknowledged and swore allegiance to the sovereignty of Y. M. and its dynasty . . . .[397]

Finally, upon Egaña's return to the Chilean mainland, similar ideas were expressed in his draft manifesto declaring the independence of the country. In it, ideas previously set forth were combined with other traditional thought. Among other statements, the manifesto mentioned that "the people of Chile decided to regain its natural rights and with them its freedom and independence,"[398] a thought which, as Jaime Eyzaguirre said, is thoroughly Scholastic, since it allows the community as the original holder of civil authority to resume this power once the ruler became a despot.[399]

Republicanism ultimately became the constitutional pattern, largely because of successive failures to establish monarchies. In New Spain it was the failure of Morelos whose political system finally ended in a consular system (the republican Constitution of Apatzingán, 1814); in the River Plate area, republicanism was strengthened in 1815, because of the failure of Director Posadas to find a candidate of the Spanish Bourbon line. The republican form was maintained at the time of the Argentine Declaration of Independence, since Belgrano failed to establish a neo-Incan Empire (1816); Pueyrredón did not succeed in having a Brazilian prince accept the throne (1817); and San Martín was unable to create a Bourbon monarchy with the future King Louis Philippe or the Prince of Lucca (1818).[400] Finally, in the old Viceroyalty of New Granada, the Federal Republic of Greater Colombia headed by Bolívar meant for many a step toward a Napoleonic empire which failed because of personal opposition by the regional chieftains.

4. The Third and Final Act: The Return of Liberalism (1820–23)

The revolt of Riego in Spain imposed on the king a return to constitutionalism: the Charter of 1812 was reintroduced, and with the years extreme liberals gained great influence, forcing a turn toward the growth of anticlericalism, with increasing Masonic influence. The Riego revolt had as its immediate effect the impossibility of sending reinforcements to Spanish America, and thus weakened the monarchy, although it was by no means the cause of the loss of overseas territories. Before the Riego revolt exploded, the Spanish cause was already lost because of its profound defects, which Giménez Fernández summarized as terrorism, absolutism, militarism, and regalism.[401] Terrorism in Spanish America had been self-defeating; absolutism failed more through its own defects than through enemy action: the Riego revolt was only the aftermath of a logical conclusion. In Spanish America the loss of Crown prestige was fatal: Ferdinand VII had to reverse his attitude from absolutism to constitutionalism, pretending that he did so of his own free will. The effect was tremendous. Besides realizing the loss of prestige of the Crown, people in the Indies were strengthened in their ideas that they too, not just the Peninsular Spaniards, were entitled to governments of their own choice. The various changes which had occurred — from absolutism to constitutionalism, and then in 1814 back to absolutism, and now in 1820 again to constitutionalism — produced confusion and a definite turn against the royalist cause of Spain. The liberals, once in power in Spain, forgot all the good counsels they had given from London, and fostered the civil war. Militarism was also destructive and in many cases had become an end in itself. Regalism found particular emphasis in very strong anticlericalism: the new regime fought the Church and religion in Spain, and ordered renewed expulsions of Jesuits, the breaking of relations with the Holy See, and the gradual closing of convents. The ultimate was reached when the Spanish Court, ruled by Masonic ministers, asked the Holy See not to recognize any Spanish American country and to appoint bishops faithful only to Madrid. Finally, their centralist policies, a continuation of the Bourbon absolutist line and of the constitutionalist period 1808–14, harmed their cause even further.

Viceroyalty of New Spain. Because of the religious sentiments of its people, New Spain was the first to react to the undignified course of the liberal rule in Madrid. The Church and the aristocracy were able with Agustín de Iturbide to obtain military cooperation from the guerrilla forces operating in the east and south of the country (Guerrero, Victoria, and Guzmán) against the reintroduction of constitutionalism as it appeared in Spanish liberal rule from 1820 to 1823, largely regalist and Masonic. The result was the Plan of Iguala of the Three Guarantees (February 24, 1821): religion, independence, and union, in which Iturbide called for the following program:

1. The Roman Catholic faith with no tolerance of any other;
2. Absolute independence from Spain and any other foreign power;
3. Union of Spaniards and Spanish Americans in New Spain,[402]

and invited Ferdinand VII or any other Spanish Bourbon to be emperor of Mexico. As Karl M. Schmitt pointed out,

> the hierarchy and the upper class were on the whole consistent in their opposition to "liberalism," even to the point of separating a conservative-controlled Mexico from a liberal-governed Spain in 1820. They tried to be consistent, too, in their loyalty to the King and to the Bourbon dynasty by offering the Mexican crown to Ferdinand VII or to a member of his family.[403]

The Plan of Iguala and the conservative *pronunciamiento* demonstrated beyond any doubt the Spanish roots of Iturbide's actions, and showed further that as late as 1821 Spanish tradition was the main factor which had moved the various countries of Spanish America in the so-called Spanish American Revolution. An example of the mood of the country was the Bishop of Puebla's sermon on August 2, 1821, in which he supported the Plan of Iguala as the bulwark of religion and monarchy against the Spanish liberals.[404]

The Plan of Iguala was to introduce constitutionalism, but of a type different from that envisioned by the liberals, since it was of a more conservative and traditionalist form highly hostile to the influence of Masonry, regalism, and centralism. But neither the absolutist Viceroy Juan Ruiz de Apodaca nor the liberal Viceroy Juan O'Donojú, his successor, was able to stem the tide. Furthermore, the Treaty of Córdoba between O'Donojú and Iturbide (August 24, 1821),[405] in which the last Spanish Viceroy accepted and amplified the Plan, did not find acceptance in Madrid, and thus the road was free for Iturbide to declare the independence of Mexico and to establish the first Mexican Empire (May 18 and July 25, 1822).[406] Hence, Mexican independence came about as a conservative, traditionalist — though not populist — reaction to liberal Spain: "Mexican independence was an act of counterrevolution."[407]

Viceroyalty of Peru. In Peru, the people opened the gates of Lima to San Martín (July 8, 1821) principally because of the influence which the Church (mainly Franciscans) exerted in favor of a break with liberal Spain.[408] The participation of the mendicant orders is mentioned in the episcopal report to the pope, sent on December 3, 1822, from Madrid by the Archbishop of Lima, Bartolomé de las Heras, who had been banished from his archbishopric. Addressed to the Nuncio Giustiniani, Archbishop of Tyre, this letter is perhaps the most significant of all the episcopal reports sent to the Holy See, and it mentions that at the time of San Martín's arrival there were in Lima four Dominican monasteries, four Franciscan, three Augustinian, and three Mercedarian, among others. It then points out the great part which the mendicant orders played in opening the gates to San Martín.[409] The members of the mendicant orders feared, from news which had been spread, that the Spanish Government would seize most of their monasteries. It should be borne in mind that San Martín — like Bolívar, Iturbide, and other patriot leaders — capitalized on the persecution of the Church by the Spanish liberals during the period 1820–23 to enlist the support of the deeply religious Spanish Americans. The liberal Spanish armies (Canterac and La Serna) were defeated even before they could meet the enemy on the battlefield.

Viceroyalty of New Granada. More than anything else it was the liberal period from 1820 to 1823 in the Peninsula which brought about the final stage in the Spanish American Revolution. In New Granada Spanish liberalism undermined the last hold left to the royalist cause: the union of religious rights with obedience to the king, in the manner Pope Pius VII had proclaimed in his encyclical of 1816.[410]

It was actually after the Riego revolt that the Spanish American bishops joined the independence movement, against the background of a liberal and regalist Spanish policy in the Indies, as in the case of such Loyalists as Rafael Lasso de la Vega (Mérida)[411] — the first republican bishop of Spanish America (though before him Friar Antonio Gómez Polanco, Bishop of Santa Marta, had declared in favor of Bolívar)[412] — and the Mercedarian Higinio Durán (Panama), as well as José Orihuela (Cuzco) and José Sebastián Goyeneche (Arequipa) in Peru.

Republicanism now gained the upper hand because it was able to satisfy the aspirations of local political groups and of military *caudillos*, but it followed in the path of the old Spanish legislation of the Indies in the sense that its laws were not always carried out, and the constitutions remained largely expressions of intellectual exercises and declarations of purely ideal objectives. The setback to political stability brought about by the fall of the Spanish Empire and its resultant Balkanization in Spanish America is best illustrated by the tragedies of Iturbide and Sucre, and the ostracism of Bolívar, San Martín, O'Higgins, and others.[413]

Scholasticism, though weak, was still a force in this last historical period. The best examples are the reasonings of the metropolitan *cabildo* of Bogotá (March 18, 1823), strongly persecuted by Morillo, and those of the neo-republican bishops Lasso de la Vega and Salvador Jiménez de Enciso.[414] The *cabildo* vindicated the right of the Colombian people to proclaim the independence of their country through the universal and simultaneous vote of its citizens, because of the oppression of the natives, the cruelty of the Spaniards, and the wounds inflicted in Spain upon the Catholic religion. Lasso de la Vega explained earlier (October 20, 1821) his conversion to republicanism: "once the oath to the constitution was given by the Catholic King, sovereignty reverted to the source whence it came, i.e., the consent and decision of the citizens; and if it reverted to the Spaniards, why not to us?"[415] Later, in a speech to the Assembly of Cúcuta, he stated:

> And since the Americas had not entered the new compact of obedience, once the King returned sovereignty to his people this people of Colombia has no obligation toward the King of Spain. For this reason I have acknowledged and given an oath of allegiance, without any scruple of conscience, to the sovereignty of the Government of Colombia and its legitimate right to independence.[416]

It is amazing how the true picture of the independence movement has been changed gradually by the Romanticists and later-nineteenth-century liberal historians, who projected their own ideology into an historical period which was as Hispanic and to a large extent still as Scholastic as the former centuries of Spanish government in the new world. In a way, this misinterpretation is not surprising: many contemporaries, like the Spanish Minister Lardizábal, mistook the Spanish American Revolution for a simple projection of the French Revolution with its terror and regicide.

The political theories with which the patriots argued were almost entirely of Spanish origin; not only the Scholastic ideas of Suárez, Molina, Mariana, and St. Thomas, or seventeenth-century Spanish political thought, but also the *Siete Partidas* of Alfonso the Learned, the *Fuero juzgo*, and the Laws of the Indies, were referred to and were all used for the end which they envisioned. The spiritual fathers of independence were all educated in colonial universities in which Scholasticism was the philosophy taught, though eighteenth-century thought was not altogether neglected. Scholastic philosophy was the intellectual basis of the great leaders of the Revolution: Moreno, Saavedra, Castelli, and Cañete in the area of the old Viceroyalty of the River Plate; Hidalgo Morelos, Abad y Queipo (even if they were forced to give up the tasks they had begun) and José Matías Delgado in the old Viceroyalty of New Spain; Torres, Peñalver, and Tenorio in the various areas of the Viceroyalty of New Granada. Their ideas came from the old roots of Salamanca, not from Paris, London, or Geneva. The military leaders were basically Hispanic, though on the surface the revolutionary language of the period — that of the French Revolution and of Napoleon — no doubt predominated at times among them. The generals such as Bolívar, San Martín, Santander, O'Higgins, Sucre, despite their revolutionary language and Napoleonic gestures, were so typically Hispanic that they could not be mistaken for anything else. Their personality, their actions, and their intellectual basis are unthinkable in a non-Hispanic country.

The two main elements of Spanish political thought remained valid until the very end of the Spanish American Revolution: faith in God and loyalty to the king. We should not ignore the fact that on two occasions the king was specifically invited to come to the Indies: the Constitution of Cundinamarca of 1811, in New Granada, and the Plan of Iguala and Treaty of Córdoba of 1821, in New Spain; and the same was also expressed for Chile in the *Catecismo político cristiano* of 1810, again showing the Spanish nature of the entire Spanish American Revolution. Also, the fundamental issue of religion in the Revolution — rarely mentioned these days — illustrates the real meaning of independence and its true Spanishness, as when the electoral college of Cundinamarca, after having proclaimed independence on July 15, 1813, solemnly declared that "Cundinamarca did not depend on any other sovereignty than that of God and the people, under the auspices of Our Lady the Virgin Mary in the mystery of her immaculate conception,"[417] or when the Plan of Iguala in 1821 incorporated religion as one of its fundamental principles.

Furlong has well summarized the situation:

> The so-called "Revolution" of May was but the final step of an evolution, and this started at the beginning of the Hispanic colonization and developed without haste and without pause through the period of two long centuries. This reality seems to us of an irrefutable logic. We maintain, however, that the basic elements of this evolution were the chairs of philosophy, theology, and law which molded [Spanish] American youth in the lecture halls of Córdoba and Chuquisaca, of Buenos Aires, of Salta, of Asunción, of La Paz and Montevideo. It was from the writings of the great Spanish thinkers whose books were the school texts or the reference and reading works in

those seats of knowledge that all the ideas and all the principles which culminated in the glorious events of 1810 germinated and flourished, particularly the great principle of the "pactum" which constituted the pivot upon which the whole revolutionary machinery revolved....

Between roughly 1612 and 1640 the influence of Suárez was the most important in the theological field; from the middle of the seventeenth century until the middle of the eighteenth century — or, to be more precise, until 1767 — his influence was all-embracing in the philosophical and legal fields, and from that date to 1810 his philosophico-juridical doctrines prevailed in an absolute way, despite the adverse campaign which was so tenaciously, intensely, and continuously waged against them.[418]

Did not Friar Servando Teresa de Mier symbolize this situation when he said positively that when he refers to the social pact of the Spanish Americans he was not speaking of Rousseau's implicit pact?[419] It could not be otherwise, since the Spanish American Revolution drew its strength from Hispanic roots, from an ancient theory reflected in the Spanish War of Independence when the people and not the Crown saved national dignity.[420] Thus, there is a great link between the Revolution and Spanish thought of the Golden Age with its extraordinary vitality, its intellectual strength, and its imposing moderation in matters of policy. Within the Spanish monarchy, much less absolute than the French or English monarchies, the *cabildos* represented the most important historical factor. Heirs to the semi-sovereign Castilian councils, they continued in Spanish America the great tradition of municipal freedom which in the Spanish American sixteenth century rose to such heights, and in the early nineteenth century began the revolution from those very seats which developed into the capitals of the independent Spanish American republics. The intellectual weapons used by the *cabildos* were those which Spanish legal and political thought had transmitted to Spanish America and which received in the Late Scholastic movement, particularly with the great writers from Vitoria to Suárez, the most impressive demonstration: resistance to tyranny and belief in Christian liberty.[421]

NOTES

[1] See Alemparte R., *El cabildo en Chile*, pp. 370–71. Alemparte gives a complete account (pp. 351–71) of the reforms undertaken by Charles III, all of which helped the future emancipation. See also Jane, pp. 44–64, esp. p. 63, and pp. 81–101; Ots Capdequí, *El estado español*, pp. 76–77; Ravignani, *Historia constitucional*, I 61–90.

[2] See Graham, pp. 43ff.

[3] See Ravignani, *Historia constitucional*, I 6. See also Majó Framis, I 1248, 1259, 1262, 1272; and Madariaga, *Bolívar*, p. xviii.

[4] P. 62.

[5] *La independencia hispanoamericana*, p. 56. With regard to the fact that foreign government models were not envisioned, see "Discurso pronunciado por el Libertador ante el Congreso de Angostura el 15 de febrero de 1819, día de su instalación," in Bolívar, *Obras* III 680.

[6] Morse, p. 166, quoting Paz, *The Labyrinth of Solitude* (New York, 1961), p. 117.

[7] Konetzke, *La condición*, pp. 33–37. See also Gómez Hoyos, II 16.
[8] Ibid.
[9] Delgado, *La independencia hispanoamericana*, pp. 19–20, esp. p. 20.
[10] Ibid.
[11] Konetzke, *La condición*, pp. 44–47, 33–37. See Delgado, *La independencia hispanoamericana*, pp. 21–26.
[12] Delgado, *La independencia hispanoamericana*, p. 21.
[13] Ibid., pp. 29–30.   [14] See ibid., pp. 30ff.   [15] Ibid., p. 30.
[16] An early example of patriotism is the case of the war of the *comuneros* in Paraguay and the execution of Antequera. A century before Bolívar, the word "patriots" was coined during this struggle (1726–35). See Madariaga, *El ocaso*, pp. 255–59.
[17] Majó Framis, I 1204–29, esp. 1206, 1226.
[18] Jane, p. 81.
[19] "Proposal of the Count of Aranda to King Charles III Concerning the Desirability of Creating Independent Kingdoms in America," in Fermín Mignone, 11. See also Majó Framis, I 1206–1208.
[20] See Robertson, "The Policy of Spain," 21–46.   [21] Parry, p. 72.
[22] See chap. IV at nn. 22–25.
[23] On the last four individuals, see Mendiburu, II 382, I 176–81, IV 159–66, IX 463–64.
[24] Giménez Fernández, *Las doctrinas populistas*, pp. 39ff.
[25] *Filiación histórica del gobierno representativo argentino*, two volumes, passim.
[26] *Historia del 25 de Mayo*, pp. 41–48, esp. pp. 43–44.
[27] II 770–71.   [28] Ibid., 774.   [29] P. 173.
[30] Ibid., p. 174.   [31] Ibid.   [32] See Masur, p. 687. See also Schoen, p. 330.
[33] Alemparte, *El cabildo en Chile*, p. 373.   [34] García Venero, pp. 55–63.
[35] "Proclama de la Junta General del Principado de Asturias. 24 de mayo," in Díaz-Plaja, pp. 51–52, and Gandía, *Historia del 25 de Mayo*, p. 425.
[36] García Venero, p. 66.   [37] Ibid.   [38] Gómez Hoyos, II 20.
[39] Pareja Paz-Soldán, p. 124.
[40] Díaz-Plaja, pp. 93–94. On Spanish American participation, see Labra, pp. 342–44.
[41] Díaz-Plaja, p. 96; Labra, p. 347.
[42] "Memorial y discurso de las razones que se ofrecen para que el Real y Supremo Consejo de Indias deva preceder en todos los actos públicos al que llaman de Frandres," in *Obras*, p. 381n65. Likewise his *Política indiana*, iv–xix, 669–71. See Ayala, *Solórzano*, pp. 164–67, 518–19, and Konetzke's paper in *Congreso Hispanoamericano de Historia*, pp. 250ff.
[43] Delgado, *La independencia hispanoamericana*, p. 56.
[44] Ibid., p. 57.
[45] *Orígenes*, p. 96.
[46] Alemparte, *El cabildo en Chile*, p. 354, with quotation from ibid., p. 28.
[47] Morse, p. 159.   [48] Ibid., p. 160.
[49] Ibid., pp. 160–61, following J. Estrada Monsalve, "El sistema político de Bolívar en la doctrina tomista," *Bolívar*, 13 (September 1952), 463–74.
[50] I 34–35. See Madariaga, *Bolívar*, p. 392, where he says: "Now, *without fidelity to the King, fidelity to Spain in Spanish America had no sense*" (emphasis added).
[51] René-Moreno, II 261–62, esp. 262n195. See also Giménez Fernández, *Las doctrinas populistas*, p. 35, and Chaves, p. 104.
[52] *Revolutions*, p. 55.   [53] Ibid., p. 57.
[54] Gandía, *Historia del 25 de Mayo*, p. 426. See too pp. 101–102 regarding the error of the so-called "mask of Ferdinand."
[55] Ibid., p. 91.   [56] Gandía, *Buenos Aires colonial*, p. 145.
[57] Delgado, *La independencia hispanoamericana*, p. 51.
[58] *Revolutions*, p. 56.
[59] *Belgrano y la independencia argentina*, I 223–31, esp. 230–31.
[60] Ibid., 231.   [61] Ibid., 232.   [62] Ibid., 233.
[63] Ibid., 234. See also Abad de Santillán, I 372.
[64] Delgado, *La independencia hispanoamericana*, pp. 51–52.
[65] Mitre, *Belgrano y la independencia argentina*, I 235.
[66] Ibid., 235–38.
[67] Giménez Fernández, *Las doctrinas populistas*, pp. 63–68.   [68] Lafuente Ferrari, p. 37.
[69] Ibid., pp. 49–50.   [70] Ibid., p. 79.   [71] Ibid., p. 104.
[72] Ibid., pp. 107–12. A more favorable point of view about Iturrigaray is expressed by Majó Framis, I 1226–28, who believes that it was an error not to support him.

[73] Lafuente Ferrari, p. 113.   [74] Ibid., pp. 119ff.   [75] Ibid., pp. 118–23.
[76] Ibid., pp. 123–24.   [77] Ibid., pp. 127–30.   [78] Ibid., pp. 134–35.
[79] Delgado, *La independencia hispanoamericana*, p. 52.
[80] Cuevas, *La nación mexicana*, p. 389. See also idem, *La iglesia en México*, V 59, and Mitre, *San Martín y la emancipación sud-americana*, I 87n51.
[81] Lafuente Ferrari, p. 158.   [82] Ibid., p. 168.
[83] Gandía, *Historia del 25 de Mayo*, p. 48.
[84] Idem, *Buenos Aires colonial*, p. 141.
[85] Ibid., p. 145. See also Ravignani, *Historia constitucional*, I 108–13, esp. 111, and Gandía, *Las ideas políticas*, II, passim, esp. pp. 184–389.
[86] Lynch, *Revolutions*, pp. 43–44. See also Gandía, *Buenos Aires colonial*, p. 152.
[87] Lynch, *Revolutions*, p. 43. See Gandía, *Las ideas políticas*, II 252ff.
[88] *Historia constitucional*, p. 117.   [89] Ibid., p. 106.
[90] Gandía, *Historia del 25 de Mayo*, p. 49.
[91] Ibid. See Ravignani, *Historia constitucional*, I 121.
[92] Ibid., 118.   [93] Gandía, *Historia del 25 de Mayo*, p. 51.   [94] Ibid., pp. 83–85.
[95] Abad de Santillán, I 406.   [96] Ibid., 409.
[97] Ibid., 408. See also Mitre, *San Martín y la emancipación sud-americana*, I 87; Lynch, *Revolutions*, pp. 52–53; Vargas Ugarte, *El episcopado*, p. 306.
[98] It is interesting to note that Alzaga was responsible for the dismissal of Viceroy Cisneros (Gandía, *Historia del 25 de Mayo*, p. 129).
[99] Abad de Santillán, I 410.   [100] Ibid., 4.   [101] Ibid., 6.
[102] Ibid.   [103] Ibid., p. 11.   [104] Gilmore, 16.
[105] Ibid., 11, 17–18.   [106] Pivel Devoto, p. 9.
[107] Ibid., p. 217. See also Schoen, p. 326.
[108] This point is held by a majority of writers, including Pivel Devoto, Mitre, Sarmiento, Juan B. Terán, Levene, and Schoen, among others; yet Ravignani feels that the viceroyalty had created links of union which were destroyed by factors which came to the fore after 1810 (*El Virreinato del Río de la Plata: Su formación histórica e institucional* [Buenos Aires, 1938]). José Nicolás Matienzo, on the contrary, believes that the *audiencia* had given the viceroyalty the same cohesion which existed in other parts of the Spanish Empire and that the peoples wished to preserve this union (*El gobierno representativo federal en la República Argentina* [Buenos Aires, 1910]) (See Pivel Devoto, pp. 191–93, 191–92nn187–89).
[109] Ibid., p. 193.
[110] Opinion of the *fiscales* Villota and Caspe, Buenos Aires, September 26, 1808, in Uruguay Museo Histórico Nacional, *Documentos relativos a la Junta Montevideana*, I 11–13.
[111] See Lynch, *Revolutions*, pp. 88ff.   [112] Ibid., p. 112.
[113] Pivel Devoto, pp. 96–121.   [114] Ibid., pp. 122–29.   [115] Ibid., pp. 136–48.
[116] Ibid., p. 151.   [117] Ibid., pp. 166–67.   [118] Ibid., p. 176.
[119] Ibid., pp. 170–71, 172–73, 176–77.   [120] Belinzón, I 63.
[121] Pivel Devoto, pp. 180–84.
[122] Lynch, *Revolutions*, p. 90. See also Pivel Devoto, pp. 177, 196–216.
[123] Belinzón, I 78.   [124] Ibid., 79.   [125] Pivel Devoto, p. 190.
[126] See Street, 479–81.   [127] Belinzón, I 79ff.   [128] Lynch, *Revolutions*, p. 91.
[129] Pivel Devoto, p. 194.   [130] Pp. 11–12.
[131] Narancio, "Las ideas políticas," 102.   [132] Ardao & Castellanos, p. 12.
[133] Ibid., pp. 12–13. The reference to Mohammed shows a certain Voltairean element, since it undoubtedly is taken from Voltaire's *Le fanatisme ou Mahomet, le prophète*, as a symbol for obscurantism and fanaticism.
[134] Narancio, "Las ideas políticas," 104.
[135] Ibid., 104–105, 129, 156–65. The original document is to be found in the Archivo Sautu of the Biblioteca Dr. Menéndez in Pergamino, Argentina.
[136] See chap. IV at n. 145.   [137] Narancio, "Las ideas políticas," 112.
[138] *Revolutions*, p. 92.   [139] Ibid., p. 91.   [140] Pivel Devoto, p. 223.
[141] Ibid., p. 238.   [142] Ibid., pp. 241–45.   [143] Ibid., p. 258.
[144] "Apuntes," in Rengger & Longchamp, *Ensayo histórico*, p. 5.
[145] Ibid., pp. 5–6.   [146] Lynch, *Revolutions*, p. 106.   [147] Ibid., p. 107.
[148] Ibid.   [149] Ibid.   [150] See chap. IV at nn. 185, 186.
[151] Alemparte, *El cabildo en Chile*, p. 390.
[152] Abad de Santillán, 404. See also Levene, *Historia del derecho argentino*, I 299, and 299n4.
[153] Gómez Hoyos, II 27–33, esp. 27, 30, 32.

154 Levene, *Historia del derecho argentino*, I 390–91; see also Fernández Almagro, *Orígenes*, p. 70, and Conde de Toreno, *Historia del levantamiento, guerra y revolución de España* (Madrid, 1862), p. 58.
155 This problem also plagues recently independent island republics in the former British West Indies.
156 Perazzo, *Cortés*, pp. 53–77.   157 Ibid., p. 56.   158 Lynch, *Revolutions*, p. 108.
159 Ibid.   160 Ibid., p. 96.   161 *Escritos*, pp. 43–62.
162 Fernández Almagro, *La emancipación*, pp. 22–29.
163 Mitre, *Historia de San Martín*, I 296–97. See further Legón & Medrano, p. 46, and Ravignani, *Asambleas constituyentes argentinas*, I 482. See also Bourquin, pp. 365–403, and O. Carlos Stoetzer, *El pensamiento político en la América española durante el período de la emancipación (1789–1825)* (2 vols.; Madrid, 1966), II 174–79.
164 Lafuente Ferrari, p. 98.   165 Ibid., p. 99.   166 Ibid.
167 Ibid., p. 100.   168 Ibid., p. 112.   169 Ibid., pp. 115–16.
170 Appendix II, in ibid., pp. 390–93.   171 Ibid., p. 121.
172 Majó Framis, p. 1227.   173 Lafuente Ferrari, p. 160.   174 Ibid., p. 161.
175 Ibid., pp. 168–71.   176 Ibid., p. 180.   177 See Majó Framis, pp. 1226–28.
178 Parkes, p. 122.   179 *La filosofía en México*, X 103–104.   180 Parkes, p. 123.
181 Fagg, p. 333.
182 Ramos, *La filosofía en México*, X 103–105, esp. 105.
183 Parkes, p. 124.   184 Ibid., p. 126.   185 Ibid., p. 127.
186 Morse, p. 160.   187 Parkes, p. 135; Fagg, p. 336.
188 Hernández y Dávalos, VI 411 (Document 531). The entire document — which mentions Suárez several times (pp. 404, 407 ["eximio Suárez"]) — shows the Scholastic and Hispanic roots with no trace whatsoever of any modernist thought. Cuevas in his *La iglesia en México*, V 91, mentions the document and his reference to Suárez' *De religione*. He says of the document that it is "... exaggerated, but is quoted herein as descriptive of the historical moment."
189 P. 1245.   190 Halperín Donghi, p. 174.   191 Furlong, "Suárez," p. 101.
192 Giménez Fernández, *Las doctrinas populistas*, pp. 66–67; Abad de Santillán, I 406.
193 Lynch, *Revolutions*, p. 52.   194 *Historia constitucional*, I 125.
195 Gandía, *Historia del 25 de Mayo*, p. 103. They included 3 members of the clergy, 3 officials, 2 members of the armed forces, 12 merchants, 2 district mayors, and 4 professionals.
196 Ibid. See also Abad de Santillán, I 407; Lynch, *Revolutions*, p. 52, whose figures are slightly different.
197 Abad de Santillán, I 408.
198 Levene, "Los sucesos de Mayo," 32. See also Abad de Santillán, I 408.
199 Abad de Santillán, I 408.   200 Ibid., 409.
201 Ibid., 408. See also Gandía, *Historia del 25 de Mayo*, pp. 93–94, 100–83, 426, among others.
202 Gandía, *Buenos Aires colonial*, p. 140. See chapter 10, pp. 139–53.
203 "Días de Mayo," *Actas del cabildo de Buenos Aires, 1810* (La Plata, 1910), 105–71, quoted in Furlong, "Suárez," p. 107.
204 Abad de Santillán, I 408–409. See Ravignani, *Historia constitucional*, I 125–47.
205 Lynch, *Revolutions*, p. 54.   206 *Historia del 25 de Mayo*, pp. 128–29.
207 Lynch, *Revolutions*, p. 54.   208 I 412.   209 *Historia constitucional*, I 132.
210 Ibid., 141, 143. See also Caillet-Bois; his thesis that the intellectual elite group in Buenos Aires sympathized with the French Revolution and made the Argentine Revolution in the image of 1789 is highly exaggerated. See the works of Levene, Martínez Paz, Ferreiro, Furlong, to name but a few.
211 *Revolutions*, p. 54; Ravignani, *Historia constitucional*, I 133 ("con evidente fraude"); Abad de Santillán, I 409 ("Se había procedido evidentemente a un falseamiento de los votos...").
212 *Revolutions*, p. 55.   213 Gandía, *Historia del 25 de Mayo*, pp. 414–15.
214 Ibid., pp. 114, 416.   215 Ibid.
216 Ibid., pp. 141ff. ("IV: La imitación del ejemplo español") and p. 279; pp. 53, 123 and 126, 139.
217 González, *Las órdenes*, p. 8.
218 Juan Hipólito Vieytes was also known for his dissemination of economic theories in the River Plate, particularly those of Adam Smith and of such Spanish reformers as Jovellanos, Campillo, Uztáriz, and Foronda. Like José da Silva Lisboa in Portuguese America, Vieytes represents in the River Plate the rise of economic thought.

[219] Gregorio Funes also showed some traces of the influence of the Enlightenment (Condillac, Mably, Rousseau) and also of Pufendorf. See also Ingenieros, I 175, 182, 183–94; Martínez Paz, *El deán Funes*, p. 100 — both agree that Funes was imbued with the ideas of the Jesuit school of thought.

[220] Furlong, *Nacimiento*, pp. 606–607, with quotation from Roberto F. Marfany, "¿Dónde está el pueblo?" *Humanidades* (La Plata), 1928, pp. 253–312.

[221] See Arnade, "Political Causes" in "Causes of Spanish-American Wars of Independence," 128–29, about economic reasons, and 130–31 about Spanish Late Scholastic thought as the basis of Spanish American emancipation. See Diffie's interesting commentary regarding the *Suarecina* thesis in the same paper (pp. 141ff.), quoting Belaúnde's denial of any relation between Late Scholastic thought and the Spanish American emancipation. On the other hand, Belaúnde admits that "undoubtedly they [eighteenth- and nineteenth-century writers in Spanish America] knew and studied the old treatise writers such as Suárez, Mariana, and Saavedra Fajardo, setting forth the principles of sovereignty and criticizing the absolute powers of the king, and chiefly the jurists who wrote especially for the Indies, such as Solórzano, Pinelo, and others . . ." (Belaúnde, *Bolívar and the Political Thought*, p. 18).

[222] Halperín Donghi, p. 21. See Gandía, *Las ideas políticas*, V 369–931, esp. 827–64, 889–97.

[223] Halperín Donghi, p. 45. [224] Ibid., p. 47. [225] Ibid., p. 82.

[226] Ibid., p. 179. [227] Ibid., p. 180. [228] Ibid., p. 181.

[229] Ibid. [230] Ibid., pp. 181–82. [231] Ibid., p. 163.

[232] Ibid., p. 173. [233] Furlong, "Suárez," p. 106.

[234] Cháves, p. 94. This is expressed in a report to the Junta of Buenos Aires from Tupiza, November 10, 1810 (Archivo General de la República Argentina, II 2).

[235] Ibid., pp. 103–104. [236] "Los sucesos de Mayo," 32.

[237] See Molinari; see also Gandía, *Historia del 25 de Mayo*, pp. 17–24, who agrees fully with Molinari; also Belaúnde, "Discurso" in Congreso Hispanoamericano de Historia, pp. 35–37, in which he made the solid statement that the propaganda for independence (free trade) which the English promised was far less a determining factor than the intrinsically Hispanic character which refused to buy freedom for material gains.

[238] Levene (ed.), "Manifiesto de la junta con motivo del fusilamiento de Liniers, y otros complicados en la conspiración de Córdoba, 9 de septiembre de 1810," *El pensamiento vivo de Mariano Moreno* (Buenos Aires, 1942), pp. 66–69. The "Manifiesto" appeared in the *Gaceta de Buenos Aires* of October 11, 1810, and was signed by the President of the Junta, Cornelio de Saavedra, and the Secretary, Mariano Moreno. See also Levene, *Moreno*, pp. 185–228.

[239] Levene, "El Congreso que acaba de convocarse y la Constitución del Estado," *El pensamiento vivo*, pp. 128–29. These statements were dated November 2, 1810, and were published in the *Gaceta de Buenos Aires* of November 13, 1810.

[240] Levene, "El Congresso," *El pensamiento vivo*, p. 142. This was dated November 28, 1810, and appeared in the *Gaceta de Buenos Aires* of December 6, 1810.

[241] *Nacimiento*, p. 631.

[242] Furlong, "Suárez," p. 102n64.

[243] Furlong, *Nacimiento*, pp. 634–35.

[244] Gros Espiell, "La formación del ideario artiguista," in Narancío, *Artigas*, p. 216. This statement is accepted with the reservations mentioned earlier, i.e., that there is no connection between Suárez and Rousseau.

[245] *Nacimiento*, p. 581. [246] Korn, pp. 110–13.

[247] Halperín Donghi, p. 127. See Jefferson Rea Spell, pp. 129, 239, 241, 301.

[248] P. 130. [249] P. 112. [250] Levene, *History of Argentina*, pp. 261–62.

[251] Ravignani, *Historia constitucional*, I 168; Abad de Santillán, I 410–11, 447–48, 450–52.

[252] Sánchez Viamonte, pp. 96–97.

[253] Ravignani, *Asambleas constituyentes argentinas*, I 3n2.

[254] Ibid., p. 4. [255] Furlong, "Suárez," p. 109.

[256] *Síntesis*, pp. 7–8. However, Levene is wrong in stating that Suárez anticipated Rousseau's *Contrat social*: there is no connection between them.

[257] Gilmore, 21. [258] Gómez Hoyos, II 407. [259] Ibid., pp. 403–404.

[260] Ibid., pp. 407–408. [261] Fagg, p. 331. [262] Gómez Hoyos, II 19.

[263] Ibid., p. 20. [264] Gilmore, 23. [265] Gómez Hoyos, II 15.

[266] Ibid., pp. 29–30. [267] Ibid., p. 31; also Giménez Fernández, p. 66.

[268] Gómez Hoyos, II 31–32. [269] Ibid., p. 36.

[270] Ibid., pp. 36–37, quoted from Eduardo Posada, *El 20 de Julio* (Bogotá, 1914), pp. 205–10.

271 Gómez Hoyos, II 39.   272 Ibid., p. 41.   273 Ibid., p. 62.
274 Ibid., p. 63. In contrast to Article 3 of the Spanish Constitution of 1812 (Cádiz) which stated that "Sovereignty resides *essentially* in the Nation . . . ," many Spanish-Americans took a Scholastic stand when they used the adjectives *radically* or *originally*.
275 Gilmore, 12.   276 Ibid., 18.   277 Gómez Hoyos, II 74n13, and p. 76.
278 Ibid., 84.   279 Ibid., 85.   280 Ibid., 94.
281 Ibid., 101.   282 Ibid., 107–108.
283 *Bolívar y el pensamiento político*, p. 17.   284 René-Moreno, II 165–66.
285 Establishment of the Junta Tuitiva (July 16, 1809) (see Arguedas, p. 180).
286 P. 320.   287 Ibid.   288 Lynch, *Revolutions*, p. 50.
289 Ibid., pp. 117–19.   290 Ibid., pp. 120–21.   291 Ibid., p. 123.
292 Pivel Devoto, pp. 25–30, esp. p. 30.   293 Ibid., p. 45.   294 Ibid., pp. 44–58.
295 Ibid., pp. 71–72.   296 Ibid., pp. 82–83, 83–95.   297 Ibid., pp. 87, 93.
298 Ibid., pp. 187–89. See Gandía, *Las ideas políticas*, pp. 164–451.
299 Pivel Devoto, pp. 254–55.   300 Ibid., p. 264.   301 Ibid., p. 267.
302 Ibid., p. 269.   303 Belinzón, I 149.
304 Ibid., p. 152. See also Street, 478–500.   305 Lynch, *Revolutions*, p. 95.
306 See Street.   307 Belinzón, I 167–68. See Street, 500–501.   308 Street, 504.
309 Belinzón, I 195.   310 Ibid.
311 Ibid., 198. See Lynch, *Revolutions*, pp. 95–96. With regard to the *Instrucciones del Año XIII* and the influence of Pufendorf and the French Revolution on this constitutional document, see "Instrucciones del año xiii," in Gros Espiell, pp. 18–20n1, and Pufendorf, II 285–86. See also "Acta de la Asamblea del 5 de abril de 1813," in Narancio, "Las ideas políticas," 128–29.
312 Belinzón, I 212.   313 Lasplaces, pp. 123–25; Belinzón, I 211.
314 Ibid., 227–31.
315 Ibid., 252–53. With regard to the Hispanic roots of Artigas, see Gros Espiell, pp. 9–26; Narancio, *El origen*; Ardao & Castellanos; and Juan A. Rebella, *Lo hispánico en la acción y en el pensamiento de Artigas* (Montevideo, 1953), besides Pivel Devoto, esp. p. 269.
316 Rengger & Longchamp, p. 47.   317 Lynch, *Revolutions*, p. 108.   318 Ibid.
319 Ibid.   320 Rengger & Longchamp, p. 48.   321 Ibid., p. 50.
322 Eyzaguirre, p. 103.
323 Ibid., p. 104. In contrast, Ricardo Donoso in his study on the *Catecismo* believed the author to be Jaime Zudáñez, thus refuting the theory of Diego Barros Arana for whom the *Catecismo* was written by Juan Martínez de Rozas. See Hanisch Espíndola: he sees sources in Plato, Aristotle, Cicero, St. Augustine, St. Thomas, Vitoria, Suárez, Mariana, Soto, Molina, Covarrubias, Domingo Antúnez de Portugal, Alfonso de Acevedo, Antonio Gómez, Juan de Matienzo, Jerónimo del Castillo y Bobadilla, Juan de Hevia Bolaños, Diego Ibáñez de Faría, Quevedo, Feijóo, but also Locke, Montesquieu and Rousseau, Grotius, Heineccius and Pufendorf (pp. 50–85).
324 Eyzaguirre, pp. 105–109.   325 Tocornal, 205–206.   326 Guzmán, I 239.
327 Eyzaguirre, p. 116.   328 Ibid., p. 123.
329 Márquez de la Plata, 397–98. This statement appears in the Bando de la Exma. Junta de Santiago of April 2, 1811, as a part of chap. iii, "El Consejo de Regencia de España y la Junta de Chile."
330 Lynch, *Revolutions*, p. 236.   331 Ibid.   332 Ibid., p. 237.
333 Gilmore, 1.   334 Ibid., 9.   335 Ibid., 10.
336 Ibid., 10–11.   337 Ibid., 8.   338 Masur, pp. 88–89.
339 Ibid., p. 90.   340 Ibid., p. 92.   341 Ibid., pp. 93–98.
342 Malagón pp. 143–44 (135–36, 140).   343 Schoen, p. 307.   344 *Obras*, I 63.
345 Gómez Hoyos, II 397.   346 Ibid., 400.   347 Ibid., 398.
348 Ibid., 403.   349 Ibid., 407ff.   350 Ibid., 408.
351 Ibid.   352 Ibid.   353 Ibid., 408–409.
354 Ibid., 509.   355 Ibid.   356 Ibid., 410.
357 Ibid., 411.   358 Ibid., 413.   359 Ibid., 415.
360 Ibid., 416.   361 Ibid., 418–19.   362 Brau, *Historia*, p. 221.
363 Masur, p. 117.   364 Giménez Fernández, *Las doctrinas populistas*, pp. 68–72.
365 Martínez Marina, *Ensayo histórico-crítico* and *Discurso*.
366 Giménez Fernández, *Las doctrinas populistas*, pp. 72ff.
367 Vargas Ugarte, *El episcopado*, pp. 434–35. See also ibid., pp. 304–305.
368 Vargas Ugarte, *Moxó y Francolí*, p. 35; see René-Moreno, II.
369 Vargas Ugarte, *El episcopado*, pp. 388–91.

³⁷⁰ Bustamante, *El Congreso*, p. 169. The four *cartas* of this edition actually refer to *cartas séptima, octava, novena*, and *décima* of Vol. II of Bustamante'*s Cuadro histórico* which follows the second revised edition of 1843-46. This first edition consisted of six volumes and was published in Mexico, 1823-32. Morelos' speech is an excellent example of the fusion of Scholastic and modern thought, since it also contains ideas of Rousseau.
³⁷¹ *El Congreso*, pp. 189-90. ³⁷² Vargas Ugarte, *El episcopado*, p. 312.
³⁷³ Giménez Fernández, *Las doctrinas populistas*, pp. 75-83.
³⁷⁴ Delgado, pp. 60-61. ³⁷⁵ See chap. V at n. 3. ³⁷⁶ Pp. 99-100.
³⁷⁷ Gandía, *Historia del 25 de Mayo*, p. 427. ³⁷⁸ Ibid., pp. 428-29.
³⁷⁹ Ibid., p. 430. ³⁸⁰ Ibid., p. 432. ³⁸¹ Ibid.
³⁸² Ibid., p. 433. ³⁸³ Ibid., pp. 433-34.
³⁸⁴ Giménez Fernández, *Las doctrinas populistas*, p. 86.
³⁸⁵ See the Manifesto of the Junta of Zitácuaro dated September 16, 1812, entitled "La Junta Suprema de la Nación a los americanos en el aniversario del día 16 de septiembre," in Bustamante, *El Congreso*, pp. 84-92, and the answers by Liceaga (actually Cos) and Rayón (ibid., pp. 92-104).
³⁸⁶ *Decreto constitucional para la libertad de la América mexicana* (see Sierra, p. 114).
³⁸⁷ Bustamente, *El Congreso*, p. 190. The re-establishment of the society was inspired by Bustamante; also Bustamante, *Cuadro histórico*, II 45-47. See proposal No. 11 of the "Propuesta de los diputados peruanos a las Cortes de Cádiz sobre igualdad de peninsulares y criollos," in Pareja Paz-Soldán, pp. 402-403, which asked for the restitution of the Society. Although this proposal was not accepted it shows the sentiments of the Spanish Americans and the true roots of their liberalism. On the other hand, it proved to be another echo of the events in the Peninsula, since the *Suprema Junta Central* had "already reinstated the Jesuits and appointed an Inquisitor-General" (Livermore, p. 355).
³⁸⁸ "Discurso pronunciado por el Libertador ante el Congreso de Angostura el 15 de febrero de 1819, día de su instalación," in Bolívar, *Obras*, III 674-97, esp. 690.
³⁸⁹ Leturia, *El ocaso*, p. 89. Leturia thinks the request that all bishops be senators actually came from Peñalver.
³⁹⁰ Ibid., pp. 91-92. ³⁹¹ Ibid., p. 92. ³⁹² Carbia, *La Revolución*, pp. 25-26.
³⁹³ Furlong, "Suárez," pp. 109-10.
³⁹⁴ Vargas Ugarte, *Moxó y Francolí*, pp. xii-xxiii, document 7 of the Appendix.
³⁹⁵ Book IV, Title 8, Law 1, and others. Soto, *De iure et iustitia*, Book I, Quest. 1, Art. 2; Suárez, *De legibus*, Book I, Ch. 7, No. 14; Solórzano Pereira, *Política indiana*, Book V, Ch. 15 (Egaña, "Memorial escrito en el presidio para dirigirse al rey Fernando VII," in *El chileno consolado*, II 8.
³⁹⁶ Indian Legislation: Book IV, Title 6, Laws 3 and 5; Book I, Title 6, Laws 24 and 28; Book II, Title 2, Law 22; Book III, Title 2, Laws 13 and 14; Solórzano Pereira, *Política indiana*, Book III, Ch. 14 (Egaña, *El chileno consolado*, II 8).
³⁹⁷ *El chileno consolado*, II 8-10. On defense of religion, see ibid., pp. 44-48.
³⁹⁸ "Apuntes para el Manifiesto que debe hacerse en la Declaración de la Independencia de Chile," in Egaña, *Escritos* p. 91; the complete text of the manifiesto appears on pp. 85-100.
³⁹⁹ Pp. 145-46.
⁴⁰⁰ The draft Constitution elaborated by the official Committee of 1813 had already declared that the form of government was the republic. Republicanism, however, declined after formal independence had been achieved in Tucumán (1816). The most impressive sign of this trend was the omission of "republic" and "people" in the Constitution of 1819 (see Sánchez Viamonte, pp. 111, 126-33). See Belgrano's statement in the secret meeting prior to the declaration of Argentine independence (July 6, 1816) in which he proposed as "the most convenient form of government a moderate monarchy" in view of the fact that "a complete change in ideas had taken place in Europe — just as before the spirit of the times was to republicanize everything, now it is to monarchize everything" (Ravignani, *Asambleas constituyentes argentinas*, I 482).
⁴⁰¹ *Las doctrinas populistas*, pp. 104-109; see also the text at pp. 241-42, above.
⁴⁰² "Plan publicado en Iguala el 24 de Febrero de 1821," pp. 186-87.
⁴⁰³ P. 311.
⁴⁰⁴ Leturia, *El ocaso*, p. 124n; see text in Alamán, V 257-61.
⁴⁰⁵ "Tratados celebrados en la Villa de Córdoba el 24 de Agosto de 1821, entre los Señores Don Juan O'Donojú, Teniente General de los Ejércitos de España y Don Agustín de Iturbide, Primer Jefe del Ejército Imperial Mexicano de las Tres Garantías," in Iturbide, pp. 252-54.
⁴⁰⁶ Parkes, p. 156; Sierra, pp. 130-31, and Cuevas, *La nación mexicana*, pp. 495-96.
⁴⁰⁷ Morse, p. 160. ⁴⁰⁸ Leturia, *La emancipación*, p. 88.

[409] Ibid., pp. 98–99; also Giménez Fernández, *Las doctrinas populistas*, p. 108. An interesting part was played by the guerrilla leader Bruno Terreros of the Franciscans who joined the struggle against the Spaniards when he realized that they used religion as a pretext. After the struggle, Bolívar asked specifically that the archbishopric of Lima take Terreros back into the Order (Paz Soldán, I 65–66).
[410] Leturia, *El ocaso*, p. 121.   [411] Groot, III 107.   [412] Ibid.
[413] Giménez Fernández, *Las doctrinas populistas*, p. 111.   [414] Ibid., p. 112.
[415] Leturia, *La emancipación*, p. 131; Leturia, *El ocaso*, p. 122.
[416] Giménez Fernández, *Las doctrinas populistas*, p. 112.   [417] Groot, II 335.
[418] *Nacimiento*, pp. 592–931; also Eyzaguirre, p. 74, who shows that Rousseau was not known in Chile until Moreno's translation arrived in Santiago in 1811.
[419] Felipe Tena Ramírez, paper read at Congreso Hispanoamericano de Historia, p. 193; also p. 194.
[420] Leturia, *El ocaso*, p. 123.
[421] Alemparte, *El cabildo en Chile*, p. 433; Eyzaguirre, p. 146.

CONCLUSION

THE SO-CALLED SPANISH AMERICAN REVOLUTION, fundamentally a civil war resulting from the Napoleonic events in the Peninsula, had profound medieval roots: it was linked to two historic developments which in turn were connected to the two medieval concepts of the *tyrannus a regimine* and the *tyrannus ab origine*, and to the medieval institution of the *cabildo*.

In the first place, the revolution was connected with the great changes which came over the Spanish Empire in the eighteenth century, since the advent of the Bourbons signified the arrival of a new Enlightened European and specifically French spirit which was opposed to a great extent to Spanish tradition. This foreign Enlightenment touched only an elite and never reached the people on both sides of the Atlantic. It aimed at putting an end to Spanish decline and proposed many reforms put into effect under King Charles III. These reforms represented, indeed, great improvements, but at the same time attempted to circumvent the extraordinary system of checks and balances which had been the essence of the Spanish government ever since it was set up in the Indies. The Bourbon reforms, such as the increasing freedom of trade — which benefited mostly foreigners — the two new viceroyalties — which increased red tape — and the introduction of the French-style *intendencia* — which affected almost every Spanish American institution — as well as the curbing of local freedoms, were not only directed against the Hispanic sense of freedom, but also hurt Spanish pride. They destroyed the idealism of the *criollos* on which this Empire had been set up.

When the Bourbon reforms also openly displayed an anticlerical and antireligious attitude with the increase of *regalismo* and the expulsion of the Jesuits (which hurt both Spanish American education and the welfare of the Indians), a danger point was reached, since it represented an attitude which by no stretch of the imagination could be linked to Spanish tradition. During the emancipation, the movement of Morelos and the Peruvian delegates to the Spanish *Cortes* asked for the return of the Jesuits. For both *peninsulares* and *criollos*, the question of Church and religion was of primary importance, but the Bourbon regime in many instances persecuted the Church and prohibited the works of Suárez, Molina, and Mariana, and seemed to follow a rationalistic (and hence un-Spanish) line. For the Spaniard of both hemispheres, Church and religion were more important than European and North American efficiency and political forms, for which they actually showed little interest. The question of Church and religion played a great role in the Spanish American Revolution: we need only to realize that Mexico became independent as a conservative reaction to liberal Spain, and that the gates of Lima were opened to San Martín as a reaction to the Spanish liberal radicalism of the early 1820s. In the final analysis, Spanish America switched to political independence in the last phase of the Revolution because it wished to remain Spanish in character and temperament, and because it seemed that Spain had lost this character through the Bourbons and the influence of European Enlightenment. Thus, the Spanish American Revolution was certainly prepared, though unwittingly, by King

Charles III and his Enlightened reforms: it represented the groundwork for independence, since Charles III's Enlightened despotism meant a departure from traditional Hispanic concepts of government. The opposition to the Bourbon policies was thus linked to the old concept of the *tyrannus a regimine* which played a role not only in the eighteenth century — the revolts of the *comuneros* in Paraguay and in New Granada — but during the Spanish American Revolution when King Ferdinand VII, who was given all opportunities — *Manifiesto de los Persas*, Sarratea's letter — refused to budge from his Enlightened Bourbon approach.

Napoleon's invasion of the Peninsula was the second historic development which triggered the revolution and which until the year 1820 represented a war, open or veiled, for a different constitutional basis in line with the old Hispanic regional traditions and with an attempt to keep a union of the Spanish world. It is only around the year 1820, at the time of the reintroduction of the Constitution of Cádiz, that sentiment switches to a definite breaking of political ties with the Peninsula.

The Spanish American Revolution was basically a Spanish affair in which foreign intellectual ideas played only a very marginal role. The beginning of the revolution in Spanish America was an echo, a projection, of the events in the Peninsula, in the defense of the legitimate rights of King Ferdinand VII and against Napoleon and his brother Joseph Bonaparte as well as the ideas of the French Revolution. The events in Spanish America reflected the reaction of the Spanish people to the Napoleonic invasion and to the disastrous policies of the *godoyistas* — true symbol of Spanish decay — and the establishment of juntas in Spanish America was a repetition of what had happened in Spain, since the Spanish Americans held the justifiable opinion that they had the same rights to establish juntas as the Peninsula. After all, the provinces or kingdoms in Spanish America, like those of the Peninsula, were linked to the Crown, as defined in the papal donations and the various royal pronouncements in the sixteenth century, and were therefore not colonies. The movement which thus began developed slowly from an autonomous sphere into a break with the mother country and complete independence in view of incomprehension of the *doceañistas*, although this had not been the ultimate goal in 1808-10.

The above historical facts centered upon a very specific current of thought. The revolution which began in 1808-10 was little influenced by the political philosophy of North America or Western Europe; it was based on the political theory of Spanish Late Scholasticism (*pactum translationis*), as set forth by Francis Suárez in his *Defensio fidei*, Luis de Molina in his *De Iustitia et iure*, and Juan de Mariana in his *De Rege et regis institutione*, among others, which became the lever for the whole movement. Authority of the kings emanated originally from the people; it reverts to them when the throne becomes vacant. The vassalage of the Indies was the tie which joined the kingdoms of the Indies, not to metropolitan Spain, the Spanish nation, or the Spanish people, but to the legitimate king of Castile and León. Hence, when King Ferdinand VII renounced the throne in Bayonne the political link was broken and the community of the people, the customary holder of sovereignty, was deemed to be the legitimate successor, who in turn had to provide for the designation of new authorities. The setting up of juntas and the arguments for freedom and popular rights were Scholastic concepts with a long tradition rooted in medieval philosophy (St. Augustine, St. Thomas), which were modernized, readjusted, and popularized through the Late Scholastic movement (Vitoria and Las Casas; Suárez, Mariana, Molina, Soto, Covarrubias, Azpilcueta, Menchaca, Báñez, Carranza, Peña, Cano; Saavedra Fajardo and Quevedo).

The application of the *pactum translationis* and the common struggle of Spaniards and Spanish Americans against the Napoleonic usurpation meant a link to the other medieval concept of the tyrant, the *tyrannus ab origine*, which allowed the people, as in the case of the *tyrannus a regimine*, to take matters into their own hands. The *pactum translationis*, however, was used by different groups for different purposes. Thus, for the Spaniards the consequence of the *pactum translationis* was simply that only the Spanish people on both sides of the Atlantic could exercise power in the absence of the king who was held prisoner in France. For the Spanish Americans, however, the application of the *pactum translationis* meant a totally different solution which was in accordance with the agreement entered into in the sixteenth century between the Spanish Crown and the conquistadors. In line with this agreement, in the absence of the legitimate king, authority returns to the various peoples of the Spanish Empire, since Spanish America never considered itself a colony and owed allegiance only to the Crown. And this loyalty to the Crown was a direct consequence of the fact that with the Discovery and Conquest the king was the personal owner of all territories in the Indies.

The Spaniards wanted all regions of the Spanish Empire to recognize the *Suprema Junta Central*, or the Regency, respectively, until the return of the king, while the Spanish Americans declared that, with the abdication in Bayonne, overseas Spain was free from all obligations toward the Peninsula and could legally establish its own governments which would solve the immediate constitutional problem of the various parts of the Spanish Empire, first in a provisional way, and then in a definitive manner.

But just as Spanish America in its totality was justified in separating from Spain when there was no longer a legitimate ruler, it was also logical and justified that the different historical regions would use this same principle, not only against Spain, but also against the capitals of the various viceroyalties, thus encouraging the Balkanization of the former Spanish Empire despite efforts by major patriots to retain at least the union of the former viceregal areas. In the last analysis, the union of the Spanish Empire was only guaranteed through the metaphysical link — the invisible and distant king; once he was gone, not even the prestige of the great leaders (Bolívar, San Martín) could stop the disintegration.

The institution which is linked to the Balkanization was the *cabildo*, another link of the revolution to the Spanish Middle Ages. The Spanish American *cabildo* evolved in the footsteps of the traditions it had inherited from medieval Castile — it thus represented the voice of genuine small republics whose extension over all the continent made up the Spanish Empire in America. This Empire was actually built on a federative basis of its many towns and provinces, a concept which had already been advanced in the sixteenth century by Juan de Castellanos and Bernardo de Vargas Machuca, and which in the Spanish American Revolution was to be revived when Miranda called for the implementation of a federation of all Spanish American *cabildos* headed by an Inca — in reality what had existed in the previous centuries with the metaphysical link to the Spanish Crown. Moreover, in view of the double meaning of the expression *pueblo*, it followed that the concept of popular sovereignty was linked to the major towns. This popular power was thus inherent in the juntas which represented the Spanish people in their struggle against Napoleon for the legitimate rights of King Ferdinand VII. It was also inherent in the Spanish American revolutionary juntas.

In true Spanish spirit and in line with the Scholastic concept of the *pactum translationis*, the Spanish American *cabildos* took over power and deposed viceroys and governors as representatives of a non-existent authority. With the exception of New Spain, Peru, and Montevideo, where the viceroys and governors, respectively, remained faithful followers of the new government in southern Spain, and where the Spanish element was politically stronger, all areas in the rest of Spanish America established revolutionary juntas. And thus, the *cabildos* of Buenos Aires, Santiago, Asunción, La Paz, Bogotá, Quito and Caracas rejected the authority of the *Suprema Junta Central* and later of the Regency, and established their own local juntas for the defense of the legitimate rights of King Ferdinand VII. The movement which began in 1808 in favor of *de facto* autonomy as a consequence of the constitutional crisis in Bayonne and the automatic reversion of civil authority to its popular source, led gradually and logically toward independent republics, and it was through the institution of the *cabildo* in the revolutionary parts of Spanish America that this evolution took place.

With the return of the king in 1814 the Spanish Crown had an opportunity to solve the constitutional problems which had arisen as a result of Bayonne. This could have been accomplished had the Crown, and especially King Ferdinand VII, understood the real causes of the events in Spanish America since 1808 — that rebellion actually meant loyalty — especially since, despite six years of political disagreements, the situation was not hopeless in 1814–15 for re-establishment of political union. The authorities in the Peninsula, however, viewed the establishment of juntas in the Indies as an act of defiance, as an echo of the French Revolution. Hence, the return of the king meant not only the resumption of absolutism but also the attempt to reconquer lost positions. And, indeed, the period 1814–20 marked the recovery of almost all lost territory except for the River Plate area. But while the war was almost won militarily, peace was not achieved, since the continuation of eighteenth-century Bourbon centralism, absolutism, and *regalismo* with persecution of dissidents through "purification tribunals" could only be detrimental to the Spanish cause.

It was not surprising, therefore, that Spanish America shifted slowly toward a complete political break with Madrid in the early 1820s when liberal Spain was weakened militarily and when the radical liberalism of the Spanish government seemed to leave no alternative. Thus, the patriots capitalized on Madrid's radical liberalism and its stand against Church and religion, and both Bolívar and San Martín took a more conservative, traditional line. For the traditional forces, which were stronger in Spanish America than in the Peninsula, it seemed that Spain was lost or that at least it was unable to resist the foreign ideological and political influences of which both absolutism and liberalism had identical roots in the Enlightenment. And hence, more and more the idea gained ground that the Spanish Americans must free themselves in order to keep their old Spanish traditional life. This was in reality the deep reason for the Spanish American Revolution.

It should not come as a surprise, then, that the Spanish American Revolution had such deep medieval roots, since Scholasticism in all its different forms

(St. Thomas, Duns Scotus, Suárez) dominated the area during the entire colonial period. Moreover, the intellectual currents of the Enlightenment which obviously had penetrated the Spanish world during the Age of Reason and which especially in the field of the modern sciences increased their hold (Copernicus, Newton, Bacon), were largely permeated by the old currents when it came to pure philosophy and political thought. This was especially true of the influence of the Spanish Enlightenment which, while calling for modernization in all the branches of the modern sciences and especially in regard to the application of useful knowledge, still clung tenaciously to Scholasticism in the humanities (Feijóo, Jovellanos).

The medieval concepts of the *tyrannus ab origine* and *tyrannus a regimine* as well as the *pactum translationis* needed no rediscovery, just as Church and religion were not suddenly found again. They existed and had been put into practice all the time even though the Bourbon regime discouraged and opposed them — revolts of the *comuneros* in Paraguay and in New Granada; the rise of the *cabildos* prior to the revolution, especially in the River Plate area. On the other hand, the new natural-law theories of the seventeenth and eighteenth centuries, many of them based on Scholasticism (Locke) or Late Scholasticism (Grotius, Pufendorf, Althusius, Thomasius, Wolff, Heineccius), and disseminated in Spanish America, made it easier for some of the traditional concepts, like popular sovereignty — even though they were quite different — to maintain and increase their hold in regard to the opposition to Bourbon centralism in line with the concept of the *tyrannus ab origine*. Thus, no doubt, in many cases the old traditions of popular sovereignty were fused with modern thought because it seemed more fashionable (Nariño, Moreno), although there is no real connection between the social contract of Suárez and that of Rousseau, and the one which was used in the establishment of juntas could not be Rousseau's, since the latter had nothing to do with the relationship of king and people. Hence, even if in some cases the modern thought of the Age of Reason appears, the so-called Spanish American Revolution is rooted in the Spanish traditions of Isidore of Seville and the Councils of Toledo, the Castilian *Cortes* and *fueros*, the *Siete Partidas* of Alfonso the Learned, and the Indian legislation, all within the general framework of medieval Scholasticism and its more modern extension, Late Scholasticism.

Obviously, the reaction to the Napoleonic events of 1808 was not the same in the entire Spanish Empire but followed more the historic development and the special circumstances of its different areas. Thus, the cultural development of New Spain, New Granada, and Peru proper had been greater than the more recently developed areas of the River Plate, which meant that the penetration of modern philosophies was deeper in the River Plate than in the former viceroyalties. It meant further that traditional thought and conservatism were stronger in the older regions of Spanish America, especially New Spain and Peru, where also the Spanish element was stronger as far as political and economic power was concerned; this was, however, also true of the city of Montevideo which followed a policy closely similar to that of Peru and New Spain in regard to the authorities in the Peninsula, however much determined by regional rivalry.

While the situation was stabilized in New Spain, despite several revolutionary attempts, and in Peru proper, where no homegrown revolution took place, this situation dictated much of the revolutionary actions. Much of the political activity in the River Plate and Chile was concerned with eliminating the old Peruvian monopoly, just as Montevideo wanted to free itself from the overlordship of Buenos Aires. On the other hand, the conservative position in the entire area of New Spain was so strong that no attempt at secession was made in the other regions of the viceroyalty. New Spain, thus, remained solidly within the royalist camp and only opted for independence in 1821 in view of the second liberal regime in the Peninsula, and Peru proper had to be liberated by outside forces. On the other hand, the River Plate had to engage in a civil war on various levels — resistance to royalist attempts (Peru, Montevideo), opposition to secession (Upper Peru, Paraguay, and *Banda Oriental*), Argentine internal troubles (city versus provinces), different ideological struggles (conservative: Saavedra; radical: Moreno, Castelli), and foreign intervention (Portugal, Brazil) — while New Granada's problems were further compounded by the unbelievable political anarchy of the *Patria boba* period.

In the last analysis economic matters and the divisions between *criollos* and *peninsulares*, of which too much has been made, played a far less important role than the typical Spanish reactions of individualism and regionalism, and the political ideology carried a greater weight than supposed economic arguments or racial discrimination. Thus, idealism found its finest expression in the application of the Scholastic political theories in line with the traditions which medieval and Renaissance Spain had transplanted to the Indies and which meant a repudiation of despotism and an exaltation of the Christian principles of charity and freedom: the echo of Isidore's principles of king and people which so clearly came to the fore in the resistance of *both* Spaniards and Spanish Americans to Napoleon's usurpation in defense of God, king, and fatherland, and which represented no *criollo* subterfuge for ulterior motives.

BIBLIOGRAPHY

Abad de Santillán, Diego. *Historia argentina.* 3 vols. Buenos Aires: Tipografía argentina, 1965.
Abud, Salomón. *Rivadavia, el organizador de la República.* Biblioteca de grandes biografías, Series A. Vol. 9. Buenos Aires: Claridad, 1945.
Acosta, José de, s.J. *Obras.* Intro. Francisco Mateos, s.J. Madrid: Biblioteca de autores españoles, 1954.
Aguado, Pedro de. *Historia de Santa Marta y Nuevo Reino de Granada.* Ed. Jerónimo Bécker. Madrid: Ratés, 1916–17.
——. *Historia de Venezuela.* Ed. Jerónimo Bécker. Madrid: Ratés, 1918–19.
Alamán, Lucas. *Historia de Méjico desde los primeros movimientos que prepararon su independencia en el año de 1808 hasta la época presente.* 5 vols. Mexico: Lara, 1849–52.
Alayza Paz Soldán, Luis. *La constitución de Cádiz, 1812: El egregio limeño Morales y Duárez.* Lima: Lumen, 1946.
Alba, Víctor. *The Mexicans: The Making of a Nation.* New York: Pegasus, 1970.
Alberini, Coriolano. *Die deutsche Philosophie in Argentinien.* Berlin: Hendrick, 1930.
Aldridge, A. Owen (ed.). *The Ibero-American Enlightenment.* Urbana: University of Illinois Press, 1971.
Alemparte R., Julio. *El cabildo en Chile colonial: Orígenes municipales de las repúblicas hispanoamericanas.* Santiago: Universidad de Chile, 1940.
——. *El cabildo de Santiago en el siglo XVI.* Santiago: Balcells, 1930.
Allen, J. W. *A History of Political Thought in the Sixteenth Century.* 3rd ed. London: Methuen, 1951.
——. "Jeremy Bentham." In F. J. C. Hearnshaw (ed.). *The Social and Political Ideas of Some Representative Thinkers of the Revolutionary Era.* New York: Barnes & Noble, 1950. Pp. 181–200.
Alvarez Requejo, Felipe. *El conde de Campomanes: Su obra histórica.* Oviedo: Gráficos Summa, 1954.
Amunátegui, Miguel Luis. *Los precursores de la independencia de Chile.* 3 vols. Santiago: Barcelona, 1909–10.
Amunátegui Solar, Domingo. *La democracia en Chile: Teatro político (1810–1910).* Santiago de Chile: Universidad de Chile, 1946.
André, Marius. *Bolivar et la démocratie.* Paris: Excelsior, 1924.
Andreas, Willy. *Das Zeitalter Napoleons und die Erhebung der Völker.* Heidelberg: Quelle & Meyer, 1955.
Angulo y Pérez, Andrés. "Instituciones de gobierno en América. Epoca carolingia." III Congreso de Cooperación Intelectual. Madrid: Instituto de Cultura Hispánica, October, 1958.
Aquinas, St. Thomas. *On Kingship: To the King of Cyprus.* Trans. Gerald B. Phelan. Ed. I. Th. Eschmann, o.p. Toronto: Pontifical Institute of Mediaeval Studies, 1949.

Arcaya, Pedro Manuel. *Personajes y hechos de la historia venezolana.* Caracas: Cosmos, 1911.
Arce, Luis A. de. *Bonaparte y Bolívar: Ensayo.* Havana: Muñoz, 1940.
Arcila-Farías, Eduardo. *Economía colonial de Venezuela.* Mexico: Fondo de cultura económica, 1946.
———. *El siglo ilustrado en América. Reformas económicas del siglo XVIII en Nueva España. Contribución al estudio de las instituciones hispanoamericanas.* Caracas: Ediciones del Ministerio de Educación. Dirección de Cultura y Bellas Artes, 1955.
Arciniegas, Germán. *Latin America. A Cultural History.* Trans. Joan MacLean. New York: Knopf, 1968.
Ardao, María Julia, and Castellanos, Aurora C. de. *Artigas: Su significación en los orígenes de la nacionalidad oriental y en la revolución del Río de la Plata.* Montevideo: "33," 1951.
Argentina. Biblioteca Nacional. *Archivo del doctor Gregorio Funes, deán de la Santa Iglesia de Córdoba.* Buenos Aires, 1944.
Arguedas, Alcides. *Historia general de Bolivia, 1809–1921.* La Paz: Arnó, 1922.
Arígita y Laza, Mariano. *El doctor navarro Don Martín de Azpilcueta y sus obras.* Pamplona: Provincial, 1895.
Arnade, Charles W.; Whitaker, Arthur P.; and Diffie, Bailey W. "Causes of Spanish-American Wars of Independence." *Journal of Inter-American Studies,* 2, No. 2 (April 1960), 125–44.
Asís, Agustín de. *Ideas sociopolíticas de Alonso Polo (El Tostado).* Seville: Escuela de Estudios Hispano-Americanos, 1955.
Ayala, Francisco Javier de. *Ideas políticas de Juan de Solórzano.* Seville: Escuela de Estudios Hispano-Americanos, 1946.
——— (ed.). *El pensamiento vivo de Saavedra Fajardo.* Biblioteca del pensamiento vivo. 2d ed. Buenos Aires: Losada, 1945.
———. *Tratado de los sofismas políticos de Jeremy Bentham.* Rosario de Santa Fe: Rosario, 1944.
Badía, Juan Fernando. "Vicisitudes e influencias de la Constitución de 1812." *Revista de Estudios Políticos,* 126 (November–December 1962), 169–228.
Báez, Cecilio. *Ensayo sobre el Dr. Francia y la dictadura en Sudamérica.* Asunción: Kraus, 1910.
Barreda y Laos, Felipe. *Vida intelectual del virreinato del Perú.* 3d ed. Lima: Universidad nacional de San Marcos, 1964.
Barros Arana, Diego. *Historia jeneral de Chile.* 16 vols. Santiago: Jover, 1884–1902.
Bataillon, Marcel. *Erasmo y España: Estudios sobre la historia espiritual del siglo XVI.* 2 vols. Mexico: Cultura Económica, 1950.
Batllori, Miguel, s.j. *El abate Viscardo. Historia y mito de la intervención de los jesuitas en la independencia de Hispanoamérica.* Instituto Panamericano de Geografía e Historia, Comisión de Historia, Comité de Orígenes de la Emancipación–Caracas. Publicación No. 10. Caracas: Imprenta de la Pontificia Universidad Gregoriana [Rome], 1953.
Bayle, Constantino, s.j. *La expansión misional de España.* Barcelona–Madrid–Buenos Aires–Rio de Janeiro: Editorial Labor, 1936.
———. *Los cabildos seculares en la América española.* Madrid: Sapientia, 1952.
———. "Un libro nuevo de Gonzalo Ximénez de Quesada." *Boletín de Historia y Antigüedades,* 19, Nos. 330–31 (April–May 1942), 338–46.

Becher, Hubert. *Die Jesuiten: Geschichte und Gestalt des Ordens.* Munich: Kösel, 1951.
Becker, Carl L. *The Heavenly City of the Eighteenth Century Philosophers.* New Haven: Yale University Press, 1932.
Belaúnde, Víctor Andrés. *Bolívar and the Political Thought of the Spanish American Revolution.* Baltimore: Johns Hopkins Press, 1938.
———. *Bolívar y el pensamiento político de la Revolución hispanoamericana.* Spanish version. Madrid: Cultura Hispánica, 1959.
Belgrano, Mario. "La era napoleónica y las colonias americanas," in Academia nacional de la historia. *Historia de la Nación Argentina (desde los orígenes hasta la organización definitiva en 1862).* 10 vols. Buenos Aires: Imprenta de la Universidad, 1936–42. V, Sec. 1, 105–23.
Belinzón, Lorenzo. *La revolución emancipadora uruguaya y sus dogmas democráticos.* 2 vols. Montevideo: Barreiro y Ramos, 1931–32.
Belloc, Hilaire. *The French Revolution.* 2d ed. London: Oxford University Press, 1956. (Reprint of 1911 ed.)
Beneyto, Juan. *Espíritu y estado en el siglo XVI.* Madrid: Aguilar, 1952.
———. *Ginés de Sepúlveda.* Madrid: Nacional, 1944.
Beneyto [Pérez], Juan. *Historia de las doctrinas políticas.* 3d ed. Madrid: Aguilar, 1958.
———. *Los orígenes de la ciencia política en España.* Madrid: Instituto de Estudios Políticos, 1949.
Benítez, Justo Pastor. *La vida solitaria del Dr. José Gaspar de Francia, Dictador del Paraguay.* Buenos Aires: Ateneo, 1937.
Bentham, Jeremy. *An Introduction to the Principles of Morals and Legislation.* Oxford: Clarendon, 1879.
———. *Works.* 11 vols. Edinburgh: Bowring, 1838–43.
Bertier de Sauvigny, G. de. *La Restauration.* Paris: Flammarion, 1955.
Bishko, Charles Julian. "The Iberian Background of Latin American History: Recent Progress and Continuing Problems." *Hispanic American Historical Review*, 36, No. 1 (February 1956), 50–80.
Bitar Letayf, Marcelo. *Economistas españoles del siglo XVIII.* Madrid: Cultura Hispánica, 1968.
Blánquez Fraile, Agustín. *Historia de España.* Barcelona: Sopena, 1933.
Blossom, Thomas. *Nariño, Hero of Colombian Independence.* Tucson: University of Arizona Press, 1967.
Bolívar, Simón. *Discursos y proclamas.* Ed. R. Blanco-Fombona. Biblioteca de grandes autores americanos. Paris: Garnier, 1913.
———. *Obras completas.* Ed. Vicente Lecuna. 2d ed. 3 vols. Havana: Lex, 1950.
Borja y Borja, Ramiro. *Las constituciones del Ecuador.* Madrid: Cultura Hispánica, 1951.
Bourquin, Maurice. *Histoire de la Sainte-Alliance.* Geneva: Georg, 1954.
Brackenridge, H. M. *Voyage to South America Performed by Order of the American Government in the Years 1817 and 1818 in the Frigate CONGRESS.* 2 vols. 2d ed. London: Miller, 1820.
Braden, Charles S. *Religious Aspects of the Conquest of Mexico.* Durham: Duke University Press, 1930.
Brandi, Karl. *Charles V: The Growth and Destiny of a Man and of a World-Empire.* Trans. C. V. Wedgwood. New York: Knopf, 1939.
Brau, Salvador. *Historia de Puerto Rico.* San Juan: Coquí, 1966.

Brau, Salvador. *La colonización de Puerto Rico.* San Juan: Instituto de Cultura Puertorriqueña, 1966.
Brinton, Crane. *English Political Thought in the Nineteenth Century.* London: Benn, 1949.
Bryce, James, Viscount. *The Holy Roman Empire.* London: Macmillan, 1950.
Bumgartner, Louis E. *José del Valle of Central America.* Durham: Duke University Press, 1963.
Burke, Edmund. *Reflexiones sobre la Revolución Francesa.* Trans. Enrique Tierno Galván. Madrid: Instituto de Estudios Políticos, 1954.
——. *Works.* 8 vols. London: Rivington, 1852.
Bushnell, David. "The Development of the Press in Great Colombia." *Hispanic American Historical Review,* 30, No. 4 (November 1950), 432–52.
——. *The Santander Regime in Gran Colombia.* Newark: University of Delaware Press, 1954.
Bustamante, Carlos María de. *El Congreso de Chilpancingo.* Vol. 20 of El Liberalismo mexicano en pensamiento y en acción. Mexico: Empresas editoriales, 1958.
——. *Cuadro histórico de la revolución [de la América] mexicana comenzada en 15 de septiembre de 1810 por el ciudadano Miguel Hidalgo y Costilla, cura del pueblo de los Dolores, en el Obispado de Michoacán.* 5 vols. Reprint of 2d ed. Mexico: Soria, 1926.
Cabanellas, Guillermo. *El Dictador del Paraguay, Dr. Francia.* Biblioteca de grandes biografías, series B. Vol. 12. Buenos Aires: Claridad, 1946.
Cabarrús, Francisco (conde) de. *Cartas sobre los obstáculos que la naturaleza, la opinión y las leyes oponen a la felicidad pública;* escritas por el conde de Cabarrús al Señor D. Gaspar de Jovellanos, y procedidos de otra al príncipe de la Paz. Havana: Arazoza y Soler, 1814.
——. *Los eruditos a la violeta.* Madrid: Pacheco, 1781.
Cadalso, José. *Cartas marruecas.* Colección clásicos castellanos. Madrid: Espasa-Calpe, 1950.
——. *Los eruditos a la violeta.* Madrid: Hernández Pacheco, 1781.
Caillet-Bois, Ricardo R. "El Río de la Plata y la Revolución Francesa 1789-1800," in Academia nacional de la historia, *Historia de la Nación Argentina (desde los orígenes hasta la organización definitiva en 1862).* 10 vols. Buenos Aires: Imprenta de la Universidad, 1936–42. V, Sec. 1, 27–51.
[Campomanes, Pedro Rodríguez de]. *Discurso sobre el fomento de la industria.* Madrid: Sancha, 1774.
——. *Discurso sobre la educación popular de los artesanos y su fomento.* Madrid: Sancha, 1775.
——. "Expediente del Obispo de Cuenca," *Biblioteca de autores españoles,* Vol. 59. Madrid, 1912.
——. "Juicio imparcial sobre el Monitorio de Parma," *Biblioteca de autores españoles,* Vol. 59. Madrid, 1912.
——. *Tratado de la regalía de España.* Paris: Hispano-Americana, 1830.
Cañal, Carlos. *San Isidoro: exposición de sus obras e indicaciones acerca de la influencia que han ejercido en la civilización española.* Seville: Andalucía moderna, 1897.
Carbia, Rómulo D. *Historia eclesiástica del Río de la Plata.* 2 vols. Buenos Aires: Alfa y Omega, 1914.

———. *Historia de la Leyenda Negra hispanoamericana.* Madrid: Consejo de la Hispanidad, 1944.
———. *La Revolución de Mayo y la Iglesia.* Buenos Aires: Huarpes, 1945.
Carlyle, Thomas. *El Dictador Francia.* Spanish ed. Asunción–Buenos Aires: Guarania, 1937.
Carr, Raymond. *Spain, 1808–1939.* Oxford: Clarendon, 1966.
Carrera y Justiz, Francisco. *Introducción a la historia de las instituciones locales de Cuba.* 2 vols. Havana: "La moderna poesía," 1905.
Carro Martínez, Antonio. *La constitución española de 1869.* Madrid: Cultura Hispánica, 1952.
Caruso, John Anthony. *The Liberators of Mexico.* New York: Pageant, 1954.
Cassirer, Ernst. *Die Philosophie der Aufklärung.* Tübingen: Mohr, 1932.
———. *Filosofía de la ilustración.* Spanish ed. by Eugenio Imaz. Mexico: Fondo de Cultura Económica, 1943.
Castellanos, Joan de. *Obras.* Ed. Carracciolo Parra-León. 2 vols. Caracas: Sur América, 1930–32.
Castro, Américo. *La realidad histórica de España.* Mexico: Porrúa, 1954.
Ceballos y Mier, Fernando de. *La falsa filosofía o el ateísmo, materialismo y demás sectas convencidas de crimen de estado contra los soberanos y sus regalías, contra los magistrados y potestades legítimas. Se combaten sus máximas sediciosas y subversivas de toda sociedad y aún de la humanidad.* 6 vols. 2d ed. Madrid: Sancha, 1774–76.
Chaves, Julio César. *Castelli: el adalid de Mayo.* Buenos Aires: Ayacucho, 1944; 2d ed. Buenos Aires: Leviatán, 1957.
Clavijero, Francisco Javier, s.J. *Storia antica del Messico.* Cesena: Biasini, 1780–81.
Collier, Simon. *Ideas and Politics of Chilean Independence, 1808–1833.* Cambridge Latin American Studies, No. I. Cambridge: Cambridge University Press, 1967.
Colombia. *Archivo Santander.* Edd. Otero d'Acosta and Luis Augusto Otero. Vol. I (1792–1818). Bogotá: Cromos, n.d.
———. Biblioteca de Historia Nacional. *Colección de documentos para la historia de Colombia (época de la independencia).* Third Series. Comp. by Sergio Elías Ortíz. Bogotá: ABC, 1966.
———. *Codificación Nacional de Colombia.* Bogotá, 1926.
Comellas, José Luis. "Las Cortes de Cádiz y la Constitución de 1812." *Revista de Estudios Políticos,* 126 (November–December 1962), 69–112.
Conde, Francisco Javier. *Teoría y sistema de las formas políticas.* Madrid: Instituto de Estudios Políticos, 1951.
Congreso Hispanoamericano de Historia. *Causas y caracteres de la independencia hispanoamericana.* Madrid: Cultura Hispánica, 1953.
Consejo de la Hispanidad. *Recopilación de leyes de los Reynos de las Indias.* 3 vols. Madrid: Gráficas Ultra, 1943.
Cordero Torres, José María. *El Consejo de Estado. Su trayectoria y perspectiva en España.* Madrid: Instituto de Estudios Políticos, 1954.
Cornevin, R. and M., *Histoire de l'Afrique des origines à nos jours.* Paris: Payot, 1964.
Corona Baratech, Carlos. *Las ideas políticas en el reinado de Carlos IV.* Madrid: O crece o muere, 1954.
Costello, Frank Bartholomew. "The Political Theory of Luis de Molina, 1535–1600." Unpublished Ph.D. diss., Georgetown University, 1959.

Cruz, Salvador. "Feijóo en Mexico: Notas de asedio," in Universidad de Oviedo, Facultad de Filosofía y Letras. *El P. Feijóo y su siglo: Ponencias y communicaciones presentadas al simposio celebrado en la Universidad de Oviedo del 28 de septiembre al 5 de octubre de 1964.* 3 vols. (Oviedo, 1966), I 47–54.

Cuesta, Luis, and Zamora Lucas, Florentino. "Los secretarios de Carlos V." *Revista de Archivos, Bibliotecas y Museos*, 64, No. 2 (June–December 1958), 415–46.

Cuevas, Mariano, s.j. *Historia de la iglesia en México.* 5 vols. 5th ed. Mexico: Patria, 1946–47.

———. *Historia de la nación mexicana.* Mexico: Talleres Modelo, 1940.

Dante Alighieri. *Tratado de Monarquía.* Trans. Angel María Pascual. Madrid: Instituto de Estudios Políticos, 1947.

Davies, Reginald Trevor. *The Golden Century of Spain.* London: Macmillan, 1937.

———. *Spain in Decline, 1621–1700.* London: Macmillan, 1957.

Davis, Harold Eugene. *Latin American Thought: An Historical Introduction.* Baton Rouge: Louisiana State University Press, 1972.

Decouflé, André; Boulanger, François; Pierrelle, Bernard-André. *Études d'histoire économique et sociale du XVIIIème siècle.* Travaux et recherches de la faculté de droit et des sciences économiques de Paris. Série "Sciences historiques," No. 9. Paris: Presses Universitaires de France, 1966.

Deforneaux, Marcelin. "Pablo de Olavide, un afrancesado en el siglo de las luces." *Estudios Americanos*, 19, No. 100 (January 1960), 23–45.

Delgado, Jaime. *La independencia de América en la prensa española.* Madrid: Seminario de problemas hispanoamericanos, 1949.

———. *La independencia hispanoamericana.* Colección Nuevo Mundo. Madrid: Cultura Hispánica, 1960.

Delpy, G. *L'Espagne et l'esprit européen: L'œuvre de Feijóo (1725–1760).* Paris: Hachette, 1936.

Dempf, Alois. *Christliche Staatsphilosophie in Spanien.* Salzburg: Pustet, 1937.

Díaz-Plaja, Fernando (ed.). *La historia de España en sus documentos. El siglo XIX.* Madrid: Instituto de Estudios Políticos, 1954.

Díaz-Plaja, Guillermo, and Monterde, Francisco. *Historia de la literatura española e historia de la literatura mexicana.* Mexico: Porrúa, 1955.

Dicey, Albert Venn. *Lectures on the Relation Between Law and Public Opinion in England During the Nineteenth Century.* 6th ed. London–New York: Macmillan, 1902.

Dombrowski, John. "A Catholic Continent Awakening." *Triumph*, 4, No. 8 (August 1969), 11–14.

Donoso, Ricardo. *Las ideas políticas en Chile.* Mexico: Cultura Económica, 1946.

Donoso Cortés, Juan. *Textos Políticos.* Biblioteca del pensamiento actual. Madrid: Rialp, 1954.

Dos Passos, John. *The Portugal Story: Three Centuries of Exploration and Discovery.* New York: Doubleday, 1969.

Driver, C. H. "John Locke," in F. J. C. Hearnshaw (ed.), *The Social and Political Ideas of Some English Thinkers of the Augustan Age, A.D. 1650–1750.* New York: Barnes & Noble, 1950. Pp. 69–96.

Ecuador. Academia Ecuatoriana. *Memoria. Número extraordinario dedicado a la memoria del Gran Mariscal Antonio José de Sucre, con motivo del centenario de la batalla de Pichincha.* Quito, 1922.

Egaña, Antonio de, s.j. *La teoría del Regio Vicariato Español en Indias.* Analecta Gregoriana. Vol. 95. Series Facultatis historiae ecclesiasticae sectio B (No. 17). Rome: Pontificia Universitas Gregoriana, 1958.
[Egaña, Juan]. *El chileno consolado en los presidios ó filosofía de la religión. Memorias de mis trabajos y reflexiones.* 2 vols. London: Calero, 1826.
——. *Escritos inéditos y dispersos.* Ed. Raúl Silva Castro. Santiago: Universitaria, 1949.
Elliott, J. H. *Imperial Spain, 1469–1716.* New York: St. Martin's, 1964.
Escalona Ramos, Alberto. *El espíritu de la Edad Media y América.* Madrid: Cultura Hispánica, 1959.
Escandel Bonet. "José Toribio Medina, historiador de la Inquisición americana." *Revista de Indias,* 13, Nos. 52–53 (April–September 1953), 361–70.
Eyzaguirre, Jaime. *Ideario y ruta de la emancipación chilena.* Colección América nuestra. Santiago: Editorial Universitaria, 1957.
Fagg, John Edwin. *Latin America: A General History.* London: Macmillan, 1969.
Faÿ, Bernard. *Revolution and Freemasonry, 1680–1800.* Boston: Little, Brown, 1935.
Feijóo, Benito Jerónimo. *Teatro crítico universal y Cartas eruditas.* Ed. Luis Sánchez Agesta. Madrid: Instituto de Estudios Políticos, 1947.
Fernández Almagro, Melchor. *La emancipación de América y su reflejo en la consciencia española.* 2d ed. Madrid: Instituto de Estudios Políticos, 1957.
——. *Orígenes del régimen constitucional en España.* Barcelona–Buenos Aires: Labor, 1928.
Fernández Alvarez, Manuel. "Pensamiento y acción en la política imperial de Carlos V." *Revista de Archivos, Bibliotecas y Museos,* 64, No. 2 (June–December 1958), 397–414.
Fernández Bonilla, Raimundo. *El tiempo como jano. Siete ensayos sobre literatura española.* New York: Iberama, 1972.
——. "La polémica filosófica (El movimiento de ilustración y de reforma en el mundo hispánico)." *Exilio: Revista de Humanidades,* 6, No. 3 (Fall 1972), 107–26.
Fisher, Lillian Estelle. *The Background of the Revolution for Mexican Independence.* Boston: Christopher, 1934.
——. "Colonial Government," in A. Curtis Wilgus (ed.), *Colonial Hispanic America.* Vol. 4, Studies in Hispanic American Affairs (Washington, D.C.: George Washington University Press, 1935), pp. 167–99.
Flynn, Gerard. *Sor Juana Inés de la Cruz.* New York: Twayne, 1971.
Fraga Iribarne, Manuel. *Las constituciones de Puerto Rico.* Madrid: Cultura Hispánica, 1953.
Frankl, Víctor. "Agustinismo y nominalismo en la filosofía de la historia según Gonzalo Jiménez de Quesada." *Estudios Americanos,* 16, Nos. 82–83 (July–August 1958), 1–32.
——. *"El Antijovio" de Gonzalo Jiménez de Quesada y las concepciones de realidad y verdad en la época de la contrareforma y del manierismo.* Madrid: Cultura Hispánica, 1963.
Friedell, Egon. *Kulturgeschichte der Neuzeit.* 2d ed. Munich: Beck, n.d.
Fueyo, Jesús. "Tomás Moro y el utopismo político." *Revista de Estudios Políticos,* 86–87 (March–June 1956), 61–108.

Fugier, André. "La era napoleónica y la guerra de la independencia española," in Academia nacional de la historia, *Historia de la Nación Argentina (desde los orígenes hasta la organización definitiva en 1862*). 10 vols. Buenos Aires: Imprenta de la Universidad, 1936–42. V. Sec. 1, 53–83.

Fülöp-Miller, René. *Leaders, Dreamers and Rebels: An Account of the Great Mass-Movements of History and of the Wish-Dreams That Inspired Them.* Trans. Eden and Cedar Paul. New York: Viking, 1935.

Furlong, Guillermo, s.j. "Francisco Suárez fué el filósofo de la revolución argentina de 1810," in Atilio Dell'Oro Maini et al., *Presencia y sugestión del filósofo Francisco Suárez: Su influencia en la Revolución de Mayo* (Buenos Aires, 1959).

——. *La Revolución de Mayo: Los sucesos–los hombres–las ideas.* Club de lectores. Buenos Aires: Balmes, 1960.

——. *Nacimiento y desarrollo de la filosofía en el Río de la Plata, 1536–1810.* Buenos Aires: Kraft, 1952.

Gaettens, Richard. *Inflationen: Das Drama der Geldentwertungen vom Altertum bis zur Gegenwart.* Munich: Pflaum, 1955.

Galdames, Luis. *A History of Chile.* Trans. Isaac Joslin Cox. The Inter-American Historical Series. Chapel Hill: University of North Carolina Press, 1941.

Gallardo, Ricardo. *Las constituciones de la República Federal de Centro-América.* 2 vols. Madrid: Instituto de Estudios Políticos, 1958.

Gálvez, Jaime. *Rosas y el proceso constitucional.* Buenos Aires: Huemul, 1961.

Gandía, Enrique de. *Buenos Aires colonial.* Buenos Aires: Claridad, 1957.

——. *Conspiraciones y revoluciones de la independencia americana.* Buenos Aires: Orientación cultural, 1960.

——. *Historia de las ideas políticas en la Argentina.* 10 vols. Buenos Aires: Depalma, 1960–68.

——. *Historia del 25 de Mayo: Nacimiento de la libertad y de la independencia argentinas.* Buenos Aires: Claridad, 1960.

——. *Napoleón y la independencia de América.* Buenos Aires: Zamora, 1955.

——. *Nueva historia de América. Las épocas de libertad y antilibertad desde la independencia.* Buenos Aires: Claridad, 1946.

Gaos, José. *El pensamiento hispanoamericano.* Mexico: Colegio de México, n.d.

García, Juan Agustín. *La ciudad indiana (Buenos Aires desde 1600 hasta mediados del siglo XVIII).* 2d ed. Buenos Aires: Estrada, 1909; new ed. Colección Argentoria, Vol. 7. Buenos Aires: Zamora, 1955.

García Bacca, Juan David. *Antología del pensamiento filosófico venezolano. (Siglos XVII–XVIII).* Introducciones sistemáticas y prólogos históricos. Selección de textos y traducción del latín al castellano. Caracas: Ediciones del Ministerio de Educación, 1954.

García Calderón, Francisco. *Latin America: Its Rise and Progress.* Trans. Bernard Miall. New York: Scribner, 1913.

García Icazbalceta, Joaquín (ed.). *Cartas de religiosos de Nueva España, 1539–1594.* 2d ed. Mexico: Chavez Hayhoe, 1941.

García Valenzuela, René. *El origen aparente de la francmasonería en Chile y la respetable logia "Filantropía chilena." Contribución al estudio de la francmasonería en Chile y sus precursores.* Santiago: Imprenta universitaria, 1949.

García Venero, Maximiano. *Historia del parlamentarismo español (1810–1833).* Madrid: Instituto de Estudios Políticos, 1946.

Gay, Peter. *The Enlightenment: An Interpretation.* I. *The Rise of Modern Paganism.* New York: Knopf, 1967.
Gierke, Otto (von). *Natural Law and the Theory of Society, 1500 to 1800.* Trans. Ernest Barker. Cambridge: Cambridge University Press, 1950.
Gil Fortoul, José. *Historia constitucional de Venezuela.* 2 vols. Berlin: Heymann, 1907–1909.
Gilmore, Robert L. "The Imperial Crisis, Rebellion, and the Viceroy: Nueva Granada in 1809." *Hispanic American Historical Review,* 40, No. 1 (February 1960), 1–24.
Giménez Fernández, Manuel. *Las doctrinas populistas en la independencia de Hispanoamérica.* Seville: Escuela de Estudios Hispano-Americanos, 1947.
———. *Instituciones jurídicas en la iglesia católica.* 2 vols. Madrid: Sociedad anónima española de traductores y autores, 1940–42.
Gmelin, Hans. *Studien zur spanischen Verfassungsgeschichte des neunzehnten Jahrhunderts.* Stuttgart: Union, 1905.
Gómez de Baquero, Eduardo. *Nacionalismo e hispanismo y otros ensayos.* Madrid: Historia nueva, 1928.
Gómez Hoyos, Rafael. *La revolución granadina de 1810: Ideario de una generación y de una época, 1781–1821.* 2 vols. Bogotá: Temis, 1962.
Gómez Robledo, Ignacio. *El origen del poder político según Francisco Suárez.* Mexico: Jus, 1948.
González, Julio V. *Filiación histórica del gobierno representativo argentino.* 2 vols. Buenos Aires: La Vanguardia, 1937–38.
González, Rubén C., o.p. *Las órdenes religiosas y la Revolución de Mayo.* Buenos Aires, 1960.
González Cárdenas, Luis. "Fray Gerónimo de Mendieta, pensador político e historiador." *Revista de Historia de América,* 28 (December 1949), 331–76.
Goytía, Víctor F. *Las constituciones de Panamá.* Madrid: Cultura Hispánica, 1954.
Graham, Richard. *Independence in Latin America.* New York: Knopf, 1972.
Grases, Pedro. *Traducciones de interés político-cultural en la época de la independencia de Venezuela.* Madrid: Guadarrama, 1961.
Green, Otis H. *Spain and the Western Tradition: The Castilian Mind in Literature from El Cid to Calderón.* 4 vols. Madison: University of Wisconsin Press, 1964–68.
———. *The Literary Mind of Medieval and Renaissance Spain.* Lexington: University Press of Kentucky, 1970.
Groot, José Manuel. *Historia eclesiástica y civil de Nueva Granada.* 3 vols. 1st ed. Bogotá: Montilla, 1869–70; 2d ed. 5 vols. Bogotá: Rivas, 1889–93.
Gros Espiell, Héctor. *Las constituciones del Uruguay.* Madrid: Cultura Hispánica, 1956.
Grossmann, Rudolf. "Das Erbe der Mönche und Conquistadoren," in Friedrich Wehner (ed.), *Idee und Wirklichkeit in Iberoamerika. Beiträge zur Politik und Geistesgeschichte.* Hamburg: Institut für Iberoamerika-Kunde, 1969. Pp. 13–24.
Guétzévich, Boris Mirkine. "La constitution de Cadix." *Revue d'histoire politique et constitutionnelle,* 3, No. 1 (January–March 1939), 48–62.
Guil Blanes, Francisco. "La filosofía en el Perú del XVII." *Estudios Americanos,* 10, No. 47 (August 1955), 167–83.

Guizot, M., and Guizot de Witt. *The History of France from the Earliest Times to 1848*. VI: *French Revolution and Directory, 1789–1799*. Trans. Robert Black. New York: Alden, 1885.

Gutiérrez, Juan María. *Noticias históricas sobre el orijen y desarrollo de la enseñanza pública superior en Buenos Aires desde la época de la estinción de la Compañía de Jesús en el año 1767 hasta poco después de fundada la Universidad en 1821*. Buenos Aires: Siglo, 1868.

Guzmán, José Javier. *El Chileno instruido en la historia topográfica, civil y política de su país*. 2 vols. Santiago: Peregrino, 1834–36.

Häfelin, Ulrich. *Die Rechtspersönlichkeit des Staates*. Tübingen: Mohr, 1959.

Hale, Charles A. *Mexican Liberalism in the Age of Mora, 1821–1853*. Caribbean Series 11. New Haven: Yale University Press, 1968.

Halévy, Elie. *The Growth of Philosophic Radicalism*. Trans. Mary Morris. Boston: Beacon, 1955.

Halperín Donghi, Tulio. *Tradición política española e ideología revolucionaria de Mayo*. Buenos Aires: Editorial Universitaria de Buenos Aires, 1961.

Hamilton, Bernice. *Political Thought in Sixteenth-Century Spain. A Study of the Political Ideas of Vitoria, Soto, Suárez, and Molina*. Oxford: Clarendon, 1963.

Hanisch, Walter, s.j. *Itinerario y pensamiento de los jesuitas expulsos de Chile (1767–1815)*. Santiago de Chile: Bello, 1972.

Hanisch Espíndola, Walter, s.j. *El catecismo político-cristiano. Las ideas y la época: 1810*. Santiago: Bello, 1970.

Hanke, Lewis. *Aristotle and the American Indians: A Study in Race Prejudice in the Modern World*. London: Hollis & Carter, 1959.

———. *Bartolomé de Las Casas: Bookman, Scholar and Propagandist*. Philadelphia: University of Pennsylvania Press, 1952.

———. "The Contribution of Bishop Zumárraga to Mexican Culture." *The Americas*, 5 (1948), 275–82.

———. *The First Social Experiments in America: A Study in the Development of Spanish Indian Policy in the Sixteenth Century*. Cambridge: Harvard University Press, 1936.

———. *The Spanish Struggle for Justice in the Conquest of America*. Philadelphia: University of Pennsylvania Press, 1949.

Hargreaves-Mawdsley, W. N. (ed.). *Spain under the Bourbons, 1700–1833: A Collection of Documents*. Columbia: University of South Carolina Press, 1973.

Haring, C. H. *El imperio hispánico en América*. Trans. Horacio Pérez Silva. Buenos Aires: Peuser, 1958.

Hartz, Louis. *The Founding of New Societies: Studies in the History of the United States, Latin America, South Africa, Canada, and Australia*. With contributions by Kenneth D. McRae, Richard M. Morse, Richard N. Rosecrance, Leonard M. Thompson. New York: Harcourt, Brace, 1964.

Hasbrouck, Alfred. "The Movement for Independence in Mexico and Central America," in A. Curtis Wilgus (ed.), *Colonial Hispanic America*. Vol. IV, Studies in Hispanic American Affairs (Washington, D.C.: George Washington University Press, 1935), pp. 413–518.

Hearnshaw, F. J. C. "Edmund Burke," in F. J. C. Hearnshaw (ed.), *The Social and Political Ideas of Some Representative Thinkers of the Revolutionary Era*. New York: Barnes & Noble, 1950. Pp. 72–99.

Heer, Friedrich. *Europäische Geistesgeschichte.* Stuttgart: Kohlhammer, 1957.
Henríquez Ureña, Pedro. *A Concise History of Latin American Culture.* Trans. Gilbert Chase. New York: Praeger, 1967.
Hera, Alberto de la. "Las leyes eclesiásticas de Indias en el siglo XVIII." *Estudios Americanos,* 16, Nos. 86–87 (November–December 1958), 239–52.
Heredia, Vicente Beltrán de. "Un precursor del maestro Vitoria. El P. Matías de Paz, o.p., y su tratado 'De Dominio Regum Hispaniae super Indos'." *La ciencia tomista,* 40 (1929), 173–90.
Hernández de Alba, Guillermo, and Lozano y Lozano, Fabio (edd.). *Documentos sobre el doctor Vicente Azuero.* Bogotá: Imprenta nacional, 1944.
Hernández y Dávalos, J. E. (ed.). *Colección de documentos para la historia de la guerra de independencia de México de 1808 a 1821.* 6 vols. Mexico: Sandoval, 1877–82.
Herold, J. Christopher. *The Age of Napoleon.* New York: American Heritage–Harper & Row, 1963.
Herr, Richard. *The Eighteenth-Century Revolution in Spain.* Princeton: Princeton University Press, 1958.
Herring, Hubert. *A History of Latin America from the Beginnings to the Present.* New York: Knopf, 1956.
Hervás y Panduro, Lorenzo. *Causas de la Revolución de Francia.* Madrid: Cisneros, 1943.
Hinojosa [y Naveros], Eduardo de. *Estudios sobre la historia del derecho español.* Madrid: Imprenta del asilo, 1903.
Höffner, Joseph. *Christentum und Menschenwürde. Das Anliegen der spanischen Kolonialethik im goldenen Zeitalter.* Trier: Paulinusverlag, 1947.
Hoenigsberg, Julio. *Santander, el clero y Bentham.* Bogotá: ABC, 1940.
Holstein, Günther. *Historia de la filosofía política.* Spanish ed. Madrid: Instituto de Estudios Políticos, 1950.
Houdaille, Jacques. *Frenchmen and Francophiles in New Spain: From 1760 to 1810.* Washington, D.C.: Catholic University of America Press, 1956.
Humboldt, Alexander von. *Ensayo político sobre el Reino de la Nueva España.* 4 vols. 6th Spanish ed. Mexico: Robredo, 1941.
———. *Essai politique sur l'île de Cuba.* 2 vols. Paris: Gide, 1826.
———. *Political Essay on the Kingdom of New Spain.* Trans. John Black. 2 vols. New York: Riley, 1871.
———. *Relation historique du voyage aux régions équinoxiales du Nouveau Continent.* 3 vols. Stuttgart: Brockhaus, 1970.
———. *Viaje a las regiones equinocciales del nuevo continente.* Vols. I–IX of Biblioteca venezolana de cultura. Trans. Lisandro Alvarado and Eduardo Röhl. 5 vols. Caracas: Escuela Técnica Industrial, 1941–42.
Humphreys, R. A., and Lynch, John (edd.). *The Origins of the Latin American Revolutions, 1808–1826.* New York: Knopf, 1965.
Ingenieros, José. *La evolución de las ideas argentinas.* 2 vols. 2d ed. Buenos Aires: Ateneo, 1951.
Instituto Panamericano de Geografía e Historia, Comisión de Historia, Comité de orígenes de la emancipación–Caracas. *Documentos Mirandinos (Prolegómenos de la emancipación iberoamericana).* Caracas: Avila Gráfica, 1950.
Insúa Rodríguez, Ramón. *Historia de la filosofía en Hispanoamérica.* Guayaquil: Universidad, 1945.

Isidore of Seville, St. *Etymologiarum sive originum, libri XX.* Ed. W. M. Lindsay. 2 vols. Oxford: Clarendon, 1911.
——. *Opera.* Ed. Faustino Arévalo, s.J. 7 vols. Venice: Fulgonius, 1797–1803.
——. *San Isidoro (Antología).* Edd. Justo Pérez de Urbel and Timoteo Ortega. Madrid: Fe, 1940.
Iturbide, Agustín de. *El Libertador. Documentos selectos de Don Agustín de Iturbide.* Ed. Mariano Cuevas, s.J. Mexico: Patria, 1947.
Jackson, Gabriel. *The Making of Medieval Spain.* New York: Harcourt Brace Jovanovich, 1972.
James, Preston E. *Latin America.* Rev. ed. New York: Odyssey, 1950.
Jane, Cecil. *Liberty and Despotism in Spanish America.* New York: Cooper Square, 1966.
Jiménez de Quesada, Gonzalo. *El Antijovio.* Bogotá: Instituto Caro y Cuervo, 1952.
——. "Indicaciones para el buen gobierno, o representación original que hace a su majestad el licenciado Gonzalo Jiménez de Quesada, conquistador de las provincias de Santa Marta y Nuevo Reino de Granada, que contiene treinta capítulos todos relativos al buen gobierno," *Boletín de historia y antigüedades,* 10, No. 162 (1923), 345–61.
Jovellanos, Gaspar Melchor de. *Informe sobre la Ley Agraria.* Intro. Valentín Andrés Alvarez. Madrid: Instituto de Estudios Políticos, 1955.
Juderías, Julián. *La leyenda negra: estudios acerca del concepto de España en el extranjero.* 13th ed. Madrid: Nacional, 1954.
Juan, Jorge, and Ulloa, Antonio de. *Noticias secretas de América.* Buenos Aires: Mar Océano, 1953.
Juretschke, Hans. "Postrimerías de Fernando VII y advenimiento del régimen liberal. Apostillas a Federico Suárez." *Razón y Fe. Revista Hispano-Americana de Cultura,* 152, No. 694 (November 1955), 325–34.
Kahle, Günter. *Militär und Staatsbildung in den Anfängen der Unabhängigkeit Mexikos.* Lateinamerikanische Forschungen, Vol. 1. Cologne–Vienna: Böhlau, 1969.
Keniston, Hayward. *Francisco de los Cobos, Secretary of the Emperor Charles V.* Pittsburgh: University of Pittsburgh Press, 1958.
King, James Ferguson. "A Royalist View of the Colored Castes in the Venezuelan War of Independence." *Hispanic American Historical Review,* 33, No. 4 (November 1953), 526–37.
——. "The Colored Castes and American Representation in the Cortes of Cádiz." *Hispanic American Historical Review,* 33, No. 1 (February 1953), 33–64.
Kirkpatrick, F. A. *Die spanischen Konquistadores.* German ed. Leipzig: Goldmann, n.d.
Klencke, Herman. *Lives of the Brothers Humboldt, Alexander and William.* New York: Longmans, Green, 1853.
Konetzke, Richard. *Colección de documentos para la historia de la formación social de Hispanoamérica, 1493–1810.* 5 vols. Madrid: Consejo Superior de Investigaciones Científicas, 1953–62.
——. *El imperio español. Orígenes y fundamentos.* Spanish trans. Felipe González Vicén. Madrid: Nueva Epoca, 1946.
——. *Entdecker und Eroberer Amerikas.* Frankfurt–Hamburg: Fischer, 1963.
——. *La condición legal de los criollos y las causas de la Independencia.* Seville: 1950.
Korn, Alejandro. *El pensamiento argentino.* Buenos Aires: Nova, 1961.

Krebs Wilckens, Ricardo. *El pensamiento histórico, político y económico del Conde de Campomanes.* Santiago: Ediciones de la Universidad de Chile, 1960.
Kropfinger-von Kügelgen, Helga; Castro Morales, Efraín; Specker, Johann. *Europäische Bücher in Neuspanien zu Ende des 16. Jahrhunderts. Ein Beitrag zur Kulturstratigraphie.* Das Mexiko-Projekt der Deutschen Forschungsgemeinschaft, Vol. 5. Wiesbaden: Steiner, 1973.
Laaths, Erwin. *Geschichte der Weltliteratur.* 4th rev. ed. Munich–Zürich; Droemer, 1953.
Labra, Rafael M. de. *España y América, 1812–1912. Estudios políticos, históricos y de derecho internacional.* Madrid: Sindicato de Publicidad, 1912.
Lacas, M. M. "A Social Welfare Organizer in Sixteenth-Century New Spain: Don Vasco de Quiroga, First Bishop of Michoacán." *The Americas,* 14 (1957–58), 57–86.
Lafinur, Juan Crisóstomo. *Curso filosófico.* Buenos Aires: Instituto de filosofía, 1938.
La Fuente, Vicente. *La corte de Carlos III.* Madrid: Ribadeneyra, 1868.
Lafuente Ferrari, Enrique. *El virrey Iturrigaray y los orígenes de la independencia de Méjico.* Madrid: Consejo Superior de Investigaciones Científicas, Instituto Gonzalo Fernández de Oviedo, 1941.
Lamas, Andrés. *Rivadavia: su obra política y cultural.* Buenos Aires: Cultura Argentina, 1915.
Lanning, John Tate. *Academic Culture in the Spanish Colonies.* London: Oxford University Press, 1940.
———. *The Eighteenth-Century Enlightenment in the University of San Carlos de Guatemala.* Ithaca: Cornell University Press, 1956.
Lanseros, Mateo. *La autoridad civil en Francisco Suárez.* Madrid: Instituto de Estudios Políticos, 1949.
Lasplaces, Alberto. *José Artigas. Protector de los pueblos libres.* Vol. 38 of Vidas españolas e hispanoamericanas del siglo xix. Madrid: Espasa-Calpe, 1933.
Lazcano y Mazón, Andrés María. *Las constituciones de Cuba.* Madrid: Cultura Hispánica, 1952.
Lea, Henry Charles. *The Inquisition in the Spanish Dependencies.* New York: Macmillan, 1908.
Lefebvre, Georges. *Napoleon: From 18 Brumaire to Tilsit, 1799–1807.* Trans. Henry F. Stockhold. New York: Columbia University Press, 1969.
———. *The Coming of the French Revolution.* Trans. R. R. Palmer. New York: Vintage, 1957.
Legón, Faustino J., and Medrano, Samuel W. *Las constituciones de la República Argentina.* Madrid: Cultura Hispánica, 1953.
Leonard, Irving A. *Baroque Times in Old Mexico.* Ann Arbor: University of Michigan Press, 1971.
———. *Books of the Brave: Being an Account of Books and of Men in the Spanish Conquest and Settlement of the Sixteenth-Century New World.* New York: Gordian, 1964.
———. "On the Lima Book Trade, 1591." *Hispanic American Historical Review,* 33, No. 4 (November 1953), 511–25.
Leturia, Pedro, S.J. *El ocaso del Patronato Real en la América Española: La acción diplomática de Bolívar, ante Pío VII (1820–1823) a la luz del archivo vaticano.* Madrid: Razón y Fe, 1925.

Leturia, Pedro, s.j. *La emancipación hispanoamericana en los informes episcopales a Pío VII.* Copias y extractos del archivo vaticano. Buenos Aires: Imprenta de la Universidad, 1935.
Levene, Ricardo. *A History of Argentina.* Trans. William Spence Robertson. New York: Russell & Russell, 1963.
———. (ed.). *El pensamiento vivo de Mariano Moreno.* Biblioteca del pensamiento vivo. Buenos Aires: Losada, 1942.
———. *Historia del derecho argentino.* 11 vols. Buenos Aires: Kraft, 1945–58.
———. *La Revolución de Mayo y Mariano Moreno.* 2 vols. Buenos Aires: Universidad, 1920–21.
———. "Los sucesos de Mayo," in Academia nacional de la historia, *Historia de la Nación Argentina (desde los orígenes hasta la organización definitiva en 1862).* 10 vols. Buenos Aires: Imprenta de la Universidad, 1936–42. V, Sec. 2. 9–52.
———. *Moreno.* Buenos Aires: Espasa-Calpe, 1945.
———. *Síntesis sobre la Revolución de Mayo.* Buenos Aires: Ferrari, 1935.
Lima, M. de Oliveira. *Dom Pedro VI no Brasil, 1808–1821.* 2 vols. Rio de Janeiro: Jornal do Commercio, 1908.
Liss, Peggy. "Jesuit Contributions to the Ideology of Spanish Empire in Mexico." *The Americas,* 29, No. 3 (January 1973), 314–33; No. 4 (April 1973), 449–70.
Livermore, Harold. *A History of Spain.* London: Allen & Unwin, 1958.
Lizárraga, Reginaldo de. *Descripción y población de las Indias.* Lima: Americana, 1908.
Lockhart, James. *Spanish Peru, 1532–1560. A Colonial Society.* Madison: University of Wisconsin Press, 1968.
Llorens Castillo, Vicente. *Liberales y Románticos. Una emigración española en Inglaterra (1823–1834).* Mexico: Colegio de México, 1954.
Llorente, Juan Antonio. *Histoire critique de l'Inquisition d'Espagne depuis son établissement par Ferdinand V jusqu'au règne de Ferdinand VII.* Trans. Alexis Pellier. 4 vols. 2d ed. Paris: Treuttel & Wurtz, 1817–18.
London, University of. Library of University College. Jeremy Bentham MSS, X (Correspondence, General and French); XII (Correspondence, U.S., Colombia, Peru, Egypt, Greece, Guatemala, 1817–25).
López Cámara, Francisco. "El Cartesianismo en Sor Juana y Sigüenza y Góngora." *Filosofía y Letras,* 20 (July–September 1950), 107–31.
López de Gómara, Francisco. *Conquista de Méjico.* Barcelona: Biblioteca clásica española, 1888.
Lowery, Woodbury. *The Spanish Settlements Within the Present Limits of the United States, 1513–1561.* New York–London: Putnam, 1921.
Lynch, John. "Intendants and Cabildos in the Viceroyalty of La Plata, 1782–1810." *Hispanic American Historical Review,* 35, No. 3 (August 1955), 337–62.
———. *Spanish Colonial Administration, 1782–1810. The Intendant System in the Viceroyalty of the Río de la Plata.* London: University of London, The Athlone Press, 1958.
———. *The Spanish-American Revolutions, 1808–1826.* New York: Norton, 1973.
Macanaz, Melchor Rafael de. *Pedimento del fiscal general Don Melchor de Macanaz sobre abusos de la dataría; provisión de beneficios; pensiones; coadjutorías; dispensas matrimoniales, espolios; vacantes; sobre el nuncio;*

derecho de los tribunales eclesiásticos; juicios posesorios y otros asuntos gravísismos. Madrid: Imprenta nacional, 1841.
Macanaz, Melchor Rafael de. *Regalías de los señores reyes de Aragón, discurso jurídico, histórico, político*. Madrid: Revista de Legislación, 1879.
Madariaga, Salvador de. *Bolívar*. English ed. New York: Pellegrini & Cudahy, 1952.
———. *El auge del imperio español en América*. Buenos Aires: Sudamericana, 1955.
———. *El ocaso del imperio español en América*. Buenos Aires: Sudamericana, 1955.
———. *Englishmen, Frenchmen, Spaniards*. London: Oxford University Press, 1949.
———. *España, ensayo de historia contemporánea*. Buenos Aires: Sudamericana, 1950.
Majó Framis, Ricardo. *Vidas de los navegantes, conquistadores y colonizadores españoles de los siglos XVI, XVII y XVIII*. 3 vols. Madrid: Aguilar, 1954.
Malagón, Javier (ed.). *Las actas de independencia de América*. Washington, D.C.: Pan American Union, 1955.
Mancini, Jules. *Bolivar et l'émancipation des colonies espagnoles: Des origines à 1815*. 2d ed. Paris: Perrin, 1912.
Manuel, Frank. *The Age of Reason*. Ithaca: Cornell University Press, 1951.
Manzano Manzano, Juan. *La incorporación de las Indias a la Corona de Castilla*. Madrid: Cultura Hispánica, 1948.
Marañón, Gregorio. *Evolución de la gloria de Feijóo*. Oviedo: Cuadernos de la Cátedra Feijóo, 1, 1955.
———. "Visión de América a través de El Ecuador." *Mundo Hispánico*, 6, No. 63 (June 1953), 19–22, 61.
Maravall, José Antonio. *El concepto de España en la Edad Media*. Madrid: Instituto de Estudios Políticos, 1954.
———. *La philosophie politique espagnole au XVIIème siècle dans ses rapports avec l'esprit de la Contre-Reforme*. Paris: Vrin, 1955.
———. "La utopía político-religiosa de los franciscanos en Nueva España." *Estudios Americanos*, 1 (January 1949), 197–227.
Marcos, Teodoro Andrés. *Los imperialismo de Juan Ginés de Sepúlveda en su "Democrates Alter."* Madrid: Instituto de Estudios Políticos, 1947.
Mariana, Juan de. *De Rege et regis institutione*. 1st ed. Toledo: Rodericus, 1599.
———. *Obras*. 2 vols. Madrid: Biblioteca de autores españoles, 1854–72.
Marías, Julián. *La España posible en tiempo de Carlos III*. Madrid: Sociedad de Estudios y Publicaciones, 1963.
Mariéjol, Jean Hippolyte. *The Spain of Ferdinand and Isabella*. Trans. Benjamin Keen. New Brunswick: Rutgers University Press, 1961.
Mariluz Urquijo, José María. *Ensayo sobre los juicios de residencia indianos*. Seville: Escuela de Estudios Hispano-Americanos, 1952.
Marín y Mendoza, Joaquín. *Historia del derecho natural y de gentes*. Madrid: Instituto de Estudios Políticos, 1950.
Markham, Clements. *The Conquest of New Granada*. Port Washington, N.Y.–London: Kennikat Press, 1971.
Márquez de la Plata, Fernando (ed.). "Documentos de la primera Junta de Gobierno de 1810." *Boletín de la academia chilena de la historia*, 5, No. 11 (1938), 106–407.

Marongiu, Antonio. *Medieval Parliaments: A Comparative Study.* Trans. and adapted by S. J. Woolf. London: Eyre & Spottiswoode, 1968.
Martin, Kingsley. *French Liberal Thought in the Eighteenth Century.* 2d ed. London: Turnstile, 1954.
Martín, Luis. *The Intellectual Conquest of Peru: The Jesuit College of San Pablo, 1568–1767.* New York: Fordham University Press, 1968.
Martínez Marina, Francisco. *Discurso sobre el origen de la monarquía y sobre la naturaleza del gobierno español.* Madrid: Instituto de Estudios Políticos, 1957.
———. *Ensayo histórico-crítico sobre la legislación y principales cuerpos legales de los reinos de León y Castilla.* 3d ed. Madrid: Sociedad literaria y tipográfica, 1845.
———. *Principios naturales de la moral, de la política y de la legislación.* Madrid: Gómez Fuentenebro, 1933.
———. *Teoría de las Cortes o grandes juntas nacionales de los reinos de León y Castilla. Monumentos de su constitución política y de la soberanía del pueblo.* 3 vols. Madrid: Fermín Villalpando, 1813.
Martínez Paz, Enrique. *El deán Funes, un apóstol de la libertad.* Córdoba: Pronsato, 1950.
———. *Sistema de filosofía del derecho.* 3d ed. Buenos Aires: Ateneo, 1940.
Mártir Rizo, Juan Pablo. *Norte de príncipes y vida de Rómulo.* Ed. José Antonio Maravall. Madrid: Instituto de Estudios Políticos, 1944.
Masur, Gerhard. *Simón Bolívar.* Albuquerque: University of New Mexico Press, 1948.
McClelland, I. L. *Benito Jerónimo Feijóo y Montenegro.* New York: Twayne, 1970.
McIlwain, Charles Howard. *The Growth of Political Thought in the West: From the Greeks to the End of the Middle Ages.* New York: Macmillan, 1953.
McPheeters, D. E. "The Distinguished Peruvian Scholar Cosme Bueno (1711–1798)." *Hispanic American Historical Review,* 35, No. 4 (November 1955), 484–91.
Meinecke, Friedrich. *Die Idee der Staatsräson in der neueren Geschichte.* Munich: Oldenbourg, 1957.
Méndez Plancarte, Alfonso, and Salcedo, Alberto G. *Obras completas de Sor Juana Inés de la Cruz.* 4 vols. Mexico and Buenos Aires: Fondo de Cultura Económica, 1951–57.
Mendiburu, Manuel de. *Diccionario histórico-biográfico del Perú.* 11 vols. Lima: Palacios, 1931–34.
Mendieta, Gerónimo de, O.F.M. *Historia eclesiástica Indiana.* 4 vols. Mexico: Chavez Hayhoe, [1945].
Menéndez y Pelayo, Marcelino. *Historia de los heterodoxos españoles.* 2 vols. Madrid: Biblioteca de autores cristianos, 1956.
Menéndez Pidal, Ramón. *Die Spanier in der Geschichte.* German ed. Munich: Rinn, n.d.
———. *El imperio hispánico y los cinco reinos.* Madrid: Instituto de Estudios Políticos, 1950.
———. *Mis páginas preferidas. Estudios lingüísticos e históricos.* Madrid: Gredos, 1957.
Merriman, Roger Bigelow. *The Rise of the Spanish Empire in the Old World and in the New.* 4 vols. New York: Macmillan, 1918.

Mexico. *México en las Cortes de Cádiz. Documentos.* Vol. 9 of El Liberalismo mexicano en pensamiento y en acción. Mexico: Empresas editoriales, 1949.

Mignone, Emilio Fermín. "The Latin America That Might Have Been." *Américas*, 26, No. 2 (February 1974), 10–11.

Millares Carlo, Agustín (ed.). "Feijóo y América." *Cuadernos Americanos*, 3 (1944), 139–60.

Miranda, Francisco de. *Diary: Tour of the United States, 1783–1784.* Ed. William Spence Robertson. New Haven: Yale University Press, 1928.

Mitre, Bartolomé. *Historia de Belgrano y de la independencia argentina.* 4th ed. 3 vols. Buenos Aires: Lajouane, 1887; 5th ed. 2 vols. Buenos Aires: "La Nación," 1902.

——. *Historia de San Martín y de la emancipación sud-americana.* 1st ed. 3 vols. Buenos Aires: "La Nación," 1887–88; 3rd ed. 5 vols. Buenos Aires: "La Nación," 1903.

Mörner, Magnus (ed.). *The Expulsion of the Jesuits from Latin America.* New York: Knopf, 1965.

Molina, Juan Ignacio, s.j. *Compendio de la historia geográfica natural y civil del Reino de Chile.* Madrid: Sancha, 1788–95.

Molinari, Diego Luis. *La representación de los hacendados de Mariano Moreno y su ninguna influencia en la vida económica del país y en los sucesos de Mayo de 1810.* 2d ed. Buenos Aires: Universidad de Buenos Aires, Facultad de Ciencias Económicas, 1939.

Monica, Sor M. *La gran controversia del siglo XVI acerca del dominio español en América.* Madrid: Cultura Hispánica, 1952.

Montiel y Duarte, Isidro Antonio. *Derecho público mexicano.* 4 vols. Mexico: Gobierno Federal, 1871–82.

Moore, John Preston. *The Cabildo in Peru Under the Bourbons: A Study in the Decline and Resurgence of Local Government in the Audiencia of Lima, 1700–1824.* Durham: Duke University Press, 1966.

——. *The Cabildo in Peru Under the Hapsburgs. A Study in the Origins and Powers of the Town Council in the Viceroyalty of Peru, 1530–1700.* Durham: Duke University Press, 1954.

Mora, José María Luis. *México y sus revoluciones.* Vols. 59–61 of Colección de escritores mexicanos. 3 vols. Mexico: Porrúa, 1950.

Moreno, Juan José. *Vida de Don Vasco de Quiroga. Primer Obispo de Michoacán.* Morelia: Martínez Mier, 1939.

Moreno, Mariano. "Prólogo." Jean Jacques Rousseau. *Del contrato social o principios del derecho político.* Obra escrita por el ciudadano de Ginebra Juan Jacobo Rousseau. Se ha reimpreso en Buenos Aires para instrucción de los jóvenes americanos. Spanish ed. (reprint). Buenos Aires: Real Imprenta de niños expósitos, 1810.

Moreno, Rafael. "Alzate y la filosofía de la ilustración." *Filosofía y Letras*, 19 (1950), 110–30.

Mornet, Daniel. *French Thought in the Eighteenth Century.* Trans. Lawrence M. Levin. New York: Prentice-Hall, 1929.

——. *Les origines intellectuelles de la Révolution Française (1715–1787).* Paris: Colin, 1933.

Morrall, John B. *Political Thought in Medieval Times.* New York: Harper, 1958.

Morse, Richard M. "The Heritage of Latin America." *The Founding of New Societies: Studies in the History of the United States, Latin America, South Africa, Canada, and Australia.* New York: Harcourt, Brace, 1964.

Moses, Bernard. *South America on the Eve of Emancipation: The Southern Spanish Colonies in the Last Half-Century of their Dependence.* New York: Cooper Square, 1965.

———. *Spain's Declining Power in South America, 1730–1806.* Berkeley: University of California Press, 1919.

———. *Spanish Colonial Literature in South America.* London–New York: Hispanic Society of America, 1922.

———. *The Intellectual Background of the Revolution in South America, 1810–1824.* New York, 1926.

———. *The Spanish Dependencies in South America: An Introduction to the History of their Civilization.* 2 vols. New York: Cooper Square, 1965.

Motten, Clement G. *Mexican Silver and the Enlightenment.* Philadelphia: University of Pennsylvania Press, 1950.

Motolinía, Toribio de. *Motolinia's History of the Indians of New Spain.* Trans. Francis Borgia Steck, o.f.m. Washington, D.C.: Academy of American Franciscan History, 1951.

Muñoz Pérez, José. "Ideas sobre comercio en el xviii español." *Estudios Americanos*, 19, No. 100 (January 1960), 47–66.

Murillo Ferrol, Francisco. *Saavedra Fajardo y la política del barroco.* Madrid: Instituto de Estudios Políticos, 1957.

Muzzey, David Seville. *The Spiritual Franciscans.* New York: American Historical Association, 1907.

Narancio, Edmundo M. (ed.). *Artigas. Estudios publicados en "El País" como homenaje al jefe de los orientales en el centenario de su muerte, 1850–1950.* Montevideo: Colombino, 1951.

———. *El origen del estado oriental.* Montevideo: L.I.G.U., 1948.

———. "Las ideas políticas en el Río de la Plata a comienzos del siglo xix." *Revista de la Facultad de Humanidades y Ciencias* (Montevideo), 14 (December 1955).

Naszalyi, Emilio. *El estado según Francisco de Vitoria.* Madrid: Cultura Hispánica, 1948.

Navarro, José Gabriel. *Los franciscanos en la conquista y colonización de América.* Madrid: Cultura Hispánica, 1955.

O'Leary, Daniel F. *Bolívar y la emancipación de Sur-América. Memorias del General O'Leary.* Trans. Simón B. O'Leary. 2 vols. Madrid: Sociedad Española de Librería, [1915].

———. *Correspondencia de extranjeros notables con el Libertador.* 2 vols. Madrid: América, 1920.

Oliveira Martins, Joaquim Pedro de. *A History of Iberian Civilization.* Trans. Aubrey F. G. Bell. London: Oxford University Press, 1930.

dell'Oro Maini, Atilio, et al. *Presencia y sugestión del filósofo Francisco Suárez. Su influencia en la Revolución de Mayo.* Buenos Aires: Kraft, 1959.

d'Ors y Rovira, Eugenio. *Cuando ya esté tranquilo.* Madrid: Renacimiento, 1930.

Ortega y Gasset, José. *Obras completas.* 6 vols. 3d ed. Madrid: Revista de Occidente, 1954.

Ortega y Medina, Juan A. *Humboldt desde México.* Mexico: Universidad Nacional Autónoma de México, 1960.

Otero, Gustavo A. "Bolívar y Bentham." *América*, 25, Nos. 93–100 (January–December 1949–50), 104–39.
Ots Capdequí, J. M. *El estado español en las Indias*. 3d ed. Mexico: Cultura Económica, 1957.
———. "Interpretación institucional de la colonización española en América," in Edgar McInnis, Gustave Lanctot, et al., *Ensayos sobre la Historia del Nuevo Mundo*. Instituto Panamericano de Geografía e Historia, Comisión de Historia, No. 31, Estudios de Historia, IV, Publicación No. 118. Mexico: Cultura, 1951. 287–314.
Pabón, Jesús. *Las ideas y el sistema napoleónicos*. Madrid: Instituto de Estudios Políticos, 1947.
Palacio Atard, Vicente. "La influencia del P. Feijóo en América," in Universidad de Oviedo, Facultad de Filosofía y Letras. *El P. Feijóo y su siglo: Ponencias y communicaciones presentadas al simposio celebrado en la Universidad de Oviedo del 28 de septiembre al 5 de octubre de 1964*. 3 vols. (Oviedo, 1966), I 22.
———. "La política internacional de Carlos III." *Estudios Americanos*, 19, No. 100 (January 1960), 99–102.
Pareja Paz-Soldán, José. *Las constituciones del Perú*. Madrid: Cultura Hispánica, 1954.
Parkes, Henry Bamford. *A History of Mexico*. 3d rev. ed. London: Eyre & Spottiswoode, 1962.
Parra-Pérez, C. *Mariño y la independencia de Venezuela. El Libertador de Oriente*. Madrid: Cultura Hispánica, 1954.
Parry, John Horace. *The Spanish Theory of Empire in the Sixteenth Century*. Cambridge: Cambridge University Press, 1940.
Pattee, R., and Rothbauer, A. M. *Spanien: Mythos und Wirklichkeit*. Graz: Styria, 1954.
Paz, Matías de. "De dominio regum Hispaniae super Indos." *Archivum Fratrum Praedicatorum*, 3 (1933), 131–81.
Paz Soldán, Mariano Felipe. *Historia del Perú independiente (1822–1827)*. Biblioteca Ayacucho. 2 vols. Madrid: América, 1919.
Pelliza, Mariano A. *Historia argentina desde su origen hasta la organización nacional*. 2 vols. Buenos Aires: Lajouane, 1910.
———. *Monteagudo, su vida y sus escritos*. Vol. I: 1785–1815; Vol. II: 1816–25. Buenos Aires: Mayo, 1880.
Penna, Mario. "Mercurino Arborio de Gattinara, gran canciller del César." III Congreso de Cooperación Intelectual. Madrid: Cultura Hispánica, October, 1958.
Peñalver, Patricio. *Modernidad tradicional en el pensamiento de Jovellanos*. Colección "Mar Adentro." Seville: Escuela de Estudios Hispano-Americanos, 1953.
Peralta, Hernán G. *El Pacto de Concordia. Orígenes del derecho constitucional de Costa Rica*. 2d ed. San José de Costa Rica: Lehmann, 1955.
Perazzo, Nicolás. *José Cortés de Madariaga*. Caracas: Ediciones del Cuatricentenario de Caracas, 1966.
Pereña Vicente, Luciano. *Misión de España en América, 1540–1560*. Madrid: Consejo Superior de Investigaciones Científicas, Instituto Francisco de Vitoria, 1956.
Pereyra, Carlos. *Humboldt en América*. Madrid: América, 1917.

Pérez-Marchand, Monelisa Lina. *Dos etapas ideológicas del siglo XVIII en México a través de los papeles de la Inquisición.* Mexico: Colegio de México, 1945.
Pérez-Prendes y Muñoz de Arracó, José Manuel. "Cortes de Castilla y Cortes de Cádiz." *Revista de Estudios Políticos,* 126 (November–December 1962), 321–431.
Pérez-Rioja, José Antonio. *Proyección y actualidad de Feijóo.* Madrid: Instituto de Estudios Políticos, 1965.
Pérez-Sarmiento, José Manuel (ed.). *Proceso de Nariño.* Cádiz: Alvarez, 1914.
Perú de Lacroix, Louis. *Diario de Bucaramanga*; estudio crítico y reproducción literalísima del manuscrito original de L. Perú de Lacroix, con toda clase de aclaraciones para discernir su valor histórico. Ed. Nicolás E. Navarro. Caracas: Americana, 1935.
Pfandl, Ludwig. *Cultura y costumbres del pueblo español de los siglos XVI y XVII: Introducción al estudio del siglo de oro.* 2d Span. ed. Trans. Félix García. Barcelona: Araluce, 1942.
———. *Philipp II. Gemälde eines Lebens und einer Zeit.* Munich: Callwey, 1951.
Phelan, John Leddy. *The Millennial Kingdom of the Franciscans in the New World — A Study of the Writings of Gerónimo de Mendieta (1525–1604).* California Publications in History, Vol. 52. Berkeley: University of California Press, 1956; 2d rev. ed. 1970.
Piccirilli, Ricardo. *Rivadavia.* Buenos Aires: Peuser, 1952.
———. *Rivadavia y su tiempo.* 2 vols. Buenos Aires: Peuser, 1943.
Picón-Salas, Mariano. *A Cultural History of Spanish America from Conquest to Independence.* Trans. Irving A. Leonard. Berkeley and Los Angeles: University of California Press, 1971.
Pinta Llorente, Miguel de la. "El sentido de la cultura española en el siglo XVIII e intelectuales de la época." *Revista de Estudios Políticos,* 68 (March–April 1953), 79–114.
Pirenne, Henri. *A History of Europe: From the Invasions to the XVI Century.* New York: University Books, 1955.
Pivel Devoto. Juan E. *Raíces coloniales de la Revolución oriental de 1811.* Montevideo: Medina, 1957.
Political Philosophers: Thomas Hobbes, John Locke, John Stuart Mill, Jean Jacques Rousseau, Henry Thoreau. New York: Carlton House, 1947.
Polt, John H. R. *Jovellanos and his English Sources: Economic, Philosophical, and Political Writings.* Transactions of the American Philosophical Society. New Series, Vol. 54, Part 7 (1964). Philadelphia: American Philosophical Society, 1964.
Porras Troconis, Gabriel. *Historia de la cultura en el Nuevo Reino de Granada.* Seville: Escuela de Estudios Hispano-Americanos, 1952.
Priestley, Herbert Ingram. *The Mexican Nation.* New York: Macmillan, 1923.
Pritchett, V. S. *The Spanish Temper.* New York: Knopf, 1954.
Pufendorf, Baron de. *Le droit de la nature et des gens, ou Système général des principes les plus importants de la morale, de la jurisprudence, et de la politique.* Trans. Jean Barbeyrac. 2 vols. 2d ed. Amsterdam: Coup, 1712.
Puy, Francisco. *El pensamiento tradicional en la España del siglo XVIII (1700–1760).* Madrid: Instituto de Estudios Políticos, 1966.
Ramos, Demetrio. "Las Cortes de Cádiz y América." *Revista de Estudios Políticos,* 126 (November–December 1962), 433–639.

Ramos, Jorge Abelardo. *América latina, un país: Su historia, su economía, su revolución.* Buenos Aires: October, 1948.
Ramos, Samuel. *Historia de la filosofía en México.* Universidad Nacional Autónoma de México. Biblioteca de filosofía mexicana, Vol. X. Mexico: Imprenta universitaria, 1943.
Rassow, Peter. *Die Kaiser-Idee Karls V. dargestellt an der Politik der Jahre 1528–1540.* Berlin: Ebering, 1932.
Ravignani, Emilio. *Asambleas constituyentes argentinas [1813–98], seguidas de los textos constitucionales, legislativos y pactos interprovinciales que organizaron políticamente la nación;* fuentes seleccionadas, coordinadas y anotadas en cumplimiento de la Ley 11.857. 6 vols. Buenos Aires: Peuser, 1937–39.
———. *Historia constitucional de la República Argentina.* 3 vols. Buenos Aires: Peuser, 1926–27.
Recaséns Siches, Luis, et al. *Latin American Legal Philosophy.* Vol. III of 20th Century Legal Philosophy Series. Cambridge: Harvard University Press, 1948.
Redmond, Walter Bernard. *Bibliography of the Philosophy in the Iberian Colonies of America.* The Hague: Nijhoff, 1972.
Reibstein, Ernst. *Johannes Althusius als Fortsetzer der Schule von Salamanca: Untersuchungen zur Ideengeschichte des Rechtsstaates und zur altprotestantischen Naturrechtslehre.* Vol. 5 of Freiburger rechts- und staatswissenschaftliche Abhandlungen. Karlsruhe: Müller, 1955.
René-Moreno, Gabriel. *Ultimos días coloniales en el Alto Perú.* Vols. IX and X of Biblioteca Boliviana. Publicación del Ministerio de Educación. 2 vols. La Paz: Renacimiento, 1940.
Rengger and Longchamps. *Ensayo histórico sobre la revolución del Paraguay;* precedida de la biografía del tirano Francia, y continuada con algunos documentos y observaciones históricas por M. A. Pelliza. Buenos Aires: Imprenta y Librería de Mayo, 1883.
———. *The Reign of Doctor Joseph Gaspard Roderick de Francia in Paraguay, Being an Account of a Six Years' Residence in that Republic from July, 1819, to May, 1825.* Trans. Johann Rudolph Rengger. London: Hurst & Chance, 1827.
Reynold, Gonzague de. *El mundo bárbaro y su fusión con el romano.* Vol. V, Part 2, of La formación de Europa. 7 vols. Madrid: Pegaso, 1955.
Ricart, Robert. *La conquista espiritual de México.* Mexico: Jus-Polis, 1947.
Río, Daniel A. del. *Pages of Glory. On Simón Bolívar, the South American Washington.* Condensed Engl. trans. of the 3d ed. [Caracas], 1966.
Ritter, Gerhard. *Die Neugestaltung Europas im 16. Jahrhundert. Die kirchlichen und staatlichen Wandlungen im Zeitalter der Reformation und der Glaubenskämpfe.* Berlin: Tempelhof, 1950.
Robertson, John Parish, and W. T. *Francia's Reign of Terror, Being the Continuation of Letters of Paraguay.* 2d ed. London: Murray, 1839.
Robertson, William Spence. "Introduction," in Francisco de Miranda, *Diary: Tour of the United States, 1783–1784,* ed. William Spence Robertson. New Haven: Yale University Press, 1928.
———. "The Policy of Spain Toward its Revolted Colonies, 1820–23." *Hispanic American Historical Review,* 6, Nos. 1–3 (February–August 1926), 21–46.

Rodríguez, Hernán. "John Locke en el Río de la Plata. Presencia de su filosofía en el pensamiento animador de la Revolución de Mayo." *Anuario del Instituto de Investigaciones históricas* (Rosario), 3, No. 3 (1958), 41–80.

Rodríguez, Mario. "The Genesis of Economic Attitudes in the Río de la Plata." *Hispanic American Historical Review*, 36, No. 2 (May 1956), 171–89.

Rodríguez Aranda, R. "La recepción y el influjo de las ideas políticas de John Locke en España." *Revista de Estudios Políticos*, 76 (July–August 1954), 115–30.

Rodríguez Casado, Vicente. "Del estado patrimonial al estado nacional." *Estudios Americanos*, 19, No. 100 (January 1960), 109–16.

———. "El intento español de 'Ilustración Cristiana'." *Estudios Americanos*, 9, No. 42 (March 1955), 141–69.

———. "La nueva sociedad burguesa en la literatura de la época de Carlos III." *Estudios Americanos*, 19, No. 100 (January 1960), 1–22.

Roig de Leuchsenring, Emilio. *La dominación inglesa en La Habana. Libro de Cabildos, 1762–1763.* Publicado bajo la dirección y con un prefacio de Emilio Roig de Leuchsenring. Havana: Molina, 1929.

Rojas, Arístides (ed.). *Miranda en la Revolución Francesa. Colección de documentos auténticos referentes a la historia del general Francisco de Miranda, durante su permanencia en Francia de 1792 a 1798.* Caracas: Gobierno Nacional, 1889.

Rojas, Armando. "La batalla de Bentham en Colombia." *Revista de historia de América*, 29 (June 1950), 37–66.

Rojas, Ricardo. *La literatura argentina. Ensayo filosófico sobre la evolución de la cultura en el Plata.* 8 vols. 2d ed. Buenos Aires: Facultad, 1924–25. (Part of Rojas, Ricardo. *Obras.* 15 vols. Buenos Aires: Facultad, 1924–25.)

———. *El santo de la espada. Vida de San Martín.* Buenos Aires: Losada, 1950.

Romanell, Patrick. *La formación de la mentalidad mexicana.* Mexico: Cultura Económica, 1954.

Romero, José Luis. *Las ideas políticas en Argentina.* 2d ed. Mexico–Buenos Aires: Cultura Económica, 1956.

Rommen, Heinrich. *Die ewige Wiederkehr des Naturrechts.* 2d ed. Munich: Kösel, 1947.

———. *Die Staatslehre des Franz Suarez, S.J.* Mönchen-Gladbach: Volksverein, 1926.

———. *The State in Catholic Thought.* St. Louis–London: Herder, 1947.

Rops, Daniel. *L'Église des révolutions. En face des nouveaux destins.* Vol. VI, Bk. 1, of Histoire de l'Église du Christ. Paris: Fayard, 1960.

Rosa, José María. *Rivadavia y el imperialismo financiero.* Buenos Aires: Orestes, 1969.

Rousseau, Jean Jacques. *Les confessions de Jean Jacques Rousseau.* Paris: Charpentier, 1886.

———. *The Social Contract or Principles of Political Right.* New York: Carlton House, n.d.

Rowe, John Howland. "The Incas under Spanish Colonial Institutions." *Hispanic American Historical Review*, 37, No. 2 (May 1957), 155–99.

Rydford, John. *Foreign Interest in the Independence of New Spain. An Introduction to the War for Independence.* Durham: Duke University Press, 1935.

Saavedra Fajardo, Diego de. *República literaria. Locuras de Europa. Política y Razón de Estado del Rey Católico Don Fernando.* Madrid: Cisneros, 1944.
Sabine, George. *A History of Political Theory.* New York, Holt: 1953.
Salaberry, Juan F. *Origen de la soberanía civil, según el P. Francisco Suárez.* Buenos Aires, 1922.
Salazar, Juan de. *Política Española.* Ed. Miguel Herrero García. Madrid: Instituto de Estudios Políticos, 1945.
San Alberto, José Antonio de. *Catecismo real . . . en que por preguntas y respuestas se enseñan catequísticamente en veinte lecciones las obligaciones que un vasallo debe a su Rey y Señor.* Madrid: Doblado, 1786.
Sánchez, Luis Alberto. *El pueblo en la revolución americana.* Buenos Aires: Américalee, 1942.
Sánchez Agesta, Luis. "Feijóo y la crisis del pensamiento político español del siglo xviii." *Revista de Estudios Políticos*, 5 (1945), 71–127.
———. *El pensamiento político del despotismo ilustrado.* Madrid: Instituto de Estudios Políticos, 1953.
———. *Historia del constitucionalismo español.* Madrid: Instituto de Estudios Políticos, 1955.
Sánchez Albornoz y Menduiña, Claudio. *España, un enigma histórico.* 2 vols. Buenos Aires: Sudamericana, 1956.
Sánchez Viamonte, Carlos. *Historia institucional de Argentina.* Mexico: Cultura Económica, 1948.
Santander, Francisco de Paula. *Cartas y mensajes [del General Francisco de Paula] Santander.* Comp. Roberto Cortázar. 10 vols. Bogotá: Voluntad, 1953.
———. *Cartas de Santander.* Ed. Vicente Lecuna. 3 vols. Venezuelan government edition. Caracas: Comercio, 1942.
Sañudo, José Rafael. *Estudios sobre la vida de Bolívar.* 2d ed. Pasto, Colombia: "Minerva nariñesa," 1931.
Sanz Cid, Carlos. *La constitución de Bayona.* Madrid: Reus, 1922.
Sarrailh, Jean. *L'Espagne éclairée de la seconde moitié du XVIIIe siècle.* Paris: Klincksieck, 1954.
Schalk, Fritz. *Spanische Geisteswelt. Vom maurischen bis zum modernen Spanien.* Baden Baden: Holle, 1957.
Scheuner, Ulrich. "Samuel Freiherr von Pufendorf," in *Die grossen Deutschen: Deutsche Biographie*, edd. Hermann Heimpel, Theodor Heuss, and Benno Reifenberg. 5 vols. Berlin: Propyläen-Verlag, 1957. V, 126–35.
Schmitt, Karl M. "The Clergy and the Independence of New Spain." *Hispanic American Historical Review*, 34, No. 3 (August 1954), 289–312.
Schoen, Wilhelm, Freiherr von. *Geschichte Mittel- und Südamerikas.* Munich: Bruckmann, 1953.
Schwarzenfeld, Gertrud von. *Charles V, Father of Europe.* Trans. Ruth Mary Bethell. Chicago: Regnery, 1957.
Schäfer, Ernesto. *El Consejo Real y Supremo de las Indias. Su historia, organización y labor administrativa hasta la terminación de la Casa de Austria.* Vol. I–Seville: Centro de Estudios de historia de América de la Universidad, 1935. Vol. II–Seville: Escuela de Estudios Hispano-Americanos, Consejo Superior de Investigaciones Científicas, 1947.

Scott, James Brown. *The Spanish Origin of International Law. I. Francisco de Vitoria and his Law of Nations.* Carnegie Endowment for International Peace. Oxford: Clarendon, 1934.
Sepúlveda, Juan Ginés de. *Democrates Segundo o de las justas causas de la guerra contra los indios.* Ed. Angel Losada. Madrid: Consejo Superior de Investigaciones Científicas, Instituto Francisco de Vitoria, 1951.
Sevilla Andrés, Diego. "La Constitución de 1812, obra de transición." *Revista de Estudios Políticos* (Madrid), 126 (November–December 1962), 113–41.
Shafer, Robert Jones. *The Economic Societies in the Spanish World (1763–1821).* Syracuse: Syracuse University Press, 1958.
Shiflett, Vance L. "Jeremy Bentham: An Appraisal of his Political Ideas and Contributions to Legal Development." Unpublished Ph.D. diss., Georgetown University, 1955.
Sierra, Justo. *Evolución política del pueblo mexicano.* Mexico: Cultura Económica, 1950.
Simonet, Francisco Javier. *Historia de los mozárabes en España, deducida de los mejores y más auténticos testimonios de los escritores christianos y árabes.* Amsterdam: Oriental, 1967 (reprint of Madrid 1897–1903 ed.).
Skalweit, Stephan. *Edmund Burke und Frankreich.* Cologne: Westdeutscher Verlag, 1956.
Solís, Ramón. "Las sociedades secretas y las Cortes de Cádiz." *Revista de Estudios Políticos*, 93 (May–June 1957), 111–22.
Solórzano Pereira, Juan de. *Emblemata centum, regio politica.* Madrid: Gazeta, 1779.
———. *De Indiarum iure, sive de iusta Indiarum Occidentalium gubernatione.* Madrid: Gazeta, 1777.
———. *Obras varias póstumas.* Madrid: Gazeta, 1776.
———. *Política indiana, sacada en lengua castellana de los dos tomos del Derecho y Gobierno municipal de las Indias Occidentales.* 1st ed. Madrid: Díaz de la Carrera, 1648.
Soto, Domingo de. *De Iustitia et iure.* Venice: Perchasinus, 1568.
Sousa, J. P. Galvão de. "Formación brasileña y problematismo hispanoamericano." *Estudios Americanos*, 9, No. 43 (April 1955), 267–87.
———. *Introdução à história do direito político brasileiro.* São Paulo: Reconquista, 1954.
Spain. *Colección de documentos inéditos relativos al descubrimiento, conquista y colonización de las posesiones españolas en América y Oceanía, sacadas en su mayor parte del Real Archivo de Indias.* Vol. III. Madrid, 1865.
———. *Diario de Sesiones de las Córtes Generales y Extraordinarias. Dieron principio el 24 de septiembre de 1810 y terminaron el 20 de septiembre de 1813.* 9 vols. Madrid: García, 1870.
Spell, Jefferson Rea. *Rousseau in the Spanish World Before 1833: A Study in Franco-Spanish Literary Relations.* Austin: University of Texas Press, 1938.
Staël, Madame de. *De l'Allemagne.* 2 vols. Paris: Garnier-Flammarion, 1968.
Stanlis, Peter James. *Edmund Burke and the Natural Law.* Ann Arbor: University of Michigan Press, 1958.
Stoetzer, O. Carlos. *El pensamiento político en la América española durante el período de la emancipación (1789–1825).* 2 vols. Madrid: Instituto de Estudios Políticos, 1966.

Street, J. "Lord Strangford and Río de la Plata, 1808–1815." *Hispanic American Historical Review*, 33, No. 4 (November 1953), 477–510.
Suárez, Federico. "Sobre las raíces de la reforma de las Cortes de Cádiz." *Revista de Estudios Políticos*, 126 (November–December 1962), 31–67.
Suárez, Francis. *Selections from Three Works of Francisco Suárez, S.J.: De Legibus, ac Deo legislatore, 1612. Defensio fidei catholicae et apostolicae adversus anglicanae sectae errores, 1613. De triplice virtute theologica, fide, spe, et charitate, 1621.* Oxford: Clarendon, 1944.
———. *Tractatus de Legibus, ac Deo legislatore.* Coimbra: Gómez de Loureyro, 1612.
———. *Tratado de las leyes y de Dios legislador.* Trans. Jaime Torrubiano Ripoll. Madrid: Reus, 1918–21.
Talmon, J. L. *The Origins of Totalitarian Democracy.* London: Secker & Warburg, 1955.
Tapia, Enrique de. *Carlos III y su época: Biografía del siglo XVIII.* Madrid: Aguilar, 1962.
Tejada, Francisco Elías de. "El pensamiento político de Fray José Antonio de San Alberto," in *Universidad de San Francisco Xavier* (Sucre, Bolivia), 16, Nos. 37–38 (January–June 1951), 175–87.
———. *El pensamiento político de los fundadores de Nueva Granada.* Seville: Escuela de Estudios Hispano-Americanos, 1955.
Terra, Helmut de. *Alexander von Humboldt und seine Zeit.* Wiesbaden: Brockhaus, 1956.
Thornton, Mary Crescentia, B.V.M. *The Church and Freemasonry in Brazil, 1872–1875: A Study in Regalism.* Washington, D.C.: Catholic University of America Press, 1948.
Tocornal, Manuel Antonio. "Memoria sobre el primer gobierno nacional leída en la sesión pública de la Universidad de Chile el 7 de noviembre de 1847," in Benjamín Vicuña Mackenna (ed.), *Historia jeneral de la República de Chile desde su independencia hasta nuestros días.* 5 vols. Santiago de Chile: Imprenta nacional, 1866–82. I (1866), 204–206.
Toreno, [José María Queipo de Llano Ruiz de Saravia], conde de. *Historia del levantamiento, guerra y revolución de España.* Vols. 6–8 of Colección de los mejores autores españoles. 3 vols. Paris: Baudry, 1838.
Trigo, Ciro Félix. *Las constituciones de Bolivia.* Madrid: Instituto de Estudios Políticos, 1958.
Troll, Carl. "Alexander von Humboldt," in *Die grossen Deutschen: Deutsche Biographie*, edd. Hermann Heimpel, Theodor Heuss, and Benno Reifenberg. 5 vols. Berlin: Propyläen-Verlag, 1957. III, 175–88.
Tudela, José (ed.). *El legado de España a América.* 2 vols. Madrid: Pegaso, 1954.
Universidad de Oviedo, *El P. Feijóo y su siglo: Ponencias y comunicaciones presentadas al simposio celebrado en la Universidad de Oviedo del 28 de septiembre al 5 de octubre de 1964.* Facultad de Filosofía y Letras. 3 vols. Oviedo: Grossi, 1966.
Universidad Nacional de La Plata. Facultad de Humanidades y Ciencias de la Educación (Depto. de Letras). *Fray Benito Jerónimo Feijóo y Montenegro. Estudios reunidos en conmemoración del II° centenario de su muerte (1764–1964).* Buenos Aires: Kraft, 1965.

Uruguay. Archivo General de la Nación. *Correspondencia del General José Artigas al Cabildo de Montevideo (1814–1816)*. *Correspondencia oficial en Copia. Gobernantes Argentinos, Artigas y Torgués al Cabildo de Montevideo (1814–1816)*. Montevideo: Botella, 1940.
———. Museo Histórico Nacional. Junta Departamental de Montevideo. *Documentos Relativos a la Junta Montevideana de Gobierno de 1808*. Montevideo: Monteverde, 1958–60.
Valle, Rafael Heliodoro. "Cartas de Bentham a José del Valle." *Cuadernos Americanos*, 1, No. 4 (July–August 1942), 127–43.
Vallenilla Lanz, Laureano. *Cesarismo democrático. Estudio sobre las bases sociológicas de la constitución efectiva de Venezuela*. 3d ed. Caracas: Garrido, 1952.
Vargas Machuca, Bernardo de. *Milicia y descripción de las Indias*. 2 vols. Madrid: Suárez, 1892 (reprint of 1st ed., 1599).
Vargas Ugarte, Rubén, s.j. *Don Benito María de Moxó y Francolí, Arzobispo de Charcas*. Buenos Aires: Instituto de Investigaciones históricas, 1931.
———. *El episcopado en los tiempos de la emancipación sudamericana*. 3d ed. Lima: Gil, 1962.
———. *Manual de estudios peruanistas*. Lima: Peruana, 1952; 4th ed. Lima: Gil, 1959.
Vázquez de Menchaca, Fernando. *Controversiarium illustrium aliarumque usu frequentium libri tres*. 4 vols. Valladolid: Cuesta, 1931–34 (reprint of 1st ed., Venice, 1564).
Vega, Pedro de (ed.). *Antología de escritores políticos del siglo de oro*. Clásicos de la política, No. 2. Madrid: Taurus, 1966.
Vergara y Vergara, José María. *Vida y escritos del General Nariño*. Publicaciones del Ministerio de Educación de Colombia. 2d ed. Bogotá: Imprenta nacional, 1946.
Vidaurre [y Encalada], Manuel [Lorenzo] de. *Cartas Americanas, políticas y morales, que contienen muchas reflecciones sobre la Guerra civil de las Américas. Escritas por el ciudadano Manuel de Vidaurre*. 2 vols. Philadelphia: Hurtel, 1823.
———. *Plan del Perú, defectos del gobierno español antiguo, necesarias Reformas. Obra escrita por el ciudadano Manuel de Vidaurre a principios del Año de 10 en Cádiz, y hoy aumentada con interesantes notas. Se dedica al Excmo. Señor Don Simón Bolívar desde Philadelphia, año de 1823*. Philadelphia: Hurtel, 1823.
Vicens Vives, Jaime. *Approaches to the History of Spain*. Berkeley: University of California Press, 1972.
Villanueva, Carlos A. *La monarquía en América*. 4 vols. Paris: Ollendorff, 1913.
Vitoria, Francisco de. *Relecciones de Indias y del derecho de la guerra, con trozos de la referente a la potestad civil*. Madrid: Espasa-Calpe, 1928.
Vizcardo y Guzmán, Juan Pablo, s.j. *Carta derijida a los españoles americanos*. London: Boyle, 1801. Appendix, Miguel Batllori, s.j. *El abate Viscardo. Historia y mito de la intervención de los jesuitas en la independencia de Hispanoamérica*. Instituto Panamericano de Geografía e Historia, Comisión de Historia, Comité de Orígenes de la Emancipación–Caracas. Publicación No. 10. Caracas: Imprenta de la Pontificia Universidad Gregoriana [Rome], 1953. Appendix, Manuel Giménez Fernández. *Las ideas populistas en la independencia de Hispanoamérica*. Seville: Escuela de Estudios Hispano-Americanos, 1947.

Vossler, Karl. *Fray Luis de León*. Buenos Aires: Espasa-Calpe, 1946.
Wagner, Henry Rapp, and Parish, Helen Rand (coll.). *The Life and Writings of Bartolomé de Las Casas*. Albuquerque: University of New Mexico Press, 1967.
Warren, Fintan B., O.F.M. *Vasco de Quiroga and his Pueblo Hospitals of Santa Fe*. Washington, D.C.: Academy of American Franciscan History, 1963.
Webster, C. K. (ed.). *Britain and the Independence of Latin America, 1812-1830. Select Documents from the Foreign Office Archives*. 2 vols. London: Oxford University Press, 1938.
Weckmann, Luis. *Las bulas alejandrinas de 1493 y la teoría política del Papado medieval: Estudio de la supremacía papal sobre islas, 1091-1491*. Publicaciones del Instituto de Historia, Series 1, No. 11. Mexico: Universidad Nacional Autónoma de México, 1949.
Whitaker, Arthur Preston (ed.). *Latin America and the Enlightenment*. New York: Appleton-Century, 1942.
———. "Las sociedades científicas latinoamericanas desde el siglo XVIII," in *Academia Colombiana de Historia*, Conferencias de 1946 y 1947, pp. 99-109.
———. "The Elhuyar Mining Missions and the Enlightenment." *Hispanic American Historical Review*, 31, No. 4 (November 1951), 557-85.
———. *The United States and Argentina*. Cambridge: Harvard University Press, 1954.
Wolf, Erik. *Grosse Rechtsdenker der deutschen Geistesgeschichte*. Tübingen: Mohr, 1944.
Zavala, Silvio. *América en el espíritu francés del siglo XVIII*. Mexico: Colegio Nacional, 1949.
———. *Ensayos sobre la colonización española en América*. Buenos Aires: Emecé, 1944.
———. *La filosofía política en la conquista de América*. Mexico: Cultura Económica, 1947.
———. *La utopía de Tomás Moro en la Nueva España*. Mexico: Porrúa, 1937.
———. *New Viewpoints on the Spanish Colonization of America*. Philadelphia: University of Pennsylvania Press, 1943.
———. *Recuerdo de Vasco de Quiroga*. Mexico: Porrúa, 1965.
———. "The American Utopia of the Sixteenth Century." *The Huntington Library Quarterly*, 10 (1947), 337-47.
———. *The Defense of Human Rights in Latin America, Sixteenth to Eighteenth Centuries*. Paris: UNESCO, 1964.
Zea, Leopoldo. "La filosofía mexicana en el siglo XIX." *Filosofía y Letras*, 27 (July-September 1947), 61-88.
Zéndegui, Guillermo de, et al. "The Rediscovery of the New World. From Columbus to Humboldt." *Americas*, 24, No. 8 (August 1972), (S) 1-24.
Zinny, Antonio. *Historia de los gobernantes del Paraguay (1535-1887)*. Buenos Aires: Mayo, 1887.

INDEX NOMINUM

Abad, Diego José, 33, 89, 90, 124, 125
Abad y Queipo, Manuel, 154, 238, 249
Abascal y Souza, José Fernando (Viceroy), 98, 155, 166, 180, 215, 226, 233, 235, 236, 241
Acevedo, Manuel Antonio de, 136
Achega, Domingo (canon), 208
Acosta, José de, 30, 35, 36, 37, 48, 99
Aguado, Pedro de, 38, 58n172
Agüero, Julián Segundo de, 244
Aguiar y Acuña, 205, 211
Aguilar, José, 48
Aguirre, Guillermo de (*oidor*), 171, 191
Aldama, Ignacio, 192, 193
Alegre, Francisco Javier, 33, 89, 90, 124, 125
Alexander VI, Pope, 16, 55n90, 164, 224
Alfonso X, the Learned (King of Castile), 5, 14n40, 20, 51, 55n91, 138, 249, 262
Alfonso XI, the Just (King of Castile), 8, 14n40, 20
Allende, Ignacio, 192, 193
Althusius, Johannes, 27, 61, 262
Altuna, Manuel Ignacio, 70
Álvarez de Cienfuegos, Nicolás, 70, 75, 107n76
Alvear, Carlos María de, 187, 221
Alzaga, Martín de, 157, 172, 173, 198, 217, 252n98
Amar y Borbon, Antonio (Viceroy), 174, 175, 176, 209, 214, 233
Amat y Junient, Manuel de (Viceroy), 80, 119
"Amor de la Patria," José, 222, 223
Apodaca, Juan Ruiz de (Viceroy), 247
Aquinas, Thomas, St., 17, 18, 20, 21, 24, 28, 31, 33, 35, 39, 40, 44, 45, 46, 47, 48, 49, 51, 52, 54n79, 55n87, 59n279, 59n285, 80, 85, 92, 93, 105, 122, 123, 124, 125, 127, 128, 131, 132, 133, 134, 135, 137, 138, 149n142, 213, 214, 215, 249, 255n323, 259, 262
Aranda, Conde de, 66, 68, 70, 98, 141, 153, 154, 188, 251n19

Aráoz, Bernabé, 234
Aráoz, Pedro Miguel, 135, 136
Arce y Miranda, Andrés de, 89
Argerich, Cosme, 196, 199
Aristotle, 17, 23, 27, 32, 33, 35, 38, 39, 40, 44, 45, 46, 50, 51, 67, 80, 90, 101, 105, 123, 124, 125, 126, 127, 128, 130, 131, 132, 135, 255n323
Arriaga, José de, 48
Arroyal, León de, 70, 107n71, 107n76, 108n80
Artigas, José Gervasio, 176, 188, 208, 217, 218, 220, 221, 255n315
Asso, Ignacio Jordán de, 66, 71
Atienza, Juan de, 48
Augustine, St., 17, 35, 38, 44, 46, 60, 85, 105, 127, 138, 213, 255n323, 259
Avendaño, Diego de, 45, 47, 48, 49
Avila, Esteban de, 46, 48
Azanza, Miguel José, 75, 156, 201
Azara, Félix de, 87
Azcuénga, Miguel, 196
Azpilcueta, Martín de, 26, 47, 52, 53n74, 59n285, 138, 139, 260

Bacon, Francis, 40, 65, 67, 89, 90, 97, 262
Báñez, Domingo, 20, 30, 37, 52, 139, 260
Baquíjano y Carrillo, José (Conde de Vistaflorida), 83, 97, 98, 99, 104, 110n183, 126
Bartolache, José Ignacio, 83, 90, 91
Baudin, Louis, 86, 96
Bayle, Pierre, 85, 99, 105, 127
Belgrano, Manuel, 85, 103, 135, 160, 167, 185, 187, 188, 196, 202, 206, 208, 216, 219, 235, 241, 244, 245, 256n400
Bellarmine, Robert (Cardinal), 24, 49, 52, 54n74, 138, 139
Bello, Andrés, 50, 122, 160, 228
Bentham, Jeremy, 71, 84
Beresford, William Carr (Colonel), 146
Berutti, Antonio Luis, 174, 234
Bodin, Jean, 29, 41, 42, 67

294 SCHOLASTIC ROOTS

Bolívar, Simón, 85, 95, 96, 111n235, 123, 155, 156, 160, 162, 166, 186, 187, 188, 194, 210, 227, 228, 229, 233, 234, 242, 243, 245, 247, 248, 249, 251n16, 257n409, 260, 261
Bossuet, Jacques, 65, 105
Bouger, Pierre, 86, 96
Boves, José Tomás, 155, 242
Bowles, Guillermo, 69
Brackenridge, Henry M., 161
Brahe, Tycho, 99, 101
Bravo, Nicolás, 194
Bucareli y Ursúa, Antonio María (Viceroy), 137–38
Bueno, Cosme, 96, 98
Bustamante, Carlos María de, 237, 242, 256n387

Caballero, José Agustín, 92
Caballero y Góngora, Antonio (Archbishop–Viceroy), 87, 139
Cabarrús, Count Francisco de, 64, 66, 70, 71, 75, 78, 108n80, 156
Cabrera, Juan de, 75, 109n99
Cadalso, José, 66, 70, 108n80
Caicedo, Luis, 209, 233
Caillés, Jaime, 17
Cajetan, Thomas de Vio (Cardinal), 21, 55n87, 138
Caldas, Francisco José de, 92, 154
Caldera, Francisco Javier, 99, 143
Calderón de la Barca, Pedro, 39, 40, 140
Calleja del Rey, Félix María, 155, 166, 193, 194, 241, 242
Calzada, General, 155, 242
Camacho, Joaquín, 92, 209, 213
Campillo y Cossío, José del, 71, 253n218
Campomanes, Pedro Rodríguez de, 66, 68, 69, 73, 77, 86, 88, 93, 104, 107n63, 107n71, 108n80, 110n183, 119, 121, 153, 206
Campostelano, Pedro, 17
Campoy, José Rafael, 90, 124
Cañete, Pedro Vicente, 132, 186, 214, 227, 233, 249
Cano, Melchor, 20, 30, 105, 124, 134, 260
Canterac, José de, 242, 247
Capmany, Antonio de, 66, 108n80
Carlota Joaquina (Queen of Portugal, sister of Ferdinand VII), 136, 167, 173, 215, 218, 233

Carmen, José Elías del, 101, 102, 133, 137
Carranza, Bartolomé, 30, 260
Carrera brothers (José Miguel, Juan José, and Luis), 233
Castellanos, Juan de, 38, 58n172, 260
Castelli, Juan José, 102, 135, 136, 155, 167, 174, 186, 187, 195, 196, 198, 201, 202, 204, 208, 216, 219, 234, 249, 263
Castro, Agustín de, 33, 89, 90, 124
Castro Barros, Pedro Ignacio de, 136, 244
Catholic rulers, 4, 6, 17, 32, 56n101, 224
Cavanilles, Antonio, 66
Cavo, Andrés, 125
Ceballos y Mier, Fernando, 75, 77, 108n99
Celis, Isidoro de, 96, 98
Celis, Miguel Rubén de, 102, 103
Cervantes de Salazar, Francisco, 32
Charles II (King of Spain), 2, 71
Charles III (King of Spain), 10, 64, 66, 69, 71, 72, 73, 76, 78, 91, 96, 104, 109n125, 115, 116, 117, 120, 147, 151, 152, 154, 157, 172, 206, 250n1, 251n19, 258, 259
Charles IV (King of Spain), 72, 73, 74, 119, 146, 155, 168, 169, 172, 173, 189
Charles V (Emperor), 2–5, 8–11, 14n49, 16, 19, 20, 22, 29, 32, 33, 37, 39, 51, 52, 53n23, 58n171, 158, 200
Chorroarín, Luis José, 102, 135, 136, 196
Cigala, Francisco Ignacio, 83, 89, 124
Cisneros, Diego, 97, 98, 154
Cisneros, Baltasar Hidalgo de (Viceroy), 173, 176, 183, 186, 195, 196, 197, 209, 215, 233, 252n98
Cisneros, Francisco Jiménez de (Cardinal), 16, 19, 21–22, 52
Clavijero, Francisco Javier, 89, 90, 91, 124, 125, 192
"Clavijo y Fajardo, José" (Alvarez de Valladares), 70, 71
Colbert, Jean Baptiste, 71, 72
Condamine, Charles de la, 86, 96
Condillac, Etienne Bonnot, 67, 69, 84, 85, 89, 90, 92, 97, 101, 102, 103, 122, 127, 135, 139, 206, 254n219
Condorcet, Marquis de, 61, 92, 122
Conquista, Conde de la, 223, 224
Copernicus, Nicolaus, 40, 92, 96, 99, 101, 262
Coriche, Cristóbal de, 83, 89
Cortés, Hernán, 11, 27, 32, 56n92, 91, 194
Cortés de Madariaga, José, 187, 227

Cos, José María, 194, 242, 256n385
Covarrubias, Diego de, 22, 30, 52, 59n278, 121, 129, 138, 139, 255n323, 260
Croix, Marqués Carlos Francisco de (Viceroy), 92, 116, 119
Cruz, Juana Inés de la (Sister), 22, 45, 90

Dombey, Joseph, 86, 96
Descartes, René, 40, 48, 60, 65, 83, 84, 89, 90, 92, 96, 97, 99, 100, 101, 102, 105, 122, 123, 126, 127, 131, 132, 133, 134, 135
Díaz de Gamarra y Dávalos, Juan Benito, 89, 90, 123
Díaz del Castillo, Bernal, 27, 32
Diderot, Denis, 61, 70, 84, 86, 92, 107n76, 122, 160
Duns Scotus, John, 32, 33, 35, 44, 45, 46, 50, 51, 93, 101, 123, 124, 127, 129, 130, 131, 132, 133, 136, 137, 262
Duquesne, José Domingo, 92

Egaña, Juan, 144, 160, 186, 188, 244, 245
Eguiara y Eguren, Juan José de, 89, 91
Elhuyar, Fausto de, 87, 91
Elhuyar, Juan José de, 87
Elío, Francisco Javier de (Governor), 172, 177, 178, 179, 180, 183, 184, 185, 217, 218, 219, 242
Elizalde Ita y Parra, Mariano Gregorio de, 89
Emparán, Vicente de (Field Marshal), 227, 233
Enríquez, Camilo, 100, 233
Erasmus, Desiderius (of Rotterdam), 19, 20, 28, 32, 48, 53n23
Escalada, Antonio José de, 196, 199
Escalada, Francisco Antonio, 196
Escalona y Agüero, Gaspar, 42
Escandón, Ignacio de, 83, 97
España, José María, 139, 144
Esquilache, Marqués de, 66
Exímenis, Francisco de, 17, 38
Eymerich, Nicolás, 17

Fabri, Manuel, 125
Falkner, Tomás, 100, 132
Farragut, Juan León, 196, 199
Febrés Oms, Andrés, 126, 127, 142
Feijóo y Montenegro, Benito Jerónimo, 45, 65, 66, 68, 69, 76, 77, 78, 79, 82, 83, 85, 88, 89, 90, 92, 93, 94, 96, 97, 100, 105, 107n43, 108n80, 123, 124, 127, 128, 130, 138, 139, 206, 255n323, 262
Ferdinand V (King of Aragon), 6, 16, 22, 28, 52, 55n90
Ferdinand VI (King of Spain), 72, 73, 113, 114
Ferdinand VII (King of Spain), 151, 155, 157, 158, 159, 162, 163, 164, 165, 166, 167, 169, 170, 171, 172, 173, 181, 182, 186, 187, 189, 190, 191, 193, 194, 195, 196, 197, 198, 201, 202, 203, 204, 207, 208, 210, 212, 213, 220, 221, 223, 224, 225, 227, 229, 230, 231, 232, 233, 235, 236, 238, 239, 240, 241, 242, 245, 246, 247, 248, 251n50, 251n54, 259, 261
Ferguson, Adam, 66, 67
Fernández, Melchor, 101, 134, 135, 196, 199
Fernández de Agüero y Echagüe, Juan Manuel, 102, 105, 121, 135, 136
Fernández de Enciso, Martín, 11, 32
Fernández de Lizardi, José Joaquín, 90
Fernández de Oviedo, Gonzalo, 32
Ferrer Gorráiz, Vicente, 71
Figueroa, Tomás de, 225
Filmer, Sir Robert, 3, 104
Finestrad, Joaquín de, 104, 121
Finísola, Vicente, 162
Flores Estrada, Alvaro, 70
Floridablanca, Conde de, 66, 68, 74, 75, 77, 119, 153, 167
Fonseca, Juan Rodríguez de (Bishop), 3, 52
Forner, Juan Pablo, 77, 108n80
Foronda, Valentín de, 70, 253n218
Fox Morcillo, Sebastián, 23
Franciz, Gaspar Rodríguez de, 184, 188, 222, 233
Franco Dávila, Pedro, 93
Franklin, Benjamin, 92, 122
French, Domingo, 174, 234
Funes, Gregorio (Dean), 102, 132, 136, 137, 199, 202, 206, 207, 242, 243, 254n219

Gálvez, José de, 87, 104, 115
García, Pantaleón, 199, 242, 243
García, Pedro Andrés, 196, 199
García Carrasco, Francisco Antonio, 233

García Ros, Governor, 140
Garcilaso de la Vega, Inca, 23, 26
Garibay, Pedro (Viceroy), 172
Gasca, Pedro de la (Bishop), 36, 239
Gassendi, Pierre, 65, 84, 90, 92, 96, 100, 101, 105, 122, 132, 133, 134, 135
Gattinara, Mercurino Arborio di, 19, 53n23
Giles of Rome (Aegidius Romanus), 17, 54n87, 127
Gillespie, Alexander, 86
Ginés de Sepúlveda, Juan, 21, 27, 28, 30, 43
Giovio, Paolo, 37, 38
Godoy, Manuel (Prince of Peace), 119, 154, 168, 169, 170, 188, 197, 198, 201, 226, 229, 259
Gómez, José Valentín, 101, 134, 135, 137
Gómez de Vidaurre Girón, Felipe, 99, 126, 143
Gorriti, Juan Ignacio, 136, 199
Goyeneche, José Manuel de, 165, 167, 198, 215, 216
Gracián, Baltasar, 16, 23, 39, 49
Gramusset, Antoine, 143
Granada, Luis de, 22, 23, 51
Grigera, Joaquín, 196, 199
Grimaldi, Marqués de, 66, 69
Grotius, Hugo, 27, 61, 62, 105, 255n323, 262
Grúa Talamanca, Miguel de la, Marqués de Branciforte (Viceroy), 119
Gual, Pedro, 139, 144
Güemes, Martín, 234
Güemes Pacheco de Padilla, Juan Vicente, Conde de Revillagigedo (Viceroy), see Revillagigedo
Guerrero, Vicente, 172, 194, 246
Guevara y Basoazábal, Andrés de, 89, 124
Guirior, Manuel de (Viceroy), 87, 119
Gundisalvo, Domingo, 17
Guridi y Alcocer, José Miguel, 213, 238
Gutiérrez, Frutos Joaquín, 175, 213

Hänke, Thaddeus, 87, 96
Heineccius, Johann Gottlieb, 84, 255n323, 262
Helvetius, 61, 67, 94, 96, 160
Herrera, Ignacio de, 209, 213, 214
Hervás y Panduro, Lorenzo, 75, 109n99
Hidalgo de Cisneros, Baltasar, see Cisneros

Hidalgo y Costilla, Miguel, 143, 145, 155, 172, 192, 193, 194, 233, 249
Hispano, Juan, 17
Hispano, Pedro (Pope John XXI), 17, 33
Hobbes, Thomas, 29, 40, 41, 61, 63, 65, 67, 96, 105, 134
Holbach, Paul Heinrich d', 85, 96, 98, 160
Hugh of St. Victor, 17
Humboldt, Alexander von, 5, 80, 84, 86, 87, 90, 91, 94, 96, 168, 211
Hume, David, 96, 127
Hurtado de Mendoza, Andrés (Viceroy), 37

Ignatius Loyola, St., 21, 22, 122
Infante, José Miguel, 223, 224
Irala, see Martínez de Irala
Iriarte, Tomás de, 71
Isabella (Queen of Castile), 6, 22, 28, 52, 53n23, 55n90, 209
Isidore of Seville, St., 18, 22, 28, 140, 262, 263
Isla, José Francisco de, 90, 108n80
Iturbide, Agustín de, 154, 155, 194, 233, 246, 247, 248
Iturrigaray y Aróstegui, José Joaquín Vicente de (Viceroy), 119, 168, 169, 170, 171, 172, 176, 180, 189, 190, 191, 192, 251n72

James I (King of England), 24
Jardine, Alexander, 66
Jesus Christ, 212, 228, 235, 236, 238
Jiménez de Cisneros, Francisco (Cardinal), see Cisneros
Jiménez de Quesada, Gonzalo 23, 37, 38, 58n172
Joan (Queen of Castile), 2
John VI (King of Portugal, Brazil, and Algarve; Dom João), 167, 219
John of Salisbury, 17
John of the Cross, St., 22
Joseph Bonaparte (King of Spain, Grand Duke of Berg), 75, 156, 157, 159, 172, 189, 214, 227, 259
Jovellanos, Gaspar Melchor de, 65, 66, 67, 68, 69, 70, 71, 75, 77, 78, 81, 83, 90, 92, 99, 108n80, 117, 119, 121, 200, 201, 206, 207, 213, 253n218, 262
Juan, Jorge, 86, 96, 113, 144

Kant, Immanuel, 63
Kepler, John, 40, 127
Keppel, Sir George (Count of Albemarle), 10

La Serna, José de, 247
Las Heras, Bartolomé de (Archbishop), 247
Labardón, Manuel de, 135
Landívar, Rafael, 90, 91
Lardizábal, Minister, 238, 248
Larraín, Tomás, 93, 131
Las Casas, Bartolomé de, 27–30, 32, 35, 36, 38, 47, 52, 56n104, 110n130, 114, 129, 209, 260
Lasso de la Vega, Rafael, 248
Ledesma, Bartolomé de, 33
Legaria, José Antonio de, 89
Leibniz, Gottfried Wilhelm von, 20, 40, 84, 97, 100, 126, 134, 135, 138
León, Luis de, 22, 23, 33, 51, 58n186
León Pinelo, Antonio de, 42, 49, 205, 211
Liendo y Goicoechea, Antonio de, 83, 92
Liniers y Brémont, Santiago de, 146, 157, 164, 165, 172, 173, 177, 178, 179, 180, 182, 183, 198, 202, 206, 217, 225
Linnaeus, Carolus, 87
Lizana y Beaumont, Francisco Javier (Archbishop, Viceroy), 172
Lizárraga, Reginaldo de, 37
Llano Zapata, José Eusebio de, 97, 98
Locke, John, 40, 61, 63, 65, 66, 67, 69, 70, 84, 89, 90, 91, 93, 97, 102, 103, 107n58, 107n76, 127, 129, 134, 135, 136, 159, 206, 212, 255n323
Lope de Vega, 51
López, Estanislao, 234
López de Gómara, Francisco, 27, 32
López de Palacios Rubios, Juan, *see* Palacios Rubios
López y Planes, Vicente, 136, 196
López Rayón, Ignacio, *see* Rayón, Ignacio López
Lorenzana, Francisco Antonio (Archbishop), 107n34, 122, 141
Lozano de Peralta, Jorge Tadeo, 92, 187, 233
Lué y Riega, Benito de la (Bishop), 174
Lull, Ramón, 17, 44, 132
Luna Pizarro, Francisco Javier, 98

Mably, Gabriel Bonnot de, 61, 69, 160, 254n219
Macanaz, Melchor Rafael de, 73, 78, 86, 90
Macchiavelli, Niccolò, 24, 37, 41, 58n185, 200
Maciel, Juan Baltasar, 85, 102, 104, 105, 121
Magariños y Ballinas, Mateo, 180, 182
Malaspina, 87, 96
Maldonado, Pedro Vicente, 93
Malebranche, Nicolas de, 84, 92, 122, 126, 134
Maneiro, Juan Luis, 90, 125
Mañer, Salvador José, 93, 94
Marchena y Ruiz de Cueto, José, 70, 107n76
Marcó del Pont, Francisco Casimiro, 166, 241, 242, 244
Mariana, Juan de, 20, 23, 26, 42, 49, 51, 52, 54n76, 68, 73, 74, 105, 109n99, 121, 128, 139, 209, 244, 249, 254n221, 255n323, 258, 259, 260
Marín, Joaquín, 75, 77, 109n99
Márquez, Juan, 52, 58n186, 59n280
Marsilius of Padua, 17
Martínez de Irala, Domingo, 11, 37
Martínez de Rozas, Juan, 186, 233, 255n323
Martínez Marina, Francisco, 70, 201, 234
Matamoros, Mariano, 193, 194
Matienzo, Juan de, 36, 42, 138, 255n323
Mazarredo, José de, 75, 156, 201
Medina, Bartolomé de, 51
Medrano, Mariano, 101, 134, 136, 199
Meléndez Valdés, Juan, 66, 70, 75, 107n76
Menchaca, *see* Vázquez de Menchaca
Méndez, Ramón Ignacio, 243
Mendieta, Gerónimo de, 27
Mendoza, Antonio de (Viceroy), 34, 35
Mercado, Tomás de, 33
Mier y Nóbrega, Servando Teresa de, 213, 250
Millás, Joaquín, 102
Miranda, Francisco de, 13, 85, 86, 94, 95, 139, 142, 144, 145, 146, 150n185, 151, 155, 185, 228, 234, 241, 242, 260
Mitre, Bartolomé, 164, 165
Mociño, José Mariano, 83, 91
Molas, Mariano Antonio, 188, 221
Molina, Juan Ignacio, 99, 126
Molina, Luis de, 20, 23, 32, 42, 49, 52, 68, 73, 109n99, 121, 128, 138, 139, 249, 255n323, 258, 259, 260

Moñino, José, *see* Floridablanca, Conde de
Monteagudo, Bernardo de, 85, 103, 122, 123, 186, 234
Montes, Toribio, 226, 229, 233
Montesquieu, Charles Louis de Sécondat, Baron de la Brède, etc., 61, 67, 69, 70, 71, 79, 84, 85, 86, 92, 96, 105, 107n76, 110n159, 122, 129, 139, 160, 200, 205, 255n323
Monteverde, Domingo de, 228, 241
Morales, Manuel, 99, 101, 102
More, Thomas, St., 28, 32, 38
Morelos y Pavón, José María, 145, 163, 172, 192, 193, 194, 233, 237, 238, 242, 245, 249, 256n370, 258
Moreno, José Ignacio, 97, 98
Moreno, Mariano, 20, 136, 146, 163, 196, 198, 201, 202, 204, 205, 207, 212, 225, 249, 254n238, 257n418, 262, 263
Morillo, Pablo, 155, 166, 210, 233, 241, 242, 248
Motolinía, Tomás de, 29, 32
Moxó y Francolí, Benito María de (Archbishop), 167, 235, 244
Muriel, Domingo, 100, 102, 132
Murillo, Pedro Domingo, 214, 215
Mutis, José Celestino, 83, 86, 87, 92, 129

Napoleon Bonaparte, 75, 79, 111n235, 147, 155, 156, 157, 159, 160, 162, 163, 164, 165, 169, 170, 172, 173, 176, 179, 181, 187, 189, 193, 197, 198, 201, 202, 219, 222, 223, 226, 227, 229, 230, 236, 240, 245, 249, 258, 259, 260, 261, 262, 263
Nariño, Antonio, 20, 93, 94, 122, 128, 129, 139, 154, 187, 205, 209, 210, 211, 213, 231, 233, 262
Navarro, Doctor, *see* Azpilcueta Martín de,
Newton, Sir Isaac, 27, 40, 65, 82, 84, 92, 96, 100, 101, 105, 108n81, 122, 127, 132, 133, 134, 135, 262
Nordenflicht, Baron von, 85, 87

Obés, Lucas José, 180, 181, 183
O'Donojú, Juan, 247
O'Farrill y Herrera, Gonzalo, 75, 156, 201
O'Higgins, Bernardo, 155, 162, 188, 233, 248, 249
Olañeta, Pedro Antonio de, 242
Olavide, Pablo de, 73, 77, 86, 95, 97, 98, 99, 126, 138
Olea, Nicolás de, 48
Oñate, Pedro de, 48
O'Reilly, Alejandro, 69

Páez, José Antonio, 241, 242
Palacios Rubios, Juan López de, 28, 55n91, 56n101
Pascal, Blaise, 39, 139
Paso, Juan José, 101, 167, 196
Paúl, Felipe Fermín, 228
Payne, Thomas, 92, 122
Paz, Matías de, 28, 55n91
Pelayo, Alvaro, 17
Peña, Juan de la, 30, 260
Peñafiel, Alonso de, 45, 47
Peñafiel, Leonardo de, 45, 47
Peñaflorida, Conde de, 70
Peñalosa, Pedro de, 75, 109n99
Peñalver, Fernando, 228, 242, 243, 249, 256n389
Peralta Barnuevo, Pedro de, 93, 96, 97, 98
Perdriel, Juan, 136
Pereira de Figueiredo, Antonio, 86
Pérez Castellanos, José María, 180, 181, 220
Pérez de Menacho, Juan, 45, 47, 48
Pérez Valiente, Pedro José, 75, 109n99
Pérez y López, Antonio Javier, 75, 77, 108n80, 109n99
Perlín, Juan, 48
Peter of Ghent, 28, 34
Pezuela, Joaquín de la, 216
Philip II (King of Spain), 2, 6, 8, 9, 22, 31, 39, 41, 52
Philip III (King of Spain), 42
Philip IV (King of Spain), 42
Philip V (King of Spain), 10, 72, 108n84, 114, 117
Picornell, Juan, 144
Piquer, Andrés, 77
Pius VII, Pope, 241, 243, 248
Plato, 44, 255n323
Pombal, Marquês de, 141
Popham, Sir Home, 146, 178
Posadas, Gervasio (Director), 243, 245
Power y Giral, Ramón, 232
Pozo y Sucre, José del, 142
Prado Portocarrero, José de, 10
Primo de Verdad y Ramos, Francisco, 171, 188, 191, 192

INDEX NOMINUM   299

Pueyrredón, Juan Martín de, 167, 188, 219, 234, 245
Pufendorf, Samuel, 27, 61, 62, 63, 70, 84, 91, 100, 101, 102, 105, 110n163, 133, 138, 220, 254n219, 255n311, 255n323, 262

Quesnay, François, 71, 160
Quevedo y Villegas, Agustín de, 93, 129, 130
Quevedo y Villegas, Francisco de, 23, 52, 138, 255n323, 260
Quintana, Manuel José de, 75, 92
Quintana, Pedro de, 16
Quintana Róo, Andrés, 194, 242
Quiroga, Vasco de, 28, 32, 38

Ramírez, Francisco, 234
Raynal, Guillaume-Thomas de, 61, 67, 71, 84, 85, 86, 87, 90, 92, 94, 110n159, 122, 139, 205
Rayón, Ignacio López, 193, 194, 256n385
Restrepo, José Félix de, 128, 129
Revillagigedo, Conde de, 71, 87, 118, 119, 168
Ribera, Lázaro de, 101, 102, 104, 121, 235
Ricla, Conde de, 10
Riego, Rafael de, 246, 248
Río, Andrés Manuel del, 91
Rivadavia, Bernardino, 103, 136, 155, 188, 196, 241
Rivarola, Pantaleón, 102, 135, 136
Rivero Araníbar, Mariano, 97, 98
Rodríguez, José Cayetano, 101, 133, 136, 242
Rodríguez, Martín, 195
Rodríguez, Simón, 95, 96, 111n232
Rodríguez de Fonseca, Bishop, see Fonseca
Rodríguez de Mendoza, Toribio, 83, 97, 98, 154
Rodríguez Peña, Nicolás, 167, 174, 201
Rodríguez Peña, Saturnino, 201, 219
Rojas, José Antonio, 85, 100, 143
Rondeau, José, 187, 216, 219, 220
Rosas, Juan Manuel de, 176, 234
Roscio, Juan Germán, 227, 228, 243
Rousseau, Jean Jacques, 24–25, 61, 63, 64, 65, 67, 69, 70, 71, 75, 77, 84, 85, 86, 89, 91, 92, 94, 95, 96, 98, 99, 100, 101, 102, 103, 105, 107n76, 110n159, 111n229, 111n232, 111n235, 121, 122, 128, 129, 138, 139, 142, 143, 144, 145, 159, 160, 199, 201, 204, 205, 206, 207, 208, 209, 212, 228, 238, 242, 244, 250, 254n219,
254n244, 254n256, 255n323, 256n370, 257n418, 262
Rubio Rodensis, Antonio, 33, 50
Ruiz de Castilla, 225, 226, 233
Ruiz de la Mota (Bishop), 19
Ruiz Huidobro, Pascual, 178, 195, 196, 217
Ruiz López, Hipólito, 83, 96

Saavedra, Cornelio de, 136, 163, 173, 174, 195, 196, 198, 201, 206, 207, 233, 234, 249, 254n238, 263
Saavedra Fajardo, Diego, 52, 129, 139, 254n221, 260
Sahagún, Bernardino de, 32
Salas, Manuel de, 99, 138
Salas, Ramón de, 70, 71
Samaniego, Félix María de, 71, 77
San Alberto, José Antonio de, 104, 121
San Martín, José de, 155, 160, 162, 166, 186, 188, 198, 216, 244, 245, 247, 248, 249, 258, 260, 261
San Martín, Tomás, 46
Sánchez Carrión, José Faustino, 98, 122
Sánchez de Arévalo, Rodríguez, 17
Santa Ana, Antonio López de, 242
Santa Cruz y Espejo, Francisco Javier Eugenio de, 83, 86, 93, 110n183, 151
Santa María, Juan de, 52, 58n185
Santander, Francisco de Paula, 188, 249
Sarmiento, Martín, 75
Sarratea, Manuel de, 163, 187, 219, 240, 241, 259
Sassenay, Bernard de, 164, 165, 179
Selva Alegre, Marqués de, 225, 233, 238
Sepúlveda, see Ginés de Sepúlveda
Servet, Miguel, 23
Sessé y Lancaster, Martín de, 83, 91
Sigüenza y Góngora, Carlos de, 45, 82, 89, 90
Smith, Adam, 66, 71, 129, 206, 253n218
Smith, Admiral Sir Sidney, 167
Sobremonte, Rafael de, Marqués de (Viceroy), 116, 138, 146, 173, 178, 182, 217
Sola, Juan Nepomuceno de, 174, 195–96
Solórzano Pereira, Juan de, 2, 42, 43, 49, 52, 105, 122, 136, 138, 139, 159, 164, 205, 209, 211, 245, 254n221
Soto, Domingo de, 20, 22, 23, 30, 33, 37, 42, 44, 51, 52, 138, 139, 245, 255n323, 260
Soto y Marne, Francisco, 83, 125
Spinoza, Baruch, 20, 40, 67, 81, 96, 127, 134

Strangford, Lord (6th Viscount), 167, 219
Suárez, Anastasio Mariano, 133, 137
Suárez, Francisco, 18, 20, 22–26, 27, 29–30, 32, 33, 35, 40, 42, 43, 44, 46, 47, 48, 49, 50, 51, 52, 54n70, 54n74, 54n75, 54n79, 68, 73, 74, 77, 108n84, 109n99, 121, 122, 123, 124, 126, 127, 128, 129, 131, 132, 133, 134, 137, 138, 139, 142, 144, 157, 159, 166, 167, 193, 194, 198, 199, 200, 201, 205, 206, 207, 209, 213, 215, 231, 242, 244, 245, 249, 250, 253n188, 254n221, 254n244, 254n256, 255n323, 258, 259, 260, 262
Suárez, Mariano, 100, 132
Sucre, Antonio José de, 226, 248, 249

Talamantes Salvador y Baeza, Melchor de, 188, 190, 191
Tanucci, Bernardo di, 69, 141
Tenorio, Ignacio (*oidor* of Quito), 186, 211, 212, 227, 233, 249
Teresa de Jesús, St., 22
Thomasius, Christian, 27, 61, 63, 262
Toledo, Francisco de (Viceroy), 29, 32, 46, 51, 143
Toro Zambrano, José de (Bishop), 138, 139
Torquemada, Juan de (Cardinal), 49, 52
Torres, Camilo, 139, 158, 175, 186, 210, 211, 212, 213, 231, 233, 249
Torres, Diego de, 48, 50
Torres Villarroel, Diego, 90, 108n80
Tupac Amarú II (José Gabriel Condorcanqui), 139, 143, 145, 216
Turgot, Anne Robert Jacques, 70, 71, 107n76

Ulloa, Antonio de, 86, 96, 113, 144
Ulloa, Bernardo de, 71, 108n80
Ulloa, Francisco de, 92
Unanúe, Hipólito, 82, 83, 96, 97, 98, 122, 123, 126
Urquijo, Mariano, 75, 119, 156
Uztáriz, Francisco Javier, 228
Uztáriz, Gerónimo de, 66, 71, 108n80, 253n218

Valdivia, Pedro de, 11, 26
Valencia, Pedro de, 21, 23, 47
Valero, Tomás, 93, 129, 130
Valle, José Cecilio del, 89, 110n183, 186

Vargas, Pedro Fermín de, 128, 129
Vargas Machuca, Bernardo de, 38, 146, 260
Vázquez de Menchaca, Fernando, 30, 47, 59n285, 121, 129, 138, 139, 260
Velasco, Bernardo de, 184, 185, 221
Velasco, Juan de, 93
Venegas, Francisco Javier de, 155, 172, 233
Vera Cruz, Alonso de la, 22, 33, 34
Vergne, Antoine Alexandre, 143, 144
Verney, Luiz Antonio, 84
Vértiz, Juan José de (Viceroy), 80, 119
Vico, Giambattista, 105
Victoria, Guadalupe (Félix Fernández), 194, 246
Vidaurre, Manuel Lorenzo de, 98
Videla del Pino, Nicolás (Bishop), 235
Vieytes, Juan Hipólito, 136, 167, 198, 219, 253n218
Vigodet, Gaspar de, 184, 217, 218
Villafañe, Diego León, 143
Villota, Celedonio (*fiscal*), 195, 214, 227, 233, 252n110
Vitoria, Francisco de, 20, 22, 23, 24, 27–30, 33, 35, 43, 47, 52, 56n101, 57n107, 77, 105, 129, 138, 139, 199, 200, 209, 250, 255n323, 260
Vives, José Luis, 19, 21, 23, 32, 48
Vizcardo y Guzmán, Juan Pablo de, 95, 142
Voltaire, 61, 65, 69, 79, 84, 85, 86, 92, 96, 98, 99, 101, 105, 110n159, 110n168, 111n254, 122, 133, 134, 139, 160, 252n133

Wall, Ricardo, 69, 137
Ward, Bernardo, 66, 69, 71
Whitelocke, John, 146
William of Auvergne, 17
Witte, Nicholas de, 58n171, 154
Wolff, Christian, 27, 84, 100, 102, 105, 126, 127, 132, 135, 262

Yáñez, Francisco Javier, 228
Yereguí, José de, 71

Zavaleta, Diego Estanislao, 101, 134, 135
Zea, Francisco Antonio, 92, 93
Zudáñez, Jaime, 154, 255n323
Zumárraga, Juan de, 32
Zúñiga, Baltasar de, Marqués de Valero (Viceroy), 119